Teacher's Edition

SRA OpenCourt READING

Level 5 • Unit 1
Cooperation and Competition

— PROGRAM AUTHORS —

Marilyn Jager Adams	Iva Carruthers	Marsha Roit
Carl Bereiter	Robbie Case	Marlene Scardamalia
Ann Brown	Jan Hirshberg	Marcy Stein
Joe Campione	Anne McKeough	Gerald H. Treadway, Jr.
	Michael Pressley	

SRA

A Division of The *McGraw-Hill* Companies

Columbus, Ohio

Acknowledgments

Grateful acknowledgment is given to the following publishers and copyright owners for permissions granted to reprint selections from their publications. All possible care has been taken to trace ownership and secure permission for each selection included. In case of any errors or omissions, the Publisher will be pleased to make suitable acknowledgments in future editions.

From GIRLS WHO ROCKED THE WORLD, copyright © 1998 by Amelie Welden. Reprinted with permission of Beyond Words Publishing, Hillsboro, Oregon. From CLASS PRESIDENT COPYRIGHT © 1990 BY JOHANNA HURWITZ. Used by permission of HarperCollins Publishers. "The Marble Champ" from BASEBALL IN APRIL AND OTHER STORIES, copyright © 1990 by Gary Soto, reprinted by permission of Harcourt, Inc. "The New Kid" © 1975 Mike Makley. "Good Sportsmanship" Copyright © 1958 by Richard Armour. Reprinted by permission of John Hawkins & Associates, Inc. From JUGGLING by Donna Gamache. Reprinted by permission of the author. From THE ABACUS CONTEST. Copyright © 1996 Priscilla Wu. Illustrations copyright © 1996 Xiao-jun Li. Used by permission of Fulcrum Publishing. Reprinted with the permission of Atheneum Books for Young Readers, a Division of Simon & Schuster Children's Publishing Division, from S.O.R. Losers by Avi. Copyright © 1984 by Avi Wortis. "The Founders of the Children's Rain Forest" from IT'S OUR WORLD, TOO! by Phillip Hoose. Copyright © 1993 by Phillip Hoose. By permission of Little, Brown and Company (Inc.).

www.sra4kids.com

SRA/McGraw-Hill

A Division of The McGraw·Hill Companies

Send all inquiries to:
SRA/McGraw-Hill
8787 Orion Place
Columbus, OH 43240-4027

Printed in the United States of America.

ISBN 0-02-684907-0

2 3 4 5 6 7 8 9 WEB 06 05 04 03 02

Welcome to

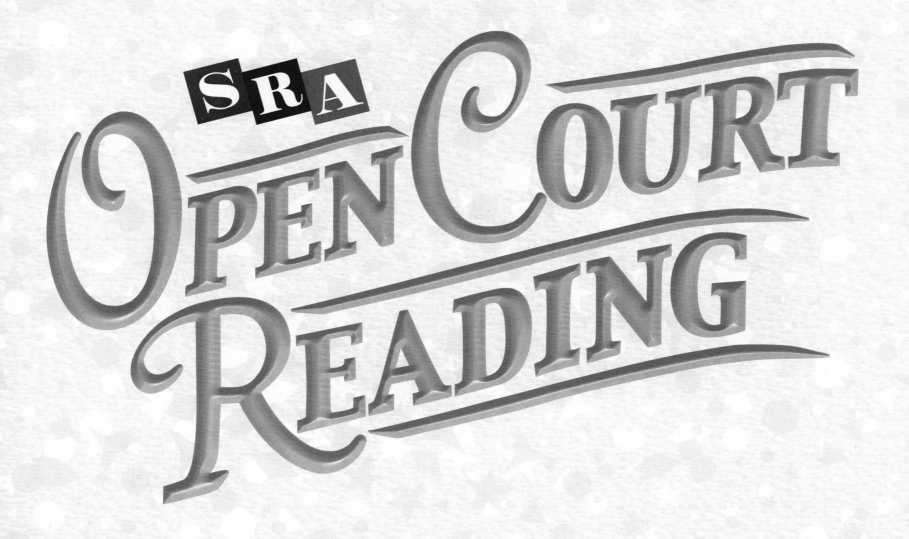

SRA OpenCourt Reading

Open Court Reading: The Most Complete, Effective Reading Program Available

Open Court Reading is the only reading program that provides:

- An **educational philosophy** based on scientific research and **nearly 40 years** of practical classroom experience
- A program that has been **proven successful in schools** nationwide
- A **well-defined plan of systematic, explicit instruction** for teaching the strategies and skills of reading
- A **partnership through training** that will help teachers and administrators successfully implement *Open Court Reading*

Open Court Reading is a **research-based** curriculum grounded in **systematic, explicit instruction** of:

- Phonemic awareness, phonics, and word knowledge
- Comprehension skills and strategies
- Inquiry skills and strategies
- Writing and language arts skills and strategies

The program creates a **literature-rich environment** that instills a passion for lifelong reading and a love of literature and the written word.

Our basic **philosophy** has remained consistent for nearly **40 years**. *Open Court Reading* has always contained the keys to teaching children how to read and read to learn.

Open Court Reading
Creates Confident Learners

Open Court Reading provides:

- Research-based instruction
- Strong authorship
- A systematic, explicit instructional plan
- Literature with a purpose
- Differentiating instruction for meeting students' individual needs

Research-Based Instruction

Open Court Reading is built on a solid foundation of nearly **40 years of research**. Test results repeatedly prove its effectiveness. Reading instruction trends may have changed; *Open Court Reading* has remained true to the fact that children learn best when taught using what has been researched and proven to work.

Open Court Reading is based on four types of research:

1. Academic
2. Most effective practices in education
3. Field testing
4. Learner verification results

Open Court Reading is the **only** program that guarantees all four.

Strong Authorship

The authors of *Open Court Reading* bring expertise in specific areas of educational research to our program. Their widely published books, journal articles, and research studies lead the field in areas such as phonemic awareness and phonics instruction and comprehension skills and strategies instruction.

Research in Action articles found throughout the program provide information showing how the work of our authors and others respected in the field of educational research have been incorporated into our program. These articles provide more information on how *Open Court Reading* works and why it is so successful.

Systematic, Explicit Instructional Plan

Students are most successful when they learn through a balance of systematic direct instruction in sound and word recognition, guided practice, and application of skills with extensive reading of decodable text and authentic literature.

Through systematic, explicit instruction, *Open Court Reading* has organized lessons in the most logical and efficient way possible for teaching children to read and write with skill and confidence. All strategies and skills are arranged from the simplest to the most complex. Because the skills build upon one another, children are able to grasp complex concepts more easily.

Open Court Reading provides more comprehensive Teacher Editions than any other program. The presentation of concepts, skills, and practice is detailed – all you need to do is follow the directions. Reading and writing strategies are delivered in a manner that has been proven through research to be the most effective.

Research in Action
Phonemic Awareness

The goal of phonemic awareness activities is to lead students to understand that spoken words are made up of chains of smaller sounds—the syllables and phonemes. Because students are accustomed to producing and hearing words as unbreakable wholes, this is not a natural insight. Nevertheless, for understanding an alphabetic language in which the letters and letter patterns represent the sub-sounds of words, it is a critical insight. After students have learned to think about words in terms of their component sounds, decoding will make sense and inventive spelling will come easily. Conversely, poorly developed phonemic awareness is believed to be the single greatest cause of reading disability. *(Marilyn J. Adams)*

Literature With a Purpose

Open Court Reading provides a **survey course of literature**, exposing students to a variety of different **writing styles** and **genres**. We guide students in understanding the strategies and skills necessary for reading text in the **real world**. Literature in *Open Court Reading* is found in:

- Big Books
- Anthologies
- Teacher Read Alouds
- Story Time Selections (Kindergarten)
- Online bibliography

In *Open Court Reading*, students read literature written by trade book authors by the middle of Grade 1. Our compilation of literature selections is so tightly woven that our students are involved in independent **Inquiry and Investigation** on complicated subjects much sooner and with more ease.

Differentiating Instruction for Meeting Individual Needs

Open Court Reading provides a variety of proven experiences for accommodating individual students' needs.

- Reteach
- Intervention
- Challenge
- English-Language Learners

Research and Results

Open Court Reading Is the Most Thoroughly Researched Program Available

Research Shows:

Students who are early independent readers:

- Learn better throughout their school years
- Become motivated readers who typically read more than children who learn to read later
- Develop increased:
  - Vocabulary
  - Understanding of abstract concepts
  - Appreciation of a diverse array of literature and writing styles
  - General knowledge

While current educational standards call for students to be reading by the end of Grade 3, *Open Court Reading* is structured to ensure that students are reading fluently and comprehending what they read **by the end of Grade 1.**

The Open Court Response:

Open Court has always included those essential concepts that research has repeatedly shown are necessary for learning to read. By using established routines throughout the program, *Open Court Reading* systematically and explicitly teaches each of these essential concepts:

- The alphabetic principle
- Print awareness
- Phonemic awareness
- Systematic, explicit phonics
- Comprehension strategies and skills
- Inquiry techniques and strategies
- The writing process and writing skills
- Spelling and vocabulary
- Grammar, usage, and mechanics

A Success Story 40 Years in the Making

Since the early 1960s, Open Court has included the fundamental elements that research has shown are necessary for teaching children how to read.

For nearly 40 years, Open Court has monitored and learned from the research that experts in the field of reading have conducted, incorporating these important findings into the programs.

SRA is proud to note that many of those same researchers hold *Open Court Reading* in high esteem as a well-balanced program that teaches students not only how to read, but also how to comprehend and make the most of reading content.

A Reading Program Rooted In Research

Academic Research

Leaders in educational research, the authors of *Open Court Reading* are experts on how children learn to read and read to learn. Together, they have created *Open Court Reading* to most effectively help expand students' reading and learning capabilities.

- **Phonemic awareness and systematic, explicit phonics** instruction is based on the work of **Dr. Marilyn Jager Adams**, author of the most frequently cited book on beginning reading, *Beginning to Read: Thinking and Learning about Print* (1990).

- **Comprehension skills and strategies** instruction is based on the work of **Dr. Ann Brown's** reciprocal teaching model and **Dr. Michael Pressley's** transactional strategy instruction model.

- **Dr. Marlene Scardamalia** lends the benefit of extensive research in the psychology of writing.

- Research conducted by **Dr. Carl Bereiter** is incorporated into the **Inquiry and Investigation** part of each lesson.

- A **Professional Development** plan has been developed and is expertly guided by **Dr. Marsha Roit**.

- The **Intervention** materials were created under the direction of **Dr. Marcy Stein**, who is widely published on the subject of special education, and **Dr. Marsha Roit** who, through her work in classrooms, brings a unique perspective to these materials.

Most Effective Practices in Education

- A comprehensive report by the **National Reading Panel** (2000) endorses the instructional model that *Open Court Reading* has used for nearly 40 years.

- Findings from studies being conducted by the **National Institute of Child Health and Human Development (NICHD)**, as well as conclusions from comprehensive reviews of beginning reading research, all indicate that effective reading instruction should include the strategies found in *Open Court Reading* for teaching children how to read.

- The **American Federation of Teachers (AFT)** reviewed current reading programs and issued a statement called *What Works*. In this statement, Open Court was identified as a program that incorporates research-based instruction and has classroom data to support its effectiveness.

- The **U.S. Department of Education's** Reading Excellence Act has awarded state grants to improve reading achievement mandating that schools choose programs that show "scientifically based research and effective practices that have been replicated effectively." Open Court has been the program of choice for schools throughout the nation who are being awarded this grant.

- An independent study (**Educational Research Analysis**, 2000) states that "*Open Court Reading* has the highest decodability, comprehensiveness, intensiveness, and consistency of any reading program." It was ranked best of all programs reviewed.

Field Testing

A study conducted by Foorman, et al. (1996) compared the effectiveness of the explicit, systematic program, Open Court, to other approaches. Results of this study found that Open Court's direct instruction approach was more effective with students at risk of reading failure than the other approaches as measured by a variety of tests, including standardized measures.

Learner Verification Results

In a study conducted by Douglas J. McRae, educational measurement specialist, Stanford/9 test scores from the STAR program were analyzed. The results of that study indicate:

- Open Court schools had higher gain scores statewide.

- Open Court provided the largest gain scores for schools with high concentration of both LEP (Limited English Proficient) and Low-SES (Socio-Economic Status) students.

- Scores show cumulative advantage over the span of two years with Open Court.

The conclusion of this study was that using Open Court made a difference. These schools (a sampling of over 150,000 students) showed greater gains than either statewide gains or gains from a demographically matched set of schools.

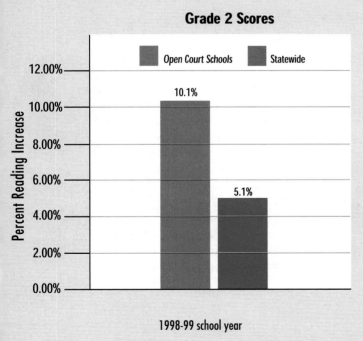

Grade 2 Scores

1998-99 school year

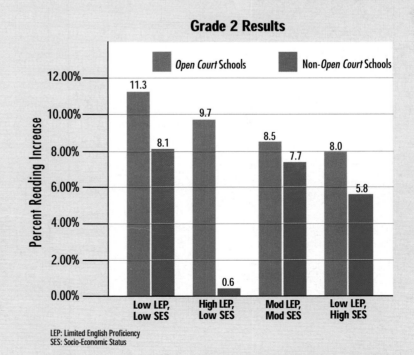

Grade 2 Results

LEP: Limited English Proficiency
SES: Socio-Economic Status

For a complete look at this study, please call 1-800-772-4543 and ask for Research Findings: The Research-Based Reading Materials You Choose May Have a Direct Impact on Your Students' Reading Performance, ISBN# R80000456.

Open Court Reading Authors
Bring Research Into Your Classroom

MARILYN JAGER ADAMS, PH.D.

Cited in the *2000 Politics of Education Yearbook* as one of the most influential people in the national reading policy arena, Dr. Adams has worked closely with a number of agencies to develop reading standards, policies, and staff development strategies.

- Author/co-author of:
  - *Beginning to Read: Thinking and Learning about Print*
  - *Preventing Reading Difficulties in Young Children*
  - *Fox in a Box* Assessment Program
  - *Phonemic Awareness in Young Children*
  - *Odyssey: A Curriculum for Thinking*
- Advisor to *Sesame Street* and *Between the Lions*

CARL BEREITER, PH.D.

An accomplished author, researcher, and professor, Dr. Bereiter has published extensively on teaching and learning.

- Invented CSILE (Computer Supported Intentional Learning Environments), the first networked collaborative learning environment in schools, with Dr. Marlene Scardamalia; the current version, *Knowledge Forum®*, is in use in 12 countries
- Co-author of:
  - *The Psychology of Written Composition*
  - *Surpassing Ourselves: The Nature and Implications of Expertise*
- Author of *Education and the Mind of the Knowledge Age*
- Professor at Centre for Applied Cognitive Science, Ontario Institute for Studies in Education
- One of 100 people honored in the Routledge Great Thinkers in Education
- Member of the National Academy of Education

JOE CAMPIONE, PH.D.

A leading researcher on cognitive development, individual differences, assessment, and the design of innovative learning environments, Dr. Campione is currently a Professor in the School of Education at University of California at Berkeley.

- Most recent work has focused on methods to restructure elementary schools
- Has created curriculums that introduce students as early as Grade 1 to the research process

IVA CARRUTHERS, PH.D.

Equipped with both hands-on and academic experience, Dr. Carruthers serves as a consultant and lecturer in both educational technology and matters of multicultural inclusion.

- President of Nexus Unlimited, Inc., a human resources development and computer services consulting firm
- Consultant, U.S. Advisory Council on the National Information Infrastructure
- Former Chairperson and Professor of the Sociology Department at Northeastern Illinois University
- Has developed software for teaching African-American history and inter-disciplinary subjects
- Co-producer of *Know Your Heritage*, a televised academic quiz show
- Has also been an elementary school teacher, high school counselor, and research historian

JAN HIRSHBERG, ED.D.

Focusing on how children learn to read and write and the logistics of teaching reading and writing in the early grades, Dr. Hirshberg is currently working as a language arts resource teacher and consultant in Alexandria, Virginia.

- Author/co-author of:
  - *Open Court 1989, Kindergarten and Grade 1 Reading and Writing Program*
  - *Collections for Young Scholars*
  - *Open Court 1995* and *2000*, reading, writing, and learning program

- Former teaching fellow, research assistant, instructor, and lecturer at the Graduate School of Education at Harvard University
- Former elementary school teacher and school district reading consultant

ANNE MCKEOUGH, PH.D.

A Professor in the Division of Applied Psychology and Chair of the Human Learning and Development program at the University of Calgary, Dr. McKeough has received a number of research awards and grants.

- Co-editor of several volumes, including:
  - *Toward the Practice of Theory Based Instruction: Current Cognitive Theories and Their Educational Promise*
  - *Teaching for Transfer: Fostering Generalization in Learning*
  - *Schools in Transition*
- Has authored numerous articles advocating the benefits of a continued and reflective partnership between teaching practices and child development research
- Current research focuses on cognitive development and developmentally based instruction

MICHAEL PRESSLEY, PH.D.

Most recently honored by the National Reading Conference as the 2000 recipient of the Oscar Causey Award for career contributions to reading research, Dr. Pressley is the Academic Director of the Masters of Education Program and Professor of Psychology at the University of Notre Dame.

- Editor of *Journal of Educational Psychology*
- Author of *Reading Instruction That Works: The Case for Balanced Teaching* and co-author of *Learning to Read: Lessons from Exemplary First-Grade Classrooms*
- An expert in comprehension instruction and in the ethnographic study of the elementary classroom experience
- Author of more than 200 scientific articles

MARSHA ROIT, ED.D.

The Director of Professional Development for SRA/McGraw-Hill, Dr. Roit spends considerable time in classrooms developing reading and writing curricula and training teachers and administrators in effective instructional practices.

- Works directly with school districts creating staff development models that support research-based instruction and its effectiveness
- Has focused research on strategy instruction with both mainstream and English-Language Learners
- Has published in a variety of professional journals, including:
  - *Exceptional Children*
  - *Journal of Learning Disabilities*
  - *The Elementary School Journal*

MARLENE SCARDAMALIA, PH.D.

A Professor at the Centre for Applied Cognitive Science and Department of Curriculum Teaching and Learning, Ontario Institute for Studies in Education, Dr. Scardamalia has conducted research and been published in the areas of cognitive development, psychology of writing, intentional learning, the nature of expertise, and educational uses of computers.

- Invented CSILE (Computer Supported Intentional Learning Environments), the first networked collaborative learning environment in schools, with Dr. Carl Bereiter; the current version, *Knowledge Forum®*, is in use in 12 countries
- Member of the U.S. National Academy of Education
- While a fellow at the Center for Advanced Study in Behavioral Sciences, headed "Cognitive Bases of Educational Reform," from which grew "Schools of Thought," a school reform program noted for its synthesis of major cognitive-based learning initiatives

MARCY STEIN, PH.D.

An Associate Professor and founding faculty member of the education program at the University of Washington, Tacoma, Dr. Stein currently coordinates At-Risk and Special Education graduate programs, and teaches in the teacher certification program. She has served as consultant to departments of education on the translation of reading research to instructional practice.

- She has published extensively on topics including:
  - Beginning and remedial reading instruction
  - Vocabulary acquisition
  - Curriculum and textbook analysis
- She has served on many national and local committees and in consultant positions, including:
  - Los Angeles Unified School District, Consultant
  - Washington State Special Education Improvement Grant Steering Committee, Invited Member
  - *Remedial and Special Education* journal, consulting editor

GERALD H. TREADWAY, JR., PH.D.

Professor at San Diego State University, Dr. Treadway teaches reading methods, balanced reading programs, and reading comprehension.

- Member of California's Reading Task Force and the Reading Credentials Task Force
- Member of California Academic Standards Commission
- Associate Director of the California Reading and Literature Project
- Contributing author to *Fox in a Box*, a diagnostic reading assessment for students in Grades K-2
- Former member and Chair of the California Curriculum Commission
- Former elementary school teacher

ANN BROWN, PH.D.

The past President of the American Education Research Association, Dr. Brown conducted a great deal of research in the area of distributed expertise in the classroom.

- Worked as a professor of math, science, and technology in the Graduate School of Education at the University of California at Berkeley
- Served on the congressional panel to monitor National Assessment of Education Progress state-by-state assessments
- Received many honors and awards in both the United States and England for her contributions to educational research

ROBBIE CASE, PH.D.

Beginning in the mid-1970s, Dr. Case conducted research on the relationship between children's learning and their cognitive development during elementary school.

- Former Professor of Education at Stanford University
- Former Director of the Laidlaw-Centre at the Institute of Child Study, University of Toronto
- Authored books and scholarly articles on cognitive development that are sold throughout the world

Open Court Reading
Instructional Plan

Systematic and Explicit

Explicit instruction is teacher-directed identification of learning goals, specific presentation to students, teacher modeling, student practice, and assessment.

Systematic instruction outlines the logical sequence of skill presentation and research-based, effective learning routines.

Teacher Modeling

Teacher modeling is key to systematic, explicit instruction. Starting in Kindergarten, teachers model a repertoire of skills and strategies students learn to apply independently. Every lesson includes multiple opportunities to model the process that good readers use. Students then practice and apply the modeled strategies to work up to independent use of the strategies.

Open Court Reading provides systematic and explicit instruction for every skill throughout the program.

1 Preparing to Read

- Sounds and letters
- Phonemic awareness
- Phonics and fluency
- Word knowledge

In Kindergarten and Grade 1, Part 1 of every lesson carefully teaches letter names, sounds, and spellings in a carefully crafted sequence that enables students to begin reading real words as soon as possible. Phonemic awareness, phonics, and fluency skills are all presented using research-based strategies that include blending and segmentation. Students quickly, efficiently, and effectively learn the sound patterns that make up English words. Practice and review of these key skills are systematically built into the curriculum to ensure mastery. In later grades, word knowledge is presented with the same careful attention. At the same time, students increase vocabulary skills through careful presentation and practice using vocabulary from the literature selection.

2 Reading and Responding

Comprehension Skills and Strategies

Part 2 of every lesson teaches specific comprehension skills and strategies in conjunction with the excellent literature that forms the core of each lesson. Comprehension strategies, such as clarifying, summarizing, and predicting, are modeled, practiced, and reviewed in the first reading of the literature.

Comprehension skills, including sequence and drawing conclusions, are modeled, practiced, and reviewed in the second reading of the literature. This comprehensive development of skills and strategies builds life-long confidence.

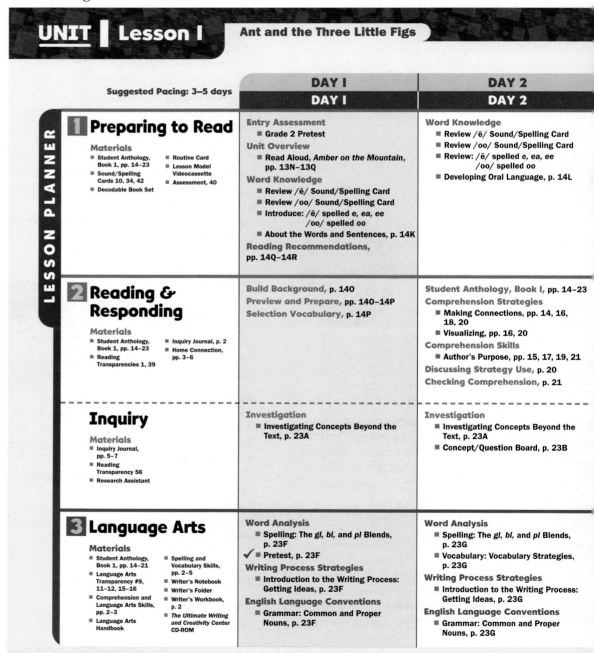

LESSON PLANNER			DAY 1	DAY 2
		Suggested Pacing: 3–5 days	DAY 1	DAY 2
	1 Preparing to Read		**Entry Assessment** ■ Grade 2 Pretest **Unit Overview** ■ Read Aloud, *Amber on the Mountain*, pp. 13N–13Q **Word Knowledge** ■ Review /ē/ Sound/Spelling Card ■ Review /oo/ Sound/Spelling Card ■ Introduce: /ē/ spelled e, ea, ee /oo/ spelled oo ■ About the Words and Sentences, p. 14K **Reading Recommendations,** pp. 14Q–14R	**Word Knowledge** ■ Review /ē/ Sound/Spelling Card ■ Review /oo/ Sound/Spelling Card ■ Review: /ē/ spelled e, ea, ee /oo/ spelled oo ■ Developing Oral Language, p. 14L
	Materials ■ Student Anthology, Book 1, pp. 14–23 ■ Sound/Spelling Cards 10, 34, 42 ■ Decodable Book Set ■ Routine Card ■ Lesson Model Videocassette ■ Assessment, 40			
	2 Reading & Responding		**Build Background, p. 14O** **Preview and Prepare,** pp. 14O–14P **Selection Vocabulary,** p. 14P	**Student Anthology, Book 1, pp. 14–23** **Comprehension Strategies** ■ Making Connections, pp. 14, 16, 18, 20 ■ Visualizing, pp. 16, 20 **Comprehension Skills** ■ Author's Purpose, pp. 15, 17, 19, 21 **Discussing Strategy Use, p. 20** **Checking Comprehension, p. 21**
	Materials ■ Student Anthology, Book 1, pp. 14–23 ■ Reading Transparencies 1, 39 ■ Inquiry Journal, p. 2 ■ Home Connection, pp. 3–6			
	Inquiry		**Investigation** ■ Investigating Concepts Beyond the Text, p. 23A	**Investigation** ■ Investigating Concepts Beyond the Text, p. 23A ■ Concept/Question Board, p. 23B
	Materials ■ Inquiry Journal, pp. 5–7 ■ Reading Transparency 56 ■ Research Assistant			
	3 Language Arts		**Word Analysis** ■ Spelling: The gl, bl, and pl Blends, p. 23F ✓ ■ Pretest, p. 23F **Writing Process Strategies** ■ Introduction to the Writing Process: Getting Ideas, p. 23F **English Language Conventions** ■ Grammar: Common and Proper Nouns, p. 23F	**Word Analysis** ■ Spelling: The gl, bl, and pl Blends, p. 23G ■ Vocabulary: Vocabulary Strategies, p. 23G **Writing Process Strategies** ■ Introduction to the Writing Process: Getting Ideas, p. 23G **English Language Conventions** ■ Grammar: Common and Proper Nouns, p. 23G
	Materials ■ Student Anthology, Book 1, pp. 14–21 ■ Language Arts Transparency #9, 11–12, 15–16 ■ Comprehension and Language Arts Skills, pp. 2–3 ■ Language Arts Handbook ■ Spelling and Vocabulary Skills, pp. 2–5 ■ Writer's Notebook ■ Writer's Folder ■ Writer's Workbook, p. 2 ■ *The Ultimate Writing and Creativity Center* CD-ROM			

UNIT 1 Lesson 1   Ant and the Three Little Figs

14E   Unit 1 Lesson 1

Ⓟ Phonics   ✓ Informal Assessment Available   ✓ Formal Assessment Available

Inquiry

Inquiry and investigation strategies are thoughtfully developed to teach students how to ask questions and find the answers to their questions. With Inquiry, students apply all of the reading, comprehension, and language arts skills they are learning in order to develop and present their investigations.

3 Language Arts

- Spelling
- Vocabulary
- Writing process strategies
- Writer's craft
- English language conventions
- Grammar, usage, and mechanics
- Listening, speaking, and viewing
- Penmanship
- Basic computer skills

Part 3 of every lesson includes systematic and explicit development of language arts skills, including the writing process, writing traits, writer's craft, and structures of writing in different genres. Each skill is explicitly taught using teacher models or models from the *Language Arts Handbook* and practiced in reading and/or writing activities. These activities show how the skill is connected to the other parts of the lesson. Like the phonics and comprehension skills, the language arts skills are added to each student's knowledge toolbox, so that students can employ appropriate skills when developing their investigations, or in other contexts.

Assessment

Continuous assessment enables teachers to gauge the progress of their students so that no student misses needed instruction.

The assessment section of *Open Court Reading* contains:

- Program Assessment
  - Teacher's Observation Log
  - Pretest
  - Midyear test
  - Posttest
- Unit Assessments
  Includes assessments for all skills taught.
  Unit Assessments contain:
  - Oral Fluency Assessments
  - Writing assessments
  - Spelling assessments
  - Vocabulary assessments
  - Listening assessments
  - Grammar, usage, and mechanics assessments
  - Comprehension assessments
  - Literature assessments
  - Class assessment record
  - Student assessment record
- Diagnostic Assessment
  Provides more focused assessment opportunities to aid in individualizing instruction.

Theme: **Sharing Stories**

DAY 2 continued / **DAY 3**	**DAY 3** / **DAY 4**	**DAY 5**
DAY 3	**DAY 4**	**DAY 5**

Phonics and Fluency P
■ Review /j/ Sound/Spelling Card
■ Introduce: Short vowels /j/ spelled ■ dge
  Compound words
■ About the Words and Sentences, p. 14M
■ Developing Oral Language, p. 14N
	Phonics and Fluency P
	■ Review /j/ Sound/Spelling Card
	■ Review: Short vowels /j/ spelled ■ dge
	  Compound words
	■ Dictation, p. 14N
	Reading a Decodable Book
	■ Decodable Book 15, p. 14N
		Review Phonics and Fluency P

Student Anthology, Book I, Second Read p. 14–23 **Supporting the Reading,** p. 21C ■ Making Connections **Meet the Author/Illustrator,** p. 22 **Theme Connections,** p. 23 **Comprehension Skills** ■ Author's Purpose, pp. 15, 17, 19, 21	**Student Anthology, Book I,** pp. 14–23 **Discussing the Selection,** p. 21A ■ Review the selection ■ Complete discussion **Review Selection Vocabulary,** p. 21B ■ View Fine Art, p. 21B **Literary Elements,** p. 21D ■ Mood	✓ **Selection Assessment,** p. 21 **Home Connection,** p. 21B **Social Studies Connection,** p. 21E ■ Main Idea in a Work of Art **Social Studies Connection,** p. 21F ■ Sharing stories about different types of food
Investigation ■ Generating Questions to Investigate, p. 23C ■ Home Connection, p. 23C	**Supporting the Investigation** ■ Alphabetical Order, p. 23D	**Investigation** ■ Concept/Question Board
Word Analysis ■ Spelling: The gl, bl, and pl Blends, p. 23H ■ Vocabulary: Vocabulary Strategies, p. 23H **Writing Process Strategies** ■ Introduction to the Writing Process: Getting Ideas, p. 23H **English Language Conventions** ■ Grammar: Common and Proper Nouns, p. 23H	**Word Analysis** ■ Spelling: The gl, bl, and pl Blends, p. 23I ■ Vocabulary: Vocabulary Strategies, p. 23I **Writing Process Strategies** ■ Introduction to the Writing Process: Getting Ideas, p. 23I **English Language Conventions** ✓ ■ Listening, Speaking, Viewing Listening: Purposes of Listening, p. 23I	**Word Analysis** ■ Spelling: The gl, bl, and pl Blends, p. 23J ✓ ■ Final Test, p. 23J ✓ ■ Vocabulary: Strategies, p. 23J **Writing Process Strategies** ■ Introduction to the Writing Process: Getting Ideas, p. 23J **English Language Conventions** ✓ ■ Penmanship: Manuscript Letters l and i, p. 23J

Open Court Reading
Literature

In-Depth Literary Theme Perspectives

The goal of *Open Court Reading* is to efficiently and effectively teach children to decode and comprehend so that they can read a variety of literature types. All of the skills development throughout the program serve this purpose. From the very beginning, the program has emphasized the quality of the literature students read and the organization of that literature around big ideas to promote understanding and discussion.

Each unit throughout the program explores a comprehensive theme. The literature in each unit of *Open Court Reading* is organized around one of two types of themes:

- **Universal themes**, such as Keep Trying, Friendship, and Survival, encourage in-depth and critical thinking.

- **Research themes**, such as Weather, Astronomy, and Ancient Civilizations, develop inquiry and research in science and social studies content areas.

Inquiry and Investigation

Throughout lessons in *Open Court Reading*, students do more than just read literature. They also ask questions, discuss, research, write about, and think about the concepts and ideas centered around the themes they read.

Quality Literature Organized into Unit Themes

	UNIT 1	UNIT 2	UNIT 3	UNIT 4
LEVEL K	**BIG BOOKS**			
	School	Shadows	Finding Friends	Wind
LEVEL 1	**BIG BOOKS**			
	Let's Read	Animals	Things That Go	Our Neighborhood at Work
LEVEL 2	**STUDENT ANTHOLOGIES**			
	Sharing Stories	Kindness	Look Again	Fossils
LEVEL 3	**STUDENT ANTHOLOGIES**			
	Friendship	City Wildlife	Imagination	Money
LEVEL 4	**STUDENT ANTHOLOGY**			
	Risks and Consequences	Dollars and Sense	From Mystery to Medicine	Survival
LEVEL 5	**STUDENT ANTHOLOGY**			
	Cooperation and Competition	Astronomy	Heritage	Making a New Nation
LEVEL 6	**STUDENT ANTHOLOGY**			
	Perseverance	Ancient Civilizations	Taking a Stand	Beyond the Notes

UNIT 5	UNIT 6	UNIT 7	UNIT 8	UNIT 9	UNIT 10
Stick to It	Red, White, and Blue	Teamwork	By the Sea		

UNIT 5	UNIT 6	UNIT 7	UNIT 8	UNIT 9	UNIT 10
Weather	Journeys	Keep Trying	Games	Being Afraid	Homes
Courage	Our Country and Its People				
Storytelling	Country Life				
Communication	A Changing America				
Going West	Journeys and Quests				
Ecology	A Question of Value				

Open Court Reading
Literature

Excellent Examples of a Variety of Literature

Interesting and high-quality literature is introduced in *Open Court Reading* as soon as students begin school. The literature provides the foundation of each lesson throughout the program. Comprehension skills and strategies, spelling and vocabulary, writing process strategies, and English language conventions all connect to the lesson selection.

Each literature selection in the Big Books and Anthologies was painstakingly selected with the following goals in mind:

- **Unique theme perspectives** encourage student inquiry. Each selection in a unit adds a new concept or idea about the theme.

- **A variety of literature** provides fiction and nonfiction genres, including novels, short stories, poems, essays, dramas, mysteries, and informational articles so students experience many different forms of literature.

- **Reading practice** includes grade-level appropriate literature.

- **Excellent examples of writing** in literature provide superior models for students' writing.

- **Classic and contemporary literature** works together to broaden students' perspectives.

- **Author Styles** offer award-winning works and different styles of writing so students develop a cultural literacy.

In addition to the literature in the Big Books and Anthologies, these components provide further exposure to literature in each unit:

- Teacher Read Alouds (K-6)
- Story Time Selections (K)
- Leveled Libraries (K-6)
- Online Bibliography (K-6)

Literature Selections Provide Foundation for Independent Inquiry and Investigation

Chart from Unit Overview found on the following page provides information on how the literature furthers theme-based study.

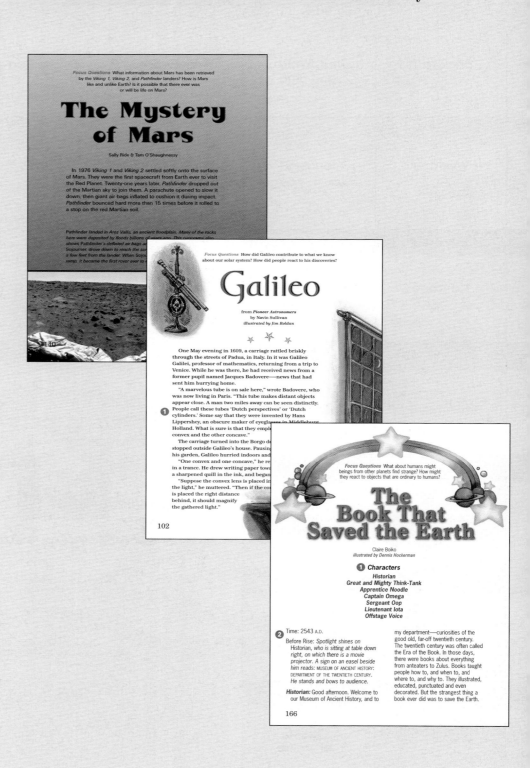

	OVERVIEW OF SELECTION	LINK TO THE THEME	UNIT INVESTIGATIONS	SUPPORTING STUDENT INVESTIGATIONS
Lesson 1 *Galileo*	■ In this biographical selection, Galileo's telescope reveals things about the heavens that eventually put him at odds with church authorities.	■ Galileo introduced many people to the faraway planets, satellites, and stars studied in astronomy.	■ Generate questions and ideas to investigate	■ Investigation activities ■ Learn to use charts
Lesson 2 *Telescopes*	■ This nonfiction selection explains how different kinds of telescopes work, including the Hubble space telescope.	■ Telescopes, the basic tools of astronomy since the 1600s, have become more powerful and sophisticated.	■ Formulate questions and problems	■ Investigation activities ■ Learn to use diagrams
Lesson 3 *The Heavenly Zoo*	■ The origins of three astrological patterns are explained by ancient myths from different cultures.	■ Lacking scientific knowledge of the stars, ancient peoples created myths to give meaning to these phenomena. ■ Constellation myths helped ancient people remember, locate, and identify stars.	■ Make conjectures	■ Investigation activities ■ Learn to use card and computer catalogs
Lesson 4 *Circles, Squares, and Daggers*	■ This nonfiction selection illustrates how Native Americans of long ago created structures to mark the cycles of seasons and the passing of time.	■ Archaeoastronomy is a field of study that combines archaeology and astronomy.	■ Establish investigation needs	■ Investigation activities ■ Learn to use outlines
Lesson 5 *The Mystery of Mars*	■ This nonfiction selection illustrates how astronomers learned a great deal about Mars from the journeys of the *Viking 1*, *Viking 2*, and *Pathfinder* spacecraft.	■ Space missions to Mars have broadened our knowledge of the field of astronomy.	■ Establish investigation plans	■ Investigation activities ■ Learn to use indices
Lesson 6 *Stars*	■ This nonfiction selection provides an introduction to the different kinds of distant objects and systems that modern astronomers investigate.	■ Nebulas, supernovas, and quasars are some of the types of stars in the universe that have been discovered through astronomy.	■ Continue investigation ■ Make informal presentations	■ Investigation activities ■ Learn note-taking skills
Lesson 7 *The Book That Saved the Earth*	■ This humorous science fiction play suggests that some aliens may not be as intelligent as we think.	■ The study of astronomy leads some to wonder what alien life-forms would think of our culture if they should discover us first.	■ Present investigation findings	■ Investigation activities ■ Self-evaluate investigations

Differentiating Instruction:
Workshop

Every Child a Reader

The instructional models in *Open Court Reading* ensure that every child has the benefit of the best reading instruction available.

Whole-Group Instruction

Every lesson begins with whole-group, teacher-directed lessons so that all children have access to the same models and information.

Differentiating Instruction: Workshop

Workshop is a period of time devoted to collaborating on investigations of unit concepts, working independently, or meeting individual needs. Workshop items and procedures are introduced to the whole group through direct-teaching sessions. Then students are released gradually from directed-teaching to work independently or in collaborative groups. Teachers work with individuals or small groups as needed during this time.

Independent Learning

As part of the Inquiry strand, the Concept/Question Board is a place for students to ask questions and find answers that will give them a better understanding of the unit theme. It is also a place to publish the results of their investigations.

Universal Access: Meeting Individual Needs

By making no assumptions about prior knowledge, *Open Court Reading* provides a variety of proven experiences that accommodate different student needs:

- **Reteach** lessons are available for those students who need extra support in all skills.

- **Intervention** lessons are for students who need more intensive support. Intervention includes controlled vocabulary selections based on unit themes and specific skill lessons to bring students up to grade level.

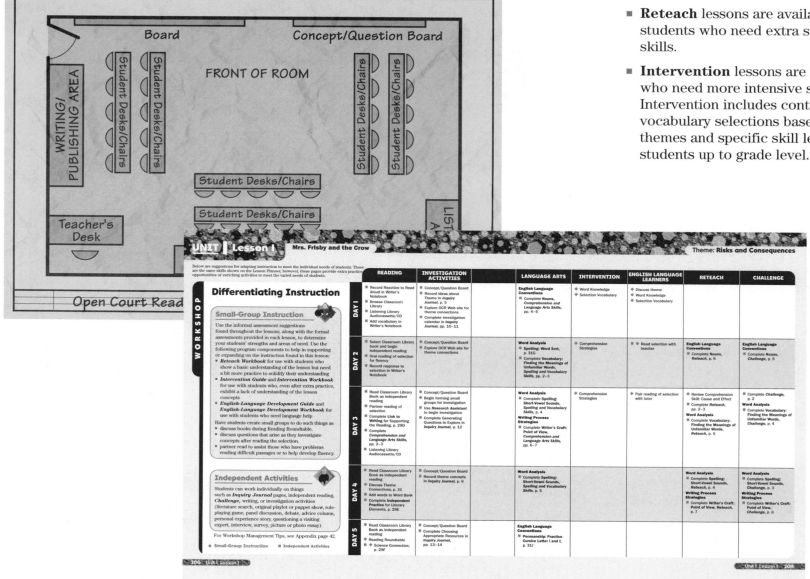

- **Challenge** activities are included to provide continued stimulation for those students working above grade level and beyond the capabilities of the average readers in the class.

- **English-Language Development** lessons address the needs of today's increasingly diverse classrooms. This instructional support complements the *Open Court Reading* lessons. Also, Home Connections Blackline Masters include parent letters in both Spanish and English to communicate classroom progress, including unit themes and activities.

Activating prior knowledge and natural inquiries with the Concept/Question Board

The *Concept/Question Board* is used throughout lessons in *Open Court Reading* to encourage students to think independently and flexibly.

At the opening of each unit, students examine a concept-related picture and discuss what about it looks familiar. Students write what they know about the concept, and post it on the *Concept* side of the board. Some questions teachers can ask to spur discussion and activate prior knowledge are provided in the Unit Overview.

Next, the class discusses what more they would like to know about the concept. The questions that come from this discussion are posted on the *Question* side of the board. Throughout the lessons in the unit, the class investigates these questions by searching for answers in the literature and in outside sources.

This ongoing learning process encourages inquiry and investigation, helping students to form independent thinking strategies, and build effective thinking habits.

A second grade Concept/Question Board from Karen Hansill in Georgia

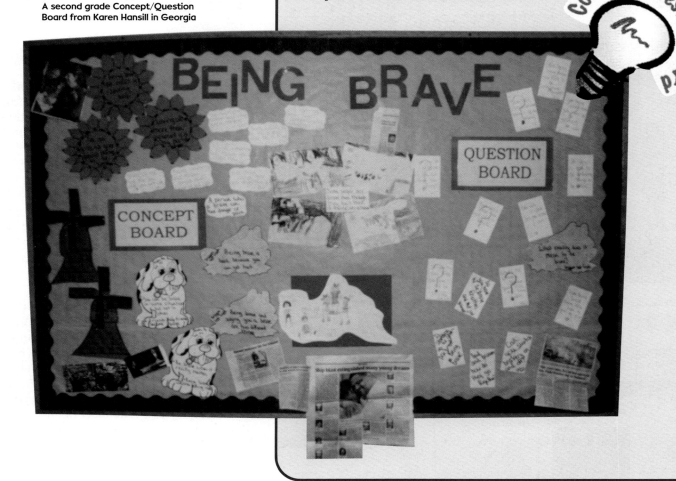

Program Components

Teacher Support (K-6)
(Teacher Editions, Online Support, Training Video Collection, Professional Development Guides)

Teacher Editions provide the information necessary for teaching systematic, explicit skills instruction centered around quality literature selections. Professional Development Guides and Lesson Model Videos offer a deeper understanding of the program, how it works, and why.

First Reader (2)
This reader contains real literature for review and reinforcement of skills is used during the Getting Started lessons at the beginning of Grade 2.

Big Books and Little Big Books (K-1)
Contain multiple literature selections and fine art to promote reading and shared reading experiences.

Story Time Selections
Trade books used to support each unit in kindergarten.

Blackline Masters and Workbooks
Sounds and Letters Skills (K), Language Arts Skills (K), Phonics Skills (1), Comprehension and Language Arts Skills (1-6), Inquiry Journal (2-6), Spelling and Vocabulary Skills (1-6), and Writer's Workbook (K-6) are used to help reinforce and practice skills taught.

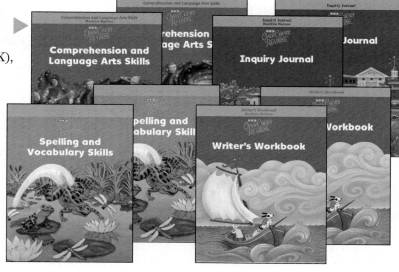

Student Anthologies (1-6)
Collections of literature based on themes. Each selection is chosen for the content it adds to the theme.

Science/Social Studies Connection Centers (K-6)
Reinforce reading across the curriculum by linking science and social studies content to the *Open Court Reading* lessons.

Technology
Alphabet Book Activities (K), Decodable Book Activities (1-3), Spelling (1-6), Writing (K-3, 4-6), Assessment (K-6), Research Assistant (2-6), and Management (K-6) CD-ROMs; Audiocassette or CD Listening Libraries (K-6), Alphabet Sound Card Stories Audiocassette or CD (K), Sound/Spelling Card Stories Audiocassette or CD (1-3), Lesson Models Video Collection (K-3), Online Bibliography (K-6), Online Teacher Support (K-6), and Leap into Phonics (K-3)

Decodable Text (K-3)
(Pre-Decodable and Decodable Books and Takehomes)

These books give students the opportunity to practice the blending strategies and high-frequency words they are learning during Part 1 of the lesson. Individual (1 copy of each book) and Classroom Sets (6 copies of each book) are available. These also come in a tear-out Takehome format in which books are made by students to use during class or to take home to practice with parents. Takehomes are available in 4-color or black & white versions.

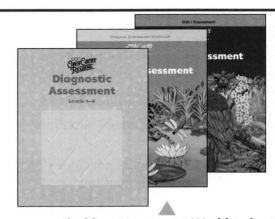

Assessment Blackline Masters or Workbooks (K-6)
Diagnostic, Program, Unit, and Standardized Test have specific assessments that help evaluate the progress of each student using various types of formal assessment.

First Reader, Second Reader (1)
These readers help transition students from reading decodable text and high-frequency sight words to reading authentic trade-book literature in the Anthologies and Leveled Classroom Libraries. Although still somewhat controlled, the text in these engaging readers about the unit theme provides students with more of the challenges found in completely uncontrolled trade-book text. They provide the perfect step between the completely controlled Decodable Text and the text found in the Anthologies.

Phonics Packages (K-3)
Contain the manipulatives necessary for teaching the phonemic awareness and phonics instruction. The Story Crafting components can also be found in the Kindergarten Reading, Phonemic Awareness, and Phonics Package.

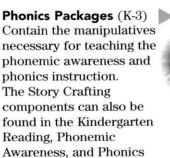

Language Arts Handbook (K-1)
Language Arts Big Book (2-6)
Contains models of the writing process, writing traits, writer's craft, and structures of writing.

Additional Literature
Selections chosen to supplement the literature in the Big Books and Anthologies can be found in Teacher Read Aloud Selections, Leveled Classroom Libraries, Online Bibliography (K-6). Leveled Libraries contain trade book selections that are leveled easy, average, and advanced and provide more information for unit investigations.

Practice Books (K-6)
(Challenge, Reteach, Intervention, English-Language Development)

For use during Differentiating Instruction in Workshop. These practice books remediate, reinforce, and extend lessons for meeting the needs of all learners in your classroom. They are available in both workbook and blackline master formats.

Every Child a Reader,
Every Teacher a Success

Every Child Deserves to Read

According to educational researchers:

- Children who learn to read by the end of Grade 1 perform better in school and beyond.
- Children who enjoy reading learn more quickly and read more.

Literacy in today's society means more than simply being able to read the billboards stretched along the interstates, sign a name to a bank account, or read a newspaper article. In today's workplaces, literacy means being able to pursue multiple tasks at one time, being able to understand written and spoken language, and even knowing how to research and solve problems.

All children, regardless of background, deserve an equal opportunity to excel. Children should be invigorated and excited about having the opportunity to acquire knowledge. This will only happen if all children are given equal access to those practices that are proven to work in the classroom.

***Open Court Reading* is *the* proven curriculum for teaching children how to read, comprehend, and gain knowledge from what they read**. The instructional plan found in *Open Court Reading* prepares our children for the reality of a literate future. The research and results that support *Open Court Reading* have shown this to be true.

When children are given the structure they need from the beginning, they move beyond that which any program or teacher can provide. Equal access is the right of every child that we are asked to educate. Every child must be taught to read fluently and independently by the end of Grade 1. With *Open Court Reading*, this is a reality, not a chance.

Every Teacher Deserves the Best Program and Support for Teaching It

The Best Program

According to the latest research, the classrooms of the most effective teachers are characterized by:

- High academic engagement
- Excellent classroom management
- Positive reinforcement and cooperation
- Explicit teaching of skills
- An emphasis on literature
- Plenty of reading and writing practice
- Matching of task demands to student competence
- Encouragement of student self-regulation
- Strong cross-curricular connections

(CELA Report Number 11007)

Only a reading program such as *Open Court Reading* can help you accomplish such a daunting list of tasks.

Open Court Reading is the only reading program that provides:

- **An educational philosophy based on scientific research and nearly 40 years of practical classroom experience**
- **A program that has been successful in classrooms nationwide**
- **A partnership through training that will help you not only successfully implement *Open Court Reading*, but also understand solid reading instruction**

What does this mean to you? **Success**, and the added assurance that the children in your classroom are getting **the best program available**.

What Open Court Means to Me

"Personally, I find your program very helpful for teaching my students. I teach at a high-risk school, and this series is not just for accelerated readers."

– Ryan Williams, Teacher

"Open Court is the most complete program that I have seen in my career."

– Linda LaMarre, Superintendent

"Open Court is not just phonics-oriented, but it includes phonics, comprehension, and writing...It is important to consider all aspects of reading instruction. If a school chooses a program that relies on phonics alone, teachers will abandon the program when they realize it does not offer the balanced instruction that Open Court does."

– Marge Thompson, Principal

"In 26 years of work in education, I have never experienced the high level of support we received from SRA. It's really amazing!"

– Lois Zercher, Assistant Superintendent

"People are always looking for quick fixes to education problems in this country and there aren't any. Open Court requires a lot of work on the part of the teacher and students, but we're happy to work hard if we're going to keep getting such great results."

– Diane Yules, Reading Specialist

For more Open Court Success Stories, call 1-800-SRA-4543 or visit SRA's web site at www.sra4kids.com.

Support for Teaching

One component of the success of *Open Court Reading* is SRA's strong commitment to professional development. SRA is dedicated not only to the education of students, but of educators as well.

During one of our many training events, you learn not only how to successfully implement *Open Court Reading*, but also how to successfully implement the best educational practices in your classroom. Our professional team of consultants are former classroom and Open Court teachers who know our program intimately. They continuously participate in professional development training in order to make sure that the information they share with you is the best and the most current.

We provide support through:

- In-service training
- On-site follow-up
- Weekend seminars
- Online training
- Summer institutes
- Professional development guides
- Training video collection

Teachers and administrators may get information about training sessions by calling the Teacher Learning Exchange at 1-800-382-7670 or by visiting www.tlexchange.com.

Lesson 1

Class President
20A

realistic fiction written by Johanna Hurwitz • *illustrated by* Richard Hull

Word Knowledge	Comprehension	Language Arts	Lesson Skills
Derivatives of Root Word *complete* Consonant Plus *r* Blends Spellings of the /er/ Sound	**Strategies:** Making Connections Predicting Summarizing **Skill:** Drawing Conclusions	The /a/ Sound Writing: Getting Ideas Nouns	

Lesson 2

The Marble Champ
36A

realistic fiction written by Gary Soto • *illustrated by* Maren Scott

Parenting's Reading Magic Award

Word Knowledge	Comprehension	Language Arts	Lesson Skills
Synonyms Regular Plurals /n/ Spelled *kn*	**Strategies:** Asking Questions Making Connections Visualizing **Skill:** Making Inferences	The /e/ Sound Prewriting Pronouns	

Lesson 3

Juggling
48A

realistic fiction written by Donna Gamache • *illustrated by* Daniel Powers

Word Knowledge	Comprehension	Language Arts	Lesson Skills
Closed Compounds Consonant Diagraph *th* S-Consonant Blends	**Strategies:** Asking Questions Predicting Making Connections **Skill:** Author's Point of View	The /o/ and /aw/ Sounds Drafting Verbs	

Getting Started

Preparing to Use

SRA

OpenCourt READING

This section provides an overview of classroom management issues and introductory activities that explain the function of the ***SRA/Open Court Reading*** program elements and how to use them.

Introductory Lessons

The major goals of the **Getting Started** introductory lessons are:

- to help students review and restart those skills learned in earlier grade levels.
- to help you obtain a clear picture of your students' strengths, needs, and prior learning.

Why a Special Getting Started Section?

Reading programs are often set up as if the first day of a new school year happens the day after the last day of the previous school year. This approach ignores the fact that students have approximately two months between the end of one school year and the beginning of the next. *SRA/Open Court Reading* recognizes this fact, and the fact that many students do little during those two months to retain and strengthen the skills and knowledge they acquired during the previous school year. This special **Getting Started** section is a quick review of important reading skills that will remind students of previous learning and get them ready for learning in the new school year.

These lessons also introduce key elements of the program, such as the Word Bank, Discussion, Writing Seminar, Concept/Question Board, and Writing Center in context.

In addition, the **Getting Started** section offers you an effective way to evaluate what your students already know and what they need to know in order to be successful in your class. This knowledge will allow you to base your reading instruction on fact rather than on assumptions, giving you and the students an opportunity to build on previous learning and to learn new and vital skills.

Most important, the **Getting Started** activities allow students to begin Unit 1 of regular instruction knowing that they possess the necessary skills.

Pacing

Whereas the *SRA/Open Court Reading Student Anthology* lessons are intended to fill three to five days, the five **Getting Started** lessons are presented in a daily lesson format and should be completed in about a week. You may spend more or less time on a specific lesson, depending on the needs of your students. If your students had the *SRA/Open Court Reading* program in the past, they should move quickly. These students should soon remember and start using the skills they learned in earlier grade levels.

The atmosphere should be relaxed, and both you and the students should view **Getting Started** as a period of rediscovery before taking on the new challenges of this grade level. Point out to students that the purposes of the lessons are, first, to review quickly what they learned the previous year, and, second, to give them a preview of the kind of wonderful stories they will read in this grade level.

Organizing Your Classroom

Reading

For students to become more than competent decoders, they must become strategic readers. That is, they must learn how to think about what they read and to use specific reading strategies and behaviors. Teachers help students become strategic readers by modeling the key reading strategies used by expert readers and by providing them with multiple opportunities to read fine literature. First-rate reading selections illustrate for students the best possible use of language and stimulate them to think about, write about, and discuss important ideas and concepts.

Oral Reading

Reading aloud is one of the best ways for students to develop their reading skills. In the course of the daily lessons, students will read orally from the ***Student Anthology*** selections. To promote students' reading growth, however, you will want multiple opportunities for oral reading. For example, you may:

- ask students to reread in pairs the anthology selections.
- set aside a period of time each day for oral reading of trade books.
- set up a home reading log, asking parents to read with their students.
- have students partner-read content area texts from other subjects your class is studying.

However you do it, you will find that every minute of oral reading by students pays off in terms of reading growth.

On a regular basis, take time to listen to students as they read favorite stories and books aloud. Listening to students read from an anthology selection provides you with information about their ability to manage the vocabulary and concepts of the text, as well as to gauge their reading fluency. Listening to students read orally allows you to evaluate their developing fluency and to identify particular areas with which they need more work. To complement these activities, you may also want to listen to students read books they have selected for themselves. This will give you insights into their taste in reading materials, their own opinion of their reading ability, as well as their reading progress.

Reading Area

Provide as many books as possible for your classroom Reading Area. During the course of the year the students will be asked to do much reading on specific subjects. Prepare your classroom ahead of time by bringing in books on the concepts or themes the students will be studying. You may choose to order the ***Leveled Classroom Library*** that accompanies the program or you may decide to provide your own library. In either case, you should encourage students to bring in books that they have enjoyed and want to share with their classmates.

Listening Area

Each selection in the ***Student Anthology*** is recorded on audiocassette and CD for use in your classroom. As you read each selection, encourage students to listen to the recording during Workshop. Provide one or two tape recorders or CD players that work both with and without earphones. In this way, individual students may listen to selections without disturbing the rest of the class. You will also be able to play the selections for the whole class if you choose.

You should also encourage students to record their own stories, then share these stories with their classmates.

Writing

Reading and writing are interwoven processes, and each helps build and strengthen the other. Throughout the year, students do a tremendous amount of writing, both independently and collaboratively. They write for an array of purposes and audiences. Extended writing includes stories and various nonfiction pieces such as research reports, biographies, persuasive papers, and letters. In addition, they write daily in the form of note taking, making lists, and making journal entries.

To assure success in writing, the students will need:

- **A Writer's Notebook**
  Each student should provide his or her own Writer's Notebook. This journal can be a three-ring binder with tabbed sections; however, a spiral notebook with sections will work also.

- **A Writing Folder**
  Students should be encouraged continually to revise and edit their writing. Each student should have a folder in which to keep this writing-in-progress. Any pocket folder will work for this purpose; however, you may choose to order the **Writing Folders** that accompany the **SRA/Open Court Reading** program. In addition to pockets to hold student writing, these folders contain a list of proofreading marks and tips for revising that students will find useful.

- **A Writing Portfolio**
  An artist's portfolio contains pieces that the artist considers the best of his or her work. Help students to develop a similar portfolio of their writing. From time to time, hold conferences with individual students so that they can show you the work they have put in their portfolios and explain what they particularly like about the pieces they have chosen to keep.

  You should keep your own portfolio for each student in which you place samples of written work that show the student's progress throughout the year.

Writing Area

The Writing Area should contain materials students can use to write and illustrate their work and to facilitate the students' efforts as they work together on unit investigations, including:

- pencil and crayons
- pens
- white paper
- colored paper
- old magazines they can cut up
- scissors
- staplers
- reference books such as dictionaries and encyclopedias.
- computers—preferably with Internet access. The SRA Home Page (see www.sra4kids.com) includes materials specifically related to the themes the students are studying.
- books on the themes the students are studying. You may choose to order the **Leveled Classroom Library** that accompanies the program. In addition, bibliographies of additional related books can be found in the unit overviews of the **Teacher's Editions.**

Inquiry: Reflection and Investigation

In **SRA/Open Court Reading**, lessons are integrated through extensive reading, writing, and discussion. In turn, the lessons are organized into learning units, with each selection in a unit adding more information or a different perspective to the students' growing knowledge of a theme or concept.

Some units allow students to expand their perspectives on universal themes such as kindness, courage, perseverance, and friendship by relating what they read to their own experiences.

Other units involve students in the research process, giving them the tools they need to discover and learn on their own and as part of a collaborative group. Inquiry activities provide students with a systematic structure for investigation that is driven by their own interests and conjectures.

All units are designed to help students:

- deepen their comprehension by enabling them to apply the skills they are learning to texts and activities of their own choosing.

- synthesize and organize what they are learning in order to present their findings to their classmates.
- determine suitable avenues of inquiry and methods of presentation.
- become more independent and responsible about their time and efforts.
- work efficiently in collaborative groups.

Concept/Question Board

One of the primary goals of *SRA/Open Court Reading* is to help you and your students form a community of learners. To do this, sharing information is essential. The Concept/Question Board is a bulletin board or chart. The students can share their growing knowledge about a unit theme or concept by posting on the Board newspaper clippings, magazine articles, information taken from the Internet, photographs, and other items that might be of interest to or help for their classmates. As the class progresses through a unit, the Board serves as the place where common interests become evident. As these interests emerge, the students can use them as the basis for forming collaborative groups to investigate ideas in greater depth.

In addition, the Board gives students an outlet for questions that arise as they read on their own. The questions can be written directly on a sheet of paper attached to the Board, or they can be written on separate slips of paper and pinned to it. Self-sticking notepads can also be used. The Concept/Question Board lets students know that questions are not problems but a way of learning. Questions thus become a springboard to further investigation. Collaborative groups can be formed around common questions.

Concept/Question Board

Cooperation and Competition

Concept | Question

The Board should change constantly, reflecting the developing and changing interests of the class. For the **Getting Started** section you can give the Board a title, such as "Reading and Writing."

Differentiating Instruction: Workshop

Workshop is integral to *SRA/Open Court Reading*. It is during this time, which you designate as a part of each class day, that students gain the experience of managing their own learning process. During Workshop, students work on their own or collaboratively to practice and review material taught in the lessons or to complete projects of their own choosing. As the students gradually take more responsibility for their work, they learn to set learning goals, to make decisions about the use of time and materials, and to collaborate with classmates. Of equal importance, Workshop gives you a designated time each day to work with students one-on-one or in small groups.

During Workshop, your students can:

- read to each other for pleasure and to increase fluency.
- work independently and in small collaborative groups on their investigations.
- work on unfinished writing projects.
- work on any unfinished projects or assignments they have.
- assess what projects they have that need work, prioritize their time, and direct their own efforts.

During Workshop, you can:

- work with individuals and small groups who have shown a need for additional instruction.
- listen to individuals read in order to assess informally their progress and help them gain fluency.
- conduct writing conferences with individual students to discuss their progress as writers.

The Reading, Listening, and Writing Areas will be used extensively during Workshop. If possible, equip these areas with furniture that is easy to move and will allow for both independent work and small group work.

Getting Started Checklist

This checklist will help you be prepared for the school year. Look back over the Getting Started section if you have any questions about these program elements.

- ○ **Organize Student Anthologies and Workbooks**
- ○ **Set Up Reading Area**
- ○ **Establish Listening Area**
- ○ **Plan for Discussions**
- ○ **Plan for Writing Notebook**
- ○ **Establish Writing Folder**
- ○ **Establish Writing Area**
- ○ **Develop Concept/Question Board**
- ○ **Plan for Workshop**

Day 1

Getting Acquainted

Have students introduce themselves to each other. Have students tell which of the other students they have had in their class before. Encourage new students to the school to tell a little about themselves—where they came from, what school they went to, etc.

Reading

Background Knowledge

To activate the students' background knowledge, have them discuss what they know about reading. List their comments on the board or on paper.

Encourage students to bring to class their favorite books or stories. Each day, invite a volunteer to read a story. You might want to tell students to practice reading their stories out loud before they read them for the class.

Listeners should be encouraged to politely ask for clarification whenever unfamiliar words or ideas are presented in the reading. Learning to ask politely for assistance should always be fostered during reading.

Discussion

Discussion is an integral part of learning. Through discussion, students are exposed to different points of view and reactions to text. They also learn to express their thoughts and opinions coherently as well as to respect the ideas and opinions of others.

Listening and responding to each other's ideas and questions is fundamental to learning. Throughout the program students are expected to listen and respond to each other—during Writing Seminar, collaborative activities, exploration of the unit concepts—not just in a discussion about a story. Talk about what a discussion is and what is expected of participants during a discussion. Students must listen to what others are saying and respond to what is being said. Students should not interrupt, raise their hands when they want to say something, ask

questions of each other, not talk while others are speaking, take turns, and respond to the question or idea rather than going off on a different or unrelated thought or tangent.

Handing off

Through a process called *handing off*, students learn to take the primary responsibility for holding and controlling a discussion. *Handing off* simply means that each student who responds in a discussion is responsible for drawing another student into the discussion.

During this initial lesson, you may want to begin a discussion by asking a question or making a statement. Have a student respond to your question, ask a question, or make a comment of his or her own, calling on another student to respond or react.

Concept/Question Board

Encourage students to add to the Concept/Question Board throughout the **Getting Started** lessons. They can write what they know about reading, writing, and learning, find articles and pictures, or add information about their favorite books.

Talk about reading and any problems the students had learning to read. Ask what they read, what they liked, and what they learned. Encourage students to ask questions as well. Write these on pieces of paper and put them on the Concept/Question Board.

Writing

The writing process will be formally introduced in the first unit. Talking about the process here will help you evaluate your students' understanding of writing. Talk about the idea that one of the most important things that good writers do is take time to think before they write. They think about what they know, what they want to write about, and whether they need to get more information. Have the students talk about reading, problems they have had, favorite stories they have read, and the like. Make a list of possible writing ideas and keep it for tomorrow. Tell the students that they will start to think about these ideas and that tomorrow you will review them and add any more ideas if the students have them.

Day 2

Reading

Ask students to share some of the stories or books they have brought in. If any of the students are ready, have them read aloud a story to the rest of the class. Start a Word Bank with any words the students have difficulty with. Tell students that the Word Bank will grow as the year goes on and that in addition to problematic words, they will add words that have to do with particular ideas or concepts and words that they particularly like.

Discussion

Quickly review what good participants do during a discussion. Remind the students of the discussion they had yesterday and how they led the discussion using *handing off*. Once again, you may have to get the students started with questions or statements such as, "That was interesting, tell me what you like best about the story." When the first student is finished responding, he or she should select the next student to continue the discussion.

Concept/Question Board

Have students place any new questions or comments they have about reading and writing on the Concept/Question Board. Be sure to note any articles, books, or pictures any of the students have brought in and put on the Board.

Writing

Writing Area

Discuss with the students the purposes of the Writing Area. Walk the students through the different materials you have in the center: pencils, crayons, markers, pens, white paper, colored paper, old magazines for ideas and illustrations, scissors, staplers, and dictionaries and a thesaurus as reference tools.

Writing Folder

Distribute the ***SRA/Open Court Reading Writing Folder*** to the students. Have the students write their names on the folders. Give the students time to look over the folders and comment on them. Tell the students that they will use these folders all year to hold the writing pieces they are working on.

If you didn't order the ***SRA/Open Court Reading Writing Folder,*** have students each bring a pocket folder to use as a writing folder.

Drafting

Review the ideas for writing that the students generated yesterday and ask if there are new ideas that they would like to add to the list. Explain to the students that after writers think about what they might want to write, they begin writing a first draft. Tell the students that they don't have to worry about this being neat or perfect. Encourage students to leave a line or two between each line they write. This will give them room to make changes later. They will have a chance to rewrite their story after they have read it and made any changes they want. The point of writing in **Getting Started** is for you to get a sense of the students' knowledge of the writing process and writing skills including spelling, grammar, and mechanics.

Have the students choose a topic from the list or a topic of their own and begin writing. As the students are writing, conference with individual students. Holding conferences with students helps them identify and solve problems. Conferences during this drafting phase help students identify and refine a topic. This is also a good time to observe students as they are writing. Remember, as you are conferencing:

- You don't have to meet with every student every day.
- Conferences should be brief.
- Don't take ownership of the student's work.
- Encourage students to identify what is good and what problems they are having.
- Leave students with a positive comment.

At the end of the writing time, have the students put their drafts in their writing folders and either put their folders in their desks or in a file box in the Writing Area.

Day 3

Reading

Give students the grade level pretest. Tell students that this test is a little different from others they have taken; they will not get a grade on this test. This test is to help you know what the students remember from last year. There will be another test like this at the end of the year that will show how much they have learned this year. If the students don't know some of the answers, tell them not to worry. There is a lot to learn about reading and writing and they will be able to meet the challenge and do it by the end of the year.

Writing

Continue Writing

Remind students of the Writing Area. During writing today, they can go to the center if they need any materials. Have the students continue the story they began yesterday. Conference with students, noting those that might have something to share during Seminar which will be introduced today. Look for students with interesting ideas, creative topics, extended sentences, etc.

Writing Seminar

Introduce the students to the idea of Seminar. Seminar is a time when the students will be able to share their work with each other. This is a time when two or three students will share their work with the class and then their classmates will have time to give feedback. Seminar participants must listen carefully and politely, just as they do during discussion and *handing off*. When the author is finished reading, the other students should say something positive about what the author wrote. They can tell what they liked and why; how the author's story made them feel good; and what the author's story reminded them of. You may need to model this in the beginning by telling what you liked about the story and why. Be sure to let students know that over the next few days everyone will have a chance to share their stories.

Differentiating Instruction: Workshop

Introduce the idea of Workshop. Workshop is a period of time each day in which the students will work collaboratively or independently to practice and review material taught in the lesson or to complete projects related to the unit theme. Tell the students that every day, there will be a time when they will be working without you on their own or in small groups. During that time, they may be working on materials that you assign or they may be partner reading, reading independently, working on writing or a unit investigation, or meeting with you.

Meet with the students and establish rules for Workshop. These might include:

- Be polite.
- Share with others.
- Use your inside voice (or whisper).
- Take only the material you need.
- When you are finished, clean up and put away the materials you used.

You may want to post these rules, review them periodically, and revise them if necessary.

Reading Area

The students have already learned about the Writing Area. Introduce the Reading Area today. In this area, students will find books, magazines, newspapers, and other reading materials. Students should be encouraged to bring in favorite books and share them in the center. Let students know they can come and choose a book any time they have free time, not just during Workshop.

Concept/Question Board

While you are not reading with the students today, give them a few minutes to add to the Concept/Question Board.

Day 4

Reading

In preparation for beginning the first unit, you might ask the students if they have read any stories about the unit theme. Encourage the students who have read such stories to retell them and tell what they thought of them. Gently encourage students to be specific in their comments. Instead of settling for "I liked the story," have the students elaborate on their thoughts by explaining what it was about the story that they liked.

Writer's Notebook

Throughout the course of the year, your students will be asked to do a tremendous amount of writing. Reading and writing are closely interwoven and each will help build and strengthen the other. In order to assure the best results and success in writing, the students will need a Writer's Notebook. Each student should provide his or her own Writer's Notebook. This notebook can be a three-ring binder with tabbed sections; however, a spiral notebook with sections works also. Use time during Getting Started to let the students prepare their Writer's Notebooks. The following sections are suggested:

- **Response Journal** in which students will write a personal response to the literature they read
- **Vocabulary** in which students will record vocabulary or spelling words they need to learn
- **Writing Ideas** in which students record ideas for future writing they want to do as well as ideas gained during brainstorming sessions
- **Personal Dictionary** in which students record concept related words or any new word they learn and want to remember

Take time to have students put together their Writer's Notebooks. If some students don't finish, have them complete their notebooks during Workshop.

Listening Area

Remind the students of the Writing Area and the materials that are there and the fact that students can use them at any time during writing, Workshop or free time. Today introduce the Listening Area. Tell students that there will be an audiocassette and CD of all the selections in their anthology.

Workshop

Review the rules for Workshop. Tell the students that today they can continue work on their stories or they may want to begin a new story. They can also go to the Reading Area, Listening Area, or complete or decorate their Writer's Notebooks. Since this is the first time students are involved in Workshop, you may want to assign students to the different areas. Circulate as students are working.

Concept/Question Board

Give students a few minutes to add to the Concept/Question Board information about what they learned today or any questions they have.

Day 5

Reading

If you have favorite stories about the unit theme, read them to the students. As you read these stories, encourage discussion about how they are alike and how they are different. Stories on the same topic generally approach the subject differently, which adds new perspectives. The ability of the students to see these different perspectives will be very important to them as they progress through their school careers.

Writing

Today you will introduce the students to revision and proofreading. Have one or two students read their stories in Seminar. As students are reading their stories, listen for short sentences that could be extended. After students have read their stories, encourage them to extend some of the sentences. Explain that extending sentences makes stories more interesting for the reader. Have students work on revising their stories by extending sentences. Show students how they can do this by putting in a carat (^) and writing their extensions in the blank lines they have left. Conference with individual students or small groups of students as they are revising their stories. At the end, have several students share sentences they have extended.

Proofreading

Today, students will also be informally introduced to proofreading. Tell students that when proofreading, if they find a mistake or problem, they should circle the word and write it correctly. Explain to students that they will proofread their stories to be sure the words are spelled correctly, that they have used capitals and punctuation correctly, and that they have used words correctly.

Sentence Lifting

Sentence Lifting is an effective and engaging way to model proofreading using sentences taken from the students' writing. Students are expected to identify and correct their own errors. Since you should use both sentences with errors and sentences without errors, the students see examples of correct writing. The focus is a positive one and helps students understand that all writers make mistakes and need to improve on their writing.

In preparation for sentence lifting, look through the students' writing folders for common errors in capitalization, punctuation, or spelling. Select some sentences that contain errors and others that don't. Copy the sentences on the board or on an overhead transparency.

Read the first sentence with a mistake. Have students identify what needs to be changed. Circle the errors and have the students tell you how to write it correctly. Help the students with spellings they are unsure of. Point out any errors that the students miss.

Give students additional time to proofread their own papers and make changes. Conference with students who need help. You may wish to spend additional time with them during Workshop.

Concept/Question Board

Give the students a few minutes to add to the Concept/Question Board information about what they learned today or any questions they have.

Workshop

Remind students that as they begin their unit investigations, they will need resources to help them. Show students what has been supplied for inquiry purposes in the Writing Area and where the supplies are kept.

By this time, students should be comfortable with the set up of the room, acquainted with you and each other, and ready to move into the anthology.

Level 5 • Unit 1

Cooperation and Competition

UNIT
I
Cooperation and Competition

Sometimes we need to cooperate with each other to get things done. Sometimes, though, we find ourselves competing with each other. Sometimes we need to do both at the same time—cooperate with teammates while competing against an opposing team. Cooperation and competition play important roles in our lives and they take on many different faces. How do you see competition and cooperation at work in your life?

18

19

Exploring the Theme

Introduction

Cooperation and competition are part of our daily lives. By the time most students reach the fifth grade, they have spent many hours working together, being part of a team, and helping others. They have also learned a great deal about competition in sports and school, among friends and foes.

This unit is designed to help students develop a deeper understanding of cooperation and competition, their contrasting and complementary natures, and how they help us reach our goals. Students will encounter story characters who struggle with issues surrounding these themes. Through these characters, they will vicariously experience and reflect upon the many faces of cooperation and competition, and learn to make them positive forces in their lives.

Teacher's Edition page numbers correspond to page numbers in the *Student Anthology.*

Investigation and Inquiry Goals

The concept goals for this unit are:

- To learn the motives and specific situations that call for cooperation and competition.
- To learn how cooperation often leads to positive outcomes.
- To learn how different characters react to competition.
- To discuss how competition and cooperation affect relationships.
- To build thematic links between the selections.

Learning Goals

Within each of the general investigation goals, a number of more specific learning goals are pursued. Students will:

- **learn to read.**
- **extend knowledge and understanding** of the complex natures of cooperation and competition and the various ways they are expressed.
- use **comprehension skills and strategies** to understand texts and relate these texts to the theme.
- **explore the theme concepts** through interviewing, debating, researching, and experiencing.
- **form and organize questions** about cooperation and competition.
- **incorporate visual aids into presentations** about chosen topics related to the theme.
- **present their ideas through various means** including written text, drawing, oral presentations, and discussion.
- **learn to use different writing formats**, such as journal entries and charts, to formulate and express what they have learned about the unit theme.

Teacher Tip The concepts of cooperation and competition raise a wide variety of questions. Model for the students asking yourself questions like the following:

- ✔ What motivates people to compete and cooperate?
- ✔ Which of these traits do I value more, or do I believe they have equal value?
- ✔ What were my own experiences related to competition and cooperation when I attended school, took part in extracurricular activities, and interacted with my family?
- ✔ What do I want my students to learn about cooperation and competition, and how can they best learn it?

Teacher Tip There are two general types of units included in the *Open Court 2002* program at all grade levels. One type of unit is the Investigation unit, which focuses on reading for information. The other type is the Inquiry unit, which focuses on a narrative exploration of some universal theme of relevance to students. We begin the fifth grade program with this latter type of unit. Students are encouraged to reflect on the theme and relate it to their own lives. They are also given a chance to learn about the literature that embodies this theme and how it is constructed. Finally, they are offered an opportunity to apply this knowledge to the task of generating a product of their own choosing.

Exploring the Theme

Supporting Student Investigations

Students are encouraged throughout *Open Court Reading* to deepen their knowledge of each of the themes presented. In learning more about cooperation and competition, students will need to talk to people about cooperation and competition as well as read stories and articles that revolve around the theme of cooperation and competition.

Encourage students to use their personal experiences to interpret the literature they read on the topic of cooperation and competition. Because it is also important for students to extend their thinking and for their views to be challenged and developed, encourage them to use this literature to reinterpret their personal experiences.

Explain to students that they will gain a better understanding of cooperation and competition. Students will be choosing from these investigation options.

- A literature search to pursue a question or idea about cooperation and competition. Discussion or writing might follow.
- A chart of story characters and their acts of cooperation and competition.
- A role-playing game to work on having members of a group cooperate during competition.
- A debate on an issue related to cooperation and competition. (Debaters would form teams. They would be required to follow some basic rules of debate, providing reasoned support for their sides of the issue.)
- An advice column dealing with problems that arise from a lack of cooperation or an excess of competition.
- An interview with someone who has direct experience with cooperation and competition, such as a team coach or an elected official.
- A picture or photo essay about cooperation and competition.

Unit Investigations

Unit investigations are student-driven and should emerge from students' interests, encouraged or ignited by reading and class discussions. The investigations should involve reading beyond program material and address the conceptual aims of the unit.

Suggested Activities

The suggested activities below are intended to support the unit investigation. Students may choose to do a personal experience story or a playlet in order to express their growing understanding of cooperation and competition. Activities that may help provide input for this project include:

- Discussions of cooperation and competition, as these concepts relate to the reading selections, students' experiences, and others' daily lives.
- Presentations of opinions on cooperation and competition, in the form of speeches, visual presentations, rewrites of the story, or comic books.
- Interviewing classmates, friends, and family members on their experiences with cooperation and competition.
- Listing activities that would not be possible without cooperation between people.
- Experiencing cooperation and competition firsthand through organization and preparation for a spelling contest.
- Debating the statement "It's not whether you win or lose, it's how you play the game."
- Listening and responding to a speaker from a nonprofit organization.

	OVERVIEW OF SELECTION	LINK TO THE THEME	UNIT ACTIVITIES	SUPPORTING STUDENT INVESTIGATIONS
Lesson I *Class President*	■ This realistic fiction selection is about two students who compete in a class election. The story illustrates that altruism can champion over self-interest.	■ Cooperative efforts tend to win more friends than competitiveness.	■ Generate questions to investigate	■ Investigation activities ■ Parts of the library
Lesson 2 *The Marble Champ*	■ This humorous fiction selection is about a girl who practices for a marble championship until her thumb muscle increases in size.	■ Commitment and practice help us succeed in competitions.	■ Formulate questions and problems	■ Investigation activities ■ Interviewing
Lesson 3 *Juggling*	■ This realistic fiction selection is about a boy who has to juggle family and team commitments. When all those affected pull together, he is able to fulfill both of his obligations.	■ Demands on our time sometimes conflict, but conflicting needs can often be met through cooperative efforts.	■ Make conjectures	■ Investigation activities ■ Note taking
Lesson 4 *The Abacus Contest*	■ This realistic fiction selection illustrates the pressures of competition and explores how competition affects individuals differently.	■ Competition can be both a worry and a stimulating challenge.	■ Establish investigation needs	■ Investigation activities ■ Using charts and diagrams
Lesson 5 *S.O.R. Losers*	■ This humorous and thoughtful fiction selection questions the assumption that the only goal of a team is to win.	■ Cooperation in competitive situations supports individuals.	■ Establish investigation plans	■ Investigation activities ■ Using multiple resources
Lesson 6 *Founders of the Children's Rain Forest*	■ This nonfiction selection chronicles the saving of a rain forest, from the beginning idea through the cooperation and planning needed to buy a large piece of rain forest land.	■ Cooperation can lead to positive results. ■ When working together to solve a problem, all people must participate. ■ Cooperation can lead to solutions of major problems.	■ Present investigation findings	■ Investigation activities ■ Using visual aids

Student Materials

Student Anthology
Pages 18–85

Inquiry Journal
Pages 5–33

Writer's Workbook
Pages 2–5

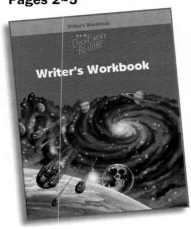

Comprehension and Language Arts Skills
Pages 2–33

Spelling and Vocabulary Skills
Pages 2–25

Language Arts Handbook

Additional Materials
- Listening Library
- Program Assessment
- Unit 1 Assessment
- Writing Folder
- Student Research Assistant
- Science/Social Studies Connection

Meeting Individual Needs
- ELD Workbook
- Intervention Workbook
- Reteach
- Challenge
- Leveled Classroom Library

Teacher Materials

Teacher's Edition, Book 1
Pages 18–99P

Home Connection
Pages 1–13

**Read Aloud
"Babe Didrikson"**
Pages 19N–19P

**Comprehension and
Language Arts Skills
Teacher's Edition**
Pages 2–33

**Spelling and Vocabulary
Skills Teacher's Edition**
Pages 2–25

**Writer's Workbook
Teacher's Edition**
Pages 2–5

Additional Materials

- Overhead Transparencies
- Teacher's Professional
  Guides
- Teacher Read Aloud
  Anthology

Meeting Individual Needs

- ELD Guide
- ELD Glossary
- Intervention Guide
- Intervention Annotated
  Bibliography
- Reteach Teacher's Edition
- Challenge Teacher's Edition

PROGRAM RESOURCES

Leveled Classroom Library*

Easy	Average	Advanced

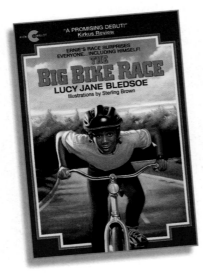

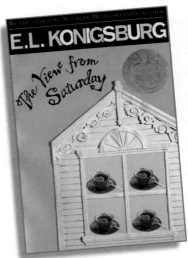

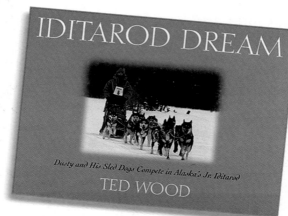

Bibliography**

Earth Keepers by Joan Anderson and George Ancona

Flood: Wrestling the Mississippi by Patricia Lauber

The Great Race by David Bouchard

Philip Hall Likes Me. I Reckon Maybe. by Bette Greene

Note: Teachers should preview any trade books and videos for appropriateness in their classrooms before recommending them to students.

* These books, which all support the unit theme Cooperation and Competition, are part of a 36-book *Leveled Classroom Library* available for purchase from SRA/McGraw-Hill.

** Check libraries or bookstores for availability.

TECHNOLOGY

Web Connections

www.sra4kids.com

Cooperation and Competition Web sites
Information about Cooperation and Competition and links to sites concerning cooperation and competition can be found at: www.sra4kids.com

CD-ROMs

* **OCR Spelling**
SRA/McGRAW-HILL, 2002

Use this software for extra spelling review in the unit.

* **Research Assistant**
SRA/McGRAW-HILL, 2002

As students continue their investigation of Cooperation and Competition, have them use the Research program to help them organize and share their findings.

* **Student Writing and Research Center**
THE LEARNING COMPANY

Students can use this word processing software to get ideas, research, draft, revise, edit, and publish their Writing Process Strategies activities in this unit.

Computer Skills

* **Basic Computer Skills**
The **SRA Basic Computer Skills** program can be used to help students develop computer skills within the context of the unit theme.

Videocassettes

* *Commodore Perry in the Land of the Shogun*
Travel with Matthew Perry on his 1853 expedition to Japan, during which he convinced both Americans and Japanese to overcome their fears of each other's differences. 26 min.

* *Jackie Robinson*
Find out about the courageous man whose spectacular baseball career paved the way for racial equality in professional sports. 19 min.

* *Meet the Caldecott Illustrator: Jerry Pinkney*
Learn about the life of this illustrator and how he works in cooperation with authors to create the images that bring text to life. 21 min.

* *Philip Hall Likes Me. I Reckon Maybe.*
Beth realizes that she's too competitive to let the boy she likes keep outdoing her. 28 min.

Audiocassette/CD-ROM

* **Listening Library: Cooperation and Competition**
SRA/McGRAW-HILL, 2002

Students will enjoy listening to the selections they have read. Have them listen during Workshop.

Titles preceded by an asterisk (✳) are available through SRA/McGraw-Hill. Other titles can be obtained by contacting the publisher listed with the title.

UNIT SKILLS OVERVIEW

	WORD KNOWLEDGE	COMPREHENSION	LITERARY ELEMENTS
Lesson 1 *Class President* **Genre: Realistic Fiction**	■ Derivative of root word *compete* ■ Consonant plus *r* blends ■ Spellings of the /er/ sound ■ Spellings of the /a/ sound	**Strategies** ■ Making Connections ■ Predicting ■ Summarizing **Skill** ■ Drawing Conclusions	■ Character Analysis
Lesson 2 *The Marble Champ* **Genre: Realistic Fiction**	■ Synonyms ■ Regular plurals ■ /n/ sound spelled *kn* ■ Spellings of the /e/ sound	**Strategies** ■ Asking Questions ■ Making Connections ■ Visualizing **Skill** ■ Making Inferences	■ Setting
Lesson 3 *Juggling* **Genre: Realistic Fiction**	■ Closed compounds ■ Consonant digraph *th* ■ *s*-consonant blends ■ Spellings of the /o/ and /aw/ sounds	**Strategies** ■ Asking Questions ■ Predicting ■ Making Connections **Skill** ■ Author's Point of View	■ Genre: Realistic Fiction
Lesson 4 *The Abacus Contest* **Genre: Realistic Fiction**	■ Math content-area words ■ /ow/ sound ■ Long e spelled *ea* ■ Spellings of the /i/ sound	**Strategies** ■ Summarizing ■ Monitoring and Clarifying ■ Predicting **Skill** ■ Sequence	■ Conflict
Lesson 5 *S.O.R. Losers* **Genre: Realistic Fiction**	■ Frequently misspelled words ■ Long e spelled *ea* ■ /ch/ sound spelled *ch* ■ Spellings of the /u/ sound	**Strategies** ■ Summarizing ■ Visualizing ■ Asking Questions **Skills** ■ Compare and Contrast ■ Author's Point of View	■ Plot/Story Structure
Lesson 6 *Founders of the Children's Rain Forest* **Genre: Narrative Nonfiction**	■ Antonyms ■ /ks/ sound spelled *x* ■ /ch/ sound spelled *tch* ■ Review of short vowels	**Strategies** ■ Asking Questions ■ Predicting ■ Monitoring and Clarifying ■ Monitoring and Adjusting Reading Speed **Skill** ■ Author's Purpose	■ Influencing Perspectives

INQUIRY	WORD ANALYSIS	WRITING PROCESS STRATEGIES	ENGLISH LANGUAGE CONVENTIONS
■ Generating Ideas to Investigate ■ Parts of the Library	**Spelling** ■ The /a/ Sound **Vocabulary** ■ Discovering Word Meanings	**Introduction to the Writing Process** ■ Getting Ideas	**Grammar, Usage, and Mechanics** ■ Nouns **Listening, Speaking, Viewing** ■ Listening: Understanding What We Hear **Penmanship** ■ Cursive Letters *i* and *t*
■ Formulating Questions and Problems ■ Interviewing	**Spelling** ■ The /e/ Sound **Vocabulary** ■ Context Clues	**Introduction to the Writing Process** ■ Prewriting	**Grammar, Usage, and Mechanics** ■ Pronouns **Listening, Speaking, Viewing** ■ Speaking: Speaking Clearly **Penmanship** ■ Cursive Letters *u* and *w*
■ Making Conjectures ■ Note Taking	**Spelling** ■ The /o/ and /aw/ Sounds **Vocabulary** ■ Word Parts	**Introduction to the Writing Process** ■ Drafting **Writer's Craft** ■ Figurative Language	**Grammar, Usage, and Mechanics** ■ Verbs **Listening, Speaking, Viewing** ■ Language: Using Appropriate Language **Penmanship** ■ Cursive Letters *r* and *s*
■ Establishing Investigation Needs ■ Using Charts and Diagrams	**Spelling** ■ The /i/ Sound **Vocabulary** ■ Dictionary Skills	**Introduction to the Writing Process** ■ Revising **Writer's Craft** ■ Sensory Description	**Grammar, Usage, and Mechanics** ■ Sentences **Listening, Speaking, Viewing** ■ Viewing: Viewing the Media **Penmanship** ■ Cursive Letters *p* and *j*
■ Establishing Investigation Plans ■ Using Multiple Resources	**Spelling** ■ The /u/ Sound **Vocabulary** ■ Thesaurus Skills	**Introduction to the Writing Process** ■ Revising **Writer's Craft** ■ Time and Order Words	**Grammar, Usage, and Mechanics** ■ Subjects and Predicates **Listening, Speaking, Viewing** ■ Interacting: Asking Questions **Penmanship** ■ Cursive Letters *a*, *c*, and *d*
■ Presenting Investigation Findings ■ Using Visual Aids	**Spelling** ■ Review Short Vowels **Vocabulary** ■ Word Mapping	**Introduction to the Writing Process** ■ Editing/Proofreading, Publishing	**Grammar, Usage, and Mechanics** ■ Review **Listening, Speaking, Viewing** ■ Presenting: Using Note Cards **Penmanship** ■ Cursive Letters *q*, *g*, and *o*

WORKSHOP

Differentiating Instruction

Explain to your students that there will be a time every day that they will be expected to work on activities. This time, called Workshop, will be devoted to collaborating on their investigations of unit concepts, working independently to meeting each of their individual needs. As students gradually take more and more responsibility during Workshop they will move from working only as a whole group to working on their own, in pairs, or in small groups independently.

Workshop assures that the needs of all students will be met, from those who require any extra help to the advanced learners. Encourage them all to become independent, self-motivated learners who

- make good use of their time.
- make decisions about activities, materials, and work.
- understand organization and care of materials.
- share and cooperate with others.
- adapt skills learned from direct teaching in self-teaching situations.

Workshop items and procedures are introduced to the whole group, through direct-teaching sessions. Then students are released gradually from directed-teaching to work independently. Early in the year, there will be the need for closer supervision than later in the year.

Students can make the best use of Workshop when

- a set of rules, such as be polite, share, and whisper, is posted and observed.
- a set of classroom materials necessary for the various activities is available.
- the physical organization of the classroom facilitates both independent and group activities.
- the teacher closely supervises this time.

Since students will be working on a variety of activities, you will be afforded time and opportunity to differentiate instruction to address the special needs of all students. At this time, you may want to reteach and reinforce previous lessons or preteach upcoming lessons with students who need help, or you might provide individual or small-group lessons related to the students' investigations.

Meeting Individual Needs

The following are examples of the types of activities that you might have going on during Workshop:

 Collaborating on Investigation Students will meet in small groups to formulate questions about the unit concept, agree on individual job assignments, and share and evaluate materials for their investigations.

 Preteaching/Reteaching If you have students who would benefit from preteaching or reteaching, you could

- help individuals or small groups either on past lessons or on the next lessons they will tackle.
- match students who could benefit from extra help with appropriate peer tutors. Strong students with average students and weaker students with you are the best matches.
- Use **Reteach** for students who show a basic understanding of the lesson but need more practice. Use **Intervention** for students who, even after extra practice, exhibit a lack of understanding of the lesson concepts.

 Independent Reading Students may find and read other books by authors featured in the unit or read the books listed in the **Leveled Classroom Library.** Students should also be reading books 30 minutes daily outside the classroom.

 Reading Roundtable During this time students may share information about additional books they have read independently and discuss how they support the unit theme or simply what they thought of them: Did they enjoy the book? Why? or Why not? Would they recommend the books? Reading Roundtable is much like a book club in which all members read the same book and share their reactions to the story or book.

 Writing Seminar This is a time students can share their writing and conference with peers.

For more information on Workshop, see the Program Appendix.

Setting Up the Classroom

Setting up your classroom to accommodate differentiating instruction activities will help assure that Workshop progresses smoothly and effectively. While setting up your classroom, keep in mind the primary activities of Workshop. Since students will be doing both independent and collaborative reading and writing, it is suggested that you provide the following space and materials:

- A reading area supplied with books and magazines.
- A writing and publishing area supplied with paper, pencils, rulers, colored markers, crayons, tape, string, and scissors.
- A listening area that includes a tape recorder (or CD-player) and audiotapes (or CDs) of stories, poems, and songs for students to hear. You might want to provide blank tapes and encourage the students to use them for writing projects or for other investigations.

Students work much better independently when there is adequate space and a sense of order. The room arrangement below is one possibility, but is not the only way to arrange your classroom, especially if space is an issue. The proposed arrangement provides for easy movement of the students, leaves a large open space on the floor for whole-class and individual activities, facilitates easy access for the teacher, and organizes the class into manageable sections. It also allows the placement of those with visual, auditory, and other impairments in advantageous positions near the front of the room. Students should not be grouped at desks or tables according to ability. They should be heterogeneously grouped.

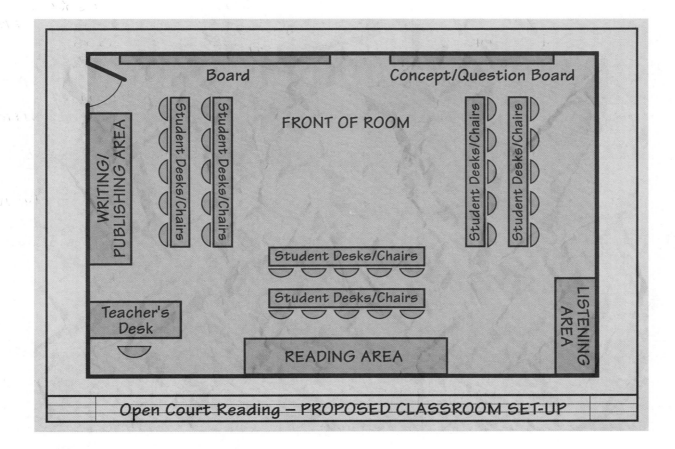

MEETING INDIVIDUAL NEEDS

	Reteach	ELL	Challenge	Intervention
Lesson 1 *Class President*	**Reading and Responding** ■ **Comprehension:** Drawing Conclusions **Language Arts** ■ **Vocabulary:** Discovering Word Meanings ■ **Spelling:** The /a/ Sound ■ **Grammar, Usage, and Mechanics:** Nouns	**Preparing to Read** ■ Preparing to Read **Reading and Responding** ■ Reading and Responding ■ Selection Vocabulary ■ Preread the Selection	**Reading and Responding** ■ **Comprehension:** Drawing Conclusions **Language Arts** ■ **Vocabulary:** Discovering Word Meanings ■ **Spelling:** The /a/ Sound ■ **Grammar, Usage, and Mechanics:** Nouns	**Preparing to Read** ■ Preparing to Read **Reading and Responding** ■ Reading and Responding ■ Selection Vocabulary ■ Preread the Selection ■ Predicting ■ Making Connections ■ Summarizing ■ Drawing Conclusions ■ Analyzing Character Traits
Lesson 2 *The Marble Champ*	**Reading and Responding** ■ **Comprehension:** Making Inferences **Language Arts** ■ **Vocabulary:** Context Clues ■ **Spelling:** The /e/ Sound ■ **Grammar, Usage, and Mechanics:** Pronouns	**Preparing to Read** ■ Word Knowledge **Reading and Responding** ■ Cultural Context ■ Selection Vocabulary ■ Preread the Selection	**Reading and Responding** ■ **Comprehension:** Making Inferences **Language Arts** ■ **Vocabulary:** Context Clues ■ **Spelling:** The /e/ Sound ■ **Grammar, Usage, and Mechanics:** Pronouns	**Preparing to Read** ■ Word Knowledge **Reading and Responding** ■ /n/ Sound Spelled *kn* ■ Selection Vocabulary ■ Preread the Selection ■ Making Connections ■ Asking Questions ■ Making Inferences
Lesson 3 *Juggling*	**Reading and Responding** ■ **Comprehension:** Author's Point of View **Language Arts** ■ **Vocabulary:** Word Parts ■ **Spelling:** The /o/ and /aw/ Sounds ■ **Grammar, Usage, and Mechanics:** Sentences ■ **Writer's Craft:** Figurative Language	**Preparing to Read** ■ Preparing to Read **Reading and Responding** ■ Word Meaning ■ Reading and Responding ■ Vocabulary ■ Preread the Selection	**Reading and Responding** ■ **Comprehension:** Author's Point of View **Language Arts** ■ **Vocabulary:** Word Parts ■ **Spelling:** The /o/ and /aw/ Sounds ■ **Grammar, Usage, and Mechanics:** Sentences ■ **Writer's Craft:** Figurative Language	**Preparing to Read** ■ Preparing to Read **Reading and Responding** ■ Consonant Digraphs ■ Reading and Responding ■ Selection Vocabulary ■ Preread the Selection ■ Predicting
Lesson 4 *The Abacus Contest*	**Reading and Responding** ■ **Comprehension:** Sequence **Language Arts** ■ **Vocabulary:** Dictionary Skills ■ **Spelling:** The /i/ Sound ■ **Grammar, Usage, and Mechanics:** Sentences ■ **Writer's Craft:** Sensory Description	**Preparing to Read** ■ Preparing to Read **Reading and Responding** ■ Reading and Responding ■ Preread the Selection ■ Summing Up and Asking Questions	**Reading and Responding** ■ **Comprehension:** Sequence **Language Arts** ■ **Vocabulary:** Dictionary Skills ■ **Spelling:** The /i/ Sound ■ **Grammar, Usage, and Mechanics:** Sentences ■ **Writer's Craft:** Sensory Description	**Preparing to Read** ■ Preparing to Read **Reading and Responding** ■ Reading and Responding ■ Preread the Selection ■ Clarifying
Lesson 5 *S.O.R. Losers*	**Reading and Responding** ■ **Comprehension:** Compare and Contrast **Language Arts** ■ **Vocabulary:** Thesaurus Skills ■ **Spelling:** The /u/ Sound ■ **Grammar, Usage, and Mechanics:** Subjects and Predicates ■ **Writer's Craft:** Time and Order Words	**Preparing to Read** ■ Preparing to Read **Reading and Responding** ■ Word Meaning ■ Cultural Context ■ Vocabulary ■ Preread the Selection ■ Asking and Answering Questions	**Reading and Responding** ■ **Comprehension:** Compare and Contrast **Language Arts** ■ **Vocabulary:** Thesaurus Skills ■ **Spelling:** The /u/ Sound ■ **Grammar, Usage, and Mechanics:** Subjects and Predicates ■ **Writer's Craft:** Time and Order Words	**Preparing to Read** ■ Preparing to Read ■ Frequently Misspelled Words **Reading and Responding** ■ Preread the Selection ■ Summarizing ■ Asking Questions
Lesson 6 *Founders of the Children's Rain Forest*	**Reading and Responding** ■ **Comprehension:** Author's Purpose **Language Arts** ■ **Vocabulary:** Word Mapping ■ **Spelling:** Review Short Vowels ■ **Grammar, Usage, and Mechanics:** Review ■ **Writers Craft:** Presentation	**Preparing to Read** ■ Word Meaning **Reading and Responding** ■ Reading and Responding ■ Preread the Selection	**Reading and Responding** ■ **Comprehension:** Author's Purpose **Language Arts** ■ **Vocabulary:** Word Mapping ■ **Spelling:** Review Short Vowels ■ **Grammar, Usage, and Mechanics:** Review ■ **Writers Craft:** Presentation	**Preparing to Read** ■ Antonyms ■ Preparing to Read **Reading and Responding** ■ Preread the Selection

Above are suggestions for adapting instruction to meet the individual needs of students. These are the same skills shown on Unit Skills Overview; however, these pages provide extra practice opportunities or enriching activities to meet the varied needs of students.

✦ **Informal Assessment**	**Progress Assessment**	✓ **Formal Assessment**	
*Comprehension Strategies, 20J, 20 *Theme Connection, 35 *Grammar, Usage, and Mechanics, 35H *Listening, Speaking, Viewing, 35I *Vocabulary, 35J *Penmanship, 35J	Comprehension and Language Arts Skills, 2–5 Reteach, 2–6 Challenge, 2–5 Spelling and Vocabulary Skills, 2–5 Inquiry Journal, 5–6, 8–9	Unit 1 Assessment ■ Lesson Assessment, 2–5 ■ Spelling Pretest, 26 ■ Spelling Final Test, 27 * Writing Process Strategies Rubrics, 35J * Research Rubrics, 20J	**Lesson 1**
*Comprehension Strategies, 36J, 36 *Theme Connection, 45 *Grammar, Usage, and Mechanics, 45H *Listening, Speaking, Viewing, 45I *Vocabulary, 45J *Penmanship, 45J	Comprehension and Language Arts Skills, 6–9 Reteach, 7–11 Challenge, 6–9 Writer's Workbook, 2 Spelling and Vocabulary Skills, 6–9 Inquiry Journal, 6, 10–14	Unit 1 Assessment ■ Lesson Assessment, 6–9 ■ Spelling Pretest, 28 ■ Spelling Final Test, 29 * Writing Process Strategies Rubrics, 45J * Research Rubrics, 36J	**Lesson 2**
*Comprehension Strategies, 48J, 48 *Theme Connection, 55 *Grammar, Usage, and Mechanics, 55H *Listening, Speaking, Viewing, 55I *Vocabulary, 55J *Penmanship, 55J	Comprehension and Language Arts Skills, 10–15 Reteach, 12–17 Challenge, 10–14 Writer's Workbook, 3 Spelling and Vocabulary Skills, 10–13 Inquiry Journal, 6, 15–19	Unit 1 Assessment ■ Lesson Assessment, 10–13 ■ Spelling Pretest, 30 ■ Spelling Final Test, 31 * Writing Process Strategies Rubrics, 55J * Research Rubrics, 48J	**Lesson 3**
*Comprehension Strategies, 58J, 58 *Theme Connection, 65 *Grammar, Usage, and Mechanics, 65H *Listening, Speaking, Viewing, 65I *Vocabulary, 65J *Penmanship, 65J	Comprehension and Language Arts Skills, 16–21 Reteach, 18–23 Challenge, 15–19 Spelling and Vocabulary Skills, 14–17 Inquiry Journal, 7, 20–23	Unit 1 Assessment ■ Lesson Assessment, 14–17 ■ Spelling Pretest, 32 ■ Spelling Final Test, 33 * Writing Process Strategies Rubrics, 65J * Research Rubrics, 58J	**Lesson 4**
*Comprehension Strategies, 66J, 66 *Theme Connection, 85 *Grammar, Usage, and Mechanics, 85H *Listening, Speaking, Viewing, 85I *Vocabulary, 85J *Penmanship, 85J	Comprehension and Language Arts Skills, 22–27 Reteach, 24–29 Challenge, 20–24 Writer's Workbook, 4 Spelling and Vocabulary Skills, 18–21 Inquiry Journal, 7, 24–27	Unit 1 Assessment ■ Lesson Assessment, 18–21 ■ Spelling Pretest, 34 ■ Spelling Final Test, 35 * Writing Process Strategies Rubrics, 85J * Research Rubrics, 66J	**Lesson 5**
*Comprehension Strategies, 86J, 86 *Theme Connection, 99 *Grammar, Usage, and Mechanics, 99H *Listening, Speaking, Viewing, 99I *Vocabulary, 99J *Penmanship, 99J	Comprehension and Language Arts Skills, 28–33 Reteach, 30–35 Challenge, 25–29 Writer's Workbook, 5 Spelling and Vocabulary Skills, 22–25 Inquiry Journal, 7, 28–33	Unit 1 Assessment ■ Lesson Assessment, 22–25 ■ Spelling Pretest, 36 ■ Spelling Final Test, 37 * Writing Process Strategies Rubrics, 99J * Research Rubrics, 86J End of Unit 1 Assessment, 38–56	**Lesson 6**

A S S E S S M E N T

Teacher's Edition page reference

Activating Prior Knowledge

Good readers relate what they know to what they are reading. As you are reading these selections, make certain you relate what you already know about cooperation and competition to what you are reading.

- What do you know about cooperation and competition before we read these pieces?
- Have you already read books about cooperation and competition?

As students read the selections, they encounter some of these ideas and new ideas as well. When they read something they already know, encourage them to make a note about this information. When they learn something new, have them be sure to notice that too. This will help students learn about cooperation and competition as they read the selections.

- Have the students recall the narrative genres an author has to choose from, including fiction and nonfiction.
- Encourage students to share any stories they have read about cooperation and competition.
- Students should get into the habit of thinking about an upcoming theme or story and activating relevant background knowledge.
- For English-language learners and others with limited language experience, exploring the concepts of cooperation and competition on the Internet may be helpful.

Read Aloud

Read aloud to students the selection "Babe Didrikson" by Amelie Welden. Prior to reading, provide students with the following background information.

- The selection is a biography, or a factual account of an actual person's life, written by someone else.
- Babe excelled in sports at a time when very few women could make careers as professional athletes.

As students listen to the Read Aloud, have them think about what competition and cooperation meant to Babe Didrikson, and how Babe's competitiveness affected her sportsmanship.

It is important for you as the teacher to let your students know that you use the comprehension strategies being taught in the program when you read. Thus, as you read "Babe Didrikson," make some predictions aloud as to what it might be about. As you are reading, let students know what questions are occurring to you, what images pop up in your mind as you are reading, and how points made in the reading relate to ideas you already know.

Toward the end of the reading, sum up for students. If you cannot sum up the selection well, let students see you go back and reread to fill in the gaps in your summary. The selection does contain some reminders for you to use these processes, because one of the most powerful ways to get students to use comprehension strategies is for them to see you using them.

About the Author

Prior to reading, provide students with the following background information.

- Amelie Welden wrote *Girls Who Rocked the World* during a publishing internship on projects designed to empower girl readers. Ms. Welden advises aspiring writers, ". . . Everyday practice improves writing skills and generates ideas. Also, reading is a great way to get inspiration and to learn about different forms and styles of writing."

Focus Questions What personality traits did Babe Didrikson possess that helped her to become a successful competitor? In what ways were Babe Didrikson's successes dependent on her ability to cooperate?

Babe Didrikson

a biography
by Amelie Welden

It was Babe's first basketball game playing for the Golden Cyclones, a semiprofessional team. They were playing the national champions, the Sun Oil team, and her teammates were nervous. But Babe wasn't nervous. She ran and passed and shot the ball, again and again and again. By the end, the Golden Cyclones had won the game. Babe had scored more baskets than the entire Sun Oil team combined! The other girls were amazed by the eighteen-year-old super-athlete, but they had no idea that Babe would become one of the greatest athletes of all time. She excelled at almost every sport she tried, including golf, track, baseball, archery, skeet shooting, swimming, diving, horseback riding, and billiards, to name just a few. Her life set an inspiring example for all female athletes who followed in her footsteps.

Mildred Ella Didrikson was born on June 26, 1914, in Port Arthur, Texas. Her family was very poor, and she and her six brothers and sisters all had to help out. Mildred picked figs and sewed potato sacks for money. Sports were her way of having fun. Early on she decided that she would be the greatest athlete ever.

As a young girl, she was such a powerful home-run hitter that kids named her "Babe" after the famous slugger Babe Ruth. Her father built a gym in the backyard, and out of all her brothers and sisters, Babe used it the most. She worked out on the gym's chin-up bars and weight-lifting equipment. She also played baseball and basketball with the kids in the neighborhood.

In high school, Babe went out for every sport open to girls. She earned a spot on the basketball team and soon became a star. Her athletic ability attracted the attention of Melvin Coombs, the manager of a company-sponsored women's basketball team. He recruited Babe to play on his team, the Golden Cyclones, and she led them to a national championship. In 1930, she was voted all-American forward.

Babe decided to try track and field next. In 1932, she competed in the Amateur Athletic Union women's national championship. Out of eight events, Babe won five, tied for first in another, and took second in another. Babe earned enough points to win the *team* title all by herself!

Her outstanding track victories at the national championship led Babe to the 1932 Olympics in Los Angeles. As she left for the games, she told reporters that she planned to "beat everybody in sight." And beat them she did. Babe won a gold medal and set the world record in the javelin throw, won another gold medal in the hurdles, and won a silver medal in the high jump!

While she was in Los Angeles, Babe played her first round of golf. Her natural ability was impressive. A few years later, Babe decided to make a career out of the sport. She practiced hard, sometimes for fifteen or sixteen hours a day, and her hard work paid off when she won the Texas Women's Amateur Golf Tournament in 1935. She remembered:

> *Weekends I put in twelve and sixteen hours a day on golf. . . .*
> *I'd drill and drill and drill on the different kinds of shots.*
> *I'd hit balls until my hands were bloody and sore. . . .*
> *After it got too late to practice any more, I went home and had my*
> *dinner. Then I'd go to bed with the golf rule book.*

In 1937, Babe met wrestler George Zaharias at a golf tournament, and the two were married in less than a year. Babe continued her golf career, winning an incredible seventeen tournaments in a row! She was the first American to win the British Women's Amateur Tournament. But Babe's biggest impact on women's golf was yet to come. In 1949, she helped to found the Ladies' Professional Golf Association. This organization sponsored professional women's golf tournaments, which attracted more and more women to the sport. Today, LPGA tournaments offer millions of dollars in prize money for professional woman golfers.

Babe wrote in her autobiography:

> *Before I was even into my teens, I knew exactly what I wanted to be*
> *when I grew up. My goal was to be the greatest athlete that ever lived.*
> *I suppose I was born with the urge to get into sports, and the ability*
> *to do pretty well at it.*
>
> *Now there's nobody who wants to win more than I do. I'll knock*
> *myself out to do it. But I've never played rough or dirty. To me good*
> *sportsmanship is just as important as winning. . . . You have to play*
> *the game the right way. If you win through bad sportsmanship, that's*
> *no real victory in my book.*

In 1953, Babe was diagnosed with cancer. She fought the disease with her usual determination, and after undergoing surgery, Babe recovered and miraculously won the U.S. Open Golf Tournament in 1954. Babe persevered like a champion for two more years, but in 1956 the cancer returned. The world's greatest athlete died at the age of 42.

Throughout her life, Babe earned prestigious awards and honors. She was the only woman to be named the Associated Press's "Woman Athlete of the Year" six times! She was also voted the "Woman Athlete of the Half Century" in 1950. Sports historians ranked her as the second most outstanding and influential athlete in American sports history, just after Babe Ruth. Babe Didrikson's legacy has passed on to today's female athletes. Her talent and determination opened doors for women to compete and succeed in the world of sports.

Discussing the Read Aloud

After finishing the Read Aloud, ask students these questions:

- What are examples of competition from Babe's life? *(Possible answer: Babe played basketball, golf, and baseball, and ran track.)*

- Which examples of competition from the previous question also involve cooperation? *(Possible answer: When Babe played basketball and baseball, she would have had to cooperate with her teammates.)*

- What are other examples of cooperation from Babe's life? *(Possible answer: Babe and her six brothers and sisters all had to help out on their farm. She also worked to help found the LPGA.)*

- How did Babe's strong competitive streak help her later in her life? *(Possible answer: Being competitive helped Babe fight her cancer so she could recover and win the U.S. Open.)*

- How does this Read Aloud relate to cooperation and competition? *(Answers will vary.)*

- What did you learn about cooperation and competition? *(Answers will vary.)*

- How did this story change your ideas about cooperation and competition? *(Answers will vary.)*

Remind students of what you asked them to think about before you read the story:

- What did cooperation and competition mean to Babe Didrikson?

- How did Babe feel about competitiveness and sportsmanship?

Also revisit the Focus Questions asked at the beginning of the Read Aloud. Discuss these questions in relation to the story. Have students tell about times when they've been competitive and cooperative in their own lives. Have students talk about the example Babe Didrikson set for young female and male athletes.

Concept/Question Board

The Concept/Question Board is a place for students to ask questions and find answers in order to have a better understanding of the unit theme. It is also a place to publish the results of their investigations.

This Board could be a standard bulletin board or a large 3-sided board placed in the front or to the side of the classroom. The Board will be a permanent place for students to ask questions, post articles or objects, add comments, and so on throughout the study of each unit theme. Students should have easy access to the Concept/Question Board, as they will need to be able to attach items to it on their own and also read what is attached.

Have a large supply of self-stick notepads or index cards and thumbtacks available. Paper cut in various shapes that represent each selection could be made available for students to use. For example, you could cut green construction paper into the shape of a leaf to represent the story, "Founders of the Children's Rain Forest." Students could write their questions, comments, or theme words on these cutout shapes, which would easily identify the story in the unit.

To begin using your Concept/Question Board, ask the students to formulate statements about what they know about the unit theme or what they believe to be important about the theme after listening to the Read Aloud. Write these statements and attach them to the Concept side of the Board. Then, write any preliminary questions they have about the unit theme and attach those to the Question side of the Board.

Another idea to help get the students started is to put up a chart or web that they can add to throughout the unit. For example, you might put up two categories—Cooperation and Competition—and as they read the selections in the unit students can post examples of each concept.

As the students progress through the unit, they can refer to the Board to learn which of their classmates have interests similar to their own. This information can be used to form groups to investigate questions and ideas about the unit theme.

Throughout the unit, have the students reread and reflect on the contributions listed on the Concept/Question Board. Have them note in their **Writer's Workbook** the contributions that mean the most to them. Suggest that they expand on the original contributions by adding their own thoughts, articles, pictures, and so on. Discuss whether the selection has provided information that might be added or that might revise existing postings.

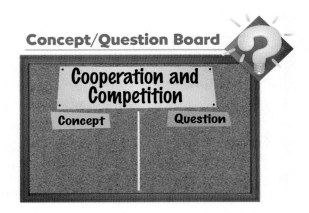

Concept/Question Board

Cooperation and Competition

Concept | Question

Setting Reading Goals

Have students examine and share their thoughts on the unit opener on *Student Anthology* pages 18–19. Remind them that good readers are always thinking when they read. Ask students what they were thinking about as they read the unit opener. Remind them that good readers browse what they are going to read before reading. Invite them to browse the selections in the unit at this time.

Tell students that good readers make predictions about what might be in the selections they are about to read. Ask them if they are making predictions about the selections or if they are asking themselves questions about the selections they are about to read. Model asking questions with any that might have occurred to you as you browsed the selections.

Explain that they will be given ample opportunity to think, read, and write about cooperation and competition. Tell them that you would like them to be thinking about the following questions:

- When is it important to be cooperative?
- When is it important to be competitive?
- What can we learn about cooperation and competition from reading stories?
- Do you already know some stories about cooperation and competition? What did they teach you?

Remind students that good readers regularly set goals when they are reading. Also make certain they know that they should get into the habit of setting reading goals for themselves, because they should know why they are reading something.

Inquiry Journal

- After the students have discussed what they think this unit might be about, have them complete page 5 in their *Inquiry Journals.*
- Have students share ideas about cooperation and competition that they would like to learn more about.

Inquiry Journal p. 5

Professional Resources

Osborn, J. & Lehr, F. (Eds.) (1998), *Literacy for all: Issues in teaching and learning.* New York: the Guilford Press.

Hoose, Phillip, *It's Our World, Too! Stories of Young People Who Are Making a Difference.* Little, Brown, and Company, 1993. Includes the personal stories of fourteen children working to improve their communities and suggestions for coordinating community service projects.

Home Connection

Distribute page 1 of *Home Connection.* This *Home Connection* is also available in Spanish on page 2.

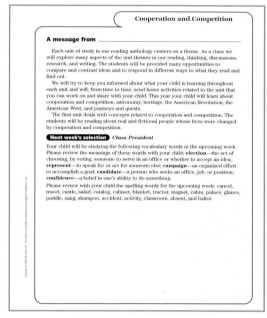

Cooperation and Competition

A message from _____

Each unit of study in our reading anthology centers on a theme. As a class we will explore many aspects of the unit themes in our reading, thinking, discussions, research, and writing. The students will be provided many opportunities to compare and contrast ideas and to respond in different ways to what they read and find out.

We will try to keep you informed about what your child is learning throughout each unit and will, from time to time, send home activities related to the unit that you can work on and share with your child. This year your child will learn about cooperation and competition, astronomy, heritage, the American Revolution, the American West, and journeys and quests.

The first unit deals with concepts related to cooperation and competition. The students will be reading about real and fictional people whose lives were changed by cooperation and competition.

Next week's selection *Class President*

Your child will be studying the following vocabulary words in the upcoming week. Please review the meanings of these words with your child: **election**—the act of choosing, by voting, someone to serve in an office or whether to accept an idea; **represent**—to speak for or act for someone else; **campaign**—an organized effort to accomplish a goal; **candidate**—a person who seeks an office, job, or position; **confidence**—a belief in one's ability to do something.

Please review with your child the spelling words for the upcoming week: cancel, travel, castle, salad, catalog, cabinet, blanket, tractor, magnet, cabin, palace, glance, paddle, sang, shampoo, accident, activity, classroom, absent, and ballot.

Home Connection p. 1

Michael Pressley on Comprehension Strategy Instruction

Instruction designed to build and support students' metacognitive skills leads to improved reading comprehension. Such instruction is most effective when teachers help students develop the strategies necessary for deep comprehension by modeling and explaining the behaviors and strategies used by expert readers as they tackle a text; by guiding students in using strategies appropriately; by asking students to apply the strategies on their own; and by gradually shifting responsibility to the students for their own learning.

Strategic reading seems to promote the development of comprehension ability most when teachers encourage students to make associations between what they read and their own experiences, to interpret, and to create summaries of what they find important in a text.

www.sra4kids.com
Web Connection
Check the Reading link of the SRA Web page for more information on Research in Reading.

Focus Questions What qualities do good leaders have? If you were running for class president, what would be your strategy for winning the election?

Class President

Johanna Hurwitz
illustrated by Richard Hull

To Delia and Bill Gottlieb
They get my vote every time!

Julio Sanchez is sure that fifth grade is going to be his best year yet. On the first day of school, his homeroom teacher Mr. Flores announces that this year the fifth grade will be electing a class president. To get ready for the election, the students are to be thinking about who might make a good leader.

In the meantime, while playing in a soccer game at recess, Julio's classmate Arthur breaks his glasses. The fifth grade pitches in to pay for the glasses by holding a bake sale. But on the day of the bake sale, Arthur's mom finds out his glasses can be replaced for free.

Now the class has two things to decide: who to elect as class president and what to do with the bake sale money no longer needed to pay for Arthur's glasses. . . .

On Monday, Arthur came to school with new glasses. Cricket came to class with a big poster that said, VOTE FOR CRICKET, THAT'S THE TICKET.

The election was going to be held on Friday. That meant there were only four days more to get ready. In the meantime, they learned about how to make a nomination and how to second it. It was going to be a really serious election.

At lunch, Cricket took out a bag of miniature chocolate bars and gave them out to her classmates. Julio took his and ate it. But it didn't mean he was going to vote for Cricket. He wondered if there was anything Lucas could give out that was better than chocolate. Nothing was better than chocolate!

20

Selection Summary

Genre: Realistic Fiction

In this excerpt from the book, *Class President*, the election for class president of the fifth grade shapes up as a two-way race between Cricket and Lucas. Julio is determined to help his friend, Lucas, get elected, but Cricket runs a strong campaign. As the competition heats up, something happens to change the course of events—Mr. Herbertson bans soccer on the playground. Julio suggests that he and the candidates persuade Mr. Herbertson to change his mind. What will the outcome of Julio's leadership be?

Some of the elements of realistic fiction are listed below. A realistic fiction selection may have one or more of these elements.

- The characters behave as people or animals do in real life.
- The setting of the story is a real place or could be a real place.
- The events of the story are based on a conflict or problem that could occur in real life.

About the Author

Johanna Hurwitz has written more than 30 books for children. As an adult, she fulfilled her childhood dream of becoming both a librarian and a writer. *Class Clowns*, which introduced Julio, Cricket, and Lucas, received Kentucky's Bluegrass Award, West Virginia's Children's Book Award, and Mississippi's Children's Book Award.

Students can read more about Johanna Hurwitz on page 34 of the ***Student Anthology.***

Other Books by Johanna Hurwitz

- *Aldo Applesauce*
- *Rip-Roaring Russell*
- *The Adventures of Ali Baba Bernstein*
- *The Hot and Cold Summer*

About the Illustrator

Richard Hull teaches illustration at Brigham Young University. He was also an art director and graphic designer with a magazine for fifteen years. He and his wife live in Orem, Utah.

Students can read more about Richard Hull on page 34 of the ***Student Anthology.***

Other Books Illustrated by Richard Hull

- *The Cat & the Fiddle & More*
- *My Sister's Rusty Bike*
- *The Alphabet from Z to A (With Much Confusion on the Way)*

Inquiry Connections

A major aim of **Open Court Reading** is knowledge building. Because inquiry is at the root of knowledge building, students are encouraged to investigate topics and questions within each selection that relate to the unit theme.

"Class President" is realistic fiction that highlights how an underdog who is cooperative can achieve more than a vocal competitive individual. Key concepts are:

- In many situations, cooperation is more productive than competition.
- Focusing on group benefits rather than individual gains is highly desirable in some situations.
- Some competition practices, such as campaigning, are fair while others, such as bribery, are not.
- Cooperation and communication are essential for leadership.

Before reading the selection:

- Point out that students may post a question, concept, word, illustration, or object on the Concept/Question Board at any time during the course of their unit investigation. Be sure that students include their name or initials on the items they post so that others will know whom to go to if they have an answer or if they wish to collaborate on a related activity.
- Students should feel free to write an answer or a note on someone else's question or to consult the Board for ideas for their own investigations throughout the unit.
- Encourage students to read about cooperation and competition at home and to bring in articles or pictures that are good examples to post on the Board.

Concept/Question Board

PROGRAM RESOURCES

Leveled Practice

Reteach
Pages 2–6

Challenge
Pages 2–5

ELD Workbook

Intervention Workbook

Leveled Classroom Library*

Have students read at least 30 minutes daily outside of class. Have them read books from the ***Leveled Classroom Library,*** which supports the unit theme and helps students develop their vocabulary by reading independently.

The Kid Who Ran for President

BY DAN GUTMAN. SCHOLASTIC, 1996.

Twelve-year-old Judson Moon is running for President of the United States— with the old lady down the street as his running mate, a first lady he's barely spoken to, and a campaign manager who swears he can sidestep the Constitution and get Judd elected. **(Easy)**

Iditarod Dream: Dusty and His Sled Dogs Compete in Alaska's Jr. Iditarod

BY TED WOOD. WALKER AND COMPANY, 1996.

Dusty shows he knows how to train and care for his Alaskan Huskie dog team, as well as drive his sled and fend off a moose, as he vies for first place in the Jr. Iditarod. **(Average)**

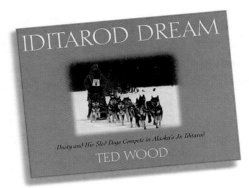

The View from Saturday

BY E. L. KONIGSBURG. ALADDIN, 1996.

Mrs. Olinski's choice of Noah, Nadia, Ethan, and Julian for her sixth grade academic team, the strange connections between the four, and their amazing academic bowl winning streak are explored. (A Newbery Medal Winner) **(Advanced)**

✳ These books, which all support the unit theme Cooperation and Competition, are part of a 36-book ***Leveled Classroom Library*** available for purchase from SRA/McGraw-Hill.
Note: Teachers should preview any trade books for appropriateness in their classrooms before recommending them to students.

TECHNOLOGY

Web Connections

www.sra4kids.com
Cooperation and Competition Web site

Audiocassette/CD

✳ **Listening Library: Cooperation and Competition**
SRA/McGRAW-HILL, 2002

Computer Skills

✳ **Basic Computer Skills**

CD-ROMs

 ✳ **Research Assistant**
SRA/McGRAW-HILL, 2002

 ✳ **Student Writing and Research Center**
THE LEARNING COMPANY

Titles preceded by an asterisk (✳) are available through SRA/McGraw-Hill. Other titles can be obtained by contacting the publisher listed with the title.

LESSON PLANNER

Suggested Pacing: 3–5 days

	DAY 1	DAY 2
	DAY 1	DAY 2

1 Preparing to Read

Materials
- Program Assessment
- Inquiry Journal, p. 5
- Routine Card 1

DAY 1

✓ Grade 5 Pretest
- *Program Assessment*, pp. 2–8

Unit Overview
- Previewing the Unit, p. 19M
- Read Aloud, pp. 19N–19P

Word Knowledge, p. 20K
- Root words and derivatives
- Consonant plus *r* blends
- Spellings of the /er/ sound
- /a/ sound spelled *a*

About the Words and Sentences, p. 20K

DAY 2

Developing Oral Language, p. 20L

2 Reading & Responding

Materials
- Student Anthology, pp. 20–35
- Reading Transparencies 1, 54
- Routine Card 1
- Program Assessment
- Unit 1 Assessment, pp. 2–5
- Science/Social Studies Connection Center Card 1
- Comprehension and Language Arts Skills, pp. 2–3
- Reteach, pp. 2–3
- Challenge, p. 2
- Home Connection, pp. 3–4
- Inquiry Journal, p. 6

DAY 1

Build Background, p. 20M

Preview and Prepare, pp. 20M–20N

Selection Vocabulary, p. 20N

Reading Recommendations, pp. 20O–20P

DAY 2

Student Anthology, pp. 20–33 — First Read

✓ Comprehension Strategies
- Making Connections, pp. 20, 22, 24, 26
- Predicting, pp. 20, 22, 24, 26, 28, 32
- Summarizing, pp. 28, 30

Discussing Strategy Use, p. 32

Discussing the Selection, p. 33A
- Review the Selection
- Complete Discussion

Inquiry

Materials
- Student Anthology, pp. 20–35
- Reading Transparency 2
- Inquiry Journal, pp. 8–9
- Research Assistant

DAY 1

Investigation
- Investigating Concepts Beyond the Text, p. 35A

DAY 2

Investigation
- Concept/Question Board, p. 35B

3 Language Arts

Materials
- Comprehension and Language Arts Skills, pp. 4–5
- Language Arts Handbook, pp. 20–22; 94–95; 146–151; 264–267; 342–343
- Language Arts Transparencies 1–5
- Spelling and Vocabulary Skills, pp. 2–5
- Student Anthology
- Student Writing and Research Center
- Unit 1 Assessment, pp. 26–27
- Challenge, pp. 3–5
- Reteach, pp. 4–6

DAY 1

Word Analysis
✓ Spelling Patterns for the /a/ Sound Pretest, p. 35F

Writing Process Strategies
- Writing Process Introduction: Getting Ideas, p. 35F

English Language Conventions
- Grammar, Usage, and Mechanics: Nouns, p. 35F

DAY 2

Word Analysis
- Spelling Patterns for the /a/ Sound, p. 35G
- Vocabulary: Discovering Word Meanings, p. 35G

Writing Process Strategies
- Writing Process: Getting Ideas, p. 35G

English Language Conventions
- Grammar, Usage, and Mechanics: Nouns, p. 35G

✓ Informal Assessment Available   ✓ Formal Assessment Available

DAY 2 continued	DAY 3	
DAY 3	**DAY 4**	**DAY 5**
General Review	General Review	Review Word Knowledge

DAY 3

Student Anthology, pp. 20–33 `Second Read`
Comprehension Skills
- Drawing Conclusions, pp. 21, 23, 25, 27, 29, 31, 33
✓ **Checking Comprehension, p. 29**
Supporting the Reading, pp. 33C–33D
- Drawing Conclusions

DAY 4

Student Anthology, pp. 34–35
- Meet the Author/Illustrator
✓ Theme Connections
Review Selection Vocabulary, p. 33B
Literary Elements, p. 33E
- Character Analysis

DAY 5

✓ **Lesson Assessment**
- *Unit 1 Assessment:* Lesson Assessment, pp. 2–5
Home Connection, p. 33B
Science Connection
- Citizenship, p 33F

Investigation
✓ **Generating Ideas to Investigate, p. 35C**

Supporting the Investigation, p. 35D
- Parts of the Library

Investigation
- Unit Investigation Continued
- Update Concept/Question Board

Word Analysis
- Spelling Patterns for the /a/ Sound, p. 35H
- Vocabulary: Discovering Word Meanings, p. 35H
Writing Process Strategies
- Writing Process: Getting Ideas, p. 35H
English Language Conventions
✓ Grammar, Usage, and Mechanics: Nouns, p. 35H

Word Analysis
- Spelling Patterns for the /a/ Sound, p. 35I
- Vocabulary: Discovering Word Meanings, p. 35I
Writing Process Strategies
- Writing Process Introduction: Getting Ideas, p. 35I
English Language Conventions
✓ Listening, Speaking, Viewing
✓ Listening: Understanding What We Hear, p. 35I

Word Analysis
✓ Spelling Patterns for the /a/ Sound Final Test, p. 35J
✓ Vocabulary: Discovering Word Meanings, p. 35J
Writing Process Strategies
✓ Writing Process Introduction: Getting Ideas for an Autobiography, p. 35J
English Language Conventions
✓ Penmanship: Cursive Letters *i* and *t*, p. 35J

Below are suggestions for differentiating instruction to meet the individual needs of students. These are the same skills shown on the Lesson Planner; however, these pages provide extra practice opportunities or enriching activities to meet the varied needs of students.

WORKSHOP

Differentiating Instruction

Small-Group Instruction

Use small-group instruction for such things as preteaching students who need this advantage; reteaching material to students having difficulty; intervening on behalf of students having extreme difficulty; instructing ELL students; and discussing students' writing projects.

Use the informal assessment suggestions found throughout the lesson along with the formal assessments provided in each lesson to determine your students' strengths and areas of need. Use the following program components to help in supporting or expanding on the instruction found in this lesson:

- **Reteach** workbook for use with those students who show a basic understanding of the lesson but need a bit more practice to solidify their understanding

- **Intervention Guide** and **Workbook** for use with those students who even after extra practice exhibit a lack of understanding of the lesson concepts

- **English-Language Development Guide** and **Workbook** for use with those students who need language help

Independent Activities

Explain to the class that during Workshop they will work alone or cooperatively in a self-directed manner. They may choose to work on **Inquiry Journal** or **Challenge** pages, independent reading, investigation activities, or writing.

For Workshop Management Tips, see Appendix pages 41–42.

♦ **Small-group Instruction**   ■ **Independent Activities**

	READING	INVESTIGATION ACTIVITIES
DAY 1	■ Record Reaction to Read Aloud in Writer's Notebook ■ Browse *Leveled Classroom Library* ■ *Listening Library Audiocassette/CD* ■ Add Vocabulary in Writer's Notebook	■ Concept/Question Board ■ Record Ideas About Theme in *Inquiry Journal*, p. 5 ■ Explore OCR Web Site for Theme Connections ■ Complete *Inquiry Journal*, p. 8
DAY 2	■ Choose *Leveled Classroom Library* Book and Begin Independent Reading ■ Oral Reading of Selection for Fluency ■ Record Response to Selection in Writer's Notebook	■ Concept/Question Board ■ Explore OCR Web Site for Theme Connections
DAY 3	■ Read *Leveled Classroom Library* Book as Independent Reading ■ Complete *Comprehension and Language Arts Skills*, pp. 2–3 ■ *Listening Library Audiocassette/CD*	■ Concept/Question Board ♦ Generate Ideas for Investigation ■ Use *Research Assistant* to Begin Investigation
DAY 4	■ Read *Level Classroom Library* Book as Independent Reading ♦ Discuss Theme Connections, p. 35 ■ Add Words to Word Bank ■ Complete *Link to Writing* for Supporting the Reading, p. 33D ■ Complete *Independent Practice* for Literary Elements, p. 33E	■ Concept/Question Board ■ Complete *Inquiry Journal*, p. 9
DAY 5	■ Read *Leveled Classroom Library* Book as Independent Reading ♦ Reading Roundtable ♦ Social Studies Connection, p. 33F	■ Concept Question/Board ■ Complete *Independent Practice* for Supporting the Investigation, p. 35D

LANGUAGE ARTS	INTERVENTION*	ENGLISH-LANGUAGE LEARNERS**	RETEACH	CHALLENGE
English Language Conventions ■ Complete Nouns, *Comprehension and Language Arts Skills,* pp. 4–5 **Writing Process Strategies** ◆ Seminar: Brainstorm, p. 35F	(30 to 45 minutes per day) ◆ Reading Words, p. 3 ◆ Preteach "Class President," pp. 4–5 ◆ Teach "Intervention Selection One," pp. 5–6 ◆ Grammar, Usage, and Mechanics, pp. 8–9	(30 to 45 minutes per day) ◆ Word Knowledge, p. 2 ◆ Activate Prior Knowledge, p. 3 ◆ Selection Vocabulary, p. 3		
Word Analysis ◆ Spelling: Word Sort, p. 35G ■ Complete Vocabulary: Discovering Word Meanings, *Spelling and Vocabulary Skills,* pp. 2–3 **Writing Process Strategies** ◆ Seminar: Planning The Approach, p. 35G	◆ Developing Oral Language, p. 3 ◆ Preteach "Class President," pp. 4–5 ◆ Teach Comprehension Strategies, p. 6 ◆ Reread "Intervention Selection One" ◆ Grammar, Usage, and Mechanics, pp. 8–9	◆ Preteach the Selection, p. 4	**English Language Conventions** ■ Complete Nouns, *Reteach,* p. 6	**English Language Conventions** ■ Complete Nouns, *Challenge,* p. 5
Word Analysis ■ Complete Spelling: The /a/ Sound, *Spelling and Vocabulary Skills,* p. 4 **Writing Process Strategies** ◆ Seminar: Getting Ideas For Informative Writing, p. 35H	◆ Dictation and Spelling, pp. 3–4 ◆ Reread "Class President" ◆ Teach "Intervention Selection Two," pp. 6–7 ◆ Writing Activity, pp. 9–10	◆ Dictation and Spelling, p. 3	**Comprehension** ◆ Review Comprehension Skill: Drawing Conclusions ■ Complete *Reteach,* pp. 2–3 **Word Analysis** ■ Complete Vocabulary: Discovering Word Meanings, *Reteach,* p. 5	**Comprehension** ■ Complete *Challenge,* p. 2 **Word Analysis** ■ Complete Vocabulary: Discovering Word Meanings, *Challenge,* p. 4
Word Analysis ■ Complete The /a/ Sound, *Spelling and Vocabulary Skills,* p. 5 **Writing Process Strategies** ◆ Seminar: Getting Ideas for a Personal Narrative, p. 35I	◆ Reread "Class President" ◆ Teach Comprehension Strategies, p. 7 ◆ Reread "Intervention Selection Two" ◆ Writing Activity, pp. 9–10	◆ Vocabulary Strategies, p. 5	**Word Analysis** ■ Complete Spelling: The /a/ Sound, *Reteach,* p. 4	**Word Analysis** ■ Complete Spelling: The /a/ Sound, *Challenge,* p. 3
Writing Process Strategies ◆ Seminar: Get Ideas for an Autobiography, p. 35J **English Language Conventions** ■ Penmanship: Cursive Letters *i* and *t,* p. 35J	◆ Repeated Readings/Fluency Check, p. 8 ◆ Informal Assessment	◆ Grammar, Usage, and Mechanics, p. 6		

*Page numbers refer to **Intervention Guide**
Page numbers refer to **English-Language Development Guide

ASSESSMENT

Formal Assessment Options

Use these summative assessments along with your informal observations to assess student progress.

Unit 1 Assessment p. 2

LESSON ASSESSMENT

Name _____ Date _____ Score _____

UNIT | Cooperation and Competition • Lesson |

Class President

Read the following questions carefully. Then completely fill in the bubble of each correct answer. You may look back at the story to find the answer to each of the questions.

1. Mr. Flores's class needed to decide who to elect for class president and
   Ⓐ where to go on their yearly field trip
   Ⓑ who to send to the principal's office
   ● how to spend the bake sale money

2. Why was soccer in the school yard canceled?
   ● Mr. Herbertson was worried about accidents.
   Ⓑ The girls wanted to jump rope instead.
   Ⓒ There wasn't enough room to play there.

Read the following questions carefully. Use complete sentences to answer the questions.

3. How did Mr. Flores respond when Cricket said, "I don't care if we can't play soccer"?
   Mr. Flores reminded Cricket that if she was president, she would be president of the whole class, not just the girls.

4. What makes Julio feel more relaxed around the principal?
   The principal remembers a couple of Julio's older brothers and says they were nice fellows.

5. How does Arthur describe Julio to the rest of the class?
   Arthur says that Julio is fair and is always doing nice things for people.

2 Unit | • Lesson | Class President • Unit | Assessment

Unit 1 Assessment p. 3

LESSON ASSESSMENT

Class President (continued)

6. Why does Lucas want to take his own name off the board?
   He wants to take his name off the board because he wants Julio to be the president.

7. What does Julio tell the class about how they should spend the bake sale money?
   He tells the class that they should spend the money in a way that everyone likes, not just the teacher.

8. What proves to Lucas that Julio will make a good president?
   Lucas sees how Julio takes charge and is not afraid when they go to talk with the principal.

Read the following questions carefully. Then completely fill in the bubble of each correct answer.

9. What caused Julio to begin to think about running for president?
   Ⓐ when he heard soccer would be canceled
   ● after he met with the principal
   Ⓒ while he made a sign for Lucas

10. Why did Cricket have a problem with Julio being nominated?
    Ⓐ Julio was nominated incorrectly.
    Ⓑ Julio did not want to be president.
    ● Cricket thought Julio was not an American citizen.

Unit | Assessment • Class President   Unit • Lesson | 3

Unit 1 Assessment p. 4

LESSON ASSESSMENT

Class President (continued)

Read the question and statement below. Use complete sentences in your answers.

Linking to the Concepts How are Cricket and Julio different in the way they would serve as president?
Answers will vary. Accept all reasonable answers.

Personal Response Suppose you were in this class. How would you feel about Cricket giving out chocolate bars in exchange for your vote? Do you think this is fair?
Answers will vary. Accept all reasonable answers.

4 Unit • Lesson | Class President • Unit | Assessment

Unit 1 Assessment p. 5

LESSON ASSESSMENT

Class President (continued)

Vocabulary

Read the following questions carefully. Then completely fill in the bubble of each correct answer.

1. To get ready for the election, the students are thinking about who might make a good leader. An **election** is a
   Ⓐ decision about how to spend class money
   ● selection of a person for office by vote
   Ⓒ discussion between a principal and a student

2. Cricket must be spending her whole allowance on the campaign, Julio thought. A **campaign** is the time when
   Ⓐ the people send in an envelope with their vote
   Ⓑ the students in a classroom take a break for lunch
   ● the people running for office try to get more supporters

3. Going to the meeting with Mr. Herbertson was a good opportunity for Cricket to represent the class. In this sentence, **represent** means
   Ⓐ learn about
   ● speak for
   Ⓒ complain about

4. Mr. Flores said the students could nominate anyone they choose, even if the candidate did not have a poster on the wall. A **candidate** is
   Ⓐ a person visiting the principal
   Ⓑ a person who likes soccer
   ● a person running for office

5. Julio felt it was his job to give Lucas confidence. To have **confidence** is to
   Ⓐ care about others
   ● believe in yourself
   Ⓒ always tell the truth

Unit | Assessment • Class President   Unit • Lesson | 5

Unit 1 Assessment p. 26

LESSON ASSESSMENT

Name _____ Date _____ Score _____

UNIT | Cooperation and Competition • Lesson | Class President

Spelling Pretest: The /a/ Sound

Fold this page back on the dotted line. Take the Pretest. Then correct any word you misspelled by crossing out the word and rewriting it next to the incorrect spelling.

1.		1.	cancel
2.		2.	travel
3.		3.	castle
4.		4.	salad
5.		5.	catalog
6.		6.	cabinet
7.		7.	blanket
8.		8.	tractor
9.		9.	magnet
10.		10.	cabin
11.		11.	palace
12.		12.	glance
13.		13.	paddle
14.		14.	sang
15.		15.	shampoo
16.		16.	accident
17.		17.	activity
18.		18.	classroom
19.		19.	absent
20.		20.	ballot

26 Unit | • Lesson | Spelling Pretest: The /a/ Sound • Unit | Assessment

---

Unit 1 Assessment p. 27

LESSON ASSESSMENT

Name _____ Date _____ Score _____

UNIT | Cooperation and Competition • Lesson | Class President

Spelling Final Test: The /a/ Sound

Look for the underlined word that is spelled wrong. Fill in the bubble of the line with the misspelled word.

1. Ⓐ He likes jazz music.
   Ⓑ Take a taxi to the airport.
   Ⓒ That flower is a pansy.
   ● Correct as is.

2. ● The trumpet is a bross instrument.
   Ⓖ We took a lantern on our camping trip.
   Ⓗ They strolled down the avenue.
   Ⓙ Correct as is.

3. Ⓐ The blanket is warm.
   Ⓑ We saw a magic show.
   Ⓒ Jogging is a good habit.
   ● Correct as is.

4. Ⓐ This is the exact amount.
   Ⓑ I will cancel the subscription.
   ● The princess lived in a palece.
   Ⓙ Correct as is.

5. Ⓐ We are out of shampoo.
   Ⓑ This is only the first draft.
   Ⓒ The painter needed a laidder.
   ● Correct as is.

6. Ⓕ Put the glasses in the cabinet.
   ● Cast your balot.
   Ⓗ Will you attend the annual picnic?
   Ⓙ Correct as is.

7. Ⓐ The valley contained many farms.
   Ⓑ She is an alto in the choir.
   Ⓒ We sang to her for her birthday.
   ● Correct as is.

8. Ⓕ The saddle fell off the horse.
   Ⓖ Do you want to take a chance?
   Ⓗ The driveway was made of gravel.
   ● Correct as is.

9. ● The classroom was dark.
   Ⓑ You were absent on Monday.
   Ⓒ She enjoyed the arts and crafts exhibit.
   Ⓙ Correct as is.

10. ● You will improve if you practace.
    Ⓖ I didn't get your address.
    Ⓗ The catalog is thick.
    Ⓙ Correct as is.

Unit | Assessment • Spelling Final Test: The /a/ Sound   Unit • Lesson | 27

Informal Comprehension Strategies Rubrics

Use the Informal Comprehension Strategies Rubrics to determine whether or not a student is using any of the strategies listed below. Note the strategies a student is using, instead of the degree to which a student might be using any particular strategy. In addition, encourage the student to tell of any strategies other than the ones being taught that he or she is using.

Predicting

- The student makes predictions about what the text is about.
- The student updates predictions during reading, based on information in the text.

Summarizing

- The student paraphrases text, reporting main ideas and a summary of what is in text.
- The student decides which parts of the text are important in his or her summary.
- The student draws conclusions from the text.
- The student makes global interpretations of the text, such as recognizing the genre.

Making Connections

- The student activates prior knowledge and related knowledge.
- The student uses prior knowledge to explain something encountered in text.
- The student connects ideas presented later in the text to ideas presented earlier in the text.
- The student notes ideas in the text that are new to him or her or conflict with what he or she thought previously.

Research Rubrics

Use the Research Rubrics to assess a student's performance throughout the stages of the investigation for each unit. The rubrics for a given lesson will match the investigation stage for that lesson. In addition, at the end of the unit you can use the rubrics to assess the groups' collaborative work as well as an individual's participation in that group.

During Workshop, assess students using the rubrics below. The rubrics range from 1–4 in most categories, with 1 being the lowest score. Record each student's score on the inside back cover of the ***Inquiry Journal.***

Formulating Research Questions and Problems

1 With help, identifies things she or he wonders about in relation to a topic.

2 Expresses curiosity about topics; with help, translates this into specific questions.

3 Poses an interesting problem or question for research; with help, refines it into a researchable question.

4 Identifies something she or he genuinely wonders about and translates it into a researchable question.

WORD KNOWLEDGE

Objectives

- Students identify derivatives that build on root words with the suffixes *-tion, -ing,* and *-or.*
- Students recognize and read blends of consonants with the letter *r* at the beginnings of words.
- Students recognize and read words with different spellings of the /er/ sound and with the /a/ sound spelled *a.*
- Students develop fluency reading words and sentences aloud.

Materials

- Program Assessment, pp. 2–8
- Routine Card 1

Routine Card

Refer to Routine 1 for the Word Knowledge procedure.

Teacher Tip SYLLABICATION To help students blend words and build fluency, use the syllabication below of the decodable multisyllabic words in the word lines.

com•pete	ac•ci•dent
com•pe•ti•tor	ac•tiv•i•ty
com•pe•ti•tion	class•room
Fri•day	ab•sent
soc•cer	bal•lot

Word Knowledge

Introduction

The Word Knowledge activities show students strategies for figuring out unfamiliar words they encounter while reading. The entire class participates in each of these activities. Use direct teaching to teach the Word Knowledge lesson. In other words, teach the words using the procedure below without varying from it. That way, students will become accustomed to the routine that they will use to study the words.

Reading the Words and Sentences

Write each word and sentence on the board. Have students read each word together. After all the words have been read, have students read each sentence in natural phrases or chunks. Use the suggestions in About the Words and Sentences to discuss the different features of listed words.

Line 1:	compete	competitor	competition	competing
Line 2:	broke	Friday	grade	proud tripped
Line 3:	soccer	hurt	whir	pertain
Line 4:	accident	activity	classroom	absent ballot
Sentence 1:	Each competitor was proud.			
Sentence 2:	She tripped while playing soccer.			
Sentence 3:	The competition is on Friday.			
Sentence 4:	There were many empty desks in the classroom because students were absent.			

About the Words and Sentences

- **Line 1:** The words include the root word *compete* and some of its derivatives. The root word means "to try to win or gain something from another or others." Have students look up its word origin in a dictionary or word origins book. (The original Lower Latin form of the word *compete* was *competere,* meaning "to seek together.") Have students discuss how the word's original meaning compares to its present-day meaning. Then have students discuss how the suffixes added to the root word *compete,* to form the words in **Line 1,** changed the root word's meaning. If necessary, explain that the suffix *-or* (or *-er*) means doer, maker, or resident. The suffix *-tion* (or *-sion*) means action, state, or result. The ending *-ing* is used to form nouns of verbs, to make gerunds, or to denote an action or process. Have students offer other words that take these suffixes (for example, *elect, elector, election, electing*). Students should identify the root word for each example and discuss its meaning and origin.

WORD KNOWLEDGE

- **Line 2:** The words contain consonant plus *r* blends. Have students offer words that have a consonant plus *r* blend at the beginning of the word (for example, *driver, president, principal, friend*).
- **Line 3:** The words illustrate different spellings for the /er/ sound. Spellings of the /er/ sound include *er, ir,* and *ur.* Have volunteers circle where these spellings occur.
- **Line 4:** The words contain the /a/ sound spelled *a,* no matter where it appears in the syllable.
- **Sentences 1–2:** Ask students to say the words with the /er/ sound *(competitor, soccer).* Then ask students to say the words that contain blends with the letter *r (proud, tripped).* Have students identify the nouns in the sentences *(competitor, soccer).*
- **Sentences 1 and 3:** Ask students to identify and say the words that have the root *compete (competitor, competition).* Have students identify the functions of these words in the sentences *(subjects).*
- **Sentence 4:** In this sentence, have students say the words that contain the /a/ sound spelled *a (classroom, absent).*

Developing Oral Language

Use direct teaching to review the words. Use the following activity to help students practice the words aloud.

- Ask a volunteer to make up a sentence containing a word from the word lines. Then have a second volunteer extend the sentence by answering the question *Who? What? Where? Why?* or *How?* The new sentence should contain the original word as well as an additional word from the word lines. Then repeat this activity using other words from the word lines.

Teacher Tip BUILDING FLUENCY
Gaining a better understanding of the spellings of sounds and the structure of words will help students as they encounter unfamiliar words in their reading. By this time in grade 5, students should be reading approximately 126 words per minute with fluency and expression. As students read, you may notice that some need work in building fluency. During Workshop, have these students choose a section of the text (a minimum of 160 words) to read several times in order to build fluency.

MEETING INDIVIDUAL NEEDS

ELL Support
For ELD strategies, use the *English-Language Development Guide,* Unit 1, Lesson 1.

Intervention Support
For intervention strategies, use the *Intervention Guide,* Unit 1, Lesson 1.

Spelling
See pages 35F–35J for the corresponding spelling lesson for the /a/ sound.

Objectives

- Students will understand the selection vocabulary before reading.
- Students will identify root words and their derivatives.
- Students will identify words beginning with consonant-plus-*r* blends.
- Students will use the comprehension strategies Predicting, Making Connections, and Summarizing as they read the story the first time.
- Students will use the comprehension skill Drawing Conclusions as they read the story the second time.

Materials

- Student Anthology, pp. 20–35
- Reading Transparencies 1, 54
- Listening Library
- Routine Card 1
- Inquiry Journal, p. 6
- Science/Social Studies Connection Center Card 1
- Home Connection, p. 3
- Comprehension and Language Arts Skills, pp. 2–3
- Program Assessment
- Unit 1 Assessment, pp. 2–5

MEETING INDIVIDUAL NEEDS

ELL Support

CULTURAL CONTEXT English-language learners may be unfamiliar with the concept of a class president. Ask English-language learners if they have been in a classroom where there was a president. If so, ask them to say what the president did. If your class does not currently have a president, talk about how the students feel a class president could be helpful.

Intervention Support

For intervention strategies, use the *Intervention Guide,* Unit 1, Lesson 1.

www.sra4kids.com
Web Connection
Students can use the connections to Cooperation and Competition in the Reading link of the SRA Web page for more background information about Cooperation and Competition.

Build Background

Activate Prior Knowledge

Tell students that good readers create links between what they already know and what they are reading. Discuss the following with students to activate their prior knowledge about the selection and about the theme of Cooperation and Competition.

- Preteach "Class President" by first determining students' prior knowledge about class elections. Ask, "What are important qualities for a class president to have? Why?"

- Ask students to think of activities that require cooperation and discuss why cooperation is important in these activities. Students should also note whether the activities also involve competition and how.

- Have students discuss other stories or books that have the theme of cooperation and competition.

Background Information

The following information may help students better understand the selection they are about to read.

- Toward the end of this selection, the main character, Julio, is nominated to run for class president. One of his potential opponents comments that Julio should not be allowed to run for class president because he is Puerto Rican. This could be a sensitive issue in your classroom and should be discussed before students read the selection.

- Have the students discuss what they know about the genre of this selection. Refer to page 20A of the *Teacher's Edition* for elements of this selection's genre.

Preview and Prepare

Browse

Tell the students that before reading each selection, they will *set purposes*, or goals, for their reading and what they want to gain from it. Doing so will give them a sense of the selection and help them to better understand what they read. Explain that before they can set purposes, they will have to *browse* the selection using the *clues*, *problems*, and *wonderings* procedure.

- Have a student read aloud the title and the names of the author and illustrator. Demonstrate how to browse. Then have students preview the selection by browsing only the first page or two of the story, so as not to spoil the ending. Discuss with them what they think this story might have to do with cooperation and competition. This allows them to activate prior knowledge relevant to the story.

- Have students search for clues that tell them something about the selection, such as the classroom setting with its upcoming election suggests that this is realistic fiction. Have them search for any problems, such as unfamiliar words or long sentences that they notice while reading. Then have them consider any questions, or wonderings they have about the story. Use **Reading Transparency 54** to record their observations as they browse.

- As students prepare to read the selection, have them browse the Focus Questions on the first page of the selection. Tell them to keep these questions in mind as they read.

Set Purposes

Have students set their own purposes for reading this selection. As they read, have students think about which characters learn something about cooperation and competition and what they learn.

Selection Vocabulary

Display **Reading Transparency 1** before reading the selection to introduce the following words and their meanings.

election:	how people vote for someone to serve in an office or approve an idea (page 20)
campaign:	an organized effort to accomplish a purpose (page 23)
represent:	speak or act for someone else (page 24)
candidate:	person who is seeking an office, job, or position (page 27)
confidence:	belief in one's ability to do something (page 27)

Have students read the words in the Word Box stopping to blend any words that they have trouble reading. Demonstrate how to decode multisyllabic words by breaking the words into syllables and blending the syllables. Then have the students try. If the word is not decodable, give the students the pronunciation.

Have students read the sentences on **Reading Transparency 1** and use the skills of context, word structure (structural analysis), or apposition to figure out the meaning of the words.

- Tell students that sometimes one can define a word by using *context clues*, or other parts of the sentence that help one figure out the word's meaning.

- One can also use his or her knowledge of *word structure* (or the word's parts, such as *suffix*, *prefix*, and *root word*).

- Sometimes one can easily define the word when the author has used *apposition*, which is when the definition is placed directly before or after the words.

Be sure students explain which skill(s) they are using and how they figured out the meanings of the words.

Clues	Problems	Wonderings
"Vote for Cricket" poster indicates an upcoming election	Pronunciation of *Julio*	Who is running for office? What office is open?

Reading Transparency 54

Teacher Tip SELECTION VOCABULARY To help students decode words, divide them into the syllables shown below. The information following each word tells how students can figure out the meaning of each word in the sentences on **Reading Transparency 1**.

e • lec • tion	context clues, word structure
rep • re • sent	context clues
cam • paign	context clues
can • di • date	context clues
con • fi • dence	context clues

Routine Card
Refer to Routine 2 for the selection vocabulary procedure. Refer to Routine 3 for the Clues, Problems, and Wonderings procedure.

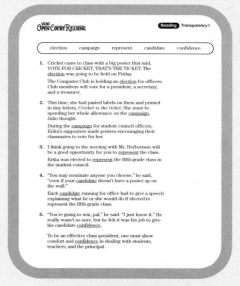

Reading Transparency 1

MEETING INDIVIDUAL NEEDS

ELL Support

For ELD strategies, use the *English-Language Development Guide,* Unit 1, Lesson 1.

Intervention Support

For intervention strategies, use the *Intervention Guide,* Unit 1, Lesson 1.

 Students will enjoy using the *Listening Library Audiocassette/CD* and listening to the selection they are about to read. Encourage them to listen to the selection during Workshop. Have students discuss with each other and with you their personal listening preferences (for example, nonfiction, poetry, drama, and so on).

 Routine Card Refer to Routine 4 for the Reading the Selection procedure.

Teacher Tip COMPREHENSION STRATEGIES Create a poster with the comprehension strategies listed. Refer to the Comprehension Strategies poster as the class reads the selection. As students are reading, ask them which of the strategies listed on the poster might be good to use at this point in the selection.

Reading Recommendations

Oral Reading

This story is natural for oral reading because of its conversational style. Students should read aloud fluently with appropriate pacing, expression, and intonation. Make sure that students attend to punctuation and read in phrases. Tell students to add a sense of feeling or anticipation as they read. Reading the selection with fluency and accuracy will help students comprehend the text. If students have trouble reading decodable words, have them break the words into sounds or syllables and then blend them together to read the words.

Have the students make use of the comprehension strategies listed below to help them understand the selection. Have them stop reading periodically or wait until they have completed the selection to discuss the reading strategies. After the students have finished reading the selection, use the "Discussing the Selection" questions on page 33A to see if they understand what they have read.

Because this is the beginning of the year, be sure to model strategy use frequently during the reading. As the year progresses and students become more confident in their use of strategies, teacher models will be replaced by prompts.

Using Comprehension Strategies First Read

Comprehension strategy instruction allows students to become aware of how good readers read. Good readers constantly check their understanding as they are reading and ask themselves questions. In addition, skilled readers recognize when they are having problems and stop to use various comprehension strategies to help them make sense of what they are reading.

During the first reading of "Class President" model and prompt the use of the following comprehension strategies. Take turns reading the story aloud with the students.

- **Making Connections** deepens students' understanding of what they read by linking it to their own past experiences and previous reading.
- **Predicting** causes readers to analyze information given about story events and characters in the context of how it may logically connect to the story's conclusion.
- **Summarizing** prompts readers to keep track of what they are reading and to focus their minds on important information.

As students read, they should be using a variety of strategies to help them understand the selection. Encourage students to use the strategies listed as the class reads the story aloud. Do this by stopping at the points indicated by the numbers in magenta circles on the reduced student page and using a particular strategy. Students can also stop periodically to discuss what they have learned and what problems they might be having.

Building Comprehension Skills

Revisiting or rereading a selection allows students to apply skills that give them a more complete understanding of the text. Some follow-up comprehension skills help students organize information. Others lead to deeper understanding—to "reading between the lines," as mature readers do. An extended lesson on the comprehension skill Drawing Conclusions can be found in the Supporting the Reading section on pages 33C–33D. This lesson is intended to give students extra practice with Drawing Conclusions. However, the Teach portion of the lesson may be used at this time to introduce the comprehension skill to students.

- **Drawing Conclusions (Introduction):** Readers draw conclusions using what they already know together with information they pull from the selection to understand the total picture in a story.

Reading with a Purpose

Have students list ways the story characters cooperate and compete throughout the selection in the Response Journal section of their Writer's Notebooks.

Teacher Tip COMPREHENSION STRATEGIES Remind students on the second day as they reread the story to summarize what they learned the first day.

Teacher Tip COMPREHENSION STRATEGIES Students' own think-alouds are always preferred to the teacher's. Encourage students to model for one another when they work out problems or as they come up with ideas when they read.

MEETING INDIVIDUAL NEEDS

ELL Support

PREREAD THE SELECTION Have English-language learners who may need help with the selection read it before the whole-class reading, using the *Listening Library Audiocassettes/CD.* As they read, help them associate what they see in the illustrations with the words in the story, so that they learn to think English words before translating them first from their native language.

Intervention Support

PREREAD THE SELECTION Preread "Class President" with students who may need help in reading the selection during the time you set aside for Workshop.

LISTENING LIBRARY During Workshop, have students listen to the selection "Class President" for a proficient, fluent model of oral reading.

COMPREHENSION

Read pages 20–35.

Comprehension Strategies

First Read

Read the story aloud, taking turns with the students. Start by modeling the use of strategies for the students.

Teacher Modeling

1 Making Connections *Good readers make connections between what they are reading and what they already know from past experience or previous reading to help them understand story events and characters.*

I connect with Julio's decision to base his vote on more than a chocolate bar. What Cricket is doing reminds me of an election where someone tries to bribe someone with money or gifts.

Teacher Modeling

2 Predicting *When reading fiction, good readers constantly make predictions about what they are reading, based on what they already know and on clues in the text. This helps them to focus on upcoming information that may be important.*

Do you think Cricket's candy bars will win her the election? I predict she will have to work harder if she wants to be class president, because it sounds like Julio is pretty serious about Lucas's campaign.

Word Knowledge

SCAFFOLDING The skills students are reviewing in Word Knowledge should help them in reading the story. This lesson focuses on root words and the suffixes *-or (-er)* and *-tion (-sion)*. Root words and derivatives with suffixes will be found in boxes similar to this one throughout the selection.

Root word	Derivative
nominate	nomination
elect	election

First Reading Recommendation

ORAL • CHORAL • SILENT

Focus Questions What qualities do good leaders have? If you were running for class president, what would be your strategy for winning the election?

Class President

Johanna Hurwitz
illustrated by Richard Hull
**To Delia and Bill Gottlieb
They get my vote every time!**

Julio Sanchez is sure that fifth grade is going to be his best year yet. On the first day of school, his homeroom teacher Mr. Flores announces that this year the fifth grade will be electing a class president. To get ready for the <u>election</u>*, the students are to be thinking about who might make a good leader.*

In the meantime, while playing in a soccer game at recess, Julio's classmate Arthur breaks his glasses. The fifth grade pitches in to pay for the glasses by holding a bake sale. But on the day of the bake sale, Arthur's mom finds out his glasses can be replaced for free.

Now the class has two things to decide: who to elect as class president and what to do with the bake sale money no longer needed to pay for Arthur's glasses. . . .

On Monday, Arthur came to school with new glasses. Cricket came to class with a big poster that said, VOTE FOR CRICKET, THAT'S THE TICKET.

The election was going to be held on Friday. That meant there were only four days more to get ready. In the meantime, they learned about how to make a <u>nomination</u> and how to <u>second</u> it. It was going to be a really serious election.

At lunch, Cricket took out a bag of miniature chocolate bars and gave them out to her classmates. Julio took his and **1** ate it. But it didn't mean he was going to vote for Cricket. He wondered if there was anything Lucas could give out that was better than chocolate. Nothing was better than chocolate!

20

Informal Assessment

Observe individual students as they read and use the Teacher Observation Log found in the ***Program Assessment Teacher's Edition,*** to record anecdotal information about each student's strengths and weaknesses.

Teacher Tip
Julio is pronounced ho͞o′ lē ō.
Flores is pronounced flō′ räs.

"If you're going to run against Cricket, we've got to get to work," Julio told Lucas on their way home. Julio wasn't very good at making posters, as Cricket and Zoe were, but he was determined to help his friend.

The next morning, a new poster appeared in Mr. Flores's classroom. It said, DON'T BUG ME. VOTE FOR LUCAS COTT. Julio had made it.

Before lunch, Mr. Flores read an announcement from the principal. "From now on, there is to be no more soccer playing in the school yard at lunchtime."

"No more soccer playing?" Julio called out. "Why not?"

Mr. Flores looked at Julio. "If you give me a moment, I'll explain. Mr. Herbertson is concerned about accidents. Last week, Arthur broke his glasses. Another time, someone might be injured more seriously."

Julio was about to call out again, but he remembered just in time and raised his hand.

"Yes, Julio," said Mr. Flores.

21

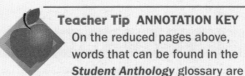

Teacher Tip ANNOTATION KEY
On the reduced pages above, words that can be found in the *Student Anthology* glossary are underlined in magenta. These words are underlined in the *Teacher's Edition* only. The magenta-encircled numbers appearing beside the text correspond to the Comprehension Strategies numbered in the column to the left.

Comprehension Skills

Second Read

COMPREHENSION

Drawing Conclusions

Introduce students to the concept of *drawing conclusions*, which means using pieces of text about a character or story event to make a statement or generalization about that character or story event. For instance, one can figure out quite a bit about a character by making note of how that character looks or behaves. Likewise, one can understand a story's events by paying attention to when and where the story takes place and how the story unfolds.

Have students read paragraph 3 on page 20. Then ask them these questions:

- What conclusion is Julio drawing about *why* Cricket is handing out the chocolate bars? *(She thinks if they eat the bars, they will vote for her.)*

- What conclusions does Julio draw about *eating* the bar? *(It doesn't mean he has to vote for her.)*

Tell the students to look for additional text clues that allow them to draw conclusions about the characters or events in the story.

Drawing Conclusions
Introduced in Grade 1.
Scaffolded throughout Grades 2–5.

REINTRODUCED: Unit 1, Lesson 1
REINFORCED: Unit 2, Lesson 1
Unit 3, Lesson 3
Unit 3, Lesson 5
Unit 4, Lesson 5
TESTED: Unit 1 Assessment

Second Reading Recommendation

ORAL • **SILENT**

COMPREHENSION

Comprehension Strategies

First Read

Teacher Modeling

❸ Making Connections *I can connect with how Julio feels. I remember being called into the principal's office when I was a student. Even though I had done nothing wrong, I was pretty nervous.*

As you are reading, be aware of how ideas and events in the text remind you of things that have happened to you. When you make such connections, tell the class about them.

Teacher Modeling

❹ Predicting *This is interesting— Julio wants Cricket to speak to the principal with him and Lucas. I predict that Cricket is going to be a big help in talking to the principal, because she wants so much to be voted class president.*

Word Knowledge

SCAFFOLDING The skills students are reviewing in Word Knowledge should help them in reading the story. This lesson focuses on words that have a consonant plus r blend at the beginning. These words will be found in boxes similar to this one throughout the selection.

Consonant plus *r* blend:
principal

Teacher Tip MAKING CONNECTIONS
Point out that each student may connect to the text in a completely different way. Assure them that this is normal and that it is impossible to connect to text in a wrong way.

"It's not fair to make us stop playing soccer just because someone *might* get hurt. Someone might fall down walking to school, but we still have to come to school every day."

Julio didn't mean to be funny, but everyone started to laugh. Even Mr. Flores smiled.

"There must be other activities to keep you fellows busy at lunchtime," he said. "Is soccer the only thing you can do?"

Lucas raised his hand. "I don't like jumping rope," he said when the teacher called on him.

All the girls giggled at that.

"You could play jacks," suggested Cricket. Everyone knew it wasn't a serious possibility, though.

"Couldn't we tell Mr. Herbertson that we want to play soccer?" asked Julio.

"You could make an appointment to speak to him, if you'd like," said Mr. Flores. "He might change his decision if you convince him that you are right."

"Lucas and I will talk to him," said Julio. "Right, Lucas?"

"Uh, sure," said Lucas, but he didn't look too sure.

❸ The principal, Mr. Herbertson, spoke in a loud voice and had eyes that seemed to <u>bore</u> right into your head when he looked at you. Julio had been a little bit afraid of Mr. Herbertson since the very first day of kindergarten. Why had he offered to go to his office and talk to him?

Mr. Flores sent Julio and Lucas down to the principal's office with a note, but the principal was out of the office at a meeting.

"You can talk to him at one o'clock," the secretary said.

22

MEETING INDIVIDUAL NEEDS

Intervention Support

PREDICTING Remind students that predicting helps them think ahead so they will be ready for new information. Reread this section with students having difficulty with predicting. Stop at sentences or paragraphs that signify some change in the action of the story, and work with students to make and revise their predictions.

22 Unit I Lesson I

At lunch, Cricket had more chocolate bars. This time, she had pasted labels on them and printed in tiny letters, *Cricket is the ticket.* She must be spending her whole allowance on the campaign, Julio thought.

After a few more days of free chocolate bars, everyone in the class would be voting for Cricket.

At recess, the girls were jumping rope. You could fall jumping rope, too, Julio thought.

Back in the classroom, Julio wished he could think up some good arguments to tell the principal. He looked over at Lucas. Lucas didn't look very good. Maybe he was coming down with the flu.

Just before one o'clock, Julio had a great idea. Cricket was always saying she wanted to be a lawyer. She always knew what to say in class. Julio figured she'd know just what to do in the principal's office, too. He raised his hand.

"Mr. Flores, can Cricket go down to Mr. Herbertson's office **4** with Lucas and me? She's running for president, so she should stick up for our class."

"Me?" Cricket said. "I don't care if we can't play soccer."

"Of course," teased Lucas. "You couldn't kick a ball if it was glued to your foot."

★ 23

Comprehension Skills

Drawing Conclusions

Have the students gather pieces of information from the text to help in *drawing conclusions* about characters and events. Ask the students to find information about Julio.

■ On page 23, Julio suggests that Cricket come speak to the principal, too. What does this tell you about Julio? *(Julio isn't afraid to ask for help in getting what he wants.)*

Have the students use the information they found to draw conclusions as they continue reading.

Word Knowledge

Consonant plus *r* blends:

printed	great
principal	Cricket
president	

COMPREHENSION

Comprehension Strategies

Teacher Modeling

5 Making Connections *I see that Julio is using a traditional Spanish pronunciation of his first name. I can connect this pronunciation to other words and names that are spelled with a j pronounced as h. I know that "jalapeño" is spelled with a j but pronounced with an h sound. Can you think of other words beginning with a j pronounced as h?*

Teacher Modeling

6 Confirming Predictions *After making a prediction, it is important to check back and see whether or not the prediction was right.*

Earlier I predicted that Cricket would be helpful when Julio talked to the principal. Cricket was no help at all! It was Julio who did all the talking. Now Cricket is taking credit for getting the principal to allow them to play soccer. I predict the other students will realize who did the persuading and that Cricket will definitely lose the election.

As you read, decide whether or not you think the predictions are on target. Come up with your own prediction based on the information in the text. As you come up with predictions, let the group know what they are. Good readers are always making predictions as they read.

Word Knowledge
Consonant plus *r* blends:

Cricket	broke
president	tripped
breath	

"Cricket," said Mr. Flores, "even if you don't want to play soccer, others in the class do. If you are elected, you will be president of the whole class, not just the girls. I think going to the meeting with Mr. Herbertson will be a good opportunity for you to <u>represent</u> the class."

So that was why at one o'clock Julio, Lucas, and Cricket Kaufman went downstairs to the principal's office.

Mr. Herbertson gestured for them to sit in the chairs facing his desk. Cricket looked as pale as Lucas. Maybe she, too, was coming down with the flu.

Julio waited for the future first woman President of the United States to say something, but Cricket didn't say a word. Neither did Lucas. Julio didn't know what to do. They couldn't just sit here and say nothing.

Julio took a deep breath. If Cricket or Lucas wasn't going to talk, he would have to do it. Julio started right in.

"We came to tell you that it isn't fair that no one can play soccer at recess just because Arthur Lewis broke his eyeglasses. Anybody can have an accident. He could have tripped and broken them getting on the school bus." Julio was amazed that so many words had managed to get out of his mouth. No one else said anything, so he went on. "Besides, a girl could fall jumping rope," said Julio. "But you didn't say that they had to stop jumping rope."

24

"I hadn't thought of that," said Mr. Herbertson.

Cricket looked alarmed. "Can't we jump rope anymore?" she asked.

"I didn't mean that you should make the girls stop jumping rope," Julio went on quickly. He stopped to think of a better example. "Your chair could break while you're sitting on it, Mr. Herbertson," he said.

Mr. Herbertson adjusted himself in his chair. "I certainly hope not," he said, smiling. "What is your name, young man?"

5 "Julio. Julio Sanchez." He pronounced it in the Spanish way with the *J* having an *H* sound.

"You have a couple of brothers who also attended this school, Julio, don't you?" asked the principal. "Nice fellows. I remember them both."

Julio smiled. He didn't know why he had always been afraid of the principal. He was just like any other person.

"Julio," Mr. Herbertson went on, "you've got a good head on your shoulders, just like your brothers. You made some very good points this afternoon. I think I can arrange things so that there will be more teachers supervising the yard during recess. Then you fellows can play soccer again tomorrow." He turned to Cricket. "You can jump rope if you'd rather do that," he said.

Cricket smiled. She didn't look so pale anymore.

Julio and Lucas and Cricket returned to Mr. Flores's classroom. "It's all arranged," said Cricket as soon **6** as they walked in the door.

25

Comprehension Skills

Second Read

Drawing Conclusions

Review with the students that drawing a conclusion means making a statement about a character, thing, or event based on information in the text. Characters in a selection can also draw conclusions based on the facts presented to them.

- Have students look carefully at the information about Mr. Herbertson on pages 24–25. What conclusion does Julio draw about Mr. Herbertson on page 25? *(that he is just like any other person)*

- What wrong conclusion had Julio originally drawn about Mr. Herbertson, and on what information did he base it? *(Julio thought Mr. Herbertson was a scary man at first because of his loud voice and stern appearance.)*

Have students find other examples of conclusions that characters in the story have drawn.

Word Knowledge
Consonant plus *r* blends:
break
brothers

Teacher Tip DRAWING CONCLUSIONS Remind students that information such as the looks and behavior of a character or the time and place of an event are helpful when drawing conclusions.

COMPREHENSION

COMPREHENSION

Comprehension Strategies

First
Read

Teacher Modeling

❼ Predicting *Julio thinks that all the girls will vote for a girl and all the boys will vote for a boy. Does this change your prediction about who will win the election? I don't think I would vote for Cricket or Lucas just because they are a boy or a girl. I still think that Cricket is going to lose. What do you think? As you come up with predictions, let the group know what they are.*

Teacher Modeling

❽ Making Connections *I see here that they are using* Robert's Rules of Order, *which is a book. I've seen this book used in very formal school meetings. It tells people how to run a formal meeting, how to decide who gets to speak first, and how long speakers get to talk.* Robert's Rules of Order *helps keep things fair for everyone. What connections can you make to the way they are running this meeting?*

Word Knowledge

Root Words:	Derivatives:
elect	election
associate	association

Teacher Tip MAKING CONNECTIONS
Have the students think of connections to the story as they are reading.
Parts of the selection may remind them of things in their lives—things that they've learned about in other selections, books they've read, or movies or television shows they've seen.

The class burst into cheers.

"Good work," said Mr. Flores.

Julio was proud that he had stood up to Mr. Herbertson. However, it wasn't fair that Cricket made it seem as if she had done all the work. She had hardly done a thing. For that matter, Lucas hadn't said anything, either. For a moment, Julio wished he hadn't offered to be Lucas's campaign manager. He wished he was the one running for class president. He knew he could be a good leader.

There was bad news on election day. Chris Willard was absent. Since there were twelve girls and twelve boys in Mr. Flores's class, it meant there were more girls than boys to vote in the election. If all the girls voted for Cricket and all the boys voted for Lucas, there would be a tie. Since one boy was absent, **❼** Lucas could be in big trouble. Julio hoped it didn't mean that Lucas had lost the election before they even voted.

Then Mr. Flores told the class that the Parent-Teacher Association was going to be holding a book fair in a few weeks. With more than seventeen dollars from the bake sale, the class could buy a good supply of paperbacks for a special classroom library. Cricket seemed to think it was a great idea, but Julio didn't think it was so hot. After all, there was a school library up one flight of stairs. Why did they need extra books, especially books the students had to pay for out of their *own* money?

26

Informal Assessment

Use the Informal Comprehension Strategies Rubrics on page 20J to determine whether a student is using the strategies being taught.

Julio thought that the class should vote on the way the money was spent. Before he had a chance to say anything, it was time for lunch.

Lunch was chicken nuggets, whipped potatoes, string beans, and Jell-O squares. Cricket and Zoe didn't even touch their lunches. Julio knew they were talking about the election. Julio clapped Lucas on the back. "You're going to win, pal," he said. "I just know it." He really wasn't so sure, but he felt it was his job to give his candidate confidence. After all, he had convinced Lucas to run for class president in the first place.

Lucas shrugged, trying to act cool. "Maybe yes, maybe no," he said. But Julio could see that he was too excited to eat much lunch, either. Julio polished off his friend's tuna-fish sandwich and his orange. "I need to keep up my strength to vote for you," he told Lucas.

Cricket had more chocolate bars. "Are you going to vote for me?" she asked everyone.

"Maybe yes, maybe no," said Julio, taking his bar.

When they returned from lunch, Mr. Flores called the class to order. It was time for the election to begin. Mr. Flores reminded **8** them about *Robert's Rules of Order*, which was the way school board and other important meetings were conducted.

"You may nominate anyone you choose," he said, "even if your candidate doesn't have a poster up on the wall. Then you

27

Comprehension Skills

Drawing Conclusions

Tell students that you have drawn the conclusion that Julio is good at thinking of the students' best interests. Have students tell you what they have read on these pages that supports this conclusion. *(Julio says that having a classroom library does not seem like a good use of class money because they can check out books for free upstairs.)*

Word Knowledge

Consonant plus *r* blends:

president

trying

COMPREHENSION

COMPREHENSION

Comprehension Strategies

First Read

Teacher Modeling

9 Summarizing *A good way to monitor your understanding of what you have read is to summarize the text's main events in your own words. If you are not able to do this, then you will know to go back and reread the parts you didn't remember or understand.*

Let's summarize the information on these pages about how an election works. First, a candidate has to be nominated. Then, someone else has to second the nomination. Once you nominate or second the nomination of a candidate, you can't nominate or second anyone else.

Let's continue reading, and as we do, remember to summarize what we are reading. Make sure you understand what you have just read. Let me know if you would like to share your summary with the group.

Teacher Modeling

10 Predicting *I had the feeling that Julio would like to run for president, but I never expected Arthur to nominate him. With Lucas and Julio both running, half of the boys might vote for Julio and half might vote for Lucas. If most of the girls vote for Cricket, she might win! I don't think all the girls will vote for Cricket, though. I don't know who will win, but I predict this will be a close race. What do you predict?*

Word Knowledge

Root word:	Derivative:
nominate	nomination
elect	election

---

can make a speech in favor of your candidate and try to convince your classmates."

9 Uh-oh, thought Julio. He was ready to nominate Lucas but he didn't know if he would be able to make a speech. He wasn't good with words, as Cricket and Lucas were.

Zoe Mitchell raised her hand. "I nominate Cricket Kaufman," she said. No surprise there. Julio wondered if Zoe had wanted to run herself.

"Does anyone second the nomination?" Mr. Flores asked.

Julio thought the class election sounded like a TV program, not the way people talked in real life.

Sara Jane seconded the nomination, and Mr. Flores wrote Cricket's name on the chalkboard.

"Are there any other nominations?" he asked.

Sara Jane raised her hand again.

"Do you have a question, Sara Jane?" asked Mr. Flores.

"Now I want to nominate Zoe Mitchell."

MEETING INDIVIDUAL NEEDS

Intervention Support

SUMMARIZING If students are having difficulty summarizing, reread the text with them, pointing out main events as necessary. Have students list the main events.

Teacher Tip SELF-EVALUATING COMPREHENSION Good readers constantly evaluate their understanding of what they read. Stop often to make sure students are doing this.

"You can't nominate someone when you have already seconded the nomination of someone else," Mr. Flores explained. "That's the way parliamentary procedure works."

Cricket looked relieved. She hadn't been expecting any competition from Zoe.

Julio raised his hand. "I nominate Lucas Cott," he said.

"Does anyone second the nomination?"

"Can I second myself?" asked Lucas.

"I'll second the nomination," said Anne Crosby from the back of the classroom.

"*Ooooh,*" giggled one of the girls. "Anne likes Lucas."

"There is no rule that girls can nominate only girls and boys nominate only boys," said Mr. Flores. He wrote Lucas's name on the board. "Are there any other nominations?" he asked.

10 Arthur Lewis raised his hand. "I want to nominate Julio Sanchez," he said.

"Julio?" Sara Jane giggled. "He's just a big goof-off."

"Just a minute," said Mr. Flores sharply. "You are quite out of order, Sara Jane. Does anyone wish to second the nomination?"

Julio couldn't believe that Arthur had nominated him. Even though Arthur had said that Julio should run for president, Julio hadn't thought he would come right out and say it in front of everyone.

Cricket raised her hand. "Julio can't run for president," she said. "He was born in Puerto Rico. He isn't an American citizen. You have to be an American citizen to be elected President. We learned that last year in social studies."

"Yeah," Lucas called out. "You also have to be thirty-five years old. You must have been left back a lot of times, Cricket."

29

Comprehension Skills

Drawing Conclusions

Remind students that they can draw conclusions to better understand the characters in the story.

■ Have students review Cricket's arguments against Julio being nominated for president on page 29. What can students conclude about Cricket from her arguments? Students should explain how they came to their conclusions. *(Students might conclude that Cricket is desperate to win the race because she tries so hard to disqualify Julio.)*

 Teacher Tip MAKING CONNECTIONS Some students might be unfamiliar with the American territory of Puerto Rico. Encourage them to look in an atlas or encyclopedia for more information.

COMPREHENSION

Comprehension Strategies

Teacher Modeling

⓫ **Summarizing** *Let's summarize again to make sure we understand how this new turn in the election occurred. Julio has now been nominated for class president. Lucas has decided not to run and has taken his name off the board. He asks everyone to vote for Julio. So now the race is between Julio and Cricket. This changes things a lot. Is there anything we should add to the summary before we go on?*

Word Knowledge

Consonant plus *r* blends:
> **president**
> **grade**
> **wrong**
> **broke**

Teacher Tip COMPREHENSION STRATEGIES Remind students to make use of their comprehension strategies to understand the story. Model behaviors good readers use, such as treating problems encountered in the text as interesting learning opportunities rather than something to be avoided or dreaded. Have students ask themselves questions about what they have just read to monitor their own comprehension. If this does not work, have them try to pinpoint exactly what is unclear to them. After the students have read the selection, use the "Discussing the Selection" questions to see if they have understood what they have read. If they have not, refer to the *Intervention Guide* for further strategies.

"Hold on," said Mr. Flores. "Are we electing a President of the United States here, or are we electing a president of this fifth-grade class?"

Cricket looked embarrassed. It wasn't often she was wrong about anything.

Julio stood up without even raising his hand. He didn't care if he was elected president or not, but there was one thing he had to make clear. "I am so an American citizen," he said. "All Puerto Ricans are Americans!"

Julio sat down, and Arthur raised his hand again. Julio figured he was going to say he had changed his mind and didn't want to nominate him after all.

"Arthur?" called Mr. Flores.

Arthur stood up. "It doesn't matter where Julio was born," he said. "He'd make a very good class president. He's fair, and he's always doing nice things for people. When I broke my glasses, he was the one who thought of going to Mr. Herbertson so that we could still play soccer at recess. That shows he would make a good president."

"But Julio is not one of the top students like Zoe or Lucas or me," Cricket said.

"He is tops," said Arthur. "He's tops in my book."

Julio felt his ears getting hot with embarrassment. He had never heard Arthur say so much in all the years that he had known him.

30

"Thank you, Arthur," said Mr. Flores. "That was a very good speech. We still need someone to second the nomination. Do I hear a second?"

Lucas raised his hand.

"I second the nomination of Julio Sanchez," he said.

Mr. Flores turned to write Julio's name on the board. Lucas was still raising his hand.

Mr. Flores turned from the board and called on Lucas again.

"Do you wish to make a campaign speech?" he asked Lucas.

"Yes, I'm going to vote for Julio, and I think everyone else should, too."

"Aren't you even going to vote for yourself?" asked Cricket.

"No," said Lucas. "I want to take my name off the board. Julio is a good leader, like Arthur said. When we went to see Mr. Herbertson, Cricket and I were scared stiff, but Julio just stepped in and did all the talking."

"Are you asking to withdraw your name from nomination, Lucas?" asked Mr. Flores.

"Yes, I am. Everyone who was going to vote for me should vote for Julio."

Julio sat in his seat without moving. He couldn't say a word. He could hardly breathe.

31

Comprehension Skills

Drawing Conclusions

Remind students that drawing conclusions means using specific ideas or events in a text to come up with and support ideas.

■ Have students review Arthur's speech on page 30. Do they agree with Arthur's ideas about Julio? What information in the text supports his ideas? *(Most students will agree with Arthur's ideas about Julio because the text provides ample support for his ideas. For example, Julio thinks the class should vote on how the money they earned is spent, he includes Cricket in the petition to the principal, and he thinks of the other students' needs as well as his own.)*

Word Knowledge
Consonant plus *r* blends:
> write
> breathe

Teacher Tip FLUENCY By this time in grade 5, good readers should be reading approximately 126 words per minute with fluency and expression. The only way to gain this fluency is through practice. Have students reread the selection to you and to each other during Workshop to help build fluency.

COMPREHENSION

COMPREHENSION

Comprehension Strategies

First Read

Teacher Modeling

12 Confirming Predictions *Let's check back and see how we did on our predictions for who would win the race. I was right that not all the girls would vote for Cricket, but Julio was right that all the boys would vote for a boy candidate. I'm glad that Julio was elected class president. I think he'll make a good leader.*

Discussing Strategy Use

While students are reading the selection, encourage them to share any problems encountered and to tell what strategies they used.

- How did they summarize the text?
- What connections did they make between the reading and what they already know?
- On what basis did they make and confirm predictions?

Remind students that good readers use all of the strategies listed above, and that they should be using them whenever they read. Make sure that students explain how using the strategies helped them better understand the selection. For example, students might say, "Predicting helped me to think ahead and stay interested in what I was reading—I wanted to see if my predictions were right."

Word Knowledge
Consonant plus *r* blends:
grade

"Are there any other nominations?" asked Mr. Flores.

Zoe raised her hand. "I <u>move</u> that the nominations be closed."

"I second it," said Lucas.

Then Mr. Flores asked the two candidates if they wanted to say anything to the class.

Cricket stood up. "As you all know," she said, "I'm going to run for President of the United States some day. Being class president will be good practice for me. Besides, I know I will do a much, much better job than Julio." Cricket sat down.

Julio stood. "I might vote for Cricket when she runs for President of the United States," he said. "But right now, I hope you will all vote for me. I think our class should make decisions together, like how we should spend the money that we earned at the bake sale. We should spend the money in a way that everyone likes. Not just the teacher." Julio stopped and looked at Mr. Flores. "That's how I feel," he said.

"If I'm president," said Cricket, "I think the money should go to the Humane Society."

"*You* shouldn't tell us what to do with the money, either," said Julio. "It should be a class decision. We all helped to earn it."

"Julio has made a good point," said Mr. Flores. "I guess we can vote on that in the future."

Mr. Flores passed out the ballots. Julio was sure he knew the results even before the votes were counted. With one boy absent, Cricket would win, twelve to eleven.

12 Julio was right, and he was wrong. All the boys voted for him, but so did some of the girls. When the votes were counted, there were fourteen for Julio Sanchez and nine for Cricket Kaufman. Julio Sanchez was elected president of his fifth-grade class.

⭐ 32

Teacher Tip COMPREHENSION STRATEGIES AND SKILLS Reread the selection with students who had difficulty understanding it. Continue modeling and prompting the use of strategies and skills as you reread the selection.

"I think you have made a good choice," said Mr. Flores. "And I know that Cricket will be a very fine vice-president."

Julio beamed. Suddenly he was filled with all sorts of plans for his class.

Mr. Flores took out his guitar. As he had said, they were going to end each week with some singing. Julio thought he had never felt so much like singing in all his life. However, even as he joined the class in the words to the song, he wished it was already time to go home. He could hardly wait to tell his family the news. Wait till he told them who was the fifth-grade class president. Julio, that's who!

At three o'clock, he ran all the way home.

33

Teacher Tip BUILDING FLUENCY

As students read, you may notice that some need work in building fluency. During Workshop, have these students choose a section of the text (a minimum of 160 words) to read several times in order to build fluency.

Formal Assessment

See pages 2–5 in *Unit 1 Assessment* to test students' comprehension of "Class President."

Comprehension Skills

COMPREHENSION

Drawing Conclusions

Remind students that conclusions they draw may not be directly stated in the story. However, conclusions should be supported by details from the story. Have students draw conclusions about the kind of president Julio will be. Make sure students support their conclusions with evidence from the text. *(Most students will conclude that Julio will be an active president that considers the entire class in his decision making. Students should note that he is already making plans for the class and that he has shown with his position on the class money that he thinks everyone should participate in decision making.)*

Checking Comprehension

Ask students the following questions to check their comprehension of the story.

- How is Cricket affected by the competition? *(She becomes desperate and tries to bribe students to vote for her.)*

- Which character puts the most effort into cooperation? Explain. *(Julio puts the most effort into cooperation by asking Cricket to join him and Lucas to talk to the principal and by saying that the class should decide as a whole how to spend their money.)*

- Of Cricket, Lucas, and Julio, do you think the best person won the election? Why? *(Most students will think the best person won because he was the only one who focused on cooperation and took seriously the job of representing the other students.*

Routine Card
Refer to Routine 5 for the *handing-off process.*

Clues	Problems	Wonderings
"Vote for Cricket" poster indicates an upcoming election	Pronunciation of *Julio*	Who is running for office? What office is open?

Reading Transparency 54

Ask students to bring in a spiral notebook or a three-ring binder that they will label Writer's Notebook. Let them know that their notebook will be divided into at least four different sections. These sections should include the following:

• Vocabulary Words—selection vocabulary words and their definitions

• Response Journal—students write their notes about a selection or a literary response to the selection

• Personal Dictionary—words that are hard to spell or any interesting words that students find in their reading can go in this section

• Writing Ideas—students write their notes, observations, and other prewriting for writing assignments

Feel free during the year to add new sections that you and your students find useful. Tell students that as they work on different ideas for writing, vocabulary words, or literary techniques, they will keep their notes in their Writer's Notebook.

Discussing the Selection

After the first read, the whole group discusses the selection and any personal thoughts, reactions, problems, or questions that it raises. To stimulate discussion, students can ask one another the kinds of questions that good readers ask themselves about a text: *How does it connect to cooperation and competition? What have I learned that is new? What did I find interesting? What is important here? What was difficult to understand? Why would someone want to read this?* It is important for students to see you as a contributing member of the group.

Routine 5 To emphasize that you are part of the group, actively participate in the *handing-off process:* Raise your hand to be called on by the last speaker when you have a contribution to make. Point out unusual and interesting insights verbalized by students so that these insights are recognized and discussed. As the year progresses, students will take more and more responsibility for the discussions of the selections.

Engage students in a discussion to determine whether they have grasped the following ideas:

■ how competition affected the characters

■ that cooperation is necessary to achieve goals

■ why Julio won the election

During this time, have students return to the clues, problems, and wonderings they noted during browsing to determine whether the clues were borne out by the selection, whether and how their problems were solved, and whether their wonderings were answered or deserve further discussion and exploration. Let the students decide which items deserve further discussion.

Also have students return to the Focus Questions on the first page of the selection. Select a student to read the questions aloud, and have volunteers answer the questions. If students do not know the answers to the questions, have them return to the text to find the answers.

You may wish to review the elements of realistic fiction with students at this time. Discuss with them how they can tell that "Class President" is realistic fiction.

Have students break into small groups to discuss how the story reflects the theme. Groups can then share their ideas with the rest of the class.

Students may wish to record personal responses to this selection. Encourage students to write about times when they won a competition through cooperation.

Review Selection Vocabulary

Have students review the definitions of the selection vocabulary words that they wrote in the vocabulary section of their Writer's Notebooks. Remind them that they discussed the meanings of these words before reading the selection. Students can use these definitions to study for the vocabulary portion of their Lesson Assessment. Have them add to the personal dictionary section of their Writer's Notebook any other interesting words that they clarified while reading. Encourage students to refer to the selection vocabulary words throughout the unit. The words from the selection are:

election   represent   candidate   campaign   confidence

Create a Word Bank for the students to help them organize the vocabulary words throughout the year. Rather than organizing the words in alphabetical order, create a Word Bank based on word origins. Headings for words to be organized in this fashion include Latin, Greek, Germanic, French, and so on. Write the vocabulary words in large black letters on colored index cards. Have students place the words under the appropriate headings on the Word Bank. Tell students that some words will fit under more than one heading. For example, one word might have a root word that was derived from the Greek and an affix that was derived from the Latin. In these cases have students underline the part of the word for which the heading applies. Encourage the students to find other words related to the unit theme and add them to the Word Bank. Have them analyze and define the meaning of each word using the information on each word part's original meaning. A full explanation of the Word Bank can be found in the Program Appendix.

Home Connection

Distribute **Home Connection,** page 3. Encourage students to discuss "Class President" with their families. Students can discuss campaign slogans and come up with their own slogans, as well as design a campaign poster or button. **Home Connection** is also available in Spanish, page 4.

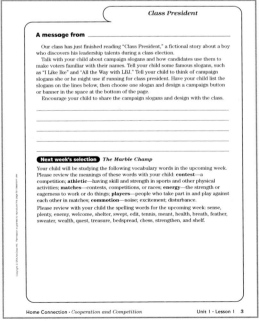

Home Connection p. 3

www.sra4kids.com
Web Connection
Some students may choose to conduct a computer search for additional books or information about cooperation and competition. Invite them to make a list of these books and sources of information to share with classmates and the school librarian. Check the Reading link of the SRA Web page for additional links to theme-related Web sites.

Teacher Tip DRAWING CONCLUSIONS You might consult the Clues, Problems, and Wonderings on *Reading Transparency 54* to come up with additional topics for drawing conclusions.

Supporting the Reading

Comprehension Skills: Drawing Conclusions

Teach Have students tell you what they know about drawing conclusions. Then explain to students that as they read, they should gather information about how characters act, what they say, and when and where the story takes place. They can put this information together to draw conclusions, or make statements, about story characters and events. Reiterate that conclusions are not directly stated, but they are based on text from the story. Emphasize that drawing conclusions allows readers to better understand characters and their motivations, as well as events, in a story.

Guided Practice Use a graphic organizer like the one below to help students organize the information needed to draw conclusions. On the board, draw three graphic organizers—one for Lucas, one for Julio, and one for Cricket—and write their names in the top boxes of the organizer. Have students provide clues from the story for each character, adding as many boxes as possible to the Clues from Story row. Finally, discuss as a class the conclusions that can be drawn about each character based on the information in the organizers.

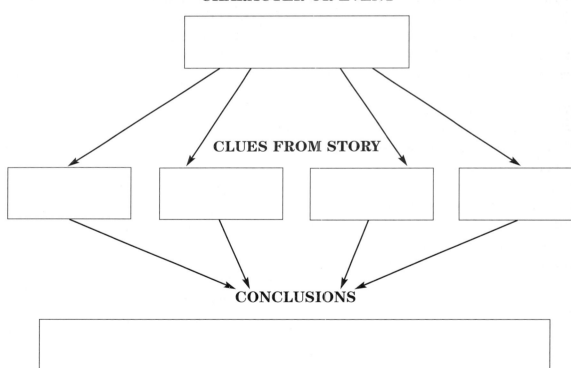

CHARACTER OR EVENT

CLUES FROM STORY

CONCLUSIONS

Independent Practice Read the **Focus** and **Identify** sections of the *Comprehension and Language Arts Skills,* page 2, with students. Guide students through the **Identify** portion, and help them come up with support from the story. Then have students complete the **Practice and Apply** portion of the *Comprehension and Language Arts Skills,* page 3, as homework.

Link to Writing Write each of the following words on separate pieces of paper: *generous, kind, happy, selfish, afraid, lonely, talkative, unhappy.* Then, have each student choose one of the words from a hat, write it down, and replace it in the hat. Students should not share their words with others. Explain that students will each write a short paragraph about a character that possesses the trait chosen. However, students cannot directly state the trait. When students have completed their paragraphs, have them exchange papers and draw conclusions about the traits presented in the paragraphs. After the conclusions have been drawn, discuss with the students the clues included in the paragraphs that led them to their conclusions.

MEETING INDIVIDUAL NEEDS

Reteach

DRAWING CONCLUSIONS Have students who need additional practice with drawing conclusions complete *Reteach,* pages 2–3.

Challenge

DRAWING CONCLUSIONS Have students who understand drawing conclusions complete *Challenge,* page 2.

Drawing Conclusions
Introduced in Grade 1.
Scaffolded throughout Grades 2–5.
REINTRODUCED: Unit 1, Lesson 1
REINFORCED: Unit 2, Lesson 1
Unit 3, Lesson 3
Unit 3, Lesson 5
Unit 4, Lesson 5
TESTED: Unit 1 Assessment

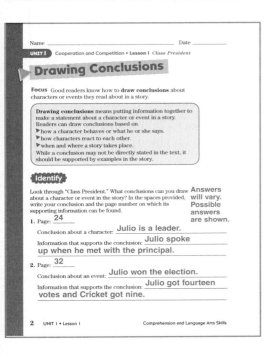
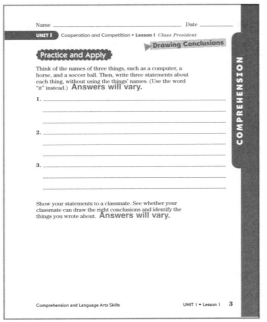

Comprehension and Language Arts Skills pp. 2–3

Teacher Tip CHARACTER ANALYSIS Remind students that as they drew conclusions during their second reading of "Class President" they were able to make generalizations about some of the characters. Have students recall these generalizations.

Teacher Tip CHARACTER ANALYSIS If necessary, define the terms *trait, motivation, conflict, relationship,* and *viewpoint* for students. A *trait* is a quality of a person or animal. *Motivation* is a reason for doing something. *Conflict* is a problem or disagreement. *Relationship,* in this context, refers to how a character relates to people around him or her. *Viewpoint* is a person's feelings or beliefs about a topic.

Teacher Tip PLOT AND THEME Review with students what they remember about *plot* and *theme* from the fourth grade. If necessary, review with them that *plot* is the progression of events in a story. Elements of plot include *exposition,* or *introduction; conflict; rising action; climax; falling action;* and *resolution. Theme* is the meaning or moral of a story.

Literary Elements

Character Analysis

Teach Have students think of ways Johanna Hurwitz made the characters in "Class President" seem like real people. Tell students that authors make characters seem real by describing their traits, motivation, conflicts, relationships, viewpoints, and changes they undergo. These are depicted through:

- what the character thinks and says.
- what the character does, and why she or he does it.
- what other characters say about the character.

Guided Practice Use the following pieces of text from the selection as examples of how an author helps his or her readers to "know" a character through traits, motivation, conflict, relationships, viewpoints, and changes he or she undergoes. Have students analyze what each reveals about Julio's character. (Possible responses are in parentheses.)

- Page 20: "At lunch, Cricket took out a bag of miniature chocolate bars and gave them out to her classmates. Julio took his and ate it. But it didn't mean he was going to vote for Cricket." (*Indicates viewpoint: Julio does not think that receiving chocolate from Cricket is reason enough to vote for her.*)
- Page 21: "Julio wasn't very good at making posters, as Cricket and Zoe were, but he was determined to help his friend." (*Indicates trait: Julio is loyal.*)
- Page 24: "Julio took a deep breath. If Cricket or Lucas wasn't going to talk, he would have to do it." (*Indicates motivation and conflict: Julio takes charge of the situation so the problem can be solved.*)
- Page 30: "'He is tops,' said Arthur. 'He's tops in my book.'" (*Indicates relationship: Julio is respected by his classmate.*)
- Pages 32–33: "Julio Sanchez was elected president of his fifth-grade class.... Julio beamed. Suddenly he was filled with all sorts of plans for his class." (*Indicates a change undergone: Julio becomes excited by the prospect of leading his class.*)

Independent Practice Have students analyze other characters from "Class President." Have students compare the motives and actions of the character with their own motives and actions, or those of people they know, especially in situations like an election or negotiation. Have them also tell how the character's motives, actions, and appearances differ from each other and how these differences are important to the story's plot and theme. (*For example, the contrast between Cricket's and Julio's characters create conflict through which the author's ideas about the qualities of good leaders are communicated.*) Finally, have students analyze how certain characters change over the course of the story, if they change, and how this corresponds with the plot's development.

Social Studies Connection: Citizenship

In "Class President," Julio points out that he is a citizen of the United States. Explain to students that United States citizens have certain privileges and rights. Point out that they have certain responsibilities, too.

Divide the class into three groups. Assign each group one of the following topics: Rights, Privileges, Responsibilities. Then have students search the library or the Internet for information about these topics. Have each group write their topic at the top of the posterboard and list aspects of the topic underneath the head. Finally, groups should present their posterboards. Have groups explain to the class each right, privilege, or responsibility listed on their posterboard. You might display the finished posters in the classroom.

Teacher Tip MATERIALS FOR ACTIVITY To complete the Social Studies Connection activity for this lesson, students will need posterboard, and markers or pencils.

Science/Social Studies Connection Center

Refer to the Science/Social Studies Connection Center Card 1 for a social studies activity that students can investigate.

Meet the Author

After students read the information about Johanna Hurwitz, discuss the following questions with them.

- Johanna Hurwitz knew she wanted to be a writer from the time she was ten years old, but she didn't have a book published until she was in her thirties. What does this tell you about her? *(Possible answer: Johanna was determined to be a writer; which made her willing to work hard to achieve her goal.)*

- Johanna Hurwitz said, "It seems all my fiction has grown out of real experiences." In what ways could writing from her own experiences make her writing better? *(Possible answer: Writing about real-life experiences enables her to give vivid details that help the reader feel like the story could really happen.)*

Meet the Illustrator

After students read the information about Richard Hull, discuss the following question with them.

- Richard Hull worked as an art director with a magazine before becoming a teacher of illustration. How do you think these different experiences have helped him to illustrate this story? *(Possible answer: He has worked with many different people, and this has helped him illustrate many different personalities.)*

Class President

Meet the Author

Johanna Hurwitz was born in New York, New York. It's not surprising that Ms. Hurwitz knew from the age of ten that she wanted to be a writer. Her parents met in a bookstore. She grew up in a New York City apartment where the walls were lined with books. Her father was a journalist and bookseller, and her mother was a library assistant.

She began her career with books working at the New York City Public Library while still in high school. She then got two degrees in Library Science. She published her first book while in her 30s and has been writing books for children ever since. In one interview she revealed, *"It seems as if all my fiction has grown out of real experiences."* She has written books about her children's love of baseball, her own childhood and summer vacations, her mother's childhood, and even her cats and their fleas!

Meet the Illustrator

Richard Hull teaches illustration at Brigham Young University. He has also worked as an art director and graphic designer with a magazine for fifteen years. Other books Mr. Hull has illustrated include *The Cat & the Fiddle & More, My Sister's Rusty Bike,* and *The Alphabet from Z to A (With Much Confusion on the Way).* He and his wife currently reside in Orem, Utah.

34

Theme Connections

Within the Selection

Record your answers to the questions below in the Response Journal section of your Writer's Notebook. In small groups, report the ideas you wrote. Discuss your ideas with the rest of your group. Then choose a person to report your group's answers to the class.

- How did the class cooperate to help Arthur? How did cooperation play a role in their effort?
- In what way are the methods that Cricket uses in the competition for class president unfair? Is competition always this way?
- Even though Julio didn't plan to run for class president, he was still nominated. What qualities did Julio have that would make him a good class president?

Beyond the Selection

- Describe a time when you or someone you know worked for the good of a group rather than the benefit of only one person.
- Think about how "Class President" adds to what you know about cooperation and competition.
- Add items to the Concept/Question Board about cooperation and competition.

Theme Connections

Within the Selection

- The class worked together to raise money to replace Arthur's glasses.
- Cricket tried to buy votes, and she took credit for getting soccer back, even though she had little to do with it. Competition is not always unfair. Lucas did not do these things.
- Julio did things for the good of others, not only for his benefit. He also supported group decisions.

Beyond the Selection

- Students may name a time when they worked on a community service project, or served on a school committee.

Have groups report and discuss their ideas with the class. As these ideas are stated, have students add them to the Concept/Question Board.

Students should record their ideas and impressions about the selections on page 6 of their *Inquiry Journals*.

Name_____ Date_____

UNIT 1 Cooperation and Competition

Recording Concept Information

As I read each selection, this is what I added to my understanding of cooperation and competition.

- "Class President" by Johanna Hurwitz
  Answers will vary.

- "The Marble Champ" by Gary Soto
  Answers will vary.

- "Juggling" by Donna Gamache
  Answers will vary.

6 UNIT 1 *Recording Concept Information • Inquiry Journal*

Inquiry Journal p. 6

Teacher Tip INQUIRY AND INVESTIGATION As students complete their discussions have them sum up what they have learned and tell how they might use this information in further investigations.

Informal Assessment

This may be a good time to observe students working in small groups and to mark your observations in the Teacher Observation Log found in the *Program Assessment Teacher's Edition.*

Objectives

- Students gain a deeper understanding of cooperation and competition.
- Students come up with questions about cooperation and competition that they would like to investigate.
- Students learn about parts of the library.

Materials

- Student Anthology, pp. 20–35
- Inquiry Journal, pp. 8–9
- Reading Transparency 2
- Research Assistant

Name_____ Date_____

UNIT 1 Cooperation and Competition

Charting Examples

As you read and investigate, you will discover many examples of cooperation and competition. Record acts from stories, newspapers, television shows, and your life in the chart below. You can check this chart periodically for investigation ideas and topics.

Answers will vary.

Acts of Cooperation	Acts of Competition

8 UNIT 1   Charting Examples • Inquiry Journal

Inquiry Journal p. 8

INVESTIGATION

Investigating Concepts Beyond the Text

In each unit, students will engage in activities of their own choosing that allow them to investigate the unit theme more thoroughly and to use the questions they have raised to do so. These investigations may relate to the current **Student Anthology** selection or to a number of selections, but they must directly relate to the theme.

To facilitate students' investigation of the unit theme, activity suggestions such as the following are provided in the Inquiry section of each lesson. Tell students that if they have activity ideas of their own that they would like to pursue, they are free to do so as an alternative to these activity suggestions. Tell students that they may work on these activities alone, in pairs, or in small groups, with an option to write about them or to present them to the group upon completion.

The activity suggestions for this lesson are:

- Have the students chart acts of cooperation and acts of competition on **Inquiry Journal,** page 8. Students may want to begin their charts by listing cooperative and competitive acts that they read about in the selection "Class President." They can continue the charts with cooperative and competitive acts from their own experiences, stories, newspapers, and television shows.

- Have students do a library search for stories involving cooperation and competition. Encourage them to update the Concept/Question Board as they acquire information that might be useful to other groups or that raises new questions about cooperation and competition.

Upon completion of their activities, have students share with the group anything new they learned about cooperation and competition through discussion and by adding information to the Concept/Question Board.

Concept/Question Board

After reading each selection, students should use the Concept/Question Board to

- post any questions they asked about a selection before reading that have not yet been answered.
- refer to as they formulate statements about concepts that apply to their investigations.
- post general statements formulated by each collaborative group.
- continue to post news articles, or other items that they find during the unit investigation.
- read and think about posted questions, articles, or concepts that interest them and provide answers to the questions.

Concept/Question Board

Cooperation and Competition

Concept   Question

Unit I Investigation Management

Lesson I	**Collaborative Investigation** **Students generate ideas for investigation.** **Supplementary Activities** **Students participate in investigation activities and learn the parts of the library.**
Lesson 2	Students formulate questions and problems for investigation.
Lesson 3	Students make conjectures.
Lesson 4	Students establish investigation needs.
Lesson 5	Students establish investigation plans.
Lesson 6	Students present investigation findings.

INVESTIGATION

Research Assistant
The Research Assistant helps students in their investigations.

www.sra4kids.com
Web Connection
Students can use the connections to Cooperation and Competition in the Reading link of the SRA Web page for more background information about cooperation and competition.

Teacher Tip INVESTIGATION ACTIVITIES To assist students in the first stages of investigation, have them frequently consult the Concept/Question Board for ideas about and examples of cooperation and competition.

Research in Action
Inquiry and Investigation

The inquiry/investigation procedure is based on the assumption that students can do research that will result in the construction of deeper knowledge. The procedure presents research as a never-ending, recursive cycle. Like real-world researchers, students produce their own questions; develop ideas or conjecture about why something is the way it is; then pursue the answers. The answers, as for real researchers, may never come. What will come are more questions. Developing the questions, pursuing the answers, developing conjectures, revising ideas, and setting off on new avenues of research and investigation are the stuff of which strong, deep knowledge and expertise are made. The web of knowledge expands in ways that no teacher or student can easily predict. *(Carl Bereiter and Marlene Scardamalia)*

INVESTIGATION

Unit 1 Investigation Possibilities

- **A literature search** to pursue a question or idea about cooperation and competition. Discussion or writing might follow.

- **A chart** of story characters and their acts of cooperation and competition.

- **A role-playing game** in which members of a group cooperate during a competition.

- **A debate on an issue** related to cooperation and competition. (Debaters would form teams. They would be required to follow some basic rules of debate, providing reasoned support for their sides of the issue.)

- **An advice column** dealing with problems that arise from a lack of cooperation or an excess of competition.

- **An interview** with someone who has direct experience with cooperation and competition, such as a team coach or an elected official.

- **A picture or photo essay** about cooperation and competition.

Reading Transparency 2

Name _____ Date _____

Cooperation and Competition **UNIT 1**

Ideas about Cooperation and Competition

Of the ideas discussed in class about cooperation and competition, these are the ones I found most interesting.
Answers will vary.

Inquiry Journal • *Ideas about Cooperation and Competition*   UNIT 1 **9**

Inquiry Journal p. 9

Formal Assessment

Use the Research Rubrics on page 20J to assess students' ability to formulate research questions and problems.

Generating Ideas to Investigate

During the course of this unit, students will be investigating the concepts of cooperation and competition. You will be guiding them through the investigation process by having them

- generate ideas to investigate.
- formulate questions and problems from their ideas.
- make conjectures as to how they might solve their problems or answer their questions.
- establish their investigation needs.
- establish their investigation plans.
- present their findings to the group.

As students progress through this investigation process, emphasize that they can use the steps of this process to investigate anything they want to know more about, whether it is related to school or to personal interests.

Tell students that they will be performing an investigation of problems and questions related to the concepts of cooperation and competition and that the purpose of their investigation is to add to the group's knowledge of the unit theme. Explain to the students that the type of investigation they will conduct will take several weeks and will require them to make important decisions about managing their time. They are free to decide what about cooperation and competition they want to investigate and with whom they want to work. At the end of the time allotted to this unit, they will present their investigation findings to the group. Display the menu of Investigation Possibilities on *Reading Transparency 2*. Tell students that these are all ideas for how they might publish their investigation findings. Tell students that these ideas are options; students are also encouraged to come up with their own ideas for publishing their findings.

Have students begin the investigation process by brainstorming problems or questions related to the concepts of cooperation and competition. Have students examine the questions they raised during discussion of the *Student Anthology* selection, their ideas about cooperation and competition posted on the Concept/Question Board, and anything they learned from the activities in Investigating the Concepts Beyond the Text. Conduct a free-floating discussion of aspects of cooperation and competition that interest the students. Then have students list the ideas they found most interesting on *Inquiry Journal,* page 9.

Parts of the Library

Teach Have students tell you what they know about the parts of the library and the many kinds of sources it contains. If necessary, give them the following information:

- Libraries contain print resources such as atlases, almanacs, dictionaries, encyclopedias, books, magazines, and newspapers.

- Atlases, almanacs, dictionaries, and encyclopedias are located in the reference section of the library. Often encyclopedias are organized in many volumes. Each volume contains information about words and topics beginning with the letters shown on its spine or cover.

- Magazines and newspapers are usually displayed in a special periodicals area in the library.

- Books are categorized according to subject matter and whether they are fiction or nonfiction.

- Many libraries also provide access to electronic resources such as periodical databases; software for atlases, dictionaries, and encyclopedias; and the Internet. These resources can often be most effectively searched using key words, which are words that describe generally the subject you are researching, like "cooperation," or "sports," or words that might be specific to the information you are seeking, like "Abraham Lincoln."

- Card catalogs list all the books in the library. Some libraries list the books on cards that are filed in small cabinet drawers. Many libraries have computerized their card catalogs. Computer catalogs can often be searched by author, title, subject, or key word, which could be a word that appears in the title, subject, or author's name.

Guided Practice Have students select a variety of subjects related to "Class President" and the key words *cooperation* and *competition*. They might also search for other realistic fiction books set in schools or that have class elections; information about local, state, or federal governments; or United States presidential elections. Let them visit the school or public library to make a list of print and electronic resources available, using the information above to help guide them in their search.

Independent Practice Have students write brief reports on their subjects based on the print and electronic resources they found in the library. Also have them describe which parts of the library were most helpful to their investigation and why.

SUPPORTING THE INVESTIGATION

Teacher Tip STUDENT WRITING AND RESEARCH CENTER Have students use the *Student Writing and Research Center CD-ROM* as they work on their investigation activities.

Objectives

Word Analysis

Spelling
- **Spelling Patterns for the /a/ Sound.** Develop understanding of spelling patterns for the /a/ sound introduced in Word Knowledge in Part 1.

Vocabulary
- Using words from "Class President," develop questions and strategies to use when determining the meaning of an unknown word.

Writing Process Strategies
- **The Process of Getting Ideas.** Learn to set writing goals and make decisions about a topic, its audience and purpose, and form of a piece of writing.

English Language Conventions

Grammar, Usage, and Mechanics
- **Nouns.** Understand correct use of nouns (common and proper) and identify them in "Class President."

Listening, Speaking, Viewing
- **Listening: Understanding What We Hear.** Students review good listening skills and learn that information can be presented in a variety of forms.

Penmanship
- **Cursive Letters *i* and *t*.** Develop handwriting skills by practicing formation of cursive *i* and *t*.

Materials

- Spelling and Vocabulary Skills, pp. 2–5
- Language Arts Handbook
- Comprehension and Language Arts Skills, pp. 4–5
- Language Arts Transparencies 1–5
- Student Anthology
- Writing Folder
- Unit 1 Assessment, pp. 26-27

MEETING INDIVIDUAL NEEDS

Reteach, Challenge, English-Language Development and *Intervention* lessons are available to support the language arts instruction in this lesson.

Research in Action

. . . Emphasis on writing activities is repeatedly shown to result in special gains in reading achievement. (*Marilyn Adams, Beginning to Read: Thinking and Learning About Print*)

OVERVIEW

Language Arts Overview

Word Analysis

Spelling The spelling activities on the following pages support the Word Knowledge introduction of the /a/ sound by developing understanding of the short *a* spelling pattern in multisyllable words.

Selection Spelling Words

These words from "Class President" contain the /a/ sound.

accident   **activity**   **classroom**   **absent**   **ballot**

Vocabulary The vocabulary activities encourage students to begin thinking about how they can approach unfamiliar words in texts and discover their meanings.

Vocabulary Skill Words

nomination   **second**   **bore**   **move**   **campaign***

*Also Selection Vocabulary.

Writing Process Strategies

This first unit covers the steps of the writing process. Each lesson focuses on one step: Getting Ideas, Prewriting, Drafting, Revising, and Editing/Proofreading and Publishing.

 Basic Computer Skills To introduce students to the computer as a writing tool, have students review basic parts of a computer and its general operation, learn about software copyrights and viruses, and show students how to delete files and folders. *Basic Computer Skills* Level 5 Lessons 1–3 teach these basic computer skills.

English Language Conventions

Grammar, Usage, and Mechanics **Nouns.** This lesson develops understanding of correct noun usage.

Listening, Speaking, Viewing **Listening: Understanding What We Hear.** The Listening, Speaking, Viewing lessons are divided into six categories: Listening, Speaking, Language, Viewing, Interacting, and Presenting. In this Listening lesson, students will develop good listening skills.

Penmanship **Cursive Letters *i* and *t*.** This lesson continues the development of handwriting skills. Students learn correct formation of *i* and *t* and then practice writing paragraphs from the literature selections.

DAY I

| Word Analysis | Writing Process Strategies | English Language Conventions |

Word Analysis

Spelling

Assessment: Pretest

Spelling Patterns for the /a/ Sound
Give students the Pretest on page 26 of *Unit 1 Assessment*. Have them proofread and correct any misspellings.

Pretest Sentences
1. **cancel**   I had to **cancel** my appointment.
2. **travel**   The space shuttle can **travel** at amazing speeds.
3. **castle**   That **castle** is nearly 400 years old.
4. **salad**   A **salad** is healthier than a hamburger.
5. **catalog**   Order that ski equipment from a **catalog.**
6. **cabinet**   The kitchen **cabinet** is a place to stack dishes.
7. **blanket**   She put a **blanket** over the sleeping child.
8. **tractor**   A **tractor** is a common sight on country roads.
9. **magnet**   A **magnet** will stick to the refrigerator door.
10. **cabin**   Laura Ingalls Wilder wrote about a log **cabin.**
11. **palace**   His home was a **palace.**
12. **glance**   I saw him **glance** at the traffic light.
13. **paddle**   We lost the canoe's **paddle.**
14. **sang**   She **sang** a solo.
15. **shampoo**   Don't get **shampoo** in your eyes.
16. **accident**   Try to avoid an **accident.**
17. **activity**   Playing soccer is a fun **activity.**
18. **classroom**   A **classroom** is a place of learning.
19. **absent**   I knew she was **absent.**
20. **ballot**   You must cast your **ballot.**

Writing Process Strategies

Introduction to the Writing Process: Getting Ideas

Decisions Before Writing

Teach

Introduce the Writing Process
Have students read *Language Arts Handbook* pages 20–21 to review what must happen before writing begins.

Ask Questions
Teacher Model: "Before I begin writing, I am going to ask myself some questions."
- Has a specific topic been assigned or is it limited in any way?
- What do I want to focus on for my topic, and what main idea do I want to communicate?

Narrow the Topic
Teacher Model: "I've been assigned to write about cooperation and competition in sports. I'll focus on the cooperation and competition that I see on my soccer team."

Guided Practice

Brainstorm
Encourage students to let key questions guide them as they brainstorm for ideas. Use *Transparency 1—Main Idea Web* to help students explore ideas.

Language Arts Handbook p. 20

English Language Conventions

Grammar, Usage, and Mechanics:
Nouns

Teach
- Have students read *Language Arts Handbook* pages 342–343 for examples of common and proper nouns, plural nouns, and capitalization of proper nouns.
- Explain that a noun is a word that names a person, place, thing, or idea.
- A common noun names any person, place, thing, or idea. A common noun is lowercase unless it begins a sentence.
- A proper noun names a particular person, place, or thing. A proper noun is always capitalized.
- Most of the time a singular noun can be made plural by adding -*s*. Other nouns are made plural by adding -*es* (*tax—taxes*), changing the *y* to *i* and adding -*es* (*celebrity—celebrities*), changing *f* to *v* and adding -*es* (*elf—elves*), or completely changing its form (*man—men*).

Independent Practice
Use *Comprehension and Language Arts Skills* pages 4–5 to practice identification and pluralization of nouns and capitalization of proper nouns.

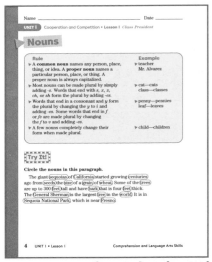

Comprehension and Language Arts Skills p. 4

DAY 2

Word Analysis

Spelling

Word Sorting

Open Word Sort Have students sort the spelling words by the number of syllables in each word. Have students explain their answers.

Vocabulary

Discovering Word Meanings

Teach

- On the board write the sentence *Her explanation made the instructions so lucid that I immediately understood what to do.* Tell students to ask the following questions about the underlined word.
  - Have you seen the word before?
  - Does the word look like any other word you know?
  - How is the word used in a sentence?
- Define *lucid* as "clear." Explain that students can often find clues about word meanings by determining how words are used in a sentence and recalling other forms and uses for the words.

Guided Practice

Assign page 2 of *Spelling and Vocabulary Skills.* Students can complete page 3 for homework.

Spelling and Vocabulary Skills p. 2

Writing Process Strategies

Introduction to the Writing Process: Getting Ideas

Decisions Before Writing

Teach

Audience and Purpose

- Emphasize the importance of **audience** and **purpose** in writing. To help students see the role that *audience* plays, ask them to think about the differences between a letter they might write to a younger cousin and a letter they might write to a favorite author. To help students see how *purpose* shapes writing, point out the differences between writing to explain a school election process and writing a personal narrative about being involved in a student election.
- Explain how purpose and audience determine the **form** of writing selected. For example, you could talk about how the purpose and audience for a **fantasy story** about talking dinosaurs would be different from the purpose and audience for a **newspaper article** about a new discovery of dinosaur bones. A dinosaur fantasy story would be written for children for the purpose of entertaining. A newspaper article would be aimed at older children and adults for the purpose of informing.
- Have students read *Language Arts Handbook* pages 264–265 for more information on audience and purpose.

Practice

Planning the Approach

Have each student imagine a writing idea that he or she could develop. Ask them to determine the following: 1) topic, 2) purpose, 3) audience, and 4) writing form. (See *Language Arts Handbook* page 21 for a partial list of writing forms.) Use *Transparency 2 Concept Map* to show how to map these decisions.

English Language Conventions

Grammar, Usage, and Mechanics: Nouns

Teach

- Review common and proper nouns. Include a review on capitalization.
- Review making singular nouns plural.
- Have students look around the room and list as many common nouns as possible. Then have them list as many proper nouns as they can (names of books, classmates, and so on). Invite students to write some of the items on the board. Have students compare their lists, checking for correct capitalization.
- Remind students that if they have any doubts about how to make nouns plural, they should refer to the dictionary.
- Tell students that when there is an alternate spelling for a plural noun, it is preferable to use the first form listed to make a plural: **tornado** *pl.* **-does** or **-dos.** Use **-does.**

Independent Practice in Reading

Have students look for common and proper nouns in "Class President." The proper nouns are mainly the names of students and teachers.

DAY 3

Word Analysis	Writing Process Strategies	English Language Conventions

Word Analysis

Spelling

Spelling Patterns for the /a/ Sound

Teach

Introduce the spelling pattern for the /a/ sound, which is *a*, no matter where the pattern falls within the word or where it is in each syllable. Have students identify words with the /a/ sound in "Class President."

Guided Practice

Have students complete page 4 from *Spelling and Vocabulary Skills*.

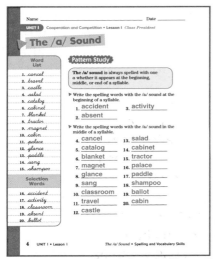

Spelling and Vocabulary Skills p. 4

Vocabulary (continued)

Discovering Word Meanings

Remind students to use their previous knowledge and examine how words are used in sentences when determining word meaning. Suggest that there are other strategies students can use to discover word meanings that take them to other sources outside the text. Ask students to think of other sources for word meanings and write a list of responses on the board. Other answers could include encyclopedias, other reference books, glossaries, the Internet, the teacher, and other adults.

Writing Process Strategies

Introduction to the Writing Process: Getting Ideas

Decisions Before Writing

Teach

Choose a Writing Form

Take students through the process of deciding on a form of writing. Have them imagine that they are to write about two different student candidates who are running for fifth-grade class president. Their purpose will be to examine the two candidates and provide straightforward information about them for an audience of students. Present them with the choices below and ask them to choose the best form of writing to use: (*Information Report*).

■ Personal Narrative
■ Play
■ Information Report

Define Writing to Inform

Information reports are written to tell people about something. For a better understanding of writing that informs, read *Language Arts Handbook* pages 94–95.

Compare and Contrast

Take students through the process of comparing and contrasting by using *Transparency 3—Venn Diagram.* Choose two subjects and have students note the important characteristics of the first subject. Next, have them note the important characteristics of the second subject that are obviously different from those of the first subject (contrast). Last, have them note the characteristics shared by the two subjects (comparison).

Guided Practice

Have each student select two subjects that lend themselves to comparison and contrast. Have students draw Venn diagrams in their Writer's Notebooks, then complete them with ideas about their subjects.

English Language Conventions

Grammar, Usage, and Mechanics:

Nouns

Teach

■ Use *Language Arts Handbook* pages 342–343 to teach how to make a singular noun plural and rules for the capitalization of proper nouns.
■ Capitalize names of places (cities, states, school, street names).
■ Capitalize family members' names and titles. (Compare *We saw **Aunt** Paula* to *Paula is my **aunt**.*)

Independent Practice in Writing

Have students each write a paragraph about a trip they would like to take and whom they would take with them. Students should include at least four names of places or people. Practice in writing names of people and places will help students with their autobiographies.

 Informal Assessment

Look for evidence that students understand the correct usage of common and proper nouns and are incorporating them into their writing.

DAY 4

Word Analysis

Spelling

Spelling Patterns for the /a/ Sound

Teach
Model the family strategy by writing *paddling* on the board and asking students to identify the spelling word that is the base word, *paddle*. Stress that the /a/ sound is spelled the same in each form of the word.

Guided Practice
Have students complete the Spelling Strategies exercises on page 5 of ***Spelling and Vocabulary Skills.***

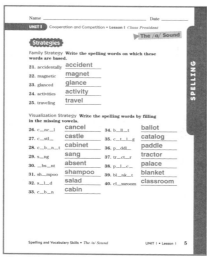

Spelling and Vocabulary Skills p. 5

Vocabulary (continued)

Discovering Word Meanings

Give students a minute to find a word in "Class President," besides the Vocabulary Skill Words, that they may have been or may still be unfamiliar with. Choose two of the students' words and, as a class, discuss the ways students could go about finding the meanings of the words. Other words chosen from "Class President" may include *miniature, candidate, parliamentary procedure,* and *withdraw.*

Writing Process Strategies

Introduction to the Writing Process: Getting Ideas
Decisions Before Writing

Teach
Choose a Writing Form

Ask students to each remember an experience that they had in which they felt strong emotion. The experience should be something that made an impression on them. Review the writing forms listed on Day 2 and challenge students to select the form that would work best. *(Personal Narrative)*

Define Personal Narrative

A personal narrative is a true story about something that happened in the writer's life. For more information, read ***Language Arts Handbook*** pages 146–151.

Focus on What Happens

Next students will need to plan a focus. Have them imagine that Cricket, the character in "Class President," wants to write about her experience of running for fifth-grade president. She would probably want to tell about the events during her campaign, the election itself, and the outcome. She would also want to tell about how she felt as the events took place and what she learned. Use ***Transparency 4—Chain-of-Events Chart*** to show students how they can use a chain of events to keep narrative writing ideas connected.

Independent Practice
Connecting Ideas

Have each student create a chain of events chart to include in his or her ***Writing Folder.*** Students may use the personal experience you had them remember earlier and fill in the chart with the events that happened. They may not use every box, but the chain should show them how to connect important events related to their experience.

English Language Conventions

Listening, Speaking, Viewing
Listening: Understanding What We Hear

Teach
- One reason for listening well is to make informed judgments based on what we've heard.
- Remind the class of the skills needed to be a good listener. We should make eye contact and face the speaker in order to give him or her our full attention. We should pay attention and concentrate on what is being said, and try not to be distracted by what's going on around us.
- Explain that we can learn information from many different sources: stories, songs, poetry, newspaper articles, etc. If we listen closely we can learn a lot of different information.
- The information we learn allows us to form our own ideas or judgments. Listening well allows us to make informed judgments.

Guided Practice
- Ask students what information they learned from "Class President." *(We learned a little about "parliamentary procedure" in meetings; we learned how to make a nomination; we learned a few requirements for becoming President of the United States; we also learned a lot about the characters in the story.)*
- Based on the information learned, have students make informed judgments about the characters and the decisions they made. For example, was Julio the best person for the job? Did Cricket make good points about why Julio should not have been class president?

 Informal Assessment

Observe whether students display good listening skills, and whether they listen for information to make informed responses.

DAY 5

| Word Analysis | Writing Process Strategies | English Language Conventions |

Word Analysis

Spelling

Assessment: Final Test

Spelling Patterns for the /a/ Sound

Teach

Repeat the Pretest for this lesson or use the Final Test on page 27 of **Unit 1 Assessment.**

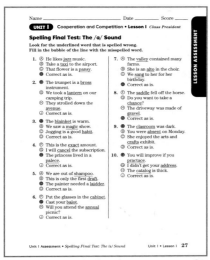

Unit 1 Assessment p. 27

Guided Practice

Have students categorize any mistakes they made on the Final Test.

Are they careless errors?
Are they lesson pattern problems?

Vocabulary

Discovering Word Meanings

Informal Assessment

■ Encourage students to use a variety of strategies for discovering word meanings throughout the year. Make sure students consider context clues and word parts when possible, instead of going straight to the dictionary for definitions.

■ Encourage students to continue identifying words they don't know as they read. Remind them that the strategies discussed throughout the week can be applied to any reading task. It would be beneficial for students to keep a record of these words and definitions in their Writer's Notebooks throughout the year.

Writing Process Strategies

Introduction to the Writing Process: Getting Ideas

Decisions Before Writing

Teach

Inspiration

Teacher Model: "I want to write a story about my own life. I'll try to remember all of the events that shaped my life and made me want to become a teacher."

Define Autobiography

An autobiography is a true story written about one's own life. For more information on *Autobiography*, see *Language Arts Handbook* pages 152–157.

The Ideas Process

Help students see that autobiographies are not just random collections of the events in a person's life. Using the example of Cricket in "Class President," have students imagine that Cricket is a real person and that thirty years after the story she achieves her goal of becoming President of the United States and wants to write an autobiography. What life events might she want to tell about? Running for fifth-grade president, losing the election, and describing what she learned might be one idea. It relates to a central theme, becoming president.

Guided Practice

Brainstorm

Show students how to use the *Main-Idea Web (Transparency 1)* to focus on topics for their autobiographies. They may come up with several themes that can be whittled down in the prewriting process later. Have them list ideas in their Writer's Notebooks.

Ordering Ideas

Use *Transparency 5—Time Line* to show students how to order events for an autobiography. In their Writer's Notebooks, have students list events from their own lives on a time line with approximate and/or actual dates.

English Language Conventions

Penmanship

Cursive Letters *i* and *t*

Teach

■ Tell students they are going to continue to learn how to write in cursive handwriting during these Penmanship lessons each week.

■ Review that all cursive letters are made of four basic types of strokes (undercurve, downcurve, overcurve, and slant line).

■ **Teacher Model:** Review the formation of lowercase cursive *i* and *t* as undercurve letters by demonstrating on the board.

i Starting point, undercurve
Slant down, undercurve to endpoint
Dot exactly above: small *i*

t Starting point, undercurve
Slant down, undercurve to endpoint
Starting point, straight across: small *t*

Guided Practice

■ **Teacher Model:** On the board, write the sentence *"A good leader knows how to listen."* to model proper letter formation.

■ Have students write a paragraph about a role model or someone they admire for general handwriting practice.

■ From "Class President," have students write two paragraphs for general handwriting practice.

Informal Assessment

Check students' handwriting to see if they have dotted their *i*'s and crossed their *t*'s.

Reading and Language Arts Skills Traces

Language Arts

WORD ANALYSIS

Spelling: The /a/ Sound

Introduced in Grade 1.
Scaffolded throughout Grades 2–5.
REINTRODUCED: Unit 1, Lesson 1, p. 35F
PRACTICED: Unit 1, Lesson 1,
pp. 35G–35I
Spelling and Vocabulary Skills,
pp. 4–5
TESTED: Unit 1, Lesson 1, p. 35J
Unit 1 Assessment

Skills Trace
Vocabulary:
Discovering Word Meanings

Introduced in Grade 1.
Scaffolded throughout Grades 2–5.
REINTRODUCED: Unit 1, Lesson 1, p. 35G
PRACTICED: Unit 1, Lesson 1,
pp. 35H–35I
Spelling and Vocabulary Skills,
pp. 2–3
TESTED: Informal Assessment, p.35J
Unit 1 Assessment

Reading

COMPREHENSION

Skills Trace
Drawing Conclusions

Introduced in Grade 1.
Scaffolded throughout Grades 2–5.
INTRODUCED: Unit 1, Lesson 1
REINFORCED: Unit 2, Lesson 1
Unit 3, Lesson 3
Unit 3, Lesson 5
Unit 4, Lesson 5
TESTED: Unit 1 Assessment

WRITING PROCESS STRATEGIES

Skills Trace
Introduction to the Writing Process:
Getting Ideas

Introduced in Grade 1.
Scaffolded throughout Grades 2–5.
INTRODUCED: Unit 1, Lesson 1, p. 35F
PRACTICED: Unit 1, Lesson 1,
pp. 35F–35J
TESTED: Unit 1 Assessment

ENGLISH LANGUAGE CONVENTIONS

Skills Trace
Grammar, Usage, and Mechanics:
Nouns

Introduced in Grade K.
Scaffolded throughout Grades 1–5.
INTRODUCED: Unit 1, Lesson 1, p. 35F
PRACTICED: Unit 1, Lesson 1, p. 35G
Unit 1, Lesson 1, p. 35H
*Comprehension and Language
Arts Skills,* pp. 4–5
TESTED: Informal Assessment, p. 35H
Unit 1 Assessment

Skills Trace
Listening, Speaking, Viewing:
**Listening: Understanding What
We Hear**

Introduced in Grade K.
Scaffolded throughout Grades 1–5.
REINTRODUCED: Unit 1, Lesson 1, p. 35I
PRACTICED: Unit 1, Lesson 1, p. 35I
TESTED: Informal Assessment, p. 35I
Unit 1 Assessment

Skills Trace
Penmanship: Cursive Letters i and t

Introduced in Grade 2.
Scaffolded throughout Grades 3–5.
REINTRODUCED: Unit 1, Lesson 1, p. 35J
PRACTICED: Unit 1, Lesson 1, p. 35J
TESTED: Informal Assessment, p. 35J

Professional Development: Comprehension

Literal Comprehension

Students' productive, literal comprehension depends in large part on their skill in *decoding*, or word recognition, and on the breadth and depth of their *vocabulary knowledge*.

What Does Research Tell Us About Decoding and Comprehension?

Much research has established that good readers are skillful at decoding words on the basis of graphophonemic, or sound/spelling, cues. To pronounce a word, these readers sound it out, blending the individual sounds represented by the word's letters. Once they have sounded it out, they can recognize what a word means, because most of the words in the materials they read are words that have been in their listening and speaking vocabularies for several years (Gough & Tunmer, 1986). In fact, researchers who have studied decoding make the point emphatically that poor word-level decoding is a critical bottleneck in the comprehension process. When a reader cannot recognize or decode a word, it is impossible for him or her to understand what the word means (Adams, 1990; Pressley, 1998).

Once readers achieve fluency, they seldom sound out words letter by letter as they read. Even when they encounter words they do not know, good readers tend to process them by recognizing common letter chunks, such as prefixes; suffixes; Latin and Greek root words; and rimes (the parts of syllables that follow the initial consonants) such as *-ight*, *-on*, *-ite*, and *-ake* (Ehri, 1992). Thus, good readers do not sound out a word such as *kite* letter by letter; rather, they blend the initial /k/ sound with what they know about the sound of the rime *-ite*. From the time children first learn to read, they are recognizing common letter chunks as wholes and using this knowledge to help them decode (Goswami, 1998).

A lack of skill in decoding words directly affects students' higher order comprehension. This is because word recognition and comprehension compete for attention: The more effort readers require to decode a word, the less attention they have left for comprehension. If readers have to struggle with words, they can easily lose track of meaning. Further, it is the words in a text that constitute the basic data with which the higher-order comprehension processes must work. When readers skip words in a text or fail to understand the words of the text, comprehension suffers (Adams, 1990).

Therefore, it is evident why the primary levels of **Open Court** emphasize the development of reading fluency rather than just the sounding out of words. Fluent readers can devote less attention to word recognition and more attention to comprehension. Most teachers have worked with young students who can sound out words—with some effort—but who do not seem to understand or remember any of what they read. All of their attention is consumed by word recognition to the exclusion of comprehension (Gough & Tunmer, 1986; LaBerge & Samuels, 1974).

* Additional information about comprehension as well as resource references can be found in the ***Professional Development Guide: Comprehension.***

SELECTION INTRODUCTION

Focus Questions What enables Lupe to accomplish her goals? Must one have natural ability in order to become good at something?

The Marble Champ

from *Baseball in April and Other Stories*
by Gary Soto
illustrated by Maren Scott

Lupe Medrano, a shy girl who spoke in whispers, was the school's spelling bee champion, winner of the reading contest at the public library three summers in a row, blue ribbon awardee in the science fair, the top student at her piano recital, and the playground grand champion in chess. She was a straight-A student and—not counting kindergarten, when she had been stung by a wasp—never missed one day of elementary school. She had received a small trophy for this honor and had been congratulated by the mayor.

But though Lupe had a razor-sharp mind, she could not make her body, no matter how much she tried, run as fast as the other girls'. She begged her body to move faster, but could never beat anyone in the fifty-yard dash.

The truth was that Lupe was no good in sports. She could not catch a pop-up or figure out in which direction to kick the soccer ball. One time she kicked the ball at her own goal and scored a point for the other team. She was no good at baseball or basketball either, and even had a hard time making a hula hoop stay on her hips.

It wasn't until last year, when she was eleven years old, that she learned how to ride a bike. And even then she had to use training wheels. She could walk in the swimming pool but couldn't swim, and chanced roller skating only when her father held her hand.

36

Selection Summary

Genre: Realistic Fiction

Lupe Medrano has won awards for her schoolwork and her nearly perfect attendance, but when it comes to sports, she's a total failure. If only she could excel at a sport, Lupe thinks, "even marbles." Suddenly inspired, Lupe borrows her brother's beautiful glass marbles and begins a routine of thumb-strengthening exercises and shooting practice. Finally, Lupe enters a marble championship and learns about the rewards of competition, hard work, and determination.

Some of the elements of realistic fiction are listed below. A realistic fiction selection may have one or more of these elements.

- The characters behave as people or animals do in real life.
- The setting of the story is a real place or could be a real place.
- The events of the story are based on a conflict or problem that could occur in real life.

About the Author

Gary Soto's life began to change when he picked up a poetry anthology and discovered that he, too, wanted to be a writer. Once a farm laborer in Fresno, California, Gary Soto is now an award-winning poet, essayist, and fiction writer for all ages. His short story collection *Baseball in April and Other Stories* was named a Best Book for Young Adults by the American Library Association.

Students can read more about Gary Soto on page 44 of the *Student Anthology.*

Other Books by Gary Soto
- *Crazy Weekend*
- *Boys at Work*
- *Local News*
- *Off and Running*
- *Neighborhood Odes* (poetry)

About the Illustrator

Maren Scott has been drawing since she was a child. Ms. Scott has won awards for both her illustrations and quilt designs. She lives in a small town in Utah with her husband and three sons.

Students can read more about Maren Scott on page 44 of the *Student Anthology.*

Also Illustrated by Maren Scott
- *Grandmother's Wonderful Wisdom*

Inquiry Connections

A major aim of **Open Court Reading** is knowledge building. Because inquiry is at the root of knowledge building, students are encouraged to investigate topics and questions within each selection that relate to the unit theme.

"The Marble Champ" is a humorous account of a young girl's transformation into a marble champion. Practice makes her thumb bigger and stronger, and she wins every match. Key concepts are:

- Competing requires commitment and practice.
- It is important to understand one's strengths and weaknesses when competing.

Before reading the selection:

- Point out that students may post a question, concept, word, illustration, or object on the Concept/Question Board at any time during the course of their unit investigation. Be sure that students include their names or initials on the items they post so that others will know whom to go to if they have an answer or if they wish to collaborate on a related activity.
- Students should feel free to write an answer or a note on someone else's question or to consult the Board for ideas for their own investigations throughout the unit.
- Encourage students to read about cooperation and competition at home and to bring in articles or pictures that are good examples to post on the Board.

Concept/Question Board

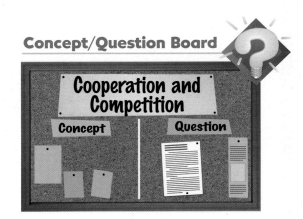

PROGRAM RESOURCES

Leveled Practice

Reteach
Pages 7–11

Challenge
Pages 6–9

ELD Workbook

Intervention Workbook

Leveled Classroom Library*

Have students read at least 30 minutes daily outside of class. Have them read books from the *Leveled Classroom Library,* which supports the unit theme and helps students develop their vocabulary by reading independently.

The Big Bike Race

BY LUCY JANE BLEDSOE. AVON, 1995.

Though a used, yellow, old clunker is the only bike his grandmother can afford to buy him, Ernie won't let the other kids' laughter hamper his determination to race and to win. **(Easy)**

Iditarod Dream: Dusty and His Sled Dogs Compete in Alaska's Jr. Iditarod

BY TED WOOD. WALKER AND COMPANY, 1996.

Dusty shows he knows how to train and care for his Alaskan Huskie dog team, as well as drive his sled and fend off a moose, as he vies for first place in the Jr. Iditarod. **(Average)**

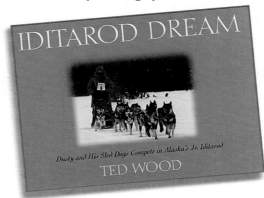

The View from Saturday

BY E. L. KONIGSBURG. ALADDIN, 1996.

Mrs. Olinski's choice of Noah, Nadia, Ethan, and Julian for her sixth grade academic team, the strange connections between the four, and their amazing academic bowl winning streak are explored. (A Newbery Medal Winner) **(Advanced)**

✳ These books, which all support the unit theme Cooperation and Competition, are part of a 36-book *Leveled Classroom Library* available for purchase from SRA/McGraw-Hill.

Note: Teachers should preview any trade books for appropriateness in their classrooms before recommending them to students.

TECHNOLOGY

Web Connections

www.sra4kids.com
Cooperation and Competition Web site

Audiocassette/CD

✳ **Listening Library:**
Cooperation and Competition
SRA/McGRAW-HILL, 2002

Computer Skills

✳ **Basic Computer Skills**

CD-ROMs

 ✳ **Research Assistant**
SRA/McGRAW-HILL, 2002

 ✳ **Student Writing and**
Research Center
THE LEARNING COMPANY

Titles preceded by an asterisk (✳) are available through SRA/McGraw-Hill. Other titles can be obtained by contacting the publisher listed with the title.

	DAY 1	DAY 2
Suggested Pacing: 3–5 days	**DAY 1**	**DAY 2**

LESSON PLANNER

1 Preparing to Read

Materials
- Routine Card 1

DAY 1

Word Knowledge, p. 36K
- Synonyms
- Regular Plurals
- /n/ Sound Spelled *kn*
- /e/ Sound Spelled *e* and *ea*

About the Words and Sentences, p. 36K

DAY 2

Developing Oral Language, p. 36L

---

2 Reading & Responding

Materials
- Student Anthology, pp. 36–47
- Reading Transparencies, 3, 54–56
- Routine Card 1
- Program Assessment
- Unit 1 Assessment, pp. 6–9
- Science/Social Studies Connection Center Cards 2–4
- Comprehension and Language Arts Skills, pp. 6–7
- Reteach, pp. 7–8
- Challenge, p. 6
- Home Connection, pp. 5–6
- Inquiry Journal, p. 6

DAY 1

Build Background, p. 36M
Preview and Prepare, pp. 36M–36N
Selection Vocabulary, p. 36N
Reading Recommendations, pp. 36O–36P
Student Anthology, pp. 36–43 [First Read]
✓ **Comprehension Strategies**
- Making Connections, p. 38
- Asking Questions, pp. 36, 38, 40
- Visualizing, p. 42

Discussing Strategy Use, p. 42
Discussing the Selection, p. 43A

DAY 2

Student Anthology, pp. 36–43 [Second Read]
Comprehension Skills
- Making Inferences, pp. 37, 39, 41, 43
✓ Checking Comprehension, p. 43
Supporting the Reading, pp. 43C–43D
- Making Inferences

Inquiry

Materials
- Student Anthology, pp. 36–47
- Inquiry Journal, pp. 10–15
- Research Assistant

Investigation
- Investigating Concepts Beyond the Text, p. 45A

Investigation
- Concept/Question Board, p. 45B

---

3 Language Arts

Materials
- Comprehension and Language Arts Skills, pp. 8–9
- Language Arts Handbook, pp. 22–25, 27–31, 344–345
- Language Arts Transparencies, 3–8, 10
- Spelling and Vocabulary Skills, pp. 6–9
- Student Anthology
- Student Writing and Research Center
- Unit 1 Assessment, pp. 28–29
- Reteach, pp. 9–11
- Challenge, pp. 7–9

Word Analysis
✓ Spelling Patterns for the /e/ Sound Pretest, p. 45F

Writing Process Strategies
- Writing Process Introduction: Prewriting, p. 45F

English Language Conventions
- Grammar, Usage, and Mechanics: Pronouns, p. 45F

Word Analysis
- Spelling Patterns for the /e/ Sound, p. 45G
- Vocabulary: Context Clues, p. 45G

Writing Process Strategies
- Writing Process: Prewriting, p. 45G

English Language Conventions
- Grammar, Usage, and Mechanics: Pronouns, p. 45G

✓Informal Assessment Available   ✓Formal Assessment Available

DAY 2 continued	DAY 3		
DAY 3	**DAY 3**	**DAY 4**	**DAY 5**
General Review		**General Review**	**Review Word Knowledge**

DAY 2 continued	DAY 4	DAY 5
Student Anthology, pp. 44–45 ■ **Meet the Author/Illustrator** ✓■ **Theme Connections**	**Review Selection Vocabulary,** p. 43B **Literary Elements,** p. 43E **Poetry,** pp. 46–47B ■ "The New Kid" ■ "Good Sportsmanship"	✓ **Lesson Assessment** ■ *Unit 1 Assessment:* Lesson Assessment, pp. 6–9 **Home Connection,** p. 43B **Science Connection** ■ Friction, p 43F
✓ **Investigation** ■ **Formulating Questions and Problems,** p. 45C	**Supporting the Investigation** ■ Interviewing, p. 45D	**Investigation** ■ Unit Investigation Continued ■ Update Concept/Question Board
Word Analysis ■ Spelling Patterns for the /e/ Sound, p. 45H ■ Vocabulary: Context Clues, p. 45H **Writing Process Strategies** ■ Writing Process: Prewriting, p. 45H **English Language Conventions** ✓■ Grammar, Usage, and Mechanics: Pronouns, p. 45H	**Word Analysis** ■ Spelling Patterns for the /e/ Sound, p. 45I ■ Vocabulary: Context Clues, p. 45I **Writing Process Strategies** ■ Writing Process: Prewriting, p. 45I **English Language Conventions** ✓■ Listening, Speaking, Viewing Speaking: Speaking Clearly, p. 45I	**Word Analysis** ✓■ Spelling Patterns for the /e/ Sound Final Test, p. 45J ✓■ Vocabulary: Context Clues, p. 45J **Writing Process Strategies** ✓■ Writing Process: Prewriting, p. 45J **English Language Conventions** ✓■ Penmanship: Cursive Letters *u* and *w*, p. 45J

Below are suggestions for differentiating instruction to meet the individual needs of students. These are the same skills shown on the Lesson Planner; however, these pages provide extra practice opportunities or enriching activities to meet the varied needs of students.

WORKSHOP

Differentiating Instruction

Small-Group Instruction

Use small-group instruction for such things as preteaching students who need this advantage; reteaching material to students having difficulty; intervening on behalf of students having extreme difficulty; collaborating with students on investigation activities; instructing ELL students; and discussing students' writing projects.

Use the informal assessment suggestions found throughout the lesson along with the formal assessments provided in each lesson to determine your students' strengths and areas of need. Use the following program components to help in supporting or expanding on the instruction found in this lesson:

- **Reteach** workbook for use with those students who show a basic understanding of the lesson but need a bit more practice to solidify their understanding

- **Intervention Guide** and **Workbook** for use with those students who even after extra practice exhibit a lack of understanding of the lesson concepts

- **English-Language Development Guide** and **Workbook** for use with those students who need language help

Independent Activities

Students can work individually on such things as:

- **Inquiry Journal** pages
- **Challenge**
- Independent reading
- **Writing**
- Investigation activities

For Workshop Management Tips, see Appendix pages 41–42.

◆ **Small-group Instruction**   ■ **Independent Activities**

	READING	INVESTIGATION ACTIVITIES
DAY 1	■ *Listening Library Audiocassette/CD* ■ Add Vocabulary in Writer's Notebook	■ Concept/Question Board ■ Explore OCR Web Site for Theme Connections ■ Complete *Inquiry Journal,* p. 10
DAY 2	■ Oral Reading of Selection for Fluency ■ Record Response to Selection in Writer's Notebook ■ *Listening Library Audiocassette/CD*	■ Concept/Question Board ■ Explore OCR Web Site for Theme Connections
DAY 3	■ Independent Reading ■ Complete *Comprehension and Language Arts Skills,* pp. 6–7	■ Concept/Question Board ■ Formulate Questions and Problems to Investigate ◆ Complete *Inquiry Journal,* p. 11 ■ Use *Research Assistant* to Help with Investigation
DAY 4	◆ Discuss Theme Connections, p. 45 ■ Add Words to Word Bank ■ Complete *Link to Writing* for Supporting the Reading, p. 43D ■ Complete *Independent Practice* for Literary Elements, p. 43E	■ Concept/Question Board ◆ Form Investigation Groups and Complete *Inquiry Journal,* p. 12
DAY 5	◆ Science Connection, p. 43F	■ Concept/Question Board ■ Complete *Inquiry Journal,* pp. 13–14, for Supporting the Investigation

LANGUAGE ARTS	INTERVENTION*	ENGLISH-LANGUAGE LEARNERS**	RETEACH	CHALLENGE
English Language Conventions ■ Complete **Pronouns,** *Comprehension and Language Arts Skills,* pp. 8–9 **Writing Process Strategies** ◆ Seminar: Prewriting a Story, p. 45F	(30 to 45 minutes per day) ◆ Reading Words, p. 12 ◆ Preteach "The Marble Champ," pp. 13–14 ◆ Teach "Intervention Selection One," pp. 14–15 ◆ Grammar, Usage, and Mechanics, pp. 17–18	(30 to 45 minutes per day) ◆ Word Knowledge, p. 7 ◆ Activate Prior Knowledge, p. 9		
Word Analysis ◆ **Spelling: Word Sort,** p. 45G ■ Complete **Vocabulary: Context Clues,** *Spelling and Vocabulary Skills,* pp. 6–7 **Writing Process Strategies** ◆ Seminar: Prewriting an Informative Report, p. 45G	◆ Developing Oral Language, p. 12 ◆ Preteach "The Marble Champ," pp. 13–14 ◆ Teach Comprehension Strategies, p. 15 ◆ Reread "Intervention Selection One" ◆ Grammar, Usage, and Mechanics, pp. 17–18	◆ Selection Vocabulary, p. 9 ◆ Preteach the Selection, p. 9	**Comprehension** ■ Complete **Making Inferences,** *Reteach,* pp. 7–8 **English Language Conventions** ■ Complete **Pronouns,** *Reteach,* p. 11	**Comprehension** ■ Complete **Making Inferences,** *Challenge,* p. 6 **English Language Conventions** ■ Complete **Pronouns,** *Challenge,* p. 9
Word Analysis ■ Complete **Spelling: The /e/ Sound,** *Spelling and Vocabulary Skills,* p. 8 **Writing Process Strategies** ◆ Seminar: Prewriting a Story, p. 45H	◆ Dictation and Spelling, pp. 12–13 ◆ Reread "The Marble Champ" ◆ Teach "Intervention Selection Two," pp. 15–16 ◆ Writing Activity, pp. 18–19	◆ Dictation and Spelling, p. 8	**Word Analysis** ■ Complete **Vocabulary: Context Clues,** *Reteach,* p. 10	**Word Analysis** ■ Complete **Vocabulary: Context Clues,** *Challenge,* p. 8
Word Analysis ■ Complete **The /e/ Sound,** *Spelling and Vocabulary Skills,* p. 9 **Writing Process Strategies** ◆ Seminar: Prewriting an Informative Report, p. 45I	◆ Reread "The Marble Champ" ◆ Teach Comprehension Strategies, p. 16 ◆ Reread "Intervention Selection Two" ◆ Writing Activity, pp. 18–19	◆ Vocabulary Strategies, p. 10	**Word Analysis** ■ Complete **Spelling: The /e/ Sound,** *Reteach,* p. 9	**Word Analysis** ■ Complete **Spelling: The /e/ Sound,** *Challenge,* p. 7
Writing Process Strategies ◆ Seminar: Prewrite for an Autobiography, p. 45J **English Language Conventions** ■ Penmanship: Cursive Letters *u* and *w,* p. 45J	◆ Repeated Readings/Fluency Check, p. 17	◆ Grammar, Usage, and Mechanics, p. 10		

*Page numbers refer to *Intervention Guide*
**Page numbers refer to *English-Language Development Guide*

Formal Assessment Options

Use these summative assessments along with your informal observations to assess student progress.

ASSESSMENT

Name _____ Date _____ Score _____

UNIT 1 Cooperation and Competition • Lesson 2

The Marble Champ

Read the following questions carefully. Then completely fill in the bubble of each correct answer. You may look back at the story to find the answer to each of the questions.

1. In the beginning of the story, you can infer that Lupe
   Ⓐ has no confidence in herself
   ● is smart but not a good athlete
   Ⓒ has nothing she is good at

2. How are marbles described in the story?
   ● rich glass treasures
   Ⓑ fragile glass insects
   Ⓒ small and colorful stars

Read the following questions carefully. Use complete sentences to answer the questions.

3. What does Lupe do to get into shape for playing marbles?
   She does push-ups on her fingertips and squeezes a rubber eraser.

4. What tips does Lupe's brother give her?
   Lupe's brother tells her to get low, aim with one eye, and place her knuckle on the ground.

5. Why does Lupe invite Rachel to join the group at the championship?
   Lupe invites Rachel to join the group because Rachel is alone.

6 Unit 1 • Lesson 2   *The Marble Champ • Unit 1 Assessment*

Unit 1 Assessment p. 6

The Marble Champ (continued)

6. What makes things difficult for Lupe when she plays marbles with Miss Baseball Cap?
   Things get difficult because the wind blows dust into Lupe's eyes and she can't see very well.

7. How did Lupe's family celebrate Lupe's victory?
   They went out for pizza and put Lupe's trophies on the table for everyone to see.

8. Why is Lupe so happy at the end of this story?
   Lupe is happy because she has always earned honors for being smart, but she has finally won an honor in sports.

Read the following questions carefully. Then completely fill in the bubble of each correct answer.

9. What is true about Lupe's last girl opponent?
   ● She is determined to win.
   Ⓑ She feels she is lucky to be there.
   Ⓒ She is angry at Lupe.

10. Whom did Lupe play after she defeated Miss Baseball Cap?
   Ⓐ the champion of last year's game
   ● the winner of the boys' division
   Ⓒ the president of the marble club

Unit 1 Assessment • *The Marble Champ*   Unit 1 • Lesson 2 **7**

Unit 1 Assessment p. 7

The Marble Champ (continued)

Read the question and statement below. Use complete sentences in your answers.

Linking to the Concepts How did Lupe's family cooperate to help her succeed?
Answers will vary. Accept all reasonable answers.

Personal Response In the past, marbles were a popular form of entertainment for young people. Why is this not true today? Why don't you play marbles?
Answers will vary. Accept all reasonable answers.

8 Unit 1 • Lesson 2   *The Marble Champ • Unit 1 Assessment*

Unit 1 Assessment p. 8

The Marble Champ (continued)

Vocabulary

Read the following questions carefully. Then completely fill in the bubble of each correct answer.

1. Lupe Medrano was winner of the reading contest at the public library three summers in a row. Another word for **contest** is
   Ⓐ imagination
   Ⓑ agreement
   ● competition

2. Lupe said nothing to her parents about her dreams of athletic glory. To be **athletic** means to be
   ● good at sports
   Ⓑ losing your marbles
   Ⓒ very intelligent

3. She signed up and was assigned her first match on baseball diamond number three. In this sentence, a **match** is
   Ⓐ something used to start fires
   ● a game at a championship
   Ⓒ a place where you practice

4. Quivering with energy, Lupe blasted two marbles out of the circle. Your **energy** is like
   Ⓐ the friends that cheer for you
   Ⓑ the skills that you have learned
   ● the power that you have

5. After the championship was over, a dog came over to see what the commotion was all about. Another word for **commotion** is
   ● excitement
   Ⓑ trouble
   Ⓒ brightness

Unit 1 Assessment • *The Marble Champ*   Unit 1 • Lesson 2 **9**

Unit 1 Assessment p. 9

Name _____ Date _____ Score _____

UNIT 1 Cooperation and Competition • Lesson 2 *The Marble Champ*

Spelling Pretest: The /e/ Sound

Fold this page back on the dotted line. Take the Pretest. Then correct any word you misspelled by crossing out the word and rewriting it next to the incorrect spelling.

1. _____		1.	*sense*
2. _____		2.	*plenty*
3. _____		3.	*enemy*
4. _____		4.	*welcome*
5. _____		5.	*swept*
6. _____		6.	*edit*
7. _____		7.	*tennis*
8. _____		8.	*meant*
9. _____		9.	*health*
10. _____		10.	*breath*
11. _____		11.	*shelter*
12. _____		12.	*sweater*
13. _____		13.	*wealth*
14. _____		14.	*quest*
15. _____		15.	*feather*
16. _____		16.	*treasure*
17. _____		17.	*bedspread*
18. _____		18.	*chess*
19. _____		19.	*strengthen*
20. _____		20.	*shelf*

28 Unit 1 • Lesson 2   *Spelling Pretest: The /e/ Sound • Unit 1 Assessment*

Unit 1 Assessment p. 28

Name _____ Date _____ Score _____

UNIT 1 Cooperation and Competition • Lesson 2 *The Marble Champ*

Spelling Final Test: The /e/ Sound

Look for the underlined word that is spelled wrong. Fill in the bubble of the line with the misspelled word.

1. Ⓐ You are no longer a teenager at age <u>twenty</u>.
   ● A pro skater is <u>stedy</u> on the ice.
   Ⓒ A proper diet promotes good <u>health</u>.
   Ⓓ Correct as is.

2. Ⓕ A <u>shelf</u> is a good place to display a trophy.
   Ⓖ Common <u>sense</u> is important to have.
   Ⓗ We wiped our feet on the <u>welcome</u> mat.
   ● Correct as is.

3. ● You can have pizza <u>insted</u> of tacos.
   Ⓑ <u>Mend</u> the hole in your shirt with this patch.
   Ⓒ Garments might come with extra <u>thread</u>.
   Ⓓ Correct as is.

4. ● I <u>dred</u> my visit to the dentist.
   Ⓖ CPR provides people with the <u>breath</u> of life.
   Ⓗ She <u>swept</u> the cobwebs off the ceilings.
   Ⓘ Correct as is.

5. Ⓐ Don't leave an <u>eggshell</u> in the cake batter.
   Ⓑ That <u>clever</u> man does division in his head.
   Ⓒ We needed a board to play <u>chess</u>.
   ● Correct as is.

6. Ⓕ You must <u>edit</u> that article by tonight.
   Ⓖ Grandmother knitted me a <u>sweater</u>.
   ● Too much <u>stres</u> could give you an ulcer.
   Ⓘ Correct as is.

7. ● I can swim under water for an <u>intire</u> minute.
   Ⓑ <u>Bread</u> is rather dry without some butter.
   Ⓒ You <u>jest</u> when you make fun of him.
   Ⓓ Correct as is.

8. Ⓕ We <u>smelled</u> the pies baking in the oven.
   Ⓖ There is <u>plenty</u> of food at the market.
   Ⓗ Exercise will <u>strengthen</u> your muscles.
   ● Correct as is.

9. Ⓐ Smooth the <u>bedspread</u> thoroughly.
   ● I <u>tresure</u> my jewelry box.
   Ⓒ A quill pen is a <u>feather</u>.
   Ⓓ Correct as is.

10. ● There is a <u>tenis</u> court at my building.
   Ⓖ I didn't <u>intend</u> to pick a fight.
   Ⓗ The opponent jabbed me with his <u>elbow</u>.
   Ⓘ Correct as is.

Unit 1 Assessment • *Spelling Final Test: The /e/ Sound*   Unit 1 • Lesson 2 **29**

Unit 1 Assessment p. 29

Informal Comprehension Strategies Rubrics

Use the Informal Comprehension Strategies Rubrics to determine whether or not a student is using any of the strategies listed below. Note the strategies a student is using, instead of the degree to which a student might be using any particular strategy. In addition, encourage the student to tell of any strategies other than the ones being taught that he or she is using.

Asking Questions

- The student asks questions about ideas or facts presented in the text and attempts to answer these questions by reading the text.

Making Connections

- The student activates prior knowledge and related knowledge.
- The student uses prior knowledge to explain something encountered in text.
- The student connects ideas presented later in the text to ideas presented earlier in the text.
- The student notes ideas in the text that are new to him or her or conflict with what he or she thought previously.

Visualizing

- The student visualizes ideas or scenes described in the text.

Research Rubrics

During Workshop, assess students using the rubrics below. The rubrics range from 1–4 in most categories, with 1 being the lowest score. Record each student's score on the inside back cover of his or her *Inquiry Journal.*

Formulating Research Questions and Problems

1 With help, identifies things she or he wonders about in relation to a topic.

2 Expresses curiosity about topics; with help, translates this into specific questions.

3 Poses an interesting problem or question for research; with help, refines it into a researchable question.

4 Identifies something she or he genuinely wonders about and translates it into a researchable question.

Objectives

- Students read and identify synonyms and use them in sentences to increase vocabulary.
- Students recognize and read regular plurals as well as identify singular forms of plurals.
- Students recognize and read words beginning with the /n/ sound spelled *kn*.
- Students recognize and read words with the /e/ sound spelled *ea*.
- Students develop fluency reading words and sentences aloud.

Materials

- Routine Card

Routine Card
Refer to Routine 1 for the Word Knowledge procedure.

Teacher Tip SYLLABICATON To help students blend words and build fluency, use the syllabication below of the decodable multisyllabic words in the word lines.

com•mo•tion	mu•scles
rack•et	knu•ckles
dis•turb•ance	trea•sure
hub•bub	bed•spread
whis•pers	strength•en
mar•bles	

MEETING INDIVIDUAL NEEDS

ELL Support

For ELD strategies, use the *English-Language Development Guide,* Unit 1, Lesson 2.

Intervention Support

For intervention strategies, use the *Intervention Guide,* Unit 1, Lesson 2.

Word Knowledge

Reading the Words and Sentences

Use direct teaching to teach the Word Knowledge lesson. Write each word and sentence on the board. Have students read each word together. After all the words have been read, have students read each sentence in natural phrases or chunks. Use the suggestions in About the Words and Sentences to discuss the different features of listed words.

Line 1:	commotion	racket	disturbance	hubbub
Line 2:	whispers	marbles	muscles	thumbs
Line 3:	knuckles	knee	knot	know
Line 4:	treasure	bedspread	chess	strengthen	shelf
Sentence 1:	The cheering fans created a racket and a hubbub.			
Sentence 2:	Playing marbles can strengthen muscles in the hands.			
Sentence 3:	When I scraped my knees and knuckles, my mom made a fuss.			
Sentence 4:	Isabel will treasure the bedspread quilted for her by her grandmother.			

About the Words and Sentences

- **Line 1:** These words are synonyms. Synonyms are words that have almost the same meanings. Have students discuss the related meanings and provide sentences for each of the words.
- **Line 2:** The words are regular plurals. Regular plurals are made by simply adding *s* to the end of a word. Have students identify the singular words.
- **Line 3:** The words contain the /n/ sound spelled *kn*. Have students offer other words that begin with the /n/ sound spelled *kn*. (*knight, knock, knife, knit*)
- **Line 4:** The words contain the /e/ sound spelled *e* and *ea*.

- **Sentence 1:** Have students read the sentence aloud. Then ask them to identify the synonyms in the sentence *(racket, hubbub)*.

- **Sentence 2:** Ask students to read the sentence aloud. Then have students identify the regular plurals in the sentence *(marbles, muscles, hands)*. Finally, ask them to give the singular forms of these words.

- **Sentence 3:** Have students identify words in the sentence that contain the /n/ sound spelled *kn*. *(knees, knuckles)* Then have students read the sentence aloud. Point out to students that both *kn* words are regular plurals.

- **Sentence 4:** Have students identify the words in the sentence that contain the /e/ sound spelled *e* and *ea*. *(Isabel, treasure, bedspread, quilted)*

Developing Oral Language

Use direct teaching to review the words and concepts. Use one or both of the following activities to help students practice the words aloud.

- Write a list of singular words on the board such as *table, head,* and *competitor.* Ask volunteers to write the regular plural forms of the words on the board. Then have them make up and say sentences using the plural forms of the words.

- Have students tell you what they know about analogies. If necessary, explain to them that an *analogy* is the comparison of one set of things to another set of things. The items in the first set are related to each other in the same way that the items in the second set are related to each other. For example, write the following analogy on the board: *commotion : racket :: disturbance : hubbub*

Tell students that words within a set have single colons between them, and double colons separate sets from each other. Have a volunteer read aloud the above analogy. If necessary, demonstrate that the above analogy says *commotion is to racket as disturbance is to hubbub.* Have students say which words in the above examples are in sets together. *(commotion and racket; disturbance and hubbub)* Then have them tell how the words in each set are related to each other. *(The words in each set are synonyms.)* Therefore, the set *commotion : racket* is like the set *disturbance : hubbub* because both sets contain synonyms.

Leave the first set on the board, but erase the second set. Supply one word for the second set, such as *champion.* Have students supply the second word for the set to complete the analogy. *(winner, victor)*

Teacher Tip BUILDING FLUENCY
Gaining a better understanding of the spelling of sounds and the structure of words will help students as they encounter unfamiliar words in their reading. By this time in grade 5, students should be reading approximately 126 words per minute with fluency and expression. As students read, you may notice that some need work in building fluency. During Workshop, have these students choose a section of the text (a minimum of 160 words) to read several times in order to build fluency.

MEETING INDIVIDUAL NEEDS

Intervention Tip

/n/ SOUND SPELLED *kn* For students who need more help with the /n/ sound spelled *kn*, explain that the *k* is silent. Say the words in Line 3 aloud, pointing out that you are pronouncing the words as if the *k* were not there. Write the following list of words on the board and have students say them aloud:

knight, knife, knockout, doorknob, knead, knell

Spelling
See pages 45F–45J for the corresponding spelling lesson for the /e/ sound.

Objectives

- Students will understand the selection vocabulary before reading.
- Students will recognize regular plurals.
- Students will use the comprehension strategies Making Connections, Asking Questions, and Visualizing as they read the story the first time.
- Students will use the comprehension skill Making Inferences as they read the story the second time.

Materials

- Student Anthology, pp. 36–45
- Reading Transparencies 3, 54, 55, 56
- Listening Library
- Routine Card 1
- Inquiry Journal, p. 6
- Science/Social Studies Connection Center Card 2
- Home Connection, pp. 5–6
- Comprehension and Language Arts Skills, pp. 6–7
- Program Assessment
- Unit 1 Assessment, pp. 6–9

MEETING INDIVIDUAL NEEDS

ELL Support

CULTURAL CONTEXT English-language learners may be unfamiliar with the game of marbles and with the vocabulary connected with it. Stage a few games. Let English-speaking players partner with English-language learners in the first few games.

Teacher Tip ACTIVATE PRIOR KNOWLEDGE Inform students that good readers typically activate what they already know about a topic before reading something new about the topic. Tell students that they should get in the habit of thinking about the topic of an upcoming selection and activating relevant background knowledge.

www.sra4kids.com
Web Connection
Students can use the connections to Cooperation and Competition in the Reading link of the SRA Web page for more background information about Cooperation and Competition.

Build Background

Activate Prior Knowledge

Discuss the following with students to find out what they may already know about the selection and have already learned about the theme of cooperation and competition.

- Preteach "The Marble Champ" by determining students' prior knowledge of the game of marbles. Have volunteers share what they know about the game's rules.
- Have students share other stories that involve marble games or playing in a championship game.
- Ask students to discuss the role of competition in "Class President" and consider the positive aspects of the concept.

Background Information

The following information may help students better understand the selection they are about to read.

- If students are not familiar with the game of marbles, tell them it is played with small, hard, round objects that may be made of stone, glass, steel, clay, or plastic. Players shoot a marble at other target marbles placed inside a circle drawn on the ground. Opponents' marbles knocked out of the ring may be kept or scored as points.
- Students might like to know that marble shooters "knuckle down" by placing the knuckle of their first finger on the ground. Then they put the marble in the joint of that finger and use their thumb to snap the marble at their opponents' marbles. Shooters try for accuracy in their aim and distance in their shots.
- Have the students discuss what they know about the genre of this selection. Refer to page 36A of the *Teacher's Edition* for elements of this selection's genre.

Preview and Prepare

Browse

- Have a student read aloud the title and the names of the author and illustrator. Demonstrate how to browse. Then have students preview the selection by browsing only the first page or two of the story, so they won't spoil its ending. This allows students to determine prior knowledge relevant to the selection. Discuss what they think this story might have to do with cooperation and competition.

- Have the students search for clues that tell them something about the story. Also, have them look for any problems, such as unfamiliar words or long sentences that they notice while reading. Use **Reading Transparency 54** to record their observations as they browse. For example, the word *champ* in the title of the selection might be a clue that the main character is going to win a contest. For the Problems column, students might point out that *marbles* is not a game with which they are familiar. They might wonder if Lupe will be good at marbles. To save time and model note taking, write students' observations as brief notes rather than complete sentences.

- As students prepare to read the selection, have them browse the Focus Questions on the first page of the selection. Tell them to keep these questions in mind as they read.

Set Purposes

Have students set their own purposes for reading this selection. As they read, have students think about how setting goals and the support and cooperation of others can lead to successful competition. Remind students that good readers have a purpose when they read. Let them know that they should make sure they know the purpose for reading whenever they read.

Selection Vocabulary

As students study vocabulary, they will use a variety of skills to determine the meaning of a word. These include context clues, word structure, and apposition. Students will apply these same skills while reading to clarify additional unfamiliar words.

Display **Reading Transparency 3** before reading the selection to introduce and discuss the following words and their meanings.

contest:	a competition (page 36)
athletic:	having skill and strength in sports and other physical activities (page 38)
match:	contest, competition, or race (page 41)
energy:	what makes someone active in work and at play (page 42)
players:	people who take part and play against each other in matches (page 42)
commotion:	noise, excitement, disturbance (p. 43)

Have students read the words in the Word Box, stopping to blend any words that they have trouble reading. Demonstrate how to decode multisyllabic words by breaking the words into syllables and blending the syllables. Then have students try. If the word in not decodable, give the students the pronunciation.

Have students read the sentences on **Reading Transparency 3** and use the skills of context, word structure (structural analysis), or apposition to figure out the meaning of the words. Be sure students explain which skill(s) they are using and how they figured out the meanings of the words.

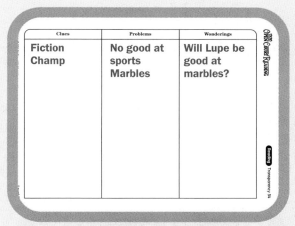

Reading Transparency 54

Teacher Tip SELECTION VOCABULARY To help students decode words, divide them into syllables shown below. The information following each word tells how students can figure out the meaning of each word on the transparency.

con•test	context clues
ath•let•ic	context clues, word structure
match•es	context clues
en•er•gy	context clues
play•ers	context clues, word structure
com•mo•tion	context clues

Routine Card
Refer to Routine 2 for the selection vocabulary procedure. Refer to Routine 3 for the Clues, Problems, and Wonderings procedure.

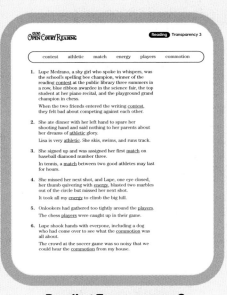

Reading Transparency 3

MEETING INDIVIDUAL NEEDS

ELL Support

VOCABULARY Check that English-language learners know the meanings of idioms and more difficult vocabulary in the story, including: *awardee, straight-A, razor-sharp, pop-up, budge, let it rip, odd-shaped, flexed, hypnotic, dead serious, quivering, slivers,* and *hard-won.* More information can be found in Unit 1, Lesson 2 of the ***English-Language Development Guide.***

Intervention Support

SELECTION VOCABULARY By now students have reviewed all the sounds and spelling needed to read the selection vocabulary words. If students are still having difficulty reading these words, reteach the vowel spellings and provide additional opportunities to read words with those spellings during the time you set aside for Workshop. Go to the ***Intervention Guide*** for additional support for students who need help with vocabulary.

 Students will enjoy using the ***Listening Library Audiocassette/CD*** and listening to the selection they are about to read. Encourage them to listen to the selection during Workshop. Have students discuss with each other and with you their personal listening preferences (for example, nonfiction, poetry, drama, and so on).

 Routine Card
Refer to Routine 4 for the Reading the Selection procedure.

 Teacher Tip COMPREHENSION STRATEGIES Let students know that they are to use comprehension strategies like good readers use them—that is, they are not supposed to wait for the teacher to remind them to use strategies, but rather are to use them on their own to understand the text.

Reading Recommendations

Oral Reading

This story lends itself to oral reading because it is an engaging, chronological narrative. Students should read aloud fluently and accurately, with appropriate pacing, expression, and intonation. Make sure that students attend to punctuation and read in phrases. Tell students to add a sense of feeling or anticipation as they read. Reading the selection with fluency and accuracy will help students comprehend the text. If students have trouble reading decodable words, have them break the words into sounds or syllables and then blend them together to read the words.

Have students make use of the comprehension strategies listed below to help them understand the selection. Have them stop reading periodically or wait until they have completed the selection to discuss the reading strategies. After the students have finished reading the selection, use the "Discussing the Selection" questions on page 43A to see if they understand what they have read.

Using Comprehension Strategies

Comprehension strategy instruction allows students to become aware of how good readers read. Good readers constantly check their understanding as they are reading and ask themselves questions. In addition, skilled readers recognize when they are having problems and stop to use various comprehension strategies to help them make sense of what they are reading.

During the reading of "The Marble Champ," model and prompt the use of the following reading strategies. Take turns reading the story aloud with students.

- **Making Connections** deepens students' understanding of what they read by linking it to their own past experiences and previous reading.
- **Asking Questions** prepares readers for what they want to learn. As they read, they should revisit the questions they have asked to see if they have been answered in the text.
- **Visualizing** helps readers understand descriptions of settings, characters, and events in a story.

As students read, they should be using a variety of strategies to help them understand the selection. Encourage students to use the strategies listed as the class reads the story aloud. Do this by stopping at the points indicated by the numbers in magenta circles on the reduced student page and using a particular strategy. Students can also stop reading periodically to discuss what they have learned and what problems they may be having.

Building Comprehension Skills

Revisiting or rereading a selection allows students to apply skills that give them a more complete understanding of the text. Some follow-up comprehension skills help students organize information. Others lead to deeper understanding—to "reading between the lines," as mature readers do. An extended lesson on the comprehension skill Making Inferences can be found in the Supporting the Reading section on pages 43C–43D. This lesson is intended to give students extra practice with Making Inferences. However, the Teach portion of the lesson may be used at this time to introduce the comprehension skill to students.

■ **Making Inferences (Introduction):** Readers make inferences by using information from the text along with personal knowledge or experience to gain a deeper understanding of characters and events.

Reading with a Purpose

Have students list positive aspects of cooperation and competition that they find throughout the selection in the Response Journal section of their Writer's Notebooks.

MEETING INDIVIDUAL NEEDS

ELL Support

PREREAD THE SELECTION Have English-language learners who may need help with the selection read it before the whole-class reading, using the *Listening Library Audiocassettes/CD*. As they read, help them associate what they see in the illustrations with the words in the story, so that they learn to think English words before translating them first from their native language.

Intervention Support

PREREAD THE SELECTION Preread "The Marble Champ" with students who may need help in reading the selection during the time you set aside for Workshop.

Research in Action
Making Connections

Good readers always relate what they read to what they already know. Many elementary-school students may not automatically make such a connection. You can do much to stimulate them to relate new information to prior knowledge by modeling the process out loud for them. *(Jan Hirshberg)*

COMPREHENSION

Read pages 36–43.

Comprehension Strategies

First Read

Read the story aloud, taking turns with the students. Start by modeling the use of strategies for the students.

Teacher Modeling

1 Asking Questions *Before and during reading, it is a good idea to ask questions as a way of identifying what you want to learn from a selection. The best questions to ask usually cannot be answered with a simple yes or no; they should begin with* Who? What? Why? When? How? *or* Where?

This story is called "The Marble Champ." I wonder who is the marble champ? Will there be some kind of contest in this story? What are some of your questions about this story?

Teacher Modeling

2 Answering Questions *As you read, it is important to revisit the questions you asked so that you can see if they have been answered. I see that one of our questions has been answered. There is going to be a championship marble contest. Have any other questions been answered yet? If you come up with a question or an answer to a question as we read, share it with the group.*

Word Knowledge

SCAFFOLDING The skills students are reviewing in Word Knowledge should help them in reading the story. This lesson focuses on regular plurals. Regular plurals will be found in boxes similar to this one throughout the selection.
Regular plurals:
whispers summers sports hips wheels

First Reading Recommendation

ORAL • CHORAL • SILENT

Focus Questions What enables Lupe to accomplish her goals? Must one have natural ability in order to become good at something?

The Marble Champ

from *Baseball in April and Other Stories*
by Gary Soto
illustrated by Maren Scott

Lupe Medrano, a shy girl who spoke in whispers, was the school's spelling bee champion, winner of the reading <u>contest</u> at the public library three summers in a row, blue ribbon awardee in the science fair, the top student at her piano recital, and the playground grand champion in chess. She was a straight-A student and——not counting kindergarten, when she had been stung by a wasp——never missed one day of elementary school. She had received a small trophy for this honor and had been congratulated by the mayor.

But though Lupe had a razor-sharp mind, she could not make her body, no matter how much she tried, run as fast as the other girls'. She begged her body to move faster, but could never beat anyone in the fifty-yard dash.

The truth was that Lupe was no good in sports. She could not catch a pop-up or figure out in which direction to kick the soccer ball. One time she kicked the ball at her own goal and scored a point for the other team. She was no good at baseball or basketball either, and even had a hard time making a hula hoop stay on her hips.

It wasn't until last year, when she was eleven years old, that she learned how to ride a bike. And even then she had to use training wheels. She could walk in the swimming pool but couldn't swim, and <u>chanced</u> roller skating only when her father held her hand.

36

Informal Assessment

Observe individual students as they read and use the Teacher Observation Log found in the *Program Assessment Teacher's Edition* to record anecdotal information about each student's strengths and weaknesses.

"I'll never be good at sports," she <u>fumed</u> one rainy day as she lay on her bed gazing at the shelf her father had made to hold her awards. "I wish I could win something, anything, even marbles."

At the word "marbles," she sat up. "That's it. Maybe I could be good at playing marbles." She hopped out of bed and rummaged through the closet until she found a can full of her brother's marbles. She poured the rich glass treasure on her bed and picked five of the most beautiful marbles.

She smoothed her bedspread and practiced shooting, softly at first so that her aim would be accurate. The marble rolled from her thumb and clicked against the targeted marble. But the target wouldn't budge. She tried again and again. Her aim became accurate, but the power from her thumb made the marble move only an inch or two. Then she realized that the bedspread was slowing the marbles. She also had to admit that her thumb was weaker than the neck of a newborn chick.

2 She looked out the window. The rain was letting up, but the ground was too muddy to play. She sat cross-legged on the bed, rolling her five marbles between her palms. Yes, she thought, I could play marbles, and marbles is a sport. At that moment she realized that she had only two weeks to practice. The playground championship, the same one her brother had entered the previous year, was coming up. She had a lot to do.

Science/Social Studies Connection Center

Refer to the Science/Social Studies Connection Center Card 2 for a science activity that students can investigate.

Teacher Tip

Lupe Medrano is pronounced loo′pā mä drä′nō.

Comprehension Skills

 Second Read

Making Inferences

Introduce students to the comprehension skill *making inferences.* Explain to the students that sometimes writers don't provide all the details in a story. Sometimes authors assume that readers have the same background information and knowledge that he or she does (though this, of course, is not always the case). Other times they are trying to be challenging or funny by making readers "read between the lines." In either case, good readers apply their own understanding of life to clues in the text to gain meaning beyond what is written on the page.

Ask the students to make inferences about characters in the story so far. Guide them to see that

- Lupe is a competitive person. We know this because she has won many scholastic awards and honors. She is unhappy because she hasn't won any sports awards and wants to be good at sports, too.

- Lupe's father has built a shelf to hold her awards because he is very proud of her accomplishments.

◆ Skills Trace ◆

Making Inferences

Introduced in Grade 2.
Scaffolded throughout Grades 3–5.

REINTRODUCED:	Unit 1, Lesson 2
REINFORCED:	Unit 2, Lesson 3
	Unit 3, Lesson 4
	Unit 5, Lesson 5
	Unit 6, Lesson 5
TESTED:	Unit 1 Assessment

Second Reading Recommendation

ORAL • **SILENT**

Comprehension Strategies

First Read

Teacher Modeling

 Making Connections *I might better understand Lupe if I can connect her with something I know or have read about. Lupe must be serious about marbles if she'd rather practice than do her homework. After all, she's a straight-A student, and she has a whole shelf of awards from school. But I know how it can be when you start doing something new. I once started playing a computer game and I didn't even notice how much time had passed while I was playing! As you are reading, be aware of how ideas or events in the text remind you of things that have happened to you. When you make such connections, tell the class about them.*

Teacher Modeling

4 Asking Questions *I am going to stop here and ask a question because I wonder why Lupe isn't telling her parents about her plan. Is she afraid that they'll make her stop practicing? Does she think she's being silly to spend time learning to play marbles? Let's read on and look for the answers to my questions. What questions do you have?*

Word Knowledge
Regular plurals:

   wrists   fingertips   hours   swirls

Teacher Tip ASKING QUESTIONS
Remind students to ask questions beginning with the words *who, what, why, where,* or *how.*

To strengthen her wrists, she decided to do twenty push-ups on her fingertips, five at a time. "One, two, three . . ." she groaned. By the end of the first set she was breathing hard, and her muscles burned from exhaustion. She did one more set and decided that was enough push-ups for the first day.

She squeezed a rubber eraser one hundred times, hoping it would strengthen her thumb. This seemed to work because the next day her thumb was sore. She could hardly hold a marble in her hand, let alone send it flying with power. So Lupe rested that day and listened to her brother, who gave her tips on how to shoot: get low, aim with one eye, and place one knuckle on the ground.

"Think 'eye and thumb'——and let it rip!" he said.

3 After school the next day she left her homework in her backpack and practiced three hours straight, taking time only to eat a candy bar for energy. With a popsicle stick, she drew an odd-shaped circle and tossed in four marbles. She used her shooter, a milky agate with hypnotic swirls, to blast them. Her thumb *had* become stronger.

4 After practice, she squeezed the eraser for an hour. She ate dinner with her left hand to spare her shooting hand and said nothing to her parents about her dreams of athletic glory.

Practice, practice, practice. Squeeze, squeeze, squeeze. Lupe got better and beat her brother and Alfonso, a neighbor kid who was supposed to be a champ.

MEETING INDIVIDUAL NEEDS

Intervention Support

MAKING CONNECTIONS If students have difficulty making connections to the text, suggest that they look through their Writer's Notebook for examples of cooperation and competition they have encountered previously.

"Man, she's bad!" Alfonso said. "She can beat the other girls for sure. I think."

The weeks passed quickly. Lupe worked so hard that one day, while she was drying dishes, her mother asked why her thumb was swollen.

"It's muscle," Lupe explained. "I've been practicing for the marbles championship."

"You, honey?" Her mother knew Lupe was no good at sports.

"Yeah. I beat Alfonso, and he's pretty good."

That night, over dinner, Mrs. Medrano said, "Honey, you should see Lupe's thumb."

"Huh?" Mr. Medrano said, wiping his mouth and looking at his daughter.

"Show your father."

"Do I have to?" an embarrassed Lupe asked.

"Go on, show your father."

Reluctantly, Lupe raised her hand and flexed her thumb. You could see the muscle.

39

Comprehension Skills

Second Read

Making Inferences

Prompt students to tell you what it means to make inferences. If necessary, remind them that it is using information from the text and their own knowledge to form a better understanding of a character, thing, or event in a story.

- We can infer that Lupe did well during practice because she says that her thumb *had* become stronger. (page 38)
- Based on Lupe's training program, we can infer that she is a very determined person.

Have students tell about people they know and share their own experiences to corroborate the inferences made above.

> ### Word Knowledge
> **Regular plurals:**
> girls   weeks

COMPREHENSION

MEETING INDIVIDUAL NEEDS

Intervention Support

MAKING INFERENCES If students are confused about making inferences, explain that people infer things all the time. For example, if we look out the window and everyone is wearing jackets and other winter gear, we infer it is cold outside. No one tells us this, but we use clues and prior knowledge to make an educated guess. Help students think of other everyday scenarios in which they make inferences.

Comprehension Strategies

First Read

Teacher Modeling

5 **Answering Questions** *Hmm. This answers my question from earlier. Both Lupe's father and mother seem to want Lupe to win the championship. So, I was wrong when I thought she didn't want to tell them about the championship because they would make her stop practicing or they would think she was being silly. I think she wanted to practice first and see if she was good at marbles before she told anyone. This seems like Lupe because she wants to do everything well.*

Word Knowledge

Regular plurals:

marbles   sports   lights

Teacher Tip MAKING INFERENCES

Because questions raised during the story may not always be answered directly, remind students that in some cases they must answer their questions by making inferences.

The father put down his fork and asked, "What happened?"

"Dad, I've been working out. I've been squeezing an eraser."

"Why?"

"I'm going to enter the marbles championship."

Her father looked at her mother and then back at his daughter. "When is it, honey?"

"This Saturday. Can you come?"

The father had been planning to play racquetball with a friend Saturday, but he said he would be there. **5** He knew his daughter thought she was no good at sports and he wanted to encourage her. He even rigged some lights in the backyard so she could practice after dark. He squatted with one knee on the ground, entranced by the sight of his daughter easily beating her brother.

40

MEETING INDIVIDUAL NEEDS

Intervention

ASKING QUESTIONS Have the students work in small groups to ask one another any questions they may have about the story so far. Remind them that some questions can be answered by what they've already read, others will be answered later on in the text, and others will require them to infer answers.

The day of the championship began with a cold blustery sky. The sun was a silvery light behind slate clouds.

"I hope it clears up," her father said, rubbing his hands together as he returned from getting the newspaper. They ate breakfast, paced nervously around the house waiting for 10:00 to arrive, and walked the two blocks to the playground (though Mr. Medrano wanted to drive so Lupe wouldn't get tired). She signed up and was assigned her first <u>match</u> on baseball diamond number three.

Lupe, walking between her brother and her father, shook from the cold, not nerves. She took off her mittens, and everyone stared at her thumb. Someone asked, "How can you play with a broken thumb?" Lupe smiled and said nothing.

She beat her first opponent easily, and felt sorry for the girl because she didn't have anyone to cheer for her. Except for her sack of marbles, she was all alone. Lupe invited the girl, whose name was Rachel, to stay with them. She smiled and said, "OK." The four of them walked to a card table in the middle of the outfield, where Lupe was assigned another opponent.

She also beat this girl, a fifth-grader named Yolanda, and asked her to join their group. They proceeded to more matches and more wins, and soon there was a crowd of people following Lupe to the finals to play a girl in a baseball cap. This girl seemed dead serious. She never even looked at Lupe.

"I don't know, Dad, she looks tough."

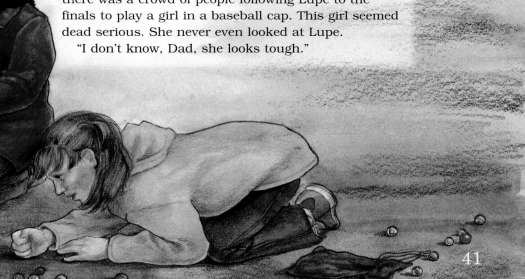

41

Comprehension Skills

Second Read

Making Inferences

Prompt students to share any unanswered questions about characters or events. Remind students that some of their questions may be answered later in the story, but others they will have to infer the answer based on clues from the text and their own prior knowledge.

- Ask students to make inferences about Lupe's family. Point them to page 40, and help them understand that Lupe has a very supportive family.

- Have students read the first sentence of the third paragraph on page 41. Help them infer from this sentence that Lupe is confident in her marbles skills.

- Have students think of times in their own lives when they have faced competition. What can they infer about Lupe's feelings based on their own experiences?

Word Knowledge

Regular plurals:
clouds   hands   blocks   nerves   wins

Teacher Tip FLUENCY By the time in grade 5, good readers should be reading approximately 126 words per minute with fluency and expression. The only way to gain this fluency is through practice. Have students reread the selection to you and to one another during Workshop to help build fluency.

COMPREHENSION

COMPREHENSION

Comprehension Strategies

First Read

Teacher Modeling

6 Visualizing *As we read about the exciting final match in the marbles championship, how many of you have had a mental picture of the action? This is called visualizing. Good readers try to visualize what they are reading as a way of making sure they understand and remember what is happening in the text.*

During the championship, I could visualize Lupe and Miss Baseball's focused faces. What pictures did you see?

Discussing Strategy Use

While they are reading the selection, have students share any problems they encountered and tell what strategies they used.

- What questions did they ask as they read?
- How did they visualize story events?
- What connections did they make between the reading and what they already know?

Remind students that good readers use all of the strategies listed above, and that they should be using them whenever they read. Make sure that students explain how using the strategies helped them better understand the selection. For example, students may say "Making connections with Lupe helped me understand how she felt."

Word Knowledge
Regular plurals:
onlookers   players   eyes   angles

Rachel hugged Lupe and said, "Go get her."

"You can do it," her father encouraged. "Just think of the marbles, not the girl, and let your thumb do the work."

The other girl broke first and earned one marble. She missed her next shot, and Lupe, one eye closed, her thumb <u>quivering</u> with <u>energy</u>, blasted two marbles out of the circle but missed her next shot. Her opponent earned two more before missing. She stamped her foot and said "Shoot!" The score was three to two in favor of Miss Baseball Cap.

The referee stopped the game. "Back up, please, give them room," he shouted. Onlookers had gathered too tightly around the <u>players</u>.

Lupe then earned three marbles and was set to get her fourth when a gust of wind blew dust in her eyes and she missed badly. Her opponent quickly scored two marbles, tying the game, and moved ahead six to five on a lucky shot. Then she missed, and Lupe, whose eyes felt scratchy when she blinked, relied on instinct and thumb muscle to score the tying point. It was now six to six, with only three marbles left. Lupe blew her nose and studied the angles. She dropped to one knee, steadied her hand, and shot so hard she cracked two marbles from the circle. She was the winner!

"I did it!" Lupe said under her breath. She rose from her knees, which hurt from bending all day, and hugged her father. He hugged her back and smiled.

42

 Teacher Tip ANSWERING QUESTIONS
Point out to students that your question from the beginning of the story has been answered: Lupe is the marble champ.

 Informal Assessment

Use the Informal Comprehension Strategies Rubrics on page 36J to determine whether a student is using the strategies being taught.

Everyone clapped, except Miss Baseball Cap, who made a face and stared at the ground. Lupe told her she was a great player, and they shook hands. A newspaper photographer took pictures of the two girls standing shoulder-to-shoulder, with Lupe holding the bigger trophy.

Lupe then played the winner of the boys' division, and after a poor start beat him eleven to four. She blasted the marbles, shattering one into sparkling slivers of glass. Her opponent looked on glumly as Lupe did what she did best—win!

The head referee and the President of the Fresno Marble Association stood with Lupe as she displayed her trophies for the newspaper photographer. Lupe shook hands with everyone, including a dog who had come over to see what the <u>commotion</u> was all about.

That night, the family went out for pizza and set the two trophies on the table for everyone in the restaurant to see. People came up to congratulate Lupe, and she felt a little embarrassed, but her father said the trophies belonged there.

Back home, in the privacy of her bedroom, she placed the trophies on her shelf and was happy. She had always earned honors because of her brains, but winning in sports was a new experience. She thanked her tired thumb. "You did it, thumb. You made me champion." As its reward, Lupe went to the bathroom, filled the bathroom sink with warm water, and let her thumb swim and splash as it pleased. Then she climbed into bed and drifted into a hard-won sleep.

Formal Assessment

See pages 6–9 in **Unit 1 Assessment** to test students' comprehension of "The Marble Champ."

Teacher Tip BUILDING FLUENCY

As students read, you may notice that some need work in building fluency. During Workshop, have these students choose a section of the text (a minimum of 160 words) to read several times in order to build fluency.

Comprehension Skills

Second Read

Making Inferences

Discuss with students any questions they have that were left unanswered and help them use their prior knowledge and clues from the text to infer answers to their questions. Ask students what they can infer about the author's feelings about competition. What about Lupe's feelings? *(Students should be able to infer that both the author and Lupe feel that competition is a positive experience that can bring people together and emphasize a person's strengths.)*

Checking Comprehension

Ask students the following questions to check their comprehension of the story.

- Why was Lupe successful in her competition with the girl in the baseball cap? *(She trained hard for two weeks, exercising her thumb, building a muscle, and practicing hitting the marbles.)*

- Why did the girl in the baseball cap and Rachel respond so differently to losing the competition? *(Answers will vary; students may mention that Rachel lost early in the contest, while the girl in the baseball cap had won many matches.)*

- How has this selection connected with your knowledge of the unit theme? *(Answers will vary—students should compare/contrast examples of cooperation and competition from this selection with their own experiences or past reading and use these connections to make a general statement about the unit theme.)*

COMPREHENSION

Routine Card
Refer to Routine 5 for the *handing-off process*.

Clues	Problems	Wonderings
Fiction Champ	No good at sports Marbles	Will Lupe be good at marbles?

Reading Transparency 54

www.sra4kids.com
Web Connection
Some students may choose to conduct a computer search for additional books or information about cooperation and competition. Invite them to make a list of these books and sources of information to share with classmates and the school librarian. Check the Reading link of the SRA Web page for additional links to theme-related Web sites.

Discussing the Selection

The whole group discusses the selection and any personal thoughts, reactions, problems, or questions that it raises. To stimulate discussion, students can ask one another the kinds of questions that good readers ask themselves about a text: *How does it connect to cooperation and competition? What have I learned that is new? What did I find interesting? What is important here? What was difficult to understand? Why would someone want to read this?* It is important for students to see you as a contributing member of the group.

Routine 5 To emphasize that you are part of the group, actively participate in the *handing-off process:* Raise your hand to be called on by the last speaker when you have a contribution to make. Point out unusual and interesting insights verbalized by students so that these insights are recognized and discussed. As the year progresses, students will take more and more responsibility for the discussion of selections.

Engage students in a discussion to determine whether they have grasped the following ideas:

- how competition affected the characters
- how cooperation helped Lupe achieve her goals
- why Lupe wanted to win a sports competition.

During this time, have students return to the clues, problems, and wonderings they noted during browsing to determine whether the clues were borne out by the selection, whether and how their problems were solved, and whether their wonderings were answered or deserve further discussion and exploration. Let the students decide which items deserve further discussion.

Also have students return to the Focus Questions on the first page of the selection. Select a student to read the questions aloud, and have volunteers answer the questions. If students do not know the answers to the questions, have them return to the text to find the answers.

You may wish to review the elements of realistic fiction with the students at this time. Discuss with them how they can tell that "The Marble Champ" is realistic fiction.

Have students break into small groups to discuss how the story reflects the theme. Groups can then share their ideas with the rest of the class.

Students may wish to record personal responses to this selection. Encourage students to record their experiences with practicing skills to gain a competitive edge.

Review Selection Vocabulary

Have students review the definitions of the selection vocabulary words that they wrote in the vocabulary section of their Writer's Notebooks. Remind them that they discussed the meanings of these words before reading the selection. Students can use these definitions to study for the vocabulary portion of their Lesson Assessment. Have them add to the personal dictionary section of their Writer's Notebook any other interesting words that they clarified while reading. Encourage students to refer to the selection vocabulary words throughout the unit. The words from the selection are:

contest   energy   athletic   matches   players

If you have created a Word Bank, have students place words under the appropriate headings on the Word Bank. Encourage the students to find other words related to the unit theme and add them to the Word Bank. Have students also use other strategies for determining the meaning and increasing their vocabulary of theme-related words. For example, have students list and define homonyms, or multiple-meaning words, homographs, and homophones having to do with cooperation and competition in the Vocabulary section of their Writer's Notebooks.

Home Connection

Distribute **Home Connection,** page 5. Encourage students to discuss "The Marble Champ" with their families. Students can set goals and discuss with their families the skills they need to achieve their goals. **Home Connection** is also available in Spanish, page 6.

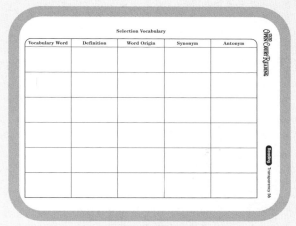

Home Connection p. 5

Teacher Tip EXPANDING VOCABULARY To help students expand their vocabulary, you may want to work with them to fill out the chart on *Reading Transparency 56* for new words in the Word Bank. Have students use multiple resources, such as a dictionary, thesaurus, and word origins book to fill in a definition, word origin, synonym, and antonym for each selection vocabulary word.

Reading Transparency 56

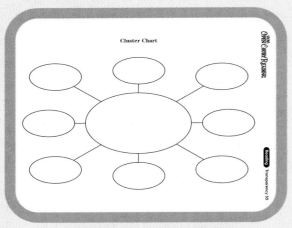

Reading Transparency 55

Supporting the Reading

Comprehension Skills: Making Inferences

Teach Have students tell what they know about making inferences. Then explain to students that good readers use their own prior knowledge to make sure of what they read about events and characters in a selection. Using text clues along with personal knowledge and experiences to more fully understand the meaning behind text is called *making inferences*. Emphasize that writers do not directly state all of the information about events or characters in a text and that it is necessary for students to infer some things as they read.

Guided Practice Use the graphic organizer on *Reading Transparency 55* to help students organize the information needed to make inferences about Lupe's relationship with her brother. Write in the center circle "Lupe's Relationship with Her Brother." Have students suggest story events and prior knowledge about brother/sister relationships to fill in the outer circles. After students have provided as much information as possible, have them make inferences about the relationship based on the information.

Independent Practice Read through the Focus and Identify sections of the *Comprehension and Language Arts Skills,* page 6, with students. Guide students through the Identify portion, and help them come up with examples found in the story. Then have students complete the **Practice** and **Apply** portions of *Comprehension and Language Arts Skills,* page 7, as homework.

Link to Writing Tell students to choose events, such as recitals, sporting events, or movies, with which they are familiar. Then have each student write a paragraph about two characters attending the chosen event. However, students should not directly state the kind of event the characters are attending. When students have finished their paragraphs, have them exchange papers with partners and make inferences about what events were described in the paragraphs. When students have made their inferences, have them discuss how they used clues from the paragraphs and their prior experiences to make these inferences.

MEETING INDIVIDUAL NEEDS

Reteach

MAKING INFERENCES Have students who need additional practice with making inferences complete *Reteach,* pages 7–8.

Challenge

MAKING INFERENCES Have students who understand making inferences complete *Challenge,* page 6.

Skills Trace
Making Inferences
Introduced in Grade 2.
Scaffolded throughout Grades 3–5.
REINTRODUCED: Unit 1, Lesson 2
REINFORCED: Unit 2, Lesson 3
Unit 3, Lesson 4
Unit 5, Lesson 5
Unit 6, Lesson 5
TESTED: Unit 1 Assessment

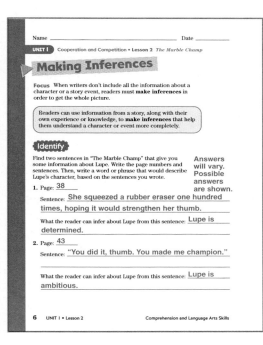

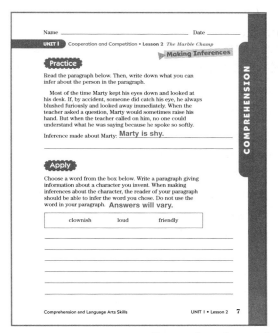

Comprehension and Language Arts Skills pp. 6–7

Teacher Tip SETTING Explain that it is important for authors to provide vivid settings so readers can visualize what is taking place. Point out that in "The Marble Champ" the author does not describe the story's setting all at once; he drops in details about when and where the action is occurring throughout the selection.

Teacher Tip PLOT To help students discuss setting as it relates to plot, tell them that the story's plot is its chain of events. The plot tells about the problem the characters have and how they solve it. In the middle of the story the characters go through one or more conflicts as they try to solve their problem. The events of the plot build to the climax, which is the highest point of interest and takes place when the problem begins to be resolved.

Literary Elements

Setting

Teach Have students share what they know about the settings of stories. Remind them, if necessary, that *setting* is the time and place in which events of a story occur.

Have students identify when and where "The Marble Champ" takes place. Help them establish that the story is set in the present, as shown by details such as the science fair, racquetball, and the attitudes about girls playing sports. Point out that the author also gives general and specific information about where Lupe lives. As an example, share some of the following details:

- Page 37, paragraph 2: "She hopped out of bed and rummaged through the closet . . . "
- Page 41, paragraph 1: "The day of the championship began with a cold blustery sky."
- Page 41, paragraph 2: "They . . . walked the two blocks to the playground . . . . "

Guided Practice Have each student find three examples of setting in the selection "Class President" and write them down on a piece of paper. Ask volunteers to share their examples with the class.

Independent Practice Have each student recall a favorite story and identify its setting. Then have students write paragraphs about how the setting affected the story and how the setting changed, if it did, as the plot developed. Have them write a second paragraph describing the similarities and differences between the settings of a selection from the **Student Anthology** and another story they have read.

Science Connection: Friction

In "The Marble Champ," Lupe realizes as she begins to practice that the bedspread is slowing down the marbles. Explain to students that the cause of the marbles slowing down was the increased friction caused by the marble rolling over the bedspread. Point out that when Lupe tried shooting marbles on a smooth floor, the marbles gained speed.

Divide the class into groups of four, and have each group member shoot a marble on a smooth surface. (You might allow students time to practice shooting marbles.) Students should record the speed of each shot and the distance the marble traveled. Then have each student shoot a marble on a carpeted surface as the other group members record the time and distance measurements. Finally, have students shoot marbles on blankets or other soft surfaces and record the measurements. When groups have gathered all of their data, have them discuss and compare the results. Groups should come to the conclusion that the rougher the surface the more friction is created when objects move across it. Students might share their data in charts or graphs with the rest of the class.

Teacher Tip MATERIALS FOR ACTIVITY To complete the Science Connection activity for this lesson, students will need marbles, a stopwatch, and a measuring stick.

Meet the Author

After students read the information about Gary Soto, discuss the following questions with them.

- Gary Soto grew up working closely with his parents, grandparents, brothers, and sisters. Lupe, from "The Marble Champ," seems to be close to her family also. Can you think of other things the character of Lupe and the author, Gary Soto, have in common? *(Possible answer: Gary Soto was never interested in school until he found a poem he liked; Lupe was never interested in sports until she started playing marbles.)*

- Why do you think that finding a poem he liked changed Gary Soto's feelings about school and learning? *(Possible answer: He found a subject in school that excited him—something that he wanted to know more about. So, learning became something he wanted to do, rather than something he was expected to do.)*

Meet the Illustrator

After the students read the information about Maren Scott, discuss the following question with them.

- Maren Scott says that it's okay to make mistakes, and that as you learn from them you get better and better at what you are trying to do. How is that similar to Lupe's experience with marbles? *(Possible answer: Lupe didn't give up on marbles the first time she tried and failed. She kept practicing until she was so good that she won the championship.)*

The Marble Champ

Meet the Author

Gary Soto was born into a Mexican-American family in Fresno, California. Growing up, he worked alongside his parents, grandparents, brothers and sister, as farm laborers in vineyards, orange groves, and cotton fields around Fresno.

As a young person, Mr. Soto was never very interested in books or schoolwork, but he decided to enroll in college anyway. He discovered he wanted to be a writer at the age of 20. In one of his classes he read a poem called "Unwanted." It had a big effect on him. He started taking poetry classes and writing his own poetry. Mr. Soto continues to write for both adults and children, and he produces short films.

Meet the Illustrator

Maren Scott lives in Utah with her husband and three sons. Besides illustrating, she also enjoys designing quilts. She has won many awards for both her art and her quilts. Ms. Scott advises young people interested in being artists to draw every day. She says, *"Draw what you see and don't be concerned about mistakes. It's okay to make mistakes; just learn from them and you'll get better and better!"*

44

Theme Connections

Within the Selection

Record your answers to the questions below in the Response Journal section of your Writer's Notebook. In small groups, report the ideas you wrote. Discuss your ideas with the rest of your group. Then choose a person to report your group's answers to the class.

- Why did Lupe care about being successful in a sports competition?
- What did Lupe do to win the marble competition? What role did her family play?
- How did Lupe treat the students she defeated in the competition? How did they respond?

Across Selections

- Which character in "Class President" is more like Lupe, Cricket or Julio? Explain why you think so.
- Compare the methods Lupe uses to win her competition with those that Cricket uses in "Class President."

Beyond the Selection

- Tell about a time when you worked hard to achieve a goal. What was your goal? Who and what helped you? What was the result of your effort?
- Think about how "The Marble Champ" adds to what you know about cooperation and competition.
- Add items to the Concept/Question Board about cooperation and competition.

45

Theme Connections

Within the Selection

- Lupe was a competitive person. She was used to winning in other things she tried.
- Lupe practiced hard. Her brother gave her tips. Her parents supported her goal.
- Lupe was a good sport. She was friendly with those she defeated. Most competitors appreciated Lupe's friendliness.

Across Selections

- Students may say that Julio and Lupe both deserved what they achieved.
- Lupe won through hard work, but Cricket used unfair methods.

Beyond the Selection

- Answers will vary.

Have groups report and discuss their ideas with the class. As these ideas are stated, have students add them to the Concept/Question Board.

Students should record their ideas and impressions about the selections on page 6 of their *Inquiry Journals*.

Name _____ Date _____

UNIT 1 Cooperation and Competition

Recording Concept Information

As I read each selection, this is what I added to my understanding of cooperation and competition.

- "Class President" by Johanna Hurwitz
  Answers will vary.

- "The Marble Champ" by Gary Soto
  Answers will vary.

- "Juggling" by Donna Gamache
  Answers will vary.

6 UNIT 1   *Recording Concept Information • Inquiry Journal*

Inquiry Journal p. 6

Teacher Tip INQUIRY AND INVESTIGATION As students complete their discussions, have them sum up what they have learned and tell how they might use this information in further investigations.

Informal Assessment

This may be a good time to observe students working in small groups and to mark your observations in the Teacher Observation Log found in the *Program Assessment Teacher's Edition.*

Objectives

- Students gain a deeper understanding of cooperation and competition.
- Students formulate questions and problems for investigation.
- Students learn how to conduct interviews.

Materials

- Student Anthology, pp. 36–47
- Research Assistant
- Inquiry Journal, pp. 10–15

INVESTIGATION

Research in Action
Inquiry and Investigation

Translated into instruction, the inquiry/investigation procedure provides enough structure so that students do not get lost or bogged down as they explore concepts, while it preserves the open-ended character of real research, which can lead to unexpected findings and to questions that students did not consider originally. To do this, the procedure follows these important principles

- Research focuses on problems, not topics.
- Conjectures guide the research, rather than the reverse.
- New information is gathered to test and revise conjectures.
- Discussion, constant feedback, and constructive criticism are important in all phases of the research, but especially so in the revising of problems and conjectures.
- The cycle of true research is essentially endless, although findings are presented from time to time; new findings give rise to new problems and conjectures, and thus to new cycles of research. *(Carl Bereiter and Marlene Scardamalia)*

Investigating Concepts Beyond the Text

To facilitate students' investigation of cooperation and competition, you might have them participate in the following activities. Tell students that if they have activity ideas of their own that they would like to pursue, they are free to do so as an alternative to these activity suggestions. Tell students that they may work on these activities alone, in pairs, or in small groups, with an option to write about them or to present them to the group upon completion.

The activity suggestions for this lesson are:

- Explain to the class that Reading Roundtable is one of the activities they may choose to participate in during Workshop. Tell them that Reading Roundtable is like a book club. In these sessions, students may form groups in which each member reads the same book and then reports back to the group to discuss how it relates to the unit theme. Students may also read books on their own and do written or oral reviews of their books for the group. Encourage students to read books on cooperation and competition from the ***Leveled Classroom Library.***

- Have students discuss the good and bad points of both cooperation and competition. Have students interview family members and friends outside the classroom to comment on these ideas. Then have students complete ***Inquiry Journal*** page 10.

Upon completion of their activities, have students share with the group anything new they learned about cooperation and competition through discussion and by adding information to the Concept/Question Board.

Inquiry Journal p. 10

Concept/Question Board

After reading each selection, students should use the Concept/Question Board to

- post any questions they asked about a selection before reading that have not yet been answered.

- refer to as they formulate statements about concepts that apply to their investigations.

- post general statements formulated by each collaborative group.

- continue to post news articles, or other items that they find during the unit investigation.

- read and think about posted questions, articles, or concepts that interest them and provide answers to the questions.

Concept/Question Board

Cooperation and Competition

Concept   Question

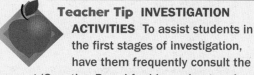

Research Assistant
The Research Assistant helps students in their investigations.

Teacher Tip INVESTIGATION ACTIVITIES To assist students in the first stages of investigation, have them frequently consult the Concept/Question Board for ideas about and examples of cooperation and competition.

www.sra4kids.com
Web Connection
Students can use the connections to Cooperation and Competition in the Reading link of the SRA Web page for more background information about cooperation and competition.

Unit I Investigation Management

Lesson I	Students generate ideas for investigation.
Lesson 2	**Collaborative Investigation** **Students formulate questions and problems for investigation.** **Supplementary Activities** **Students participate in investigation activities and learn how to interview.**
Lesson 3	Students make conjectures.
Lesson 4	Students establish investigation needs.
Lesson 5	Students establish investigation plans.
Lesson 6	Students present investigation findings.

Name_____ Date_____

Cooperation and Competition **UNIT I**

Formulating Questions and Problems

A good question or problem to investigate:
Answers will vary.

Why this is an interesting question or problem:
Answers will vary.

Some other things I wonder about this question or problem:
Answers will vary.

Inquiry Journal • *Formulating Questions and Problems*   UNIT I   **11**

Formulating Questions and Problems *(continued)*

My investigation group's question or problem:
Answers will vary.

What our investigation will contribute to the rest of the class:
Answers will vary.

Some other things I wonder about this question or problem:
Answers will vary.

12   UNIT I   *Formulating Questions and Problems* • Inquiry Journal

Inquiry Journal pp. 11–12

Formal Assessment

Use the Research Rubrics on page 36J to assess students' ability to formulate research questions and problems.

INVESTIGATION

Formulating Questions and Problems

Tell students that, to continue the investigation process, they must narrow the ideas about cooperation and competition that interest them into investigation problems or questions. Model for them how to do this. For example, have them consider the difference between the idea of athletic competitions and the problem, How do athletes prepare for competitions? Explain to them that if they choose to investigate the topic of athletic competitions, it will be very difficult to choose what about athletic competitions to investigate and that this will make it hard for them to organize their findings. Choosing a specific question or problem that interests them will help them focus their investigation and advance their understanding. Explain to the students that a good investigation problem or question will not only require them to consult multiple sources, but will add to the group's knowledge of cooperation and competition, be engaging, and generate further questions. As a group, have students generate a list of potential investigation problems and questions. When they have completed their lists, assign *Inquiry Journal* page 11.

Then have students present the problems or questions that interest them the most to the group. This will lead to the creation of investigation groups to work on selected problems. Have students present their proposed problems, along with reasons for investigating them, allowing open discussion of how promising and interesting various proposed problems are. To aid the formation of groups, have students record and initial their problems on the board. During the discussion, draw arrows between problems to link ones that are related. Have students take notes on who has similar interests to their own. When all of the students have had a chance to propose questions and problems, have them form investigation groups based on shared interests.

During Workshop, have each group meet to agree on an investigation problem. Tell them that they will be required to state the problem that they will be working on and tell how working on that problem will contribute to the class's knowledge. Have them record this in their *Inquiry Journal* page 12.

Interviewing

Teach Ask students what they know about interviewing. If necessary, tell students that interviewing involves asking a person questions and writing down or tape-recording his or her opinions, information, or personal accounts.

Write these rules for interviewing on the board and discuss them:

- Contact the person and ask for permission to conduct an interview. Explain the reason for the interview and tell how long the interview will take.

- Read books or consult other sources of background information on the topic to help generate questions for the interview.

- Think of questions to ask that will help you get the information you need.

- Write down your questions in the order you want to ask them.

- Speak clearly, using an appropriate volume and speed. Listen carefully and be polite.

- Take notes as the person answers your questions, even if you use a tape recorder.

- Be polite after the interview, too. Thank the person you interviewed for his or her time.

- Read your notes as soon after the interview as possible.

Guided Practice Have students imagine that they are reporters for the school newspaper who will interview Lupe Medrano after winning the marble championship. Tell them to concentrate on the questions they want to ask Lupe, particularly about cooperation and competition. Allow time for students to present their questions and discuss them. After the discussion, ask students whether they want to change or add any questions.

Independent Practice Have students conduct interviews with someone they know, such as a family member, friend, or a schoolmate. Have students read and organize information from multiple sources about cooperation and competition to help them generate questions for their interviews.

For more practice with interviewing, have students complete *Inquiry Journal*, pages 13–14.

SUPPORTING THE INVESTIGATION

Teacher Tip INTERVIEWING
Explain to students that when interviewing they should avoid asking questions that can be answered with a "yes" or "no."

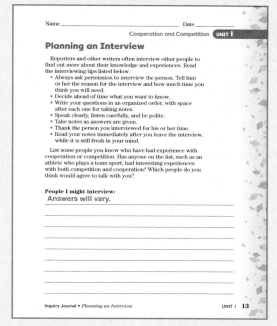

Inquiry Journal pp. 13–14

OVERVIEW

Objectives

Word Analysis

Spelling
- **Spelling Patterns for the /e/ Sound.** Develop understanding of spelling patterns for the /e/ sound introduced in Word Knowledge in Part 1.

Vocabulary
- Using words from "The Marble Champ," develop an understanding of discovering word meanings based on context clues.

Writing Process Strategies
- **The Prewriting Process.** Learn the process of focusing the topic or events, collecting information, selecting resources, organizing ideas, mapping story events, building action, and developing characters to generate effective expository and narrative writing.

English Language Conventions

Grammar, Usage, and Mechanics
- **Pronouns.** Understand correct use of pronouns and identify them in "The Marble Champ."

Listening, Speaking, Viewing
- **Speaking: Speaking Clearly.** Practice speaking clearly at an appropriate volume and rate.

Penmanship
- **Cursive Letters *u* and *w*.** Develop handwriting skills by practicing formation of cursive *u* and *w*.

Materials

- Spelling and Vocabulary Skills, pp. 6–9
- Language Arts Handbook
- Comprehension and Language Arts Skills, pp. 8–9
- Writer's Workbook, p. 2
- Transparencies 3–8; 10
- Student Anthology
- Writing Folder
- Unit 1 Assessment, pp. 28–29

MEETING INDIVIDUAL NEEDS

Reteach, Challenge, English-Language Development and *Intervention* lessons are available to support the language arts instruction in this lesson.

Research in Action

Remember: *children learn to spell pattern by pattern, not word by word. (J. Richard Gentry and Jean Wallace Gillet*, Teaching Kids to Spell)

Language Arts Overview

Word Analysis

Spelling The spelling activities on the following pages support the Word Knowledge introduction of the /e/ sound by developing understanding of the spelling patterns for short *e*.

Selection Spelling Words

These words from "The Marble Champ" contain the /e/ sound.

| treasure | bedspread | chess | strengthen | shelf |

Vocabulary Students will be introduced to the concept of context clues. Students will also be introduced to specific kinds of context clues, including direct definitions, restatements, and comparisons/contrasts.

Vocabulary Skill Words

| fumed | rummaged | agate | entranced | quivering |

Writing Process Strategies

This Writing Process Strategies lesson looks at the prewriting process and guides students through the steps of prewriting so that they understand how to plan and prepare for drafting.

Basic Computer Skills To introduce students to the computer as a writing tool, show students how to identify different types of software, learn about computer operating systems, and how to use the computer's calculator. *Basic Computer Skills* Level 5 Lessons 4–6 teach these basic computer skills.

English Language Conventions

Grammar, Usage, and Mechanics **Pronouns.** This lesson develops understanding of correct pronoun usage. Students will identify pronouns, including antecedents and possessives.

Listening, Speaking, Viewing **Speaking: Speaking Clearly.** In this Speaking lesson, students will practice speaking clearly, making sure to say each full word at an appropriate volume and rate.

Penmanship **Cursive Letters *u* and *w*.** This lesson continues the development of handwriting skills. Students learn correct formation of *u* and *w* and then practice writing paragraphs from the literature selection.

DAY 1

| Word Analysis | Writing Process Strategies | English Language Conventions |

Word Analysis

Spelling

Assessment: Pretest

Spelling Patterns for the /e/ Sound
Give students the Pretest on page 28 of *Unit 1 Assessment*. Have them proofread and correct any misspellings.

Pretest Sentences
1. **sense** A bird can **sense** that her young are in danger.
2. **plenty** There are **plenty** of things to do.
3. **enemy** It is better to make a friend than an **enemy.**
4. **welcome** Parades **welcome** home Olympic athletes.
5. **swept** The floor hasn't been **swept.**
6. **edit** Can you **edit** the paper?
7. **tennis** Wimbledon is a **tennis** tournament.
8. **meant** I **meant** to get some milk at the store.
9. **health** Good **health** is important.
10. **breath** The sprinters are out of **breath.**
11. **shelter** Many people have no **shelter.**
12. **sweater** A **sweater** will keep the chill away.
13. **wealth** The family acquired much **wealth.**
14. **quest** A knight will go on a **quest.**
15. **feather** A parrot **feather** is quite colorful.
16. **treasure** Ancient tombs may have **treasure.**
17. **bedspread** Her **bedspread** matches the curtains.
18. **chess** **Chess** is a game of strategy.
19. **strengthen** Lift weights to **strengthen** your arms.
20. **shelf** The cookie jar is on the top **shelf.**

Writing Process Strategies

Introduction to the Writing Process: Prewriting

Targeting the Topic

Teach

- Have students read *Language Arts Handbook* pages 22–24 on targeting the topic.
- Refer to the web on *Language Arts Handbook* page 22. Help students see how aspects of a broad topic form branching clusters of related topics, from which smaller circles sprout. These smaller circles are the subjects that form the basis of specific topics, or *controlling ideas.*
- As a class, try converting these broad topics—*The Ice Age, mountains, school, the West Coast,* and *wild animals*—to more specific ones.

Guided Practice

Focusing the Events of a Story
Have students work from a general story idea to one that has specific, related events. Use *Transparency 6— Problem-Resolution Chart* to show students how to organize story ideas. Have them describe in their Writer's Notebooks how they would apply *problem → actions to solve problem → resolution* to a story idea of their own.

Language Arts Handbook p. 22

English Language Conventions

Grammar, Usage, and Mechanics:

Pronouns

Teach

- Use *Language Arts Handbook* pages 344–345 for examples of pronoun usage.
- Explain that a pronoun is a word used in place of one or more nouns. *Maria lost the report. She had written it for English class.* **She** is the pronoun replacing **Maria,** the antecedent.
- Some commonly used pronouns are *I, my, mine, me, we, our, ours, us, he, him, his, she, her, hers, it, its, you, your, yours, they, their, theirs,* and *them.*
- *It's* means "it is" and can never be used correctly for *its* (possessive). Possessive pronouns never have an apostrophe (*ours, hers, yours, theirs, whose*).
- Talk about yourself last. *She and **I** like music. He gave the CD to Sam and **me.***

Independent Practice

Use *Comprehension and Language Arts Skills* pages 8–9 to practice the identification and correct usage of pronouns.

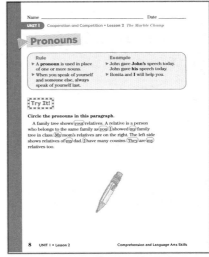

Comprehension and Language Arts Skills p. 8

DAY 2

Word Analysis

Spelling

Word Sorting

Open Word Sort Have students sort the spelling words by the spelling patterns for the /e/ sound. Have students explain their answers.

Vocabulary

Context Clues

Teach

- Write *context clues* on the board and explain that the term means information about a word that you discover in the text.
- On the board, write *The room was dark when we entered, but we soon lit some candles to <u>illuminate</u> the space.* Ask students to use context clues to come up with a definition for *illuminate,* which means "to light."

Guided Practice

Assign page 6 of *Spelling and Vocabulary Skills.* Students can complete page 7 of *Spelling and Vocabulary Skills* for homework.

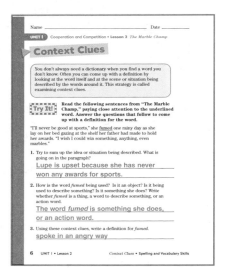

Spelling and Vocabulary Skills p. 6

Writing Process Strategies

Introduction to the Writing Process: Prewriting

Collecting Information

Teach

Ask students where they would look to find information for a report. Write down their ideas (magazines, newspapers, encyclopedias and other reference books, the Internet). Point out the difficulty of finding information from a regular reference book for some subjects. Have students read *Language Arts Handbook* page 25 on collecting information.

Organizing Information

Emphasize the importance of staying centered on a topic once material is in hand. Have students read *Language Arts Handbook* pages 26–29 to learn how to break up information into manageable parts related to a subject.

Guided Practice

Show *Transparency 7—Expository Structure* and have students choose topics about which they are already knowledgeable. Have students map out subtopics and key points to work through in the process of planning a writing project. Have them add this to their *Writing Folders.*

Language Arts Handbook p. 25

English Language Conventions

Grammar, Usage, and Mechanics:
Pronouns

Teach

- Review correct pronoun usage.
- Write the following sentences, minus the bracketed words, on the board. Have students suggest corrections.
  - Carla and me [I] went to the movies.
  - Us [We] learned about World War II.
  - Them [They] came from Norway.
  - Him [He] and me [I] learned how them [they] farmed in Minnesota.
  - Her mother and us [we] rode in they're [their] new car.
  - Its [It's] a bright-blue sports car.

Independent Practice in Reading

Have students look for pronouns in "The Marble Champ." Because there is quite a lot of dialogue in the story, many pronouns are found in the first person *(I).* Others are in the third person *(she, her).*

DAY 3

Word Analysis	Writing Process Strategies	English Language Conventions

Word Analysis

Spelling

Spelling Patterns for the /e/ Sound

Teach

Introduce the spelling patterns for the /e/ sound, which are *e* and *ea*. The pattern *ea* can also spell the long e sound, but in the case of words like *head* and *dead*, spells the short e sound. Have students generate a list on the board of words with *ea* spelling the short e sound and words with *ea* spelling the long e sound.

Guided Practice

Have students complete page 8 from *Spelling and Vocabulary Skills*.

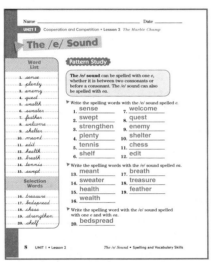

Spelling and Vocabulary Skills p. 8

Vocabulary (continued)

Context Clues

■ Write *An agate is a playing marble with swirls or stripes of color.* Explain that sometimes the meaning of a word is revealed directly in the sentence.

■ Write *She was entranced, or made to stare with great wonder, by the sight.* Explain that the meaning of a word is sometimes stated after the word.

■ Write *He wasn't calm and steady, but was quivering with excitement.* Explain that sometimes the meaning of a word is contrasted with the opposite meaning.

Writing Process Strategies

Introduction to the Writing Process: Prewriting

Organizing Story Writing

Teach

Tell students that story writing calls for a unique kind of planning. Have students read *Language Arts Handbook* pages 27–28 on organizing story writing. Make sure students understand that stories and most types of narrative writing have common elements. Emphasize to students that awareness of these elements will help them plan stories that are interesting and complete.

Story Elements

■ **Characters** (who is in the story)
■ **Setting** (the time and place of the story)
■ **Conflict** (the problem that characters face)
■ **Key Events** (working through the problem, important things that happen)
■ **Resolution** (how the problem is solved)

Story Titles

Point out that titles do not have to be obvious descriptions of topics. Emphasize the way in which clever or intriguing titles can spark the curiosity and interest of readers. As a class, think of examples from children's literature (*Mrs. Frisby and the Rats of NIMH, The Wheel on the School, Roll of Thunder Hear My Cry, And Now Miguel*).

Guided Practice

Mapping Narrative Elements

Show *Transparency 8—Story Map* and have students map out the story elements of a published story. Have students use "The Marble Champ" or another recently read story. Tell students to include the map in their *Writing Folders*.

English Language Conventions

Grammar, Usage, and Mechanics:

Pronouns

Teach

■ Use *Language Arts Handbook* pages 344–345 to review pronoun use.
■ When a pronoun is used as a subject, use *I, he, she, it, you, we,* or *they*.
■ Use possessive pronouns before nouns: *my, your, her, his, our, your, its, their*.
■ Use these pronouns by themselves: *mine, yours, hers, his, its, ours, yours, theirs*.
■ Be clear about to whom you are referring.
Unclear: *When Latrice met Angela for dinner, she had steak.*
Clear: *When Latrice and Angela met for dinner, Latrice had steak.*

Independent Practice in Writing

Tell students to each write a paragraph about a time they did something of which they were proud. Have them include a pronoun in each sentence.

Informal Assessment

Look for evidence that the students are progressing in understanding correct pronoun usage and that they are correctly incorporating pronouns into their work.

DAY 4

| Word Analysis | Writing Process Strategies | English Language Conventions |

Word Analysis

Spelling

Spelling Patterns for the /e/ Sound

Teach

Model the rhyming strategy by writing *health* on the board and asking students for the spelling word that rhymes, *wealth*. Note that both have the same spelling pattern.

Practice

Have students complete the Spelling Strategies exercises on page 9 of ***Spelling and Vocabulary Skills.***

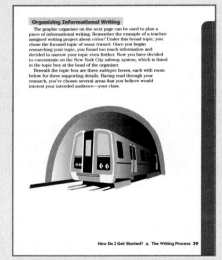

Spelling and Vocabulary Skills p. 9

Vocabulary (continued)

Context Clues

Remind students of the different kinds of context clues, including direct definitions, restatements, and comparisons/contrasts. Have students scan later stories in their anthologies to find a word they don't know. Ask for an example or two and write the sentence or sentences containing the word on the board. Ask students to identify context clues and, as a class, come up with a definition.

Writing Process Strategies

Prewriting

Organizing Writing

Teach

Read ***Language Arts Handbook*** pages 29–31 on organizing informational writing.

Organizing Informational Writing

As a class, plan an information report on the topic of how to play the marble game described in "The Marble Champ." Glean information from the illustrations and descriptions of the game in the story. Use ***Transparency 7—Expository Structure*** to show how to map out subtopics and key points. **Possible Subtopics:** 1) *Conditioning the Thumb and Wrist*, 2) *Game Layout and Number of Players*, 3) *Rules of the Game*.

Guided Practice

Mapping Story Action

Use ***Transparency 10—Web*** to show students how to map an information report.

Language Arts Handbook p. 29

English Language Conventions

Listening, Speaking, Viewing

Speaking: Speaking Clearly

Teach

- Remind the class that when we speak clearly, we are able to express our thoughts and ideas. We should speak slowly and make sure to say each full word. We should also speak loudly enough to be heard without shouting.
- Remind the class that when we speak this way, we demonstrate that we have thought about what we are saying and why we want to say it. People will take us more seriously if they can understand what we are saying.

Guided Practice

- Break the class into small groups. Within their groups, have students take turns speaking about something they have read, focusing on one of the following aspects: a summary of what it was about, a description of its situations or characters, or a description of how the text made them feel.
- Remind the students that the groups should not have to talk over neighboring groups in order to be heard. They should talk just loudly enough for their own group members to hear; anything louder would be disruptive.
- If a member of the group is speaking too fast to be understood or is not pronouncing each full word, the other members of the group should politely interrupt and correct the speaker.

Informal Assessment

Observe whether students are able to discuss the texts in a clear, coherent way. Students should be able to listen to one another and identify good speaking skills.

DAY 5

Word Analysis

Spelling

Assessment: Final Test
Spelling Patterns for the /e/ Sound

Teach
Repeat the Pretest for this lesson or use the Final Test on page 29 of *Unit 1 Assessment*.

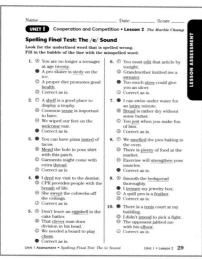

Unit 1 Assessment p. 29

Guided Practice
Have students categorize any mistakes they made on the Final Test.

Are they careless errors?
Are they lesson pattern problems?

Vocabulary (continued)

Context Clues

Informal Assessment

- Encourage students periodically to continue tackling unfamiliar words by searching for context clues in the sentences and paragraphs surrounding these words. Occasionally remind students that context clues can help them determine the exact definition of a word as it is used in that particular instance.
- Remind students to continue keeping a list of new and unfamiliar words and definitions in their Writer's Notebook.

Writing Process Strategies

Introduction to the Writing Process: Prewriting
Organizing the Autobiography

Teach
Mapping Elements
As a class, talk about how one or more of these graphic organizers may be used to plan the components of an autobiography *(Transparency 3—Chain of Events, Transparency 5—Time Line,* and *Transparency 8—Story Map).*
Introduce *Transparency 5—Time Line,* and show students how it may be used to explore key events in their own lives for their autobiographies.

Guided Practice
- In their Writer's Notebooks, have students re-create time lines and fill them out with information about important events in their lives.
- Have students do the prewriting activities on page 2 of their *Writer's Workbooks.*

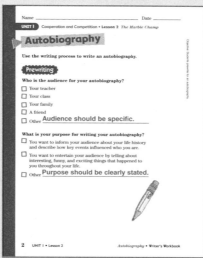

Writer's Workbook p. 2

English Language Conventions

Penmanship
Cursive Letters *u* and *w*

Teach
- Review how all cursive letters are made of four basic types of strokes (undercurve, downcurve, overcurve, and slant line).
- Remind students it is important for all their letters to slant to the right.
- **Teacher Model:** Review formation of lowercase cursive *u* and *w* as undercurve letters.

u Starting point, undercurve
Slant down, undercurve
Slant down, undercurve: small *u*

w Starting point, undercurve
Slant down, undercurve, slant down, undercurve, small curve to right: small *w*

Guided Practice
- **Teacher Model:** On the board, write the sentence *"When Jessica was the new kid in town, she quickly made friends."* to model proper letter formation and slant. Draw slanted lines through letters to demonstrate proper slant.
- Have students write a paragraph about how they might handle being in a new situation, such as a new school, for general handwriting practice.
- From "The New Kid," have students write two paragraphs for general handwriting practice.

Informal Assessment
Check students' handwriting for proper slant.

LESSON WRAP-UP

Reading and Language Arts Skills Traces

Language Arts

WORD ANALYSIS

Skills Trace

Spelling: The /e/ Sound
Introduced in Grade 1.
Scaffolded throughout Grades 2–5.
REINTRODUCED: Unit 1, Lesson 2, p. 45F
PRACTICED: Unit 1, Lesson 2,
pp. 45G–45I
Spelling and Vocabulary Skills,
pp. 8–9
TESTED: Unit 1, Lesson 2, p. 45J
Unit 1 Assessment

Skills Trace

Vocabulary:
Context Clues
Introduced in Grade 1.
Scaffolded throughout Grades 2–5.
REINTRODUCED: Unit 1, Lesson 2, p. 45G
PRACTICED: Unit 1, Lesson 2,
pp. 45H–45I
Spelling and Vocabulary Skills,
pp. 6–7
TESTED: Informal Assessment, p. 45J
Unit 1 Assessment

Reading

COMPREHENSION

Skills Trace

Making Inferences
Introduced in Grade 2.
Scaffolded throughout Grades 3–5.
REINTRODUCED: Unit 1, Lesson 2
REINFORCED: Unit 2, Lesson 3
Unit 3, Lesson 4
Unit 5, Lesson 5
Unit 6, Lesson 5
TESTED: Unit 1 Assessment

WRITING PROCESS STRATEGIES

Skills Trace

Introduction to the Writing Process:
Prewriting
Introduced in Grade 1.
Scaffolded throughout Grades 2–5.
INTRODUCED: Unit 1, Lesson 2, p. 45F
PRACTICED: Unit 1, Lesson 2,
pp. 45F–45J
Writer's Workbook, p. 2
TESTED: Unit 1 Assessment

ENGLISH LANGUAGE CONVENTIONS

Skills Trace

Grammar, Usage, and Mechanics:
Pronouns
Introduced in Grade K.
Scaffolded throughout Grades 1–5.
INTRODUCED: Unit 1, Lesson 2, p. 45F
PRACTICED: Unit 1, Lesson 2, p. 45G
Unit 1, Lesson 2, p. 45H
*Comprehension and Language
Arts Skills,* pp. 8–9
TESTED: Informal Assessment, p. 45H
Unit 2 Assessment

Skills Trace

Listening, Speaking, Viewing:
Speaking: Speaking Clearly
Introduced in Grade K.
Scaffolded throughout Grades 1–5.
REINTRODUCED: Unit 1, Lesson 2, p. 45I
PRACTICED: Unit 1, Lesson 2, p. 45I
TESTED: Informal Assessment, p. 45I

Skills Trace

Penmanship: Cursive Letters u and w
Introduced in Grade 2.
Scaffolded throughout Grades 3–5.
REINTRODUCED: Unit 1, Lesson 2, p. 45J
PRACTICED: Unit 1, Lesson 2, p. 45J
TESTED: Informal Assessment, p. 45J

Professional Development: Inquiry

How Does the Inquiry/Investigation Procedure Differ from Conventional Research Instruction?

In conventional elementary school classrooms, *research* generally means having students collect information and prepare a paper. They conduct their research by following a procedure that usually involves a series of steps such as the following: (1) select a topic, (2) narrow the topic, (3) collect materials, (4) take notes, (5) organize notes, (6) make an outline, (7) write the paper, (8) present the paper.

Topic selection usually means choosing from a list of topics suggested or directed by the teacher. The remainder of the steps usually requires students to locate encyclopedia entries or articles easily found in a library or on the Internet—then write down information from them (Schack, 1993).

Although this procedure may result in the preparation of an adequate paper, it does not constitute *research* in any meaningful or useful sense. Indeed, it gives students a distorted and depressing idea of what real research is all about.

Ample evidence exists that elementary school students *can* do descriptive, historical, and experimental research that seeks answers to real questions or solutions to real problems (Schack, 1993). To do this kind of work, however, students need a better research procedure than the one provided by the traditional approach.

The inquiry/investigation procedure is based on the assumption that students *can* do research that will result in the construction of deeper knowledge. The procedure presents research as a never-ending, recursive cycle. Like real-world researchers, students produce their own questions, develop ideas or conjectures about why something is the way it is, then pursue the answers.

The answers, as for real researchers, may never come. What will come are more questions. Developing the questions, pursuing the answers, developing conjectures, revising ideas, and setting off on new avenues of research and exploration are the stuff of which strong, deep knowledge and expertise are made. The web of knowledge expands in ways that no teacher or student can predict easily.

Translated into instruction, the inquiry/investigation procedure provides enough structure that students do not get lost or bogged down as they explore concepts, while it preserves the open-ended character of real research, which can lead to unexpected findings and to questions that students did not consider originally. To do this, the procedure follows these important principles (Bereiter & Scardamalia, 1993):

- Research focuses on problems, not topics.
- Conjectures guide the research rather than the reverse.
- New information is gathered to test and revise conjectures.
- Discussion, constant feedback, and constructive criticism are important in all phases of the research, especially in the revising of problems and conjectures.
- The cycle of true research is essentially endless, although findings are presented from time to time; new findings give rise to new problems and conjectures, and thus to new cycles of research.

* Additional information about inquiry and investigation as well as resource references can be found in the *Professional Development Guide: Inquiry and Investigation.*

Objectives

- Students will read and comprehend the poem.
- Students will demonstrate an understanding of the poetry element of Rhyme.
- Students will demonstrate an understanding of the presentation skill Dramatic Interpretation.

Materials

- Student Anthology, pp. 46–47
- Listening Library
- Science/Social Studies Connection Center Cards 3–4

Activating Prior Knowledge

- Preteach this lesson by asking students to discuss what they know about baseball and good sportsmanship. Encourage students to share experiences from their own lives.

Reading the Poems

- Read each poem aloud. Then have volunteers read each stanza aloud. Have them emphasize the rhythm of the language as they read. Remind readers to enunciate clearly and use an appropriate volume and speaking rate. Other students should listen carefully to the words and focus on the images they bring to mind.

- In the time you designate for Workshop, encourage students to listen to the recording of the poems on the **Listening Library Audiocassette/CD.**

Reading Recommendation

ORAL • SILENT

Focus Questions How do the Oak Street Tigers feel about the new kid? What does this poem say about how to put together a winning team?

The New Kid

Mike Makley

illustrated by Tony Caldwell

Our baseball team never did very much,
we had me and PeeWee and Earl and Dutch.
And the Oak Street Tigers always got beat
until the new kid moved in on our street.

The kid moved in with a mitt and a bat
and an official New York Yankee hat.
The new kid plays shortstop or second base
and can outrun us all in any race.

The kid never <u>muffs</u> a grounder or fly
no matter how hard it's hit or how high.
And the new kid always acts quite polite,
never yelling or spitting or starting a fight.

We were playing the league champs just last week;
they were trying to break our winning streak.
In the last inning the score was one-one,
when the new kid swung and hit a home run.

A few of the kids and their parents say
they don't believe that the new kid should play.
But she's good as me, Dutch, PeeWee, or Earl,
so we don't care that the new kid's a girl.

46

Science/Social Studies Connection Center

Refer to the Science/Social Studies Connection Center Card 3 for a social studies activity that students can investigate.

Focus Questions Why is it important to have good sportsmanship? What are the qualities of a good sport?

Good Sportsmanship

Richard Armour
illustrated by Tony Caldwell

Good sportsmanship we hail, we sing,
  It's always pleasant when you spot it.
There's only one unhappy thing:
  You have to lose to prove you've got it.

47

Science/Social Studies Connection Center

Refer to the Science/Social Studies Connection Center Card 4 for a social studies activity that students can investigate.

Writer's Notebook

Have the students write the following question in their Writer's Notebook:

■ What lesson do these poems teach about cooperation and competition?

Then have students write their answers to the questions in the response section of their Writer's Notebooks.

Meet the Poet

Richard Armour was a worldwide lecturer and held faculty positions as dean, trustee, and professor of English at universities across the United States. He authored over a dozen children's books, more than 6,000 prose and verse magazine contributions, and over 40 adult nonfiction, poetry, humor, and satire books. ("Good Sportsmanship" appears in his book, *Night with Armour*.) In addition to his many scholarly achievements, the American Film Festival awarded him second prize for his children's educational film, "On Your Marks: A Package of Punctuation," and he was named Author of the Year by PEN, Stanford University, and the Los Angeles Public Library Association. He believed it was his "mission" to make poetry accessible to children. "One thing that keeps me going is their letters, in which they thank me for taking the dullness out of study, [and for] making learning fun."

Teacher Tip LIMERICKS Students may enjoy writing a limerick. A limerick is a short and witty form of verse. The poem contains five short lines. The first, second, and fifth lines rhyme. Lines three and four are shorter and rhyme with each other. The following is an example of a limerick:

There was an Old Man who said, "Do
Tell me *how* I should add two and two?
  I think more and more
  That it makes about four—
But I fear that is almost too few."

author unknown

ELEMENTS OF POETRY

Teacher Tip POETRY ELEMENTS

Tell students that poetry is a special kind of writing in which the sounds and meanings of words are combined to create ideas and feelings. Have students identify these and other elements of poetry:

- Poetry is written in lines and stanzas. Sentences are sometimes broken into parts to create two or more lines. Several lines can be grouped in a poem to form a stanza.

- Some poems have a rhythm, or meter. In poetry, a rhythmic pattern of accented and unaccented syllables is called meter. Not all poems have meter.

- Sounds, words, or phrases may be repeated. Alliteration is a form of sound repetition.

Elements of Poetry

As students study poetry, they will learn that there are many elements that make up a poem. Have students look at "The New Kid" and "Good Sportsmanship" and discuss the following element with them.

Rhyme

Explain to students that rhyme is the repetition of similar sounds at the ends of words or lines in poetry. Have students look at both poems and provide examples of rhyming words from each. Discuss with students how rhyme affects the rhythmic and musical qualities of poetry.

Tell students that the rhyme of an entire poem is called a rhyme scheme. Explain that rhyme schemes are marked using lowercase letters of the alphabet. The first rhyme is marked *a;* the second *b;* and so on. Demonstrate marking the rhyme scheme of "Good Sportsmanship" on the board or on a transparency *(abab).* Then challenge students to mark the rhyme scheme of "The New Kid." You might help them get started by marking the first stanza with them. *(aabb)*

Writing

Students can respond to poetry and practice new elements by writing poems themselves. Have students work in pairs to think of rhyming words. Then have pairs collaborate to compose a rhyming poem about cooperation and competition in a sporting event.

Presentation

Dramatic Interpretation

Have students tell you what they know about *dramatic interpretation*. If necessary, explain that dramatic interpretation is the acting out of events in a story or poem in a way that expresses their meanings. Tell students that they will be enacting the events in the poem "The New Kid." Have students break into groups. Each group will need actors for the parts of the narrator, PeeWee, Dutch, Earl, and the new kid. The narrator will read the poem as he or she and the other students mime the events the poem describes.

Allow students to outline the events of the poem. Then, have them practice their movements and interpretations, event by event. Finally, groups can present their dramatic interpretations to the class.

As groups present their dramatic interpretations, other students should take notes on the interpretations. When all groups have performed, lead a class discussion on the interpretations noting the similarities and differences between those done by different groups. Address how watching the poem acted out as it was read added to or changed their understanding of the ideas in the poem.

Humor

Tell students that humor is the funny part of something or that which makes people laugh. Have students discuss elements of humor, or what it is that makes some things funny. If students have a hard time putting a finger on why they laugh at certain things, you may want to offer the following elements of humor.

- Irony—when something happens that is the opposite of what you expect

- Absurdity—when something happens that does not seem to make sense with its surroundings

- Wit—an imaginative connection made between two seemingly different things

- Timing—the ability to pick the "right moment" to say something witty, absurd, or ironic; this usually involves an element of surprise.

Have students reread the poem "Good Sportsmanship" and discuss how the author used each of the above elements to make his poem humorous. (See the Teacher Tip to the right for examples of how elements of humor are used in the poem.) Then, have students write humorous poems of their own to present to the class. After each presentation, have students discuss the elements of humor they recognized.

LISTENING/SPEAKING/VIEWING

Teacher Tip ELEMENTS OF HUMOR You may want to offer students the following to illustrate the elements of humor:

- **Irony:** A tow truck towing another tow truck down the highway
- **Absurdity:** A person playing football wearing a wedding dress
- **Wit:** "I have not failed. I've just found 10,000 ways that won't work."—Thomas Edison
- **Timing:** Tell students that timing is often associated with stand-up comedy—just when you think the comedian is going to say one thing, he or she says something completely unexpected.

Teacher Tip TYING HUMOR TO THE SELECTION If students are having difficulty tying the elements of humor to the poem "Good Sportsmanship," you may want to offer the following:

- The idea of having to lose to be a good sport is **ironic** because most people want to be considered a good sport, but few want to lose.
- The idea of having to lose in order to win, as is the case with good sportsmanship, is **absurd**.
- The author's ability to connect the ideas of winning and losing in the manner he did is an example of **wit**.
- The fact that there is an unexpected twist at the ending of the poem is an example of **timing**.

Teacher Tip TEACHER CONFERENCING You may want to hold individual conferences with students to help them develop ideas for their humorous poems and to ensure that the content of their poems is appropriate for presentation to the class.

Selection Summary

Genre: Realistic Fiction

When Kyle's gym teacher, Mr. Braden, discovers Kyle's talent as a volleyball player, Mr. Braden begins a campaign to recruit Kyle for the school team. But Kyle has another commitment, his paper route, that takes up all of his after-school time. The money Kyle earns from his paper route is very important to his family's income. Kyle's dilemma is this: How can he juggle responsibility to his job and mother and still contribute to his school's team? The solution comes when some teachers and students cooperate to help Kyle juggle his schedule.

Some of the elements of realistic fiction are listed below. A realistic fiction selection may have one or more of these elements.

- The characters behave as people or animals do in real life.
- The setting of the story is a real place or could be a real place.
- The events of the story are based on a conflict or problem that could occur in real life.

SELECTION INTRODUCTION

About the Author

DONNA GAMACHE is a writer and teacher who lives in a Manitoba, Canada village. Interested in writing since she was young, some of her favorite topics are nature, sports, and farm life. Her own three sons played sports and often had difficulty juggling sports and their other responsibilities. Mrs. Gamache's advice to students who want to write is to read widely, then start writing. "Writing is a learned process which takes practice," Mrs. Gamache says. "Students need to realize that re-writing is a necessity. Even professional writers must re-write and re-write."

Also by Donna Gamache

- *Spruce Woods Adventure*

About the Illustrator

DANIEL POWERS studied art history and received an MFA in illustration at Marywood University in Pennsylvania. Other children's books he has illustrated include *Jiro's Pearl*, which was awarded Pick of the List by the American Bestsellers Association; *From the Land of the White Birch*, which received the Original Art Award from the Society of Illustrators; and *Dear Katie, The Volcano Is a Girl*, which earned him an artist-in-residency from the Kalani Honua Institute for Cultural Studies.

Students can read more about Daniel Powers on page 54 of the **Student Anthology.**

Also Illustrated by Daniel Powers
- *Henrietta*
- *Toil in the Soil*

Inquiry Connections

A major aim of **Open Court Reading** is knowledge building. Because inquiry is at the root of knowledge building, students are encouraged to investigate topics and questions within each selection that relate to the unit theme.

"Juggling" is realistic fiction about a young boy who faces the conflicting demands of his family's needs and the needs of his school volleyball team. The key concepts to be explored are

- conflicting needs can often be met through cooperative efforts.
- a team effort is effective in both sports and everyday life.
- cooperation is essential if we are to compete successfully.

Before reading the selection:

- Point out that students may post a question, concept, word, illustration, or object on the Concept/Question Board at any time during the course of their unit investigation. Be sure that students include their names or initials on the items they post so that others will know whom to go to if they have an answer or if they wish to collaborate on a related activity.

- Students should feel free to write an answer or a note on someone else's question or to consult the Board for ideas for their own investigations throughout the unit.

- Encourage students to read about cooperation and competition at home and to bring in articles or pictures that are good examples to post on the Board.

Concept/Question Board

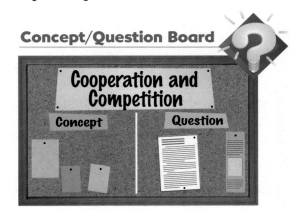

PROGRAM RESOURCES

Leveled Practice

Reteach
Pages 12–17

Challenge
Pages 10–14

ELD Workbook

Intervention Workbook

Leveled Classroom Library*

Have students read at least 30 minutes daily outside of class. Have them read books from the ***Leveled Classroom Library,*** which supports the unit theme and helps students develop their vocabulary by reading independently.

The Big Bike Race
BY LUCY JANE BLEDSOE. AVON, 1995.

Though a used, yellow, old clunker is the only bike his grandmother can afford to buy him, Ernie won't let the other kids' laughter hamper his determination to race and to win. **(Easy)**

The Wheel on the School
BY MEINDERT DEJONG. HARPER TROPHY, 1972.

When Lina begins to wonder why the storks no longer come to the village of Shora, she spurs the five other children to action, and they set out to bring the storks back to Shora. (A Newbery Medal Winner) **(Average)**

A World in Our Hands
BY THE YOUNG PEOPLE OF THE WORLD. TRICYCLE, 1995.

Edited by a team of 12 to 21 year olds and composed of drawings, poems and essays by young people from many countries, this book presents a history of the UN and hope for its future achievements. **(Advanced)**

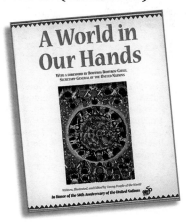

✱ These books, which all support the unit theme Cooperation and Competition, are part of a 36-book ***Leveled Classroom Library*** available for purchase from SRA/McGraw-Hill.
  Note: Teachers should preview any trade books for appropriateness in their classrooms before recommending them to students.

TECHNOLOGY

Web Connections

www.sra4kids.com
Cooperation and Competition Web site

Audiocassette/CD

✱**Listening Library:**
Cooperation and Competition
SRA/McGRAW-HILL, 2002

Computer Skills

✱ **Basic Computer Skills**

CD-ROMs

 ✱ **Research Assistant**
SRA/McGRAW-HILL, 2002

 ✱ **Student Writing and Research Center**
THE LEARNING COMPANY

Titles preceded by an asterisk (✱) are available through SRA/McGraw-Hill. Other titles can be obtained by contacting the publisher listed with the title.

LESSON PLANNER

		DAY 1	DAY 2
Suggested Pacing: 3–5 days		**DAY 1**	**DAY 2**

1 Preparing to Read

Materials
- Routine Card 1

DAY 1

Word Knowledge, p. 48K
- Closed Compounds
- Consonant Digraph *th*
- S-Consonant Blends
- /o/ and /aw/ Sounds Spelled *o*

About the Words and Sentences, p. 48K

DAY 2

Developing Oral Language, p. 48L

2 Reading & Responding

Materials
- Student Anthology, pp. 48–55
- Reading Transparencies 4–5, 54
- Routine Card 1
- Program Assessment
- Unit 1 Assessment, pp. 10–13
- Science/Social Studies Connection Center Card 5
- Comprehension and Language Arts Skills, pp. 10–11
- Reteach, pp. 12–13
- Challenge, p. 10
- Home Connection, pp. 7–8
- Inquiry Journal, p. 6

DAY 1

Build Background, p. 48M
Preview and Prepare, pp. 48M–48N
Selection Vocabulary, p. 48N
Reading Recommendations, pp. 48O–48P
Student Anthology, pp. 48–53 [First Read]
- ✓ Comprehension Strategies
  - Asking Questions, p. 48
  - Predicting, pp. 48, 50, 52
  - Making Connections, p. 50
Discussing Strategy Use, p. 52
Discussing the Selection, p. 53A

DAY 2

Student Anthology, pp. 48–53 [Second Read]
Comprehension Skills
- Author's Point of View, pp. 49, 51, 53
- ✓ Checking Comprehension, p. 53
Supporting the Reading, pp. 53C–53D
- Author's Point of View

Inquiry

Materials
- Student Anthology, pp. 48–57
- Inquiry Journal, pp. 15–19
- Research Assistant

DAY 1

Investigation
- Investigating Concepts Beyond the Text, p. 55A

DAY 2

Investigation
- Concept/Question Board, p. 55B

3 Language Arts

Materials
- Comprehension and Language Arts Skills, pp. 12–15
- Language Arts Handbook, pp. 32–37, 272–275, 286–289, 346–347
- Language Arts Transparencies 2, 4
- Spelling and Vocabulary Skills, pp. 10–13
- Student Anthology
- Student Writing and Research Center
- Writer's Workbook
- Unit 1 Assessment, pp. 30–31
- Reteach, pp. 14–17
- Challenge, pp. 11–14

DAY 1

Word Analysis
- ✓ Spelling Patterns for the /o/ and /aw/ Sounds Pretest p. 55F

Writing Process Strategies
- Writing Process Introduction: Drafting p. 55F

English Language Conventions
- Grammar, Usage, and Mechanics: Verbs p. 55F

DAY 2

Word Analysis
- Spelling Patterns for the /o/ and /aw/ Sounds, p. 55G
- Vocabulary: Word Parts, p. 55G

Writing Process Strategies
- Writing Process: Drafting, p. 55G

English Language Conventions
- Grammar, Usage, and Mechanics: Verbs, p. 55G

✓Informal Assessment Available   ✓Formal Assessment Available

| DAY 2 continued | DAY 3 | |
DAY 3	DAY 4	DAY 5
General Review	**General Review**	**Review Word Knowledge**
Student Anthology, pp. 54–55 ■ **Meet the Illustrator** ✓■ **Theme Connections**	**Review Selection Vocabulary, p. 53B** **Literary Elements, p. 53E** ■ **Genre: Realistic Fiction** **Student Anthology, pp. 56–57** ■ **Fine Art**	✓ **Lesson Assessment** ■ *Unit 1 Assessment:* **Lesson Assessment, pp. 10–13** **Home Connection, p. 53B** **Science Connection** ■ **The Circulatory System, p. 53F**
✓ **Investigation** ■ **Making Conjectures, p. 55C**	**Supporting the Investigation** ■ **Note Taking, p. 55D**	**Investigation** ■ **Unit Investigation Continued** ■ **Update Concept/Question Board**
Word Analysis ■ **Spelling Patterns for the /o/ and /aw/ Sounds, p. 55H** ■ **Vocabulary: Word Parts, p. 55H** **Writing Process Strategies** ■ **Writing Process: Drafting, p. 55H** **English Language Conventions** ✓■ **Grammar, Usage, and Mechanics: Verbs, p. 55H**	**Word Analysis** ■ **Spelling Patterns for the /o/ and /aw/ Sounds, p. 55I** ■ **Vocabulary: Word Parts, p. 55I** **Writing Process Strategies** ■ **Writing Process: Drafting, p. 45I** **English Language Conventions** ✓■ **Listening, Speaking, Viewing Language: Using Appropriate Language, p. 45I**	**Word Analysis** ✓■ **Spelling Patterns for the /o/ and /aw/ Sounds Final Test, p. 55J** ✓■ **Vocabulary: Word Parts, p. 55J** **Writing Process Strategies** ✓■ **Writing Process: Drafting, p. 55J** **English Language Conventions** ✓■ **Penmanship: Cursive Letters *r* and *s*, p. 55J**

Below are suggestions for differentiating instruction to meet the individual needs of students. These are the same skills shown on the Lesson Planner; however, these pages provide extra practice opportunities or enriching activities to meet the varied needs of students.

WORKSHOP

Differentiating Instruction

Small-Group Instruction

Use small-group instruction for such things as collaborating with students on investigation activities.

Use the informal assessment suggestions found throughout the lesson along with the formal assessments provided in each lesson to determine your students' strengths and areas of need. Use the following program components to help in supporting or expanding on the instruction found in this lesson:

- **Reteach** workbook for use with those students who show a basic understanding of the lesson but need a bit more practice to solidify their understanding

- **Intervention Guide** and **Workbook** for use with those students who even after extra practice exhibit a lack of understanding of the lesson concepts

- **English-Language Development Guide** and **Workbook** for use with those students who need language help

Independent Activities

Students can work individually on such things as:

- **Inquiry Journal** pages
- Independent reading
- Investigation activities
- **Challenge**
- Writing

During this time students may discuss unit theme-related questions, problems, and conjectures related to their investigations. They may also complete activities that allow them to investigate questions that interest them.

For Workshop Management Tips, see Appendix pages 41–42.

◆ **Small-group Instruction**   ■ **Independent Activities**

	READING	INVESTIGATION ACTIVITIES
DAY 1	■ Browse *Leveled Classroom Library* ■ *Listening Library Audiocassette/CD* ■ Add Vocabulary in Writer's Notebook ■ Record Response to Selection in Writer's Notebook	■ Concept/Question Board ■ Explore OCR Web Site for Theme Connections ■ Complete *Inquiry Journal,* pp. 15–16
DAY 2	■ Choose *Leveled Classroom Library* Book and Begin Independent Reading ■ Oral Reading of Selection for Fluency ■ *Listening Library Audiocassette/CD* ■ Complete *Comprehension and Language Arts Skills,* pp. 10–11	■ Concept/Question Board ■ Explore OCR Web Site for Theme Connections
DAY 3	■ Read *Leveled Classroom Library* Book as Independent Reading ◆ Discuss Theme Connections, p. 55 ■ Complete *Link to Writing* for Supporting the Reading, p. 53D	■ Concept/Question Board ◆ Make Conjectures About Solutions to Investigation Problems. ■ Use *Research Assistant* to Help with Investigation
DAY 4	■ Read *Leveled Classroom Library* Book as Independent Reading ■ Add Words to Word Bank ■ Complete *Independent Practice* for Literary Elements, p. 53E	■ Concept/Question Board ■ Complete *Inquiry Journal,* p. 17
DAY 5	■ Read *Leveled Classroom Library* Book as Independent Reading ◆ Reading Roundtable ◆ Social Studies Connection, p. 53F	■ Concept Question/Board ■ Practice Note Taking in *Inquiry Journal,* pp. 18–19

LANGUAGE ARTS	INTERVENTION*	ENGLISH-LANGUAGE LEARNERS**	RETEACH	CHALLENGE
English Language Conventions ■ Complete Verbs, *Comprehension and Language Arts Skills,* pp. 12–13 **Writing Process Strategies** ◆ Seminar: Drafting Expository Writing, p. 55F	(30 to 45 minutes per day) ◆ Reading Words, p. 21 ◆ Preteach "Juggling," pp. 22–23 ◆ Teach "Intervention Selection One," pp. 23–24 ◆ Grammar, Usage, and Mechanics, p. 26	(30 to 45 minutes per day) ◆ Word Knowledge, Closed Compounds, p. 11 ◆ Word Knowledge, Consonant Digraph *th*, p. 11 ◆ Activate Prior Knowledge, p. 13		
Word Analysis ◆ Spelling: Word Sort, p. 55G ■ Complete Vocabulary: Word Parts, *Spelling and Vocabulary Skills,* pp. 10–11 **Writing Process Strategies** ◆ Seminar: Drafting a Paragraph, p. 55G	◆ Developing Oral Language, p. 21 ◆ Preteach "Juggling," pp. 22–23 ◆ Teach Comprehension Strategies, p. 24 ◆ Reread "Intervention Selection One" ◆ Grammar, Usage, and Mechanics, p. 26	◆ Selection Vocabulary, p. 13 ◆ Preteach the Selection, p. 14	**Comprehension** ◆ Review Comprehension Skill: Author's Point of View ■ Complete *Reteach,* pp. 12–13 **English Language Conventions** ■ Complete Verbs: *Reteach,* p. 16	**Comprehension** ■ Complete *Challenge,* p. 10 **English Language Conventions** ■ Complete Verbs, *Challenge,* p. 13
Word Analysis ■ Complete **Spelling: The /o/ and /aw/ Sounds,** *Spelling and Vocabulary Skills,* p. 12 **Writing Process Strategies** ◆ Seminar: Drafting a Summary, p. 55H	◆ Dictation and Spelling, pp. 21–22 ◆ Reread "Juggling" ◆ Teach "Intervention Selection Two," pp. 24–25 ◆ Writing Activity, pp. 27–28	◆ Word Knowledge, Consonant Blends, p. 12 ◆ Dictation and Spelling, p. 12	**Word Analysis** ■ Complete Vocabulary: Word Parts, *Reteach,* p. 15	**Word Analysis** ■ Complete Vocabulary: Word Parts, *Challenge,* p. 12
Word Analysis ■ Complete **The /o/ and /aw/ Sounds,** *Spelling and Vocabulary Skills,* p. 13 **Writing Process Strategies** ◆ Seminar: Drafting a Personal Narrative, p. 55I	◆ Reread "Juggling" ◆ Teach Comprehension Strategies, p. 25 ◆ Reread "Intervention Selection Two" ◆ Writing Activity, pp. 27–28	◆ Vocabulary Strategies, p. 14	**Word Analysis** ■ Complete **Spelling: The /o/ and /aw/ Sounds,** *Reteach,* p. 14	**Word Analysis** ■ Complete **Spelling: The /o/ and /aw/ Sounds,** *Challenge,* p. 11
Writing Process Strategies ■ Complete **Writer's Craft: Figurative Language,** *Comprehension and Language Arts Skills,* pp. 14–15 ◆ Seminar: Draft an Autobiography, p. 55J **English Language Conventions** ■ Penmanship: Cursive Letters *r* and *s,* p. 55J	◆ Repeated Readings/Fluency Check, pp. 25–26 ◆ Informal Assessment	◆ Grammar, Usage, and Mechanics, p. 15	**Writing Process Strategies** ■ Complete **Writer's Craft: Figurative Language,** *Reteach,* p. 17	**Writing Process Strategies** ■ Complete **Writer's Craft: Figurative Language,** *Challenge,* p. 14

*Page numbers refer to *Intervention Guide*
**Page numbers refer to *English-Language Development Guide*

ASSESSMENT

Formal Assessment Options

Use these summative assessments along with your informal observations to assess student progress.

Unit 1 Assessment p. 10

Name _____ Date _____ Score _____

UNIT I Cooperation and Competition · **Lesson 3**

LESSON ASSESSMENT

Juggling

Read the following questions carefully. Then completely fill in the bubble of each correct answer. You may look back at the story to find the answer to each of the questions.

1. Why did Kyle play volleyball poorly in gym?
   Ⓐ So other kids could make the team.
   Ⓑ So everyone would leave him alone.
   Ⓒ So someone would help him with his papers.

2. Why can't Kyle go to volleyball practice?
   Ⓐ He has to deliver papers.
   Ⓑ He has to get home to study.
   Ⓒ He has other sports to play.

Read the following questions carefully. Use complete sentences to answer the questions.

3. Why does Kyle need the paper route?
   Kyle needs the money from his paper route to help his mother.

4. How does Kyle feel about everybody bugging him to join the team?
   Kyle feels angry and frustrated because he can't join even though he wants to.

5. Why does Kyle get angry with his mother?
   She thinks Kyle should join the team, too.

10 Unit I · Lesson 3   Juggling · Unit I Assessment

Unit 1 Assessment p. 11

Juggling (continued)

6. Why does Mr. Braden call Kyle's mother on the telephone?
   Mr. Braden wants Kyle to join the volleyball team.

7. How do you know Kyle is responsible?
   He chooses to work instead of joining the volleyball team.

8. What is the climax of this story?
   The climax of the story is when Mr. Braden and Dave make their offers to help Kyle juggle his time.

Read the following questions carefully. Then completely fill in the bubble of each correct answer.

9. The setting of this story is probably
   Ⓐ a school today
   Ⓑ a school long ago
   Ⓒ a school in the far future

10. From which point of view is this story written?
   Ⓐ third-person
   Ⓑ first-person
   Ⓒ unknown writer

Unit I Assessment · Juggling   Unit I · Lesson 3 11

Unit 1 Assessment p. 12

Juggling (continued)

Read the questions below. Use complete sentences in your answers.

Linking to the Concepts How do the coach and Dave cooperate to give Kyle a chance to play?
Answers will vary. Accept all reasonable answers.

Personal Response How would you feel if a coach and your friends were pressuring you to join a team or club?
Answers will vary. Accept all reasonable answers.

12 Unit I · Lesson 3   Juggling · Unit I Assessment

Unit 1 Assessment p. 13

Juggling (continued)

Vocabulary

Read the following questions carefully. Then completely fill in the bubble of each correct answer.

1. In gym class on Monday, Kyle hit seven straight serves just over the net, hard and fast. A **serve** is
   Ⓐ when you hit the ball by mistake
   Ⓑ when you let other people hit the ball for you
   Ⓒ when you put the ball into play

2. One student says to Kyle, "Where's your school spirit?" If you have school **spirit** you
   Ⓐ cheer for all of the schools
   Ⓑ want your school teams to win
   Ⓒ go straight home after school

3. Kyle had taken a second paper route because he and his mother had no money to **spare**. This means Kyle and his mother
   Ⓐ had only cash
   Ⓑ had a little extra
   Ⓒ had nothing extra

4. The next day, Kyle deliberately hit all his serves low into the net and messed up several setups. **Deliberately** means
   Ⓐ on purpose
   Ⓑ accidentally
   Ⓒ as a joke

5. Mr. Braden asks Kyle if he can juggle his time and join the team. In this sentence **juggle** means
   Ⓐ do two things at once
   Ⓑ learn to throw three balls
   Ⓒ serve the ball so it wiggles

Unit I Assessment · Juggling   Unit I · Lesson 3 13

Unit 1 Assessment p. 30

Name _____ Date _____ Score _____

UNIT I Cooperation and Competition · Lesson 3 Juggling

Spelling Pretest: The /o/ and /aw/ Sounds

Fold this page back on the dotted line. Take the Pretest. Then correct any word you misspelled by crossing out the word and rewriting it next to the incorrect spelling.

1. _____	1. congress
2. _____	2. topic
3. _____	3. promise
4. _____	4. proper
5. _____	5. collar
6. _____	6. common
7. _____	7. comet
8. _____	8. cause
9. _____	9. broad
10. _____	10. caught
11. _____	11. awful
12. _____	12. ought
13. _____	13. fought
14. _____	14. brought
15. _____	15. thought
16. _____	16. volleyball
17. _____	17. office
18. _____	18. lockers
19. _____	19. intercom
20. _____	20. offered

30 Unit I · Lesson 3   Spelling Pretest: The /o/ and /aw/ Sounds · Unit I Assessment

---

Unit 1 Assessment p. 31

Name _____ Date _____ Score _____

UNIT I Cooperation and Competition · Lesson 3 Juggling

Spelling Final Test: The /o/ and /aw/ Sounds

Look for the underlined word that is spelled wrong. Fill in the bubble of the line with the misspelled word.

1. Ⓐ She taght the third grade for thirty years.
   Ⓑ A comet is an amazing sight.
   Ⓒ I thought that play was very entertaining.
   Ⓓ Correct as is.

2. Ⓐ There is popcorn on the movie theater floor.
   Ⓑ I feel so awful, I think I have the flu.
   Ⓒ We stoped cheering when the player tripped.
   Ⓓ Correct as is.

3. Ⓐ Congress is not in session every day of the year.
   Ⓑ The animal in the trap faught for freedom.
   Ⓒ I can't get the cap off of the bottle.
   Ⓓ Correct as is.

4. Ⓐ You need the propper papers to cross the border.
   Ⓑ Can you scan the broad expanse of the canyon?
   Ⓒ It feels good to do an honest day's work.
   Ⓓ Correct as is.

5. Ⓐ You can't play volleyball without a net.
   Ⓑ Announcements are often given on an intercom.
   Ⓒ An elevator can be found in the main loby.
   Ⓓ Correct as is.

6. Ⓐ That black banana is definitely routten.
   Ⓑ Much business is conducted at the office.
   Ⓒ A good report has an interesting topic.
   Ⓓ Correct as is.

7. Ⓐ Living near an airport can mean constant noise.
   Ⓑ I boght that sweater from a catalog.
   Ⓒ His uncle is always described as jolly.
   Ⓓ Correct as is.

8. Ⓐ He can't comment on the position of the senator.
   Ⓑ The dog slipped out of its coller.
   Ⓒ This is a promise I intend to keep.
   Ⓓ Correct as is.

9. Ⓐ A cold makes it hard to breathe through your nostril.
   Ⓑ He caught the soccer ball.
   Ⓒ These are new buildings and quite maudern.
   Ⓓ Correct as is.

10. Ⓐ You really ought to try the dessert.
    Ⓑ Snow in February is a common sight.
    Ⓒ Press pawse on the tape recorder.
    Ⓓ Correct as is.

Unit I Assessment · Spelling Final Test: The /o/ and /aw/ Sounds   Unit I · Lesson 3 31

Informal Comprehension Strategies Rubrics

Use the Informal Comprehension Strategies Rubrics to determine whether or not a student is using any of the strategies listed below. Note the strategies a student is using, instead of the degree to which a student might be using any particular strategy. In addition, encourage the student to tell of any strategies other than the ones being taught that he or she is using.

Making Connections

- The student activates prior knowledge and related knowledge.
- The student uses prior knowledge to explain something encountered in text.
- The student connects ideas presented later in the text to ideas presented earlier in the text.
- The student notes ideas in the text that are new to him or her or conflict with what he or she thought previously.

Asking Questions

- The student asks questions about ideas or facts presented in the text and attempts to answer these questions by reading the text.

Predicting

- The student makes predictions about what the text is about.
- The student updates predictions during reading, based on information in the text.

Research Rubrics

During Workshop, assess students using the rubrics below. The rubrics range from 1–4 in most categories, with 1 being the lowest score. Record each student's score on the inside back cover of the ***Inquiry Journal.***

Making Conjectures

1 Offers conjectures that are mainly expressions of fact or opinion. ("I think the Anasazi lived a long time ago." "I think tigers should be protected.")

2 Offers conjectures that partially address the research question. ("I think germs make you sick because they get your body upset." "I think germs make you sick because they multiply really fast.")

3 Offers conjectures that address the research question with guesses. ("I think the Anasazi were wiped out by a meteor.")

4 Offers reasonable conjectures that address the question and that can be improved through further research.

Objectives

- Students read and identify closed compounds.
- Students recognize and read words with *th* digraphs.
- Students recognize and read words with *s*-consonant blends and use the words in sentences.
- Students recognize and read words with the /o/ and /aw/ sounds spelled *o*.
- Students develop fluency reading words and sentences aloud.

Materials

- Routine Card 1

Teacher Tip SYLLABICATION To help students blend words and build fluency, use the syllabication below of the decodable multisyllabic words in the word lines.

ev•er•y•one	lock•ers
vol•ley•ball	of•fice
home•work	in•ter•com
af•ter•noon	of•fered

MEETING INDIVIDUAL NEEDS

ELL Support

For ELD strategies, use the *English-Language Development Guide,* Unit 1, Lesson 3.

Intervention Tip

For intervention strategies, use the *Intervention Guide,* Unit 1, Lesson 3.

Routine Card
Refer to Routine 1 for the Reading the Words and Sentences procedure.

WORD KNOWLEDGE

Word Knowledge

Reading the Words and Sentences

Use direct teaching to teach the Word Knowledge lesson. Write each word and sentence on the board. Have students read each word together. After all the words have been read, have students read each sentence in natural phrases or chunks. Use the suggestions in About the Words and Sentences to discuss the different features of listed words.

Line 1:	everyone	volleyball	homework	afternoon
Line 2:	then	those	both	truth
Line 3:	stop	spin	most	speak
Line 4:	lockers	office	intercom	offered
Sentence 1:	Most students do their homework in the afternoon.			
Sentence 2:	Everyone saw both sport stars at the game yesterday.			
Sentence 3:	The volleyball spins and then skips across the net.			
Sentence 4:	Our lockers are down the hall from the principal's office.			

About the Words and Sentences

- **Line 1:** The words are closed compounds, which are formed by joining together two words. They are considered "closed" because there is no space between the two words.
- **Line 2:** The words have the consonant digraph *th.* Digraphs are formed when two letters are placed together, creating only one sound.
- **Line 3:** These words contain *s*-consonant blends. Invite students to think of other words that contain these blends and use these words in sentences.
- **Line 4:** The words contain the /o/ and /aw/ sounds spelled *o.*

- **Sentences 1 and 3:** Ask students to read both sentences aloud. Then have students identify the closed compounds (*everyone, homework, afternoon, volleyball*) and the words containing the digraph *th* (*their, the, then*).

- **Sentence 2:** Have students identify the *s* consonant blends in the sentence (*sport, stars*). Then, have volunteers read the sentence aloud. Challenge students to add more *s* consonant blends to the sentence, and have them read their sentences aloud. For example, *Everyone spied both sports stars speaking at the stadium yesterday.*

- **Sentence 4:** Have students identify the words that contain the /o/ and /aw/ sounds spelled *o* (*lockers, office*).

Developing Oral Language

Use direct teaching to review the words. Use the following activity to help students practice the words aloud.

- Tell students they will be constructing a class story out loud. Each student will contribute one sentence that builds on every previous sentence to create a story. The story should make sense, so students will have to construct their sentences thoughtfully. Have a volunteer begin the class story by using a word from lines 1–4 aloud in a sentence. Then have a second student add a second sentence to the story, also using a word from lines 1–4. Continue in this fashion until the class has constructed a coherent story. This activity can be repeated by starting a new story with a different word.

Teacher Tip BUILDING FLUENCY
Gaining a better understanding of the spellings of sounds and structure of words will help students as they encounter unfamiliar words in their reading. By this time in grade 5 students should be reading approximately 126 words per minute with fluency and expression. As students read, you may notice that some need work in building fluency. During Workshop, have these students choose a section of text (a minimum of 160 words) to read several times in order to build fluency.

MEETING INDIVIDUAL NEEDS

ELL Support

WORD MEANING Make sure that English-language learners understand the meaning of the words on the word lines before you do the exercises with them. Use pictures, photos, and bilingual dictionaries.

Intervention Tip

CONSONANT DIGRAPHS For students who need more help with the consonant digraph *th*, explain that when the letter *t* and the letter *h* are used together, they make a single sound. Demonstrate the *th* sound as it is pronounced in *then* and *those.* Contrast how *th* sounds when used in *both* and *truth.* Brainstorm with students to generate a list of words that contain the consonant digraph *th*. Have students say each word aloud and use each in a sentence.

Spelling
See pages 55F–55J for the corresponding spelling lesson for the /o/ and /aw/ sounds.

Objectives

- Students will understand the selection vocabulary before reading.
- Students will identify words containing the digraph *th*.
- Students will use the comprehension strategies Asking Questions, Predicting, and Making Connections as they read the story the first time.
- Students will use the comprehension skill Author's Point of View as they read the story the second time.

Materials

- Student Anthology, pp. 48–55
- Reading Transparencies 4, 5, 54
- Listening Library
- Routine Card 1
- Inquiry Journal, p. 6
- Home Connection, pp. 7–8
- Comprehension and Language Arts Skills, pp. 10–11
- Program Assessment
- Unit 1 Assessment, pp. 10–13

MEETING INDIVIDUAL NEEDS

ELL Support

For ELD strategies, use the *English-Language Development Guide,* Unit 1, Lesson 3.

Intervention Support

For intervention strategies, use the *Intervention Guide,* Unit 1, Lesson 3.

www.sra4kids.com
Web Connection
Students can use the connections to cooperation and competition in the Reading link of the SRA Web page for more background information about cooperation and competition.

Build Background

Activate Prior Knowledge

Discuss the following with students to find out what they may already know about the selection and have already learned about the theme of cooperation and competition.

- Preteach "Juggling" by discussing what students know about the art of juggling, as well as what they know about "juggling" as a metaphor for balancing activities and time.
- Have students discuss what they know about the game of volleyball.

Background Information

- Some students might not be familiar with the concept of a paper route. Tell them that students their own age often do this job, riding their bicycles to deliver the daily newspaper to people's homes.
- Tell students that spiking a volleyball requires a player to hit the ball hard straight down over the net. Spiked balls are extremely difficult to return.
- Have the students discuss what they know about the genre of this selection. Refer to page 48A of the *Teacher's Edition* for elements of this selection's genre.

Preview and Prepare

Browse

- Have a student read aloud the title and the names of the author and illustrator. Demonstrate how to browse. Then have students preview the selection by browsing the first page or two of the story. This allows them to activate prior knowledge relevant to the story. Discuss what they think this story might have to do with cooperation and competition.
- Have the students search for clues that tell them something about the story. Also, have them look for any problems, such as unfamiliar words or long sentences that they notice while reading. Use *Reading Transparency 54* to record their observations as they browse. For example, the characters playing volleyball in the illustrations might be a clue that the main character plays volleyball. For the Problems column, students might point out that they are not familiar with the volleyball terms *serves* and *setups*. They might wonder why Kyle doesn't give up his paper route to join the team. To save time and model note taking, write students' observations as brief notes rather than complete sentences.

- As students prepare to read the selection, have them browse the Focus Questions on the first page of the selection. Tell them to keep these questions in mind as they read.

Set Purposes

Have students set their own purposes for reading. As they read, have students think about what each character learns about cooperation and competition. Remind students that good readers have a purpose when they read. Let them know that they should make sure they know the purpose for reading whenever they read.

Selection Vocabulary

As students study vocabulary, they will use a variety of skills to determine the meaning of a word. These include context clues, word structure, and apposition. Students will apply these same skills while reading to clarify additional unfamiliar words. After students have finished reading the selection, use the "Discussing the Selection" questions on page 53A to see if they understand what they have read.

Display ***Reading Transparency 4*** before reading the selection to introduce and discuss the following words and their meanings.

serve:	in volleyball and tennis, a way of putting the ball into play by sending it over the net (page 48)
juggle:	to handle more than one object or activity at a one time; perform a clever trick (page 48)
spare:	left over, remaining; extra (page 50)
spirit:	enthusiasm; loyalty (page 51)
deliberately:	when something is done on purpose or intentionally (page 52)

Have students read the words in the Word Box, stopping to blend any words that they have trouble reading. Demonstrate how to decode multisyllabic words by breaking the words into syllables and blending the syllables. Then have students try. If the word is not decodable, give the students the pronunciation.

Have students read the sentences on ***Reading Transparency 4*** and use the skills of context, word structure (structural analysis), or apposition to figure out the meanings of the words. Be sure students explain which skill(s) they are using and how they figured out the meanings of the words.

Clues	Problems	Wonderings
volleyball juggling paper route realistic fiction	serves setups	Why doesn't Kyle give up his route to join the team?

Reading Transparency 54

Teacher Tip

SELECTION VOCABULARY To help students decode words, divide them into the syllables shown below. The information following each word tells how students can figure out the meaning of each word.

serves:	context clues
jug•gle:	context clues
spare:	context clues
spir•it:	context clues
de•lib•er•ate•ly:	context clues

Routine Card

Refer to Routine 2 for the selection vocabulary procedure. Refer to Routine 3 for the Clues, Problems, and Wonderings procedure.

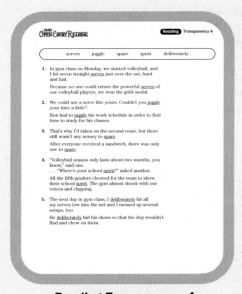

Reading Transparency 4

MEETING INDIVIDUAL NEEDS

ELL Support

VOCABULARY Check that English-language learners know the meanings and idioms and more difficult vocabulary in the story including: *junior, paper route, salary, persuade, spike the ball, shrill, setups, intercom,* and *pestering.* More information can be found in Unit 1, Lesson 3, of the *English-Language Development Guide.*

Intervention Support

SELECTION VOCABULARY By now students have reviewed all the sounds and spelling needed to read the selection vocabulary words. If students are still having difficulty reading these words, reteach the vowel spellings and provide additional opportunities to read words with those spellings during the time you set aside for Workshop. Go to the *Intervention Guide* for additional support for students who need help with vocabulary.

Teacher Tip DEVELOPING VOCABULARY During oral reading, have students develop their vocabularies by listening for unfamiliar words as they follow along in the text. Have them quickly jot down the page and paragraph number where each unfamiliar word appears so that they can find it and look it up later. Also, have students jot down pronunciations and text locations for words they would not have recognized had they been reading silently—some difficult words students will comprehend when they hear them pronounced, even if they cannot identify them by their spellings. After reading, have students work together to clarify and confirm meanings and pronunciations of the words they have listed.

Routine Card
Refer to Routine 4 for the Reading the Selection procedure.

Reading Recommendations

Oral Reading

This story lends itself to oral reading because of its reliance on dialogue. As students read aloud, have them read expressively at an appropriate pace in natural phrases and chunks. Make sure they enunciate their words and use appropriate intonations. Reading the selection with fluency and accuracy will help students comprehend the text. If students have trouble reading decodable words, have them break the words into sounds or syllables and then blend them together to read the words. After students have finished reading the selection, use the "Discussing the Selection" questions on page 53A to see if they understand what they have read.

Using Comprehension Strategies

Comprehension strategy instruction allows students to become aware of how good readers read. Good readers constantly check their understanding as they are reading and ask themselves questions. In addition, skilled readers recognize when they are having problems and stop to use various comprehension strategies to help them make sense of what they are reading.

During the reading of "Juggling," model and prompt the use of the following reading strategies:

- **Asking Questions** prepares readers for what they want to learn.
- **Predicting** causes readers to analyze information given about story events and characters in the context of how it may logically connect to the story's conclusion.
- **Making Connections** deepens students' understanding of what they read by linking it to their own past experiences and previous reading.

As students read, they should be using a variety of strategies to help them understand the selection. Encourage students to use the strategies listed as the class reads the story aloud. Do this by stopping at the points indicated by the numbers in magenta circles on the reduced student page and using a particular strategy. Students can also stop reading periodically to discuss what they have learned and what problems they may be having.

Building Comprehension Skills

Revisiting or rereading a selection allows students to apply skills that give them a more complete understanding of the text. Some follow-up comprehension skills help students organize information. Others lead to deeper understanding—to "reading between the lines," as mature readers do. An extended lesson on the comprehension skill Author's Point of View can be found in the Supporting the Reading section on pages 53C–53D. This lesson is intended to give students extra practice with Author's Point of View. However, the Teach portion of the lesson may be used at this time to introduce the comprehension skill to students.

■ **Author's Point of View (Introduction):** Readers identify who is telling the story, whether it's the main character speaking from a first-person point of view, or a narrator speaking from a third-person point of view.

Reading with a Purpose

Have students list the positive results of cooperation they find in the selection in the Response Journal section of their Writer's Notebooks.

MEETING INDIVIDUAL NEEDS

ELL Tip

PREREAD THE SELECTION Have English-language learners who may need help with the selection read it before the whole-class reading, using the *Listening Library Audiocassette/CD*. As they read, help them associate what they see in the illustrations with the words in the story, so that they learn to think English words before translating them first from their native language.

Intervention Tip

PREREAD THE SELECTION Preread "Juggling" with students who may need help in reading the selection during the time you set aside for Workshop.

LISTENING LIBRARY During Workshop, have students listen to the selection "Juggling" for a proficient, fluent model of oral reading. After students have listened to the *Listening Library Audiocassette/CD,* have them discuss their personal preferences of the literature and nonfiction selections read. Ask them what other things they have listened to on the radio, CDs, or audiocassettes. Have them tell what kinds of things they like listening to.

Read pages 48–53.

Comprehension Strategies

First Read

Read the story aloud, taking turns with the students. Start by modeling the use of strategies for the students.

Teacher Modeling

❶ Asking Questions *This is a good place to stop and ask a question because I have found something I don't understand. Kyle seems to want to play volleyball and Mr. Braden is asking him to join the team. What's wrong with Kyle? Why doesn't he just join the team? Maybe I need to read a bit more carefully.*

Oh, I see. He has a paper route at the same time the practices are being held.

Teacher Modeling

❷ Predicting *Good readers predict what will happen next and then confirm or revise their predictions as they go. It is important for all predictions to be firmly based on both the text and one's own knowledge and experiences.*

Kyle has a dilemma. From what we have read about him so far, Kyle seems like a very conscientious and level-headed person. Based on that, I predict that he'll just explain his situation to Mr. Braden so that he'll understand why Kyle can't play.

Word Knowledge

SCAFFOLDING The skills students are reviewing in Word Knowledge should help them in reading the story. This lesson focuses on words containing the digraph *th*. Digraph *th* words will be found in boxes similar to this one throughout the selection.

Digraph *th* words:

without   three   that   this

First Reading Recommendation

ORAL • CHORAL • SILENT

Focus Questions What does "juggling" have to do with cooperation? What important lesson does Kyle learn by the end of the story?

Juggling

Donna Gamache
illustrated by Daniel Powers

In gym class on Monday, we started volleyball, and I hit seven straight <u>serves</u> just over the net, hard and fast. Mr. Braden called me over at the end of the class.

"You've got a good serve, Kyle," he said. "How about coming out for the junior team?"

❶ "Sorry, Mr. Braden," I said, without looking at him. "I'm busy every afternoon." I knew the practices were three times a week, right after school, and that's when I delivered papers. I'd started a paper route two years ago when I was ten, but this year I'd taken over a second route—a long one, too. I never finished delivering before 5:30.

"Well, think about it," Mr. Braden called as I left for my next class. "We could use a serve like yours. Couldn't you <u>juggle</u> your time a little?"

48

Writer's Craft

Figurative Language Point out the sentence, "Couldn't you juggle your time a little?" Tell students this is an example of figurative language. Although time cannot physically be juggled, the idiom is still understood. The phrase also serves as the basis for the title of the story. Explain to students that they too can use figurative language to enliven their writing. See Writer's Craft lesson on page 55J.

Informal Assessment

Observe individual students as they read and use the Teacher Observation Log found in the *Program Assessment Teacher's Edition* to record anecdotal information about each student's strengths and weaknesses.

My friend Dave was waiting for me outside the gym door. "Did Mr. Braden ask you to join the team?" he asked.

I nodded. "I told him I was busy."

"You're a lot better than I am," said Dave as we got books from our lockers. "I wish you'd join. We need good servers."

Our next class was math, but it was hard to keep my mind on fractions and percentages. I kept thinking about how good it felt to hit that ball and see it sail over the net. Somehow I managed a spin on the ball that made it hard to hit back.

I'd have loved to say yes to Mr. Braden, but I couldn't afford to. I needed that paper route—or rather, my mom and I *both* needed it. We lived alone in a basement apartment about three blocks from school, and Mom worked at the Cramer Clothing

49

COMPREHENSION

Comprehension Skills

Second Read

Author's Point of View

Introduce students to the concept of *author's point of view*. Point out that this refers to the kind of narrator that the writer uses to tell the story. In a *first-person* narrative, the story is told by a character in the story. In a *third-person narrative*, the story is told by someone outside of the story.

- "In gym class on Monday, *we* started volleyball, and *I* hit seven straight serves…" (page 48)
- "*My* friend Dave was waiting for *me* outside the gym door." (page 49)

Explain that these examples show that this story is being told from a first-person point of view. A third-person point of view would have used the words *he* and *his*, instead of *I* and *my*. Have students find other examples that show this story is being narrated in the first person.

Point out that the reader will learn the most about what Kyle (the narrator) thinks, feels, and does. Knowing whose point of view is being expressed helps the reader understand the story's message.

Skills Trace

Author's Point of View

Introduced in Grade 2.
Scaffolded throughout Grades 3–5.

REINTRODUCED:	Unit 1, Lesson 3
REINFORCED:	Unit 1, Lesson 5
	Unit 3, Lesson 1
	Unit 3, Lesson 4
	Unit 3, Lesson 5
TESTED:	Unit 1 Assessment

Second Reading Recommendation

ORAL • **SILENT**

Science/Social Studies Connection Center

Refer to the Science/Social Studies Connection Center Card 5 for a social studies activity that students can investigate.

Teacher Tip PROBLEM SOLVING
During reading, encourage discussion of possible solutions to the main character's time conflict. Have students reflect on how the solutions will affect the parties to whom the main character feels responsible.

COMPREHENSION

Comprehension Strategies

First Read

Teacher Modeling

3 Making Connections *Kyle seems pretty upset. I understand why he feels this way because I can connect his situation with things that have happened to me. There have been times in my life when I've had to give up doing something fun because I'd already promised to do something else. How do you connect with Kyle?*

Teacher Modeling

4 Confirming Predictions
Nobody seems to understand why Kyle isn't joining the team. And Kyle hasn't explained things to Mr. Braden yet like I predicted he would. I am revising my prediction—I think that Kyle is going to make everyone so angry at him that they won't want him to join the team at all.

As we continue reading, see if you can predict what is going to happen next. Maybe some of you will share your predictions with us.

Word Knowledge

Digraph *th* words:

   that   months   clothing   there

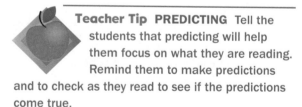

Teacher Tip PREDICTING Tell the students that predicting will help them focus on what they are reading. Remind them to make predictions and to check as they read to see if the predictions come true.

Factory sewing winter jackets. She didn't earn that much money, and most months her whole salary went for food and rent. Any clothing or school supplies had to come out of what I earned delivering papers. That's why I'd taken on the second route, but there still wasn't any money to spare.

The next day in gym class, Mr. Braden watched me again, and when class ended, he called out loudly, "Think about joining the team, Kyle."

Everyone heard him, and soon several other boys started trying to persuade me. "We haven't got any strong servers," said Jason. "Come on and help us out."

"I bet you could learn to spike the ball," said Billy. "You're tall enough."

They didn't seem to hear me when I mentioned my paper routes.

50

MEETING INDIVIDUAL NEEDS

Intervention Support

PREDICTING Have the students keep a list of the main ideas as they read. Then they can refer to them as they make and revise predictions.

Informal Assessment

Use the Informal Comprehension Strategies Rubrics on page 48J to determine whether a student is using the strategies being taught.

"We finish at 5:15," Jason persisted.

"I'm sorry!" I said. "I can't make the practices." It wouldn't have been so bad if I didn't *want* to play on the team.

"Volleyball season only lasts about two months, you know," said one.

"Where's your school spirit?" asked another.

"Leave me alone!" I finally snapped.

I decided I'd have to see Mr. Braden and tell him the truth—that I couldn't *afford* to play volleyball. But that night I found he'd phoned my mother. I knew right away something was up, but she didn't say anything until we'd finished our spaghetti.

"Your gym teacher called," she said then. "He says he wants you on the volleyball team, but you turned him down."

"Did he tell you the practice times?" I said sharply.

"Yes."

"Then you know why I said no."

Mom sighed. "I told him about the paper routes. He said the practices are over by 5:15."

"My papers have to be delivered by then," I reminded her. "And when there are games, they'll play later than that." I knew my voice was shrill, but I couldn't help it. Everyone was pushing me to do something I already wanted to do, but *couldn't*.

But Mom didn't quit. I guess she knew how much I really wanted to play. "Maybe you could get someone else to deliver the papers on those nights."

51

③

④

Comprehension Skills

Author's Point of View

Remind students that in first-person point of view the narrator is a character in the story who is involved in the action. Also tell students that first-person point of view allows readers to know first-hand how a character feels and what a character thinks. Provide the following examples from the story:

- "It wouldn't have been so bad if I didn't *want* to play on the team." (page 51)

- "I knew right away something was up..." (page 51)

Word Knowledge
Digraph *th* words:
months   truth   something   then   they   those

Teacher Tip FLUENCY By this time in grade 5, good readers should be reading approximately 126 words per minute with fluency and expression. The only way to gain this fluency is through practice. Have students reread the selection to you and to one another during Workshop to help build fluency.

COMPREHENSION

Comprehension Strategies

First Read

Teacher Modeling

5 Confirming Predictions

I am glad my original prediction that Kyle would explain to Mr. Braden why he couldn't play on the team came true after all, and even more glad that Mr. Braden had a solution to the problem.

Discussing Strategy Use

While they are reading the selection, have students share any problems they encountered and tell what strategies they used.

- What questions did they ask as they read?

- What connections did they make between the reading and what they already know?

- On what basis did they make and confirm predictions?

Remind students that good readers use all of the strategies listed above and that they should be using them whenever they read. Make sure students explain how using the strategies helped them better understand the selection. For example, students might say, "Asking questions helped me to know what I needed to find out in this story."

Word Knowledge
Digraph *th* words:
    three   anything   other   thought

"I'd have to pay someone nearly twenty dollars a week to do both routes three times," I said. Abruptly, I shoved my chair back from the table and stamped into my room. I flung myself on the bed and I didn't go out to help Mom with the dishes, either.

The next day in gym class, I <u>deliberately</u> hit all my serves low into the net and I messed up several setups, too. I saw Mr. Braden looking at me in a funny way, but he didn't say anything then. I kept away from Dave all day and ignored the other boys from the team.

At 3:30 I grabbed my homework from my locker and was just heading out the door when my name was called on the intercom. "Kyle Kreerson, please report to Mr. Braden's office."

I thought about ignoring the announcement, but I didn't want to get into trouble. When I reached the office, I saw that Dave was already there. I didn't give Mr. Braden time to speak. I just started right in. "Mr. Braden," I said, "I'm sorry I can't join your team. Will you please stop asking me about it? And ask the other guys to stop <u>pestering</u> me? I'd join if I could. But I *can't!* O.K.?!"

52

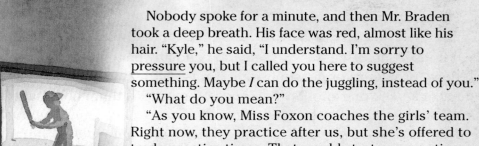

Nobody spoke for a minute, and then Mr. Braden took a deep breath. His face was red, almost like his hair. "Kyle," he said, "I understand. I'm sorry to pressure you, but I called you here to suggest something. Maybe *I* can do the juggling, instead of you."

"What do you mean?"

"As you know, Miss Foxon coaches the girls' team. Right now, they practice after us, but she's offered to trade practice times. That would start our practices at 5:15."

"I'm not finished with my routes by then," I said sharply.

"If you had some help, you could be, right? Dave is offering to help you."

"I can't afford to pay him," I insisted.

"I don't want to be paid," Dave said.

"Then why do it?"

Dave shrugged. "Because I want to. Because I want you on the team. And because you're my friend."

"Enough reasons?" asked Mr. Braden.

I looked at them both for a moment and I felt good for the first time in four days. "When do we start?" I smiled. **5**

53

 Formal Assessment

See pages 10–13 in *Unit 1 Assessment* to test students' comprehension of "Juggling."

 Teacher Tip BUILDING FLUENCY
As students read, you may notice that some need work in building fluency. During Workshop, have these students choose a section of text (a minimum of 160 words) to read several times in order to build fluency.

Comprehension Skills

Second Read

Author's Point of View

Review the concept of first- and third-person points of view with students. Then have students identify examples from the text that indicate it is told from the first-person point of view.

- "I looked at them both for a moment and I felt good for the first time in four days." (page 53)

- "I smiled." (page 53)

Checking Comprehension

Ask students the following questions to check their comprehension of the story.

- How did Kyle help his family? (*He made money delivering papers.*)

- How did the girls' team cooperate so that Kyle could play volleyball? (*They switched practice times with the boys' team.*)

- Give other examples of how characters in this story worked together. (*Answers will vary but may include that Dave helped out on Kyle's paper route.*)

- How has this selection connected with your knowledge of the unit theme? (*Answers will vary—students should compare/contrast examples of cooperation and competition from this selection with their own experiences or past reading and use these connections to make a general statement about the unit theme.*)

Word Knowledge
Digraph *th* words:
     breath   something   they   them

COMPREHENSION

Routine Card
Refer to Routine 5 for the *handing-off process.*

Clues	Problems	Wonderings
volleyball juggling paper route realistic fiction	serves setups	Why doesn't Kyle give up his route to join the team?

Reading Transparency 54

www.sra4kids.com
Web Connection
Some students may choose to conduct a computer search for additional books or information about cooperation and competition. Invite them to make a list of these books and sources of information to share with classmates and the school librarian. Check the Reading link of the SRA Web page for additional links to theme-related Web sites.

Discussing the Selection

The whole group discusses the selection and any personal thoughts, reactions, problems, or questions that it raises. To stimulate discussion, students can ask one another the kinds of questions that good readers ask themselves about a text: *How does it connect to cooperation and competition? What have I learned that is new? What did I find interesting? What is important here? What was difficult to understand? Why would someone want to read this?* It is important for students to see you as a contributing member of the group.

Routine 5 To emphasize that you are part of the group, actively participate in the *handing-off process:* Raise your hand to be called on by the last speaker when you have a contribution to make. Point out unusual and interesting insights verbalized by students so that these insights are recognized and discussed. As the year progresses, students will take more and more responsibility for the discussion of selections.

Engage students in a discussion to determine whether they have grasped the following ideas:

- how cooperation affected Kyle
- that cooperation often leads to helping others
- why Kyle could not give up his paper route to be a part of the team

During this time, have students return to the clues, problems, and wonderings that they noted during browsing to determine whether the clues were borne out by the selection, whether and how their problems were solved, and whether their wonderings were answered or deserve further discussion and exploration. Let the students decide which items deserve further discussion.

Also have students return to the Focus Questions on the first page of the selection. Select a student to read the questions aloud, and have volunteers answer the questions. If students do not know the answers to the questions, have them return to the text to find the answers.

You may wish to review the elements of realistic fiction with the students at this time. Discuss with them how they can tell that "Juggling" is realistic fiction.

Have students break into small groups to discuss how the story reflects the theme. Groups can then share their ideas with the rest of the class.

Students may wish to record personal responses to this selection. Encourage students to record their experiences with cooperating in order to solve a time conflict or another problem.

Review Selection Vocabulary

Have students review the definitions of the selection vocabulary words that they write in the Vocabulary section of their Writer's Notebooks. Remind them that they discussed the meanings of these words before reading the selection. Students can use these definitions to study for the Vocabulary portion of their Lesson Assessment. Have them add to the Personal Dictionary section of their Writer's Notebook any other interesting words that they clarified while reading. Encourage students to refer to the selection vocabulary words throughout the unit. The words from the selection are:

Teacher Tip VOCABULARY Have students write sentences using the selection vocabulary words. In order to provide additional help in remembering words, students can write synonyms or antonyms for the words if it is appropriate. Some students may even draw something to help them remember the meanings of the words.

deliberately   serves   spirit   juggle   spare

If you have created a Word Bank, have students place words under the appropriate headings on the Word Bank. Encourage the students to find other words related to the unit theme and add them to the Word Bank.

View Fine Art

Artist Pyramid by **Josef Hegenbarth** is found on page 57 of the ***Student Anthology.*** This is a picture of a team of acrobats who are working together to form a pyramid. To carry off this balancing act, the acrobats must have complete trust in each other, and work in total cooperation. Have students discuss how acrobats' cooperation is similar to the cooperation that made it possible for Kyle, in "Juggling," to balance his responsibilities.

Artist Pyramid. Josef Hegenbarth. Oil on canvas. Private collection ©2001 Josef Hegenbarth/Licensed by VAGA, New York, NY.

Catcher on the Line. Robert Riggs. Oil on canvas. Private collection.

57

Student Anthology p. 57

Home Connection

Distribute ***Home Connection,*** page 7. Encourage students to discuss "Juggling" with their families. Students can make schedules with their families to help organize their time. ***Home Connection*** is also available in Spanish, page 8.

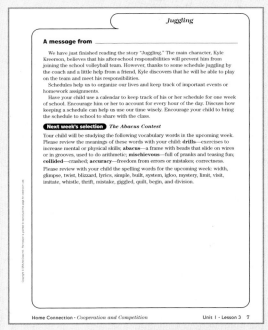

Home Connection p. 7

Author's Point of View	"Class President"	"The Marble Champ"	"Juggling"
1. From what point of view is the story told?			
2. Does the story focus on a particular character? If so, which one?			
3. What do you learn about the characters' feelings and thoughts?			
4. Are the feelings and thoughts directly stated? Or did you have to make inferences about them?			

Reading Transparency 5

Supporting the Reading

Comprehension Skills: Author's Point of View

Teach Have students tell you what they know about author's point of view. Then tell them that before writers begin a story, they must decide from whose point of view it will be told. Stories told by a character are written in first-person point of view. Use of pronouns such as *I, we, us,* and *my* in the telling of a story is an indicator that it is in first person. First-person point of view allows readers to really know one character—what he or she thinks and how he or she feels. Stories told by an outside storyteller are written in third-person point of view. Use of pronouns such as *he, she, it, they, him, her,* and *them* in the telling of a story is an indicator that it is in third person. Third-person point of view can show the feelings and thoughts of any character in the story. However, third-person narrators often focus on the thoughts and feelings of one character.

Guided Practice Use the chart on *Reading Transparency 5* to help students organize information about author's point of view for "Class President," "The Marble Champ," and "Juggling." Lead students through the stories to answer the questions in the chart. When students have completed the chart, discuss how first- and third-person point of view are similar and different. Then ask students to discuss how they think an author's choice of first- or third-person point of view affects the overall feeling, effect, or quality of the story.

Independent Practice Read through the **Focus** and **Identify** sections of *Comprehension and Language Arts Skills,* page 10 with students. Then have students complete the **Practice and Apply** portion of *Comprehension and Language Arts Skills,* page 11 as homework.

Link to Writing Have students think of a time in their lives when they were extremely excited about doing something or going somewhere. Have each student write a paragraph in the first-person point of view about the time. Then, challenge students to write about the event from the third-person point of view. When students have completed the exercise, have them discuss the differences between the first-person and the third-person paragraphs.

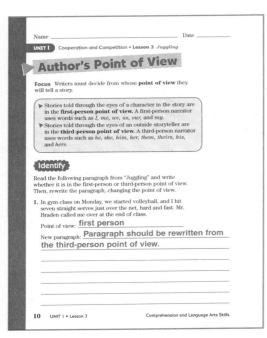

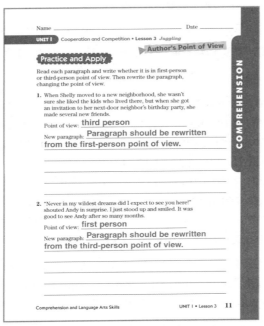

Comprehension and Language Arts Skills pp. 10–11

MEETING INDIVIDUAL NEEDS

Reteach

AUTHOR'S POINT OF VIEW Have students who need additional practice with identifying author's point of view complete *Reteach,* pages 12–13.

Challenge

AUTHOR'S POINT OF VIEW Have students who understand author's point of view complete *Challenge,* page 10.

Skills Trace
Author's Point of View
Introduced in Grade 2.
Scaffolded throughout Grades 3–5.

REINTRODUCED:	Unit 1, Lesson 3
REINFORCED:	Unit 1, Lesson 5
	Unit 3, Lesson 1
	Unit 3, Lesson 4
	Unit 3, Lesson 5
TESTED:	Unit 1 Assessment

Literary Elements

Genre: Realistic Fiction

Teach Have students tell you what they know about fiction in general. Students should be able to respond that fiction tells a story or stories about characters and events that are not real. Then have students tell you what they know about the genre *realistic fiction*. If necessary, tell them that realistic fiction involves stories with characters and settings that are true to life and events that could really happen. Review the following characteristics of realistic fiction with students.

- The characters behave as people or animals do in real life. Their feelings and thoughts are often described.
- The setting of the story is real or could be a real place.
- The events in the story could happen in real life.

Have students share examples of realistic fiction they have read.

Guided Practice Have students skim the selection "Juggling" for examples showing that the selection is realistic fiction. Draw a three-column chart on the board with the headings *Characters*, *Setting*, and *Events*. Have students fill in the chart with examples of realistic characters, settings, and events from the story. Have them discuss what makes the items in the chart realistic. Then have students compare and contrast the characters, settings, and events in this story with those in other realistic fiction selections they have read in the **Student Anthology** and on their own.

Independent Practice Have the students look through their **Writing Folders** for stories they can revise to be made more realistic. They might work with a partner and review each other's revised stories for realistic elements.

Science Connection:
The Circulatory System

Teacher Tip MATERIALS FOR ACTIVITY To complete the Science Connection activity for this lesson, students will need a stopwatch, pens or pencils, and paper.

Remind the students of Kyle's physical activity in "Juggling." *(He played volleyball.)* Ask the students what probably happened to Kyle's heart rate when he played volleyball. Prompt them to tell you that his heart rate increased when he played volleyball. Have students participate in this demonstration of how heart rate increases during physical activity. Have students create a two-column chart with the headings "Resting Pulse" and "Active Pulse." Then have students divide into groups of three or four members. Have group members take each other's resting pulses, using a stopwatch to determine the number of times each person's heart beats in a minute. Have groups record each group member's resting pulse under the appropriate chart heading. Then, have group members march in place for three minutes. After three minutes have passed, have group members take each other's pulses again and note on the chart how their pulses have changed. Afterward, have each group use the completed chart to find the average difference between the resting and active pulse rates for each team.

Challenge the students to find out why a person's heart rate increases during physical activity. Divide the students into two groups. Have the first group conduct library or Internet research to find out how blood circulates through the heart, lungs and body. Have the second group conduct research to determine the part that circulating blood plays in the exchange of oxygen and carbon dioxide in the lungs and the tissues of the body.

Have the groups present the results of their findings to each other. Encourage each group to create visual aids that show how the process they have been assigned works. Then, based on the combined results, have students answer this question: Why did Kyle's heartbeat increase when he played volleyball? *(Since his muscles were working harder, they needed more oxygen, which is supplied by the blood. So, his heart beat faster to pump more blood.)*

Meet the Illustrator

After the students read the information about Daniel Powers, discuss the following questions with them.

- What do you think Daniel Powers teaches the children in the schools of Zuñi Pueblo? *(Possible answer: The book doesn't say what he teaches them, but it probably has to do with art. Maybe he goes into the schools as a special speaker, because he only goes there a couple of times each year.)*

- After reading the titles of other books he has illustrated, what do you think are his favorite things to illustrate? *(Possible answer: From the book titles, it sounds as if some of the other stories he has illustrated may have to do with things in nature. It would make sense if he enjoyed doing nature illustrations because one of his favorite hobbies is to go hiking with his wife.)*

Juggling

Meet the Illustrator

Daniel Powers always loved drawing and painting, but he did not go to art school until recently. Mr. Powers lives in the high desert country of New Mexico and enjoys hiking there with his wife and two dogs. A couple of times a year he works with children in the schools of the nearby Zuñi Pueblo. He has illustrated many children's books including *Jiro's Pearl*, *From the Land of the White Birch*, and *Dear Katie, The Volcano is a Girl*.

54

Theme Connections

Within the Selection

Record your answers to the questions below in the Response Journal section of your Writer's Notebook. In small groups, report the ideas you wrote. Discuss your ideas with the rest of your group. Then choose a person to report your group's answers to the class.

- In what way is Kyle a cooperative member of his family?
- How did the cooperation of the girls' volleyball team help solve Kyle's problem?
- How will Dave's help in delivering papers aid both Kyle and the team? Why did Dave offer to help Kyle?

Across Selections

- Compare how Dave, in this story, and Julio, in "Class President," cooperate for the benefit of the group.
- In what way are the families in this story and "The Marble Champ" alike?

Beyond the Selection

- Think about how "Juggling" adds to what you know about cooperation and competition.
- Add items to the Concept/Question Board about cooperation and competition.

Theme Connections

Within the Selection

- He willingly works to earn money for the family.
- The girls' team cooperated by trading practice times with the boys' team.
- Dave's help allowed Kyle to meet his family commitment and improved the team's chances of success. He wants to help both his friend and the team.

Across Selections

- Both Dave and Julio make an individual contribution that helps the group.
- Both families support their children's efforts.

Beyond the Selection

Students should record their ideas and impressions about the selections on page 6 of their ***Inquiry Journals.***

Name _____ Date _____

UNIT 1 Cooperation and Competition

Recording Concept Information

As I read each selection, this is what I added to my understanding of cooperation and competition.

- "Class President" by Johanna Hurwitz
  Answers will vary.

- "The Marble Champ" by Gary Soto
  Answers will vary.

- "Juggling" by Donna Gamache
  Answers will vary.

6 UNIT 1 *Recording Concept Information • Inquiry Journal*

Inquiry Journal p. 6

Teacher Tip INQUIRY AND INVESTIGATION Have groups report and discuss their ideas with the class. As these ideas are stated, have students add them to the Concept/Question Board. As students complete their discussions, have them sum up what they have learned and tell how they might use this information in further investigations.

Informal Assessment

This may be a good time to observe students working in small groups and to mark your observations in the Teacher Observation Log found in the ***Program Assessment Teacher's Edition.***

Objectives

- Students gain a deeper understanding of the results of cooperation.
- Students make conjectures about their investigation problems.
- Students practice note-taking skills.

Materials

- Student Anthology, pp. 48–57
- Inquiry Journal, pp. 15–19
- Research Assistant

INVESTIGATION

Name_____ Date_____

Cooperation and Competition **UNIT I**

Time Management

Often large tasks can be accomplished by one person, but two or three people can finish the task much quicker. In the chart below, list in the first column several large tasks that you do at home or at school. In the second column, list the approximate time it takes you to complete each task by yourself. In the third column, list the approximate time the task would take if you had help. In the last column, calculate the amount of time you would save on each task if you had help. **Answers will vary.**

Task	Time Alone	Time with Help	Saved Time

Inquiry Journal • Time Management   UNIT I   **15**

Time Management *(continued)*

Review the chart on the previous page, and record below the amount of time you would save if you had help with your tasks. Then, on the lines provided, write a paragraph about how you would spend the time that you saved. Include details about when you would use the time and where you would spend it. **Answers will vary.**

Total Time Saved: _____

How I Would Spend My Time: _____

_____

_____

_____

_____

_____

_____

_____

_____

_____

_____

_____

_____

_____

_____

_____

_____

_____

16 UNIT I   Time Management • Inquiry Journal

Inquiry Journal pp. 15–16

Investigating Concepts Beyond the Text

To facilitate students' investigation of cooperation and competition, you might have them participate in the following activities. Tell students that if they have activity ideas of their own that they would like to pursue, they are free to do so as an alternative to these activity suggestions. For example, students may want to pursue activities of their own choosing that relate more directly to the problems and questions they are investigating with their groups. Tell students that they may work on these activities alone, in pairs, or in small groups, with an option to write about them or to present them to the group upon completion.

The activity suggestions for this lesson are:

- Point out to students that in the selection "Juggling," Kyle becomes more and more frustrated as he tries to solve his problems by himself. However, when others help him, everything works out. Have students list activities that would not be possible without cooperation between people. Then, have students discuss times when they couldn't solve a problem by themselves, but, with the help of others, they could. Once students have discussed their experiences, have them complete *Inquiry Journal* pages 15–16.

- Have students consult at least three different sources for ideas on how people cooperate to solve problems. Tell students that these sources can be fiction, nonfiction, audio, and visual.

Upon completion of their activities, have students share with the group anything new they learned about cooperation and competition through discussion and by adding information to the Concept/Question Board.

Concept/Question Board

After reading each selection, students should use the Concept/Question Board to

- post any questions they asked about a selection before reading that have not yet been answered.
- refer to as they formulate statements about concepts that apply to their investigations.
- post general statements formulated by each collaborative group.
- continue to post news articles, or other items that they find during the unit investigation.
- read and think about posted questions, articles, or concepts that interest them and provide answers to the questions.

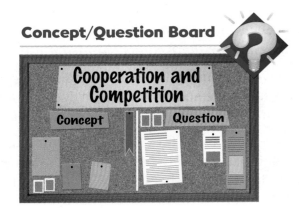

Concept/Question Board

Cooperation and Competition

Concept | Question

Unit I Investigation Management

Lesson I	Students generate ideas for investigation.
Lesson 2	Students formulate questions and problems for investigation.
Lesson 3	**Collaborative Investigation** **Students make conjectures.** **Supplementary Activities** **Students participate in investigation activities and learn how to take notes.**
Lesson 4	Students establish investigation needs.
Lesson 5	Students establish investigation plans.
Lesson 6	Students present investigation findings.

Research Assistant
The Research Assistant helps students in their investigations.

Teacher Tip EXPLORATION ACTIVITIES To help students focus their exploration, have them frequently consult the Concept/Question Board for ideas about and examples of cooperation and competition.

Research in Reading
Schema Theory

The *system* of understandings, or knowledge structures, that a student brings to learning about a concept is more important than facts he or she may know or not know. This view of learning is known as *schema theory*. According to schema theory, knowledge (*schema*) is an huge network of abstract mental structures that represent our understanding of the world. A general category of schema includes slots for all the features included in the category. Each of us has many *schemata* (plural). Relationships among our schemata are like webs, with each schema interconnected to many others. Our schemata grow and change as we acquire new information through experience and reading. *Richard C. Anderson and P. David Pearson.* "A schema-theoretic view of basic processes in reading." Handbook of Reading Research.

Name_____ Date_____

Cooperation and Competition **UNIT I**

Making Conjectures

Our question or problem:

Answers will vary.

_____

_____

_____

_____

_____

Conjecture (my first theory or explanation):

Answers will vary.

_____

_____

_____

_____

_____

_____

_____

_____

As you collect information, your conjecture will change.
Return to this page to record your new theories or
explanations about your question or problem.

Inquiry Journal • *Making Conjectures*   UNIT I   **17**

Inquiry Journal p. 17

Formal Assessment

Use the Research Rubrics on page 48J to
assess students' ability to make conjectures.

Making Conjectures

Tell students that their investigations of their stated problems and questions will be more productive if they first form conjectures as to how their problems might be solved or their questions answered. Explain to the students that a *conjecture* is a kind of educated guess, an explanation that we suggest for something before we have a great deal of evidence. Conjectures may be proved right, proved wrong, or modified in some way by evidence uncovered in the investigation process.

If students are unsure of how to make conjectures, it will be helpful to have group discussions featuring modeling of conjectures. For this, you might choose a problem that has already been suggested for investigation but has not been chosen by any group. (Using such a problem, the whole class can engage in conjecturing without taking anything away from the individual group's project.) For example, you might present the problem, *How do athletes prepare for competitions?* Then model conjectures such as, *They prepare for their competitions by practicing alone and with teammates.*

Have students get into their investigation groups to discuss conjectures they have for the solution to their investigation problem. Have group members write their conjectures on ***Inquiry Journal,*** page 17.

Tell students as they begin their investigations, they will revisit their conjectures and revise them based on new information, if necessary. Explain to the students that they will continuously return to the previous phases of investigation to assess how their problems and the conjectures have changed and what new information they need.

Note Taking

Teach Tell students to talk about times when they have taken notes and how the notes have helped them. Tell them that note taking will help them to plan their activities. It will also help them to keep track of and organize information they obtain during their investigations.

Write the following guidelines for note taking on the board.

- Organize your notes under subject headings.
- Write notes in your own words.
- Summarize the most important information.
- Keep your notes short. Use abbreviations, key phrases and short sentences.
- Put an author's or speaker's exact words within quotation marks. Include the author's or speaker's name. If the quotation comes from a written work, include the work's title and the page numbers from which the quote material was taken.
- Write neatly and clearly.

Tell students that as they discuss investigation topics, they should take notes on important ideas and questions that arise. Tell students that these notes will help them to recall important and interesting aspects of their topics when they begin their investigations.

Tell them that once investigation begins, they should take notes also, to help them remember important conversations they have had and stories they read about cooperation and competition. Tell them that having everything down on paper will make it easier later to organize their information for their activities.

Guided Practice Have students think about the following question for investigation: Who cooperates to help Kyle solve his problem in "Juggling"? Tell them to skim the selection and take notes on characters and how they cooperated. Tell students to use abbreviations and key phrases and to sum up the information in a sentence or two.

Apply Have students write a brief report on the question investigated above. Remind them to base their reports on their notes. For more practice with note taking, have students complete *Inquiry Journal,* pages 18–19.

SUPPORTING THE INVESTIGATION

Teacher Tip NOTE TAKING You may wish to remind students of the way you have been making notations on the Clues, Problems, and Wonderings transparency when they browse a selection. Point out that, except for very formal papers that require exact quotes or extensive outlines, they should use short, incomplete sentences that convey the thought quickly.

Inquiry Journal pp. 18–19

Objectives

Word Analysis

Spelling
- **Spelling Patterns for the /o/ and /aw/ Sounds.** Develop understanding of spelling patterns for the /o/ and /aw/ sounds introduced in Word Knowledge in Part 1.

Vocabulary
- Develop an understanding of discovering word meanings by examining parts of words, such as roots, prefixes, and suffixes.

Writing Process Strategies
- **The Process of Drafting.** Learn the importance of writing from a plan, creating paragraphs from ideas, staying focused, and adding interest and imagery in the drafting phase of the writing process.

English Language Conventions

Grammar, Usage, and Mechanics
- **Verbs.** Understand the correct use of verbs and identify them in "Juggling."

Listening, Speaking, Viewing
- **Language: Using Appropriate Language.** Determine what kind of language is appropriate for different settings and audiences.

Penmanship
- **Cursive Letters *r* and *s*.** Develop handwriting skills by practicing formation of cursive *r* and *s*.

Materials

- Spelling and Vocabulary Skills, pp. 10–13
- Language Arts Handbook
- Comprehension and Language Arts Skills, pp. 12–15
- Writer's Workbook, p. 3
- Language Arts Transparencies 2, 4
- Student Anthology
- Writing Folder
- Unit 1 Assessment, pp. 30–31

MEETING INDIVIDUAL NEEDS

Reteach, Challenge, English-Language Development and *Intervention* lessons are available to support the language arts instruction in this lesson.

Research in Action

The mind travels faster than the pen; consequently, writing becomes a question of learning to make occasional wing shots, bringing down the bird of thought as it flashes by. *(William Strunk, Jr. and E.B. White,* The Elements of Style*)*

Language Arts Overview

Word Analysis

Spelling The spelling activities on the following pages support the Word Knowledge introduction of the /o/ and /aw/ sounds by developing understanding of their spelling patterns.

Selection Spelling Words

These words from "Juggling" contain the /o/ and /aw/ sounds.

v<u>o</u>lleyball   l<u>o</u>ckers   <u>o</u>ffice   interc<u>o</u>m   <u>o</u>ffered

Vocabulary The vocabulary activities introduce the idea of discovering word meanings by examining the different parts of an unfamiliar word.

Vocabulary Skill Words

shrill   deliberately*   abruptly   pestering   persuade

Also Selection Vocabulary.

Writing Process Strategies

This Writing Process Strategies lesson shows how to use drafting techniques for writing about defined topics as well as for drafting autobiographies.

 Basic Computer Skills To learn basic computer skills for writing, have students review keyboarding basics, demonstrate correct fingering for the **Home** keys and practice keying the **H, E, I,** and **R, O, T, N,** and **G** keys; show students how to use the left **Shift** and **Period** keys. *Basic Computer Skills* Level 5 Lessons 7–11 teach these keyboarding skills.

English Language Conventions

Grammar, Usage, and Mechanics **Verbs.** This lesson develops understanding of correct verb usage. Students identify action, state-of-being, and auxiliary verbs.

Listening, Speaking, Viewing **Language: Using Appropriate Language.** In this Language lesson, students will review the importance of knowing what kind of language is appropriate for different settings.

Penmanship **Cursive Letters *r* and *s*.** This lesson continues the development of handwriting skills. Students learn correct formation of *r* and *s* and then practice writing paragraphs from the literature selection.

DAY 1

| Word Analysis | Writing Process Strategies | English Language Conventions |

Spelling

Assessment: Pretest

Spelling Patterns for the /o/ and /aw/ Sounds

Give students the Pretest on page 30 of **Unit 1 Assessment.** Have them proofread and correct any misspellings.

Pretest Sentences

1. **congress**   There are senators in **Congress.**
2. **topic**   A paragraph should have a **topic** sentence.
3. **promise**   Breaking a **promise** is a serious offense.
4. **proper**   The **proper** response is to say thank you.
5. **collar**   The dog doesn't have a **collar.**
6. **common**   Red is a **common** color for a sports car.
7. **comet**   Halley's **Comet** will appear in the sky.
8. **cause**   The **cause** of a fire can be hard to determine.
9. **broad**   The Mississippi River is rather **broad.**
10. **caught**   She had **caught** a cold.
11. **awful**   The storm created **awful** driving conditions.
12. **ought**   He **ought** to try out for the choir.
13. **fought**   Siblings often recall that they **fought.**
14. **brought**   Settlers **brought** supplies in wagons.
15. **thought**   People **thought** the sun revolved around Earth.
16. **volleyball**   Spikes and sets are moves in **volleyball.**
17. **office**   The President works in the Oval **Office.**
18. **lockers**   Our **lockers** are metal.
19. **intercom**   She heard her name on the **intercom.**
20. **offered**   I **offered** to take her home.

Introduction to the Writing Process: Drafting

Getting It Down on Paper

Teach

Introduce the Drafting Process

■ Read **Language Arts Handbook** pages 32–33 on drafting. Define **draft:** the first rough copy of a report or story.

Teacher Model: Drafting

Teacher:

"I want to write about cooperation and competition in our school." To emphasize the importance of completing the prewriting step, have students help you fill in ideas in a graphic organizer such as **Transparency 2—Concept Map.** Save what you write so that it can be reworked into paragraphs on Day 2. Have fun with the drafting and encourage input from students as you write.

Guided Practice

Have students use any of the graphic organizers they practiced with earlier to write a short draft about another subject. Choose a topic that does not require research such as "Cooperation in the Story 'Juggling.'"

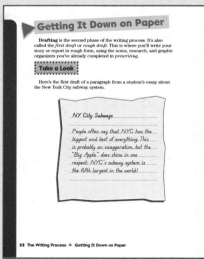

Language Arts Handbook p. 32

Grammar, Usage, and Mechanics:

Verbs

Teach

■ Use **Language Arts Handbook** pages 346–347 for examples of the correct use of verbs.

■ Explain that a verb is a word that shows action or conveys a state of being.

■ An action verb tells what the person or thing in a sentence is doing. The action can be seen or unseen. *Understand* is a verb in which the action is unseen.

■ State-of-being verbs do not show action. They convey a condition of existence. *Adam is the goalie of the team.*

■ An auxiliary, or helping, verb helps the main verb tell about an action or express a state of being: *Tomas and Rachel **are studying.***

■ Common auxiliary verbs include *do, did, does, am, is, are, was, were, being, been, have, has, had, may, might, must, can, could, will, would, shall,* and *should.*

Independent Practice

Use **Comprehension and Language Arts Skills** pages 12–13 to practice forming the correct tenses of verbs.

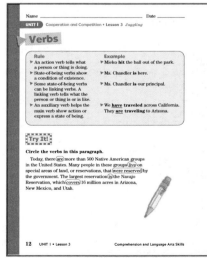

Comprehension and Language Arts Skills p. 12

DAY 2

Word Analysis

Spelling

Word Sorting

Open Word Sort Have students sort the spelling words by the /o/ and /aw/ sounds. Have students explain their answers.

Vocabulary

Word Parts

Teach

■ Write the compound word *outcast* on the board. Have students break the word into two words and discuss the meaning of each part. Define *outcast*.

■ Review the different word parts. Define prefixes and suffixes as units of meaning before and after a root and roots as units of meaning at the core of a word.

■ Write the word *misinform* on the board and have students think of other words they know with the prefix *mis*, such as *misspell* or *mistake*. Define *mis*, and then have students define *misinform*. Repeat the same process with the words *faultless* and *audible*.

Guided Practice

Assign page 10 of **Spelling and Vocabulary Skills.** Students can do page 11 of **Spelling and Vocabulary Skills** for homework.

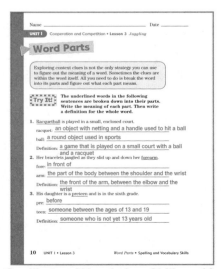

Spelling and Vocabulary Skills p. 10

Writing Process Strategies

Introduction to the Writing Process: Drafting

Turning Notes into Paragraphs

Teach

■ Read **Language Arts Handbook** pages 34–35 on creating paragraphs.

■ Discuss with students what makes up a paragraph. Define *paragraph*: a group of two or more sentences that tell about the same thing. Make sure students understand that a paragraph has a topic sentence and one or more supporting sentences. New ideas are developed in separate paragraphs.

Teacher Model: Creating Paragraphs

Form your paragraphs from the draft written with the class on Day 1 of this lesson. Put a sentence in the paragraph that clearly does not belong. If students do not catch it, point out the sentence and explain that it doesn't belong because it does not support the topic sentence.

Guided Practice

Have students create paragraphs from the draft they wrote on Day 1. Have them include the paragraphs in their **Writing Folders.**

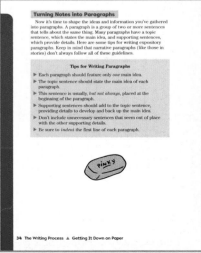

Language Arts Handbook p. 34

English Language Conventions

Grammar, Usage, and Mechanics:
Verbs

Teach

■ Review main and auxiliary verbs.

■ Write the following sentences on the board and have students identify the verbs. (Tell students that sometimes a helping verb is separated from the main verb.)

  • I do exercises every morning. [do]
  • Serena did well on the test. [did]
  • The band has marched in a parade. [has marched]
  • He has often been late this spring. [has been]
  • Have you written the letter? [have written]

■ Remind students that there are regular verbs that undergo spelling changes when *ed* is added *(plot + ed = plotted)*. There are also irregular verbs that create their past forms in some way other than by adding *ed* or *d (grow, grew, grown)*. Dictionaries will show the irregular forms of the entry word.

Independent Practice in Reading

Have students search for verbs in "Juggling." The story is written in the past tense, so most of the text will have past and past participle verbs. The dialogue is mostly in the present tense.

DAY 3

Word Analysis	Writing Process Strategies	English Language Conventions

Spelling

Spelling Patterns for the /o/ and /aw/ Sounds

Teach

Explain the spelling patterns for the /o/ and /aw/ sounds, which are *o*, *ough*, *augh*, *aw*, *au*, and *oa*. Have students skim later stories in their **Student Anthologies** for other words with the /o/ and /aw/ sounds and spelling patterns and share them with the class.

Guided Practice

Have students complete page 12 of **Spelling and Vocabulary Skills** to reinforce the spelling patterns for the /o/ and /aw/ .

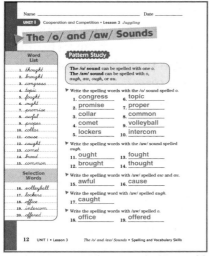

Spelling and Vocabulary Skills p. 12

Vocabulary (continued)

Word Parts

Write the following prefixes and suffixes on the board. Discuss the meaning of each one (*one*, *opposite*, *most*, *without*, and *state of*) and challenge students to list words that contain each prefix and suffix. Remind students that these word units always have the same meaning.

uni   de   est   less   ness

Introduction to the Writing Process: Drafting

Transition Words

Teach

- Read **Language Arts Handbook** pages 36–37. See **Language Arts Handbook** pages 272–275 for additional information on transition words.
- Emphasize that transition words perform the important function of connecting sentences and paragraphs to each other so that ideas flow smoothly.

Teacher Model: Transition Words

Write a two-paragraph description of the front of your classroom. Use transition words showing location and any others that link sentences and paragraphs. (Example: "**Above** the blackboard, I see …") Encourage input from students.

Independent Practice

Have students each write a two-paragraph summary of the events in "Juggling" to include in their **Writing Folders**. Tell students to be sure to include transition words within each paragraph and to show the connection between paragraphs through the use of transition words. Make sure students have access to the **Language Arts Handbook** list of transition words, page 36.

Grammar, Usage, and Mechanics:

Verbs

Teach

- Use **Language Arts Handbook** pages 346–347 to teach which verbs are action verbs and which verbs are state-of-being verbs.
- The **Language Arts Handbook** also addresses active and passive voice. Remind students that writing in the active voice usually makes writing clearer and stronger.
- Remind students that using verbs other than state-of-being verbs and verbs such as *said*, *went*, and *looked* makes writing more vivid and interesting. *She said, "Stop. There's a car coming." She shrieked, "Stop. There's a car coming."*

Independent Practice in Writing

Have students each write a paragraph about the illustration on page 49 in the story "Juggling." Direct them to describe the scene using action, state-of-being, and auxiliary verbs.

 Informal Assessment

Look for evidence that students are progressing in using verbs correctly in their writing.

DAY 4

| Word Analysis | Writing Process Strategies | English Language Conventions |

Spelling

Spelling Patterns for the /o/ and /aw/ Sounds

Teach

Model the pronunciation strategy by writing the word *modern* on the board and drawing a line between the two syllables, *mod* and *ern*.

Guided Practice

Have students complete the Spelling Strategies exercises on page 13 of *Spelling and Vocabulary Skills.*

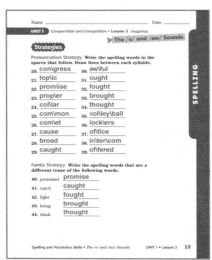

Spelling and Vocabulary Skills p. 13

Vocabulary (continued)

Word Parts

Write the following words from "Juggling" on the board. Instruct students to find these words in the story. Break the words into parts and discuss the meaning of each part. Then come up with a definition for each word.

deliberately   abruptly   pestering

Deliberately means "on purpose." *Abruptly* means "suddenly." *Pestering* means "bothering."

Introduction to the Writing Process: Drafting

Getting the Ideas Down

Teach

Keep It Interesting

Point out that as students draft they should try to keep their writing interesting. Suggest to students that they add questions, anecdotes, examples, intriguing facts, and suspenseful items aimed at capturing and holding the reader's interest.

Stay Focused

Drafting allows writers to be as interesting as possible with one topic. Emphasize that the limitations of topic need not be restricting. With well-laid plans, students can focus freely on their topic without being distracted by unrelated ideas.

Include Basic Elements

Remind students that in drafting, nothing is permanent. The later revision process will allow them to add, delete, and change anything they want. While they draft, however, they will want to remember to provide details and transition words to link paragraphs as well as including a resolution or conclusion that brings the action to an end or summarizes important ideas.

Independent Practice

Have students each draft in their Writer's Notebooks a personal narrative about a time when they helped out a friend or a friend helped them (as Dave helped Kyle in the story "Juggling"). Students may draft on paper, or if you have computers in your classroom, have students draft using word processing software. Students should include their drafts in their **Writing Folders**.

Listening, Speaking, Viewing

Language: Using Appropriate Language

Teach

- In Reading and Responding we discussed predicting. Knowing where we are going to speak can help us predict what kind of words to use.
- Remind the class that our language changes when we are presented with different situations, audiences, and purposes. Our vocabulary or word choice changes; we discuss different topics; we make different examples.
- Explain that language is a part of our speaking skills, but that the two are not the same thing. One of our speaking skills should be knowing how to speak and what kind of language to use. When we talk about our language changing, we mean the words we use. We still speak clearly, slowly, and at an appropriate volume; we simply use different words.

Guided Practice

- Refer to the story "Juggling." When Mr. Braden first asks Kyle to join the volleyball team, Kyle calmly tells him that he can't. Kyle reacts differently when his mother asks him about joining the team. How are the two situations different, and why does Kyle change the way he speaks? *(Kyle must speak more formally to his teacher than he speaks to his mother. Kyle is in a public, more formal place.)*
- Did Kyle speak to Mr. Braden appropriately when he was called into his office? Could he have spoken to a close friend this way?

 Informal Assessment

- Observe whether students understand how and when to change their speech style.

DAY 5

Word Analysis	Writing Process Strategies	English Language Conventions

Word Analysis

Spelling

Assessment: Final Test
Spelling Patterns for the /o/ and /aw/ Sounds

Teach
Repeat the Pretest for this lesson or use the Final Test on page 31 of **Unit 1 Assessment.**

Unit 1 Assessment p. 31

Guided Practice
Have students categorize any mistakes they made on the Final Test.

Are they careless errors?
Are they lesson pattern problems?

Vocabulary (continued)

Word Parts

Informal Assessment

- Remind students to continue identifying prefixes, suffixes, and roots so they can recall their meanings as they find them in unfamiliar words. Call attention to various prefixes, suffixes, and roots that are encountered in future selections. Have students review pages 10 and 11 in **Spelling and Vocabulary Skills** if they need to review these concepts.
- Encourage students to record suffixes, prefixes, and roots and their meanings in their Writer's Notebook.

Writing Process Strategies

Drafting

Writer's Craft
Figurative Language

Read **Language Arts Handbook** pages 286–289 on using figurative language.
- Point out that figures of speech make writing interesting and enjoyable to read because they create vivid pictures in readers' minds.
- Remind students that figurative language uses comparisons that rely on audience experience.
- As a class, come up with new examples of each type of figurative language: *simile, metaphor, personification, hyperbole,* and *idiom.*

Independent Practice
- For practice using figurative language, have students complete **Comprehension and Language Arts Skills** pages 14–15. Also have students do the drafting activity on Writer's Workbook page 3.
- Show students **Transparency 5— Time Line.** Have them each use a time line to organize their autobiographies around a theme. Have students include their drafts in their **Writing Folders.**

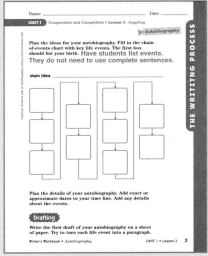

Writer's Workbook p. 3

English Language Conventions

Penmanship
Cursive Letters *r* and *s*

Teach
- Remind students it is important to have all their letters slant to the right. Tell them that proper slant makes their writing more legible.
- **Teacher Model:** Review the formation of lowercase, cursive *r* and *s* as undercurve letters by demonstrating on the board.

r Starting point, undercurve
Slant right
Slant down, undercurve: small *r*

s Starting point, undercurve
Curve down and back, undercurve: small *s*

Guided Practice
- **Teacher Model:** Write the sentence "Sometimes my favorite sport is wrestling." on the board to model proper letter formation and slant. Draw slanted lines through the letters to demonstrate proper slant.
- From "Juggling," have students write two paragraphs for general handwriting practice.
- Have students draw slanted lines through their words to check for proper slant.

Informal Assessment

Check students' handwriting for legibility and consistent slant.

Reading and Language Arts Skills Traces

Language Arts

WORD ANALYSIS	WRITING PROCESS STRATEGIES	ENGLISH LANGUAGE CONVENTIONS

Skills Trace
Spelling: The /o/ and /aw/ Sounds

Introduced in Grade 1.
Scaffolded throughout Grades 2–5.
REINTRODUCED: Unit 1, Lesson 3, p. 55F
PRACTICED: Unit 1, Lesson 3,
pp. 55G–55I
Spelling and Vocabulary Skills,
pp. 12–13
TESTED: Unit 1, Lesson 3, p. 55J
Unit 1 Assessment

Skills Trace
Vocabulary: Word Parts

Introduced in Grade 1.
Scaffolded throughout Grades 2–5.
REINTRODUCED: Unit 1, Lesson 3, p. 55G
PRACTICED: Unit 1, Lesson 3,
pp. 55H–55I
Spelling and Vocabulary Skills,
pp. 10–11
TESTED: Informal Assessment, p. 55J
Unit 1 Assessment

Skills Trace
Introduction to the Writing Process: Drafting

Introduced in Grade 1.
Scaffolded throughout Grades 2–5.
INTRODUCED: Unit 1, Lesson 3, p. 55F
PRACTICED: Unit 1, Lesson 3,
pp. 55F–55J
Writer's Workbook, p. 3
TESTED: Unit 1 Assessment

Skills Trace
Writer's Craft: Figurative Language

Introduced in Grade 2.
Scaffolded throughout Grades 3–5.
INTRODUCED: Unit 1, Lesson 3, p. 55J
PRACTICED: Unit 1, Lessons 3, p. 55J
Comprehension and Language Arts Skills, pp. 14–15
TESTED: Unit 1 Assessment

Skills Trace
Grammar, Usage, and Mechanics: Verbs

Introduced in Grade K.
Scaffolded throughout Grades 1–5.
INTRODUCED: Unit 1, Lesson 3, p. 55F
PRACTICED: Unit 1, Lesson 3, p. 55G
Unit 1, Lesson 3, p. 55H
Comprehension and Language Arts Skills, pp. 12–13
TESTED: Informal Assessment, p. 55H
Unit 1 Assessment

Skills Trace
Listening, Speaking, Viewing: Language: Using Appropriate Language

Introduced in Grade K.
Scaffolded throughout Grades 1–5.
REINTRODUCED: Unit 1, Lesson 3, p. 55I
PRACTICED: Unit 1, Lesson 3, p. 55I
TESTED: Informal Assessment, p. 55I

Skills Trace
Penmanship: Cursive Letters r and s

Introduced in Grade 3.
Scaffolded throughout Grades 4–5.
REINTRODUCED: Unit 1, Lesson 3, p. 55J
PRACTICED: Unit 1, Lesson 3, p. 55J
TESTED: Informal Assessment, p. 55J

Reading

COMPREHENSION

Skills Trace
Author's Point of View

Introduced in Grade 2.
Scaffolded throughout Grades 3–5.
REINTRODUCED: Unit 1, Lesson 3
REINFORCED: Unit 1, Lesson 5
Unit 3, Lesson 1
Unit 3, Lesson 4
Unit 3, Lesson 5
TESTED: Unit 1 Assessment

Professional Development: Writing

Becoming Real Writers: What It's All About

The writing classroom is changing, and adjusting to this change is one of many challenges facing today's teachers. Instruction now encourages the expression of ideas and feelings, the development of fluency, the building of knowledge, the sharing of learning, and the development of confidence and self-esteem. ***Open Court Reading*** sees every child as a writer and an author. This program provides not only opportunities for independent writing in every lesson, but also for feedback in teacher and peer writing conferences and in Seminar, where authors interact with peers while reading and discussing each other's writing.

What has caused this change in writing instruction? Much of our insight comes from our growing understanding of what good writers do. They have ownership of their work and are actively involved in the process from start to finish. The same should be true for the young authors in our classrooms.

What Do Successful Writers Do?

Writers spend time thinking about and planning their topics. They choose their own topics from a number of sources including their interests; what they care about, dream about, or have experienced; and what they have yet to learn. Writers consider their audience and develop and conduct research, if necessary, before they ever begin writing.

- Writers draft or put their ideas into words. They get their ideas down on paper, often in a rough form.

- Writers revise and revisit their work. They take another look to see if it makes sense and to see if it says what they want it to say. They check to be sure the meaning is clear for the reader.

- Writers edit their work. Good writers recognize the importance of writing conventions—grammar, mechanics, and spelling—that allow the reader to understand and enjoy published works.

- Writers go public with their works. They publish their work in books, newspapers, magazines, anthologies, and so on.

Writing is a recursive process as authors move back and forth through writing activities—from planning to drafting to revising and back—to create their final pieces. It is a process of thinking, experimenting, and evaluating.

All writers need feedback throughout the writing process. They need reactions to ideas, drafts, and revisions before it is too late to make changes. ***Open Court Reading's*** writing conferences and Seminar support young authors and provide opportunities for feedback about work in progress.

How Can We Create Environments That Nurture Our Young Authors?

- Inspire even our youngest students to communicate, even if it is only through drawings and invented spellings.

- Set aside blocks of time each day for writing—time in which students can think about ideas, read about their topics, draft, reflect upon, and publish their pieces.

- Provide opportunities for students to experiment with different types of writing, to take risks, to learn from their mistakes, and to get reactions from others throughout the process.

- Provide constructive feedback to help students recognize and solve problems, to grow in their understanding, and to become independent writers.

* Additional information about writing as well as resource references can be found in the ***Professional Development Guide: Writing.***

Viewing the Theme Through Fine Art

Students can use the artworks on these pages to explore the unit theme of cooperation and competition in images rather than words. Encourage them to talk about their impressions of the artworks and how each artwork might relate to the unit theme of cooperation and competition.

Below is some background information about each of the artworks. Share with students whatever you feel is appropriate for enhancing students' understanding of the unit concept as well as their enjoyment of each artwork. You might encourage students to find out more about artists and artistic styles that interest them.

Small Roman Abacus

Calculi or *abaculi* were the common names used for the abacus, an instrument used to make arithmetic calculations. There were originally three types of abaci used by the Romans: a table marked for counters, the primitive board, and a grooved plate with sliding beads, the last to be developed.

Small Roman Abacus is made of a metal plate, possibly bronze, on which the small disks slide. Each disk is assigned a value, which is determined by its position on the plate. The values of ones, tens, and hundreds are most commonly used.

Footballers

RUSKIN SPEAR (1911–   ) was born in London and studied at the Hammersmith School of Art and the Royal College of Art. He is best known for his still lifes, cityscapes, and stocky figures portrayed in a loosely painted technique.

Fine Art

Cooperation and Competition

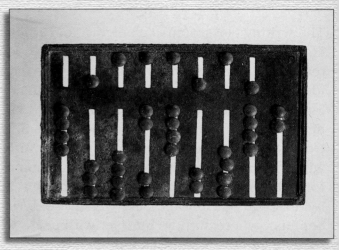

Small Roman Abacus. Museo Nazionale Romano Delle Terme, Rome, Italy.

Footballers. **Ruskin Spear.** Private collection.

56

Artist Pyramid. **Josef Hegenbarth.** Oil on canvas. Private collection ©2001 Josef Hegenbarth/Licensed by VAGA, New York, NY.

Catcher on the Line. **Robert Riggs.** Oil on canvas. Private collection.

57

Footballers portrays three young men who are captured in a moment of jubilation, perhaps after a successful play or game. In England, *football* is the name for soccer. These three men depended on the cooperation of their teammates to successfully compete in the game.

Artist Pyramid

JOSEF HEGENBARTH was born in Kamenice, Germany, in 1884. He began his career as a freelance artist creating cartoonlike illustrations for a variety of magazines. From 1946 to 1949, he was a professor at the Akademie der Bildenden Künste.

Artist Pyramid depicts 17 acrobats working together to form a human pyramid. The acrobats appear to completely trust their teammates. Imagine the teamwork and cooperation that must take place for this type of stunt to be successful.

Catcher on the Line

ROBERT RIGGS (1896–1970) was born in Decatur, Illinois. Dramatic scenes such as circus acts, emergency wards, and prize fights were his favorite subject matter. Although he is best known as a skilled lithographer (a printing technique) he also created several dramatic paintings in oils.

Catcher on the Line reveals the quick action play on the sideline near the dugout. The young boys are ready to catch the ball if the player should miss, as his teammates encourage him on the catch. Notice how the action has been stilled and the viewpoint is from a stadium seat to the right of the catcher.

Selection Summary

Genre: Realistic Fiction

Gao Mai, a young girl living in a small Taiwanese city, is intent on winning a class contest. The author takes us through her perceptions and feelings on the day of the contest. What will Gao Mai do if her best friend wins? What if neither of them wins? Friendships, family, and personal expectations, as well as handling feelings of disappointment, anxiety, and competition, are explored in this thoughtful story.

Some of the elements of realistic fiction are listed below. A realistic fiction selection may have one or more of these elements.

- The characters behave as people or animals do in real life.
- The setting of the story is a real place or could be a real place.
- The events of the story are based on a conflict or problem that could occur in real life.

About the Author

PRISCILLA WU'S first book is *The Abacus Contest.* She lives in Reno, Nevada, with her family. Wu has been a Montessori teacher and recently completed graduate course work in counseling and marriage therapy at the University of Nevada.

Students can read more about Priscilla Wu on page 64 of the *Student Anthology*.

About the Illustrator

YOSHI MIYAKE was born in Tokyo and educated as a scientist. A correspondence course led to her interest in art. Ms. Miyake went on to study at the American Academy of Art in Chicago, where she now lives.

Students can read more about Yoshi Miyake on page 64 of the *Student Anthology.*

Other Books Illustrated by Yoshi Miyake

- *What Makes it Rain?: The Story of Raindrops*
- *Rachel Carson: Friend of the Earth*
- *Mozart: Young Music Genius*
- *Moshi Moshi*

Inquiry Connections

A major aim of *Open Court Reading* is knowledge building. Because inquiry is at the root of knowledge building, students are encouraged to investigate topics and questions within each selection that relate to the unit theme.

"The Abacus Contest" is realistic fiction about a young girl's competitive approach to a contest that she lost the previous year. The key concepts explored are:

- Competition sometimes causes feelings of anxiety.
- Competition can be a stimulating challenge.
- Competitions affect individuals differently.

Before reading the selection:

- Point out that students may post a question, concept, word, illustration, or object on the Concept/Question Board at any time during the course of their unit investigation. Be sure that students include their names or initials on the items they post so that others will know whom to go to if they have an answer or if they wish to collaborate on a related activity.
- Students should feel free to write an answer or a note on someone else's question or to consult the Board for ideas for their own investigations throughout the unit.
- Encourage students to read about cooperation and competition at home and to bring in articles or pictures that are good examples to post on the Board.

Concept/Question Board

PROGRAM RESOURCES

Leveled Practice

Reteach
Pages 18–23

Challenge
Pages 15–19

ELD Workbook

Intervention Workbook

Leveled Classroom Library*

Have students read at least 30 minutes daily outside of class. Have them read books from the *Leveled Classroom Library,* which supports the unit theme and helps students develop their vocabulary by reading independently.

The Big Bike Race

BY LUCY JANE BLEDSOE. AVON, 1995.

Though a used, yellow, old clunker is the only bike his grandmother can afford to buy him, Ernie won't let the other kids' laughter hamper his determination to race and to win. **(Easy)**

Iditarod Dream: Dusty and His Sled Dogs Compete in Alaska's Jr. Iditarod

BY TED WOOD. WALKER AND COMPANY, 1996.

Dusty shows he knows how to train and care for his Alaskan Huskie dog team, as well as drive his sled and fend off a moose, as he vies for first place in the Jr. Iditarod. **(Average)**

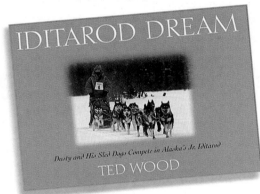

The View from Saturday

BY E.L. KONIGSBURG. ALADDIN, 1996.

Mrs. Olinski's choice of Noah, Nadia, Ethan, and Julian for her sixth grade academic team, the strange connections between the four, and their amazing academic bowl winning streak are explored. (A Newbery Medal Winner) **(Advanced)**

＊ These books, which all support the unit theme Cooperation and Competition, are part of a 36-book *Leveled Classroom Library* available for purchase from SRA/McGraw-Hill.

Note: Teachers should preview any trade books for appropriateness in their classrooms before recommending them to students.

TECHNOLOGY

Web Connections

www.sra4kids.com
Cooperation and Competition Web site

Audiocassette/CD

＊ **Listening Library:**
Cooperation and Competition
SRA/McGRAW-HILL, 2002

Computer Skills

＊ **Basic Computer Skills**

CD-ROMs

＊ **Research Assistant**
SRA/McGRAW-HILL, 2002

＊ **Student Writing and Research Center**
THE LEARNING COMPANY

Titles preceded by an asterisk (＊) are available through SRA/McGraw-Hill. Other titles can be obtained by contacting the publisher listed with the title.

LESSON PLANNER

Suggested Pacing: 3–5 days

	DAY 1	DAY 2
	DAY 1	DAY 2

1 Preparing to Read

Materials
- Routine Card 1

DAY 1

Word Knowledge, p. 58K
- Content-Area Words
- /ow/ Sound Spelled *ou*
- Long e Spelled *ea*
- /i/ Sound Spelled *i*

About the Words and Sentences, p. 58K

DAY 2

Developing Oral Language, p. 58L

2 Reading & Responding

Materials
- Student Anthology, pp. 58–65
- Reading Transparencies 6, 54, 56–57
- Routine Cards 1
- Intervention Guide
- Program Assessment
- Inquiry Journal, p. 7
- Unit 1 Assessment, pp. 14–17
- Comprehension and Language Arts Skills, pp. 16–17
- Reteach, pp. 18–19
- Challenge, p. 15
- Home Connection, pp. 9–10
- Science/Social Studies Connection Center Card 6

DAY 1

Build Background, p. 58M
Preview and Prepare, pp. 58M–58N
Selection Vocabulary, p. 58N
Reading Recommendations, pp. 58O–58P
Student Anthology, pp. 58–63 [First Read]
✓ **Comprehension Strategies**
- Summarizing, p. 58
- Monitoring and Clarifying, p. 60
- Predicting, pp. 58, 62

Discussing Strategy Use, p. 62
Discussing the Selection, p. 63A

DAY 2

Student Anthology, pp. 58–63 [Second Read]
Comprehension Skills
- Sequence, pp. 59, 61, 63
✓ **Checking Comprehension, p. 63**
Supporting the Reading, pp. 63C–63D
- Sequence

Inquiry

Materials
- Student Anthology, pp. 58–65
- Inquiry Journal, pp. 20–23
- Reading Transparencies 2, 58
- Research Assistant

DAY 1

Investigation
- Investigating Concepts Beyond the Text, p. 65A

DAY 2

Investigation
- Concept/Question Board, p. 65B

3 Language Arts

Materials
- Comprehension and Language Arts Skills, pp. 18–21
- Language Arts Handbook, pp. 38–40, 43, 363
- Language Arts Transparencies 11–15, 26
- Spelling and Vocabulary Skills, pp. 14–17
- Student Anthology
- Student Writing and Research Center
- Writing Folder
- Unit 1 Assessment, pp. 32–33
- Reteach, pp. 20–23
- Challenge, pp. 16–19

DAY 1

Word Analysis
✓ Spelling Patterns for the /i/ Sound Pretest, p. 65F
Writing Process Strategies
- Writing Process Introduction: Revising, p. 65F
English Language Conventions
- Grammar, Usage, and Mechanics: Sentences, p. 65F

DAY 2

Word Analysis
- Spelling Patterns for the /i/ Sound, p. 65G
- Vocabulary: Using the Dictionary, p. 65G
Writing Process Strategies
- Writing Process: Revising, p. 65G
English Language Conventions
- Grammar, Usage, and Mechanics: Sentences, p. 65G

✓ Informal **Assessment Available**   ✓ Formal **Assessment Available**

DAY 2 continued	DAY 3	
DAY 3	**DAY 4**	**DAY 5**
General Review	**General Review**	**Review Word Knowledge**
Student Anthology, pp. 64–65 ■ **Meet the Author/Illustrator** ✓■ **Theme Connections**	**Review Selection Vocabulary, p. 63B** **Literary Elements, p. 63E** ■ **Conflict**	✓ **Lesson Assessment** ■ *Unit 1 Assessment:* **Lesson Assessment, pp. 14–17** **Home Connection, p. 63B** **Science Connection** ■ **The Steps of Digestion, p. 63F**
Investigation ✓■ **Establishing Investigation Needs, p. 65C**	**Supporting the Investigation** ■ **Using Charts and Diagrams, p. 65D**	**Investigation** ■ **Unit Investigation Continued** ■ **Update Concept/Question Board**
Word Analysis ■ **Spelling Patterns for the /i/ Sound, p. 65H** ■ **Vocabulary: Using the Dictionary, p. 65H** **Writing Process Strategies** ■ **Writing Process: Revising, p. 65H** **English Language Conventions** ✓■ **Grammar, Usage, and Mechanics: Sentences, p. 65H**	**Word Analysis** ■ **Spelling Patterns for the /i/ Sound, p. 65I** ■ **Vocabulary: Using the Dictionary, p. 65I** **Writing Process Strategies** ■ **Writing Process: Revising, p. 65I** **English Language Conventions** ✓■ **Listening, Speaking, Viewing Viewing: Viewing the Media, p. 65I**	**Word Analysis** ✓■ **Spelling Patterns for the /i/ Sound Final Test, p. 65J** ✓■ **Vocabulary: Using the Dictionary, p. 65J** **Writing Process Strategies** ■ **Writing Process: Revising, p. 65J** **English Language Conventions** ✓■ **Penmanship: Cursive Letters *p* and *j*, p. 65J**

Below are suggestions for differentiating instruction to meet the individual needs of students. These are the same skills shown on the Lesson Planner; however, these pages provide extra practice opportunities or enriching activities to meet the varied needs of students.

WORKSHOP

Differentiating Instruction

Small-Group Instruction

Use the informal assessment suggestions found throughout the lesson along with the formal assessments provided in each lesson to determine your students' strengths and areas of need. Use the following program components to help in supporting or expanding on the instruction found in this lesson:

- **Reteach** workbook for use with those students who show a basic understanding of the lesson but need a bit more practice to solidify their understanding

- **Intervention Guide** and **Workbook** for use with those students who even after extra practice exhibit a lack of understanding of the lesson concepts

- **English-Language Development Guide** and **Workbook** for use with those students who need language help

Independent Activities

Have students prepare and deliver oral responses to the literature they have been reading with Reading Roundtable groups. Have them summarize significant events and details and describe several ideas or images about cooperation and competition that were communicated by the literary work. Tell them that they should use textual evidence, such as quoted passages from the literary work, to support any conclusions about cooperation and competition they have drawn from their reading.

For Workshop Management Tips, see Appendix pages 41–42.

◆ **Small-group Instruction**   ■ **Independent Activities**

	READING	INVESTIGATION ACTIVITIES
DAY 1	■ *Listening Library Audiocassette/CD* ■ Add Vocabulary in Writer's Notebook ■ Record Response to Selection in Writer's Notebook	■ Concept/Question Board ■ Explore OCR Web Site for Theme Connections
DAY 2	■ Oral Reading of the Selection for Fluency ■ *Listening Library Audiocassette/CD* ■ Complete *Comprehension and Language Arts Skills*, pp. 16–17	■ Concept/Question Board ■ Explore OCR Web Site for Theme Connections
DAY 3	■ Independent Reading ◆ Discuss Theme Connections, p. 65 ■ Complete *Link to Writing* for Supporting the Reading, p. 63D	■ Concept/Question Board ◆ Establish Investigation Needs ■ Use *Research Assistant* to Help with Investigation
DAY 4	■ Add Words to Word Bank ■ Complete *Independent Practice* for Literary Elements, p. 63E	■ Concept/Question Board ■ Complete *Inquiry Journal*, pp. 20–22
DAY 5	◆ Reading Roundtable ◆ Science Connection, p. 63F	■ Concept/Question Board ■ Practice Organizing Information in *Inquiry Journal*, p. 23

LANGUAGE ARTS	INTERVENTION*	ENGLISH-LANGUAGE LEARNERS**	RETEACH	CHALLENGE
English Language Conventions ■ Complete **Kinds of Sentences,** *Comprehension and Language Arts Skills,* pp. 18–19 **Writing Process Strategies** ◆ Seminar: Revise by Adding Material, p. 65F	(30 to 45 minutes per day) ◆ Reading Words, p. 30 ◆ Preteach "The Abacus Contest," pp. 31–32 ◆ Teach "Intervention Selection One," pp. 32–33 ◆ Grammar, Usage, and Mechanics, p. 35	(30 to 45 minutes per day) ◆ Word Knowledge, p. 16 ◆ Activate Prior Knowledge, p. 17		
Word Analysis ◆ Spelling: Word Sort, p. 65G ■ Complete **Vocabulary: Using the Dictionary,** *Spelling and Vocabulary Skills,* pp. 14–15 **Writing Process Strategies** ◆ Seminar: Revise by Deleting Material, p. 65G	◆ Developing Oral Language, p. 30 ◆ Preteach "The Abacus Contest," pp. 31–32 ◆ Teach Comprehension Strategies, p. 33 ◆ Reread "Intervention Selection One" ◆ Grammar, Usage, and Mechanics, p. 35	◆ Selection Vocabulary, p. 18 ◆ Preteach the Selection, p. 17	**Comprehension** ◆ Review Comprehension Skill: Sequence ■ Complete *Reteach,* pp. 18–19 **English Language Conventions** ■ Complete **Kinds of Sentences,** *Reteach,* p. 22	**Comprehension** ■ Complete *Challenge,* p. 15 **English Language Conventions** ■ Complete **Kinds of Sentences,** *Challenge,* p. 18
Word Analysis ■ Complete **Spelling: The /i/ Sound,** *Spelling and Vocabulary Skills,* p. 16 **Writing Process Strategies** ◆ Seminar: Revise by Consolidating Material, p. 65H	◆ Dictation and Spelling, pp. 30–31 ◆ Reread "The Abacus Contest" ◆ Teach "Intervention Selection Two," pp. 33–34 ◆ Writing Activity, pp. 36–37	◆ Dictation and Spelling, p. 17	**Word Analysis** ■ Complete **Vocabulary: Using the Dictionary,** *Reteach,* p. 21	**Word Analysis** ■ Complete **Vocabulary: Using the Dictionary,** *Challenge,* p. 17
Word Analysis ■ Complete **The /i/ Sound,** *Spelling and Vocabulary Skills,* p. 17 **Writing Process Strategies** ◆ Seminar: Revise by Rearranging Material, p. 65I	◆ Reread "The Abacus Contest" ◆ Teach Comprehension Strategies, p. 34 ◆ Reread "Intervention Selection Two" ◆ Writing Activity, pp. 36–37	◆ Vocabulary Strategies, p. 19	**Word Analysis** ■ Complete **Spelling: The /i/ Sound,** *Reteach,* p. 20	**Word Analysis** ■ Complete **Spelling: The /i/ Sound,** *Challenge,* p. 16
Writing Process Strategies ■ Complete **Writer's Craft: Sensory Description,** *Comprehension and Language Arts Skills,* pp. 20–21 ◆ Seminar: Revise an Autobiography, p. 65F–65I **English Language Conventions** ■ Penmanship: Cursive Letters *p* and *j,* p. 65J	◆ Repeated Readings/Fluency Check, pp. 34–35	◆ Grammar, Usage, and Mechanics, p. 19	**Writing Process Strategies** ■ Complete **Writer's Craft: Sensory Description,** *Reteach,* p. 23	**Writing Process Strategies** ■ Complete **Writer's Craft: Sensory Description** *Challenge,* p. 19

*Page numbers refer to *Intervention Guide*
**Page numbers refer to *English-Language Development Guide*

ASSESSMENT

Formal Assessment Options

Use these summative assessments along with your informal observations to assess student progress.

Unit 1 Assessment p. 14

Name _____ Date _____ Score _____

UNIT 1 Cooperation and Competition • Lesson 4

LESSON ASSESSMENT

The Abacus Contest

Read the following questions carefully. Then completely fill in the bubble of each correct answer. You may look back at the story to find the answer to each of the questions.

1. Which of these happened first in the story?
   Ⓐ Gao Mai walked through the market.
   ● Gao Mai dreamed she broke the abacus.
   Ⓒ Gao Mai competes in the abacus contest.

2. Where does Gao Mai sleep?
   Ⓐ in a hammock with a blanket
   Ⓑ in a large wooden bed
   ● on the floor under a quilt

Read the following questions carefully. Use complete sentences to answer the questions.

3. What do you think Gao Mai's dream at the beginning of the story means?
   The dream probably means she is worried about Li Zhi beating her at the abacus contest again.

4. Why do you think the author described Gao Mai's breakfast?
   The author probably described Gao Mai's breakfast to give the reader an idea of Gao Mai's culture.

5. What is the market like that Gao Mai sees on her way to school?
   The market that Gao Mai sees on her way to school has things like fresh fish and sugar cane right on the street.

14 Unit 1 • Lesson 4   The Abacus Contest • Unit 1 Assessment

---

Unit 1 Assessment p. 15

The Abacus Contest (continued)

LESSON ASSESSMENT

6. During the abacus contest, what does Gao Mai pull apart with shaking hands?
   Gao Mai pulls apart the two pages of her book that are stuck together.

7. What does Gao Mai worry about during recess?
   She worries that her father will be disappointed that she has not won the contest.

8. What is the unusual situation Mr. Wang tells the class about at the end of the story?
   The unusual situation is that Li Zhi and Gao Mai have tied for first place in the contest.

Read the following questions carefully. Then completely fill in the bubble of each correct answer.

9. How did the girls respond to the contest's ending in a tie?
   ● They burst out laughing.
   Ⓑ They both looked confused.
   Ⓒ They burst out crying.

10. Which of these is true about Li Zhi pulling Gao Mai's ponytail?
   Ⓐ It is an example of being mean.
   ● It is a gesture of friendly teasing.
   Ⓒ It is a way of slowing Gao Mai down.

Unit 1 Assessment • The Abacus Contest   Unit 1 • Lesson 4 15

Unit 1 Assessment p. 16

The Abacus Contest (continued)

LESSON ASSESSMENT

Read the questions and statements below. Use complete sentences in your answers.

Linking to the Concepts Gao Mai and Li Zhi are good friends but they compete fiercely against one another. Is this unusual? Do you have a friend against whom you enjoy competing?
Answers will vary. Accept all reasonable answers.

_____
_____
_____
_____
_____
_____
_____

Personal Response Li Zhi loves to play practical jokes. How do you feel about practical jokes?
Answers will vary. Accept all reasonable answers.

_____
_____
_____
_____
_____
_____
_____
_____
_____

16 Unit 1 • Lesson 4   The Abacus Contest • Unit 1 Assessment

---

Unit 1 Assessment p. 17

The Abacus Contest (continued)

LESSON ASSESSMENT

Vocabulary

Read the following questions carefully. Then completely fill in the bubble of each correct answer.

1. Based on the story, which of these is most like an **abacus**?
   ● a calculator
   Ⓑ a television
   Ⓒ a ruler

2. Li Zhi loved practical jokes and you could tell from her mischievous look that she might try one at any moment. **Mischievous** means
   Ⓐ jealous
   ● playful
   Ⓒ foolish

3. To win the abacus contest, the students needed both speed and accuracy. **Accuracy** is
   Ⓐ quickness
   ● correctness
   Ⓒ thoughtfulness

4. When the two girls finish their booklets, they jump up from their seats and collide with each other. To **collide** means to
   ● bump into
   Ⓑ trip over
   Ⓒ jump around

5. During a few of her timed drills, Gao Mai was even faster than her father with the abacus. In this sentence, a **drill** is for
   Ⓐ measuring
   Ⓑ digging
   ● practicing

Unit 1 Assessment • The Abacus Contest   Unit 1 • Lesson 4 17

Unit 1 Assessment p. 32

Name _____ Date _____ Score _____

UNIT 1 Cooperation and Competition • Lesson 4 The Abacus Contest

LESSON ASSESSMENT

Spelling Pretest: The /i/ Sound

Fold this page back on the dotted line. Take the Pretest. Then correct any word you misspelled by crossing out the word and rewriting it next to the incorrect spelling.

1. _____	1. _width_
2. _____	2. _glimpse_
3. _____	3. _twist_
4. _____	4. _blizzard_
5. _____	5. _lyrics_
6. _____	6. _simple_
7. _____	7. _built_
8. _____	8. _system_
9. _____	9. _igloo_
10. _____	10. _mystery_
11. _____	11. _limit_
12. _____	12. _visit_
13. _____	13. _imitate_
14. _____	14. _whistle_
15. _____	15. _thrift_
16. _____	16. _mistake_
17. _____	17. _giggled_
18. _____	18. _quilt_
19. _____	19. _begin_
20. _____	20. _division_

32 Unit 1 • Lesson 4   Spelling Pretest: The /i/ Sound • Unit 1 Assessment

---

Unit 1 Assessment p. 33

Name _____ Date _____ Score _____

UNIT 1 Cooperation and Competition • Lesson 4 The Abacus Contest

LESSON ASSESSMENT

Spelling Final Test: The /i/ Sound

Look for the underlined word that is spelled wrong. Fill in the bubble of the line with the misspelled word.

1. Ⓐ You have to use <u>thrift</u> when living on a budget.
   ● The train <u>wistle</u> signals the arrival at the station.
   Ⓒ We heard a <u>cricket</u> chirping all night.
   Ⓓ Correct as is.

2. ● The story of Hercules is a <u>mith</u>.
   Ⓑ How big can an <u>igloo</u> be?
   Ⓒ He scanned the <u>image</u> and saved it on the computer.
   Ⓓ Correct as is.

3. Ⓐ Sweeping a <u>chimney</u> is a dirty job.
   Ⓑ The fried <u>chicken</u> was hot and crispy.
   Ⓒ The wall forms a <u>division</u> between classrooms.
   Ⓓ Correct as is.

4. Ⓕ Our fingers are sometimes called <u>digits</u>.
   ● The Statue of Liberty was <u>bilt</u> over a hundred years ago.
   Ⓗ Even a soft <u>tissue</u> hurt her red nose.
   Ⓘ Correct as is.

5. Ⓐ I felt out of place, like a <u>misfit</u>.
   Ⓑ It is dangerous to drive in a <u>blizzard</u>.
   Ⓒ Each <u>mistake</u> was marked with a red pen.
   ● Correct as is.

6. ● Fry the eggs in this <u>skuillet</u>.
   Ⓖ We received a <u>visit</u> from a hungry raccoon.
   Ⓗ A <u>ribbon</u> will really enhance the gift wrap.
   Ⓘ Correct as is.

7. Ⓐ Measure the <u>width</u> of the yard for planting.
   Ⓑ I hope that dark cloud doesn't begin to <u>twist</u>.
   ● Copy the song <u>lirics</u> and sing along.
   Ⓓ Correct as is.

8. ● We couldn't wait for the game to <u>beguin</u>.
   Ⓖ A <u>quilt</u> has many tiny, decorative stitches.
   Ⓗ Don't be too <u>timid</u> to raise your hand in class.
   Ⓘ Correct as is.

9. Ⓐ The field was full of <u>thistle</u>.
   Ⓑ His <u>guilt</u> was evident by the look on his face.
   Ⓒ Parents must put <u>limits</u> on their children.
   ● Correct as is.

10. Ⓕ The <u>simple</u> melody was very memorable.
   ● We learned about the circulatory <u>sistem</u> in health class.
   Ⓗ It is hard to <u>admite</u> that we are guilty.
   Ⓘ Correct as is.

Unit 1 Assessment • Spelling Final Test: The /i/ Sound   Unit 1 • Lesson 4 33

Informal Comprehension Strategies Rubrics

Use the Informal Comprehension Strategies Rubrics to determine whether or not a student is using any of the strategies listed below. Note the strategies a student is using, instead of the degree to which a student might be using any particular strategy. In addition, encourage the student to tell of any strategies other than the ones being taught that he or she is using.

Predicting

- The student makes predictions about what the text is about.
- The student updates predictions during reading, based on information in the text.

Summarizing

- The student paraphrases text, reporting main ideas and a summary of what is in text.
- The student decides which parts of the text are important in his or her summary.
- The student draws conclusions from the text.
- The student makes global interpretations of the text, such as recognizing the genre.

Monitoring and Clarifying

- The student notes characteristics of the text, such as whether it is difficult to read or whether some sections are more challenging or more important than others.
- The student shows awareness of whether he or she understands the text and takes appropriate action, such as rereading, in order to understand the text better.
- The student rereads to reconsider something presented earlier in the text.
- The student recognizes problems during reading, such as a loss of concentration, unfamiliar vocabulary, or lack of sufficient background knowledge to comprehend the text.

Research Rubrics

During Workshop, assess students using the rubrics below. The rubrics range from 1–4 in most categories, with 1 being the lowest score. Record each student's score on the inside back cover of his or her *Inquiry Journal*.

Recognizing Information Needs

1 Identifies topics about which more needs to be learned. ("I need to learn more about the brain.")

2 Identifies information needs that are relevant though not essential to the research question. ("To understand how Leeuwenhoek invented the microscope, I need to know what size germs are.")

3 Identifies questions that are deeper than the one originally asked. (Original question: "How does the heart work?" Deeper question: "Why does blood need to circulate?")

Objectives

- Students recognize root words and suffixes of mathematics content-area words.
- Students recognize and read words with the /ow/ sound spelled *ou*.
- Students recognize and read words with the long e sound spelled *ea*.
- Students recognize and read words with the /i/ sound spelled *i*.
- Students develop fluency reading words and sentences aloud.

Materials

- Routine Card 1

Teacher Tip SYLLABICATION To help students blend words and build fluency, use the syllabication below of the decodable multisyllabic words in the word lines.

ad • di • tion	teach • er
sub • trac • tion	breath • ing
mul • ti • pli • ca • tion	fea • ture
di • vi • sion	mis • take
cal • cu • la • tion	gig • gled
an • nounce	be • gin

MEETING INDIVIDUAL NEEDS

ELL Support

For ELD strategies, use the *English-Language Development Guide,* Unit 1, Lesson 4.

Intervention Support

For intervention strategies, use the *Intervention Guide,* Unit 1, Lesson 4.

Routine Card
Refer to Routine 1 for the Reading the Words and Sentences procedure.

Word Knowledge

Reading the Words and Sentences

Use direct teaching to teach the Word Knowledge lesson. Write each word and sentence on the board. Have students read each word together. After all the words have been read, have students read each sentence in natural phrases or chunks. Use the suggestions in About the Words and Sentences to discuss the different features of listed words.

Line 1:	addition subtraction multiplication calculation
Line 2:	bounce loud round announce
Line 3:	teacher bead breathing feature
Line 4:	mistake giggled quilt begin division
Sentence 1:	The teacher showed the students how to do subtraction.
Sentence 2:	The multiplication game is played with a round bead and a game board.
Sentence 3:	The players are breathing hard as they bounce the ball.
Sentence 4:	It is easy to make a mistake when you are doing a long division problem.

About the Words and Sentences

- **Line 1:** These are content-area words dealing with mathematics. Point out that the words are roots plus the suffix *-tion* or *-sion*. Ask students to identify the root words (*add, subtract, multiply, calculate*). Then explain that the suffix *-tion* means action, result, or state. Challenge students to identify the part of speech of the root words (*verbs*), and discuss how the addition of the suffixes changes the part of speech (*nouns*).

- **Line 2:** The words have the /ow/ sound, as in *shout*, spelled *ou*. Have students offer other words with this spelling of the /ow/ sound.

- **Line 3:** The words focus on long e spelled *ea*. Invite students to think of other words with this spelling of the long e sound.

- **Line 4:** The words review the /i/ sound spelled *i*.

- **Sentences 1–2:** Have students identify the mathematics content-area words and words with the long e sound spelled *ea (subtraction, multiplication, teacher, bead)*. Ask students to provide the root words for the mathematics words *(subtract, multiply)*. Then, have students read the sentences aloud.

- **Sentence 2–3:** Have students identify the words with the /ow/ sound spelled *ou (round, bounce)*. Then, have students read the sentences aloud. Challenge students to add *ou* words to the third sentence and read it aloud again. *(The players are breathing hard as they bounce the ball off the ground around the house.)*

- **Sentence 4:** Have students identify the words that contain the /i/ sound spelled *i (it, is, mistake, doing, division)*. Point out that the word *division* is also a math content-area word.

Developing Oral Language

Use direct teaching to review the words. Use the following activity to help students practice the words aloud.

- On the board, list some of the words from Lines 1–4. Create a class paragraph using the words from the list. Start by having a student choose a word and use it in a sentence. Then have another student create a related sentence using another word from the list. Continue the activity to see how many words from the list the students can use to create a cohesive paragraph.

Teacher Tip BUILDING FLUENCY
Gaining a better understanding of the spellings of sounds and structure of words will help students as they encounter unfamiliar words in their reading. By this time in grade 5 students should be reading approximately 126 words per minute with fluency and expression. As students read, you may notice that some need work in building fluency. During Workshop, have these students choose a section of the text (a minimum of 160 words) to read several times in order to build fluency.

Spelling
See pages 65F–65J for the corresponding spelling lesson for the /i/ sound.

Objectives

- Students will understand the selection vocabulary before reading.
- Students will identify words containing the long e sound spelled *ea*.
- Students will use the comprehension strategies predicting, summarizing, and clarifying as they read the story the first time.
- Students will use the comprehension skill sequence as they read the story the second time.

Materials

- Student Anthology, pp. 58–65
- Reading Transparency 6, 54, 56, 57
- Listening Library
- Routine Card 1
- Inquiry Journal, p. 7
- Home Connection, pp. 9–10
- Comprehension and Language Arts Skills, pp. 16–17
- Program Assessment
- Unit 1 Assessment, pp. 14–17
- Science/Social Studies Connection Center Card 6

MEETING INDIVIDUAL NEEDS

ELL Support

For ELD strategies, use the *English-Language Development Guide,* Unit 1, Lesson 4.

Intervention Support

For intervention strategies, use the *Intervention Guide,* Unit 1, Lesson 4.

www.sra4kids.com
Web Connection
Students can use the connections to cooperation and competition in the Reading link of the SRA Web page for more background information about Cooperation and Competition.

Build Background

Activate Prior Knowledge

Discuss the following with students to find out what they may already know about the selection and have already learned about the theme of cooperation and competition.

- Preteach "The Abacus Contest" first determining students' prior knowledge about using an abacus. Ask students if they know what it is used for. *(calculating equations)*
- Ask students whether they are familiar with the story they are about to read, and if so, to tell a little about it. Remind students, however, not to give away the ending of the selection.
- Have students share other stories that involve timed contests or intense competition.

Background Information

The following information may help the students better understand the selection they are about to read.

- An abacus is a device usually made of beads strung on wires. If possible, bring one to class and allow the students to handle it. It is sometimes used in Asian countries such as Taiwan, China, and Japan to add and subtract. Ask volunteers to point out these countries on a world map or globe.
- Discuss the word *honor,* and talk about the importance of this in regard to family.
- The game *jian zhi* seems similar to a game played in the United States with a small leather beanbag. Have a few students research *jian zhi* to find out the rules and its origin. Have them summarize their findings in a report for the class and then demonstrate how the game is played.
- Be aware that Gao Mai's motivation to succeed may be a sensitive issue in your classroom. Emphasize that this story is a positive illustration of how people who are in competition with each other can maintain their friendship.
- Have the students discuss what they know about the genre of this selection. Refer to page 58A of the *Teacher's Edition* for elements of this selection's genre.

Preview and Prepare

Browse

- Have a student read aloud the title. Point out and read the names of the author and illustrator to students. Demonstrate how to browse. Then have them preview the selection by browsing the first page or two of the story. This allows them to activate prior knowledge relevant to the story. Discuss what they think this story might have to do with cooperation and competition.

- Have the students search for clues that tell them something about the story. Also, have them look for any problems, such as unfamiliar words or long sentences, that they notice while reading. Use **Reading Transparency 54** to record their observations as they browse. For example, the phrase *big day* may be a clue that the story takes place the day of the contest. For the Problems column, students might point out that they are not familiar with the word *abacus.* They might wonder where the story takes place. To save time and model note taking, write students' observations as brief notes rather than complete sentences.

- As students prepare to read the selection, have them browse the Focus Questions on the first page of the selection. Tell them to keep these questions in mind as they read.

Set Purposes

Have students set their own purposes for reading. Also, as they read, have students think about friendship in competitive situations and how this can teach them new lessons. Remind students that good readers have a purpose when they read. Let them know that they should make sure they know the purpose for reading whenever they read.

Selection Vocabulary

As students study vocabulary, they will use a variety of skills to determine the meaning of a word. These include context clues, word structure, and apposition. Students will apply these same skills while reading to clarify additional unfamiliar words.

Display **Reading Transparency 6** before reading the selection to introduce and discuss the following words and their meanings.

abacus:	a tool used to figure math problems by sliding counters (page 58)
drills:	exercises to increase your mental or physical skills (page 59)
mischievous:	full of pranks and teasing fun (page 60)
collided:	crashed (page 61)
accuracy:	being without mistakes (page 63)

Have students read the words in the Word Box. Demonstrate how to decode multisyllabic words by reading them syllable by syllable. Then have students try. If the word is not decodable, give the students the pronunciation.

- Have students read the sentences on **Reading Transparency 6** and use the skills of context, word structure (structural analysis), or apposition to figure out the meanings of the words. Be sure students explain which skill(s) they are using and how they figured out the meanings of the words.

Reading Transparency 54

Teacher Tip

SELECTION VOCABULARY To help students decode words, divide them into the syllables shown below. The information following each word tells how students can figure out the meaning of each word.

a • ba • cus:	context clues
drills:	context clues
mis • chie • vous:	context clues, word structure
book • lets:	context clues, word structure
col • lid • ed:	context clues, word structure
ac • cur • a • cy:	context clues, word structure

Routine Card

Refer to Routine 2 for the selection vocabulary procedure. Refer to Routine 3 for the Clues, Problems, and Wonderings procedure.

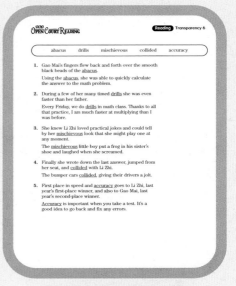

Reading Transparency 6

Teacher Tip COMPREHENSION STRATEGIES Refer to the Comprehension Strategies poster as the class reads the selection. As students are reading, ask them which of the strategies listed on the poster might be good to use at this point in the selection.

Routine Card
Refer to Routine 4 for the Reading the Selection procedure.

Reading Recommendations

Oral Reading

Because of unfamiliar word pronunciations in this selection, oral reading is recommended. For your convenience, Teacher Tips on the pronunciations of foreign words and names in the selection are featured beside and below the reduced *Student Anthology* pages in the *Teacher's Edition.* As students read aloud, have them read expressively at an appropriate pace in natural phrases and chunks. Make sure students enunciate their words and use appropriate intonations.

Reading the selection with fluency and accuracy will help students comprehend the text. If students have trouble reading decodable words, have them break the words into sounds or syllables and then blend them together to read the words.

After students have finished reading the selection, use the "Discussing the Selection" questions on page 63A to see if they understand what they have read.

Using Comprehension Strategies

Comprehension strategy instruction allows students to become aware of how good readers read. Good readers constantly check their understanding as they are reading and ask themselves questions. In addition, skilled readers recognize when they are having problems and stop to use various comprehension strategies to help them make sense of what they are reading.

During the reading of "The Abacus Contest," model and prompt the use of the following reading strategies:

- **Summarizing** prompts readers to keep track of what they are reading and to focus their minds on important information.
- **Monitoring and Clarifying** prompts readers to track and immediately clear up any unfamiliar ideas or words, using context, structural analysis, apposition, or other resources. Stop and check the students' understanding when something is unclear.
- **Predicting** causes readers to analyze information given about story events and characters in the context of how it may logically connect to the story's conclusion.

As students read, they should be using a variety of strategies to help them understand the selection. Encourage students to use the strategies listed as the class reads the story aloud. Do this by stopping at the points indicated by the numbers in magenta circles on the reduced student page and modeling for the students the use of a particular strategy.

Building Comprehension Skills

Revisiting or rereading a selection allows students to apply skills that give them a more complete understanding of the text. Some follow-up comprehension skills help students organize information. Others lead to deeper understanding—to "reading between the lines," as mature readers do. An extended lesson on the comprehension skill Sequence can be found in the Supporting the Reading section on pages 63C–63D. This lesson is intended to give students extra practice with sequence. However, the Teach portion of the lesson may be used at this time to introduce the comprehension skill to students.

- **Sequence (Introduction):** Readers use time words and order words in the text in order to follow the author's line of thought.

Reading with a Purpose

Have students list ways competition affects individuals and friendships in the Response Journal section of their Writer's Notebooks.

COMPREHENSION

Read pages 58–63.

Comprehension Strategies

First Read

Read the story aloud, taking turns with the students. Start by modeling the use of strategies for the students.

Teacher Modeling

1 Predicting *What a nightmare! Gao Mai must be afraid that Li Zhi will be angry with her for competing against her in the abacus contest. I predict that Li Zhi will not be angry with Gao Mai because they have always been friends. What do you predict?*

Teacher Modeling

2 Summarizing *Let's stop and summarize what we've just read to help us remember what happened and who everyone is. Let's see, Gao Mai woke up from a bad dream the day of the abacus contest at school. Her father and mother reminded her that she has improved since last year when Gao Mai's best friend, Li Zhi, won. Let's continue reading, and as we do, remember to summarize what we are reading.*

Writer's Craft

Sensory Description Point out the description of the abacus beads and the smell of the rice. Tell students that the words smooth, steamy, and overcooked add precision to the descriptions and help the reader feel more connected to the story. Explain to students that using sensory details can help pull their readers into their writing. See Writer's Craft lesson on page 65J.

First Reading Recommendation

ORAL • CHORAL • SILENT

Focus Questions Why is Gao Mai nervous about the upcoming abacus contest? Is it possible to be friends with one's rival?

The Abacus Contest

Priscilla Wu
illustrated by Yoshi Miyake

Gao Mai's fingers flew back and forth over the smooth black beads of the abacus.

Suddenly a wire snapped. The beads bounced onto the desk and rolled across the floor.

Gao Mai fell to her knees and crawled around after them. Just as she reached for the last bead, her best friend Li Zhi kicked it away from her hand. The other children giggled. Gao Mai's face burned.

Gao Mai opened her eyes wide and sat up in alarm. What an awful dream!

The comforting aroma of steamy, overcooked rice drifted in from the next room. She pushed aside the heavy quilt, got up from the floor and put on her school uniform.

"Are you ready for the big day?" Gao Mai's mother asked her as she came into the main room of the apartment. Gao Mai sat down at the table and helped herself to dried meat, eel and pickled cucumber.

58

Informal Assessment

Observe individual students as they read and use the Teacher Observation Log found in the *Program Assessment Teacher's Edition* to record anecdotal information about each student's strengths and weaknesses.

Teacher Tip SUMMARIZING If students are having problems with summarizing, remind them that summaries include only main and supporting information about a selection. Trivial and repetitive information should be left out of their summaries.

The dream was fresh in her mind. "I'm not sure," she said.

"Remember what I told you," said Gao Mai's father. "Imagine the abacus is part of you." He smiled at her. "You did so well when we practiced."

It was true. During a few of her many timed drills she was even faster than her father. And he used the abacus every day at the bank.

"Don't worry," said her mother. "You're one of the best abacus students in your class."

"But what about Li Zhi?" asked Gao Mai. "She's beaten me every year."

❷ "Last time it was only by one second. You've improved so much, I'm sure you'll win. Besides," continued her mother, as she lit the incense on the altar where the family ancestors were honored, "you were born under the lucky sign of the horse. I went to the temple yesterday and said a special prayer for you."

Gao Mai looked at her watch. "I have to go."

"Good luck," said her mother.

"Good luck," said her father. "I'll be thinking about you all morning."

Gao Mai ran downstairs to the street and walked quickly through the open market. One farmer had spread a piece of burlap on the pavement and piled it high with cut sugarcane. Her mouth watered as she thought of sucking the sweet juice from the snowy white center. Gao Mai glanced at the fish swimming around in a shallow metal pan. Tonight they would be on someone's plate, maybe even her own.

59

Teacher Tip PRONUNCIATION
Some students may be confused because of the culturally diverse names and references in this selection. Tell the students how to pronounce the names properly: *Gao Mai* is pronounced **gou mī**, and *Li Zhi* is pronounced **lē djē**. Invite the students to share what they know about Taiwan's culture.

Comprehension Skills

Second Read

Sequence

Introduce students to the concept of *sequence*. Tell the students that writers often place story events in a certain sequence, or order. This helps the reader locate and recall important events and understand how one event relates to another. Writers often use *time words* and *order words* to help readers follow the sequence.

- "Good Luck," said her father. "I'll be thinking about you all *morning*." (page 59)

- "*Tonight* they will be on someone's plate, maybe even her own." (page 59)

Explain to students that these words give clues to tell what time of day it is.

Word Knowledge

SCAFFOLDING The skills students are reviewing in Word Knowledge should help them in reading the story. This lesson focuses on words with the long e spelled *ea*. Long e words will be found in boxes similar to this one throughout the selection.

Long e spelled *ea*:

    beaten   dream

Skills Trace

Sequence

Introduced in Grade 2.
Scaffolded in Grades 3–5.

REINTRODUCED:	Unit 1, Lesson 4
REINFORCED:	Unit 4, Lesson 2
	Unit 5, Lesson 3
	Unit 6, Lesson 1
TESTED:	Unit 1 Assessment

Second Reading Recommendation

ORAL • **SILENT**

COMPREHENSION

COMPREHENSION

Comprehension Strategies

 First Read

Teacher Modeling

❸ Monitoring and Clarifying *It is important to monitor your reading for words and ideas that you don't understand and clarify them right away. This way, you avoid confusion further into your reading. Jian zhi is an unfamiliar game to me. I remember we talked about how this game is played before we began reading the selection. You kick something called a jian zhi into the air, and the more times you can kick it before it hits the ground, the more points you have. I can clarify this game a little more by connecting it to a game I know that seems similar, one that is played with a small, round bean bag.*

Teacher Modeling

❹ Monitoring and Clarifying
This is another phrase I don't understand. Ni Hao must be a Taiwanese phrase. I can clarify it with context clues. Because the teacher is asking a question first thing in the morning and the class has just stood up to greet him, I think it might mean, "How is everyone today?"

What else should be clarified before we go on?

Word Knowledge
Long e spelled *ea*:
reached   beaten   leaned   teacher

Teacher Tip
Kun Pei is pronounced **ko͞on pī.**
Da Wei is pronounced **da wā.**
Jian zhi is pronounced **zhyan djē.**
Ni hao is pronounced **nē hou.**

❸ She reached the school just as the bell rang. Outside her classroom some boys were playing jian zhi. Her classmate, Kun Pei, scored one point after another by kicking the jian zhi into the air over and over again without letting it hit the ground.

Gao Mai walked into the classroom and Kun Pei yelled: "I won!"

During last year's abacus contest Li Zhi had beaten Kun Pei by four seconds, and Gao Mai had beaten him by three seconds. Today she was hoping to beat both of them.

Gao Mai watched Li Zhi's braids bounce as she tapped everyone on the way to her desk. She knew Li Zhi loved practical jokes and could tell by her <u>mischievous</u> look that she might play one at any moment. Gao Mai smiled while thinking of jokes they had played on their classmates together. Last week they had even played one on Li Zhi's mother. Yesterday Li Zhi had invited her to come over after school today so that they could think of a trick to play on her brother, Da Wei.

"Don't forget who won last year," said Li Zhi, sitting down behind her. She tugged on Gao Mai's ponytail and giggled.

"That was last year." Gao Mai leaned away and said, "If you pull my hair again, I'm not going to your house today."

Li Zhi leaned forward to grab Gao Mai's ponytail but only caught the tip. Gao Mai started to say: That's it, I'm not going to your house today. But the teacher arrived and the class stood up to greet him.

❹ "Ni hao?" said Mr. Wang. "While everyone is nice and fresh, we'll begin with the abacus contest." He passed out <u>booklets</u> filled with addition, subtraction, multiplication and division problems.

 60

MEETING INDIVIDUAL NEEDS

Intervention Support

CLARIFYING Have students identify parts of the text that are unclear. If they are having difficulty with clarifying, have them share ideas with a partner on how best to clear up anything that is confusing.

COMPREHENSION

"Open to the first page and begin with number one. When all the exercises are completed, return your booklet to my desk and I'll write the final time. Ready?" He paused. "Begin!"

Gao Mai's left hand moved down the column of numbers rapidly, wrote the answers and turned the test pages. The fingers on her right hand flew back and forth among the smooth, black beads of the abacus.

In a few minutes she was writing the last answer to the addition problems. Gao Mai began subtracting and a moment later heard pages turning. Everyone was right behind her!

She worked carefully. It was easy to make a subtraction mistake, especially when exchanging a higher bead for lesser ones.

After finishing the last subtraction problem she heard Li Zhi's page turn.

Gao Mai frantically turned to the multiplication but two pages were stuck together. She pulled them apart with shaking hands.

Barely breathing, Gao Mai sped through the multiplication and division. Finally she wrote down the last answer, jumped from her seat and collided with Li Zhi.

(61)

Comprehension Skills

Sequence

Review with students the concept of sequence. Ask students to list several time words and order words. Then, have students identify time words and order words in the text.

- "*In a few minutes* she was writing the last answer to the addition problems." (page 61)
- "Gao Mai *began* subtracting and *a moment later* heard pages turning." (page 61)

Word Knowledge
Long e spelled *ea*:
beads   easy   breathing   seat

Teacher Tip CHARACTERIZATION
During reading, have students discuss ways the author allows readers to understand what kind of people the characters are through their reactions to story events.

Teacher Tip FLUENCY By this time in grade 5, good readers should be reading approximately 126 words per minute with fluency and expression. The only way to gain this fluency is through practice. Have students reread the selection to you and to one another during Workshop to help build fluency.

Science/Social Studies Connection Center
Refer to the Science/Social Studies Connection Center Card 6 for a science activity that students can investigate.

Comprehension Strategies

First Read

Teacher Modeling

⑤ Predicting *It looks as if Gao Mai and Li Zhi are going to lose, just because they ran into each other. I don't think that's fair at all. I predict that the teacher will take that into account. Let's keep reading to find out.*

As we continue reading, see if you can predict what is going to happen next. Maybe some of you will share your predictions with us.

Teacher Modeling

⑥ Confirming Predictions *I see that my prediction was correct. The teacher looked at how many they got right and their time to decide the winner. It was fair after all.*

The prediction I made at the beginning of the selection also came true: Li Zhi is not angry with Gao Mai. They're going to spend time together after school.

Discussing Strategy Use

While students are reading the selection, encourage them to share any problems encountered and to tell what strategies they used.

- Where did they pause in reading to summarize?
- How did they clarify confusing passages?
- What predictions did they make?

Make sure students explain how using the strategies helped them better understand the selection. For example, students might say, "Clarifying words I didn't understand right away helped me to understand the whole story."

⑤ Two desks in front of them, Kun Pei rushed up and dropped his booklet on the teacher's desk.

"Oh, no!" yelled Li Zhi. "It's not fair!" She and Gao Mai dropped their booklets on the desk immediately after him.

"Quiet down, everyone," said the teacher.

Gao Mai returned to her desk and <u>slumped</u> in the seat, unaware of the other students handing in their booklets. Her bad dream had come true.

"Time for recess," said Mr. Wang, "while I check the answers."

Gao Mai was the last to go outside.

"Come on," yelled Ping Mei, wanting her to come and jump rope. But she shook her head. Across the playground, Li Zhi motioned for her to come and play tag with some of their friends. But Gao Mai turned away.

As he kicked the jian zhi into the air, Kun Pei bragged to a group of boys about winning the abacus contest. Gao Mai thought of her father's jian zhi at home on top of the TV. Father! Gao Mai knew he'd be disappointed that she hadn't won. The bell rang and everyone piled back into the classroom.

She heard Li Zhi behind her, laughing. "Hurry up, slowpoke!" she said, pushing past her.

Gao Mai secretly wished she could be carefree, like Li Zhi.

MEETING INDIVIDUAL NEEDS

ELL

SUMMING UP AND ASKING QUESTIONS
These are valuable tools for English-language learners and should be used even more often than by other students.

◆ Informal Assessment

Use the Informal Comprehension Strategies Rubrics on page 58J to determine whether a student is using the strategies being taught.

Mr. Wang stood up with the winning certificates in his hand. "Third-place winner of this year's abacus contest is Zong Zong."

The class applauded and a small girl with thick glasses walked quickly to the front of the room and shook hands with the teacher.

"The second-place certificate goes to Kun Pei," Mr. Wang continued.

Kun Pei came forward, looking as if he were about to cry.

"You were first to get your booklet in," Mr. Wang said as he handed him a certificate. "But one answer was wrong."

Gao Mai was confused. She turned around and looked into Li Zhi's bewildered face.

"Now," began the teacher, "we have an unusual situation—one that has never happened to me before. First place in speed and accuracy goes to Li Zhi, last year's first-place winner, and also to Gao Mai, last year's second-place winner."

Gao Mai turned and looked at Li Zhi. They burst out laughing and hurried to the front of the room.

"Here's a first-place certificate for both of you," said Mr. Wang.

As Gao Mai shook hands with the teacher, she decided it was a good day to go to Li Zhi's, after all.

(6)

Teacher Tip BUILDING FLUENCY
As students read, you may notice that some need work in building fluency. During Workshop, have these students choose a section of the text (a minimum of 160 words) to read several times in order to build fluency.

Formal Assessment
See pages 14–17 in the *Unit 1 Assessment* book to test students' comprehension of "The Abacus Contest."

Comprehension Skills

Second Read

Sequence

Point out that the sequence of events in this story is recorded in chronological, or time, order. Have students identify the order in which the teacher distributed the winning certificates.

- "Third-place winner of this year's abacus contest is Zong Zong."
- "The second-place certificate goes to Kun Pei."
- "First place in speed and accuracy goes to Li Zhi . . . and also to Gao Mai . . ."

Checking Comprehension

Ask students the following questions to check their comprehension of the story.

- How is Gao Mai like Lupe from "The Marble Champ" and Cricket from "Class President"? How is she different? *(Answers will vary but might include that Gao Mai is driven like the other characters but less ruthless than Cricket.)*
- What would have happened to Gao Mai and Li Zhi if Gao Mai had lost again? Would they still be good friends? *(Answers will vary but may include that the girls' humor and mutual response would protect the friendship.)*
- How has this selection connected with your knowledge of the unit theme? *(Answers will vary—students should compare/contrast examples of cooperation and competition from this selection with their own experiences or past reading and use these connections to make a general statement about the unit theme.)*

COMPREHENSION

Routine Card
Refer to Routine 5 for the
handing-off process.

Clues	Problems	Wonderings
big day realistic fiction	abacus pickled eel altar incense culturally diverse names and words	Where does the story take place? Why is it a "big day"?

SRA OPEN COURT READING
Reading Transparency 54

Reading Transparency 54

www.sra4kids.com
Web Connection
Some students may choose to
conduct a computer search for
additional books or information
about cooperation and competition. Invite them
to make a list of these books and sources of
information to share with classmates and the
school librarian. Check the Reading link of the
SRA Web page for additional links to theme-
related Web sites.

Discussing the Selection

The whole group discusses the selection and any personal thoughts, reactions, problems, or questions that it raises. To stimulate discussion, students can ask one another the kinds of questions that good readers ask themselves about a text: *How does it connect to cooperation and competition? What have I learned that is new? What did I find interesting? What is important here? What was difficult to understand? Why would someone want to read this?* It is important for students to see you as a contributing member of the group.

Routine 5 To emphasize that you are part of the group, actively participate in the *handing-off process:* Raise your hand to be called on by the last speaker when you have a contribution to make. Point out unusual and interesting insights verbalized by students so that these insights are recognized and discussed. As the year progresses, students will take more and more responsibility for the discussion of selections.

Engage students in a discussion to determine whether they have grasped the following ideas:

- how competition affected Gao Mai
- how competition affected Gao Mai's friendship with Li Zhi

During this time, have students return to the clues, problems, and wonderings that they noted during browsing to determine whether the clues were borne out by the selection, whether and how their problems were solved, and whether their wonderings were answered or deserve further discussion and exploration. Let the students decide which items deserve further discussion.

Also have students return to the Focus Questions on the first page of the selection. Select a student to read the questions aloud, and have volunteers answer the questions. If students do not know the answers to the questions, have them return to the text to find the answers.

You may also wish to review the elements of realistic fiction with the students at this time. Discuss with them how they can tell that "The Abacus Contest" is realistic fiction.

Have students break into small groups to discuss how the story reflects the theme. Groups can then share ideas with the rest of the class.

Writer's Notebook
Students may wish to record their thoughts about and reactions to this selection. Encourage students to write about how competition has affected their friendships.

Teacher Tip SELECTION VOCABULARY Encourage students to use the selection vocabulary words in their writing and investigation projects for the unit theme.

Review Selection Vocabulary

Have students review the definitions of the selection vocabulary words that they wrote in the vocabulary section of their Writer's Notebooks. Remind them that they discussed the meanings of these words before reading the selection. Students can use these definitions to study for the Vocabulary portion of their Lesson Assessment. Have them add to the Personal Dictionary section of their Writer's Notebook any other interesting words that they clarified while reading. Encourage students to refer to the selection vocabulary words throughout the unit. The words from the selection are:

abacus   drills   mischievous   collided   accuracy

If you have created a Word Bank, have students place words under the appropriate headings on the Word Bank. Encourage the students to find other words related to the unit theme and add them to the Word Bank.

View Fine Art

This example of an abacus that was used by early Romans can also be found on page 56. This type of mathematical tool for calculating equations has been used for hundreds of years by a variety of cultures. Have students share their experiences with using or seeing abacuses. Does this abacus look similar to or different from others they have seen?

Student Anthology p. 56

Home Connection

Distribute **Home Connection,** page 9. Encourage students to discuss "The Abacus Contest" with their families. Students can discuss the use of modern equipment vs. the use of older equipment with their families. **Home Connection** is also available in Spanish, page 10.

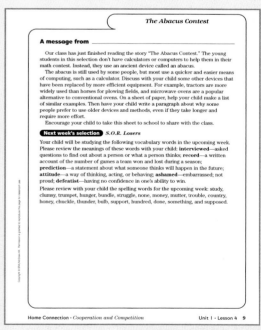

Home Connection p. 9

Teacher Tip TIME WORDS AND ORDER WORDS Before you give students the list of time words and order words, challenge students to list as many as possible on their own. Then ask students why it is important to use these kinds of words in writing.

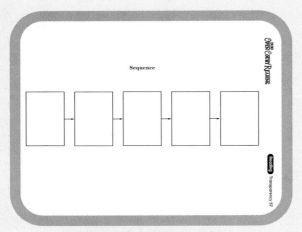

Sequence

Reading Transparency 57

Supporting the Reading

Comprehension Skills: Sequence

Teach Have students tell you what they know about sequence. Then tell them that, to help readers make sense of what they read, writers show the sequence, or order, of events by using time words and order words. Time words include *yesterday, today, tomorrow, this afternoon, morning, night, minute, suddenly,* and *last year,* to name a few. Order words include *first, second, last, after, before, next, finally,* and *then.*

Guided Practice To help students visualize the order of events in "The Abacus Contest," use the flowchart on ***Reading Transparency 57.*** Ask students to provide the main events of the story, and then have them order the events in the flowchart. Discuss how the author made the order of events clear.

Independent Practice Read through the **Focus** and **Identify** sections of *Comprehension and Language Arts Skills,* page 16 with students. Guide students through the **Identify** portion, and help them come up with examples found in the story. Then have students complete the **Practice** and **Apply** portions of *Comprehension and Language Arts Skills,* page 17, as homework.

Link to Writing Have students think of a time in their lives when they completed a task, such as making cookies with a friend or family member or putting together a puzzle. Describe the process of the task using order words. When students have completed their descriptions, have them discuss how the order words clarified the sequence of events.

Comprehension and Language Arts Skills pp. 16–17

Research in Action
Writing

Reading and writing go hand-in-hand. Students should always be encouraged to notice and comment on outstanding writing as they are reading. Students should be encouraged to use these ideas in their own writing. *(Marlene Scardamalia)*

Skills Trace
Sequence

Introduced in Grade 1.
Scaffolded throughout Grades 2–5.
REINTRODUCED: Unit 1, Lesson 4
REINFORCED: Unit 4, Lesson 2
Unit 5, Lesson 3
Unit 6, Lesson 1
TESTED: Unit 1 Assessment

Literary Elements

Conflict

Teach Have students tell you what they know about *conflict*. If necessary, explain to students that conflict is a struggle a main character has during a story. Tell students that most stories focus on a struggle and its outcome. Share the following information about conflict with students.

- If a conflict is external, the character struggles with an outside force, such as another person or nature.
- If a conflict is internal, the character struggles with something inside himself or herself. Characters often struggle over choices to be made or how to behave.
- Usually a conflict is introduced at the beginning of a story and resolved at the end of the story.

Guided Practice Ask students to identify the conflicts in "The Abacus Contest." *(Possible answers include Gao Mai's anxiety over the contest and Gao Mai's competition with her best friend.)* Then have students tell whether the conflicts are internal or external. *(Gao Mai's anxiety is internal and her competition with Li Zhi is external.)* Finally, have students explain how each conflict is resolved. *(Both conflicts are resolved when the two friends tie for first place in the contest.)*

Independent Practice Have students review "Class President" and "Juggling" and identify the main conflict in each. Students should also note whether the conflicts are internal or external, and how they are resolved. Have students choose an event from one of the stories, such as the meeting with Mr. Herbertson or the election in "Class President," or Kyle's amazing performance as a server in gym class in "Juggling." Have students write paragraphs describing the main conflict of the story their event is from, and how this event contributed either to the development or to the solution of the story's conflict.

Science Connection: The Steps of Digestion

Remind students of Gao Mai's breakfast of pickled cucumber, eel, dried meat, and rice in "The Abacus Contest." After Gao Mai eats her breakfast, the story moves on to her abacus contest. Though she may have thought little about it, Gao Mai's digestive system would have been hard at work digesting her food while she feverishly worked the abacus beads.

Divide the students into several groups. Instruct the groups to research the digestive system using the library or their science textbooks. Assign each group the task of creating a poster diagramming one of the following parts of the digestive system: the teeth and mouth; esophagus; stomach; small and large intestines; and colon. Have students label each organ with its function and order in the sequence of digestion. Once the posters have been created, have each group present their poster, sharing their knowledge of the digestive system with the rest of the class.

Teacher Tip MATERIALS FOR ACTIVITY To complete the Science Connection activity for this lesson, students will need posterboard, markers, and colored pencils.

Meet the Author

After the students read the information about Priscilla Wu, discuss the following questions with them.

- Priscilla Wu's father, grandfather, and grandmother were writers. How do you think this influenced her decision to become one? *(Possible answer: Writing has special memories for her, as does sitting around with her family telling stories. She wanted to share her talents with others, especially her children.)*

- "Writing is very hard work, but the hard work makes a difference," says Priscilla Wu. Why do you think she believes this? *(Possible answer: She doesn't want others to be discouraged about their writing. The pleasure and pride that come from writing are from all the effort she puts into it.)*

Meet the Illustrator

After the students read the information about Yoshi Miyaki, discuss the following questions with them.

- Yoshi Miyake didn't study art in college. She studied science. Why do you think she moved to Chicago to study art after college? *(Possible answer: The correspondence class she took made her realize that she wanted to be an artist, so she followed her dream and became one.)*

The Abacus Contest

Meet the Author

Priscilla Wu comes from a family full of writers. Her father and grandfather write books, and her grandmother had some articles published in a newspaper. Says Priscilla, *"My dad, I remember him in the basement pounding away on a typewriter. . . . And from my dad's side—he was from the South—there was a tradition of storytelling. I grew up with many stories, or tall tales. . . . And I did the same thing with my own children. We had a lot of storytelling. We used to sit around in the dark at night, and sometimes, rather than read a story, we would tell stories."* Priscilla went on to become a writer herself, but not because writing came easily to her. *"I wasn't a very good writer in school. I've had to work very hard, and I think it is important to let students know that working hard* does *make a difference."*

Meet the Illustrator

Yoshi Miyake was born in Tokyo, Japan. She graduated from the Tokyo Metropolitan University with a degree in chemistry. While in college, she took a correspondence class in art. After graduation, she moved to Chicago to attend the American Academy of Art. She later opened a gallery called American West. Her long-time interest in Native American culture, and her study of the Blackfoot and Sioux languages inspired the theme of this gallery. Yoshi Miyake is the illustrator of more than a dozen children's books.

64

Theme Connections

Within the Selection

Record your answers to the questions below in the Response Journal section of your Writer's Notebook. In small groups, report the ideas you wrote. Discuss your ideas with the rest of your group. Then choose a person to report your group's answers to the class.

- How did the attitude of Gao Mai's parents toward the contest affect her own attitude?
- Why did Gao Mai feel it was unfair for Kun Pei to have his test booklet turned in before hers?
- What might have happened to Gao Mai's friendship with Li Zhi if there had been no tie?

Across Selections

- In what way is Gao Mai's attitude toward the abacus competition similar to Lupe's in "The Marble Champ"? In what way is it different?
- Compare the way Gao Mai responds to her parents' interest in the abacus competition with the way Lupe responds to hers.

Beyond the Selection

- Tell about a time when you competed against a friend. How did you feel? How did it affect your friendship?
- Think about how "The Abacus Contest" adds to what you know about cooperation and competition.
- Add items to the Concept/Question Board about cooperation and competition.

65

Theme Connections

Within the Selection

- Gao Mai's parents are confident in her, so she doesn't want to disappoint them.
- Kun Pei got his paper in first because Gao Mai and Li Zhi collided, not because he finished first.
- Their friendship is probably strong enough to last. After all, they were friends despite Li Zhi's victory in the competition the prior year.

Across Selections

- Both Gao Mai and Lupe are determined to win, but Gao Mai's friendship with her closest competitor complicates her competition.
- Gao Mai feels added pressure, but Lupe does not.

Beyond the Selection

- Answers will vary.

Students should record their ideas and impressions about the selections on page 7 of their **Inquiry Journals.**

- "The Abacus Contest" by Priscilla Wu
  Answers will vary.

- "S.O.R. Losers" by Avi
  Answers will vary.

- "Founders of the Children's Rain Forest" by Phillip Hoose
  Answers will vary.

Inquiry Journal • *Recording Concept Information*　　　UNIT I　**7**

Inquiry Journal p. 7

Teacher Tip INQUIRY AND INVESTIGATION Have groups report and discuss their ideas with the class. As these ideas are stated, have students add them to the Concept/Question Board. As students complete their discussions, have them sum up what they have learned and tell how they might use this information in further investigations.

✓ **Informal Assessment**

This might be a good time to observe students working in small groups and to mark your observations in the Teacher Observation Log found in the *Program Assessment Teacher's Edition.*

Objectives

- Students gain a deeper understanding of cooperation and competition.
- Students establish investigation needs.
- Students practice using charts and diagrams.

Materials

- Student Anthology, pp. 58–65
- Inquiry Journal, pp. 20–23
- Research Assistant
- Reading Transparency 2, 58

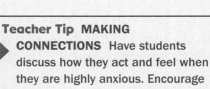

Teacher Tip MAKING CONNECTIONS Have students discuss how they act and feel when they are highly anxious. Encourage them to think of ways they can incorporate realistic emotions in their unit activities.

INVESTIGATION

Investigating Concepts Beyond the Text

To facilitate students' investigation of cooperation and competition, you might have them participate in the following activities. Tell students that if they have activity ideas of their own that they would like to pursue, they are free to do so as an alternative to these activity suggestions. For example, students may want to pursue activities of their own choosing that relate more directly to the problems and questions they are investigating with their groups. Tell students that they may work on these activities alone, in pairs, or in small groups, with an option to write about them or to present them to the group upon completion.

The activity suggestions for this lesson are:

- Give students a firsthand experience with cooperation and competition by testing their knowledge in a class spelling contest. Set a date for the contest, provide materials to study, and have the students decide as a group what rules will govern the contest. Tell students to have family members and friends help them read and organize the information in the study materials to help them prepare for the contest.

  Conduct the contest. After the contest has been completed, have the class discuss what the contest taught them about cooperation and competition. Students may want to comment on how cooperation was demonstrated when the rules for the contest were decided as a class and when family members and friends helped them to prepare. Students also may wish to discuss how competing made them feel (for example, focused, anxious, or excited).

Upon completion of their activities, have students share with the group anything new they learned about cooperation and competition through discussion and by adding information to the Concept/Question Board.

Concept/Question Board

After reading each selection, students should use the Concept/Question Board to

- post any questions they asked about a selection before reading that have not yet been answered.
- refer to as they formulate statements about concepts that apply to their investigations.
- post general statements formulated by each collaborative group.
- continue to post news articles, or other items that they find during the unit investigation.
- read and think about posted questions, articles, or concepts that interest them and provide answers to the questions.

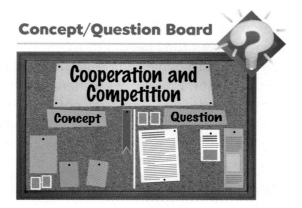

Concept/Question Board

Research Assistant

The Research Assistant helps students in their investigations.

www.sra4kids.com
Web Connection
Students can use the connections to Cooperation and Competition in the Reading link of the SRA Web page for more background information about cooperation and competition.

Teacher Tip INVESTIGATION ACTIVITIES To help students focus their investigation, have them frequently consult the Concept/ Question Board for ideas about and examples of cooperation and competition.

Unit I Investigation Management

Lesson I	Students generate ideas for investigation.
Lesson 2	Students formulate questions and problems for investigation.
Lesson 3	Students make conjectures.
Lesson 4	**Collaborative Investigation** **Students establish investigation needs.** **Supplementary Activities** **Students participate in investigation activities and learn to use charts and diagrams.**
Lesson 5	Students establish investigation plans.
Lesson 6	Students present investigation findings.

Name_____ Date_____
UNIT I Cooperation and Competition
Project Planning
Use the calendar to help schedule your cooperation and competition unit investigation. Fill in the dates. Make sure that you mark any days you know you will not be able to work. Then choose the date on which you will start and the date on

Sunday	Monday	Tuesday	Wednesday

20 UNIT I   *Project Planning • Inquiry Journal*

Inquiry Journal p. 20

Name_____ Date_____
UNIT I Cooperation and Competition
Establishing Investigation Needs
My group's question or problem:
Answers will vary.

Knowledge Needs—Information I need to find or figure out in order to investigate the question or problem: Answers will vary.
A. ____
B. ____
C. ____
D. ____
E. ____

Source	Useful?	How?
Encyclopedias		
Books		
Magazines		
Newspapers		
Videotapes, filmstrips, and so on		
Television		
Interviews, observations		
Museums		
Other:		

22 UNIT I   *Establishing Investigation Needs • Inquiry Journal*

Inquiry Journal p. 22

INVESTIGATION

Establishing Investigation Needs

By now, the students should have produced conjectures regarding their chosen investigation problems and discussed them in their investigation groups. A whole-class discussion of these conjectures may now be conducted, in which problems and conjectures are briefly presented and all students have a chance to contribute suggestions, constructive criticisms, and questions. These ideas should help the investigation groups establish what knowledge and resources they will need to acquire for their investigations.

To help groups get started in identifying the information they need to find or figure out in order to investigate their problems, you might focus on one of the conjectures that came out of the previous discussion. Pose questions, such as *What facts will we need to decide whether or not this conjecture is right? Where can we look for these facts? What would an expert on this problem know that we do not know?* Tell students that the manner in which they want to present their investigation findings to the group might also affect the resources they need. For example, a student who decides to make a poster might want to collect photographs and illustrations from magazines to place on the poster. Encourage students to begin thinking of interesting ways to present the information they collect. You may want to display again the Unit 1 Investigation Possibilities menu on *Reading Transparency 2* to get students started. Encourage them to come up with their own presentation ideas, as well. Then have them complete *Inquiry Journal,* page 22.

Then outline a schedule for students of how much time will be available until the first presentation will be due. Most projects should be completed at the time you finish the unit. Inform the students, however, that some projects take longer. Help groups set goals for their investigations on the calendar in their *Inquiry Journal,* pages 20–21. Tell them that their goals should include due dates for obtaining certain information and time for organizing and publishing their findings. Tell them to make note of their accomplishments each day. This will help them monitor their progress and will enable you to help them manage their time. Suggest that they record dates on the calendar in pencil, since schedules often need to be revised.

Using Charts and Diagrams

Teach Explain to students that charts and diagrams can be useful for organizing information quickly and easily. Charts and graphs can display a lot of information in a small place. Explain that different charts are used for different purposes. Remind students that they used a flowchart in studying about Sequence. Remind them also of the Clues/Problems/Wonderings chart they use before reading each selection. Discuss how these charts help them to organize and understand information quickly. Introduce students to the Venn Diagram. Display *Reading Transparency 58.* Explain that Venn diagrams are used to compare and contrast two things. Qualities that are individual to each thing are written in the outer circles; similarities are placed in the overlap.

Guided Practice Label the circles on the Venn Diagram "Gao Mai" and "Li Zhi." Using the Venn Diagram, have students compare and contrast the competitive personalities of Gao Mai and Li Zhi from "The Abacus Contest." After the diagram is completed, discuss the results. Point out that the Venn Diagram contains a lot of information about Gao Mai and Li Zhi's similarities and differences, and all can be seen at a glance.

Independent Practice Have students think of ways they can organize information from their investigations using charts and diagrams.

For more practice with organizing information using charts and diagrams, have students complete *Inquiry Journal,* page 23.

Teacher Tip STUDENT WRITING AND RESEARCH CENTER Have students use the *Student Writing and Research Center CD-ROM* as they work on their investigation activities.

Teacher Tip USING A COMPUTER Encourage students to use *Basic Computer Skills* to learn how to use a computer to write a report.

SUPPORTING THE INVESTIGATION

Inquiry Journal p. 23

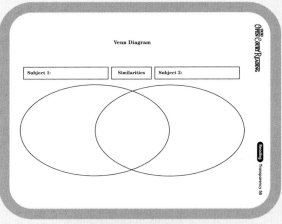

Reading Transparency 58

Objectives

Word Analysis

Spelling
- **Spelling Patterns for the /i/ Sound.** Develop understanding of spelling patterns for the /i/ sound introduced in Word Knowledge in Part 1.

Vocabulary
- Using words from "The Abacus Contest," practice using the dictionary to explore word meanings.

Writing Process Strategies
- **The Process of Revising.** Learn to revise by adding, deleting, consolidating, rearranging, and clarifying writing material and ideas. Learn to use proofreading marks during the revising process.

English Language Conventions

Grammar, Usage, and Mechanics
- **Sentences.** Understand kinds of sentences, ending punctuation of sentences, and capitalization of the first word in a sentence and identify them in "The Abacus Contest."

Listening, Speaking, Viewing
- **Viewing: Viewing the Media.** Develop viewing skills through examining the content of visual media messages.

Penmanship
- **Cursive Letters *p* and *j*.** Develop handwriting skills by practicing formation of cursive *p* and *j*.

Materials

- Spelling and Vocabulary Skills, pp. 14–17
- Language Arts Handbook
- Comprehension and Language Arts Skills, pp. 18–21
- Language Arts Transparencies 11–15, 26
- Student Anthology
- Unit 1 Assessment, pp. 32–33

MEETING INDIVIDUAL NEEDS

Reteach, Challenge, English-Language Development and *Intervention* lessons are available to support the language arts instruction in this lesson.

Research in Action

. . . instruction designed to develop children's sensitivity to spellings and their relations to pronunciations should be of paramount importance . . . (*Marilyn Adams*, Beginning to Read: Thinking and Learning About Print)

Language Arts Overview

Word Analysis

Spelling The spelling activities on the following pages support the Word Knowledge introduction of the /i/ sound by developing understanding of the spelling patterns for short *i*.

Selection Spelling Words

These words from "The Abacus Contest" contain the /i/ sound.

mistake   **giggled**   **quilt**   **begin**   **division**

Vocabulary The vocabulary activities encourage use of a dictionary to determine more than just one definition for an unknown word.

Vocabulary Skill Words

abacus   **aroma**   **incense**   **mischievous***   **frantically**

*Also Selection Vocabulary.

Additional Materials

On Days 3 and 4, students will need dictionaries.

Writing Process Strategies

This Writing Process Strategies lesson includes instruction on the revision process for both a drafted essay and student autobiographies.

Basic Computer Skills To learn basic computer skills for writing, have students practice keying the **U** and **C**, **W** and right **Shift** keys, **B** and **Y**, **M** and **X**, **P** and **V**, **Q** and **Comma**, and **Z** and **Colon** keys. *Basic Computer Skills* Level 5 Lessons 12–15 teach these keyboarding skills.

English Language Conventions

Grammar, Usage, and Mechanics **Sentences.** This lesson develops understanding of kinds of sentences and their correct capitalization and ending punctuation. Students will identify the kinds of sentences and practice using them in writing.

Listening, Speaking, Viewing **Viewing: Viewing the Media.** This is the first of the Viewing lessons. Students will examine a magazine advertisement provided by the teacher and interpret its message.

Penmanship **Cursive Letters *p* and *j*.** This lesson continues the development of handwriting skills. Students learn correct formation of *p* and *j* and then practice writing paragraphs from the literature selections.

DAY 1

Word Analysis	Writing Process Strategies	English Language Conventions

Spelling

Assessment: Pretest

Spelling Patterns for the /i/ Sound
Give students the Pretest on page 32 of *Unit 1 Assessment.* Have them proofread and correct any misspellings.

Pretest Sentences
1. **width**   Measure the **width** of the room.
2. **glimpse**   I caught a **glimpse** of the taxi.
3. **twist**   I had to **twist** my hair to put it into a bun.
4. **blizzard**   The electricity might go off during a **blizzard.**
5. **lyrics**   What are the **lyrics** of the song?
6. **simple**   The furniture had a **simple** design.
7. **built**   The pyramids in Egypt were **built** without modern equipment.
8. **system**   Nine planets make up our solar **system.**
9. **igloo**   An **igloo** is made of ice.
10. **mystery**   Read a **mystery** novel.
11. **limit**   The speed **limit** is different in many states.
12. **visit**   Grandparents appreciate an occasional **visit.**
13. **imitate**   Some comedians like to **imitate** famous people.
14. **whistle**   The referee blows the **whistle.**
15. **thrift**   Take old clothes to a **thrift** store.
16. **mistake**   A **mistake** can be positive.
17. **giggled**   We **giggled** when we saw his hat blow away.
18. **quilt**   A **quilt** is a precious gift.
19. **begin**   You may **begin** your tests.
20. **division**   Did you learn **division?**

Introduction to the Writing Process: Revising

Adding Material

Teach

■ Have students read *Language Arts Handbook* pages 38–39. Go over with students what revising involves: changing what is written to make it clearer, interesting, and more enjoyable to read.

• Show *Transparency 26— Proofreading Marks* and go over the marks commonly used in revising *(add, delete, transpose).*

Guided Practice

Show students *Transparency 11— Adding Copy* and go over ways to improve a draft by adding copy. Have students each draft an essay about a time when they put pressure on themselves as Gao Mai did in "The Abacus Contest." Have students revise by adding precise words that support the story line and then place their drafts in their *Writing Folders.*

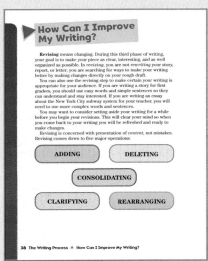

Language Arts Handbook p. 38

Grammar, Usage, and Mechanics:

Sentences

Teach

■ Refer to *Language Arts Handbook* page 363 for examples of the four kinds of sentences.

■ Explain that there are four kinds of sentences as listed below.

• A **declarative** sentence makes a statement. It always ends with a period. *She wrote her friend a letter.*

• An **interrogative** sentence asks a question. It ends with a question mark. *Did she put a stamp on the envelope?*

• An **imperative** sentence gives a command or makes a request. It usually ends with a period. Sometimes it ends with an exclamation point. *Please bring me that plate. Do it now!*

• An **exclamatory** sentence expresses a strong feeling. It ends with an exclamation point. *What a fabulous touchdown!*

Independent Practice

Have students complete *Comprehension and Language Arts Skills,* pages 18–19, for practice on kinds of sentences.

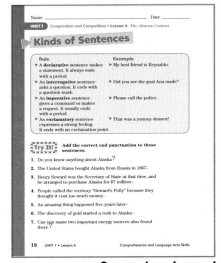

Comprehension and Language Arts Skills p. 18

DAY 2

Word Analysis

Spelling

Word Sorting

Open Word Sort Have students sort the spelling words by their spelling patterns for the /i / sound. Have students explain their answers.

Vocabulary

Dictionary Skills

Teach

■ Write the following dictionary entry on the board. Point out the multiple definitions, the example sentence, the syllable breakdown, the pronunciation, the part of speech, and the other forms of the word.

> **distribute** 1. To give out in shares: *The teacher distributed new books to the class.* 2. To spread something out over a large area; scatter: *The farm machines distributed seed over the plowed field.* **dis trib ute** (di strib´ ūt) *verb*, **distributed, distributing**.

Guided Practice

Assign page 14 of *Spelling and Vocabulary Skills.* Students can complete page 15 of *Spelling and Vocabulary Skills* for homework.

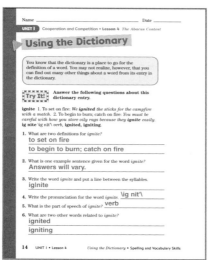

Spelling and Vocabulary Skills p. 14

Writing Process Strategies

Introduction to the Writing Process: Revising

Deleting Material

Teach

■ Read *Language Arts Handbook* page 40. Remind students that their goal in the revising process is to change what they have written to make it clearer, more interesting, and enjoyable to read. One way to do this is by deleting material from their drafts. Explain that they should delete words and sentences if doing so will improve a draft for any of the following reasons.

• A sentence or perhaps an entire paragraph strays from the subject.

• Too many sentences have been used to say what could have been said with just a few words.

• The word choice and content is inappropriate for the audience.

• Words have been repeated.

■ For the last two items, *substitutions* may be in order. For example, if students are writing for a younger audience who will not understand some of the words they used, they can substitute simpler words for the more difficult words. Repeated words sometimes occur when a word is used twice by accident and can easily be deleted. Other times, a word is used repeatedly because it is the subject or has a strong connection to it. If a word is used over and over so that it is tiresome to read, synonyms may be used.

■ Another strategy for revising is *sentence lifting.* (See Appendix page 31 for more information.)

Guided Practice

Show students *Transparency 12—Deleting Copy* and go over the reasons and ways to delete material. Have students delete copy from the drafts they wrote last week.

English Language Conventions

Grammar, Usage, and Mechanics:
Sentences

Teach

■ Review the four kinds of sentences, their ending punctuation, and capitalizing the first word in a sentence.

■ Write the following sentences on the board and have students suggest ending punctuation. Have a student read aloud each sentence with the proper inflection and emphasis.

• Take this envelope to the office [.]

• Can you hear me in the back of the room [?]

• I like your handwriting [.]

• I can't believe that movie [!]

• Tell me about your weekend [.]

• There is a school election on Friday [.]

• Is Molly having a party [?]

• What a blast we had last time [!]

■ Remind students that some statements sound like questions, but they do not directly ask a question. Only a direct question has a question mark. *I wonder why Sara is late. Why is Sara late?*

Practice in Reading

Have students look for the four kinds of sentences (declarative, interrogatory, imperative, and exclamatory) in "The Abacus Contest." Most of the interrogative and exclamatory sentences are in dialogue.

DAY 3

| Word Analysis | Writing Process Strategies | English Language Conventions |

Word Analysis

Spelling

Spelling Patterns for the /i/ Sound

Teach

Explain the spelling patterns for the /i/ sound, which are *i, y,* and *ui.* Have students locate words with these spelling patterns in the selection "The Abacus Contest."

Guided Practice

Have students complete page 16 from *Spelling and Vocabulary Skills* to reinforce the spelling patterns for short *i*.

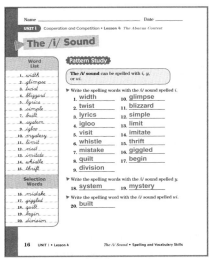

Spelling and Vocabulary Skills p. 16

Vocabulary (continued)

Dictionary Skills

Write the words *aroma, incense, mischievous,* and *frantically* from "The Abacus Contest" on the board. Depending on the availability of dictionaries, have students as a class or in groups examine dictionary entries and look for definitions, parts of speech, pronunciations, syllable breakdowns, and different forms of the word. Students may need to be told that *frantically* is a form of the word *frantic.* The answers may be written on paper among groups or on the board.

Writing Process Strategies

Introduction to the Writing Process: Revising

Consolidating Material

Teach

Have students read *Language Arts Handbook,* page 41. Go over with students what *consolidate* means: to join together, unite, or combine. When students consolidate what they have written, they should focus on keeping their ideas unified. Tell students that they can consolidate what they've written when they spot any of the following in a draft:

- Ideas are scattered throughout. → Keep one idea to a paragraph and make sure that each paragraph follows logically to the next.
- The draft is longer than the length that was assigned. → Use fewer words to make points or to tell the story.
- The draft rambles on without introducing any new ideas. Readers will lose interest if what they are reading is repetitious and appears to ramble. → Condense ideas in writing so readers feel that what they're reading is worth their time.

Guided Practice

Show students *Transparency 13—Consolidating* and go over how to consolidate material. Have students consolidate copy from the draft they wrote last week.

English Language Conventions

Grammar, Usage, and Mechanics: Sentences

Teach

- Use *Language Arts Handbook* page 363 to teach the four kinds of sentences.
- Use the correct ending punctuation in sentences.
- Capitalize the first word in all sentences.

Independent Practice in Writing

Tell the students to each write a paragraph about "The Abacus Contest" using at least three of the four kinds of sentences.

Informal Assessment

Look for evidence that students are progressing in their understanding of the four different kinds of sentences and their correct end punctuation and capitalization. Make sure that students are using variety in their sentence choice.

DAY 4

Word Analysis	Writing Process Strategies	English Language Conventions

Word Analysis

Spelling

Spelling Patterns for the /i/ Sound

Teach
Review with students the concept that the /i/ sound can be spelled with an *i*, a *y*, or with *ui*. Model the rhyming strategy by writing the word *lift* on the board and asking students what spelling word rhymes.

Guided Practice
Have students complete the Spelling Strategies exercises on page 17 of *Spelling and Vocabulary Skills.*

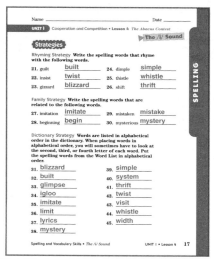

Spelling and Vocabulary Skills p. 17

Vocabulary (continued)

Dictionary Skills
Give students one minute to find an unfamiliar word in one of the later stories in the **Anthology**. If all students have access to dictionaries, have students write down all the information they can about their chosen word including pronunciation, part of speech, multiple forms and definitions, and syllable breakdown. If not all students have access to dictionaries, ask one or two to volunteer their words and write the entries on the board for class discussion.

Writing Process Strategies

Introduction to the Writing Process: Revising
Rearranging Material

Teach
- Have students read **Language Arts Handbook** page 43 on rearranging material. Tell students that sometimes the material that they have is useful; it is simply in the wrong place. By rearranging what they already have written, they can strengthen their writing so that ideas cohere, or stick together, better. Explain that they can rearrange material for the following reasons.
  - The concluding sentence or another sentence in a paragraph works better as the topic sentence.
  - A sentence supports one paragraph better than the one it's in.
  - Sentences in the conclusion for the entire piece would work better in the introduction, or the other way around.
  - The strongest points or the most exciting events appear too early in a report or story. Move the strongest points closer to the conclusion and climactic events closer to the resolution.
- Students may find single words or entire paragraphs that can be rearranged for other reasons. The important thing is to have students look for ways to strengthen what they have written by rearranging the text they have.

Guided Practice
Use **Transparency 14—Rearranging** to show students how to improve what they have written by rearranging text. If you have computers with word processing software, go over *cut and paste* with them. Have students rearrange text in the draft they wrote last week.

English Language Conventions

Listening, Speaking, Viewing
Viewing: Viewing the Media

Teach
- In Reading and Responding we learned about clarifying. Here we will clarify what magazine advertisements tell us.
- Remind the class that illustrations add to the meaning of a story, but when there is an illustration with no or few words, we must learn how to interpret what the image is saying.
- Explain that we need to pay attention to the details of an image, just like we pay attention to the details of a story. (*What objects are in the illustration? What words, if any, are included?*)
- Explain that the media, such as television commercials and magazine advertisements, use images to send a message. How people interpret that message influences how they think about a particular object or product. We should be able to interpret these kinds of images in order to make our own judgements.

Guided Practice
- Provide the class with magazine advertisements. Look for images that have few, if any, words. Give each student his/her own advertisement.
- Instruct the student to study the image. (*Look at the object/s displayed; look at the background.*) Have students ask themselves what kind of message the image is giving. (*This is bad; this is good; this will make you rich; this will make you young.*)
- Ask students what kind of picture they would make if they wanted to convince someone to eat a healthy lunch. (*It might show nutritious foods such as vegetables, deli sandwiches, and milk.*)

 Informal Assessment

Observe whether students are able to interpret the main idea from a media message.

DAY 5

Word Analysis	Writing Process Strategies	English Language Conventions

Spelling

Assessment: Final Test
Spelling Patterns for the /i/ Sound

Teach
Repeat the Pretest for this lesson or use the Final Test on page 33 of **Unit 1 Assessment**.

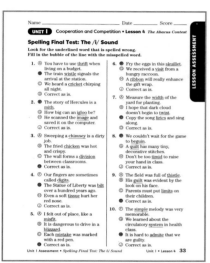

Unit 1 Assessment p. 33

Guided Practice
Have students categorize any mistakes they made on the Final Test.

Are they careless errors?
Are they lesson pattern problems?

Vocabulary (continued)

Dictionary Skills

Informal Assessment

- Encourage students to look at all parts of a dictionary entry for information concerning a word. Periodically check students' dictionary skills by having them find more than just the definition for a word. Have students refer to page 14 of **Spelling and Vocabulary Skills** if they need to review the parts of a dictionary entry.
- Tell students that as they continue to list unfamiliar words and their definitions in their Writer's Notebooks, they may want to add part of speech, pronunciation, or related words.

Introduction to the Writing Process: Revising
Clarifying

Teach

Writer's Craft
Sensory Description

Help students understand that sensory details add clarity and precision to writing. Point out the use of sensory detail in "The Abacus Contest." On page 58, the abacus beads are described as smooth and black. On page 59, note the description of the sugarcane.

- As a class, come up with some examples of sensory description.
- Point out that including sensory details is just one of the ways to add clarity to writing.

Other ways to add **clarity** to writing include the following.

- Fix sentences so that they are easier to understand.
- Add explanations and examples.
- Use transition words.
- Change language so that it fits the audience and purpose. Use **Transparency 15—Clarifying** to show the various ways in which writing can be made clearer.

Independent Practice
Have students complete **Comprehension and Language Arts Skills** pages 20–21 for practice on using sensory description.

Penmanship
Cursive Letters *p* and *j*

Teach
- Explain to students that not all letters have loops, and to make loops only in letters that require them.
- **Teacher Model:** Review the formation of lowercase, cursive *p* and *j* as undercurve letters by demonstrating on the board. Point out that these letters both have loops.

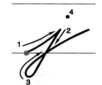

p Starting point, undercurve
Slant, loop back
Overcurve
Curve back, undercurve: small *p*

j Starting point, undercurve
Slant down
Loop back
Overcurve to endpoint
Dot exactly above: small *j*

Guided Practice
- On the board, write the sentence *"The playful puppy is just jogging down the street."* to model proper letter formation and loops.
- **Teacher Model:** For general handwriting practice, have students write a paragraph about what it feels like to win or lose an important game.
- From "The Abacus Contest," have students write two paragraphs for general handwriting practice.

Informal Assessment

Check students' handwriting for letters that should be looped. Make sure all loops below the baseline close below the baseline.

Reading and Language Arts Skills Traces

Language Arts

WORD ANALYSIS

Skills Trace

Spelling: The /i/ Sound

Introduced in Grade 1.
Scaffolded throughout Grades 2–5.
REINTRODUCED: Unit 1, Lesson 4, p. 65F
PRACTICED: Unit 1, Lesson 4,
pp. 65G–65I
Spelling and Vocabulary Skills,
pp. 16–17
TESTED: Unit 1, Lesson 4, p. 65J
Unit 1 Assessment

Skills Trace

Vocabulary: Dictionary Skills

Introduced in Grade 1.
Scaffolded throughout Grades 2–5.
REINTRODUCED: Unit 1, Lesson 4, p. 65G
PRACTICED: Unit 1, Lesson 4,
pp. 65H–65I
Spelling and Vocabulary Skills,
pp. 14–15
TESTED: Informal Assessment, p. 65J
Unit 1 Assessment

Reading

COMPREHENSION

Skills Trace

Sequence

Introduced in Grade 1.
Scaffolded throughout Grades 2–5.
REINTRODUCED: Unit 1, Lesson 4
REINFORCED: Unit 4, Lesson 2
Unit 5, Lesson 3
Unit 6, Lesson 1
TESTED: Unit 1 Assessment

WRITING PROCESS STRATEGIES

Skills Trace

Introduction to the Writing Process: Revising

Introduced in Grade 1.
Scaffolded throughout Grades 2–5.
INTRODUCED: Unit 1, Lesson 4, p. 65F
PRACTICED: Unit 1, Lessons 4, 5,
pp. 65F–65J; 85F–85J
TESTED: Unit 1 Assessment

Skills Trace

Writer's Craft: Sensory Detail

Introduced in Grade K.
Scaffolded throughout Grades 1–5.
INTRODUCED: Unit 1, Lesson 4, p. 65J
PRACTICED: Unit 1, Lesson 4, p. 65J
*Comprehension and Language
Arts Skills,* pp. 20–21
TESTED: Unit 1 Assessment

ENGLISH LANGUAGE CONVENTIONS

Skills Trace

Grammar, Usage, and Mechanics: Sentences

Introduced in Grade K.
Scaffolded throughout Grades 1–5.
INTRODUCED: Unit 1, Lesson 4, p. 65F
PRACTICED: Unit 1, Lesson 4, p. 65G
Unit 1, Lesson 4, p. 65H
*Comprehension and Language
Arts Skills,* pp. 18–19
TESTED: Informal Assessment, p. 65H
Unit 1, Lesson 4
Unit 1 Assessment

Skills Trace

Listening, Speaking, Viewing: Viewing: Viewing the Media

Introduced in Grade 3.
Scaffolded throughout Grades 4–5.
REINTRODUCED: Unit 1, Lesson 4, p. 65I
PRACTICED: Unit 1, Lesson 4, p. 65I
TESTED: Informal Assessment, p. 65I

Skills Trace

Penmanship: Cursive Letters p and j

Introduced in Grade 3.
Scaffolded throughout Grades 4–5.
REINTRODUCED: Unit 1, Lesson 4, p. 65J
PRACTICED: Unit 1, Lesson 4, p. 65J
TESTED: Informal Assessment, p. 65J

Professional Development: Assessment

The Changing Face of Reading Assessment

Reading assessment has moved away from being based predominantly on multiple-choice items and toward requiring students to be more active, or *constructive*, in responding. Formal, standardized assessment is being supplemented by teacher observations, samples of students' work, and other activities that can be used to infer achievement and reading progress. The new, or *alternative*, forms of assessment are called by several names, including *authentic* assessment and *performance-based* assessment. Whatever the name, the idea behind alternative assessment is that testing should be an integral part of instruction, not the end purpose of learning (Reichel, 1994). Alternative assessments include portfolio assignments, written responses to reading, oral fluency or miscue analysis, word reading, cloze passages, and a variety of other assessments that are useful in guiding instruction and showing how well students can read (Pearson, DeStefano, & García, 1998; Tierney, Carter, & Desai, 1991).

One reason for the shift in reading assessment is that traditional, standardized tests provide relatively little instructional guidance (García & Pearson, 1994; Shepard, 1989; Stallman & Pearson, 1990). Although alternative assessments have shortcomings that prevent their widespread use for accountability purposes, they provide a great deal of meaningful instructional guidance (Pearson et al., 1998). A second reason for the shift is a new concept of reading. The traditional perspective of reading was more or less that students either did or did not read and comprehend what they read. Recent views of reading interpret reading as a more dynamic act that includes a variety of skills and active processing by the reader—processing that reflects the reader's background, prior knowledge, preferences, and so forth (Anderson & Pearson, 1984; Rumelhart, 1985).

Assessment, whether traditional or alternative, is only a sample of behavior from which conclusions can be drawn and generalizations made. In the case of a traditional test, the behavior sample is a single event that occurs in a relatively short duration of time. In alternative assessment, the sample is drawn over a longer time period and involves complex thinking, problem solving, and continuous feedback (Wiggins, 1993). Students construct responses instead of choosing one correct answer; solve a problem or apply principles instead of responding to text by choosing an answer, usually from four options, that is "more correct" than the others; and apply several skills at once, rather than depending on an isolated skill.

Although alternative assessments have enjoyed increasing popularity, their widespread use has been limited by a number of factors. They are difficult to score and are highly susceptible to subjective interpretation. The time and effort involved mean they cost more to develop and to score. They lack the rigor of traditional assessments. Finally, for certain students, alternative assessments may be just as unfair as traditional assessments. For example, students who are good at presenting their ideas may be overrated when compared to students who comprehend what they read just as well but cannot present their ideas as clearly as other students (Mehrens, 1992; Pearson et al., 1998).

* Additional information about assessment as well as resource references can be found in the ***Professional Development Guide: Assessment.***

SELECTION INTRODUCTION

Focus Questions Should one always try to be a winner?
Is it ever better to lose a competition than to win one?

S.O.R. LOSERS

from the book by Avi
illustrated by Kate Flanagan

Ed Sitrow and his friends have a big problem. All students at
South Orange River Middle School are required to play one sport
per year—only Ed is no jock and neither are his friends. Playing
a sport is sure to mean only one thing for them—total
humiliation. Somehow, they manage to slip through their first
year at S.O.R. without playing a sport. But when the school
catches on, they make up a special soccer team just for Ed's
crowd. This soccer team is anything but typical at a school
positively famous for its winning teams and all-star athletes. Mr.
Lester, the history teacher, has volunteered to be their coach. Little
does the team know that they'll be making history of their own.

I should have guessed what was going to happen next when
this kid from the school newspaper <u>interviewed</u> me. It went
this way.

NEWSPAPER: How does it feel to lose every game?
ME: I never played on a team that won, so I can't compare.
    But it's . . . interesting.
NEWSPAPER: How many teams have you been on?
ME: Just this one.
NEWSPAPER: Do you want to win?
ME: Wouldn't mind knowing what it feels like. For the <u>novelty</u>.
NEWSPAPER: Have you figured out why you lose all the time?
ME: They score more goals.
NEWSPAPER: Have you seen any improvement?
ME: I've been too busy.

66

Selection Summary

Genre: Realistic Fiction

A requirement at South Orange River Middle School
is that all students participate in a sport. A soccer
team is formed of all the students who escaped
playing sports their first year at school. Everyone on
the team is good at something—except soccer or
any sport. This first-person account truly illustrates
that it's not whether you win or lose, it's how you
play the game.

Some of the elements of realistic fiction are listed
below. A realistic fiction selection may have one or
more of these elements.

- The characters behave as people or animals do in
  real life.
- The setting of the story is a real place or could be
  a real place.
- The events of the story are based on a conflict or
  problem that could occur in real life.

About the Author

AVI, once an assistant professor and librarian, is a prolific writer who has written more than two dozen books despite his lifelong battle with a writing dysfunction called dysgraphia. Among the honors he has received are the following: the Scott O'Dell Award for Historical Fiction for *The Fighting Ground;* the Christopher Award for *Encounter at Easton;* the Newbery Honor Medal for *Nothing but the Truth;* and an Edgar Award Nomination for *Something Upstairs: A Tale of Ghosts.* In addition to these awards, *The True Confessions of Charlotte Doyle* was named a Newbery Honor Book; *Wolf Rider* was honored as the ALA Best Book for Young Adults; and *S.O.R. Losers* was given the Parent's Choice "Remarkable Citation."

Students can read more about Avi on page 84 of the *Student Anthology.*

Other Books by Avi
- *Who Stole the Wizard of Oz?*
- *A Place Called Ugly*
- *Shadrach's Crossing*

About the Illustrator

KATE FLANAGAN graduated from Tufts University with a degree in fine arts. A former assistant editor and book reviewer for *The Horn Book Magazine,* Flanagan works as a freelance illustrator.

Students can read more about Kate Flanagan on page 84 of the *Student Anthology.*

Other Books Illustrated by Kate Flanagan
- *Kids Pumpkin Projects*
- *The Very Lonely Bathtub*
- *My Gum is Gone*

Inquiry Connections

A major aim of **Open Court Reading** is knowledge building. Because inquiry is at the root of knowledge building, students are encouraged to investigate topics and questions within each selection that relate to the unit theme.

"S.O.R. Losers" is humorous realistic fiction about a group of nonathletic students forced to play soccer and expected to commit to winning. Instead, they decide to be true to their own beliefs and interests. The key concepts are:

- The desire to win is taken as a given in our society.
- Not everyone wants to compete and excel in sports.
- Cooperation within competitive situations facilitates decision making and supports individuals.

Before reading the selection:

- Point out that students may post a question, concept, word, illustration, or object on the Concept/Question Board at any time during the course of their unit investigation. Be sure that students include their names or initials on the items they post so that others will know whom to go to if they have an answer or if they wish to collaborate on a related activity.
- Students should feel free to write an answer or a note on someone else's question or to consult the Board for ideas for their own investigations throughout the unit.
- Encourage students to read about cooperation and competition at home and to bring in articles or pictures that are good examples to post on the Board.

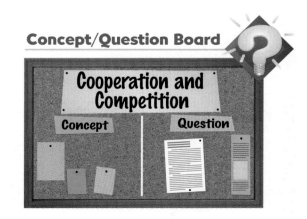

Concept/Question Board

Cooperation and Competition

Concept | Question

PROGRAM RESOURCES

Leveled Practice

Reteach
Pages 24–29

Challenge
Pages 20–24

ELD Workbook

Intervention Workbook

Leveled Classroom Library*

Have students read at least 30 minutes daily outside of class. Have them read books from the *Leveled Classroom Library,* which supports the unit theme and helps students develop their vocabulary by reading independently.

The Kid Who Ran for President

BY DAN GUTMAN. SCHOLASTIC, 1996.

Twelve-year-old Judson Moon is running for President of the United States—with the old lady down the street as his running mate, a first lady he's barely spoken to, and a campaign manager who swears he can sidestep the Constitution and get Judd elected. **(Easy)**

The Wheel on the School

BY MEINDERT DEJONG. HARPER TROPHY, 1972.

When Lina begins to wonder why the storks no longer come to the village of Shora, she spurs the five other children to action, and they set out to bring the storks back to Shora. (A Newbery Medal Winner) **(Average)**

The View from Saturday

BY E. L. KONIGSBURG. ALADDIN, 1996.

Mrs. Olinski's choice of Noah, Nadia, Ethan, and Julian for her sixth grade academic team, the strange connections between the four, and their amazing academic bowl winning-streak are explored. (A Newbery Medal Winner) **(Advanced)**

* These books, which all support the unit theme Cooperation and Competition, are part of a 36-book *Leveled Classroom Library* available for purchase from SRA/McGraw-Hill.

Note: Teachers should preview any trade books for appropriateness in their classrooms before recommending them to students.

TECHNOLOGY

Web Connections

www.sra4kids.com
Cooperation and Competition Web site

Audiocassette/CD

* **Listening Library: Cooperation and Competition**
SRA/McGRAW-HILL, 2002

Computer Skills

* **Basic Computer Skills**

CD-ROMs

* **Research Assistant**
SRA/McGRAW-HILL, 2002

* **Student Writing and Research Center**
THE LEARNING COMPANY

Titles preceded by an asterisk (*) are available through SRA/McGraw-Hill. Other titles can be obtained by contacting the publisher listed with the title.

	DAY 1	**DAY 2**
Suggested Pacing: 3–5 days	**DAY 1**	**DAY 2**

LESSON PLANNER

1 Preparing to Read

Materials
- Routine Card 1

DAY 1

Word Knowledge, p. 66K
- Frequently Misspelled Words
- Long e Spelled *ea*
- /ch/ Sound Spelled *ch*
- /u/ Sound Spelled *u*

About the Words and Sentences, p. 66K

DAY 2

Developing Oral Language, p. 66L

---

2 Reading & Responding

Materials
- Student Anthology, pp. 66–85
- Reading Transparencies, 7, 54, 58–59
- Routine Card 1
- Program Assessment
- Unit 1 Assessment, pp. 18–21
- Comprehension and Language Arts Skills, pp. 22–23
- Reteach, pp. 24–25
- Challenge, p. 20
- Home Connection, pp. 11–12

DAY 1

Build Background, p. 66M
Preview and Prepare, pp. 66M–66N
Selection Vocabulary, p. 66N
Reading Recommendations, pp. 66O–66P
Student Anthology, pp. 66–76 [First Read]
✓ **Comprehension Strategies**
- Summarizing, pp. 72, 76
- Visualizing, pp. 66, 68, 70, 74
- Asking Questions, pp. 68, 70, 74

DAY 2

Student Anthology, pp. 76–83 [First Read]
✓ **Comprehension Strategies**
- Visualizing, p. 78
- Asking Questions, pp. 76, 80, 82
Discussing Strategy Use, p. 82
Discussing the Selection, p. 83A

Inquiry

Materials
- Student Anthology, pp. 66–85
- Inquiry Journal, pp. 24–27
- Research Assistant

DAY 1

Investigation
- Investigating Concepts Beyond the Text, p. 85A

DAY 2

Investigation
- Concept/Question Board, p. 85B

---

3 Language Arts

Materials
- Comprehension and Language Arts Skills, pp. 24–27
- Language Arts Handbook
- Language Arts Transparencies, 16–18, 20
- Spelling and Vocabulary Skills, pp. 18–21
- Student Anthology
- Student Writing and Research Center
- Writer's Workbook, p. 4
- Writing Folder
- Unit 1 Assessment, pp. 34–35
- Reteach, pp. 26–29
- Challenge, pp. 19–24

DAY 1

Word Analysis
✓ Spelling Patterns for the /u/ Sound Pretest, p. 85F
Writing Process Strategies
- Writing Process Introduction: Revising, p. 85F
English Language Conventions
- Grammar, Usage, and Mechanics: Subjects and Predicates, p. 85F

DAY 2

Word Analysis
- Spelling Patterns for the /u/ Sound, p. 85G
- Vocabulary: Using a Thesaurus, p. 85G
Writing Process Strategies
- Writing Process: Revising, p. 85G
English Language Conventions
- Grammar, Usage, and Mechanics: Subjects and Predicates, p. 85G

✓ **Informal** Assessment Available   ✓ **Formal** Assessment Available

DAY 2 continued	**DAY 3**	
DAY 3	**DAY 4**	**DAY 5**

General Review	**General Review**	**Review Word Knowledge**

Student Anthology, pp. 66–75 [Second Read]	**Student Anthology, pp. 76–83** [Second Read]	✔ **Lesson Assessment**
Comprehension Skills	**Comprehension Skills**	▪ *Unit 1 Assessment:* Lesson Assessment, pp. 18–21
▪ **Compare and Contrast, pp. 67, 69, 71**	▪ **Compare and Contrast, pp. 79, 81, 83**	**Home Connection, p. 83B**
▪ **Author's Point of View, pp. 73, 75**	▪ **Author's Point of View, p. 77**	**Science Connection**
	✔ **Checking Comprehension, p. 83**	▪ **Cellular Respiration, p 83F**
	Supporting the Reading, pp. 83C–83D	
	▪ **Compare and Contrast**	
	Student Anthology, pp. 84–85	
	▪ **Meet the Author/Illustrator**	
	✔ ▪ **Theme Connections**	
	Review Selection Vocabulary, p. 83B	
	Literary Elements, p. 83E	
	▪ **Plot/Story Structure**	

Investigation	**Supporting the Investigation**	**Investigation**
✔ ▪ **Establishing Investigation Plans, p. 85C**	▪ **Using Multiple Sources, p. 85D**	▪ **Unit Investigation Continued**
		▪ **Update Concept/Question Board**

Word Analysis	**Word Analysis**	**Word Analysis**
▪ **Spelling Patterns for the /u/ Sound, p. 85H**	▪ **Spelling Patterns for the /u/ Sound, p. 85I**	✔ ▪ **Spelling Patterns for the /u/ Sound Final Test, p. 85J**
▪ **Vocabulary: Using a Thesaurus, p. 85H**	▪ **Vocabulary: Using a Thesaurus, p. 85I**	✔ ▪ **Vocabulary: Using a Thesaurus, p. 85J**
Writing Process Strategies	**Writing Process Strategies**	**Writing Process Strategies**
▪ **Writing Process: Revising, p. 85H**	▪ **Writing Process: Revising, p. 85I**	▪ **Writing Process: Revising, p. 85J**
English Language Conventions	**English Language Conventions**	**English Language Conventions**
✔ ▪ **Grammar, Usage, and Mechanics: Subjects and Predicates, p. 85H**	✔ ▪ **Listening, Speaking, Viewing Interacting: Ask Questions, p. 85I**	✔ ▪ **Penmanship: Cursive Letters *a, c,* and *d*, p. 85J**

Below are suggestions for differentiating instruction to meet the individual needs of students. These are the same skills shown on the Lesson Planner; however, these pages provide extra practice opportunities or enriching activities to meet the varied needs of students.

WORKSHOP

Differentiating Instruction

Small-Group Instruction

Use small-group instruction for such things as preteaching students who need this advantage and reteaching material to students having difficulty.

Use the informal assessment suggestions found throughout the lesson along with the formal assessments provided in each lesson to determine your students' strengths and areas of need. Use the following program components to help in supporting or expanding on the instruction found in this lesson:

- *Reteach* workbook for use with those students who show a basic understanding of the lesson but need a bit more practice to solidify their understanding

- *Intervention Guide* and *Workbook* for use with those students who even after extra practice exhibit a lack of understanding of the lesson concepts

- *English-Language Development Guide* and *Workbook* for use with those students who need language help

Independent Activities

The students may investigate their ideas and questions by using information from their investigation groups. They may use sources available to them. Some students may need larger blocks of time to complete certain aspects of their investigation of the concepts surrounding cooperation and competition. Some students may be well into the stage of organizing their findings. Others may need a gentle reminder from you to organize their time or prioritize tasks according to an approaching deadline.

For Workshop Management Tips, see Appendix pages 41–42.

◆ **Small-group Instruction**　■ **Independent Activities**

	READING	INVESTIGATION ACTIVITIES
DAY 1	■ Browse *Leveled Classroom Library* ■ *Listening Library Audiocassette/CD* ■ Add Vocabulary in Writer's Notebook	■ Concept/Question Board ■ Explore OCR Web site for Theme Connections ■ Complete Winning and Losing Poll in *Inquiry Journal*, pp. 24–25
DAY 2	■ Choose *Leveled Classroom Library* Book and Begin Independent Reading ■ Oral Reading of Selection for Fluency ■ *Listening Library Audiocassette/CD* ■ Record Response to Selection in Writer's Notebook	■ Concept/Question Board ■ Explore OCR Web site for Theme Connections
DAY 3	■ Read *Leveled Classroom Library* Book as Independent Reading ■ *Listening Library Audiocassette/CD*	■ Concept/Question Board ◆ Establish Investigation Plans ■ Use *Research Assistant* to Help with Investigation
DAY 4	■ Read *Leveled Classroom Library* Book as Independent Reading ■ *Listening Library Audiocassette/CD* ■ Complete *Comprehension and Language Arts Skills*, pp. 22–23 ◆ Discuss Theme Connections, p. 85 ■ Add Words to Word Bank ■ Complete **Independent Practice** for Literary Elements, p. 83E	■ Concept/Question Board ■ Complete *Inquiry Journal*, p. 26 ■ Carry Out Job Assignments
DAY 5	■ Read *Leveled Classroom Library* Book as Independent Reading ■ Complete **Link to Writing** for Supporting the Reading, p. 83D ◆ Reading Roundtable ■ Science Connection, p. 83F	■ Concept/Question Board ■ Practice Organizing Sources in *Inquiry Journal*, p. 27

LANGUAGE ARTS	INTERVENTION*	ENGLISH-LANGUAGE LEARNERS**	RETEACH	CHALLENGE
English Language Conventions ■ Complete **Subjects and Predicates,** *Comprehension and Language Arts Skills,* pp. 24–25 **Writing Process Strategies** ◆ Seminar: Revising for Ideas, p. 85F	(35 to 40 minutes per day) ◆ Reading Words, p. 39 ◆ Preteach "S.O.R. Losers," pp. 40–41 ◆ Teach "Intervention Selection One," pp. 41–42 ◆ Grammar, Usage, and Mechanics, p. 45	(35 to 40 minutes per day) ◆ Work Knowledge, p. 20 ◆ Activate Prior Knowledge, p. 21		
Word Analysis ◆ Spelling: Word Sort, p. 85G ■ Complete **Vocabulary: Using the Thesaurus,** *Spelling and Vocabulary Skills,* pp. 18–19 **Writing Process Strategies** ◆ Seminar: Revising for Organization, p. 85G	◆ Developing Oral Language, p. 39 ◆ Preteach "S.O.R. Losers," pp. 40–41 ◆ Teach Comprehension Strategies, p. 42 ◆ Reread "Intervention Selection One" ◆ Grammar, Usage, and Mechanics, p. 45	◆ Selection Vocabulary, p. 21 ◆ Preteach the Selection, p. 21	**English Language Conventions** ■ Complete **Subjects and Predicates,** *Reteach,* p. 28	**English Language Conventions** ■ Complete **Subjects and Predicates,** *Challenge,* p. 23
Word Analysis ■ Complete **Spelling: The /u/ Sound,** *Spelling and Vocabulary Skills,* p. 20 **Writing Process Strategies** ◆ Seminar: Revising for Word Choice, p. 85H	◆ Dictation and Spelling, pp. 39–40 ◆ Reread "S.O.R. Losers" ◆ Teach "Intervention Selection Two," pp. 43–44 ◆ Writing Activity, pp. 46–47	◆ Dictation and Spelling, p. 20	**Word Analysis** ■ Complete **Vocabulary: Using the Thesaurus,** *Reteach,* p. 27	**Comprehension** ◆ Drawing Conclusions **Word Analysis** ■ Complete **Vocabulary: Using the Thesaurus,** *Challenge,* p. 22
Word Analysis ■ Complete **The /u/ Sound,** *Spelling and Vocabulary Skills,* p. 21 **Writing Process Strategies** ◆ Seminar: Revising for Sentence Fluency, p. 85I	◆ Reread "S.O.R. Losers" ◆ Teach Comprehension Strategies, p. 44 ◆ Reread "Intervention Selection Two" ◆ Writing Activity, pp. 46–47	◆ Vocabulary Strategies, p. 23	**Comprehension** ◆ Review Comprehension Skill: Compare and Contrast ■ Complete *Reteach,* pp. 24–25 **Word Analysis** ■ Complete **Spelling: The /u/ Sound,** *Reteach,* p. 26	**Comprehension** ◆ Complete *Challenge,* p. 20 **Word Analysis** ■ Complete **Spelling: The /u/ Sound,** *Challenge,* p. 21
Writing Process Strategies ■ Complete **Writer's Craft: Time and Order Words,** *Comprehension and Language Arts Skills,* pp. 26–27 ◆ Seminar: Revise an Autobiography, p. 85J **English Language Conventions** ■ Penmanship: Cursive Letters *a, c,* and *d,* p. 85J	◆ Repeated Readings/ Fluency Check, pp. 44–45	◆ Grammar, Usage, and Mechanics, p. 24	**Writing Process Strategies** ■ Complete **Writer's Craft: Time and Order Words,** *Reteach,* p. 29	**Writing Process Strategies** ■ Complete **Writer's Craft: Time and Order Words,** *Challenge,* p. 24

*Page numbers refer to *Intervention Guide*
**Page numbers refer to *English-Language Development Guide*

Formal Assessment Options

Use these summative assessments along with your informal observations to assess student progress.

Page 18:

LESSON ASSESSMENT

Name _____ Date _____ Score _____

UNIT I Cooperation and Competition • Lesson 5

S.O.R. Losers

Read the following questions carefully. Then completely fill in the bubble of each correct answer. You may look back at the story to find the answer to each of the questions.

1. From which point of view is this story told?
   Ⓐ second-person
   Ⓑ third-person
   ● first-person

2. How did the team help Hays?
   Ⓐ They carried him off the field.
   ● They cheered so he wouldn't feel bad.
   Ⓒ They gave him a shirt with his name on it.

Read the following questions carefully. Use complete sentences to answer the questions.

3. Why did people want the S.O.R. Losers to win?
   People thought they felt bad losing all the time.

4. What was the biggest difference between the S.O.R. Losers' team and the Parkville team?
   The Parkville team thought it was important to win, and the S.O.R. Losers did not.

5. Why weren't the S.O.R. Losers concerned about sports?
   They were good at other things besides sports.

18 Unit I • Lesson 5   S.O.R. Losers • Unit I Assessment

Unit 1 Assessment p. 18

Page 19:

S.O.R. Losers *(continued)*

LESSON ASSESSMENT

6. What do the teachers think is so unusual about the S.O.R. Losers' attitudes?
   The teachers think it is strange that the teammates do not care if they lose.

7. Why does the crowd think that the S.O.R. Losers have a chance to beat Parkville?
   The crowd thinks the S.O.R. Losers have a chance to beat Parkville because Parkville hasn't won a game either.

8. How does South Orange River Middle School encourage the S.O.R. Losers to win?
   They encourage them by making banners for the lunch room and holding a pep rally before the game.

Read the following questions carefully. Then completely fill in the bubble of each correct answer.

9. Who is Ed Sitrow?
   Ⓐ the coach of the team
   Ⓑ the author of the story
   ● the narrator of the story

10. What was unusual about the team picture of the S.O.R. Losers?
    ● The players had their backs to the camera.
    Ⓑ The players stood on each other's shoulders.
    Ⓒ The players from the other team were in it.

Unit I Assessment • S.O.R. Losers   Unit I • Lesson 5   19

Unit 1 Assessment p. 19

Page 20:

S.O.R. Losers *(continued)*

LESSON ASSESSMENT

Read the question and statement below. Use complete sentences in your answers.

Linking to the Concepts What can you conclude from the interview at the beginning of the story?
Answers will vary. Accept all reasonable answers.

Personal Response In this story, the S.O.R. Losers don't care if they lose. How do you feel about this attitude?
Answers will vary. Accept all reasonable answers.

20 Unit I • Lesson 5   S.O.R. Losers • Unit I Assessment

Unit 1 Assessment p. 20

Page 21:

S.O.R. Losers *(continued)*

LESSON ASSESSMENT

Vocabulary

Read the following questions carefully. Then completely fill in the bubble of each correct answer.

1. At the beginning of the story, Ed is interviewed by someone from the school newspaper. To be **interviewed** means
   ● to be asked questions
   Ⓑ to be made fun of
   Ⓒ to be left alone

2. Mr. Tillman thinks the S.O.R. Losers might be encouraging a defeatist attitude in the school. A **defeatist** attitude is a
   Ⓐ supportive attitude
   ● losing attitude
   Ⓒ winning attitude

3. Ed read somewhere that records are made to be broken. In this sentence, a **record** is
   Ⓐ a front page newspaper article
   Ⓑ a recording of music played at games
   ● a team's history of wins and losses

4. The newspaper reporter wants Ed to make a prediction about the big game. When you make a **prediction**, you
   ● tell what you think will happen
   Ⓑ explain why something happened
   Ⓒ show how to do something well

5. In this story, what is an **attitude**?
   Ⓐ whom you hang around with
   ● how you feel about something
   Ⓒ when people do not like sports

Unit I Assessment • S.O.R. Losers   Unit I • Lesson 5   21

Unit 1 Assessment p. 21

Page 34:

LESSON ASSESSMENT

Name _____ Date _____ Score _____

UNIT I Cooperation and Competition • Lesson 5 *S.O.R. Losers*

Spelling Pretest: The /u/ Sound

Fold this page back on the dotted line. Take the Pretest. Then correct any word you misspelled by crossing out the word and rewriting it next to the incorrect spelling.

1. _____   1. _study_
2. _____   2. _clumsy_
3. _____   3. _trumpet_
4. _____   4. _trouble_
5. _____   5. _hunger_
6. _____   6. _none_
7. _____   7. _bundle_
8. _____   8. _struggle_
9. _____   9. _money_
10. _____   10. _mutter_
11. _____   11. _country_
12. _____   12. _honey_
13. _____   13. _chuckle_
14. _____   14. _thunder_
15. _____   15. _bulb_
16. _____   16. _support_
17. _____   17. _hundred_
18. _____   18. _done_
19. _____   19. _something_
20. _____   20. _supposed_

34 Unit I • Lesson 5   Spelling Pretest: The /u/ Sound • Unit I Assessment

Unit 1 Assessment p. 34

Page 35:

LESSON ASSESSMENT

Name _____ Date _____ Score _____

UNIT I Cooperation and Competition • Lesson 5 *S.O.R. Losers*

Spelling Final Test: The /u/ Sound

Look for the underlined word that is spelled wrong. Fill in the bubble of the line with the misspelled word.

1. Ⓐ I enjoy living out in the country.
   Ⓑ A volcano can spew ash when it erupts.
   Ⓒ A blueberry muffin sounds good for breakfast.
   Ⓓ Correct as is.

2. Ⓕ A suffix comes at the end of a word.
   Ⓖ The math problem took me duble the time it took her.
   Ⓗ It is impossible to win a campaign without support.
   Ⓙ Correct as is.

3. Ⓐ The sun setting over the lake is luvely.
   Ⓑ I had to chuckle to myself.
   Ⓒ The actor is often in the public eye.
   Ⓓ Correct as is.

4. Ⓕ Bundle up when you visit Alaska.
   Ⓖ The sound of the trumpet signals the king's arrival.
   Ⓗ She shares a bank account with her husband.
   Ⓙ Correct as is.

5. Ⓐ Maybe your brother will loan you money.
   Ⓑ Is the orator done addressing the crowd?
   Ⓒ The thonder became more distant as the storm passed.
   Ⓓ Correct as is.

6. Ⓕ I felt someone tugging at my sleeve.
   Ⓖ Blowing a buble takes practice.
   Ⓗ Our hunger grew as the afternoon went on.
   Ⓙ Correct as is.

7. Ⓐ How much lomber do we need to build a tree house?
   Ⓑ Alice taught her sister to count to a hundred.
   Ⓒ The salesman can recommend a good product.
   Ⓓ Correct as is.

8. Ⓕ You should try to studdy French in France.
   Ⓖ Claire was embarrassed when her zipper came undone.
   Ⓗ You can eat the seeds of a pumpkin.
   Ⓙ Correct as is.

9. Ⓐ None of the days in August were chilly.
   Ⓑ Don't mutter, but speak loudly and clearly.
   Ⓒ The jar is on the shelf above the soup.
   Ⓓ Correct as is.

10. Ⓕ Moles dig tunnels.
    Ⓖ Put some huney in your tea.
    Ⓗ A teacher will instruct you how to play the piano.
    Ⓙ Correct as is.

Unit I Assessment • Spelling Final Test: The /u/ Sound   Unit I • Lesson 5   35

Unit 1 Assessment p. 35

Informal Comprehension Strategies Rubrics

Use the Informal Comprehension Strategies Rubrics to determine whether or not a student is using any of the strategies listed below. Note the strategies a student is using, instead of the degree to which a student might be using any particular strategy. In addition, encourage the student to tell of any strategies other than the ones being taught that he or she is using.

Asking Questions

- The student asks questions about ideas or facts presented in the text and attempts to answer these questions by reading the text.

Summarizing

- The student paraphrases text, reporting main ideas and a summary of what is in text.
- The student decides which parts of the text are important in his or her summary.
- The student draws conclusions from the text.
- The student makes global interpretations of the text, such as recognizing the genre.

Visualizing

- The student visualizes ideas or scenes described in the text.

Research Rubrics

During Workshop, assess students using the rubrics below. The rubrics range from 1–4 in most categories, with 1 being the lowest score. Record each student's score on the inside back cover of his or her *Inquiry Journal.*

Revising Problems and Conjectures

1 No revision.

2 Produces new problems or conjectures with little relation to earlier ones.

3 Tends to lift problems and conjectures directly from reference material.

4 Progresses to deeper, more refined problems and conjectures.

Finding Needed Information

1 Collects information loosely related to topic.

2 Collects information clearly related to topic.

3 Collects information helpful in advancing on a research problem.

4 Collects problem-relevant information from varied sources and notices inconsistencies and missing pieces.

5 Collects useful information, paying attention to the reliability of sources and reviewing information critically.

Objectives

- Students recognize frequently misspelled words and review their correct spellings.
- Students recognize and read words with the long e sound spelled *ea*.
- Students recognize and read words with the /ch/ sound spelled *ch*.
- Students recognize and read words with the /u/ sound spelled *u*.
- Students develop fluency reading words and sentences aloud.

Materials

- Routine Card 1

Routine Card
Refer to Routine 1 for the Word Knowledge procedure.

Teacher Tip SYLLABICATION To help students blend words and build fluency, use the syllabication below of the decodable multisyllabic words in the word lines.

los•er	sup•port
be•lieve	hun•dred
trea•son	hun•ger
de•feat	sup•posed
cham•pi•on•ship	

MEETING INDIVIDUAL NEEDS

ELL Support

For ELD strategies, use the *English-Language Development Guide,* Unit 1, Lesson 5.

Intervention Support

For intervention strategies, use the *Intervention Guide,* Unit 1, Lesson 5.

WORD KNOWLEDGE

Word Knowledge

Reading the Words and Sentences

Use direct teaching to teach the Word Knowledge lesson. Write each word and sentence on the board. Have students read each word together. After all the words have been read, have students read each sentence in natural phrases or chunks. Use the suggestions in About the Words and Sentences to discuss the different features of listed words.

Line 1:	loser believe caught through
Line 2:	treason leave defeat scream
Line 3:	championship cheer chant chair
Line 4:	support hundred hunger supposed
Sentence 1:	I believe that I caught you going through the fence.
Sentence 2:	We will defeat your team before you leave the school.
Sentence 3:	At the championship, the students cheered and chanted so loudly that it was difficult to hear anything else.
Sentence 4:	Cheerleaders are supposed to show support for their team by leading cheers.

About the Words and Sentences

- **Line 1:** These words are frequently misspelled. Review the words and their meanings and spellings with the students.
- **Line 2:** The words focus on long e spelled *ea*. Have students offer other words that contain this spelling of the long e sound.
- **Line 3:** The words have the /ch/ sound spelled *ch*. Have students offer words that contain this spelling of the /ch/ sound somewhere other than the beginning of the word (for example, *inch, branch,* and *wrench*).
- **Line 4:** The words contain the /u/ sound spelled *u*.

- **Sentence 1:** Have students read the sentence aloud. Then ask students to identify the frequently misspelled words. Finally, read each sentence to students, and have them write it as you speak. Check students' spellings of the words *believe*, *caught*, and *through*.

- **Sentence 2:** Have students read the sentence aloud and identify the words that contain the long e sound spelled *ea (defeat, team, leave)*.

- **Sentence 3:** Have students identify the words containing the /ch/ sound spelled *ch (championship, cheered, chanted)*. Then, have them read the sentence aloud.

- **Sentence 4:** Have students notice the words in the sentence that contain the /u/ sound spelled *u (supposed, support)*. Point out that the letter *u* is in a closed syllable and therefore has the /u/ sound.

Developing Oral Language

Use direct teaching to review the words. Use one or both of the following activities to help students practice the words aloud.

- Challenge students to use as many words as possible from Lines 1–4 in a single sentence that makes sense. Ask volunteers to read their sentences aloud.

- Give a clue for one of the words in Lines 1–4. For example, for the word *defeat*, you might give the following clue: "What word means to *beat another team* and has the same vowel sound as *weave*?" Have the students identify the word. Then have students choose a word from lines 1–4 for classmates to identify. Have them come up with and present to the class a clue similar to the example given. Let the class identify the word. Challenge students to include words from lines 1–4 in their clues.

Teacher Tip BUILDING FLUENCY
Gaining a better understanding of the spellings of sounds and structure of words will help students as they encounter unfamiliar words in their reading. By this time in grade 5 students should be reading approximately 126 words per minute with fluency and expression. As students read, you may notice that some need work in building fluency. During Workshop, have these students choose a section of text (a minimum of 160 words) to read several times in order to build fluency.

MEETING INDIVIDUAL NEEDS

ELL Support

WORD MEANING Make sure that English-language learners understand the meanings of the words on the word lines before you do the exercises with them. Use pictures, photos, and bilingual dictionaries. Go to the *English-Language Development Guide* for additional support for students who need help with blending.

Intervention Tip

FREQUENTLY MISSPELLED WORDS Make a list of frequently misspelled words. Write them on the board, and have the students write them down on paper. Then erase the words and ask students to put their lists away. Say each word aloud, and have students write down the words. Continue to work with students on words that they misspell. For students who need more help, see Unit 1, Lesson 5, of the *Intervention Guide*.

Spelling
See pages 85F–85J for the corresponding spelling lesson for the /u/ sound.

Objectives

- Students will understand the selection vocabulary before reading.
- Students will identify words containing the /ch/ sound spelled *ch*.
- Students will identify words containing the long e sound spelled *ea*.
- Students will use the comprehension strategies Visualizing, Asking Questions, and Summarizing as they read the story the first time.
- Students will use the comprehension skills Compare and Contrast and Author's Point of View as they read the story the second time.

Materials

- Student Anthology, pp. 66–85
- Reading Transparencies 7, 54, 58, 59
- Listening Library
- Routine Card 1
- Inquiry Journal, p. 7
- Home Connection, pp. 11–12
- Comprehension and Language Arts Skills, pp. 22–23
- Program Assessment
- Unit 1 Assessment, pp. 18–21

MEETING INDIVIDUAL NEEDS

ELL Support

CULTURAL CONTEXT Ask English-language learners to talk about what kind of sports are most popular with children in their first culture.

Teacher Tip ACTIVATE PRIOR KNOWLEDGE Inform students that good readers typically activate what they already know about a topic before reading something new about the topic. Tell students that they should get in the habit of thinking about the topic of an upcoming selection and activating relevant background knowledge.

www.sra4kids.com
Web Connection
Students can use the connections to cooperation and competition in the Reading link of the SRA Web page for more background information about Cooperation and Competition.

Build Background

Activate Prior Knowledge

Discuss the following with students to find out what they may already know about the selection and have already learned about the theme of cooperation and competition.

- Preteach "S.O.R. Losers" by first determining students' knowledge of playing team sports. Have students share their experiences with playing on school sports teams.
- Have students share other stories that involve team sports.
- Ask students whether they have heard the saying, "It's not important whether you win or lose, it's how you play the game." Have students discuss this saying, focusing on the following questions: *Where have you heard this saying? Do you agree or disagree with its message? How is the American culture, or way of life, reflected in this saying? How is this saying reflective of other cultures?*

Background Information

The following information may help the students better understand the selection they are about to read.

- Tell students that "S.O.R. Losers" is set in a junior high school.
- Some students may be unfamiliar with soccer, so allow time for those students who play soccer to give a brief overview of the rules of the game.
- Explain that the story includes various kinds of humor, such as understatement and sarcasm, and help students identify examples as they read.
- Have students tell what they know about the genre of this selection. Refer to page 66A of the **Teacher's Edition** for elements of this selection's genre.

Preview and Prepare

Browse

- Have a student read aloud the title. Point out and read the names of the author and illustrator to students. Demonstrate how to browse. Then have them preview the selection by browsing the first page or two of the story. This allows them to activate prior knowledge relevant to the story. Discuss what they think this story might have to do with cooperation and competition.

■ Have the students search for clues that tell them something about the story. Also, have them look for any problems, such as unfamiliar words or long sentences, that they notice while reading. Use ***Reading Transparency 54*** to record their observations as they browse. For example, the word *losers* may be a clue that the story is about a losing team. For the Problems column, students might point out that they don't know what S.O.R. stands for. They might wonder why the team always loses. To save time and model note taking, write students' observations as brief notes rather than complete sentences.

Set Purposes

Have students set their own purposes for reading the selection. As they read, have students think about what the characters learn about winning and losing. Remind students that good readers have a purpose when they read. Let them know that they should make sure they know the purpose for reading whenever they read.

Selection Vocabulary

As students study vocabulary, they will use a variety of skills to determine the meaning of a word. These include context clues, word structure, and apposition. Students will apply these same skills while reading to clarify additional unfamiliar words.

Display ***Reading Transparency 7*** before reading the selection to introduce and discuss the following words and their meanings.

interviewed:	asked questions to find out about a person or what a person thinks (page 66)
record:	a written account of the number of games the team won and lost during the season (page 67)
prediction:	what someone thinks will happen in the future (page 67)
attitude:	how someone acts or behaves to show his or her feelings or thoughts (page 68)
ashamed:	embarrassed; not proud (page 75)
defeatist:	having no confidence to win (page 78)

Have students read the words in the Word Box, stopping to blend any words that they have trouble reading. Demonstrate how to decode multisyllabic words by breaking the words into syllables and blending the syllables. Then have the students try. If the word is not decodable, give the students the pronunciation.

Have students read the sentences on ***Reading Transparency 7*** and use the skills of context, word structure (structural analysis) or apposition to figure out the meanings of the words. Be sure students explain which skill(s) they are using and how they figured out the meanings of the words.

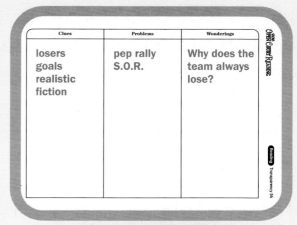

Reading Transparency 54

Teacher Tip SELECTION VOCABULARY To help students decode words, divide them into the syllables shown below. The information following each word tells how students can figure out the meaning of each word on the transparency.

in • ter • viewed	context clues, word structure
rec • ord	context clues
pre • dic • tion	context clues, word structure
at • ti • tude	context clues
a • shamed	context clues, word structure, apposition
de • feat • ist	word structure, apposition

Routine Card
Refer to Routine 2 for the selection vocabulary procedure. Refer to Routine 3 for the Clues, Problems, and Wonderings procedure.

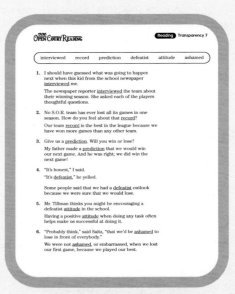

Reading Transparency 7

MEETING INDIVIDUAL NEEDS

ELL Support

VOCABULARY Check that English-language learners know the meanings of idioms and more difficult vocabulary in the story, including: *tension; interviewed; to lose every game; prediction; a pep rally; terminal illness; supportive; bribe; blocking; team captain; the school chant; the pits; beneath the pits; disown; a complete vote of no confidence; ironed-on press letters; being rejected; final pointers; the ref; we broke up at that; penalty; stolen ball; sore losers.* Explain and show pictures as needed. Model example sentences and help English-speaking students make their own sentences.

Students will enjoy using the *Listening Library Audiocassette/CD* and listening to the selection they are about to read. Encourage them to listen to the selection during Workshop. Have students discuss with each other and with you their personal listening preferences (for example, nonfiction, poetry, drama, and so on).

Routine Card
Refer to Routine 4 for the Reading the Selection procedure.

Teacher Tip COMPREHENSION STRATEGIES Let students know that good readers are using Summarizing, Visualizing, and Asking Questions all the time. Students should use these strategies whenever they read.

Reading Recommendations

Oral Reading

This contemporary selection contains a lot of dialogue, so students may enjoy reading it aloud as classmates listen. As students read aloud, have them read expressively at an appropriate pace in natural phrases and chunks. Make sure students enunciate and use appropriate intonations.

Reading the selection with fluency and accuracy will help students comprehend the text. If students have trouble reading decodable words, have them break the words into sounds or syllables and then blend them together to read the words.

After students have finished reading the selection, use the "Discussing the Selection" questions on page 83A to see if they understand what they have read.

Using Comprehension Strategies

Comprehension strategy instruction allows students to become aware of how good readers read. Good readers constantly check their understanding as they are reading and ask themselves questions. In addition, skilled readers recognize when they are having problems and stop to use various comprehension strategies to help them make sense of what they are reading.

During the reading of "S.O.R. Losers," model and prompt the use of the following reading strategies:

- **Summarizing** prompts readers to keep track of what they are reading and to focus their minds on important information.
- **Visualizing** helps readers to understand descriptions of settings, characters, and events in a story.
- **Asking Questions** prepares readers for what they want to learn.

As students read, they should be using a variety of strategies to help them understand the selection. Encourage students to use the strategies listed as the class reads the story aloud. Do this by stopping at the points indicated by the numbers in magenta circles on the reduced student page and using a particular strategy. Students can also stop reading periodically to discuss what they have learned and what problems they may be having.

Building Comprehension Skills

Revisiting or rereading a selection allows students to apply skills that give them a more complete understanding of the text. Some follow-up comprehension skills help students organize information. Others lead to deeper understanding—to "reading between the lines," as mature readers do. An extended lesson on the comprehension skill Compare and Contrast can be found in the Supporting the Reading section on pages 83C–83D. This lesson is intended to give students extra practice with Compare and Contrast. However, the Teach portion of the lesson may be used at this time to introduce the comprehension skill to students.

- **Compare and Contrast (Introduction):** Comparing and contrasting unfamiliar thoughts, ideas, or things with familiar thoughts, ideas, and things gives readers something within their own experience base to use in understanding the selection.

- **Author's Point of View (Review):** Readers identify who is telling the story, whether it is the main character speaking from a first-person point of view or a narrator speaking from a third-person point of view.

Reading with a Purpose

Have students list ways a person's interests can affect his or her competitive spirit in the Response Journal section of their Writer's Notebooks, based on what they read in the selection.

ELL Tip

PREREAD THE SELECTION Have English-language learners who may need help with the selection read it before the whole-class reading, using the *Listening Library Audiocassette/CD.* As they read, help them associate what they see in the illustrations with the words in the story, so that they learn to think English words instead of translating them first from their native language.

Intervention Tip

PREREAD THE SELECTION Preread "S.O.R. Losers" with students who may need help in reading the selection during the time you set aside for Workshop.

 Students will enjoy using the *Listening Library Audiocassette/CD* and listening to the selection they are about to read. Encourage them to listen to the selection during Workshop. Have students discuss with each other and with you their personal listening preferences (for example, nonfiction, poetry, drama, and so on).

This selection is broken into two parts. On the first day, read pages 66–76. On the second day, read pages 76–83.

Comprehension Strategies

 First Read

Teacher Modeling

1 Visualizing *I think the answers Ed gives to the newspaper reporter's questions are pretty funny. But the reporter doesn't seem to think so. She just keeps asking more questions. When I visualize her face during this scene, I picture her looking very serious. I wonder if Ed is laughing or smiling as he answers, or if he is putting on a serious face. What do you think Ed looks like as he answers the reporter's questions? Good readers are always getting images in their heads about what they read. If you get a good one, tell the class about it.*

Word Knowledge

SCAFFOLDING The skills students are reviewing in Word Knowledge should help them in reading the story. This lesson focuses on words with the long e spelled *ea*. Long e words will be found in boxes similar to this one throughout the selection.

Long e spelled *ea*:

team

Teacher Tip FORMAT Some students might be confused by the interview format at the beginning of this story. Show them newspaper or magazine interviews with similar formatting.

First Reading Recommendation

ORAL • CHORAL • SILENT

Focus Questions Should one always try to be a winner? Is it ever better to lose a competition than to win one?

S.O.R. LOSERS

from the book by Avi
illustrated by Kate Flanagan

Ed Sitrow and his friends have a big problem. All students at South Orange River Middle School are required to play one sport per year—only Ed is no jock and neither are his friends. Playing a sport is sure to mean only one thing for them—total humiliation. Somehow, they manage to slip through their first year at S.O.R. without playing a sport. But when the school catches on, they make up a special soccer team just for Ed's crowd. This soccer team is anything but typical at a school positively famous for its winning teams and all-star athletes. Mr. Lester, the history teacher, has volunteered to be their coach. Little does the team know that they'll be making history of their own.

I should have guessed what was going to happen next when this kid from the school newspaper <u>interviewed</u> me. It went this way.

NEWSPAPER: How does it feel to lose every game?
ME: I never played on a team that won, so I can't compare. But it's . . . interesting.
NEWSPAPER: How many teams have you been on?
ME: Just this one.
NEWSPAPER: Do you want to win?
ME: Wouldn't mind knowing what it feels like. For the <u>novelty</u>.
NEWSPAPER: Have you figured out why you lose all the time?
ME: They score more goals.
NEWSPAPER: Have you seen any improvement?
ME: I've been too busy.

66

 Informal Assessment

Observe individual students as they read and use the Teacher Observation Log found in the *Program Assessment Teacher's Edition* to record anecdotal information about each student's strengths and weaknesses.

NEWSPAPER: Busy with what?

ME: Trying to stop their goals. Ha-ha.

NEWSPAPER: From the scores, it doesn't seem like you've been too successful with that.

ME: You can imagine what the scores would have been if I wasn't there. Actually, I'm the tallest.

NEWSPAPER: What's that have to do with it?

ME: Ask Mr. Lester.

NEWSPAPER: No S.O.R. team has ever lost all its games in one season. How do you feel about that <u>record</u>?

ME: I read somewhere that records are made to be broken.

NEWSPAPER: But how will you feel?

ME: Same as I do now.

NEWSPAPER: How's that?

ME: Fine.

NEWSPAPER: Give us a <u>prediction</u>. Will you win or lose your last game?

ME: As captain, I can promise only one thing.

NEWSPAPER: What's that?

(1) ME: I don't want to be there to see what happens.

67

Comprehension Skills

Second Read

Compare and Contrast

Explain to students that writers often compare and contrast characters, events, settings, and ideas in order to add interest and to help readers understand a text more deeply. To *compare* means to tell how two or more things are similar. To *contrast* means to tell how two or more things are different. Have students reread the interview on pages 66–67, and help them understand the following:

- The interviewer is comparing Ed's soccer team to all other S.O.R. teams.

- Ed's attitude toward the interview is in direct contrast with that of the interviewer because he isn't taking the interview seriously and she is.

Word Knowledge

Long e spelled *ea*:

      team   season

Skills Trace

Compare and Contrast

Introduced in Grade 1.
Scaffolded throughout Grades 2–5.

REINTRODUCED:	Unit 1, Lesson 5
REINFORCED:	Unit 2, Lesson 5
	Unit 2, Lesson 6
	Unit 3, Lesson 2
	Unit 4, Lesson 3
TESTED:	Unit 1 Assessment

Second Reading Recommendation

ORAL • **SILENT**

Comprehension Strategies

 First Read

Teacher Modeling

2 Asking Questions *It's good to stop and ask questions when you encounter a word you don't know or a word that is used strangely. I wonder what Ed means when he says "Maybe we should defect?" You don't often hear the word "defect" used the way Ed has here. If we don't find out what Ed means by reading a little farther, we should look up the word to see what he's suggesting he and Saltz do. First we should pay close attention to see if the answer is in the story.*

3 Answering Questions *We don't have to read far before our question is answered. It looks like Ed was joking that they should leave the country to avoid the game. "Defect" must mean to abandon your own country for another one, in this case one without any sports! Let's keep reading to see if this gets brought up again.*

> ### Word Knowledge
> **Long e spelled *ea*:**
> **teacher   defeatist   sneak   mean**

Teacher Tip ASKING QUESTIONS
Remind students to look for the answers to their questions as they read. In some cases, the answer may not be in the text. In such instances, students should infer the answer from the information they do have.

Naturally, they printed all that. Next thing I knew some kids decided to hold a pep rally.

"What for?" asked Radosh.

"To fill us full of pep, I suppose."

"What's pep?"

Hays looked it up. "Dash," he read.

Saltz shook his head.

"What's dash?" asked Porter.

"Sounds like a deodorant soap," said Eliscue.

And then Ms. Appleton called me aside. "Ed," she said, sort of whispering (I guess she was embarrassed to be seen talking to any of us), "people are asking, 'Do they *want* to lose?'"

"Who's asking?"

"It came up at the last teachers' meeting. Mr. Tillman thinks you might be encouraging a <u>defeatist</u> attitude in the school. And Mr. Lester . . ."

"What about him?"

"He doesn't know."

It figured. "Ms. Appleton," I said, "why do people care so much if we win or lose?"

"It's your . . . <u>attitude</u>," she said. "It's so unusual. We're not used to . . . well . . . not winning sometimes. Or . . . not caring if you lose."

"Think there's something the matter with us?" I wanted to know.

"No," she said, but when you say "no" the way she did, slowly, there's lots of time to sneak in a good hint of "yes." "I don't think you *mean* to lose."

"That's not what I asked."

"It's important to win," she said.

"Why? We're good at other things. Why can't we stick with that?"

But all she said was, "Try harder."

68

 Informal Assessment

Use the Informal Comprehension Strategies Rubrics on page 66J to determine whether a student is using the strategies being taught.

COMPREHENSION

I went back to my seat. "I'm getting nervous," I mumbled.

"About time," said Saltz.

❷ "Maybe we should defect."

"Where to?"

❸ "There must be some country that doesn't have sports."

Then, of course, when my family sat down for dinner that night it went on.

"In two days you'll have your last game, won't you," my ma said. It was false cheerful, as if I had a terminal illness and she wanted to pretend it was only a head cold.

"Yeah," I said.

"You're going to win," my father announced.

"How do you know?" I snapped.

"I sense it."

"Didn't know you could tell the future."

"Don't be so smart," he returned. "I'm trying to be supportive."

"I'm sick of support!" I yelled and left the room.

69

Comprehension Skills

Second Read

Compare and Contrast

Explain to students that some comparisons and contrasts are directly stated. Some words that signal comparisons are *both, like, as, also, too,* and *neither . . . nor.* Some words that signal contrasts are *different, instead of, but, rather than,* and *unlike.*

Tell students that comparisons and contrasts can sometimes be implied, or not directly stated. Ask students to explain the two things being contrasted in the following:

■ "It's your . . . attitude," she said. "It's so unusual. We're not used to . . . well . . . not winning sometimes. Or . . . not caring if you lose." (page 68) *(The attitude of the current soccer team and that of all other students or other athletic students are being contrasted.)*

> **Word Knowledge**
> **Long e spelled *ea*:**
> seat

MEETING INDIVIDUAL NEEDS
Challenge

DRAWING CONCLUSIONS Have the students work in small groups to write and act out the scene at the pep rally. Have them imagine what Ed's team will say to the rest of the school about why they keep losing and how it's okay with them. Then have students use the conclusions they draw in the exercise to predict how the rest of the school will react to what Ed's team says.

COMPREHENSION

Comprehension Strategies

First Read

Teacher Modeling

4 Asking Questions *Ed seems to be very upset, so we need to ask why he would feel this way. Is he upset because people are bugging him, or is there a part of him that feels bad because he's losing?*

Ed says he feels fine about losing. Is that really true? We should pay close attention to Ed's feelings as we continue to read. If you come up with any other questions or any answers to questions we've already asked, share them with the group.

Teacher Modeling

5 Visualizing *Visualizing the events in a story can help us connect with its characters. They made poor Ed speak in front of everyone without even giving him any warning. From the way he was talking, I imagine he looked pretty nervous. I can visualize him standing up on a stage in front of everyone in the cafeteria and looking very small up there by himself. I would hate it if I were in that position. How do you visualize this part of the story?*

Word Knowledge

SCAFFOLDING The skills students are reviewing in Word Knowledge should help them in reading the story. This lesson focuses on words with the /ch/ sound spelled *ch. Ch* words will be found in boxes similar to this one throughout the selection.

Ch words:

> lunch

Twenty minutes later I got a call. Saltz.

"Guess what?" he said.

"I give up."

"Two things. My father offered me a bribe."

"To lose the game?"

"No, to win it. A new bike."

"Wow. What did you say?"

"I told him I was too honest to win a game."

"What was the second thing?"

"I found out that at lunch tomorrow they are doing that pep rally, and worse. They're going to call up the whole team."

I sighed. "Why are they doing all this?" I asked.

"Nobody loves a loser," said Saltz.

"Why?" I asked him, just as I had asked everybody else.

"Beats me. Like everybody else does." He hung up.

I went into my room and flung myself on my bed and stared up at the ceiling. A short time later my father came into the room. "Come on, kid," he said, "I was just trying to be a pal."

"Why can't people let us lose in peace?"

"People think you feel bad."

4 "We feel *fine!*"

"Come on. We won't talk about it any more. Eat your dinner."

I went.

Next day, when I walked into the school eating area for lunch there was the usual madhouse. But there was also a big banner across the front part of the room:

> ***Make the Losers Winners***
> ***Keep Up the Good Name of***
> ***S.O.R.***

70

MEETING INDIVIDUAL NEEDS

Intervention Support

SUMMARIZING Review with students that it is a good idea to summarize frequently when reading a story that has many characters or events, or covers a long period of time. Reread this part of the selection with students having difficulty with its main ideas.

I wanted to start a food fight right then and there.

I'm not going through the whole bit. But halfway through the lunch period, the president of the School Council, of all people, went to the microphone and called for attention. Then she made a speech.

"We just want to say to the Special Seventh-Grade Soccer Team that we're all behind you."

"It's in front of us where we need people," whispered Saltz. "Blocking."

The president went on. "Would you come up and take a bow." One by one she called our names. Each time one of us went up, looking like <u>cringing</u> but grinning worms, there was some general craziness, hooting, foot stomping, and an occasional milk carton shooting through the air.

The president said: "I'd like the team captain, Ed Sitrow, to say a few words."

5 What could I do? Trapped, I cleared my throat. Four times. "Ah, well . . . we . . . ah . . . sure . . . hope to get there . . . and . . . you know . . . I suppose . . . play and . . . you know!"

71

Comprehension Skills

Compare and Contrast

Review with students the definitions of compare and contrast. Then, ask students to recall words that indicate comparisons or contrasts. Help them understand the contrast in the following:

■ "Make the *Losers Winners*" (page 70)

Word Knowledge

Ch words:

     lunch   speech   each

Teacher Tip *WRITING SKILLS*
Some students might enjoy writing cheers for Ed's team. Encourage them to write cheers expressing Ed's indifference about winning.

COMPREHENSION

Comprehension Strategies

First Read

Teacher Modeling

6 Summarizing *Let's stop and quickly sum up what's happened so far. This will help us check our understanding of the events up to this point. Ed's team has lost all its soccer games this season, but they don't seem to care. The rest of the school really cares. The newspaper prints an article about his team, the teachers bring it up in a meeting, and the students decide to hold a pep rally. That's a lot of pressure on Ed and his team. Can you add anything to this summary?*

Let's continue reading, and as we do, remember to summarize what we are reading. Make sure you understand what you have just read. Let me know if you would like to share your summary with the group.

Word Knowledge

Long e spelled *ea*:

> seats   beating   beneath

Teacher Tip ANSWERING QUESTIONS Remind the students to look for the answers to the questions they ask as they read. The answer to the question asked in the strategy exercise on page 70 is answered on lines 10–15 of page 73.

The whole room stood up to cheer. They even began the school chant.

"Give me an S! Give me an O . . . "

After that we went back to our seats. I was madder than ever. And as I sat there, maybe two hundred and fifty kids filed by, thumping me hard on the back, shoulder, neck and head, yelling, "Good luck! Good luck!" They couldn't fool me. I knew what they were doing: beating me.

6 "Saltz," I said when they were gone and I was merely numb, "I'm calling an emergency meeting of the team."

Like thieves, we met behind the school, out of sight. I looked around. I could see everybody was feeling rotten.

"I'm sick and tired of people telling me we have to win," said Root.

"I think my folks are getting ready to disown me," said Hays. "My brother and sister too."

"Why can't they just let us lose?" asked Macht.

"Yeah," said Barish, "because we're not going to win."

"We might," Lifsom offered. "Parkville is supposed to be the pits too."

"Yeah," said Radosh, "but we're beneath the pits."

"Right," agreed Porter.

For a moment it looked like everyone was going to start to cry.

"I'd just like to do my math," said Macht. "I like that."

There it was. Something clicked. "Hays," I said, "you're good at music, right."

"Yeah, well, sure—rock 'n' roll."

"Okay. And Macht, what's the lowest score you've pulled in math so far?"

"A-plus."

"Last year?"

"Same."

72

MEETING INDIVIDUAL NEEDS

Intervention

ASKING QUESTIONS Read students small portions of the text, then stop and ask a question about what they have read. Breaking the text into small chunks will help students get used to asking questions.

"Lifsom," I went on, getting excited, "how's your painting coming?"

"I just finished something real neat and . . ."

"That's it," I cut in, because that kid can go on forever about his painting. "Every one of us is good at something. Right? Maybe more than one thing. The point is, *other* things."

"Sure," said Barish.

"Except," put in Saltz, "sports."

We were quiet for a moment. Then I saw what had been coming to me: "That's *their* problem. I mean, we are good, good at *lots* of things. Why can't we just plain stink in some places? That's got to be normal."

"Let's hear it for normal," chanted Dorman.

"Doesn't bother me to lose at sports," I said. "At least, it didn't bother me until I let other people make me bothered."

"What about the school record?" asked Porter. "You know, no team ever losing for a whole season. Want to be famous for that?"

"Listen," I said, "did we want to be on this team?"

"No!" they all shouted.

73

Teacher Tip WRITING DESCRIPTIONS
Have the students write descriptions of new sporting events that would combine physical activity with the strengths of Ed's teammates. One example might be a bicycle race in which the riders complete both the course and a painting in order to win. Another example could be an obstacle course that required one to solve math equations in order to pass from obstacle to obstacle.

Comprehension Skills

Author's Point of View

Point out that *author's point of view* tells what kind of narrator the writer uses to tell the story. In a *first-person narrative*, one of the characters tells the story. In the *third-person narrative*, the story is told by someone outside of the story.

■ "*We* were quiet for a moment. Then *I* saw what had been coming to *me*: 'That's their problem . . .'" (page 73)

Explain that this example shows that the story is told from a first-person point of view. A third-person point of view would have used the words *he*, *him*, and *their* instead of *I*, *me*, and *we*. The story is told in this point of view so that the reader will be allowed to know what the narrator, Ed, is thinking. The story would be quite different from another point of view—readers wouldn't know how the "S.O.R. Losers" felt about "losing." They would only know what an outside narrator thought they felt. This point of view also helps readers really get to know Ed's personality.

> ### Word Knowledge
> *Ch* word:
>
> **chanted**

Skills Trace
Author's Point of View
Introduced in Grade 2.
Scaffolded throughout Grades 3–5.
REINTRODUCED: Unit 1, Lesson 3
REINFORCED: Unit 1, Lesson 5
Unit 3, Lesson 1
Unit 3, Lesson 4
Unit 3, Lesson 5
TESTED: Unit 1 Assessment

COMPREHENSION

Comprehension Strategies

 First Read

Teacher Modeling

7 Asking Questions *That's a good question Radosh is asking. Why are sports so important? Are they more important than painting or writing a poem or doing math? What do you think?*

When I think about what we read, I can see that Ed and his team don't think so. I wonder how Ed and his team can make the rest of the school understand that. Let's keep reading.

Teacher Modeling

8 Visualizing *The ability to visualize helps readers better understand and enjoy the selection. Right now, I am visualizing the secret meeting between Ed and his friends behind the school building. I can imagine how miserable they feel at first, knowing that it means so much to everyone else that they be winners in soccer when they know they never will be. But, I can also picture their growing excitement as they figure out that they don't need to be good at soccer because they are all good at other things.*

Remember that good readers are always getting images in their heads about what they read. If you get a good one, tell the class about it.

Word Knowledge

Ch words:

much   cheer

Teacher Tip ASKING AND ANSWERING QUESTIONS Remind the students to jot down whatever questions they have to help them remember to look for the answers to their questions as they read.

"I can see some of it," I said. "You know, doing something different. But I don't like sports. I'm not good at it. I don't enjoy it. So I say, so what? I mean if Saltz here writes a stinko poem—and he does all the time—do they yell at him? When was the last time Mr. Tillman came around and said, 'Saltz, I *believe* in your being a poet!'"

"Never," said Saltz.

7 "Yeah," said Radosh. "How come sports is so important?"

"You know," said Dorman, "maybe a loser makes people think of things *they* lost. Like Mr. Tillman not getting into pro football. Us losing makes him remember that."

"Us winning, he forgets," cut in Eliscue.

"Right," I agreed. "He needs us to win for *him*, not for us. Maybe it's the same for others."

74

MEETING INDIVIDUAL NEEDS

ELL

ASKING AND ANSWERING QUESTIONS Read a short passage to English-language learners and have them ask questions about the most important point in the passage. Provide help as needed in stating questions, suggesting that they include words such as *Who? What? When? Why? How?* and *Where?* as appropriate.

"Yeah, but how are you going to convince them of that?" said Barish.

"By not caring if we lose," I said.

"Only one thing," put in Saltz. "They say this Parkville team is pretty bad too. What happens if we, you know, by mistake, win?"

That set us back a moment.

"I think," suggested Hays after a moment, "that if we just go on out there, relax, and do our best, and not worry so much, we'll lose."

8 There was general agreement on that point.

"Do you know what I heard?" said Eliscue.

"What?"

"I didn't want to say it before, but since the game's a home game, they're talking about letting the whole school out to cheer us on to a win."

"You're kidding."

He shook his head.

There was a long, deep silence.

"Probably think," said Saltz, "that we'd be <u>ashamed</u> to lose in front of everybody."

I took a quick count. "You afraid to lose?" I asked Saltz.

"No way."

"Hays?"

"No."

"Porter?"

"Nope."

And so on. I felt encouraged. It was a complete vote of no confidence.

"Well," I said, "they just might see us lose again. With Parkville so bad I'm not saying it's automatic. But I'm not going to care if we do."

"Right," said Radosh. "It's not like we're committing <u>treason</u> or something. People have a right to be losers."

We considered that for a moment. It was then I had my most brilliant idea. "Who has money?"

"What for?"

"I'm your tall captain, right? Trust me. And bring your soccer T-shirts to me in the morning, early."

75

COMPREHENSION

Comprehension Skills

Author's Point of View

Remind students that using a first-person point of view limits the author to showing only that character's thoughts and feelings. Point out the following passages.

- "I felt encouraged." (page 75)
- "It was then I had my most brilliant idea." (page 75)

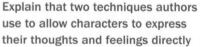

Long e spelled *ea:*
treason

Teacher Tip CHARACTERIZATION
Explain that two techniques authors use to allow characters to express their thoughts and feelings directly are using dialogue and telling the story from a first-person point of view.

Comprehension Strategies

 First Read

Teacher Modeling

9 Summarizing *I think this is a good time to stop reading for today. When you take a break in the middle of a story like this, it is a good idea to summarize everything you have read so far. Everyone seems to want Ed's team to win, except the team itself. The pressure put on Ed and the team almost gets to them, but in a secret meeting, the team agrees not to care if they lose their last game. Finally, Ed collects money from the team members and asks them to bring him their soccer shirts. I wonder what this last detail is all about? It seems like Ed has some secret plan he won't tell the others about. We'll have to read more tomorrow to find out what Ed is planning!*

Teacher Modeling

10 Asking Questions *Now Ed is sneaking into the home ec room so we can't see what he's doing. I wonder what they did with the T-shirts in there? Maybe we'll find out when the game starts. After all, they have to put on those T-shirts sooner or later!*

Teacher Modeling

11 Answering Questions *My question about the shirts from earlier has been answered. Ed and Saltz added letters. I knew we'd see the shirts when the team got dressed for the game. I think adding "Losers" to the team's shirts was a bit of a risk. I hope the team likes the change! Let's read on. Remember to share any questions you have with the class.*

Word Knowledge

Long e spelled *ea*:
    mean   leaned   beat   sneaked

I collected about four bucks and we split up. I held Saltz back.

"What's the money all about?" he wanted to know. "And the T-shirts."

9 "Come on," I told him. "Maybe we can show them we really mean it."

When I woke the next morning, I have to admit, I was excited. It wasn't going to be an ordinary day. I looked outside and saw the sun was shining. I thought, "Good."

For the first time I *wanted* a game to happen.

I got to breakfast a little early, actually feeling happy.

"Today's the day," Dad announced.

"Right."

"Today you'll really win," chipped in my ma.

"Could be."

My father leaned across the table and gave me a tap. "Winning the last game is what matters. Go out with your head high, Ed."

"And my backside up if I lose?" I wanted to know.

"Ed," said my ma, "don't be so hard on yourself. Your father and I are coming to watch."

"Suit yourselves," I said, and beat it to the bus.

As soon as I got to class Saltz and I collected the T-shirts. "What are you going to do with them?" the others kept asking.

"You picked me as captain, didn't you?"

"Mr. Lester did."

"Well, this time, trust *me*."

10 When we got all the shirts, Saltz and I sneaked into the home ec room and did what needed to be done. Putting them into a bag so no one would see, we went back to class.

"Just about over," I said.

"I'm almost sorry," confessed Saltz.

"Me too," I said. "And I can't figure out why."

76

Teacher Tip SUMMARIZING Since this story has been divided into two parts, have students summarize what has happened so far before they begin reading the second part.

"Maybe it's—the team that loses together, really stays together."

"Right. Not one fathead on the whole team. Do you think we should have gotten a farewell present for Mr. Lester?"

"Like what?"

"A begging cup."

It was hard getting through the day. And it's impossible to know how many people wished me luck. From all I got it was clear they considered me the unluckiest guy in the whole world. I kept wishing I could have banked it for something important.

But the day got done.

It was down in the locker room, when we got ready, that I passed out the T-shirts.

Barish held his up. It was the regular shirt with "S.O.R." on the back. But under it Saltz and I had ironed on press letters. Now they all read:

11 S.O.R.
LOSERS

Comprehension Skills

Author's Point of View

Remind the students that using a first-person point of view limits the author to showing only that character's thoughts and feelings. Have students find examples of this fact in the text, such as the following.

- "When I woke the next morning, I have to admit, I was excited." (page 76)

- "For the first time I wanted a game to happen." (page 76)

- "My father leaned across the table and gave me a tap." (page 76)

Explain that the author is showing story events through Ed's eyes and sharing how Ed feels.

> ### Word Knowledge
> **Long e spelled *ea*:**
> clear

Teacher Tip OBSERVING STUDENTS
Observe students' nonverbal reactions as they read—a puzzled frown, a long pause, a look of surprise, a smile. When you see such reactions, ask students to share their questions and comments.

Comprehension Strategies

First Read

Teacher Modeling

12 Visualizing *I know that happy beads are a kind of necklace made of glass or wooden beads. I think the reason people wear them is so that they can rub the beads together and remind themselves to have a good attitude. Now that I've made that connection, I think that if Mr. Tillman is shaking them furiously, they are not doing him much good. Can you visualize how Mr. Tillman must have looked?*

Teacher Modeling

13 Visualizing *Ed and his team have reached the crucial moment, where they will be either winners or losers in this final competition between "horribles." For this reason, I am visualizing what it must be like to be walking out onto the soccer field with them in their "S.O.R. Loser" jerseys with all those people watching. Ed says that the crowd starts getting a little crazy when it begins to sense that he and his team don't care if they win or lose. I think I would be a little scared of all those victory-obsessed fans myself. What do you see in this scene?*

Word Knowledge
Long e spelled *ea:*
    defeatist   reasons

Teacher Tip DISCUSSION If a new or unexpected idea is generated during discussion, have students comment on it.

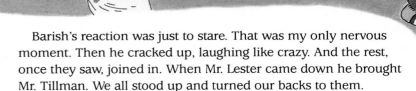

Barish's reaction was just to stare. That was my only nervous moment. Then he cracked up, laughing like crazy. And the rest, once they saw, joined in. When Mr. Lester came down he brought Mr. Tillman. We all stood up and turned our backs to them.

"Oh, my goodness," moaned Mr. Lester.

12 "That's sick," said Mr. Tillman. "Sick!" His happy beads shook furiously.

"It's honest," I said.

"It's <u>defeatist</u>," he yelled.

"Mr. Tillman," I asked, "is that true, about your trying out for pro football?"

He started to say something, then stopped, his mouth open. "Yeah. I tried to make it with the pros, but couldn't."

"So you lost too, right?"

"Yeah," chimed in Radosh, "everyone loses sometime."

"Listen here, you guys," said Mr. Tillman, "it's no fun being rejected."

"Can't it be okay to lose sometimes? You did. Lots do. You're still alive. And we don't dislike you because of that."

"Right. We got other reasons," I heard a voice say. I think it was Saltz.

Mr. Tillman started to say something, but turned and fled.

Mr. Lester tried to give us a few final pointers, like don't touch the ball with our hands, only use feet, things that we didn't always remember to do.

"Well," he said finally, "I enjoyed this."

"You did?" said Porter, surprised.

"Well, not much," he admitted. "I never coached anything before. To tell the truth, I don't know anything about soccer."

"Now you tell us," said Eliscue. But he was kidding. We sort of guessed that before.

78

Comprehension Skills

Second Read

Compare and Contrast

Have students identify the comparisons or contrasts in the following items:

- "As we ran onto the field, we were met with something like a roar." (page 79)

- "The big difference was their faces. Stiff and tight. You could see, they *wanted* to win. Had to win. We were relaxed and fooling around." (page 79)

Word Knowledge

Ch word:

chanting

Just as we started out onto the field, Saltz whispered to me, "What if we win?"

"With our luck, we will," I said.

And on we went.

As we ran onto the field we were met with something like a roar. Maybe the whole school wasn't there. But a lot were. And they were chanting, "Win! Win! Win!"

13 But when they saw the backs of our shirts, they really went wild. Crazy. And you couldn't tell if they were for us or against us. I mean scary . . .

Oh yes, the game . . .

We had been told that Parkville was a team that hadn't won a game either. They looked it. From the way they kicked the ball around—tried to kick the ball around—it was clear this was going to be a true contest between horribles.

The big difference was their faces. Stiff and tight. You could see, they *wanted* to win. Had to win. We were relaxed and fooling around. Having a grand old time.

Not them.

79

Comprehension Strategies

First Read

Teacher Modeling

14 Asking Questions *Here Ed has prompted us to ask a question by telling us that something has happened, but not what. This makes me wonder what "it" could possibly be. The way he refers to it, it sounds important. We'll have to keep reading to find out what it is!*

Word Knowledge

Ch words:

coach   each

Teacher Tip ASKING QUESTIONS Inform students that they should keep asking questions and trying to answer them as they read.

Research in Action
Strategy Use

Modeling should always be used to get the children started, but it should stop as soon as they think independently at the level you have demonstrated. They show you they can do this by thinking aloud themselves during the reading lesson. Once you have turned the thinking aloud over to the children, your involvement should be limited to tactful shaping of their comments to improve their appropriateness.

(Jan Hirshberg)

The ref blew his whistle and called captains. I went out, shook hands. The Parkville guy was really tense. He kept squeezing his hands, rubbing his face. The whole bit.

The ref said he wanted the usual, a clean, hard game, and he told us which side we should defend. "May the best team win," he said. A believer!

Anyway, we started.

(I know the way this is supposed to work. . . . There we are, relaxed, having a good time, not caring really what goes on, maybe by this time, not even sweating the outcome. That should make us, in television land—winners. Especially as it becomes very clear that Parkville is frantic about winning. Like crazy. They have a coach who screams himself red-faced all the time. Who knows. Maybe he's going to lose his job if they lose.)

Well . . .

A lot of things happened that game. There was the moment, just like the first game, when their side, dressed in stunning scarlet, came plunging down our way. Mighty Saltz went out to meet them like a battleship. True to form (red face and wild) he gave a mighty kick, and missed. But he added something new. Leave it to my buddy Saltz. He swung so hard he sat down, sat down on the ball. Like he was hatching an egg.

We broke up at that. So did everyone else. Except the Parkville coach. He was screaming, "Penalty! Penalty!"

So they got the ball. And, it's true, I was laughing so much they scored an easy goal. It was worth it.

"Least you could have done is hatched it," I yelled at Saltz.

"I think they allow only eleven on a team," he yelled back.

Then there was the moment when Porter, Radosh and Dorman got into a really terrific struggle to get the ball–from each other. Only when they looked up did they realize with whom they were struggling. By that time, of course, it was too late. Stolen ball.

80

There was the moment when Parkville knocked the ball out of bounds. Macht had to throw it in. He snatched up the ball, held it over his head, got ready to heave it, then–dropped it.

It was a close game though. The closest. By the time it was almost over they were leading by only one. We were actually in the game.

And how did the crowd react? They didn't know what to do. Sometimes they laughed. Sometimes they chanted that "Win! Win!" thing. It was like a party for them.

14 Then it happened . . .

Macht took the ball on a pass from Lifsom. Lifsom <u>dribbled</u> down the right side and flipped it toward the middle. Hays got it fairly well, and, still driving, shot a pass back to Radosh, who somehow managed to snap it easy over to Porter, who was right near the side of the goal.

Porter, not able to shoot, knocked the ball back to Hays, who charged toward the goal–only some Parkville guy managed to get in the way. Hays, screaming, ran right over him, still controlling the ball.

Comprehension Skills

Compare and Contrast

Have students point out the comparisons and contrasts in the following text.

- "There was the moment, just like the first game, when their side, dressed in stunning scarlet, came plunging down our way." (page 80)

- "He swung so hard he sat down, sat down on the ball. Like he was hatching an egg." (page 80)

Word Knowledge
Long e spelled *ea*:
    heave   leading   easy   screaming

Teacher Tip FLUENCY By this time in grade 5, good readers should be reading approximately 126 words per minute with fluency and expression. The only way to gain this fluency is through practice. Have students reread the selection to you and to one another during Workshop to help build fluency.

Comprehension Strategies

First Read

Teacher Modeling

15 **Answering Questions** *I think we know now what "it" is. Hays missed an easy shot, and started to feel bad about it. But Ed and the team chanted "S.O.R. Loser" to remind Hays that it was about having fun, not about winning or losing.*

I think I can answer my question from earlier, about whether there is a part of Ed that feels bad about losing. Since Ed started chanting "S.O.R. Loser" to keep Hays from feeling bad, it looks like he doesn't feel bad at all. And it looks like the whole team feels the same as Ed!

Discussing Strategy Use

While they are reading the selection, have students share any problems they encountered and tell what strategies they used.

- What questions did they ask as they read?
- How did they summarize the text?
- What did they visualize as they were reading?

Remind students that good readers use all of the strategies listed above and that they should be using them whenever they read. Make sure that students explain how using the strategies helped them understand the selection better. For example, students might say, "Visualizing helped me understand things that happened during the games."

Word Knowledge

Long e spelled *ea:*
mean   cleanest   screaming   meanwhile

I stood there, astonished. "They've gotten to him," I said to myself. "He's flipped."

I mean, Hays was like a wild man. Not only had he the cleanest shot in the universe, he was desperate.

And so . . . he tripped. Fell flat on his face. Thunk!

Their goalie scooped up the ball, flung it downfield and that was the end of that.

As for Hays, he picked himself up, slowly, too slowly. The crowd grew still.

You could see it all over Hays. Shame. The crowd waited. They were feeling sorry for him. You could feel it. And standing there in the middle of the field—everything had just stopped— everybody was watching Hays—the poor guy began to cry.

That's all you could hear. His sobs. He had failed.

Then I remembered. "SOR LOSER!" I bellowed.

At my yell, our team snapped up their heads and looked around.

"SOR LOSER!" I bellowed again.

The team picked up the words and began to run toward Hays, yelling, cheering, screaming, "SOR LOSER! SOR LOSER! SOR LOSER!"

Hays, stunned, began to get his eyes up.

Meanwhile, the whole team, and I'm not kidding, joined hands and began to run in circles around Hays, still giving the chant.

The watching crowd, trying to figure out what was happening, finally began to understand. And they began to cheer!

 15 "SOR LOSER   SOR LOSER   SOR LOSER!"

As for Hays, well, you should have seen his face. It was like a Disney nature-film flower blooming. Slow, but steady. Fantastic! There grew this great grin on his face. Then he lifted his arms in victory and he too began to cheer. He had won—himself.

82

Right about then the horn blared. The game was over. The season was done. Losers again. Champions of the <u>bloody</u> bottom.

We hugged each other, screamed and hooted like teams do when they win championships. And we were a lot happier than those Parkville guys who had won.

In the locker room we started to take off our uniforms. Mr. Lester broke in.

"Wait a minute," he announced. "Team picture."

We trooped out again, lining up, arm in arm, our *backs* to the camera. We were having fun!

"English test tomorrow," said Saltz as he and I headed for home. "I haven't studied yet. I'll be up half the night."

"Don't worry," I said. "For *that*, I believe in you."

"You know what?" he said. "So do I."

And he did. <u>Aced</u> it. *Our* way.

83

Teacher Tip BUILDING FLUENCY
As students read, you may notice that some need work in building fluency. During Workshop, have these students choose a section of text (a minimum of 160 words) to read several times in order to build fluency.

Formal Assessment

See pages 18–21 in the *Unit 1 Assessment* to test students' comprehension of "S.O.R. Losers."

Comprehension Skills

Compare and Contrast

Help students identify the comparisons in the following:

- "As for Hays, well, you should have seen his face. It was like a Disney nature-film flower blooming." (page 82)

- "We hugged each other, screamed and hooted like teams do when they win championships." (page 83)

Checking Comprehension

Ask students the following questions to check on their comprehension of the story.

- Why was it so important to everyone else that Ed's team win a soccer game? *(They were more competitive than the team.)*

- What if Ed and his friends had cared about winning? Is it possible they might have won some games then? *(With the team's ability to cooperate, they might have won.)*

- Would Ed and his friends have cared more about winning if they had been competing for an award in something they did better, such as an art contest or a quiz show? *(Such a competition would have had more meaning for the team.)*

- How has this selection connected with your knowledge of the unit theme? *(Answers will vary—students should compare/contrast examples of cooperation and competition from this selection with their own experiences or past reading and use these connections to make a general statement about the unit theme.)*

COMPREHENSION

2 Reading & Responding   S.O.R. Losers

Routine Card
Refer to Routine 5 for the
handing-off process.

Clues	Problems	Wonderings
losers goals realistic fiction	pep rally S.O.R.	Why does the team always lose?

Reading Transparency 54

www.sra4kids.com
Web Connection
Some students may choose to conduct a computer search for additional books or information about cooperation and competition. Invite them to make a list of these books and sources of information to share with classmates and the school librarian. Check the reading link of the SRA Web page for additional links to theme-related Web sites.

Discussing the Selection

 The whole group discusses the selection and any personal thoughts, reactions, problems, or questions that it raises. To stimulate discussion, students can ask one another the kinds of questions that good readers ask themselves about a text: *How does it connect to cooperation and competition? What have I learned that is new? What did I find interesting? What is important here? What was difficult to understand? Why would someone want to read this?* It is important for students to see you as a contributing member of the group.

Routine 5 To emphasize that you are part of the group, actively participate in the *handing-off process:* Raise your hand to be called on by the last speaker when you have a contribution to make. Point out unusual and interesting insights verbalized by students so that these insights are recognized and discussed. As the year progresses, students will take more and more responsibility for the discussion of selections.

Engage students in a discussion to determine whether they have grasped the following ideas.

- how cooperation affected competition
- why the characters on the soccer team did not care about winning
- that it is okay not to be competitive in everything

During this time, have students return to the clues, problems, and wonderings that they noted during browsing to determine whether the clues were borne out by the selection, whether and how their problems were solved, and whether their wonderings were answered or deserve further discussion and exploration. Let the students decide which items deserve further discussion.

Also have students return to the Focus Questions on the first page of the selection. Select a student to read the questions aloud, and have volunteers answer the questions. If students do not know the answers to the questions, have them return to the text to find the answers.

You may also wish to review the elements of realistic fiction with the students at this time. Discuss with them how they can tell that "S.O.R. Losers" is realistic fiction.

 Have students break into small groups to discuss how the story reflects the theme. Groups can then share ideas with the rest of the class.

 Students may wish to record their thoughts about and reactions to this selection. Encourage students to write about how the members of the soccer team are different from most competitors.

Review Selection Vocabulary

Have students review the definitions of the selection vocabulary words that they wrote in the vocabulary section of their Writer's Notebooks. Remind them that they discussed the meanings of these words before reading the selection. Students can use these definitions to study for the vocabulary portion of their Lesson Assessment. Have them add to the personal dictionary section of their Writer's Notebook any other interesting words that they clarify while reading. Encourage students to refer to the selection vocabulary words throughout the unit. The words from the selection are:

interviewed   record   prediction   ashamed   defeatist   attitude

If you have created a Word Bank, have students place words under the appropriate headings on the Word Bank. Encourage the students to find other words related to the unit theme and add them to the Word Bank.

Home Connection

Distribute ***Home Connection,*** page 11. Encourage students to discuss "S.O.R. Losers" with their families. Students can discuss a chart to compare and contrast the S.O.R. and Parkville teams. ***Home Connection*** is also available in Spanish, page 12.

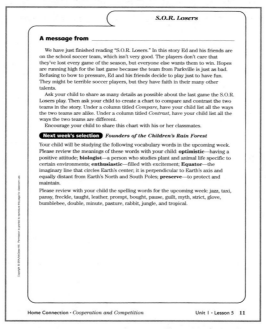

S.O.R. Losers

A message from _____

We have just finished reading "S.O.R. Losers." In this story Ed and his friends are on the school soccer team, which isn't very good. The players don't care that they've lost every game of the season, but everyone else wants them to win. Hopes are running high for the last game because the team from Parkville is just as bad. Refusing to bow to pressure, Ed and his friends decide to play just to have fun. They might be terrible soccer players, but they have faith in their many other talents.

Ask your child to share as many details as possible about the last game the S.O.R. Losers play. Then ask your child to create a chart to compare and contrast the two teams in the story. Under a column titled *Compare,* have your child list all the ways the two teams are alike. Under a column titled *Contrast,* have your child list all the ways the two teams are different.

Encourage your child to share this chart with his or her classmates.

Next week's selection *Founders of the Children's Rain Forest*

Your child will be studying the following vocabulary words in the upcoming week. Please review the meanings of these words with your child: **optimistic**—having a positive attitude; **biologist**—a person who studies plant and animal life specific to certain environments; **enthusiastic**—filled with excitement; **Equator**—the imaginary line that circles Earth's center; it is perpendicular to Earth's axis and equally distant from Earth's North and South Poles; **preserve**—to protect and maintain.

Please review with your child the spelling words for the upcoming week: jazz, taxi, pansy, freckle, taught, leather, prompt, bought, pause, guilt, myth, strict, glove, bumblebee, double, minute, pasture, rabbit, jungle, and tropical.

Home Connection · *Cooperation and Competition*   Unit 1 · Lesson 5   11

Home Connection p. 11

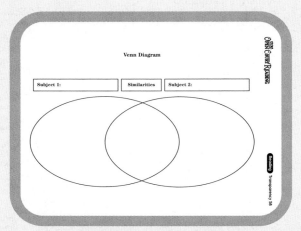

Reading Transparency 58

Supporting the Reading

Comprehension Skills: Compare and Contrast

Teach Have students tell you what they know about comparing and contrasting. Then tell them that writers often use comparison and contrast to help readers understand ideas and to highlight certain characteristics of things being described. To *compare* means to tell how two or more things are similar. Some words that signal comparison are *both, like, as, also, too,* and *neither . . . nor.* To *contrast* means to tell how two or more things are different. Some words that signal contrast are *different, instead of, but, rather than,* and *unlike.*

Guided Practice To help students practice and organize comparisons and contrasts from "S.O.R. Losers," use the Venn diagram on **_Reading Transparency 58._** Explain that contrasts will be included in the outer circles and comparisons, or similarities, will be included in the overlap. Label the first circle "Attitude of S.O.R. Losers" and the second circle "Attitude of Others." Label the overlap "Similarities." Have students help you fill in the diagram. After completing the diagram, have students discuss how the author's use of comparisons and contrasts helped them to better understand ideas presented in the text.

Independent Practice Read through the **Focus** and **Identify** sections of *Comprehension and Language Arts Skills,* page 22 with students. Guide students through the **Identify** portion, and have them come up with examples found in the story. Then have students complete the **Practice** and **Apply** portions of *Comprehension and Language Arts Skills,* page 23 as homework.

Link to Writing Explain to students that when a writer organizes a piece by comparison and contrast, he or she usually uses one of two kinds of organization. The material can be organized point by point, or each topic can be thoroughly addressed separately. Have students choose two of their favorite hobbies and compare and contrast them. They might organize their notes in a Venn diagram. Then they can decide how they will organize their writing.

MEETING INDIVIDUAL NEEDS

Reteach

COMPARE AND CONTRAST Have students who need additional practice with compare and contrast complete *Reteach,* pages 24–25.

Challenge

COMPARE AND CONTRAST Have students who understand compare and contrast complete *Challenge,* page 20.

Skills Trace
Compare and Contrast
Introduced in Grade 1.
Scaffolded in Grades 2–5.
REINTRODUCED: Unit 1, Lesson 5
REINFORCED: Unit 2, Lesson 5
Unit 2, Lesson 6
Unit 3, Lesson 2
Unit 4, Lesson 3
TESTED: Unit 1 Assessment

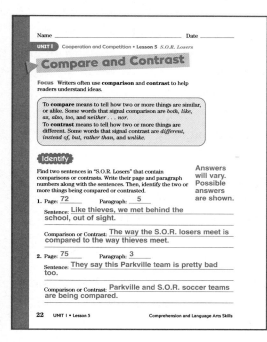
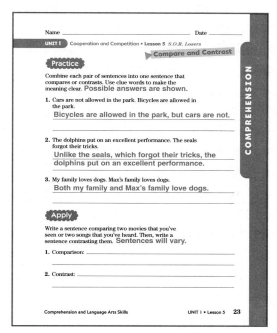

Comprehension and Language Arts Skills pp. 22–23

Teacher Tip PLOT Explain to students that not only is the problem introduced in the beginning of a story but also the characters and the setting.

Teacher Tip PLOT AND CHARACTER Tell students that plot and character are closely related because the plot is driven along by the actions of the characters as they try to solve their problems. Students may find it helpful to plot the changes they see in characters like Ed or Mr. Lester as the plot develops. A diagram similar to the one in *Reading Transparency 59* can be used.

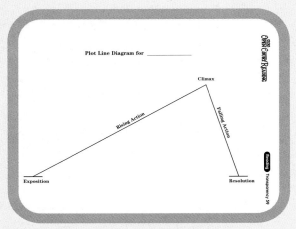

Reading Transparency 59

Literary Elements

Plot/Story Structure

Teach Have the students tell you what they know about plot. If necessary, tell them that the sequence of events in a story is called the plot. The plot introduces a problem and follows the characters as they deal with it.

Share the following elements of plot with the students.

- A plot usually has a beginning, a middle, and an end.
- A problem that one or more main characters have is usually introduced at the beginning of a story.
- In the middle of a story, the characters go through one or more conflicts as they try to solve the problem. Excitement occurs when the conflicts take place. This excitement contributes to the story's rising action, or build of suspense.
- The highest point of interest in the story takes place when the character begins to solve the problem. This is called the climax.
- After the climax, the resolution occurs. The resolution tells how the problem was resolved and ties up any loose ends in the story. The events that take place after the story's climax are part of the story's falling action, or decline from suspense to a sense of calm.

Guided Practice Display *Reading Transparency 59,* Plot Line Diagram. Have the students summarize "S.O.R. Losers" briefly. Let them tell about the problem Ed and his friends had, how they struggled with it, how they solved it, and how the story ended. As the students discuss the story, add their responses to the appropriate spot on the plot line.

Independent Practice Have the students look through the selections they read prior to "S.O.R. Losers" in Unit 1. Have them choose one of the selections, and ask them to diagram the plot line for that story.

Science Connection: Cellular Respiration

Remind students of what they learned in the Science Connections for "Juggling": Physical activity requires that more oxygen, and therefore more blood, be pumped to the body. Challenge students to hypothesize about why a person's muscles need more oxygen when he or she is, for example, playing soccer. Challenge them also to find out about how that oxygen is used by the cells in the rest of a person's body.

Tell the students to research cellular respiration using library sources or their science textbooks. Have them look for answers to the following questions:

- What does cellular respiration do for the body?
- What conditions must be present for respiration to occur?
- What are the waste products of cellular respiration?
- In what types of organisms does cellular respiration take place?

Have students write a short report based on their findings. To challenge students, have them expand the scope of their reports by incorporating information about circulation that they learned in the "Juggling" Science Connection.

Meet the Author

After the students read the information about Avi, discuss the following questions with them.

- Why do you suppose Avi loved to read so much when he didn't much care for school otherwise? *(Possible answer: He might have liked to read because it allowed him to escape into new places he had never been before.)*

- Why do you think Avi would not allow his dysgraphia to keep him from eventually writing his own children's books? *(Possible answer: His love of reading books made him want to be able to tell stories too, so he was willing to work hard to reach his goal.)*

Meet the Illustrator

After the students read the information about Kate Flanagan, discuss the following questions with them.

- What experiences has Kate Flanagan had that might have contributed to her illustrations for "S.O.R. Losers?" *(Possible answer: She plays soccer, which would help her to know what equipment soccer players wear and how a soccer field is set up.)*

S.O.R. LOSERS

Meet the Author

Avi was born in New York City and raised in Brooklyn. His twin sister Emily nicknamed him Avi when they were children. To this day, Avi is the only name he uses. He was shy, uninterested in sports, and not a very good student. He failed at one school and nearly "flunked out" of another one before anybody realized he suffered from dysgraphia. This learning disability made writing very difficult for Avi. It caused him to reverse letters in words or spell them incorrectly. Reading, however, was not a problem. Though he hated Fridays in school because they were spelling test days, he loved Fridays because they were library days. He read everything he could find and even started his own library of favorite books.

Meet the Illustrator

Kate Flanagan graduated from Tufts University with a degree in fine arts. She was the assistant editor and a book reviewer for *The Horn Book Magazine*, a journal of children's literature, until leaving to have her first child. She now lives with her husband, three children, a cat and two fire-bellied toads in New Haven, Connecticut, where she is a free-lance illustrator. Some of the books she has illustrated include *Kids' Pumpkin Projects* (Williamson), *The Very Lonely Bathtub* and *My Gum Is Gone* (both Magination Press).

When she is not drawing, Kate enjoys quilting and sports. She runs in local road races, plays soccer and softball, and is a member of the Lady Lightning, a women's ice hockey team.

84

Theme Connections

Within the Selection

Record your answers to the questions below in the Response Journal section of your Writer's Notebook. In small groups, report the ideas you wrote. Discuss your ideas with the rest of your group. Then choose a person to report your group's answers to the class.

- Why were so many people at South Orange River Middle School surprised by the soccer team's attitude about losing?
- How did other students in the school cooperate to help the team? Why did they do so?
- How did cooperation among team members change the S.O.R. Losers? How did it affect their game?

Across Selections

- Compare the students on the S.O.R. Losers with Lupe in "The Marble Champ." Which other story characters from this unit are similar to the S.O.R. Losers?
- What other story about a sports team have you read in this unit? How are the S.O.R. Losers different from that team?

Beyond the Selection

- Think about how "S.O.R. Losers" adds to what you know about cooperation and competition.
- Add items to the Concept/Question Board about cooperation and competition.

85

Theme Connections

Within the Selection

- Many people assume that everyone cares about sports and winning in sports.
- As a show of support, huge numbers of schoolmates come to the final game.
- It didn't make them winners, but it did make them a team, and they had fun.

Across Selections

- Just like Lupe, the students on the S.O.R. Losers team are good students with little athletic talent. Students may say that the characters in "The Abacus Contest" reminded them of the players.
- "Juggling" has a volleyball team. The S.O.R. Losers are different because they don't care about winning their games.

Beyond the Selection

Students should record their ideas and impressions about the selections on page 7 of their ***Inquiry Journals.***

- "The Abacus Contest" by Priscilla Wu
  Answers will vary.

- "S.O.R. Losers" by Avi
  Answers will vary.

- "Founders of the Children's Rain Forest" by Phillip Hoose
  Answers will vary.

Inquiry Journal • *Recording Concept Information*　　　UNIT I　7

Inquiry Journal p. 7

DAY 3

Word Analysis

Spelling

Spelling Patterns for the /u/ Sound

Teach
Explain the spelling patterns for the /u/ sound, which are *u*, *o-consonant-e*, and *ou*. Have students recall other words besides the lesson spelling words with these patterns and make a list on the board.

Guided Practice
Have students complete page 20 from *Spelling and Vocabulary Skills* to reinforce the spelling patterns for the /u/ sound.

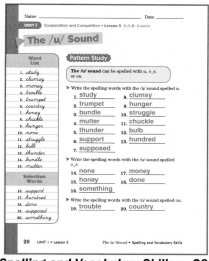

Spelling and Vocabulary Skills p. 20

Vocabulary (continued)

Thesaurus Skills
Remind students that the synonyms listed for a word in the thesaurus can have slightly different meanings. On the board, write the word *illustrate* above the synonyms *demonstrate* and *draw*, and the word *model* above the synonyms *shape* and *copy*. Explain that the two words below each main word are both synonyms, but obviously have different meanings. Have students write and share sentences containing each synonym.

Writing Process Strategies

Introduction to the Writing Process: Revising
Revising for Word Choice

Teach
■ Introduce making changes in word choice by using ***Transparency 18—Revising for Word Choice***. Emphasize to students the importance of using exact words for descriptions and ideas. Precise language communicates the meanings and impressions intended by the writer. When changing a draft to improve word choice, students may find these tips helpful:
- Work toward accuracy and clarity with word selection.
- Use words to create mental pictures.
- Verbs contribute most when they are precise.
- Language should be simple, yet used in an expert way.
- Language should be natural and avoid striving to impress.
- Use words and phrases that will stick in your readers' minds.
- Words should impact readers by triggering connections, memories, reflections, and insights.

Independent Practice
Have students use the tips above to revise the words and phrases used in their writing from Days 1 and 2.

English Language Conventions

Grammar, Usage, and Mechanics:
Subjects and Predicates

Teach
■ Use *Language Arts Handbook* pages 352–353 to teach identification and use of subjects and predicates, including compound subjects, compound predicates, and inverted order of the subject and predicate.
■ Compound subjects are linked by a conjunction and share the same verb.
■ Compound predicates are linked by a conjunction and share the same subject.

Guided Practice in Writing
■ Have students each write sentences, one with a compound subject, one with a compound predicate, and one with inverted order. Have some students write their sentences on the board for the other students to identify the subjects and predicates.
■ Remind students that checking sentences for correct usage of subjects and predicates is an important part of proofreading their autobiographies. Suggest that a variety of sentence lengths and an occasional inverted-order sentence adds interest to writing.

 Informal Assessment

Look for evidence that students are progressing in their understanding of simple and complete subjects and predicates and are incorporating these in their writing.

DAY 4

| Word Analysis | Writing Process Strategies | English Language Conventions |

Word Analysis

Spelling

Spelling Patterns for the /u/ Sound

Teach

Model the meaning strategy exercise for students by giving them the words *uphold*, *carry*, and *stand by* and having them identify the word *support* from the spelling list as a synonym.

Guided Practice

Have students complete the Spelling Strategies exercises on page 21 of *Spelling and Vocabulary Skills*.

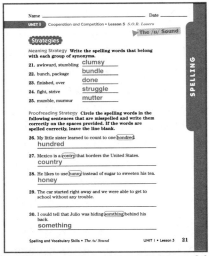

Spelling and Vocabulary Skills p. 21

Vocabulary (continued)

Thesaurus Skills

Write the following sentences on the board and state that the underlined word, a synonym for the bold word following the sentence, is not exactly the right word. Have students find a more correct synonym for the bold word.

That hole in the back of your sleeve is not very <u>remarkable</u>. **noticeable**

The class president is often one of the most <u>attractive</u> students in the school. **popular**

The caffeine in coffee will often <u>improve</u> a sleepy person. **revive**

Writing Process Strategies

Introduction to the Writing Process: Revising

Revising for Sentence Fluency

Teach

Have students read *Language Arts Handbook* page 45 on conferencing with classmates. Go over the tips for successful peer conferencing. Remind students of the importance of being positive and specific when reviewing a peer's work and also of the need to be open to suggestions from classmates about their own work. Tell students that having others look at their work is a great way to get a new point of view. They don't have to use every idea, but they will want to use those that will improve their writing.

Introduce revising for sentence fluency. Describe sentence fluency for students: carefully constructed sentences with a built-in sense of rhythm and grace. Have students think about how their writing would sound if it were read aloud. They should try to ensure that the following features are present when revising for sentence fluency:

- Varied sentence beginnings, lengths, and structure
- Creatively phrased ideas
- A natural, appealing rhythm
- Minimal repetition and redundancy

Independent Practice

Have students revise either their drafts on "S.O.R. Losers" or other drafts while focusing on the tips for sentence fluency.

English Language Conventions

Listening, Speaking, Viewing

Interacting: Asking Questions

Teach

- In Reading and Responding we discussed the importance of asking questions. Here we will talk about how asking questions helps us learn what we want to know.
- Remind the students that everyone has strengths and weaknesses. There are certain things we are good at and certain things we are not good at. The S.O.R. Losers are examples of this.
- Interacting includes speaking with one another, asking questions, answering questions, giving feedback or advice, and drawing conclusions.
- Interacting with one another is also a way to practice speaking skills and the rules of conversation. Speak clearly to one another and listen carefully, alternating between speaking and listening.

Guided Practice

- Break the class into groups. Have the students take turns asking each other one thing they are good at doing and one thing they would like to be able to do better.
- Ask students to draw a conclusion about someone's strength by asking themselves what the person did to become good at it. Encourage them to share their ideas. (*If basketball is a strength, that student probably practices a lot.*)

 **Informal Assessment**

Observe whether students have difficulty asking and answering questions with one another.

DAY 5

Word Analysis	Writing Process Strategies	English Language Conventions

Spelling

Assessment: Final Test
Spelling Patterns for the /u/ Sound

Teach
Repeat the Pretest for this lesson or use the Final Test on page 35 of *Unit 1 Assessment*.

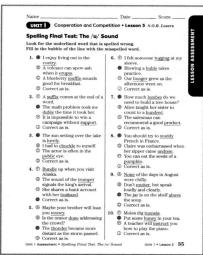

Unit 1 Assessment p. 35

Guided Practice
Have students categorize any mistakes they made on the Final Test.

Are they careless errors?

Are they lesson pattern problems?

Vocabulary (continued)

Thesaurus Skills

Informal Assessment

- Periodically check to see that students are using a thesaurus to discover word meanings and to find appropriate words when writing.
- Remind students to keep adding words to their Writer's Notebooks. Encourage them to continue using the thesaurus to find synonyms for unfamiliar words, or when they are writing, to find just the right word to convey meanings.

Introduction to the Writing Process: Revising

Revising the Autobiography

Writer's Craft
Time and Order Words

- Ask students if they can think of transition words that show **time** or **when things happened** (*now, this morning, today, tonight, yesterday*).
- Ask students if they can think of transition words that show **order**. These words show **when events happened in relationship to one another** (*before, first, second, during, next, then, later.*) Use *Comprehension and Language Arts Skills* pages 26–27 for practice organizing by time and order.

Teach
Introduce *revising for voice* by showing *Transparency 20—Revising for Voice*. Students may follow these tips when revising for voice:

- The writing should show a strong concern for the audience and topic.
- The writing should show enthusiasm and originality.
- Narrative writing should display a personal touch, and expository writing should be thought-provoking.

Independent Practice
Have students complete *Writer's Workbook* page 4.

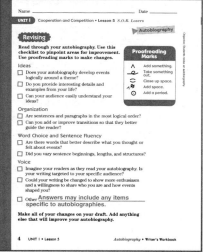

Writer's Workbook p. 4

Penmanship
Cursive Letters *a*, *c*, and *d*

Teach
- Explain to students that by making their letters all slant to the right, their writing will be more legible.
- **Teacher Model:** review the formation of lowercase cursive *a*, *c*, and *d* as downcurve letters by demonstrating on the board.

a   Starting point, downcurve
Undercurve to starting point
Slant down, undercurve: small *a*

c   Starting point, downcurve
Undercurve: small *c*

d   Starting point, downcurve
Undercurve past starting point
Slant down, undercurve: small *d*

Guided Practice
- **Teacher Model:** On the board, write the sentences "Lucky wasn't always so lucky. He lost at dominoes." to model proper letter formation and slant.
- For general handwriting practice have students write a paragraph about a team on which they play or a club to which they belong.
- From "S.O.R. Losers," have students write two paragraphs for general handwriting practice.

Informal Assessment
Check students' handwriting for consistent slant and legibility.

Reading and Language Arts Skills Traces

Language Arts

WORD ANALYSIS

Skills Trace

Spelling: The /u/ Sound
Introduced in Grade 1.
Scaffolded throughout Grades 2–5.
REINTRODUCED: Unit 1, Lesson 5, p. 85F
PRACTICED: Unit 1, Lesson 5,
pp. 85G–85I
Spelling and Vocabulary Skills,
pp. 20–21
TESTED: Unit 1, Lesson 5, p. 85J
Unit 1 Assessment

Skills Trace

Vocabulary: Thesaurus Skills
Introduced in Grade 1.
Scaffolded throughout Grades 2–5.
REINTRODUCED: Unit 1, Lesson 5, p. 85G
PRACTICED: Unit 1, Lesson 5,
pp. 85H–85I
Spelling and Vocabulary Skills,
pp. 18–19
TESTED: Informal Assessment, p. 85J
Unit 1 Assessment

Reading

COMPREHENSION

Skills Trace

Compare and Contrast
Introduced in Grade 1.
Scaffolded throughout Grades 2–5.
INTRODUCED: Unit 1, Lesson 5
REINFORCED: Unit 2, Lesson 5
Unit 2, Lesson 6
Unit 3, Lesson 2
Unit 4, Lesson 3
TESTED: Unit 1 Assessment

WRITING PROCESS STRATEGIES

Skills Trace

Introduction to the Writing Process: Revising
Introduced in Grade 1.
Scaffolded throughout Grades 2–5.
INTRODUCED: Unit 1, Lesson 4, p. 65F
PRACTICED: Unit 1, Lessons 4 & 5,
pp. 65F–65J; pp. 85F–85J
TESTED: Unit 1 Assessment

Skills Trace

Writer's Craft: Orders of Writing
Introduced in Grade K.
Scaffolded throughout Grades 1–5.
INTRODUCED: Unit 1, Lesson 5, p. 85J
PRACTICED: Unit 1, Lesson 5, p. 85J
*Comprehension and Language
Arts Skills,* pp. 26–27
TESTED: Unit 1 Assessment

COMPREHENSION

Skills Trace

Author's Point of View
Introduced in Grade 2.
Scaffolded throughout Grades 3–5.
REINTRODUCED: Unit 1, Lesson 3
REINFORCED: Unit 1, Lesson 5
Unit 3, Lesson 1
Unit 3, Lesson 4
Unit 3, Lesson 5
TESTED: Unit 1 Assessment

ENGLISH LANGUAGE CONVENTIONS

Skills Trace

Grammar, Usage, and Mechanics: Subjects and Predicates
Introduced in Grade 3.
Scaffolded throughout Grades 4–5.
INTRODUCED: Unit 1, Lesson 5, p. 85F
PRACTICED: Unit 1, Lesson 5, p. 85G
Unit 1, Lesson 5, p. 85H
*Comprehension and Language
Arts Skills,* pp. 24–25
TESTED: Informal Assessment, p. 85H
Unit 1 Assessment

Skills Trace

Listening, Speaking, Viewing: Interacting: Asking Questions
Introduced in Grade K.
Scaffolded throughout Grades 1–5.
REINTRODUCED: Unit 1, Lesson 5, p. 85I
PRACTICED: Unit 1, Lesson 5, p. 85I
TESTED: Informal Assessment, p. 85I

Skills Trace

Penmanship: Cursive Letters a, c, and d
Introduced in Grade 2 *(a, d)* and Grade 3 *(c)*.
Scaffolded throughout Grades 3–5
and Grades 4–5.
INTRODUCED: Unit 1, Lesson 5, p. 85J
PRACTICED: Unit 1, Lesson 5, p. 85J
TESTED: Informal Assessment, p. 85J

Professional Development: Comprehension

What Does Research Tell Us about Comprehension Strategies and Strategy Instruction?

Comprehension strategies instruction has been studied extensively in the past quarter century. The earliest studies focused on particular *individual comprehension strategies*. These studies were followed by investigations of *repertoires of comprehension strategies* that students can be taught to coordinate as they read.

Individual Comprehension Strategies

For many years, researchers thought that text comprehension could be improved if students were taught to use a particular strategy, with the particular strategy differing from researcher to researcher. The strategies proposed included creating mental images to represent events in a narrative, constructing mental summaries of text during reading, relating prior knowledge to the text, and seeking clarifications of passages and unknown words (Haller, Child, & Walberg, 1988; Pearson & Dole, 1987; Pearson & Fielding, 1991; Pressley, Johnson, Symons, McGoldrick, & Kurita, 1989). The researchers who proposed and examined these strategies usually had reasons to believe that students were not already using strategies as they read, or that they were not using them systematically and completely.

Indeed, this research validated the value of a variety of individual strategies, including:

- prior knowledge activation (Levin & Pressley, 1981);
- construction of mental images to represent text (Gambrell & Bales, 1986; Gambrell & Jawitz, 1993; Oakhill & Patel, 1991; Pressley, 1976);

- analysis of stories into their story grammar components (identification of characters, settings, problems, attempts at problem resolutions, and resolutions) (Idol, 1987; Idol & Croll, 1987; Short & Ryan, 1984);
- question generation (Oakhill, 1993; Rosenshine, Meister, & Chapman, 1996); and
- summarization (Ambruster et al., 1987; Bean & Steenwyk, 1984; Berkowitz, 1986 ; Taylor, 1982; Taylor & Beach, 1984).

In short, researchers validated specific strategies that readers can apply *before reading* (making predictions based on prior knowledge), *during reading* (generating mental images), and *after reading* (summarization) (Levin & Pressley, 1981).

However, as researchers developed more sophisticated models of how readers process information, they came to understand that good readers do not rely just on single strategies as they read; rather, they activate and use multiple strategies to make sense of text (Brown, Bransford, Ferrara, & Campione, 1983; Levin & Pressley, 1981). Not surprisingly, researchers next began to look at comprehension instruction that combined a set, or repertoire, of strategies that could promote reading competence from the beginning to the end of a reading.

* Additional information about comprehension as well as resource references can be found in the ***Professional Development Guide: Comprehension.***

SELECTION INTRODUCTION

Focus Questions How can ordinary people make a difference worldwide? Do they need to possess any special abilities?

FOUNDERS OF THE CHILDREN'S RAIN FOREST

from *It's Our World, Too!*
by Phillip Hoose
illustrated by Jim Effler

It all began in the first week of school when Eha Kern, from the Fagervik School, in the Swedish countryside, showed her forty first- and second-grade students pictures of hot, steamy jungles near the Equator. It was there, she said, that half the types of plants and animals in the whole world could be found. She read to them about monkeys and leopards and sloths, about snakes that can paralyze your nerves with one bite, about strange plants that might hold a cure for cancer, about the great trees that give us oxygen to breathe and help keep the earth from becoming too hot.

And then she told them that the world's rain forests were being destroyed at the rate of one hundred acres a *minute*. In the past thirty years, she said, nearly half the world's rain forests have been cut down, often by poor people who burn the wood for fire. Sometimes forests are cleared to make pastures for cattle that are slaughtered and sold to hamburger chains in the U.S. and Europe. Sometimes the trees are sold and shipped away to make furniture and paper. More often they are just stacked up and burned. At this rate, there might not be any rain forests left in thirty years!

The children were horrified. The creatures of the rain forest could be gone before the students were even old enough to have a chance to see them. It didn't matter that they lived thousands of miles away in cold, snowy Sweden. It seemed to them that their future was being chopped and cleared away.

86

Selection Summary

Genre: Narrative Nonfiction

When Eha Kern introduced her first- and second-grade classes to the rain forest, they fell in love and decided they wanted to help save a rain forest. When one of her students suggested they buy one, Kern was skeptical. However, when she discussed the matter with American biologist Sharon Kinsman, Kinsman introduced her to Monte Verde, which was for sale. Through much planning and cooperation, the students were able to raise a significant amount of money and get their message across the world to help save the rain forest.

Some of the elements of nonfiction are listed below. A narrative nonfiction selection may have one or more of these elements.

- Its purpose is to share information with the reader.
- It often includes facts about real people and events.
- The information is presented as a narrative or story.
- It often presents events in the order in which they happened.
- It may be organized by topics and include diagrams, maps, or illustrations to help the reader understand the subject better.
- The factual information can be checked by referring to other sources.

About the Author

PHILLIP HOOSE is a staff member of the Nature Conservancy and a founding member of the Children's Music Network. He has also written about the Indiana Hoosiers Basketball team and about racial barriers in American sports. With his daughter Hannah he co-wrote the children's book *Hey Little Ant*.

Students can read more about writer Phillip Hoose on page 98 of the *Student Anthology*.

Other Books by Phillip Hoose

- *We Were There Too: Young People in U.S. History*
- *Hoosiers: The Fabulous Basketball Life of Indiana*
- *Necessities: Racial Barriers in American Sports*

About the Illustrator

JIM EFFLER has illustrated several children's books about animals. Jim's work has won awards from Art Directors' Clubs and the Society of Illustrators. He lives in Cincinnati, Ohio, with his wife Debbie and daughters, Jenna and Ariana.

Students can read more about illustrator Jim Effler on page 98 of the *Student Anthology*.

Other Books Illustrated by Jim Effler

- *How Do Flies Walk Upside Down?: Questions and Answers About Insects*
- *Bamboo Valley: A Story of a Chinese Bamboo Forest*
- *Do Tarantulas Have Teeth?: Questions and Answers About Poisonous Creatures*

Inquiry Connections

A major aim of **Open Court Reading** is knowledge building. Because inquiry is at the root of knowledge building, students are encouraged to investigate topics and questions within each selection that relate to the unit theme.

"Founders of the Children's Rain Forest" is narrative nonfiction that chronicles the saving of a rain forest, from the beginning idea through the cooperation and planning needed to buy a large piece of rain forest land. The key concepts are

- cooperation can lead to positive results.
- when working together to solve a problem, all people must participate.
- no ideas are bad—everything should at least be considered.
- cooperation can lead to solutions of major problems.

Before reading the selection:

- Point out that students may post a question, concept, word, illustration, or object at any time during the course of their unit investigation. Be sure that students include their names or initials on the items they post so that others will know whom to go to if they have an answer or if they wish to collaborate on a related activity.
- Students should feel free to write an answer or a note on someone else's question or to consult the Board for ideas for their own investigations throughout the unit.
- Encourage students to read about cooperation and competition at home and to bring in articles or pictures that are good examples to post on the Board.

Concept/Question Board

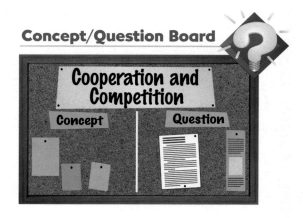

PROGRAM RESOURCES

Leveled Practice

Reteach
Pages 30–35

Challenge
Pages 25–29

ELD Workbook

Intervention Workbook

Leveled Classroom Library*

Have students read at least 30 minutes daily outside of class. Have them read books from the *Leveled Classroom Library,* which supports the unit theme and helps students develop their vocabulary by reading independently.

The Kid Who Ran for President

BY DAN GUTMAN. SCHOLASTIC, 1996.

Twelve-year-old Judson Moon is running for President of the United States—with the old lady down the street as his running mate, a first lady he's barely spoken to, and a campaign manager who swears he can sidestep the Constitution and get Judd elected. **(Easy)**

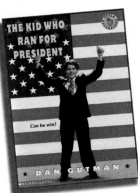

The Wheel on the School

BY MEINDERT DEJONG. HARPER TROPHY, 1972.

When Lina begins to wonder why the storks no longer come to the village of Shora, she spurs the five other children to action, and they set out to bring the storks back to Shora. **(Average)**

A World in Our Hands

BY THE YOUNG PEOPLE OF THE WORLD. TRICYCLE, 1995.

Edited by a team of 12–21 year olds and composed of drawings, poems, and essays by young people from many countries, this book presents a history of the UN and hope for its future achievements. **(Advanced)**

＊ These books, which all support the unit theme Cooperation and Competition, are part of a 36-book *Leveled Classroom Library* available for purchase from SRA/McGraw-Hill.

Note: Teachers should preview any trade books for appropriateness in their classrooms before recommending them to students.

TECHNOLOGY

Web Connections

www.sra4kids.com
Cooperation and Competition Web site

Audiocassette/CD

＊**Listening Library:
Cooperation and Competition**
SRA/McGRAW-HILL, 2002

Titles preceded by an asterisk (＊) are available through SRA/McGraw-Hill. Other titles can be obtained by contacting the publisher listed with the title.

Computer Skills

＊ **Basic Computer Skills**

CD-ROMs

＊**Research Assistant**
SRA/McGRAW-HILL, 2002

＊**OCR Spelling**
SRA/McGRAW-HILL, 2002

＊**Student Writing and Research Center**
THE LEARNING COMPANY

	DAY 1	**DAY 2**
Suggested Pacing: 3–5 days	**DAY 1**	**DAY 2**

LESSON PLANNER

1 Preparing to Read

Materials
- Routine Card 1

DAY 1

Word Knowledge, p. 86K
- Antonyms
- /ks/ Sound Spelled *x*
- /ch/ Sound Spelled *tch*
- Review /a/, /o/, /i/, and /u/ Sound Spellings

About the Words and Sentences, p. 86K

DAY 2

Developing Oral Language, p. 86L

2 Reading & Responding

Materials
- Student Anthology, pp. 86–99
- Reading Transparencies 8, 54, 56, 60
- Routine Card 1
- Program Assessment
- Unit 1 Assessment, pp. 22–25
- Science/Social Studies Connection Center Cards 7–8
- Comprehension and Language Arts Skills, pp. 28–29
- Reteach, pp. 30–31
- Challenge, p. 25
- Home Connection, pp. 13–14
- Inquiry Journal, p. 7

DAY 1

Build Background, p. 86M
Preview and Prepare, pp. 86M–86N
Selection Vocabulary, p. 86N
Reading Recommendations, pp. 86O–86P
Student Anthology, pp. 86–97 — First Read
✓ Comprehension Strategies
- Asking Questions, pp. 90, 92, 94
- Predicting, pp. 88, 92
- Monitoring and Clarifying, pp. 88, 92, 94, 96
- Monitoring and Adjusting Reading Speed, p. 86
Discussing Strategy Use, p. 96
Discussing the Selection, p. 97A

DAY 2

Student Anthology, pp. 86–97 — Second Read
Comprehension Skills
- Author's Purpose, pp. 87, 89, 91, 93, 95, 97
✓ Checking Comprehension, p. 97
Supporting the Reading, pp. 97C–97D
- Author's Purpose

Inquiry

Materials
- Student Anthology, pp. 86–99
- Inquiry Journal, pp. 5, 28–31
- Research Assistant
- Reading Transparency 57

DAY 1

Investigation
- Investigating Concepts Beyond the Text, p. 99A

DAY 2

Investigation
- Concept/Question Board, p. 99B

3 Language Arts

Materials
- Comprehension and Language Arts Skills, pp. 30–33
- Language Arts Handbook
- Language Arts Transparencies 21–26, 28, 34
- Unit 1 Assessment, pp. 36–37
- Spelling Software
- Spelling and Vocabulary Skills, pp. 22–25
- Student Anthology
- Student Writing and Research Center
- Writing Folder
- Writer's Workbook, p. 5
- Reteach, pp. 32–35
- Challenge, pp. 26–29

DAY 1

Word Analysis
✓ Short-Vowel Spelling Patterns Pretest, p. 99F

Writing Process Strategies
- Writing Process Introduction: Editing/Proofreading, p. 99F

English Language Conventions
- Grammar, Usage, and Mechanics: Review Nouns, Pronouns, Verbs, Sentences, Subjects, and Predicates, p. 99F

DAY 2

Word Analysis
- Short-Vowel Spelling Patterns, p. 99G
- Vocabulary: Word Mapping, p. 99G

Writing Process Strategies
- Writing Process: Editing/Proofreading, p. 99G

English Language Conventions
- Grammar, Usage, and Mechanics: Review Nouns, Pronouns, Verbs, Sentences, Subjects, and Predicates, p. 99G

✓ **Informal** Assessment Available   ✓ **Formal** Assessment Available

DAY 2 continued	**DAY 3**	
DAY 3	**DAY 4**	**DAY 5**
General Review	**General Review**	**Review Word Knowledge**
Student Anthology, pp. 98–99 ■ Meet the Author/Illustrator ✓ ■ Theme Connections	**Review Selection Vocabulary, p. 97B** **Literary Elements, p. 97E** ■ Influencing Perspectives	✓ **Lesson Assessment** ■ *Unit 1 Assessment:* **Lesson Assessment, pp. 22–25** **Home Connection, p. 97B** **Science Connection** ■ Habitat, p. 97F ■ Photosynthesis, p. 97F
Investigation ✓ ■ Presenting Investigation Findings, p. 99C	**Supporting the Investigation** ■ Using Visual Aids, p. 99D	**Investigation** ■ Unit Investigation Continued ■ Update Concept/Question Board **Unit Wrap-Up**
Word Analysis ■ Short-Vowel Spelling Patterns, p. 99H ■ Vocabulary: Word Mapping, p. 99H **Writing Process Strategies** ■ Writing Process: Editing/Proofreading, p.99H **English Language Conventions** ✓ ■ Grammar, Usage, and Mechanics: Review Nouns, Pronouns, Verbs, Sentences, Subjects, and Predicates, p. 99H	**Word Analysis** ■ Short-Vowel Spelling Patterns, p. 99I ■ Vocabulary: Word Mapping, p. 99I **Writing Process Strategies** ■ Writing Process: Publishing, p. 99I **English Language Conventions** ✓ ■ Listening, Speaking, Viewing Presenting: Using Note Cards, p. 99I	**Word Analysis** ✓ ■ Short-Vowel Spelling Patterns Final Test, p. 99J ✓ ■ Vocabulary: Word Mapping, p. 99J **Writing Process Strategies** ✓ ■ Writing Process: Publishing, p. 99J **English Language Conventions** ■ Penmanship: Cursive Letters *q, g,* ✓ and *o,* p. 99J ✓✓ **Unit Wrap-Up**

Below are suggestions for differentiating instruction to meet the individual needs of students. These are the same skills shown on the Lesson Planner; however, these pages provide extra practice opportunities or enriching activities to meet the varied needs of students.

WORKSHOP

Differentiating Instruction

Small-Group Instruction

Use small-group instruction for such things as discussing students' writing projects.

Use the informal assessment suggestions found throughout the lesson along with the formal assessments provided in each lesson to determine your students' strengths and areas of need. Use the following program components to help in supporting or expanding on the instruction found in this lesson:

- **Reteach** workbook for use with those students who show a basic understanding of the lesson but need a bit more practice to solidify their understanding

- **Intervention Guide** and **Workbook** for use with those students who even after extra practice exhibit a lack of understanding of the lesson concepts

- **English-Language Development Guide** and **Workbook** for use with those students who need language help

Independent Activities

Students should be working in their collaborative groups to complete investigations of cooperation and competition. Each group might conference together to make sure that all areas of their investigation have been considered. They should be considering how they want to share their information with the rest of the class. Those groups that want to present their investigations orally may want to use this time to practice their presentations either by themselves or for another group to get feedback.

For Workshop Management Tips, see Appendix pages 41–42.

◆ **Small-group Instruction**   ■ **Independent Activities**

	READING	INVESTIGATION ACTIVITIES
DAY 1	■ Browse *Leveled Classroom Library* ■ *Listening Library Audiocassette/CD* ■ Add Vocabulary in Writer's Notebook	■ Concept/Question Board ■ Complete *Inquiry Journal*, pp. 28–29 ■ Explore OCR Web site for Theme Connections
DAY 2	■ Choose *Leveled Classroom Library* Book and Begin Independent Reading ■ Oral Reading of Selection ■ Record Response to Selection in Writer's Notebook	■ Concept/Question Board ■ Explore OCR Web site for Theme Connections
DAY 3	■ Read *Leveled Classroom Library* Book as Independent Reading ■ Complete *Comprehension and Language Arts Skills*, pp. 28–29	■ Concept/Question Board ◆ Wrap Up Compilation of Investigation Findings ■ Use *Research Assistant* to Help with Investigations
DAY 4	■ Read *Leveled Classroom Library* Book as Independent Reading ◆ Discuss Theme Connections, p. 99 ■ Add Words to Word Bank ■ Complete **Link to Writing** for Supporting the Reading, p. 97D ■ Complete **Independent Practice** for Literary Elements, p. 97E	■ Concept/Question Board ◆ Begin Presentations of Investigation Findings
DAY 5	■ Read *Leveled Classroom Library* Book as Independent Reading ◆ Reading Roundtable ■ Science Connections, p. 97F	■ Concept/Question Board ◆ Continue Presentations of Investigation Findings ■ Complete *Inquiry Journal*, pp. 30–31, for Supporting the Investigation

LANGUAGE ARTS	INTERVENTION*	ENGLISH-LANGUAGE LEARNERS**	RETEACH	CHALLENGE
English Language Conventions ■ Complete **Review,** *Comprehension and Language Arts Skills,* pp. 30–31 **Writing Process Strategies** ◆ Seminar: Editing and Proofreading, p. 99F	(30 to 45 minutes per day) ◆ Reading Words, p. 49 ◆ Preteach "Founders of the Children's Rain Forest," pp. 50–51 ◆ Teach "Intervention Selection One," pp. 51–52 ◆ Grammar, Usage, and Mechanics, pp. 54–55	(30 to 45 minutes per day) ◆ Word Knowledge, /ks/ Spelled _x, p. 25 ◆ Activate Prior Knowledge, p. 27 ◆ Selection Vocabulary, p. 27		
Word Analysis ◆ Spelling: Word Sort, p. 99G ■ Complete **Vocabulary: Word Mapping,** *Spelling and Vocabulary Skills,* pp. 22–23 **Writing Process Strategies** ◆ Seminar: Editing and Proofreading, p. 99G	◆ Developing Oral Language, p. 49 ◆ Preteach "Founders of the Children's Rain Forest," pp. 50–51 ◆ Teach Comprehension Strategies, p. 52 ◆ Reread "Intervention Selection One" ◆ Grammar, Usage, and Mechanics, pp. 54–55	◆ Preteach the Selection, p. 26	**Comprehension** ■ Complete **Author's Purpose,** *Reteach,* pp. 30–31 **English Language Conventions** ■ Complete **Review,** *Reteach,* p. 34	**Comprehension** ■ Complete **Author's Purpose,** *Challenge,* p. 25 **English Language Conventions** ■ Complete **Review,** *Challenge,* p. 28
Word Analysis ■ Complete **Spelling: The Short-Vowel Sounds,** *Spelling and Vocabulary Skills,* p. 24 **Writing Process Strategies** ◆ Seminar: Edit and Proofread an Autobiography, p. 99H	◆ Dictation and Spelling, pp. 49–50 ◆ Reread "Founders of the Children's Rain Forest" ◆ Teach "Intervention Selection Two," pp. 52–53 ◆ Writing Activity, pp. 55–56	◆ Word Knowledge, /ch/ Spelled _tch, p. 25 ◆ Dictation and Spelling, p. 26	**Word Analysis** ■ Complete **Vocabulary: Word Mapping,** *Reteach,* p. 33	**Word Analysis** ■ Complete **Vocabulary: Word Mapping,** *Challenge,* p. 27
Word Analysis ■ Complete **The Short-Vowel Sounds,** *Spelling and Vocabulary Skills,* p. 25 **Writing Process Strategies** ■ Complete **Writer's Craft: Presentation,** *Comprehension and Language Arts Skills,* pp. 32–33 ◆ Seminar: Correcting Grammar, p. 99I	◆ Reread "Founders of the Children's Rain Forest" ◆ Teach Comprehension Strategies, p. 53 ◆ Reread "Intervention Selection Two" ◆ Writing Activity, pp. 55–56	◆ Grammar, Usage, and Mechanics, Review, p. 28	**Word Analysis** ■ Complete **Spelling: The Short-Vowel Sounds,** *Reteach,* p. 32	**Word Analysis** ■ Complete **Spelling: The Short-Vowel Sounds,** *Challenge,* p. 26
Writing Process Strategies ◆ Seminar: Publish an Autobiography, p. 99J **English Language Conventions** ■ Penmanship: Cursive Letters *q, g,* and *o,* p. 99J	◆ Repeated Readings/Fluency Check, p. 54	◆ Grammar, Usage, and Mechanics, Subjects and Predictions, p. 28	**Writing Process Strategies** ■ Complete **Writer's Craft: Presentation,** *Reteach,* p. 35	**Writing Process Strategies** ■ Complete **Writer's Craft: Presentation,** *Challenge,* p. 29

*Page numbers refer to *Intervention Guide*
**Page numbers refer to *English-Language Development Guide*

ASSESSMENT

Formal Assessment Options

Use these summative assessments along with your informal observations to assess student progress.

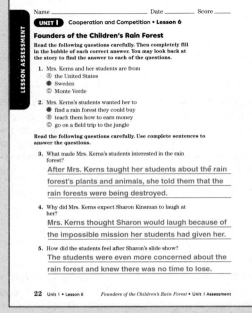

Unit 1 Assessment p. 22

Unit 1 Assessment p. 23

Unit 1 Assessment p. 24

Unit 1 Assessment p. 25

Unit 1 Assessment p. 36

Unit 1 Assessment p. 37

Informal Comprehension Strategies Rubrics

Use the Informal Comprehension Strategies Rubrics to determine whether or not a student is using any of the strategies listed below. Note the strategies a student is using, instead of the degree to which a student might be using any particular strategy. In addition, encourage the student to tell of any strategies other than the ones being taught that he or she is using.

Predicting

- The student makes predictions about what the text is about.
- The student updates predictions during reading, based on information in the text.

Monitoring and Clarifying

- The student notes characteristics of the text, such as whether it is difficult to read or whether some sections are more challenging or more important than others.
- The student shows awareness of whether he or she understands the text and takes appropriate action, such as rereading, in order to understand the text better.
- The student rereads to reconsider something presented earlier in the text.
- The student recognizes problems during reading, such as a loss of concentration, unfamiliar vocabulary, or lack of sufficient background knowledge to comprehend the text.

Research Rubrics

During Workshop, assess students using the rubrics below. The rubrics range from 1-4 in most categories, with 1 being the lowest score. Record each student's score on the inside back cover of his or her *Inquiry Journal.*

Communicating Research Progress and Results

(This rubric may apply to oral, written, or multimedia reports.)

1 Reporting is sparse and fragmentary.

2 Report is factual; communicates findings but not the thinking behind them.

3 Report provides a good picture of the research problem, of how original conjectures were modified in light of new information, and of difficulties and unresolved issues.

4 A report that not only interests and informs the audience but also draws helpful commentary from them.

Overall Assessment of Research

1 A collection of facts related in miscellaneous ways to a topic.

2 An organized collection of facts relevant to the research problem.

3 A thoughtful effort to tackle a research problem, with some indication of progress toward solving it.

4 Significant progress on a challenging problem of understanding.

1 Preparing to Read

Objectives

- Students will identify antonym pairs and provide antonyms of their own.
- Students will recognize and read words with the /ks/ sound spelled *x*.
- Students will recognize and read words with the /ch/ sound spelled *tch*.
- Students recognize and read words with the /a/ sound spelled *a*, the /o/ sound spelled *o*, the /i/ sound spelled *i*, and the /u/ sound spelled *u*.
- Students develop fluency reading words and sentences aloud.

Materials

- Routine Card 1

 Teacher Tip SYLLABICATION To help students blend words and build fluency, use the syllabication below of the decodable multisyllabic words in the word lines.

ex•pen•sive	min•ute
ox•y•gen	pas•ture
ex•plained	rab•bit
ex•pect•ed	jun•gle
twitch•ing	trop•i•cal

Routine Card
Refer to Routine 1 for the Reading the Words and Sentences procedure.

WORD KNOWLEDGE

Word Knowledge

Reading the Words and Sentences

Use direct teaching to teach the Word Knowledge lesson. Write each word and sentence on the board. Have students read each word together. After all the words have been read, have students read each sentence in natural phrases or chunks. Use the suggestions in About the Words and Sentences to discuss the different features of listed words.

Line 1: hot   cold   more   less   cheap   expensive
Line 2: oxygen   explained   expected   expression
Line 3: twitching   watch   latch   itch
Line 4: minute   pasture   rabbit   jungle   tropical
Sentence 1: The swimmer expected to need more oxygen under water.
Sentence 2: The fire was hot, but the air was cold.
Sentence 3: I watched the twitching tail of my cat.
Sentence 4: Some scientists study in a tropical setting, like a jungle in South America.

About the Words and Sentences

- **Line 1:** The word sets are antonyms. Antonyms are two words that mean the opposite of each other. Have students identify the pairs and offer other antonyms of the words.
- **Line 2:** The words have the /ks/ sound spelled *x*. Point out that this spelling of the /ks/ sound is always preceded by a short vowel.
- **Line 3:** These words contain the /ch/ sound spelled *tch*. Invite students to think of other words that contain this spelling of the /ch/ sound.
- **Line 4:** The words review the /a/ sound spelled *a*, the /o/ sound spelled *o*, the /i/ sound spelled *i*, and the /u/ sound spelled *u*.

- **Sentence 1:** Have students identify the words that have the /ks/ sound spelled *x (expected, oxygen)*. Then, have students read the sentence aloud.

- **Sentence 2:** Have students identify the antonyms in this sentence *(hot, cold)*. Challenge students to come up with additional antonym pairs with the same definitions *(scorching, freezing)*. Then, have students read the sentence aloud as it is and then with their own antonym pairs substituted.

- **Sentence 3:** Have students identify the words that have the /ch/ sound spelled *tch (watched, twitching)*. Then have students read the sentence aloud.

- **Sentence 4:** Have students notice the words in the sentence that contain the /o/ sound spelled *o* and the /u/ sound spelled *u (study, tropical, jungle)*. Point out that these short-vowel sounds are in closed syllables.

Developing Oral Language

Use direct teaching to review the words. Use the following activity to help students practice the words aloud.

- Ask students to tell you what they know about analogies. If necessary, remind students that analogies are used to compare the relationships between two words. Give them the example "hot : cold :: go : stop" *(hot is to cold as go is to stop)*. In this case, "hot" and "cold" have the same relationship to each other (antonyms) as "go" and "stop" do. Have students use a set of words from line 1 and a set of their own words to offer aloud analogies using antonyms. Challenge students to present the first three words of an analogy to the class, and have the class fill in the final word. Presenters should select a word from line one or a word of their own choice as the first word, a synonym or antonym of that word for the second word, and another word from line one as the third word. Once a volunteer has completed the analogy, have the class determine whether the words in the two sets were synonyms or antonyms.

Teacher Tip BUILDING FLUENCY
Gaining a better understanding of the spellings of sounds and structure of words will help students as they encounter unfamiliar words in their reading. By this time in grade 5 students should be reading approximately 126 words per minute with fluency and expression. As students read, you may notice that some need work in building fluency. During Workshop, have these students choose a section of text (a minimum of 160 words) to read several times in order to build fluency.

MEETING INDIVIDUAL NEEDS

ELL Support

WORD MEANING Make sure that English-language learners understand the meaning of the words on the word lines before you do the exercises with them. Use pictures, photos, and bilingual dictionaries. Go to the *English-Language Development Guide* for additional support for students who need help with blending.

Intervention Tip

ANTONYMS Make a list of words. Next to each word, write an antonym and a synonym. Say the words aloud to students. Ask them to tell you which word is the antonym and how they know. If necessary, remind students that antonyms are words that have opposite meanings. For students who need more help, see Unit 1, Lesson 6, of the *Intervention Guide.*

Spelling
See pages 99F–99J for the corresponding spelling lesson for the /a/, /o/, /i/, and /u/ sounds.

Objectives

- Students will understand the selection vocabulary before reading.
- Students will identify antonym pairs as they read.
- Students will identify words containing the /ks/ sound spelled *x*.
- Students will use the comprehension strategies Asking Questions, Monitoring and Adjusting Reading Speed, Predicting and Clarifying as they read the story the first time.
- Students will use the comprehension skill Author's Purpose as they read the story the second time.

Materials

- Student Anthology, pp. 86–99
- Reading Transparencies 8, 54, 56, 60
- Listening Library
- Routine Card 1
- Inquiry Journal, p. 7
- Home Connection, pp. 13–14
- Comprehension and Language Arts Skills, pp. 28–29
- Program Assessment
- Unit 1 Assessment, pp. 22–25
- Science/Social Studies Connection Center Cards 7–8

MEETING INDIVIDUAL NEEDS

ELL Support

For ELD strategies, use the *English-Language Development Guide,* Unit 1, Lesson 6.

Intervention Support

For intervention strategies, use the *Intervention Guide,* Unit 1, Lesson 6.

www.sra4kids.com
Web Connection
Students can use the connections to Cooperation and Competition in the Reading link of the SRA Web page for more background information about Cooperation and Competition.

Build Background

Activate Prior Knowledge

Discuss the following with students to find out what they may already know about the selection and have already learned about the theme of cooperation and competition.

- Preteach "Founders of the Children's Rain Forest" by first determining students' prior knowledge about ecology. Ask students what they know about preserving the environment.
- Have students share any other stories that involve rain forests or Sweden.
- Tell students to review what they have learned about cooperation and competition from the previous selections in this unit and from personal experiences.

Background Information

The following information may help the students better understand the selection they are about to read.

- By the time a rain forest tree is one hundred years old, it has provided enough oxygen for a human being to breathe for twenty years.
- More than one-quarter of the medicinal drugs prescribed in the United States come from rain forest plants.
- Most of the plants that have cancer-fighting properties grow in tropical rain forests.
- Though tropical rain forests cover only a small part of the earth, half the world's plants and animal species are found within them.
- Many foods come from rain forests. Both coffee and chocolate are products of the rain forest.
- Have students what they know about the genre of this selection. Refer to page 86A of the *Teacher's Edition* for elements of this selection's genre.

Preview and Prepare

Browse

- Have a student read aloud the title and the names of the author and illustrator. Demonstrate how to browse. Then have them browse the entire selection. This allows them to activate prior knowledge relevant to the selection. Discuss what they think this story might have to do with cooperation and competition.

- Have the students search for clues that tell them something about the story. Also, have them look for any problems, such as unfamiliar words or long sentences, that they notice while reading. Use **Reading Transparency 54** to record their observations as they browse. For example, the words *rain forest* may be a clue that the selection will have an ecology theme. For the Problems column, students might point out that they don't know how to stop the destruction of the rain forests. They might wonder how children will *found* a rain forest. To save time and model note taking, write students' observations as brief notes rather than complete sentences.

- As students prepare to read the selection, have them browse the Focus Questions on the first page of the selection. Tell them to keep these questions in mind as they read.

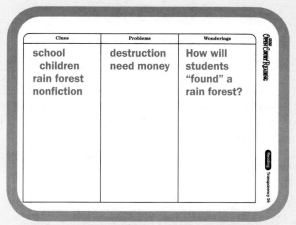

Clues	Problems	Wonderings
school children rain forest nonfiction	destruction need money	How will students "found" a rain forest?

Reading Transparency 54

Set Purposes

Have the students set their own purposes for reading. As they read, have students consider how important cooperation was in founding the Children's Rain Forest. Remind students that good readers have a purpose when they read. Let them know that they should make sure they know the purpose for reading whenever they read.

Selection Vocabulary

As students study vocabulary, they will use a variety of skills to determine the meaning of a word. These include context clues, word structure, and apposition.

- Students will apply these same skills while reading to clarify additional unfamiliar words.

Display **Reading Transparency 8** before reading the selection to introduce and discuss the following words and their meanings.

Equator: the imaginary line that circles Earth's center; it is perpendicular to Earth's axis and equally distant from Earth's North and South poles (p. 86)

biologist: a person who studies plant and animal life specific to certain environments (p. 88)

enthusiastic: filled with excitement (p. 90)

preserve: to protect and maintain (p. 97)

optimistic: having a positive outlook (p. 97)

Have students read the words in the Word Box, stopping to blend any words that they have trouble reading. Demonstrate how to decode multisyllabic words by breaking the words into syllables and blending the syllables. Then have the students try. If the word is not decodable, give the students the pronunciation.

Have students read the sentences on **Reading Transparency 8** and use the skills of context, word structure (structural analysis) or apposition to figure out the meaning of the words. Be sure students explain which skill(s) they are using and how they figured out the meanings of the words.

Teacher Tip SELECTION VOCABULARY To help students decode words, divide them into the syllables shown below. The information following each word tells how students can figure out the meaning of each word on the transparency.

E·qua·tor	context clues
bi·ol·o·gist	context clues, word structure
en·thu·si·as·tic	context clues
pre·serve	context clues
op·ti·mis·tic	context clues

Routine Card
Refer to Routine 2 for the selection vocabulary procedure. Refer to Routine 3 for the Clues, Problems, and Wonderings procedure.

Reading Transparency 8

Teacher Tip COMPREHENSION STRATEGIES Let students know that good readers are to use comprehension strategies like good readers use them—that is, they are not supposed to wait for the teacher to remind them to use strategies, but rather are to use them on their own to understand the text.

Routine Card
Refer to Routine 4 for the Reading the Selection procedure.

Reading Recommendations

Oral Reading

This engaging selection is fast-paced and contains dialogue, so students might enjoy reading it aloud as classmates listen. As students read aloud, have them read expressively, at an appropriate pace, in natural phrases and chunks. Make sure students enunciate and use appropriate intonations.

Reading the selection with fluency and accuracy will help students comprehend the text. If students have trouble reading decodable words, have them break the words into sounds or syllables and then blend them together to read the words. After students have finished reading the selection, use the "Discussing the Selection" questions on page 97A to see if they understand what they have read.

Using Comprehension Strategies

Comprehension strategy instruction allows students to become aware of how good readers read. Good readers constantly check their understanding as they are reading and ask themselves questions. In addition, skilled readers recognize when they are having problems and stop to use various comprehension strategies to help them make sense of what they are reading.

During the reading of "Founders of the Children's Rain Forest," model and prompt the use of the following comprehension strategies. Take turns reading the story aloud with students.

- **Asking Questions** prepares readers for what they want to learn.
- **Predicting** causes readers to analyze information given about story events and characters in the context of how it may logically connect to the story's conclusion.
- **Monitoring and Clarifying** prompts students to track and immediately clear up unfamiliar words and ideas by using context, word structure, apposition, and outside resources. Stop and check the students' understanding when something is unclear.
- **Monitoring and Adjusting Reading Speed** prompts readers to assess the difficulty level of a text and adapt their reading pace accordingly.

As students read, they should be using a variety of strategies to help them understand the selection. Encourage students to use the strategies listed as the class reads the story aloud. Do this by stopping at the points indicated by the numbers in magenta circles on the reduced student page and using a particular strategy. Students can also stop reading periodically to discuss what they have learned and what problems they may be having.

Building Comprehension Skills

Revisiting or rereading a selection allows students to apply skills that give them a more complete understanding of the text. Some follow-up comprehension skills help students organize information. Others lead to deeper understanding—to "reading between the lines," as mature readers do. An extended lesson for the comprehension skill Author's Purpose can be found in the Supporting the Reading section on pages 97C–97D. This lesson is intended as extra practice with Author's Purpose. However, it may be used at this time to introduce the comprehension skill to students.

■ **Author's Purpose (Introduction):** Readers identify the author's reason for writing the piece in order to obtain some prior idea of what the author is going to say.

Reading with a Purpose

Have students focus on the "domino effect" created by the cooperation and enthusiasm of one group of people and list their thoughts on this in the Response Journal sections of their Writer's Notebooks.

COMPREHENSION

Read pages 86–97.

Comprehension Strategies

First Read

Read the story aloud, taking turns with the students. Start by modeling the use of strategies for the students.

Teacher Modeling

1 Monitoring and Adjusting Reading Speed *Good readers skim a text before reading it to decide what they want to learn from it and how difficult the text will be to understand. As I skim this selection, I can see that it is nonfiction and it contains information I might want to know about fundraising. Also, I see that there are some words that might be difficult to read. So that I will comprehend all of the facts in this piece, I will need to adjust my reading rate to a slower pace.*

Word Knowledge

SCAFFOLDING The skills students are reviewing in Word Knowledge should help them in reading the story. This lesson focuses on words with the /ks/ sound spelled *x*. These words will be found in boxes similar to this one throughout the selection.

/ks/ spelled *x*:

oxygen

First Reading Recommendation

ORAL • CHORAL • SILENT

Focus Questions How can ordinary people make a difference worldwide? Do they need to possess any special abilities?

FOUNDERS OF THE CHILDREN'S RAIN FOREST

from *It's Our World, Too!*
by Phillip Hoose
illustrated by Jim Effler

1

It all began in the first week of school when Eha Kern, from the Fagervik School, in the Swedish countryside, showed her forty first- and second-grade students pictures of hot, steamy jungles near the Equator. It was there, she said, that half the types of plants and animals in the whole world could be found. She read to them about monkeys and leopards and sloths, about snakes that can paralyze your nerves with one bite, about strange plants that might hold a cure for cancer, about the great trees that give us oxygen to breathe and help keep the earth from becoming too hot.

And then she told them that the world's rain forests were being destroyed at the rate of one hundred acres a *minute*. In the past thirty years, she said, nearly half the world's rain forests have been cut down, often by poor people who burn the wood for fire. Sometimes forests are cleared to make pastures for cattle that are slaughtered and sold to hamburger chains in the U.S. and Europe. Sometimes the trees are sold and shipped away to make furniture and paper. More often they are just stacked up and burned. At this rate, there might not be any rain forests left in thirty years!

The children were horrified. The creatures of the rain forest could be gone before the students were even old enough to have a chance to see them. It didn't matter that they lived thousands of miles away in cold, snowy Sweden. It seemed to them that their future was being chopped and cleared away.

86

Informal Assessment

Observe individual students as they read and use the Teacher Observation Log found in the *Program Assessment Teacher's Edition* to record anecdotal information about each student's strengths and weaknesses.

Teacher Tip SELF-EVALUATING COMPREHENSION Good readers constantly evaluate their understanding of what they read. Stop often to make sure students are doing this.

During the autumn, as the sunlight weakened and the days became short, the Fagervik children continued to think about the rain forest. Whenever they went on walks past the great fir trees on the school grounds, they imagined jaguars crouched in the limbs just above them, their long tails twitching impatiently.

They begged Mrs. Kern to help them think of something—anything—they could do to rescue the creatures of the tropics. And then one afternoon during a music lesson, a student named Roland Tiensuu asked suddenly, "Can't we just *buy* some rain forest?"

The lesson stopped. It was a simple, clear idea that all the others understood at once. The class began to cheer, and then they turned to their teacher. "Please, Mrs. Kern," they said. "Please, won't you find us a forest to buy?"

87

COMPREHENSION

Comprehension Skills

Author's Purpose

Explain to students that writers always have a reason for writing. The author's purpose may be to inform, explain, entertain, or persuade. Tell students that an author can have more than one purpose for writing. Also, explain that the author's purpose affects the details, descriptions, pictures, and dialogue included in the story. Point out the following passages and ask students what the purpose of each is:

- Page 86: "In the past thirty years, she said, nearly half the world's rain forests have been cut down, often by poor people who burn the wood for fire." *(to inform)*

- Page 86: "The children were horrified. . . . It didn't matter that they lived thousands of miles away in cold, snowy Sweden." *(to entertain)*

Help students understand that the first passage is informative and the second is more for entertainment value.

Word Knowledge
Antonyms:
    short   long

Author's Purpose
Introduced in Grade 2.
Scaffolded throughout Grades 3–5.

REINTRODUCED:	Unit 1, Lesson 6
REINFORCED:	Unit 3, Lesson 1
	Unit 6, Lesson 4
TESTED:	Unit 1 Assessment

Second Reading Recommendation

ORAL • **SILENT**

COMPREHENSION

Comprehension Strategies

Teacher Modeling

2 Monitoring and Clarifying
Let's stop for a second and clarify what just happened. Roland suggested that the class buy a rain forest. Then he asked Mrs. Kern to find one for them to buy. Mrs. Kern didn't know where to look for a rain forest for sale, but she happened to meet an American biologist who had one for sale.

Teacher Modeling

3 Predicting *Good readers make predictions about what will happen later in a work. They base those predictions on clues from the text. So far, we know that the students want to buy a rain forest and Mrs. Kern has found one for them to buy. I think that the students will try to buy the rain forest that Ms. Kinsman is showing them. I predict that they will have to organize some kind of fund-raiser.*

As we continue reading, see if you can predict what is going to happen next. Maybe some of you will share your predictions with us.

Word Knowledge

/ks/ sound spelled *x:*
     expected   **expression**

Teacher Tip SELF-MONITORING Tell students to remember that they need to check their own understanding of a selection as they are reading. Encourage them to ask themselves questions, such as *Does what I am reading make sense? How well do I understand this? What is the most important point?*

"PLEASE BUY MINE."

Mrs. Kern had no idea how to find a rain forest for sale. But then, the very weekend after Roland's idea, she was introduced to an American <u>biologist</u> named Sharon Kinsman. As they chatted, Ms. Kinsman explained that she had been working in a rain forest called Monte Verde, or Green Mountain.

When Mrs. Kern told Ms. Kinsman of the nearly impossible mission her students had given her, she expected the biologist to laugh. Instead her expression turned serious. "Oh," she said quickly, "please buy mine."

Ms. Kinsman said that some people in Monte Verde were trying desperately to buy land so that more trees wouldn't be cut. Much land had already been protected, but much more was needed. Land was cheap there, she said—only about twenty-five dollars per acre.

Ms. Kinsman agreed to visit the Fagervik School. She would bring a map and slides of the Monte Verde forest and tell the children where they could send money to buy rain forest land. When Mrs. Kern told the children what had happened, they didn't even seem surprised. As they put it, "We knew you would find one."

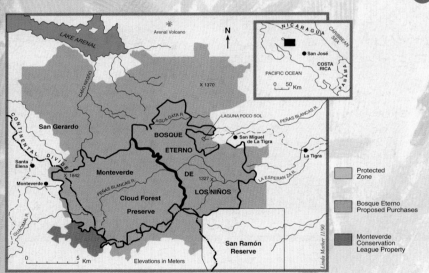

Here is a map of the Children's Rain Forest.

88

Informal Assessment

Use the Informal Comprehension Strategies Rubrics on page 86J to determine whether a student is using the strategies being taught.

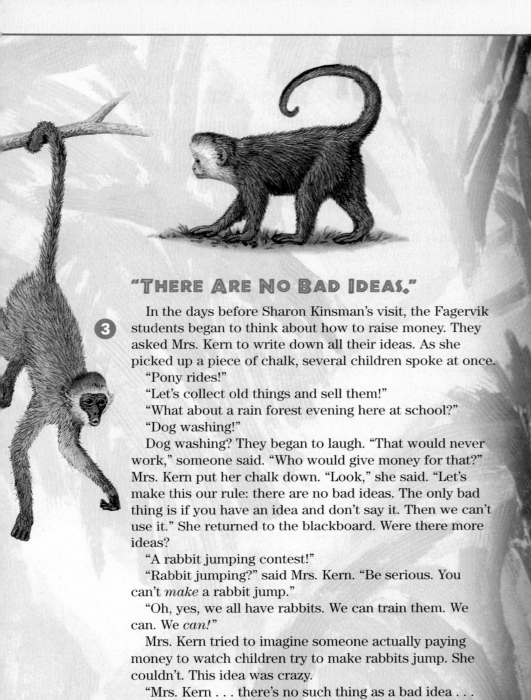

"THERE ARE NO BAD IDEAS."

3 In the days before Sharon Kinsman's visit, the Fagervik students began to think about how to raise money. They asked Mrs. Kern to write down all their ideas. As she picked up a piece of chalk, several children spoke at once.

"Pony rides!"

"Let's collect old things and sell them!"

"What about a rain forest evening here at school?"

"Dog washing!"

Dog washing? They began to laugh. "That would never work," someone said. "Who would give money for that?" Mrs. Kern put her chalk down. "Look," she said. "Let's make this our rule: there are no bad ideas. The only bad thing is if you have an idea and don't say it. Then we can't use it." She returned to the blackboard. Were there more ideas?

"A rabbit jumping contest!"

"Rabbit jumping?" said Mrs. Kern. "Be serious. You can't *make* a rabbit jump."

"Oh, yes, we all have rabbits. We can train them. We can. We *can!*"

Mrs. Kern tried to imagine someone actually paying money to watch children try to make rabbits jump. She couldn't. This idea was crazy.

"Mrs. Kern . . . there's no such thing as a bad idea . . . remember?" She did. "Rabbit jumping," she wrote, dutifully putting her doubts aside.

89

Comprehension Skills

Author's Purpose

Review with students the possible author's purposes: to inform, explain, persuade, and entertain. Reiterate that authors include certain descriptions for different purposes. Help students see that the following passages both explain how the students went about finding a way to make money and entertain the readers.

- Page 89: "In the days before Sharon Kinsman's visit, the Fagervik students began to think about how to raise money."

- Page 89: "Rabbit jumping?" said Mrs. Kern. "Be serious. You can't *make* a rabbit jump."

Word Knowledge

SCAFFOLDING The skills students are reviewing in Word Knowledge should help them in reading the story. This lesson focuses on antonyms. Antonym pairs will be found in boxes similar to this one throughout the selection.
Antonyms:

old	new
bad	good

COMPREHENSION

Comprehension Strategies

First Read

Teacher Modeling

4 Asking Questions *The students were very excited to have Ms. Kinsman visit. I wonder how they reacted after they saw all of her slides. Do you think they will be even more interested in raising money? Do you have any other questions about the selection so far?*

Word Knowledge

Antonyms:

many	few
preserve	destroy

Science/Social Studies Connection Center

Refer to the Science/Social Studies Connection Center Card 7 for a science activity that students can investigate.

GIANT SPIDERS AND DEADLY SNAKES

On November 6, 1987, Sharon Kinsman arrived at the Fagervik School. She was just as enthusiastic as the students. They put on skits for her about rain forests and showed her the many books they had written about tropical creatures. Then at last, it was her turn to show them slides of the Monte Verde forest.

First she unfolded a map of the forest and pointed to the area their money could preserve from cutting. She told them that 400 bird species live in the forest, more than in all of Sweden, as well as 490 kinds of butterflies and 500 types of trees. Monte Verde is also the only home in the world, she said, for the golden toad, a creature that seems to glow in the dark.

Then she showed her slides. As the room became dark, **4** the students were swept into a hot, steamy jungle half the world away. The slides took them sloshing along a narrow, muddy trail, crisscrossed with roots and vines. A dark canopy of giant trees, thick with bright flowering plants, closed in above them.

They saw giant spiders and deadly snakes. Ms. Kinsman's tape recorder made the forest ring with the shriek of howler monkeys calling to each other and with the chattering of parrots above the trees. They saw the golden toad, the scarlet macaw, and the red-backed poison-arrow frog.

90

And they saw the forest disappearing, too. They saw hard-muscled men, their backs glistening with sweat, pushing chain saws deep into the giant trees. They could almost smell the smoke of burning tree limbs and feel the thunder of thick, brown trunks crashing down. Behind great piles of ragged wood, the tropical sky was hazy with smoke. Time seemed very short.

When the lights came on, the students were back in Sweden, but they were not the same. Now they had seen their forest—and the danger it faced. There was no time to lose. Mrs. Kern had inspired them with a problem, and Roland had given them an idea they could work with. Sharon Kinsman had shown them their target. Now it was up to them.

91

Comprehension Skills

Author's Purpose

Review with students the possible author's purposes. Also, reiterate that an author can have more than one purpose. Then, ask students to suggest the possible purposes for the following passages.

- Page 90: "Monte Verde is also the only home in the world," she said, "for the golden toad, a creature that seems to glow in the dark." *(to inform)*

- Page 90: "As the room became dark, the students were swept into a hot, steamy jungle half the world away." *(to entertain)*

Help students understand that the first passage informs readers, whereas the second passage explains how the students feel.

Word Knowledge

Antonyms:

disappearing	appearing
giant	small
same	different

Teacher Tip AUTHOR'S PURPOSE
Tell students that they should try to figure out the author's purpose whenever they are reading.

COMPREHENSION

Comprehension Strategies

 First Read

Teacher Modeling

5 Confirming Predictions
Earlier I predicted that the students would organize a fund-raiser so that they could buy a rain forest. As I predicted, the students are having a rain forest evening to make money to buy their own.

Teacher Modeling

6 Predicting *Based on the information about the fund-raiser, I predict that the students will make a lot of money for the rain forest. However, I think that they will need more money if they want to buy a large piece of land. As you read, decide whether or not you think the predictions are on target. Come up with your own prediction based on the information in the text. As you come up with predictions, let the group know what they are. Good readers are always making predictions as they read.*

Teacher Modeling

7 Monitoring and Clarifying
Let's go over this. The students came up with ideas and tried them. What exactly were the ideas they proposed? They wrote to people for donations, and they asked the king to come see them perform.

Word Knowledge

Antonyms:

later	earlier
quickly	slowly
shout	whisper

 Teacher Tip PREDICTING Jot down students' predictions so that they can be referred to again later.

"WE KNEW WHAT WE WANTED."

5

Two weeks later, more than a hundred people crowded into an old schoolhouse near the Fagervik School for a rain forest evening. Students stood by the door and collected ten crowns (about $1.50) from each person. Special programs cost another crown. Even though it was winter, rain splattered steadily onto the roof, just as it must have been raining in the Monte Verde forest. To the students, rain was a good sign.

First they performed a play containing a dramatic scene in which trees of the rain forest were cut and creatures killed. That way guests would understand the problem they were trying to help solve. As the applause died down, the children passed an old hat around, urging audience members to drop money in it.

Then they sold rain forest books and rain forest poems. "We were not afraid to ask for money," remembers Maria Karlsson, who was nine. "We knew what we wanted was important." One boy stood at a table keeping track of how much they were making. Whenever a classmate would hand over a fresh delivery of cash, he would count it quickly and shout above the noise, "Now we've got two hundred crowns!!" "Now it's three hundred!!"

6

92

 **Science/Social Studies Connection Center**

Refer to the Science/Social Studies Connection Center Card 8 for a science activity that students can investigate.

Comprehension Skills

Author's Purpose

Point out the following passages to students:

- "The evening's total came to 1,600 crowns, or about $240. . . . They needed more." (page 93)

- "Someone else wrote to the king of Sweden and asked if he would watch them perform plays about the rain forest. He said yes." (page 93)

Ask students what they think were the author's purposes for including these passages. *(Answers will vary; have students explain the reasoning behind their answers.)*

Here are the children from the Fagervik School in Sweden who started a multimillion-dollar effort to preserve rain forest habitats for endangered plants and animals.

The evening's total came to 1,600 crowns, or about $240. The next day, they figured out that they had raised enough money to save about twelve football fields worth of rain forest. It was wonderful . . . but was it enough space for a sloth? A leopard? They all knew the answer. They needed more.

They filled up another blackboard with ideas and tried them out. Everything seemed to work. Mrs. Kern brought in a list of prominent people who might make donations. Two girls wrote a letter to the richest woman on the list. A few days later, a check arrived. Someone else wrote to the king of Sweden and asked if he would watch them perform plays about the rain forest. He said yes.

7

```
+-------------------------------------+
|          Word Knowledge             |
| Antonyms:                           |
|          next         previous      |
|          wonderful    horrible      |
|          richest      poorest       |
+-------------------------------------+
```

93

COMPREHENSION

Comprehension Strategies

 First Read

Teacher Modeling

8 Answering Questions *Earlier I asked whether the students would be more interested in raising money after they met with Ms. Kinsman. They were definitely more interested. In fact, they were so interested that when they didn't make enough money during their first event they decided to use other ways of making more money.*

Teacher Modeling

9 Monitoring and Clarifying
The selection begins in the autumn when the students hear about the rain forests. Now it is midwinter, and they have raised over one thousand dollars and have purchased a large portion of a rain forest. I realize now that they have only worked on this for a few months. They really worked hard together to solve their problem.

Word Knowledge

/ks/ sound spelled *x:*
         box

Teacher Tip SELF-MONITORING Tell students to remember that they need to check their own understanding of a selection as they are reading. Encourage them to ask themselves questions, such as *Does what I am reading make sense? How well do I understand this? What is the most important point?*

One day they went to a recording studio and made a tape of their rain forest songs. From the very beginning, Mrs. Kern and a music teacher had been helping them write songs. They started with old melodies they liked, changing them a little as they went along. As soon as anybody came up with a good line, they sang it into a tape recorder so they would't forget it by the end of the song. They rehearsed the songs many times on their school bus before recording them, then designed a cover and used some of their money to buy plastic boxes for the tapes. Within months, they had sold five hundred tapes at ten dollars each.

The more they used their imaginations, the more money **8** they raised. They decided to have a fair. "We had a magician and charged admission," remembers Lia Degeby, who was eight. "We charged to see who could make the ugliest face. We had a pony riding contest. We had a market. We had a lady with a beard. We had the strongest lady in the world. We tried everything." The biggest money maker of all was the rabbit jumping contest, even though each rabbit sat still when its time came to jump! Even carrots couldn't budge them. One simply flopped over and went to sleep, crushing its necklace of flowers.

Soon they needed a place to put all the money they had earned. Mrs. Kern's husband, Bernd, helped them form an organization called Barnens Regnskog, which means Children's Rain Forest. They opened a bank account with a post office box where people could continue to mail donations.

94

By midwinter, they had raised $1,400. The children addressed an envelope to the Monte Verde Cloud Forest Protection League, folded a check inside, and sent it on its way to Costa Rica. Weeks later, they received a crumpled package covered with brightly colored stamps. It contained a map of the area that had been bought with their money. A grateful writer thanked them for saving nearly ninety acres of Costa Rican rain forest.

In the early spring, the Fagervik students performed at the Swedish Children's Fair, which led to several national television appearances. Soon schools from all over Sweden were joining Barnens Regnskog and sending money to Monte Verde. At one high school near Stockholm, two thousand students did chores all day in the city and raised nearly $15,000. And inspired by the students, the Swedish government gave a grant of $80,000 to Monte Verde.

95

Comprehension Skills

Second Read

Author's Purpose

Explain to students that the passage below explains what they did with the money they earned.

- "The children addressed an envelope to the Monte Verde Cloud Forest Protection League, folded a check inside, and sent it on its way to Costa Rica." (page 95)

Ask students what the second paragraph on this page explains. Help them understand that it explains how others got involved in the effort to save Monte Verde.

Word Knowledge

Antonyms:

later	earlier
several	few

Teacher Tip FLUENCY By this time in grade 5, good readers should be reading approximately 126 words per minute with fluency and expression. The only way to gain this fluency is through practice. Have students reread the selection to you and to one another during Workshop to help build fluency.

COMPREHENSION

COMPREHENSION

Comprehension Strategies

First Read

Teacher Modeling

10 Monitoring and Clarifying

Let's stop and clarify what has happened. The children who visited the rain forest presented a $25,000 check to the staff of Monte Verde. Because of the work the Fagervik children started, the staff was able to establish the Eternal International Children's Rain Forest.

Discussing Strategy Use

While they are reading the selection, have students share any problems they encountered and tell what strategies they used.

- What questions did they ask about confusing words or passages?
- How did they clarify confusing passages?
- What predictions did they make?
- How did they adjust their reading speed?

Remind students that good readers use all of the strategies listed above and that they should be using them whenever they read. Make sure that students explain how using the strategies helped them better understand the selection. For example, "Reading more slowly when I came across confusing sections and hard words helped me make sure I understood before reading on."

Word Knowledge

/ks/ spelled *x*:

next

"I THINK OF MY FUTURE."

After another year's work, the children of Fagervik had raised $25,000 more. The families who could afford it sent their children to Costa Rica to see Monte Verde. Just before Christmas, ten Fagervik children stepped off the plane, blinking in the bright Costa Rican sunlight. It was hot! They stripped off their coats and sweaters, piled into a bus, and headed for the mountains.

A few hours later, the bus turned onto a narrow, rocky road that threaded its way through steep mountains. The children looked out upon spectacular waterfalls that fell hundreds of feet. Occasionally they glimpsed monkeys swinging through the trees.

Ahead, the mountaintops disappeared inside a dark purple cloud. For a few moments they could see five rainbows at once. Soon it began to rain.

The next morning, they joined ten Costa Rican children and went on a hike through the Monte Verde rain forest. Sometimes the thick mud made them step right out of their boots. But it didn't matter. "There were plants everywhere," says Lia. "I saw monkeys and flowers."

96

On Christmas day, the children of the Fagervik School proudly presented the staff of the Monte Verde Cloud Forest with their check for $25,000. They said it was a holiday present for all the children of the world.

10 The Monte Verde Conservation League used their gift, and funds that had been donated by other children previously, to establish what is now known as El Bosque Eterno de los Niños, or the Eternal International Children's Rain Forest. It is a living monument to the caring and power of young people everywhere. So far, kids from twenty-one nations have raised more than two million dollars to <u>preserve</u> nearly 33,000 acres of rain forest, plenty of room for <u>jaguars</u> and <u>ocelots</u> and <u>tapirs</u>. The first group of Fagervik students have now graduated to another school, but the first- and second-graders who have replaced them are still raising great sums of money. The school total is now well over $50,000.

The Fagervik students continue to amaze their teacher. "I never thought they could do so much," Mrs. Kern says. "Sometimes I say to them, 'Why do you work so hard?' They say, 'I think of my future.' They make me feel <u>optimistic</u>. When I am with them, I think maybe anything can be done."

Here is a view of a Monte Verde rain forest.

97

Formal Assessment

See pages 22–25 in the *Unit 1 Assessment* to test students' comprehension of "Founders of the Children's Rain Forest."

Comprehension Skills

Author's Purpose

Remind students that authors can have more than one purpose for writing a text. Help students see that the author's purposes of this text might be

- **to inform:** to make people aware of the work the children did to save the rain forest
- **to explain:** to explain how the founders of the Eternal International Children's Rain Forest began their quest
- **to persuade:** although this text is not meant to persuade, the author wants readers to agree it is important to save the rain forests

Checking Comprehension

Ask students the following questions to check their comprehension of the story.

- What sparked the children's interest in the rain forest? *(Mrs. Kern taught a class about rain forests and explained that they were being rapidly destroyed.)*
- What did the children decide to do to save the rain forest? *(They decided to buy a rain forest, and they held fund-raisers to make money.)*
- How did the children succeed? *(They were able to buy a rain forest, and their example led other children to help save rain forests.)*
- How has this selection connected with your knowledge of the unit theme? *(Answers will vary, but students should compare the results of cooperation in this selection with those from other selections in this unit and with their own prior knowledge.)*

Routine Card
Refer to Routine 5 for the *handing-off process.*

Clues	Problems	Wonderings
school children rain forest nonfiction	destruction need money	How will students "found" a rain forest?

Reading Transparency 54

www.sra4kids.com
Web Connection
Some students may choose to conduct a computer search for additional books or information about cooperation and competition. Invite them to make a list of these books and sources of information to share with classmates and the school librarian. Check the Reading link of the SRA Web page for additional links to theme-related Web sites.

Discussing the Selection

The whole group discusses the selection and any personal thoughts, reactions, problems, or questions that it raises. To stimulate discussion, students can ask one another the kinds of questions that good readers ask themselves about a text: *How does it connect to cooperation and competition? What have I learned that is new? What did I find interesting? What is important here? What was difficult to understand? Why would someone want to read this?* It is important for students to see you as a contributing member of the group.

Routine 5 To emphasize that you are part of the group, actively participate in the *handing-off process:* Raise your hand to be called on by the last speaker when you have a contribution to make. Point out unusual and interesting insights verbalized by students so that these insights are recognized and discussed. As the year progresses, students will take more and more responsibility for the discussion of selections.

Engage students in a discussion to determine whether they have grasped the following ideas:

- how cooperation led to positive results
- how cooperation among a small group leads to cooperation among a larger group
- how first- and second-grade students were able to save a rain forest

During this time, have students return to the clues, problems, and wonderings that they noted during browsing to determine whether the clues were borne out by the selection, whether and how their problems were solved, and whether their wonderings were answered or deserve further discussion and exploration. Let the students decide which items deserve further discussion.

Also have students return to the Focus Questions on the first page of the selection. Select a student to read the questions aloud, and have volunteers answer the questions. If students do not know the answers to the questions, have them return to the text to find the answers.

You may also wish to review the elements of narrative nonfiction with students. Discuss with them how they can tell that "Founders of the Children's Rain Forest" is narrative nonfiction.

Have students break into small groups to discuss how the story reflects the theme. Groups can then share ideas with the rest of the class.

Students may wish to record their thoughts about and reactions to this selection. Encourage students to write about how the members of the class saw great results through cooperation.

Review Selection Vocabulary

Have students review the definitions of the selection vocabulary words that they wrote in the vocabulary section of their Writer's Notebooks. Remind them that they discussed the meanings of these words before reading the selection. Students can use these definitions to study for the vocabulary portion of their Lesson Assessment. Have them add to the personal dictionary section of their Writer's Notebook any other interesting words that they clarify while reading. Encourage students to refer to the selection vocabulary words throughout the unit. The words from the selection are:

optimistic   **Equator**   **biologist**   **preserve**   **enthusiastic**

If you have created a Word Bank, have students place words under the appropriate headings on the Word Bank. Encourage the students to find other words related to the unit theme and add them to the Word Bank.

Home Connection

Distribute **Home Connection,** page 13. Encourage students to discuss "Founders of the Children's Rain Forest" with their families. Students can then explore options for them to help save rain forest land and investigate organizations that are doing so now. **Home Connection** is also available in Spanish, page 14.

Home Connection p. 13

Teacher Tip SELECTION VOCABULARY Encourage students to identify words from the selection vocabulary that connect with what they are learning in the Spelling and Vocabulary lessons for this selection.

Teacher Tip AUTHOR'S PURPOSE
Help students understand author's purpose by introducing them to texts with different purposes. For example, you might tell them that the fictional stories in this unit were written to entertain, and news articles are written to inform.

Author's Purpose

Purposes of "_____"

inform

entertain

explain

persuade

Reading Transparency 60

Supporting the Reading

Comprehension Skills: Author's Purpose

Teach Have students tell you what they know about author's purpose. Then tell them that writers always have a reason for writing. They may want *to inform, to entertain, to explain,* or *to persuade.* In addition, they may have more than one purpose for writing. The author's purpose affects the details, descriptions, pictures, dialogue, and form of writing. For example, a writer trying to persuade an audience might write an editorial or an advertisement and include information that supports his or her view. If the purpose is to entertain, one might write a novel and include elements such as humor, drama, and descriptive language. If the purpose is to explain, one might write directions on how to complete a process and include words that indicate the order in which the steps of the process should be carried out. If the purpose is to inform, one might write a report that includes general information about a certain topic. Have students think of other types of writing for which the author's purpose may be to inform, to entertain, to explain, or to persuade.

Guided Practice Explain to students that a selection might have several purposes, but one or two purposes are usually predominant. Have students use the chart on **Reading Transparency 60** to identify descriptions, details, pictures, and dialogue from the selection "Founders of the Children's Rain Forest" that support each of the purposes listed. When they have finished the chart, discuss which purpose or purposes are the most predominant.

Then discuss why the literary form the author chose for this selection, as well as the details listed on the chart, are appropriate for those purposes. Discuss also how any of these might have changed if the author's primary purpose had been different.

Independent Practice Read through the **Focus** and **Identify** sections of *Comprehension and Language Arts Skills,* page 28, with students. Guide students through the **Identify** portion, and help them come up with examples found in the story. Then have students complete the **Practice** and **Apply** portions of *Comprehension and Language Arts Skills,* page 29, as homework.

Link to Writing Have students think of an issue that they feel strongly about. Then, challenge them to write a letter to the editor of a local newspaper for the purpose of persuading others to take their side of the issue. You might show students examples of letters to the editor before they begin writing.

MEETING INDIVIDUAL NEEDS

Reteach

AUTHOR'S PURPOSE Have students who need additional practice with author's purpose complete *Reteach,* pages 30–31.

Challenge

AUTHOR'S PURPOSE Have students who understand author's purpose complete *Challenge,* page 25.

Skills Trace
Author's Purpose
Introduced in Grade 2.
Scaffolded throughout Grades 3–5.
REINTRODUCED: Unit 1, Lesson 6
REINFORCED: Unit 3, Lesson 1
Unit 6, Lesson 4
TESTED: Unit 1 Assessment

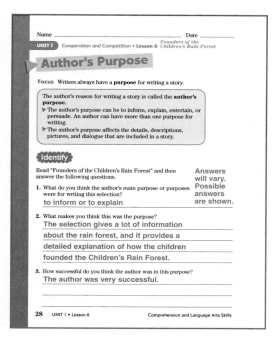
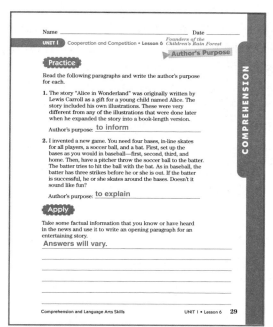

Comprehension and Language Arts Skills pp. 28–29

Literary Elements

Influencing Perspectives

Teach Have students tell you what they know about author techniques for influencing how their readers feel about a given topic. If necessary, tell students that authors might use vivid descriptions, include certain details, or choose words that have positive or negative associations to influence readers. Also, a writer might present a biased opinion, and only present his or her side of an issue.

Guided Practice Ask students what their feelings are about the rain forests and the children that founded the Monte Verde organization after reading the selection. Then, have students review the selection "Founders of the Children's Rain Forest" and look for the use of techniques that influenced their perspective. For example, students may mention that the author's portrayal of the Fagervik children's excitement about and success with their rain forest project persuades readers to take an interest in preserving rain forests. Record examples of these techniques and have students tell how each influenced them.

Independent Practice Have students review one of the other selections in Unit 1 and record the techniques the writer used to influence readers. Discuss whether the writer was successful in influencing students.

Science Connection: Habitat

Ask students if they know what *habitat* is. Remind them that *habitat* is what we call the natural environment of an animal or plant. In the selection, the rain forest habitat supported many animals. When rain forest is destroyed, the animals lose their homes and often die off. Encourage discussion of animals that lived in the students' area, but now have lost their habitat, or have them discuss other endangered animals. Then have students express their thoughts on posters.

■ Ask students to consider the following: What caused the loss of habitat? Why couldn't animals survive the change? Could the animals have adapted to the new habitat? How? Could the animals be brought back? Would the community want the animals to come back? If so, what could be done to encourage their return?

■ Tell each student to choose one animal and create a poster, using posterboard and paints or colored markers. Subject matter for the posters might include pictures of the animals and their habitats, reasons the animals have lost their habitat, whether the students would like to see the animals come back to their area, and if so, what could be done to bring them back.

■ Have students share finished posters with the class.

Science Connection: Photosynthesis

Remind the students that there may be plants in the rain forest that scientists have yet to discover. Have the students draw and color a plant they think might be found in the rain forest. Tell students to include the plant's leaves and roots in their drawings.

Next, write the following words on the board: carbon dioxide, oxygen, sugar, water, sunlight, and chlorophyll. Tell students that each of these things plays a part in photosynthesis, which is the process by which plants make their own food. Each is either taken in, given off, or found inside the plant.

Using the Internet, the library, or their science textbooks, have students research photosynthesis. Once students have discovered the part each word listed on the board plays in the process, have them turn their plant drawings into photosynthesis diagrams by adding each word in its proper place and showing with arrows where elements enter or leave the plant (for example, water flows in through the roots).

Last, have the students evaluate their original plants in light of what they've learned. What could they change to make their plants more successful in the rain forest? Do the plants have enough leaves? Are they green? Can their roots gather enough water? Would they get enough sunlight?

Teacher Tip MATERIALS FOR ACTIVITIES To complete the first Science Connection activity for this lesson, students will need posterboard, paints, and markers. To complete the second Science Connection activity for this lesson, students will need paper, pens, pencils, markers, and crayons.

Meet the Author

After students read the information about Phillip Hoose, discuss the following questions with them.

- Why do you think Phillip Hoose chose to write about children helping the rain forest? *(Possible answer: He works for something called Nature Conservancy. He probably cares about the environment and wants other people to care too.)*

- What do you think Phillip Hoose would say to you if he saw you squashing ants? *(Possible answer: He might tell you to stop doing it, but he might ask you why you think it is okay to squash bugs.)*

Meet the Illustrator

After students read the information about Jim Effler, discuss the following question with them.

- Jim Effler's illustrations for "Founders of the Children's Rain Forest" are very detailed. How might Mr. Effler have researched these tropical animals for his illustrations? *(Possible answer: He could have looked up pictures of the animals in the library or on the Internet, or he could have gone to a zoo to see what they look like.)*

FOUNDERS OF THE CHILDREN'S RAIN FOREST

Meet the Author

Phillip Hoose likes to spend time with his family. When his daughter Hannah was younger, the Hooses had a family band in which they sang and wrote songs. One of their songs, "Hey Little Ant," later became a book by the same title. Phillip and Hannah got the idea for the song when they saw Hannah's younger sister squashing ants in their driveway. The book asks readers to question whether or not it is right to kill bugs.

Mr. Hoose has made a career out of his love of nature and music. He is a staff member of the Nature Conservancy and a founding member of the Children's Music Network.

Meet the Illustrator

Jim Effler has been drawing since he was two years old. That was back in 1958!

He has illustrated several children's books about animals. Jim's work has won awards from Art Directors' Clubs and the Society of Illustrators. He lives in Cincinnati with his wife Debbie and daughters, Jenna and Ariana.

98

Theme Connections

Within the Selection

Record your answers to the questions below in the Response Journal section of your Writer's Notebook. In small groups, report the ideas you wrote. Discuss your ideas with the rest of your group. Then choose a person to report your group's answers to the class.

- How did Mrs. Kern discourage competition among students as they brainstormed ways to raise money? Why did she do this?
- How did the students prove that the small contributions of many people can make a difference?
- Students carried out many different plans to earn money for the Children's Rain Forest. In what ways did students use competition as a way to raise money?

Across Selections

- Compare the cooperative efforts of students in Fagervik School with those of students in "Class President."
- Which character or characters from the other stories you have read in this unit would be most likely to lead this movement? Explain why you think so.

Beyond the Selection

- Tell about a time when you have seen people successfully work together to solve a problem that is too big for one person to solve.
- Think about how "Founders of the Children's Rain Forest" adds to what you know about cooperation and competition.
- Add items to the Concept/Question Board about cooperation and competition.

99

Theme Connections

Within the Selection

- She told them "There are no bad ideas." She knew this was the best way to generate creative ideas.
- The first fund-raiser earned $240. This success encouraged students to continue. Each time they involved more people and raised more money.
- They held a pony-riding contest, a rabbit race, and a contest to see who could make the ugliest face.

Across Selections

- Students of Fagervik School, just like those in "Class President," worked to raise money for a good cause.
- Students may say Julio, because he had good leadership skills.

Beyond the Selection

- Answers will vary.

Students should record their ideas and impressions about the selections on page 7 of their *Inquiry Journals.*

Teacher Tip INQUIRY AND INVESTIGATION Have groups report and discuss their ideas with the class. As these ideas are stated, have students add them to the Concept/ Question Board. As students complete their discussions, have them sum up what they have learned and tell how they might use this information in further investigations.

Informal Assessment

This may be a good time to observe students working in small groups and to mark your observations in the Teacher Observation Log found in the *Program Assessment Teacher's Edition.*

- "The Abacus Contest" by Priscilla Wu
  Answers will vary.

- "S.O.R. Losers" by Avi
  Answers will vary.

- "Founders of the Children's Rain Forest" by Phillip Hoose
  Answers will vary.

Inquiry Journal • *Recording Concept Information*   UNIT I   **7**

Inquiry Journal p. 7

INVESTIGATION

Objectives

- Students gain a better understanding of the results of cooperation.
- Students present their investigation findings.

Materials

- Student Anthology, pp. 86–99
- Research Assistant
- Inquiry Journal, pp. 28–31

Name _____ Date _____

UNIT I   Cooperation and Competition

Finding a Cause

The first step in working as a class to support a cause is to find a cause in which all of you are interested. In the first column, write any causes that are of personal interest to you. (For example, your cause may be finding families for homeless pets.) In the second column, list the names of any organizations that support the causes. (For example, an organization that helps place pets in homes is the Humane Society.) Then, in the third column, write the reasons you think each cause is important. When you have completed the chart, compare and discuss your charts with your classmates. Then, as a class, decide which cause or organization to support. Answers will vary.

Causes	Organizations	Reasons

28   UNIT I   *Finding a Cause • Inquiry Journal*

After you have decided with the class which cause or organization to support, choose a fundraiser that you would like to host. Write the name of the fundraiser in the first box. Then, list the pros (strengths or good points) and cons (weaknesses or bad points) of the fundraiser you chose. When you have finished, share your chart with others in the class. Then, as a class, you can decide the kind of fundraiser to host and begin planning. Answers will vary.

Fundraiser:	
Pros	Cons

Inquiry Journal • *Finding a Cause*   UNIT I   29

Inquiry Journal pp. 28–29

Investigating Concepts Beyond the Text

To facilitate students' investigation of cooperation and competition, you might have them participate in the following activities. Tell students that if they have activity ideas of their own that they would like to pursue, they are free to do so as an alternative to these activity suggestions. For example, students may want to pursue activities of their own choosing that relate more directly to the problems and questions they are investigating with their groups. Tell students that they may work on these activities alone, in pairs, or in small groups, with an option to write about them or to present them to the group upon completion.

The activity suggestions for this lesson are:

- Students may be interested in finding a cause of their own to support. Have them complete *Inquiry Journal,* pages 28–29, to establish where their interests lie and what kind of fundraiser they might host to raise money for their cause.

- You might invite a person from a nonprofit organization to speak in the class about the origins of the organization and the cooperation that is needed to keep the organization running. In preparation for the speaker
  - have students prepare any questions they might want to ask.
  - encourage students to take notes on what the speaker says so that they will recall the main ideas and supporting details in the speech.
  - have students note any unfamiliar words or ideas that they hear in the speech and clarify them afterward.
  - remind students to listen attentively to the speaker, making eye contact and facing the speaker.

Following the speaker's talk, allow some time for students to respond to the speaker by asking questions and making contributions that are relevant to what he or she said. After the session with the speaker, discuss the speech as a class to ensure students comprehended all the main points. At that time, have students identify, analyze, and critique any persuasive techniques the speaker used (e.g. promises, dares, flattery, or glittering generalities) and their interpretations of the speaker's verbal and nonverbal messages, purposes, and perspectives.

Have students identify any logical fallacies in the speaker's presentation.

Upon completion of their activities, have students share with the group anything new they learned about cooperation and competition through discussion and by adding information to the Concept/Question Board.

Concept/Question Board

After reading each selection, students should use the Concept/Question Board to

- post any questions they asked about a selection before reading that have not yet been answered.
- refer to as they formulate statements about concepts that apply to their investigations.
- post general statements formulated by each collaborative group.
- continue to post news articles, or other items that they find during the unit investigation.
- read and think about posted questions, articles, or concepts that interest them and provide answers to the questions.

Concept/Question Board

Cooperation and Competition

Concept   Question

Research Assistant

The Research Assistant helps students in their investigations.

Teacher Tip REVIEW To help students retain the information they learned while studying this theme, allow them time to review the Concept/Question Board. Invite students to discuss how their knowledge increased while studying this unit.

Unit 1 Investigation Management

Lesson 1	Students generate ideas for investigation.
Lesson 2	Students formulate questions and problems for investigation.
Lesson 3	Students make conjectures.
Lesson 4	Students establish investigation needs.
Lesson 5	Students establish investigation plans.
Lesson 6	**Collaborative Investigation** **Students present investigation findings.** **Supplementary Activities** **Students participate in investigation activities and learn to use visual aids.**

INVESTIGATION

Formal Assessment

Use the Research Rubrics on page 86J to assess students' research and ability to communicate their progress and results.

Informal Assessment

As students give oral presentations, note your observations as to the organization of their presentations. For example,

- Is it apparent that the presenters prepared for the presentation?
- Is the presentation focused and organized?
- If the presentation is informational, does it contain a controlling idea developed and clarified with simple facts, details, examples, and explanations?
- If the presentation is narrative, do the presenters establish a situation, plot, point of view, and setting with descriptive words and phrases?
- Are visual aids, technology, or demonstrations effectively used to support the presentation?

Also note your observations of students' ability to speak effectively. For example,

- Do they use strategies to speak clearly?
- Do they use both verbal and nonverbal strategies to engage the audience?
- Do they correctly use grammar, sentence structure, and sentence variety in speech?
- Do they use language appropriate to the situation, audience, and purpose of the presentation?
- Do they use appropriate words to shape reactions, perceptions, and beliefs?

Finally, observe audience members and note their use of listening strategies and their ability to comprehend, respond to, and evaluate the presentations.

Presenting Investigation Findings

By now, students should be in the midst of carrying out their job assignments and discovering information to contribute to their investigation projects. Tell students that it is time for them to begin compiling their findings to present to the group, either orally or in written form. Some students may not feel that their findings are conclusive enough to present. Tell them that most true investigations are essentially endless, although findings are presented from time to time. New findings give rise to new problems and conjectures, and therefore to new cycles of investigation.

You may want to meet with the whole class as needed
- to arrange schedules and update calendars;
- to discuss problems that students are encountering with their investigation findings;
- to hear discussions of interesting findings
- to provide guidance to ensure that groups progress through the investigation process—obtaining information; revising problems, conjectures, needs, and plans (perhaps with input resulting from a presentation to the class); and proceeding to a further cycle of problem, conjecture, and so forth.

Have students compile their findings into their chosen presentation format during Workshop and as homework. Encourage those who will be making oral presentations or demonstrations to practice a few times before presenting to the group. Then, allow time for groups to present their investigation projects.

Tell students who will be making oral presentations to be sure that they speak clearly, being mindful that the rate and volume at which they speak is appropriate for the audience. Tell them that they should also use nonverbal strategies to engage their audience, such as making eye contact, incorporating hand gestures, and practicing good posture. Tell audience members that they should use listening strategies to help them comprehend what they are hearing. They should face the speaker, making eye contact with him or her, and take notes on information that they find interesting or would like to know more about.

Following each presentation, allow students time to respond to the speaker or speakers. Have them ask questions and paraphrase parts of the presentation to confirm their understanding. Have them contribute new ideas and share conclusions they have come to as a result of the presented material. Have them also offer feedback, telling what they especially liked about the presentation or offering constructive criticism. Allow presenters to respond to this feedback. Finally, have students share new problems or questions raised by the presented material that have not previously been discussed. Then have the students add information to the Concept/Question Board. Encourage interested students to continue investigating and learning about their problems.

Using Visual Aids

Teach Ask students what they know about visual aids and their uses. Then explain that visual aids provide a means of presenting a lot of information in a small space. They also help clarify or add to information that is presented in text.

Write the following descriptions on the board:

- A **table** is a kind of visual aid in which data is found by matching horizontal and vertical categories.
- **Charts** can take many forms and organize a variety of information. For example, **flowcharts** show the order of events or steps, **cluster charts** organize ideas around a main idea, and **pie charts** show percentages.
- **Illustrations,** or drawings or photographs, help make concepts clearer or provide interest to the audience.
- **Diagrams** illustrate concepts or processes.

Guided Practice Have students flip through the pages of "Founders of the Children's Rain Forest" and look at the illustrations. Ask students why they think the illustrator chose those certain events to illustrate. What do they add to the text? How do they help make information more accessible and usable? Discuss what other events in the text would work well in illustration.

Independent Practice Have students chart the main events of "Founders of the Children's Rain Forest." Discuss the kind of chart they should use (flowchart) and why. Display ***Reading Transparency 57.*** Have students discuss which events were the five most important. Have students chart the events in a five-box flowchart. For additional practice using visual aids, have students complete ***Inquiry Journal,*** pages 30–31.

Have students think of ways to incorporate visual aids into their presentations.

SUPPORTING THE INVESTIGATION

Teacher Tip VISUAL AIDS Encourage students to use visual aids to enhance their investigation presentations.

Teacher Tip STUDENT WRITING AND RESEARCH CENTER Have students use the *Student Writing and Research Center CD-ROM* as they work on their investigation activities.

Teacher Tip USING A COMPUTER Encourage students to use *Basic Computer Skills* to learn how to use a computer to write a report.

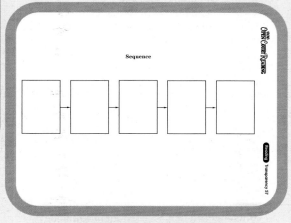

Reading Transparency 57

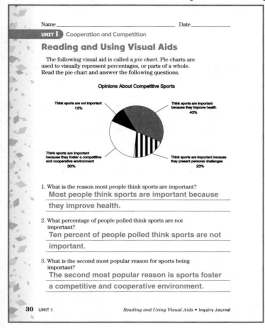

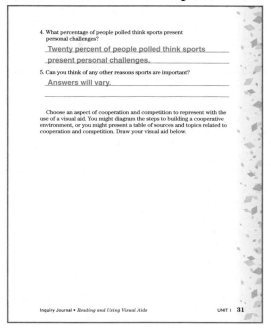

Inquiry Journal pp. 30–31

Objectives

Word Analysis

Spelling
- **Short-Vowel Spelling Patterns.** Review the various spelling patterns for the /a/, /e/, /o/, /aw/, /i/, and /u/ sounds.

Vocabulary
- Review strategies for discovering word meanings. Introduce word mapping as a way to relate words and ideas and draw on previous knowledge.

Writing Process Strategies
- **The Process of Editing/Proofreading and Publishing.** Learn aspects of the publishing process including presenting work to others for review, exploring publishing formats, and doing a final evaluation of audience and purpose.

English Language Conventions

Grammar, Usage, and Mechanics
- **Review.** Review correct use of nouns, pronouns, and verbs; kinds of sentences and their ending punctuation; and subjects and predicates.

Listening, Speaking, Viewing
- **Presenting: Using Note Cards.** Learn the value of note cards as a speaking aid as well as how to use them for a presentation.

Penmanship
- **Cursive Letters *q*, *g*, and *o*.** Develop handwriting skills by practicing formation of cursive *q*, *g*, and *o*.

Materials

- Spelling and Vocabulary Skills, pp. 22–25
- Language Arts Handbook
- Comprehension and Language Arts Skills, pp. 30–33
- Writer's Workbook, p. 5
- Language Arts Transparencies 21–26; 28; 34
- Spelling Software
- Student Anthology
- Unit 1 Assessment, pp. 36–37

MEETING INDIVIDUAL NEEDS

Reteach, Challenge, English-Language Development and *Intervention* lessons are available to support the language arts instruction in this lesson.

Research in Action

In short, whereas good spellers seem to spell visually and read phonetically, poorer spellers seem to spell phonetically and read visually. (*Marilyn Adams*, Beginning to Read: Thinking and Learning About Print)

OVERVIEW

Language Arts Overview

Word Analysis

Spelling The spelling activities on the following pages support the Word Knowledge introduction of the short-vowel sounds by reinforcing the spelling patterns for /a/, /e/, /o/, /aw/, /i/, and /u/.

Selection Spelling Words

These words from "Founders of the Children's Rain Forest" contain short-vowel sounds.

m<u>i</u>nute   p<u>a</u>sture   r<u>a</u>bbit   j<u>u</u>ngle   tr<u>o</u>pical

Vocabulary The vocabulary activities incorporate a review of strategies for defining unfamiliar words with an introduction of semantic word mapping.

Vocabulary Skill Words

equator*   biologist*   species   optimistic*   prominent

*Also Selection Vocabulary.

Additional Materials

On Day 4, each student will need a thesaurus and a dictionary.

Writing Process Strategies

This Writing Process Strategies lesson has students editing/proofreading for correct grammar, usage, and mechanics on various drafts in their Writer's Notebooks, ***Writing Folders,*** and on their autobiographies.

 Basic Computer Skills To learn basic computer skills for writing, have students practice striking the Number and Symbol keys. ***Basic Computer Skills*** Level 5 Lessons 17–18 teach these keyboarding skills.

English Language Conventions

Grammar, Usage, and Mechanics **Review.** This lesson reviews correct noun, pronoun, and verb use; kinds of sentences; and subjects and predicates. Students will practice these skills in their writing.

Listening, Speaking, Viewing **Presenting: Using Note Cards.** In this Presenting lesson, students will learn how using note cards can help as a speaking aid, and will discuss what they could include on the cards for the different parts of their presentations.

Penmanship **Cursive Letters *q*, *g* and *o*.** This lesson continues the development of handwriting skills. Students learn correct formation of *q*, *g* and *o* and then practice writing paragraphs from the literature selections.

DAY I

Word Analysis	Writing Process Strategies	English Language Conventions

Word Analysis

Spelling

Assessment: Pretest

Short-Vowel Spelling Patterns
Give students the Pretest on page 36 of *Unit 1 Assessment*. Have them proofread and correct any misspellings.

Pretest Sentences

1. **jazz**   She is in a **jazz** band.
2. **double**   He was seeing **double** after being hit in the head.
3. **freckle**   The sun will often bring out a **freckle.**
4. **glove**   Did someone lose a **glove?**
5. **pause**   A yield sign signals you to **pause.**
6. **bumblebee**   A **bumblebee** floats from flower to flower.
7. **myth**   The story of Paul Bunyan is a **myth.**
8. **leather**   Shoes are made of **leather.**
9. **strict**   Keep to a **strict** exercise schedule.
10. **taxi**   Hailing a **taxi** can be a difficult job.
11. **prompt**   We expect **prompt** service.
12. **bought**   The United States **bought** Alaska from Russia.
13. **pansy**   A **pansy** is a small, delicate flower.
14. **taught**   Annie Sullivan **taught** the blind and deaf Helen Keller.
15. **guilt**   A jury will determine the **guilt** of a person.
16. **minute**   Can you hold your breath for a **minute?**
17. **rabbit**   A **rabbit** is likely to nibble on lettuce.
18. **tropical**   A toucan is a brightly-colored **tropical** bird.
19. **jungle**   A **jungle** contains many species of plants.
20. **pasture**   They cleared land for a **pasture** for their livestock.

Writing Process Strategies

Introduction to the Writing Process: Editing/Proofreading

Making It Correct

Teach

Read *Language Arts Handbook* pages 46–47 on editing. Encourage the use of dictionaries for checking on spelling and word usage.

- Show *Transparency 21— Conventions, Capitalization* and point out how correct capitalization helps readers see when sentences begin and when the writer is referring to specific nouns.
- Show *Transparency 22— Conventions,* focusing on *End Marks* and discuss the importance of letting readers know when sentences end and what type of sentence they are reading.
- Show *Transparency 26— Proofreading Marks.* Proofreading marks may be used as tools to help students make the editing process neat, clear, and quick.

Independent Practice

Have students practice editing a page in their *Writing Folders* utilizing proofreading marks from *Transparency 26.*

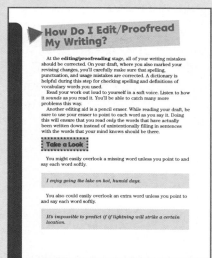

Language Arts Handbook p. 46

English Language Conventions

Grammar, Usage, and Mechanics:

Review

Teach

- Use *Language Arts Handbook* pages 342–347; 352–353; and 363 for examples of nouns, pronouns, verbs, kinds of sentences, and subjects and predicates.
- Review that a noun is a word that names a person, place, thing, or idea.
- Review common and proper nouns.
- Review capitalization of proper nouns.
- Review the difference between words and possessive pronouns that are often confused (*it's, its; you're, your*).
- Review auxiliary verbs.
- Review the four kinds of sentences (*declarative, interrogative, imperative, exclamatory*) and the ending punctuation of each.
- Review subject and predicate sentence structure.

Independent Practice

Use *Comprehension and Language Arts Skills* pages 30–31 to practice pluralizing nouns and identifying pronouns, verb forms, ending punctuation for different kinds of sentences, and subjects and predicates.

Comprehension and Language Arts Skills p. 30

DAY 2

Word Analysis

Spelling

Word Sorting

Open Word Sort Have students sort the spelling words by their short vowel sounds. Have students explain their answers.

Vocabulary

Word Mapping

Teach

- Write the word *orchestra* on the board and have students make a list of all the related terms they can think of, which might include *drum, violin, conductor, baton, auditorium, theater, concertmaster, trumpet,* and *trombone.* Then put these words into categories. These might include *instruments, people, places to perform,* etc. Write these categories around the main word and draw lines to connect them to the main word. Then list the corresponding terms under each category.

Guided Practice

Assign page 22 of **Spelling and Vocabulary Skills.** Students can complete page 23 of **Spelling and Vocabulary Skills** for homework.

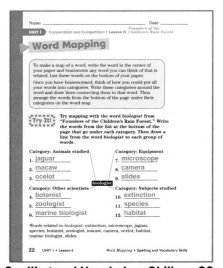

Spelling and Vocabulary Skills p. 22

Writing Process Strategies

Introduction to the Writing Process: Editing/Proofreading
Making It Correct, Writing on a Computer

Teach

- Have students read **Language Arts Handbook** page 48 and go over the editing checklist.
- Use **Transparency 23—Conventions,** focusing on **Internal Punctuation.** Point out that commas, semicolons, and colons help organize writing into distinct ideas and let readers know when thoughts or items are separate and when to pause.
- Use **Transparency 24—Conventions,** focusing on **Spelling.** Discuss how incorrect spelling distracts the reader and may sometimes lead to misunderstanding. Remind students to use a dictionary or thesaurus when they are unsure of the spelling of a word.
- Discuss how to edit computer drafts of documents. Review these tips for computer editing: 1) Increase the type size for easier reading, 2) Open documents to fill as much of the computer screen as possible, 3) Make corrections as mistakes are seen and read the changes aloud, 4) Read through the printed hard copy to catch additional mistakes.

Independent Practice

Have students practice editing/ proofreading drafts from their **Writing Folders.** If you have a classroom computer, let students practice editing drafts of a document on it.

English Language Conventions

Grammar, Usage, and Mechanics:
Review

Teach

- Review common and proper nouns. Include a review on capitalization.
- Write this sentence on the board: *Brad drove.* Have students come up to the board and add modifiers to the subject and the predicate to make the sentence more detailed and interesting.
- Review naming yourself last *(Brad and I drove),* as this is a sentence structure that will probably appear many times in their autobiographies.
- Review being clear about the antecedents of pronouns.

Independent Practice in Reading

- Have students look for nouns (common and proper) in "Founders of the Children's Rain Forest." The proper nouns are mainly the names of people and geographic locations.

DAY 3

Word Analysis	Writing Process Strategies	English Language Conventions

Word Analysis

Spelling

Short-Vowel Spelling Patterns

Teach
Review all short-vowel patterns, including *a* for /a/; *e* and *ea* for /e/; *o, au, oa, augh, aw,* and *ough* for /o/ and /aw/; *i, y,* and *ui* for /i/; and *u, o-consonant-e,* and *ou* for /u/. Divide students into groups and assign each one a vowel sound. Have each group look for words with their assigned spelling patterns in different sections of a newspaper.

Guided Practice
Have students complete page 24 from *Spelling and Vocabulary Skills*.

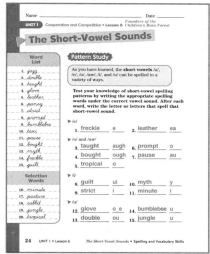

Spelling and Vocabulary Skills p. 24

Vocabulary (continued)

Word Mapping
Write the following words from "Founders of the Children's Rain Forest" on the board. Briefly discuss their definitions and ask students for synonyms and antonyms. Under each main word, list synonyms and antonyms such as *positive, hopeless, famous,* and *hidden* in separate columns.

optimistic   prominent

Writing Process Strategies

Introduction to the Writing Process: Editing/Proofreading
Correcting Grammar

Teach
- Show **Transparency 25—Conventions** focusing on **Grammar**. Discuss with students the importance of subject-verb agreement. Remind students when editing to make sure singular verbs have singular subjects and plural verbs have plural subjects. Point out that they can sometimes trust their own ear to decide subject-verb agreement. For help determining tricky agreement for compound subjects and indefinite pronouns, they may refer to **Language Arts Handbook** pages 368–369.
- Discuss common sentence structure problems and point out to students that ridding their writing of awkward sentences in the editing process will give it another boost toward clarity and readability. Encourage students to look for and fix these types of awkward sentences in the editing process:
  - **Sentence fragments:** groups of words that lack a subject, verb, or both and do not express a complete thought.
  - **Run-on sentences:** two or more sentences written as though they are one.
  - **Rambling sentences:** sentences that go on and on with too many conjunctions connecting what could be read more easily as separate sentences.

See **Language Arts Handbook** pages 360–362 for specific examples of awkward sentences along with ways to correct them.

Independent Practice
Have students focus on capitalization, punctuation, and grammar as they proofread their autobiographies in their **Writing Folders**.

English Language Conventions

Grammar, Usage, and Mechanics: Review

Teach
- Use **Language Arts Handbook** pages 342–347, 352–353, and 363 to review common and proper nouns, plural nouns, capitalization of proper nouns, pronouns, verbs, kinds of sentences, ending punctuation, and subjects and predicates.
- Remind students that writing in the active voice makes their writing clearer and stronger.
- Remind students to use precise verbs (*strolled* rather than *walked*) in their autobiographies.

Independent Practice in Writing
Remind students that checking for proper noun capitalization, correct pronoun use, and correct use of ending punctuation in sentences is an important part of editing their autobiographies.

 Informal Assessment

Check to see that students are progressing in their understanding and usage of the skills learned in this unit.

DAY 4

Word Analysis	Writing Process Strategies	English Language Conventions

Word Analysis

Spelling

Short-Vowel Spelling Patterns

Teach

Model the family strategy exercise by explaining that the short i spelling pattern in *instinct* is the same in *instinctive, instinctual,* and *instinctively.*

Guided Practice

Have students complete the Spelling Strategies exercises on page 25 of *Spelling and Vocabulary Skills*.

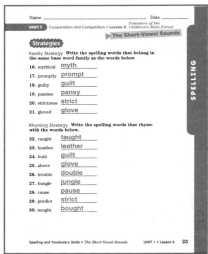

Spelling and Vocabulary Skills p. 25

Vocabulary (continued)

Word Mapping

- Divide students into groups of at least four and assign one of the words below to each group. Part of the group will define the word from context by locating it in "Founders of the Children's Rain Forest." Another part will define the word based on word parts and roots. The other two parts of the group will look up the word in the dictionary or thesaurus. Have students share their definitions.

equator	dramatic
conservation	spectacular
enthusiastic	admission
paralyze	

Writing Process Strategies

Introduction to the Writing Process: Publishing

Final Decisions

Teach

- Go over what the publishing step involves: preparing writing to share with an audience and deciding how the writing will be shared.
- Before they create the final copies of what they have written, encourage students to share their writing with another person. The new reader may be able to catch mechanical and grammatical errors that students missed in their final review. The new reader may also be able to point out any confusing sentences and paragraphs.
- Read *Language Arts Handbook* pages 50–55 and discuss formats for publishing various types of writing:
  - Letters written to friends, relatives, newspapers, school or government officials, authors and other people that students admire
  - Plays, oral presentations, and introductions at school programs
  - Short stories, book reviews, letters, riddles, and poems for a school newsletter or for children's magazines

Guided Practice

Have students review their autobiographies to see whether what they have written meets their intended audience and purpose.

Writer's Craft
Presentation

- Tell students that good writers are concerned not only with the content of their writing, but also the look of their writing. Tell students that bullets, charts, graphs, and illustrations can help their writing stand out. Have students complete *Comprehension and Language Arts Skills* pages 32–33 for practice on presentation.

English Language Conventions

Listening, Speaking, Viewing
Presenting: Using Note Cards

Teach

- Explain how giving a good presentation requires the speaker to stay on topic and present the points in a logical order. Note cards are small pieces of paper with the important points of a presentation written on them. The speaker can put them in order and look at them briefly during the presentation to help remember what to say.
- Explain how points from the beginning would be on the first cards, followed by points from the middle, and then points from the end of the presentation.
- Remind students that note cards can help the speaker remember what to say. Students should not read straight from their cards during a presentation. Even when using note cards, the speaker must speak clearly and look at the audience.

Guided Practice

- Tell students that if they were going to tell their whole school how to play volleyball, they might want a set of note cards to help them with the presentation.
- What would they include on the note cards? (*Main points such as how many people are on a team, what the rules are, how each team scores a point.*)
- Ask students if they think using note cards would help them with the presentation.

 Informal Assessment

Observe whether students understand how note cards can help when giving a presentation, and whether they understand what type of information to write on them.

DAY 5

Word Analysis	Writing Process Strategies	English Language Conventions

Word Analysis

Spelling

Assessment: Final Test
Short-Vowel Spelling Patterns

Teach
Repeat the Pretest for this lesson or use the Final Test on page 37 of *Unit 1 Assessment*.

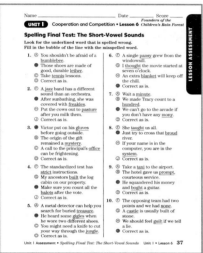

Unit 1 Assessment p. 37

Practice
Have students categorize any mistakes they made on the Final Test.

Are they careless errors?
Are they lesson pattern problems?

Vocabulary (continued)

Word Mapping

 Informal Assessment

- Remind students to continue using all the strategies discussed in this unit as they encounter unfamiliar words. Students should continue using the dictionary, but know that context and word parts are other useful details that can provide the full meaning for unfamiliar words.
- Encourage the continued recording of words in their Writer's Notebooks.

Writing Process Strategies

Introduction to the Writing Process: Publishing
Final Decisions

Teach
- Go over **Transparencies 28** and **34** and discuss the things students have applied and can still apply to their autobiographies.
- Have students use **Tips for Writing an Autobiography** on page 157 of the **Language Arts Handbook**.

Guided Practice
Have students complete page 5 of their **Writer's Workbooks**. Then, have them neatly type or print final copies of their autobiographies and share them.

 Formal Assessment

Share the rubric with students before they begin the assignment to give them a foundation on which to base their work.
Total Point Value 10
1. The published piece matches its audience and purpose. (2 points)
2. Sentences and paragraphs are smooth and transition well. (2 points)
3. The writing stays on topic. (3 points)
4. Grammar, usage, and mechanics conventions have been followed. (3 points)

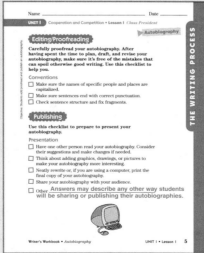

Writer's Workbook p. 5

English Language Conventions

Penmanship
Cursive Letters *q*, *g* and *o*

Teach
- **Teacher Model:** Review lowercase cursive *q*, *g*, and *o* as downcurve letters.

q Starting point, downcurve
Undercurve to starting point
Slant down and loop back
Undercurve: small *q*

g Starting point, downcurve
Undercurve to starting point
Slant down and loop forward
Overcurve: small *g*

o Starting point, downcurve
Undercurve
Small curve to right: small *o*

- Remind students that they should make loops only for letters that require them, and that the loop in *q* and *g* should close below the baseline.

Guided Practice
- **Teacher Model:** On the board, write the sentence "The ground quickly became wet." to model proper letter formation and loops that close below the baseline.
- From "Founders of the Children's Rain Forest," have students copy two paragraphs for general handwriting practice.

 Informal Assessment

Check students' handwriting for legibility and letters that are looped that should *not* be looped.

Reading and Language Arts Skills Traces

Language Arts

WORD ANALYSIS

Skills Trace

Spelling: Review Short Vowels

Introduced in Grade 1.
Scaffolded throughout Grades 2–5.
REINTRODUCED: Unit 1, Lesson 6, p. 99F
PRACTICED: Unit 1, Lesson 6,
pp. 99G–99I
Spelling and Vocabulary Skills,
pp. 24–25
TESTED: Unit 1, Lesson 6, p. 99J
Unit 1 Assessment

Skills Trace

Vocabulary: Word Mapping

Introduced in Grade 1.
Scaffolded throughout Grades 2–5.
REINTRODUCED: Unit 1, Lesson 6, p. 99G
PRACTICED: Unit 1, Lesson 6,
pp. 99H–99I
Spelling and Vocabulary Skills,
pp. 22–23
TESTED: Informal Assessment, p. 99J
Unit 1 Assessment

Reading

COMPREHENSION

Skills Trace

Author's Purpose

Introduced in Grade 2.
Scaffolded throughout Grades 3–5.
REINTRODUCED: Unit 1, Lesson 6
REINFORCED: Unit 3, Lesson 1
Unit 6, Lesson 4
TESTED: Unit 1 Assessment

WRITING PROCESS STRATEGIES

Skills Trace

**Introduction to the Writing Process:
Editing/Proofreading and Publishing**

Introduced in Grade 1.
Scaffolded throughout Grades 2–5.
INTRODUCED: Unit 1, Lesson 6, p. 99F
PRACTICED: Unit 1, Lesson 6,
pp. 99F–99J
TESTED: Formal Assessment
Unit 1, Lesson 6, p. 99J
Unit 1 Assessment

Skills Trace

Writer's Craft: Transition Words

Introduced in Grade K.
Scaffolded throughout Grades 1–5.
INTRODUCED: Unit 1, Lesson 6, p. 99I
PRACTICED: Unit 1, Lesson 6, p. 99I
*Comprehension and Language
Arts Skills,* pp. 32–33
TESTED: Unit 1 Assessment

ENGLISH LANGUAGE CONVENTIONS

Skills Trace

**Grammar, Usage, and Mechanics:
Unit 1 Review**

Introduced in Grade 3.
Scaffolded throughout Grades 4–5.

Skills Trace

**Listening, Speaking, Viewing:
Presenting: Using Note Cards**

Introduced in Grade 2.
Scaffolded throughout Grades 3–5.
REINTRODUCED: Unit 1, Lesson 6, p. 99I
PRACTICED: Unit 1, Lesson 6, p. 99I
TESTED: Informal Assessment, p. 99I

Skills Trace

**Penmanship: Cursive Letters
q, g, and o**

Introduced in Grade 2 *(q, g)* and Grade 3 *(o).*
Scaffolded throughout Grades 3–5
and Grades 4–5.
REINTRODUCED: Unit 1, Lesson 6, p. 99J
PRACTICED: Unit 1, Lesson 6, p. 99J
TESTED: Informal Assessment, p. 99J

Professional Development: Inquiry

What Does the Inquiry/Investigation Procedure Look Like in the Classroom?

In the classroom the inquiry/investigation procedure takes students through a recursive cycle that involves many steps. Students may go through these steps several times before coming to the end of their research. In real research the cycle can go on for years, and in some cases for lifetimes.

The steps in the recursive cycle of research are:

1. Decide on a problem or question to research.
2. Formulate an idea or conjecture about the problem.
3. Identify needs and make plans.
4. Reevaluate the problem or question based on what has been learned.
5. Revise the idea or conjecture.
6. Make presentations.
7. Identify new needs and make new plans.

Real research is not motivated by a general interest or by curiosity about a topic. It is motivated by a problem or question. Being interested in a topic helps, because it leads to the identification of better problems and to more motivation to pursue them.

When the procedure is first introduced, students may require some help in formulating problems or questions, especially if they are accustomed to doing conventional, topic-centered research for the purpose of writing papers. For example, a student who has written only on topics such as "meteors" or "crocodiles," and who was rewarded for this work with praise and good grades, will be tempted to tackle similar broad topics. It is easy to find information about broad topics. It is also easy to divide this information into categories, then turn it into an encyclopedia-style paper. If these students are urged to formulate a question or problem, they might come up with something like: "What is a meteor?" This is merely a broad topic with a question mark.

In the inquiry/investigation procedure, students generate problems and questions after some discussion but *before* consulting reference materials. This approach tends to bring out ideas that students wonder about or wish to understand. In contrast, if students consult reference sources before discussion, they will likely come up with questions that the reference source has already answered or problems in which they have no real interest.

Having students generate problems or questions before consulting sources allows them to bring their own conjectures into play. Young students often ask questions that show a naive understanding of how things work. Questions such as "What is gravity made of?" and "What keeps the gravity inside Earth?" reveal the belief that gravity is a *substance*—something that can be seen and touched. Because these questions are based on false premises, they are unanswerable. However, encouraging students to investigate their questions can help them understand what gravity is— that it is *not* a substance; indeed, it is not an identifiable *thing* at all. They may be pleased to learn that this bothered Isaac Newton just as it bothers them.

Occasionally, students may select problems that are too hard for them. This is sure to happen if being "too hard" means that students cannot find definitive answers to their questions. Given this definition, most real research questions are too hard. When this occurs, teachers should remind students that the criterion of success is not finding answers but making progress. As noted previously, traditional schooling is based on question-answer dialogues. Students and teachers alike come to believe that success is measured only by correct answers. It takes patience and effort to shift the criterion of success from answers to progress, but it is an important move toward building a community of scholars.

* Additional information about inquiry and investigation as well as resource references can be found in the ***Professional Development Guide: Inquiry and Investigation.***

Review the Concepts

After all the groups have presented their findings, lead students in a large group discussion about the unit activities. Ask students which part of the investigation they enjoyed most. Which part was the most challenging? What part of their investigations can they use in their everyday lives?

Review with students the following key concepts.

- Cooperation between people allows them to do things that would not otherwise have been possible.
- A competitive spirit enables one to accomplish many things.
- Competition can be negative when a competitor uses unfair tactics to get what he or she wants.
- Many activities, such as playing team sports and running for an election, require a balance of cooperation and competition.

Tips for Reviewing Concepts

- As always, students' ideas should determine the discussion.
- Remind students that they can continue to investigate cooperation and competition even though they have completed the unit.

Have students refer to page 5 of their *Inquiry Journals* to remind themselves of what their ideas about cooperation and competition were when the unit began and also of what they expected to learn from the unit. Ask them to describe the new ideas they have acquired and the new information they have learned.

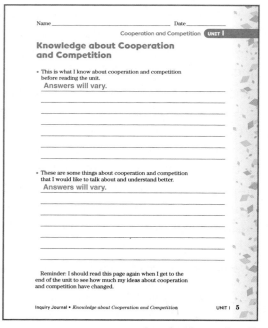

Inquiry Journal p. 5

Evaluating the Unit

- Have students conduct an evaluation of the unit selections, identifying those selections they found most interesting and those they found least interesting.
- Have students evaluate the different activities in which they participated throughout the unit. Which activities did they find the most enjoyable and informative?
- Ask students to evaluate the overall unit. Have them answer questions such as the following: How well did the unit cover the theme? Which selections added something new to your knowledge of cooperation and competition?
- Have students suggest ideas related to cooperation and competition to explore further, possibly beginning with any questions left on the Concept/Question Board.

Concept/Question Board

Cooperation and Competition

Concept   Question

Evaluating Participation

In their small groups, have students discuss the unit activity. Encourage them to talk about the importance of teamwork. Have the groups consider the following: What things did we do well as a team? What things could we do better next time? Why is teamwork important?

Throughout this unit investigation into cooperation and competition, you have been informally assessing student progress. Go over your notes to see who has been contributing to the group's investigation and how students have helped each other during this process. Talk with each group to get their feedback about how they felt working as a team. Use your observation notes, feedback from the group, and Research Rubrics to assess the groups as well as individual participation in groups. Record each student's score in the inside back cover of their *Inquiry Journals*.

Research Rubrics

Collaborative Group Work (this rubric is applied to groups, not individuals)

1 Group members work on separate tasks with little interaction.

2 Work-related decisions are made by the group, but there is little interaction related to ideas.

3 Information and ideas are shared, but there is little discussion concerned with advancing understanding.

4 The group clearly progresses in its thinking beyond where individual students could have gone.

Participation in Collaborative Inquiry (this rubric is applied to individual students)

1 Does not contribute ideas or information to team or class.

2 Makes contributions to Concept/Question Board or class discussions when specifically called upon to do so.

3 Occasionally contributes ideas or information to other students' inquiries.

4 Takes an active interest in the success of the whole class's knowledge-building efforts.

 Progress Assessment

Self-Evaluation

- Give students the opportunity to evaluate their personal learning experiences during this unit by completing *Inquiry Journal*, pages 32–33.

- The students could also complete the self-evaluation questions on the *Research Assistant CD-ROM*.

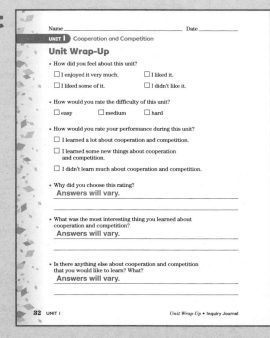

Inquiry Journal pp. 32–33

ASSESSMENT

Formal Assessment

Use these summative assessments along with your informal observations to assess student mastery.

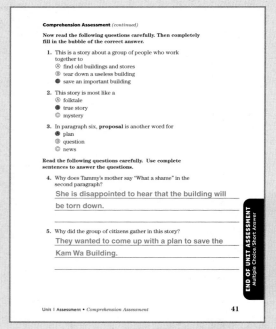

Unit 1 Assessment p. 38

Unit 1 Assessment p. 39

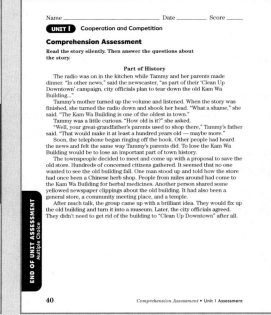

Unit 1 Assessment p. 40

Unit 1 Assessment p. 41

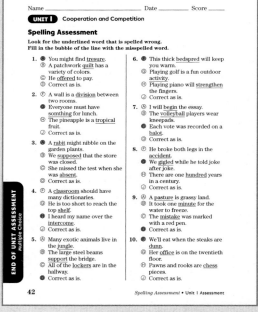

Unit 1 Assessment p. 42

Unit 1 Assessment p. 43

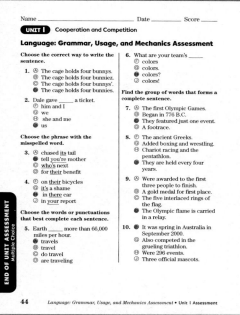

Name _____ Date _____ Score _____

UNIT 1 Cooperation and Competition

Language: Grammar, Usage, and Mechanics Assessment

Choose the correct way to write the sentence.

1. Ⓐ The cage holds four bunnys.
   Ⓑ The cage holds four bunniez.
   Ⓒ The cage holds four bunnys'.
   Ⓓ The cage holds four bunnies.

2. Dale gave _____ a ticket.
   Ⓕ him and I
   Ⓖ we
   Ⓗ she and me
   Ⓙ us

Choose the phrase with the misspelled word.

3. Ⓐ chased its tail
   Ⓑ tell you're mother
   Ⓒ who's next
   Ⓓ for their benefit

4. Ⓕ on their bicycles
   Ⓖ it's a shame
   Ⓗ in there car
   Ⓙ in your report

Choose the words or punctuations that best complete each sentence.

5. Earth _____ more than 66,000 miles per hour.
   Ⓐ travels
   Ⓑ travel
   Ⓒ do travel
   Ⓓ are traveling

6. What are your team's _____
   Ⓕ colors
   Ⓖ colors.
   Ⓗ colors?
   Ⓙ colors!

Find the group of words that forms a complete sentence.

7. Ⓐ The first Olympic Games.
   Ⓑ Began in 776 B.C.
   Ⓒ They featured just one event.
   Ⓓ A footrace.

8. Ⓕ The ancient Greeks.
   Ⓖ Added boxing and wrestling.
   Ⓗ Chariot racing and the pentathlon.
   Ⓙ They are held every four years.

9. Ⓐ Were awarded to the first three people to finish.
   Ⓑ A gold medal for first place.
   Ⓒ The five interlaced rings of the flag.
   Ⓓ The Olympic flame is carried in a relay.

10. Ⓕ It was spring in Australia in September 2000.
    Ⓖ Also competed in the grueling triathlon.
    Ⓗ Were 296 events.
    Ⓙ Three official mascots.

END OF UNIT ASSESSMENT — Multiple Choice

44   *Language: Grammar, Usage, and Mechanics Assessment • Unit 1 Assessment*

Unit 1 Assessment p. 44

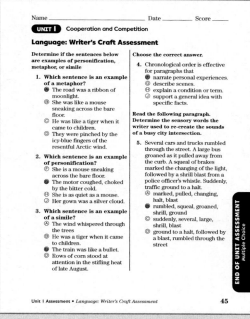

Name _____ Date _____ Score _____

UNIT 1 Cooperation and Competition

Language: Writer's Craft Assessment

Determine if the sentences below are examples of personification, metaphor, or simile.

1. **Which sentence is an example of a metaphor?**
   Ⓐ The road was a ribbon of moonlight.
   Ⓑ She was like a mouse sneaking across the bare floor.
   Ⓒ He was like a tiger when it came to children.
   Ⓓ They were pinched by the icy-blue fingers of the resentful Arctic wind.

2. **Which sentence is an example of personification?**
   Ⓕ She is a mouse sneaking across the bare floor.
   Ⓖ The motor coughed, choked by the bitter cold.
   Ⓗ She is as quiet as a mouse.
   Ⓙ Her gown was a silver cloud.

3. **Which sentence is an example of a simile?**
   Ⓐ The wind whispered through the trees
   Ⓑ He was a tiger when it came to children.
   Ⓒ The train was like a bullet.
   Ⓓ Rows of corn stood at attention in the stifling heat of late August.

Choose the correct answer.

4. Chronological order is effective for paragraphs that
   Ⓕ narrate personal experiences.
   Ⓖ describe scenes.
   Ⓗ explain a condition or term.
   Ⓙ support a general idea with specific facts.

Read the following paragraph. Determine the sensory words the writer used to re-create the sounds of a busy city intersection.

5. Several cars and trucks rumbled through the street. A large bus groaned as it pulled away from the curb. A squeal of brakes marked the changing of the light, followed by a shrill blast from a police officer's whistle. Suddenly, traffic ground to a halt.
   Ⓐ marked, pulled, changing, halt, blast
   Ⓑ rumbled, squeal, groaned, shrill, ground
   Ⓒ suddenly, several, large, shrill, blast
   Ⓓ ground to a halt, followed by a blast, rumbled through the street

END OF UNIT ASSESSMENT — Multiple Choice

Unit 1 Assessment • Language: Writer's Craft Assessment   45

Unit 1 Assessment p. 45

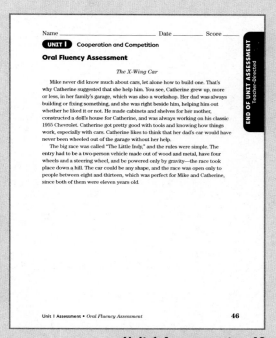

Name _____ Date _____ Score _____

UNIT 1 Cooperation and Competition

Oral Fluency Assessment

The X-Wing Car

Mike never did know much about cars, let alone how to build one. That's why Catherine suggested that she help him. You see, Catherine grew up, more or less, in her family's garage, which was also a workshop. Her dad was always building or fixing something, and she was right beside him, helping him out whether he liked it or not. He made cabinets and shelves for her mother, constructed a doll's house for Catherine, and was always working on his classic 1955 Chevrolet. Catherine got pretty good with tools and knowing how things work, especially with cars. Catherine likes to think that her dad's car would have never been wheeled out of the garage without her help.

The big race was called "The Little Indy," and the rules were simple. The entry had to be a two-person vehicle made out of wood and metal, have four wheels and a steering wheel, and be powered only by gravity—the race took place down a hill. The car could be any shape, and the race was open only to people between eight and thirteen, which was perfect for Mike and Catherine, since both of them were eleven years old.

END OF UNIT ASSESSMENT — Teacher-Directed

Unit 1 Assessment • Oral Fluency Assessment   46

Unit 1 Assessment p. 46

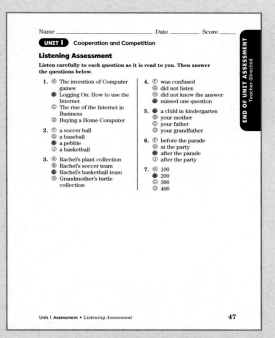

Name _____ Date _____ Score _____

UNIT 1 Cooperation and Competition

Listening Assessment

Listen carefully to each question as it is read to you. Then answer the questions below.

1. Ⓐ The invention of Computer games
   Ⓑ Logging On: How to use the Internet
   Ⓒ The rise of the Internet in Business
   Ⓓ Buying a Home Computer

2. Ⓕ a soccer ball
   Ⓖ a baseball
   Ⓗ a pebble
   Ⓙ a basketball

3. Ⓐ Rachel's plant collection
   Ⓑ Rachel's soccer team
   Ⓒ Rachel's basketball team
   Ⓓ Grandmother's turtle collection

4. Ⓕ was confused
   Ⓖ did not listen
   Ⓗ did not know the answer
   Ⓙ missed one question

5. Ⓐ a child in kindergarten
   Ⓑ your mother
   Ⓒ your father
   Ⓓ your grandfather

6. Ⓕ before the parade
   Ⓖ at the party
   Ⓗ after the parade
   Ⓙ after the party

7. Ⓐ 100
   Ⓑ 200
   Ⓒ 300
   Ⓓ 400

END OF UNIT ASSESSMENT — Teacher-Directed

Unit 1 Assessment • Listening Assessment   47

Unit 1 Assessment p. 47

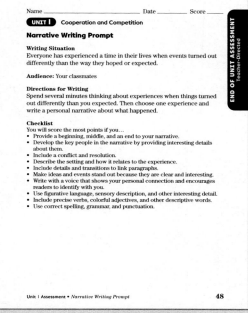

Name _____ Date _____ Score _____

UNIT 1 Cooperation and Competition

Narrative Writing Prompt

Writing Situation
Everyone has experienced a time in their lives when events turned out differently than the way they hoped or expected.

Audience: Your classmates

Directions for Writing
Spend several minutes thinking about experiences when things turned out differently than you expected. Then choose one experience and write a personal narrative about what happened.

Checklist
You will score the most points if you...
• Provide a beginning, middle, and an end to your narrative.
• Develop the key people in the narrative by providing interesting details about them.
• Include a conflict and resolution.
• Describe the setting and how it relates to the experience.
• Include details and transitions to link paragraphs.
• Make ideas and events stand out because they are clear and interesting.
• Write with a voice that shows your personal connection and encourages readers to identify with you.
• Use figurative language, sensory description, and other interesting detail.
• Include precise verbs, colorful adjectives, and other descriptive words.
• Use correct spelling, grammar, and punctuation.

END OF UNIT ASSESSMENT — Teacher-Directed

Unit 1 Assessment • Narrative Writing Prompt   48

Unit 1 Assessment p. 48

Also included:

- Writing Rubrics (Four Point and Six Point)
- Writing Portfolio Assessment and Rubrics
- Directions for Listening Assessment
- Teacher's Record of Oral Fluency
- Formal Assessment Record

Pronunciation Key

a as in **a**t	**ô** as in b**ou**ght and r**a**w	**ə** as in **a**bout, chick**e**n, penc**i**l, cann**o**n, circ**u**s
ā as in l**a**te		
â as in c**a**re	**oi** as in c**oi**n	
ä as in f**a**ther	**o͞o** as in b**oo**k	**ch** as in **ch**air
e as in s**e**t	**o͞o** as in t**oo**	**hw** as in **wh**ich
ē as in m**e**	**or** as in f**or**m	**ng** as in ri**ng**
i as in **i**t	**ou** as in **ou**t	**sh** as in **sh**op
ī as in k**i**te	**u** as in **u**p	**th** as in **th**in
o as in **o**x	**ū** as in **u**se	**t͟h** as in **th**ere
ō as in r**o**se	**ûr** as in t**ur**n, g**er**m, l**ear**n, f**ir**m, w**or**k	**zh** as in trea**s**ure

The mark (´) is placed after a syllable with a heavy accent, as in **chicken** (chik´ ən).

The mark (ˈ) after a syllable shows a lighter accent, as in **disappear** (dis´ ə pēr´).

628

Glossary

A

abacus (a´ bə kəs) *n.* A tool used to figure math problems by sliding counters.

abandon (ə ban´ dən) *v.* Leave something behind forever.

accomplish (ə kom´ plish) *v.* Do something successfully.

accuracy (a´ kyə rə sē) *n.* Freedom from errors or mistakes; correctness.

ace (ās) *v.* To easily get all or most answers correct.

acquit (ə kwit´) *v.* Conduct oneself well, even in a stressful situation.

adjacent (ə jā´ sənt) *adj.* Next to; touching.

adjourn (ə jûrn´) *v.* Bring to a temporary end; end for the present.

admission (ad mish´ ən) *n.* The price paid to attend an event.

adobe (ə dō´ bē) *n.* Sun-dried brick.

adventure (ad ven´ chər) *n.* A fun or exciting experience.

agate (a´ gət) *n.* A striped marble.

aimlessly (ām´ ləs lē) *adv.* Without purpose or direction.

alder (ôl´ dər) *n.* A tree in the birch family.

align (ə līn´) *v.* To place in a straight line.

alignment (ə līn´ mənt) *n.* The arrangement of things in a straight line.

altitude (al´ tə to͞od) *n.* How high something is above Earth.

amiss (ə mis´) *adv.* Wrong; not as expected.

ample (am´ pəl) *adj.* More than enough.

ancestor (an´ ses tər) *n.* A person from whom one is descended.

anticipation (an tis´ ə pā´ shən) *n.* A feeling of looking forward to something.

apparatus (a´ pə ra´ təs) *n.* A piece of equipment that has a particular use.

appetite (ap´ ə tīt) *n.* Desire for food.

apprehension (ap´ ri hen´ shən) *n.* Fear.

apprentice (ə pren´ tis) *v.* To bind oneself to a craft worker in order to learn a trade.—*n.* A person learning a trade or an art.

apt (apt´) *adj.* Inclined; likely.

arc (ärk) *v.* To move in a curved line. —*n.* A curve.

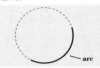
arc

Word Derivations

Below are some words related to *arc*.

arcade	arcading	arcing
arcaded	arced	arcs

archaeoastronomy (är´ kē ō ə stron´ ə mē) *n.* The study of ancient astronomical observatories.

629

---

archaeology   bice

> **Pronunciation Key:** at; lāte; câre; fäther; set; mē; it; kīte; ox; rōse; ô in bought; coin; bo͞ok; to͞o; form; out; up; ūse; tûrn; ə sound in about, chicken, pencil, cannon, circus; chair; **hw** in **wh**ich; ring; shop; thin; t͟here; **zh** in treasure.

archaeology or **archeology** (är´ kē ol´ ə jē) *n.* The scientific study of people of the past by digging up things they left behind.

Word History

Archaeology, or **archeology,** came into English in the year 1837. It is from the Latin word *archaeologia,* meaning "knowledge gained through the study of ancient objects." This Latin word's origins are with the Greek words *archē,* meaning "beginning," and *logos,* meaning "word."

arm (ärm) *v.* Prepare for war; make weapons ready for use.

aroma (ə rō´ mə) *n.* A smell or odor, usually pleasant.

artifice (är´ tə fis) *n.* A clever trick in the way a story's plot is constructed.

artisan (är´ tə zən) *n.* A person who works at a craft that requires artistic skill or working with the hands.

ascend (ə send´) *v.* To climb up; to rise.

ashamed (ə shāmd´) *adj.* Embarrassed; not proud.

astronomical (as´ trə nom´ i kəl) *adj.* Having to do with the study of the stars and planets.

astronomy (ə stron´ ə mē) *n.* The scientific study of stars and planets.

athletic (ath le´ tik) *adj.* Having skill and strength in sports and other physical activities.

atmosphere (at´ mə sfir´) *n.* The gases that surround a planet or moon.

attendant (ə ten´ dənt) *n.* A person who waits on someone.

attitude (a´ tə to͞od´) *n.* A way of thinking, acting, or behaving.

avert (ə vûrt´) *v.* To avoid.

B

bamboo (bam´ bo͞o´) *n.* A tropical, grass plant with long, stiff, hollow stems.

bandana (ban dan´ ə) *n.* A large, colorful handkerchief.

barrack (bar´ ək) *n.* A building where soldiers live.

bastion (bas´ chən) *n.* A part of a fortified structure that juts out so that defenders can fire at attackers from several angles.

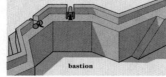
bastion

beanie (bē´ nē) *n.* A small bill-less cap worn on the crown of the head.

bedclothes (bed´ klōz) *n.* Items used to cover a bed, such as sheets, blankets, and quilts.

bedrock (bed´ rok) *n.* Solid rock.

benevolent (bə nev´ ə lənt) *adj.* Kind; generous.

berate (bi rāt´) *v.* To scold harshly.

bice (bīs) *adj.* Blue or blue-green.

630

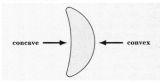

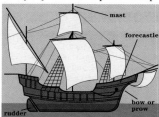

biologist (bī o′ lə jəst) *n.* A person who studies plant and animal life specific to certain environments.

blemish (blem′ ish) *n.* A stain; a defect.

blintze (blints) *n.* Cheese or fruit wrapped in a thin pancake.

bloody (blu′ dē) *adj.* A word used to indicate an extremely negative feeling.

body (bo′ dē) *n.* An object such as a star or asteroid.

bombard (bom′ bärd) *n.* A leather jug or bottle.

booklet (boŏk′ lət) *n.* A small book, usually with a paper cover.

bore (bor) *v.* To drill into; to pierce.

bow (bou) *n.* The front part of a ship.

mast

forecastle

bow or prow

rudder

Word History

Bow came into English about 500 years ago. It probably came from the Dutch word *boech*, meaning "bow" or "shoulder." It is also related to *bōg*, a word meaning "bough" (a large tree branch) that dates back more than 800 years.

boycott (boi′ kot′) *v.* Join with others in refusing to buy from or deal with a person, nation, or business.

brazen (brā′ zən) *adj.* Bold; cocky.

breach (brēch) *n.* A violation of a law or agreement.

break (brāk) *v.* To tame a horse.

breakwater (brāk′ wô′ tər) *n.* Any structure that protects a harbor or beach from damage by waves.

brocade (brō kād′) *n.* Woven cloth that has a raised pattern.

bronc (bronk) *n.* A wild or poorly broken horse.

brushpopper (brush′ po pər) *n.* A person who works in an area covered with low-growing bushes and weeds.

bulldog (boŏl′ dôg′) *v.* To wrestle a steer, usually by grabbing its horns and twisting its neck.

buttress (bu′ tris) *n.* A structure built outside a wall to give the wall support.

c

cairn (kârn) *n.* A pile of stones left as a landmark or a monument.

cairn

calculation (kal′ kyə lā′ shən) *n.*
1. Counting, computing, or figuring.
2. The result of counting, computing, or figuring.

campaign (kam pān′) *n.* A series of actions planned and carried out to bring about a particular result; an organized effort to accomplish a purpose.

Pronunciation Key: at; l**āte**; c**âre**; f**ä**ther; s**et**; m**ē**; **it**; k**ī**te; **ox**; r**ō**se; **ô** in b**ou**ght; c**oi**n; b**oŏk**; t**oō**; f**or**m; **out**; **up**; **ūse**; t**ûr**n; **ə** sound in **a**bout, chick**e**n, penc**i**l, cann**o**n, circ**u**s; **chair**; **hw** in **wh**ich; ri**ng**; **sh**op; **th**in; **th**ere; **zh** in trea**s**ure.

candidate (kan′ də dāt′) *n.* A person who is seeking an office, job, or position.

canyon (kan′ yən) *n.* A deep, narrow valley with high, steep sides.

capable (kā′ pə bəl) *adj.* Skilled or able to do something well.

capsule (kap′ səl) *n.* The top part of a rocket that is self-contained and holds astronauts and equipment.

capsize (kap′ sīz) *v.* To turn upside down.

captivity (kap ti′ və tē) *n.* Being held as prisoner.

carbon dating (kär′ bən dā′ ting) *v.* Using carbon 14 to find out the age of old material.

carcass (kär′ kəs) *n.* The body of a dead animal.

caribou (kar′ ə boō′) *n.* A reindeer.

cease (sēs) *v.* Bring an activity or action to an end.

celandine (sel′ ən dīn′) *n.* A plant in the buttercup family with single yellow flowers.

celestial (sə les′ chəl) *adj.* Relating to the sky.

ceremonial (ser′ ə mō′ nē əl) *adj.* Having to do with a formal celebration.

chance (chans) *v.* To take a risk and try something difficult.

challenge (chal′ ənj) *n.* Something that may be difficult to do.

chaparral (shap′ ə ral′) *n.* An area thick with shrubs and small trees.

cheder (kā′ dər) *n.* Religious school for teaching Judaism.

chives (chīvz) *n.* A food seasoning made from the leaves of a plant related to the onion.

cinder (sin′ dər) *n.* Ash or a piece of partially burnt coal or wood.

circumference (sər kum′ fər əns) *n.* The line that defines a circle.

claim (klām) *n.* A section of land declared as belonging to one person or group of people.

clamber (klam′ bər) *v.* To climb with difficulty.

clarify (klâr′ ə fī′) *v.* To make something clear; to explain.

cloister (kloi′ stər) *n.* A place where religious people live away from the world; a convent or a monastery.

cobbler (kob′ lər) *n.* A person who repairs shoes and boots.

collards (käl′ ərds) *n.* A green, leafy vegetable.

collide (kə līd′) *v.* Crash.

colonel (kûr′ nəl) *n.* A military officer; ranking between lieutenant and general.

commence (kə mens′) *v.* To begin.

Word History

Commence came into English about 600 years ago. It came from the French word *comencer*, and its assumed origin is the Latin word *cominitiare*. This Latin word is a derivative of *initiare*, meaning "to initiate." (Also note that the word *commence* contains the *-ence* suffix, which in this word means "the action of" or "the process of.")

commission (kə mi′ shən) *n.* An important task or assignment.

commotion (kə mō′ shən) *n.* Noise; excitement; disturbance.

communal (kə mū′ nəl) *adj.* Public; shared by all.

compassion (kəm pash′ ən) *n.* Sympathy; pity.

composition (kom′ pə zish′ ən) *n.* What something is made of.

comrade (kom′ rad′) *n.* Friend; companion.

concave (kon kāv′) *adj.* Curved inward; hollow; like the inner curve of a contact lens.

conceive (kən sēv′) *v.* 1. To start something with a certain point of view. 2. To understand.

conciliatory (kən sil′ ē ə tor′ ē) *adj.* Causing peace to be made.

condense (kən dens′) *v.* Change the physical state of something from a gas to a liquid or solid.

confederation (kən fe′ də rā′ shən) *n.* The act of joining states together for a common purpose.

confetti (kən fet′ ē) *n.* Tiny pieces of colored paper that are thrown during celebrations.

confidence (kon′ fə dəns) *n.* A belief in one's ability to do something.

confine (kən fīn′) *v.* 1. To limit. 2. To keep in a place.

confounded (kon foun′ did) *adj.* Darned.

confront (kən frunt′) *v.* To face.

congress (kong′ gris) *n.* An assembly of people who make laws.

constellation (kon′ stə lā′ shən) *n.* A group of stars that form shapes in the sky.

constituent (kən stich′ wənt) *n.* A voter in a particular area.

constitution (kon′ sti toō′ shən) *n.* The basic principles used to govern a state, country, or organization.

content (kən tent′) *adj.* Happy or satisfied.

contest (kon′ test) *n.* A competition.

convention (kən ven′ shən) *n.* A formal meeting for some special purpose.

convex (kon veks′) *adj.* Curved outward; like the outer curve of a contact lens.

concave ⟶ ⟵ convex

conveyor belt (kən vā′ ər belt′) *n.* A device with a large looping belt used to move objects.

cordially (kor′ jə lē) *adv.* Sincerely; pleasantly.

corn pone (korn′ pōn′) *n.* Baked or fried corn bread.

cotangent (kō tan′ jənt) *n.* A term used in trigonometry.

course (kors) *v.* To flow.

cradleboard (krād′ l bord′) *n.* A wooden frame that Native American women wore on their backs to carry their babies.

ANTHOLOGY GLOSSARY

Pronunciation Key: **at**; **lāte**; **câre**; **fäther**; **set**; **mē**; **it**; **kīte**; **ox**; **rōse**; **ô** in b**ou**ght; **coin**; b**ŏŏk**; t**ōō**; f**or**m; **out**; **up**; **ūse**; **tûrn**; ə sound in **a**bout, chick**e**n, penc**i**l, cann**o**n, circ**u**s; **chair**; **hw** in **wh**ich; ri**ng**; **sh**op; **thin**; **th**ere; **zh** in trea**s**ure.

cringe (krinj) *v.* To back away from something unpleasant; to physically shrink because of fear or excessive humility.

croaker-sack (krō´ kər sak) *n.* A sack usually made of burlap.

cultivate (kul´ tə vāt´) *v.* To till the ground; to grow crops.

curvilinear (kur´ və li´ nē ər) *adj.* Having rounded or curving lines.

D

decipher (dē sī´ fər) *v.* To read or translate something written in code; decode.

deduction (di duk´ shən) *n.* A fact or conclusion figured out by reasoning.

defeatist (di fē´ təst) *adj.* Expecting and accepting that one will lose or be defeated.

defect (di fekt´) *v.* To leave one's home country for another.

defiance (di fī´ əns) *n.* Bold refusal to obey or respect authority.

dehydration (dē´ hī drā´ shən) *n.* Loss of water in the body.

delegation (del´ i gā´ shən) *n.* A group of people chosen to act for others; representatives.

deliberately (di li´ bə rət lē) *adv.* On purpose; meaning to.

Word History

Deliberately came into English about 500 years ago. It is the adverb form of the word *deliberate*, which came from the Latin word *deliberare*, meaning "to consider carefully." It is assumed that the Latin word *libra*, meaning "pound" or "scale," is also in its word history. This brings to mind the modern figure of speech "to weigh one's options." (Also note that *deliberately* contains the *-ly* suffix, which in this word means "in the manner of being.")

delta (del´ tə) *n.* Land formed at the mouth of a river by sediment carried in the water.

demolish (di mol´ ish) *v.* To do away with.

denounce (di nouns´) *v.* Openly condemn; declare disapproval.

deposits (di poz´ its) *n.* Valuables put away for safekeeping, as in a bank.

depredation (dep´ ri dā´ shən) *n.* The act of attacking and robbing.

descent (di sent´) *n.* A coming from a higher place to a lower one.

desert (dez´ ərt) *n.* A place where little or no rain falls.

deserted (də zər´ təd) *adj.* Not lived in; abandoned.

desist (di sist´) *v.* To stop.

desolation (des´ ə lā´ shən) *n.* Deserted condition.

desperation (des´ pə rā´ shən) *n.* A hopeless feeling, when you are ready to try anything to help the situation.

despotism (des´ pə ti´ zəm) *n.* A government run by a tyrannical ruler.

dialect (dī´ ə lekt´) *n.* A form of language that is spoken in a particular area or by a particular group of people.

---

diligence (dil´ i jens) *n.* Steady effort put forth to accomplish a task.

Word History

Diligence came into English about 600 years ago. It is a derivative of the word *diligent*, which has origins in the French word *diligere*, meaning "to love" or "to esteem." *Diligere* can also be divided into the word parts *di-*, meaning "apart," and *legere*, meaning "to select." (Also note that *diligence* contains the *-ence* suffix, which in this word means "the quality of" or "the state of.")

diminish (di min´ ish) *v.* To decrease; to lessen; to get smaller.

din (din) *n.* Clamor; uproar; racket.

diplomacy (di plō´ mə sē) *n.* The handling of relations between nations.

discernible (di sûrn´ ə bəl) *adj.* Easy to recognize as different.

disconsolately (dis kon´ sə lit lē) *adv.* In a very unhappy way; hopelessly.

disembodied (dis´ em bod´ ēd) *adj.* Without a body.

dismay (dis mā´) *n.* A sudden feeling of disappointment.

disown (di sōn´) *v.* To deny a connection to; to refuse to admit a relationship to.

distinct (di stingkt´) *adj.* 1. Clear; plain. 2. Separate.

district (dis´ trikt) *n.* A region that is part of some larger entity such as a city or county.

document (dok´ yə mənt) *n.* A written or printed statement that gives official proof and information about something.

dogie (dō´ gē) *n.* A calf with no mother.

domesticated (də mes´ ti kāt´ əd) *adj.* Able to exist closely with humans.

downpour (doun´ por´) *n.* A heavy rain.

dramatization (dram´ ə tə zā´ shən) *n.* An acting out of a story.

draught (draft) *n. chiefly British.* A liquid that is drunk; a dose.

dribble (dri´ bəl) *v.* In soccer, to move a ball down the field with a series of short, controlled kicks.

drill (dril) *n.* An exercise to increase mental or physical skills.

drought (drout) *n.* Dry weather that lasts a very long time.

dubiously (doo´ bē əs lē) *adv.* In a doubtful way.

dumpling (dum´ pling) *n.* A small pocket of dough filled with a meat or vegetable mixture and cooked by steaming or boiling it.

dwindle (dwin´ dl) *v.* To get smaller gradually.

E

eclipse (i klips´) *v.* To become more important than; to cover over.

ecstatically (ek stat´ ik lē) *adv.* With great joy.

eddy (ed´ ē) *n.* A small, circling current of water.

edible (ed´ ə bəl) *adj.* Eatable.

election (i lek´ shən) *n.* The act of choosing, by voting, someone to serve in an office, or whether to accept an idea.

elector (i lek´ tər) *n.* A qualified voter.

embarrassed (im bar´ əsd) *adj.* Feeling bad or silly about something one has done.

Pronunciation Key: **at**; **lāte**; **câre**; **fäther**; **set**; **mē**; **it**; **kīte**; **ox**; **rōse**; **ô** in b**ou**ght; **coin**; b**ŏŏk**; t**ōō**; f**or**m; **out**; **up**; **ūse**; **tûrn**; ə sound in **a**bout, chick**e**n, penc**i**l, cann**o**n, circ**u**s; **chair**; **hw** in **wh**ich; ri**ng**; **sh**op; **thin**; **th**ere; **zh** in trea**s**ure.

embellish (em bel´ ish) *v.* To make something better or more beautiful by adding to it.

emphatically (em fat´ ik lē) *adv.* With spoken firmness or force.

employee (em ploi ē´) *n.* One who works for pay.

encampment (en kamp´ mənt) *n.* A camp; a temporary stopping place.

encompass (en kum´ pəs) *v.* To include.

encounter (en koun´ tər) *v.* To meet by chance.

endurance (en dûr´ əns) *n.* The power to put up with hardships or difficulties.

energy (e´ nər jē) *n.* The strength or eagerness to work or do things.

enthusiastic (in thōō´ zē as´ tik) *adj.* Filled with excitement.

Equator (i kwā´ tər) *n.* The imaginary line that circles Earth's center; it is perpendicular to Earth's axis and equally distant from Earth's North and South Poles.

equinox (ē´ kwə noks´) *n.* The two times of the year when day and night are equal in length.

era (er´ ə) *n.* A period of time or of history, often beginning or ending with an historical event.

ermine (ûr´ min) *n.* A valuable white fur; the winter white fur coat of some weasels.

escort (e skort´) *v.* To go with and help or protect.

establish (i stab´ lish) *v.* To settle in a place.

Word Derivations

Below are some words related to *establish*.
establishable   establisher   establishment
established   establishes

estate (i stāt´) *n.* A large piece of land owned by one individual or family.

eternal (i tûr´ nl) *adj.* Everlasting; always; endless.

ewe (ū) *n.* A female sheep.

excursion (ik skûr´ zhən) *n.* A pleasure trip; an outing.

exhausted (ig zô´ stəd) *adj.* Very tired.

explorer (ik splor´ ər) *n.* A person who goes to a place one knows nothing about.

extraordinary (ik stror´ dən âr´ ē) *adj.* Unusual or amazing.

F

facility (fə sil´ ə tē) *n.* A place, such as a building, that serves a certain purpose.

Fahrenheit (fâr´ ən hīt) *adj.* Relating to a system for measuring temperature where water freezes at 32 degrees and water boils at 212 degrees.

fare (fâr) *n.* The cost to ride a bus, taxi, or other means of transportation.

feat (fēt) *n.* An act or deed that shows great courage, strength, or skill.

federal (fed´ ər əl) *adj.* Formed by an agreement of states or provinces to join together as one nation.

feisty (fī´ stē) *adj.* Having a lively and aggressive personality.

Page 637

fervently (fûr´ vənt lē) *adv.* With great feeling; with emotion.

fidelity (fi del´ i tē) *n.* Faithfulness to duties or promises.

fife (fīf) *n.* A musical instrument like a flute that makes a high, clear sound and is often used with drums in a marching band.

floe (flō) *n.* A large sheet of floating ice.

flounder (floun´ dər) *v.* To struggle. —*n.* A type of flatfish that is good to eat.

forlornly (for lorn´ lē) *adv.* Sadly; hopelessly.

Word History

Forlornly is the adverb form of the word *forlorn*, which came into English more than 800 years ago. It is a derivative of the word *forlēosan*, which means "to lose." (Also note that *forlornly* contains the *-ly* suffix, which in this word means "in the manner of being.")

formation (for mā´ shən) *n.* A particular arrangement.

foundry (foun´ drē) *n.* A place where metal is melted and formed.

frantic (fran´ tik) *adj.* Very worried and afraid.

frantically (fran´ ti klē) *adv.* Quickly in a worried way.

frequency (frē´ kwən sē) *n.* The number of times something happens within a set period of time.

frigate (frig´ it) *n.* A type of tropical seabird with a hooked beak, webbed feet, and long wings and tail feathers.

fume (fūm) *v.* To mumble something in an angry or irritated way.

furrow (fûr´ ō) *n.* A trench cut by a plow.

fuse (fūz) *v.* To join together by melting.

G

gable (gā´ bəl) *n.* A part of a wall that is enclosed by sloping sides of a roof, making a triangle-shaped section on a building.

galaxy (gal´ ək sē) *n.* A large group of stars, dust, and gas.

gallinipper (gal´ ə nip´ ər) *n. informal.* Any of several insects that sting or bite.

garrison (gâr´ i sən) *n.* A military post or station.

genuine (jen´ yə wən) *adj.* Real.

geologist (jē o´ lə jist) *n.* A person who studies the solid matter on a moon or planet.

ginger (jin´ jər) *n.* A strong tasting spice made from ground ginger root.

gizzard (gi´ zərd) *n.* Intestine.

globular (glob´ yə lər) *adj.* Having the shape of a globe.

gore (gor) *v.* To pierce with an animal's horn or tusk.

gourd (gord) *n.* A melon-shaped fruit that can be dried and used as a bowl.

grenadier (gren´ ə dēr´) *n.* A soldier on foot; an infantry soldier.

groschen (grō´ shən) *n.* A form of money worth $1/100$ of a schilling. (A schilling is worth about $7 1/2$ cents.)

grozing iron (grō´ zing ī´ ərn) *n.* A steel tool for cutting glass.

grueling (grōō´ ə ling) *adj.* Very difficult or exhausting.

guide (gīd) *v.* Lead someone along a path or to show the way.

Page 638

Pronunciation Key: at; lāte; câre; fäther; set; mē; it; kīte; ox; rōse; ô in bought; coin; bŏŏk; tōō; form; out; up; ūse; tûrn; ə sound in about, chicken, pencil, cannon, circus; chair; hw in which; ring; shop; thin; there; zh in treasure.

H

haberdasher (ha´ bər da´ shər) *n. chiefly British.* One who sells men's clothing.

haint (hānt) *n.* A ghost.

hamlet (ham´ lit) *n.* A small village.

haughtily (hô´ təl ē) *adv.* In an overly proud way.

headquarters (hed´ kwor´ tərz) *n.* A center of operations where leaders work and give orders; a main office.

healer (hē´ lər) *n.* A doctor.

heavens (he´ vəns) *n.* The sky as viewed from earth.

hemisphere (hem´ ə sfir) *n.* Half of a sphere that results from cutting it through the center with a horizontal plane.

hesitate (hez´ ə tāt) *v.* Pause.

high-falutin' (hī´ fə lōō´ tn) *adj.* Appealing to a higher class of people; fancy; showy.

hogan (hō´ gôn) *n.* A Navaho dwelling.

homespun (hōm´ spən) *adj.* Made at home.

hone (hōn) *v.* To sharpen.

honor (ä´ nər) *v.* Show respect.

horizon (hə rī´ zən) *n.* A line formed in the distance by an apparent meeting of Earth and sky.

horizontal (hor´ ə zon´ tl) *adj.* Along a line parallel to the horizon.

hospitable (hos pi´ tə bəl) *adj.* Kind and generous to guests.

hover (huv´ ər) *v.* To hang in the air.

Word History

Hover came from an older English word, *hoven*, which may have come into use as many as 800 years ago. Since the earliest records of this word, it has always had the same meaning.

humanity (hū man´ ə tē) *n.* People; all human beings.

hypotenuse (hī po´ tə nōōs´) *n.* In a right triangle, the side opposite the right angle.

I

ice floes (īs´ flōz´) *n.* Large sheets of floating ice.

immigrant (i´ mi grənt) *n.* A person who comes to live in a country in which he or she was not born.

impeach (im pēch´) *v.* Accuse of misconduct.

imperial (im pir´ ē əl) *adj.* Part of, or belonging to, a king's empire.

impetuous (im pech´ wəs) *adj.* Acting or done too quickly, without planning or thought.

impoverished (im pov´ risht) *adj.* Living in poverty.

impressed (im prest´) *adj.* Made to form a high opinion of someone or something.

inexorable (in ek´ sər ə bəl) *adj.* Absolute; unyielding.

infallibility (in fal´ ə bil´ ə tē) *n.* Assuredness or certainty of success.

Page 639

inferno (in fûr´ nō) *n.* A place of extreme, almost unbearable, heat.

infirm (in fûrm´) *adj.* Weak; feeble; insecure.

ingenious (in jēn´ yəs) *adj.* Clever; skillful.

Word History

Ingenious came into English about 500 years ago. It comes from the Latin word *ingenium*, which means "natural capacity." Some meanings of the word *capacity* are "the amount that can be held in a space" and "ability or power." (Also note that *ingenious* contains the *in-* prefix, which in this word means "within," and the *-ous* suffix, which in this word means "having" or "possessing.")

ingot (ing´ gət) *n.* A piece of metal in the shape of a bar or a block.

ingratiate (in grā´ shē āt´) *v.* To put oneself in the good graces of others.

innovation (in´ ə vā´ shən) *n.* The act of creating something new or original.

insignificant (in´ sig ni´ fə kənt) *adj.* Not important.

intelligence (in tel´ ə jəns) *n.* 1. A network of people and resources working to gather secret information about an enemy. 2. The secret information about an enemy gathered by a spy.

intensity (in ten´ si tē) *n.* Great strength.

internal (in tûr´ nəl) *adj.* On the inside.

interplanetary (in´ tər pla´ nə târ´ ē) *adj.* Shared between the planets.

interrogation (in ter´ ə gā´ shən) *n.* Questioning.

interview (in´ tər vū´) *v.* Ask questions to find out about a person or what a person thinks.

intimacy (in´ tə mə sē) *n.* A closeness.

intricate (in´ tri kit) *adj.* Tangled; complicated.

investment (in vest´ mənt) *adj.* Using money to make a profit.

irrepressible (ir´ i pres´ ə bəl) *adj.* Unwilling to be controlled.

J

jabber (ja´ bər) *v.* Talk a lot and very fast.

journeyman (jûr´ nē mən) *n.* A person who has completed an apprenticeship and can now work in a trade under another person.

juggle (ju´ gəl) *v.* Handle more than one object or activity at one time; perform a clever trick.

juniper (jōō´ nə pər) *n.* An evergreen shrub with purple berries.

K

karate (kə rä´ tē) *n.* An Asian art of self-defense.

kasha (kä´ shə) *n.* A soft food made from a grain, usually buckwheat.

kayak (kī´ ak) *n.* A light Eskimo canoe having a wooden or bone framework and covered with skins.

kayak

Pronunciation Key: **at**; **lāte**; **câre**; **fäther**; **set**; **mē**; **it**; **kīte**; **ox**; **rōse**; **ô** in b**ou**ght; **coin**; b**ōō**k; t**ōō**; f**or**m; **out**; **up**; **ūse**; t**ûrn**; **ə** sound in **a**bout, chick**e**n, penc**i**l, cann**o**n, circ**u**s; **chair**; **hw** in **wh**ich; ri**ng**; **sh**op; **th**in; **th**ere; **zh** in trea**s**ure.

keelboat (kēl´ bōt) *n.* A shallow boat built with a keel, or long beam, on the bottom.

kiln (kiln) *n.* An oven for firing glass, or heating it at very high temperatures, in order to make the color permanent.

kosher (kō´ shər) *adj.* Proper or acceptable according to Jewish law.

L

lambent (lam´ bənt) *adj.* Glowing softly.

lance (lans) *n.* A long-shafted spear.

lariat (lâr´ ē ət) *n.* A rope tied with a movable loop at one end, used to catch cows and horses; a lasso.

learned (lûrnd) *v.* Past tense of **learn:** To gain new knowledge or skill. —*adj.* (lûr´ nid) Educated.

legendary (lej´ ən der´ ē) *adj.* From a story that has been passed down from a people's earlier times.

legislature (lej´ i slā´ chər) *n.* A group of people who make or pass laws.

levee (le´ vē) *n.* An embankment built along a river to keep the river from overflowing.

levity (le´ və tē) *n.* A lighthearted attitude.

lieutenant (lōō ten´ ənt) *n.* An officer in the armed forces.

lull (lul) *n.* A period of reduced noise or violence.

lumber (lum´ bər) *n.* Wood that has been cut into boards of various sizes for building.

lunar (lōō´ nər) *adj.* Relating to the moon.

luxurious (lug zhŏŏr´ ē əs) *adj.* Grand; rich; elegant.

lynx (lingks) *n.* A wildcat; a bobcat.

M

macaw (mə kô´) *n.* A large parrot that has bright colors and a long tail.

magnification (mag´ nə fi kā´ shən) *n.* The amount of enlargement possible; the amount something is enlarged.

magnificent (mag ni´ fə sənt) *adj.* Outstanding or inspiring.

mallet (ma´ lət) *n.* A type of hammer with a head made of wood or other soft material.

manager (ma´ ni gər) *n.* A person who takes care of or organizes something, like an office or a sports team.

maneuvering (mə nōō´ vər ing) *n.* Planning and then acting according to plans.

manic (man´ ik) *adj.* Overly excited.

mantel (man´ təl) *n.* A shelf over a fireplace.

marrow (mar´ ō) *n.* 1. The soft substance in the hollow parts of bones. 2. The center; the core.

mast (mast) *n.* A pole that supports the sails of a ship or boat. See illustration of **bow.**

640

---

match (mach´) *n.* A contest, competition, or race.

Maya or **Mayan** (mä´ yə) or (mä´ yən) *n.* A member of a people who built an ancient civilization in Mexico and Central America. **Mayan** *adj.* Having to do with the civilization of the Mayas.

medley (med´ lē) *n.* A mixture; a jumble.

melodrama (mel´ ə drä´ mə) *n.* A play that exaggerates emotions and encourages the audience to be sympathetic.

menial (mē´ nē əl) *adj.* Humble; lowly; boring; tedious.

merciful (mûr´ si fəl) *adj.* Forgiving.

mesa (mā´ sə) *n.* A small, high plateau that stands alone, like a mountain with a flat top.

mesa

mesquite (me skēt´) *n.* A spiny shrub or tree in the legume, or pea and bean, family.

meteorite (mē´ tē ə rīt´) *n.* A piece of matter from the solar system that hits a planet or moon's surface.

microbes (mī´ krōbz) *n.* Living things that can only be seen with a microscope.

militia (mə lish´ ə) *n.* A group of citizens trained to fight and help in emergencies.

mill (mil) *n.* A factory.

mischievous (mis´ chə vəs) *adj.* Causing trouble in a playful way.

mission (mish´ ən) *n.* A special job or task.

module (mä´ jəl) *n.* A separate part of a rocket that is self-contained and serves a specific purpose.

monarch (mon´ ərk) *n.* A ruler; a king or a queen.

morale (mə ral´) *n.* The level of one's confidence.

morose (mə rōs´) *adj.* Sullen; gloomy.

mossback (môs´ bak) *n.* A wild bull or cow.

move (mōōv) *v.* To make a motion or a suggestion to act on something in a meeting.

muck (muk) *v.* To clean out.

muff (muf) *v.* To do an action poorly; to miss; to mess up.

musket (mus´ kət) *n.* A weapon, used in early American battles, which was aimed and fired from the shoulder. It fired a small, lead ball.

muster (mus´ tər) *v.* To work up; to gather a group in preparation for battle.

myriad (mir´ ē əd) *n.* An immense number; many.

mystified (mis´ tə fīd´) *adj.* Bewildered; baffled; puzzled.

mythology (mi thol´ ə jē) *n.* A collection of legends or fables.

N

nation (nā´ shən) *n.* A group of people living in a particular area under one government.

nebula (ne´ byə lə) *n.* Glowing clouds of gas and dust amidst the stars.

641

Pronunciation Key: **at**; **lāte**; **câre**; **fäther**; **set**; **mē**; **it**; **kīte**; **ox**; **rōse**; **ô** in b**ou**ght; **coin**; b**ōō**k; t**ōō**; f**or**m; **out**; **up**; **ūse**; t**ûrn**; **ə** sound in **a**bout, chick**e**n, penc**i**l, cann**o**n, circ**u**s; **chair**; **hw** in **wh**ich; ri**ng**; **sh**op; **th**in; **th**ere; **zh** in trea**s**ure.

netherworld (neth´ ər wûrld´) *n.* The region below the ground; hell.

nomination (no´ mə nā´ shən) *n.* A proposal that someone could hold a government position or office.

Word History

Nomination is a derivative of the word *nominate*, which came into English about 500 years ago. It came from a derivation of the Latin word *nomen*, which means "name." (Also note that the word *nomination* contains the *-ation* suffix, which means "connected to the process of.")

novelty (no´ vəl tē) *n.* Something new or different.

nuclear reaction (nōō´ klē ər rē ak´ shən) *n.* A process in which the centers or cores of atoms are changed.

nugget (nug´ ət) *n.* A solid lump of gold.

nylon (nī´ lon´) *adj.* A synthetic fiber that is strong and durable.

O

obliterate (ə blit´ ə rāt´) *v.* To destroy completely; to rub out; to erase.

Word Derivations

Below are some words related to *obliterate.*

obliterated	obliterating	obliterative
obliterates	obliteration	obliterator

oblong (ob´ lông) *adj.* Being longer than it is wide.

obscure (əb skyŏŏr´) *adj.* Not well known. —*v.* To hide; to cover up.

observatory (əb zûr´ və tor´ē) *n.* A place that is designed for astronomers to study the stars.

observatory

ocelot (o´ sə lot´) *n.* A small wildcat with black spots and a yellow coat.

optical (op´ ti kəl) *adj.* Having to do with sight.

optimism (op´ tə miz´ əm) *n.* The belief that everything will happen for the best.

optimistic (op´ tə mis´ tik) *adj.* Having a positive outlook.

organic (or gan´ ik) *adj.* Produced by living things; was once alive.

organism (or´ gə niz´ əm) *n.* Any living thing.

ornery (or´ nə rē) *adj.* Mean; grouchy; irritable.

oxlip (oks´ lip) *n.* A flowering herb with pale-colored flowers.

P

pantomime (pan´ tə mīm´) *v.* Use bodily movements or facial expressions, instead of speech, to tell a story.

parched (pärcht) *adj.* Very hot and dry.

642

Page 643

parliamentary procedure (pär′ lə men′ trē prə sē′ jər) *n.* A formal way to hold or conduct a meeting, following certain rules.

particle (pär′ ti kəl) *n.* A very small piece or portion of something.

partisan (pär′ tə zən) *n.* A committed supporter of a party, cause, person, or idea.

passion (pash′ ən) *n.* A strong liking or enthusiasm for something.

patchwork quilt (pach′ wûrk′ kwilt′) *n.* A blanket made from scraps of material sewn together.

peevishly (pē′ vish lē) *adv.* With irritation or lack of patience.

perimeter (pə rim′ i tər) *n.* The distance around the boundary of something.

persecute (pûr′ si kūt′) *v.* To torment; to oppress; to treat badly.

perspective (pər spek′ tiv) *n.* A way of looking at things in relation to each other.

Word History

Perspective came into English about 600 years ago. It came from the Latin word *perspectivus*, meaning "of sight" or "optical." This Latin word came from a derivation of *perspicere*, which can be broken into the word parts *per-*, meaning "through," and *specere*, meaning "to look." (Also note that the word *perspective* contains the *-ive* suffix, which means "performs the action of.")

persuade (pər swād′) *v.* To get others to think as you do about a subject or topic.

Word Derivations

Below are some words related to *persuade*.

persuaded	persuading	persuasively
persuader	persuasion	persuasiveness
persuades	persuasive	

pester (pes′ tər) *v.* To bother; to annoy.

petition (pə ti′ shən) *v.* Submit a formal request to someone in authority.

petroglyph (pe′ trə glif′) *n.* A drawing or word carved into a rock.

peyote (pā ō′ tē) *n.* A cactus plant.

piñon (pin′ yən) *n.* A kind of pine tree with edible seeds.

pity (pi′ tē) *v.* Feel sorry for.

plateau (pla tō′) *n.* A tract of high, flat land; a tableland.

player (plā′ ər) *n.* A person who takes part in, and plays against another person in, a match.

plummet (plum′ it) *v.* Fall suddenly.

pogrom (pō′ grəm) *n.* An organized attack on Jews in Russia in the late 1800s. Pogroms were encouraged by the Russian government at that time.

ponder (pon′ dər) *v.* To think about.

portage (pôr täzh′) *n.* The act of carrying boats and supplies from one waterway to another.

portage

Page 644

Pronunciation Key: at; **lāte**; **câre**; **fäther**; **set**; **mē**; **it**; **kīte**; **ox**; **rōse**; **ô** in **b**ought; **coin**; **bŏŏk**; **tōō**; **form**; **out**; **up**; **ūse**; **tûrn**; **ə** sound in **a**bout, chick**e**n, penc**i**l, cann**o**n, circ**u**s; **chair**; **hw** in **wh**ich; **ring**; **shop**; **thin**; **th**ere; **zh** in trea**s**ure.

portal (por′ təl) *n.* An entryway.

posterity (po ster′ ə tē) *n.* Future generations.

poultice (pōl′ tis) *n.* A wad of something soft and moist that is placed over a wound to heal it.

prairie (prâr′ ē) *n.* A large area of level or rolling land with grass and few or no trees.

prankster (prangk′ stər) *n.* A person who plays tricks on people for fun.

preamble (prē′ am′ bəl) *n.* The section of text at the beginning of a law document that states why the document was written.

precarious (pri kâr′ ē əs) *adj.* Lacking security or stability.

precaution (pri kô′ shən) *n.* Care taken beforehand.

prediction (pri dik′ shən) *n.* A statement about what someone thinks will happen in the future.

preserve (pri zərv′) *v.* 1. Protect and maintain. 2. Prepare food so that it can be eaten in the future.

pressure (pre′ shər) *v.* To force.

prevail (pri vāl′) *v.* To persuade.

primary (prī′ mâr ē) *adj.* Main.

prime (prīm) *n.* The most successful or important period of time.

primitive (prim′ ə tiv) *adj.* 1. Living in the ways of long ago. 2. In the earliest stages of development.

procedure (prə sē′ jər) *n.* The steps to follow in carrying out a routine or method.

proclaim (prō klām′) *v.* To announce publicly.

procure (prə kyūr′) *v.* Obtain by making a special effort.

profound (prə found′) *adj.* Deep.

prominence (prom′ ə nəns) *n.* Fame; importance.

prominent (prom′ ə nənt) *adj.* Famous; well-known.

proportions (prə por′ shənz) *n.* Amounts.

prospect (pros′ pekt′) *v.* Look for gold.

provisions (prə vizh′ ənz) *n.* Supplies, especially food or tools.

ptarmigan (tär′ mi gən) *n.* A bird also known as a grouse.

pun (pun) *n.* A joke made by using words that sound almost the same but have different meanings.

pungent (pun′ jənt) *adj.* Sharp or strong smelling or tasting.

Q

quarantine (kwor′ ən tēn′) *adj.* Involving the isolation of people from others to prevent the spreading of disease.

quiver (kwi′ vər) *v.* To shake slightly.

R

racquetball (ra′ kət bôl′) *n.* A sport played with a racket and small rubber ball in an enclosed room.

Page 645

radiation (rā′ dē ā′ shən) *n.* Emitted energy that can be harmful.

radical (ra′ di kəl) *n.* A person who favors extreme changes or reforms.

rampart (ram′ pärt) *n.* A wall used as a defense for a city.

rancid (ran′ sid) *adj.* Stale; unpleasant.

rapscallion (rap skal′ yən) *n.* A rascal; a scamp.

ratification (rat′ ə fi kā′ shən) *n.* The formal approval of a law or laws.

ration (rash′ ən) *n.* A limited share of food.

ravage (ra′ vij) *v.* To damage heavily.

ravine (rə vēn′) *n.* A narrow, steep-sided valley worn into the earth by running water.

rebellion (ri bel′ yən) *n.* An uprising against a ruling authority; an act of defiance.

recede (ri sēd′) *v.* To go backward; to back away.

Word Derivations

Below are some words related to *recede*.

receded	recession	recessionary
receding	recessional	recessive
recess		

recognize (re′ kig nīz′) *v.* Know that you have seen someone or something before.

recoil (ri koil′) *v.* To spring back from.

reconciliation (rek′ ən sil′ ē ā′ shən) *n.* A restoration of agreement between two or more parties.

record (re′ kərd) *n.* A written account of the number of games a team won or lost during its season.

refracting (ri frak′ ting) *adj.* Passing through an object and changing direction, as a light ray passing into a lens at one angle and coming out at a different angle.

regard (re gärd′) *n.* Thought or care.

regiment (rej′ ə mənt) *n.* A large body of soldiers.

register (re′ jə stər) *v.* Officially record in order to protect.

rehearse (ri hûrs′) *v.* Practice.

remedy (rem′ ə dē) *n.* A cure; something that will make a sickness better.

remote (ri mōt′) *adj.* Far away and separate from others.

renounce (ri nouns′) *v.* To give up; to reject.

represent (re′ pri zent′) *v.* Speak or act for someone else.

resonance (rez′ ə nəns) *n.* Richness of sound; echoing.

resource (rē′ sors) *n.* Something that can be used.

reunion (rē ūn′ yən) *n.* A coming or bringing together of family, friends, or other groups of people.

reverie (rev′ ə rē) *n.* A daydream.

revolution (rev′ ə lōō′ shən) *n.* The overthrow of a system of government and the setting up of a new system of government.

revolutionize (re′ və lōō′ shə nīz′) *v.* Cause dramatic change.

rice paper (rīs′ pā′ pər) *n.* A thin paper produced from the stems of rice plants.

riddle (rid′ əl) *n.* A puzzle that appears as a statement or question.

Pronunciation Key: at; lāte; câre; fäther; set; mē; it; kīte; ox; rōse; ô in bought; coin; bŏŏk; tōō; form; out; up; ūse; tûrn; ə sound in about, chicken, pencil, cannon, circus; chair; hw in which; ring; shop; thin; ŧħere; zh in treasure.

ritual (rich´ ŏŏ əl) *n.* A ceremony of worship; an act always performed on certain occasions.

roam (rōm) *v.* Wander.

rocker (ro´ kər) *n.* A device used to separate gold from sand and dirt.

rotate (rō´ tāt) *v.* To revolve; to turn around; to spin.

rowdy (rou´ dē) *adj.* Rough; disorderly.

rudder (rud´ ər) *n.* A broad, flat blade at the rear of a ship used to steer. See illustration of **bow.**

rutting (rut´ ing) *n.* Mating.

S

saber (sā´ bər) *n.* A heavy sword with a curved blade.

sabotage (sab´ ə täzh´) *v.* To damage purposely.

salutary (sal´ yə ter´ ē) *adj.* Favorable; positive.

salutation (sal´ yə tā´ shən) *n.* Greeting.

samovar (sam´ ə vär´) *n.* A decorative metal container with a spigot, or faucet, often used in Russia to heat water for tea.

Word History

Samovar came into English in the year 1830. It is a Russian word formed by joining the word parts *samo-*, meaning "self," and *varit'*, which means "to boil."

scallion (skal´ yən) *n.* A type of onion.

scout (skout) *v.* Go ahead of the group, while on a journey, to look for information.

scowl (skoul) *v.* Frown.

scythe (sīŧħ) *n.* A tool with a long, curved blade for cutting grass or grain by hand.

scythe

sear (sēr) *v.* To roast; to burn.

seclude (si klōōd´) *v.* To keep away from others.

second (se´ kənd) *v.* To verbally agree with a motion or suggestion to do something in a meeting.

sect (sekt) *n.* A group of people bound together by common beliefs or ideals.

secure (sə kyŏŏr´) *adj.* Safe from harm or danger.

sentinel (sent´ nəl) *n.* A person who stands watch; a guard.

serve (sûrv) *v.* In volleyball and tennis, a way of putting the ball into play by sending it over the net.

shamefaced (shām´ fāst) *adj.* Embarrassed.

sharecropper (shâr´ krop´ ər) *n.* A farmer who gives part of his or her crop as rent to the owner of the land.

shlemiel (shlə mēl´) *n. slang.* A fool who is both awkward and unlucky.

646

shmendrick (shmen´ drik) *n. slang.* A nincompoop; a nobody.

short circuit (short´ sûr´ kət) *n.* A condition in which the path of an electrical current is obstructed.

shrill (shril) *adj.* High-pitched; piercing.

shroud (shroud) *n.* A covering for a dead body.

shy (shī´) *adj.* 1. Lacking; falling short. 2. Secretive; protective.

simultaneously (sī´ məl tā´ nē əs lē) *adv.* At exactly the same time.

singsong (sing´ sông´) *adj.* Having a repetitive musical sound.

skeeter (skē´ tər) *n. informal.* A mosquito.

slaughter (slô´ tər) *n.* The killing of a large number of animals.

slew (slōō) *n.* Many.

slump (slump) *v.* To sit with drooping shoulders.

Word History

Slump came into English in the year 1887. Its origins are probably in the Scandinavian languages. It is related to the Norwegian word *slumpa*, which means "to fall."

smithy (smith´ ē) *n.* A blacksmith's shop; a place where horseshoes are made.

solar system (sō´ lər sis´ təm) *n.* The sun and all the planets and other bodies that revolve around it.

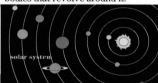

solar system

solder (sod´ ər) *v.* To join metal pieces together by using a highly heated liquid metal at a joint without heating the pieces themselves.

solitary (sol´ i ter´ ē) *adj.* Alone; single.

solstice (sol´ stis) *n.* The day of the year when the sun appears the farthest north and the day when it appears the farthest south in the sky.

sombre (som´ bər) *adj.* Dark or gloomy.

sovereign (so´ vrən) *adj.* Independent; self-governed.

span (span) *v.* To stretch across.

spar (spär) *n.* A pole or beam which supports the rigging on a ship; a mast.

spare (spâr) *adj.* Left over; remaining; extra.

spasm (spaz´ əm) *n.* A seizure; a fit.

spawn (spôn) *v.* To lay eggs and deposit them in water.

spectral (spek´ trəl) *adj.* Ghostly, eerie.

speculation (spek´ yə lā´ shən) *n.* Thinking about a subject; pondering.

spew (spū) *v.* To pour out; to squirt out.

spike (spīk) *v.* To forcefully hit a volleyball down the other side of the net.

spirit (spir´ ət) *n.* Enthusiasm; loyalty.

spirits (spir´ its) *n.* A liquid containing alcohol.

spooked (spōōkt) *adj.* Scared.

stance (stans) *n.* A person's mental position on a subject.

647

Pronunciation Key: at; lāte; câre; fäther; set; mē; it; kīte; ox; rōse; ô in bought; coin; bŏŏk; tōō; form; out; up; ūse; tûrn; ə sound in about, chicken, pencil, cannon, circus; chair; hw in which; ring; shop; thin; ŧħere; zh in treasure.

staple (stā´ pəl) *n.* A basic, or necessary, food.

stockyard (stok´ yärd´) *n.* A place where livestock such as cattle, sheep, horses, and pigs that are to be bought or sold, slaughtered, or shipped are held.

Stonehenge (stōn´ henj) *n.* A group of large stones in England placed in circular formations around 3,500 years ago, possibly as an astronomical calendar.

Stonehenge

straddle (stra´ dəl) *v.* To sit with one's legs on each side of an object.

stroke (strōk) *n.* A sudden attack of illness caused by a blocked or broken blood vessel in or leading to the brain.

succession (sək sesh´ ən) *n.* One thing happening right after another.

substitute (sub´ stə tōōt) *n.* Anything that could take the place of something else.

succulent (suk´ yə lənt) *adj.* Juicy; tasty.

sufficient (sə fish´ ənt) *adj.* Enough.

suffocate (suf´ ə kāt´) *v.* To smother; to choke.

sull (sul) *v.* To balk; to stop suddenly and refuse to move.

summon (sum´ ən) *v.* Ask to come.

supple (sup´ əl) *adj.* Easily bent; not stiff.

sway (swā) *v.* To influence.

T

tan (tan) *v.* To turn animal hides into leather.

Word History

Tan came into English about 600 years ago, from the French word *tanner*, a derivation of the Latin word *tanum* or *tannum*. The Latin word means "tanbark," a type of bark that contains an astringent, or drying, substance used in the making of leather.

tangled-up (tang´ gəld up´) *adj.* Mixed-up and stuck together.

tantrum (tan´ trəm) *n.* A screaming, crying fit of childish anger.

tapir (tā´ pər) *n.* An animal similar to a pig, but with a long, flexible nose.

tariff (târ´ əf) *n.* A fee charged by a government on imports and exports.

teeming (tē´ ming) *adj.* Overflowing; swarming.

terminal (tûr´ mə nəl) *adj.* Eventually ending in death.

terrace (târ´ əs) *n.* A raised area with a series of level steps or surfaces cut into the side.

terrain (tə rān´) *n.* An area of land that is thought of in terms of its physical features.

tethered (teŧħ´ ərd) *adj.* Tied by rope to a fixed object.

648

thresh (thresh) *v.* To separate grain from the stalk by beating it.

tidal flat (tī′ dəl flat) *n.* A flat area of land that is sometimes covered by tidal waters.

timpani (tim′ pə nē) *n.* A type of drum.

tipi (tē′ pē) *n.* A tent of the Native Americans of the Plains; a tepee.

Word History

Tipi, or tepee, came into English in the year 1743. It is a Native American word, meaning "to dwell," that originated with the Dakota tribe.

toboggan (tə bog′ ən) *n.* A long, narrow sled.

tome (tōm) *n.* One volume of a set of books.

tract (trakt) *n.* A large area of land.

traditional (trə di′ shən əl) *adj.* Passed from one generation to another.

traitor (trā′ tər) *n.* A person who betrays his or her country.

tranquility (tran kwil′ ə tē) *n.* Calmness.

transcribe (tran skrīb′) *v.* To change from one recorded form to another; to translate.

treason (trē′ zən) *n.* The act of betraying someone's trust.

treaty (trē′ tē) *n.* A formal agreement between two countries.

trek (trek) *n.* A long, slow journey.

trench (trench) *n.* A ditch; a long, narrow channel cut in the earth.

tributary (trib′ yə ter′ ē) *n.* A stream or river that flows into a larger one.

tribute (trib′ ūt) *n.* Praise, honor, or gifts given to show respect or to show thanks.

trifling (trī′ fling) *adj.* Small and unimportant.

trinket (tring′ kit) *n.* A small or cheap piece of jewelry.

tripod (trī′ pod) *n.* A three-legged table or stand.

tripod

troop (trōōp) *n.* Soldiers.

tsar (zär) *n.* An emperor of Russia before 1918.

tsarina (zä rē′ nə) *n.* An empress of Russia before 1918.

tumult (tōō′ mult) *n.* A great disorder; an uproar.

tundra (tun′ drə) *n.* A large, treeless plain in the arctic regions.

tunic (tōō′ nik) *n.* A short coat.

tyranny (tir′ ə nē) *n.* The unjust use of power; harsh or cruel government.

U

unaccountably (un′ ə koun′ tə blē) *adv.* In a way that cannot be explained.

unalienable (un′ āl′ yə nə bəl) *adj.* Not capable of being given or taken away.

unanimity (ū′ nə ni′ mə tē) *n.* A condition of complete agreement.

Pronunciation Key: at; lāte; câre; fäther; set; mē; it; kīte; ox; rōse; ô in bought; coin; bŏŏk; tōō; form; out; up; ūse; tûrn; ə sound in about, chicken, pencil, cannon, circus; chair; hw in which; ring; shop; thin; thére; zh in treasure.

unison (ū′ nə sən) *n.* Behaving the same way at the same time. **in unison** *idiom.* Two or more people saying or doing the same thing at the same time.

universe (ū′ nə vers′) *n.* Everything that exists, including the earth, the planets, the stars, and all of space.

unquenchably (un kwench′ ə blē) *adv.* Endlessly; in a persistent way.

V

vain (vān) *adj.* Conceited.

vagabond (va′ gə bond′) *n.* One who wanders from place to place.

valiant (val′ yənt) *adj.* Brave; fearless.

variable (vâr′ ē′ ə bəl) *adj.* Likely to change.

velocity (və los′ i tē) *n.* Speed.

vindicate (vin′ di kāt′) *v.* To prove innocent.

vintage (vin′ tij) *n.* The grapes or wine produced in a vineyard in one year.

vintner (vint′ nər) *n.* A person who makes wine for a living.

visible (vi′ zə bəl) *adj.* Able to be seen or noticed.

vocation (vō kā′ shən) *n.* An occupation; a profession.

voyage (voi′ ij) *n.* A journey by water.

W

water buffalo (wô′ tər buf′ ə lō′) *n.* A kind of oxen with large curved horns and a bluish-black hide. Water buffaloes are trained to work in rice fields in Asia.

whim (hwim) *n.* An impulsive thought, idea, or desire.

whopper (hwop′ ər) *n. informal.* A big lie.

wince (wins) *v.* To flinch; to start back from.

windlass (wind′ ləs) *n.* A roller turned with a handle used for lifting heavy weights.

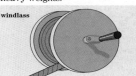

windlass

winnow (win′ ō) *v.* To remove the chaff, or husks, from grain.

wrath (rath) *n.* Anger; rage.

Y

yarn (yärn) *n.* A made-up story.

yield (yēld) *v.* To give in; to stop arguing.

Z

Zulu (zōō′ lōō) *n.* A person from KwaZulu Natal in South Africa.

Program Appendix

The Program Appendix includes a step-by-step explanation of procedures for research-based, effective practices in reading instruction that are repeatedly used throughout *SRA/Open Court Reading.* These practices may also be used in other instructional materials.

Table of Contents

Reading Materials and Techniques

Different reading materials and techniques are appropriate at different stages of reading development. The purpose of this section is to discuss different types of reading materials and how they may be used most effectively.

Reading Big Books

Purpose

Many students come from homes where they are read to often, but a significant number of other students have not had this valuable experience. Big Books (Levels K and 1) offer all students crucial opportunities to confirm and expand their knowledge about print and reading. They are especially useful for shared reading experiences in the early grades.

The benefits of reading Big Books include engaging even nonreaders in:

- unlocking the books' messages.
- developing print awareness.
- participating in good reading behaviors.
- observing what a good reader does: remarking on the illustrations and the title, asking questions about the content and what might happen, making predictions, and clarifying words and ideas.
- promoting the insight that a given word is spelled the same way every time it occurs as high-frequency words are pointed out.
- reinforcing the correspondence between spoken and written words and spelling patterns.
- enjoying the illustrations and connecting them to the text to help students learn to explore books for enjoyment and information.
- interpreting and responding to literature and expository text before they can read themselves.

Procedure for Reading Big Books

During the first reading of the Big Books, you will model reading behaviors and comprehension strategies similar to those that will later be taught formally. During the second reading, you will address print awareness and teach comprehension skills such as classifying and categorizing or sequencing, which help the reader organize information. In addition, you will teach skills such as making inferences and drawing conclusions, which help the reader focus on the deeper meaning of the text. At first, teachers should expect to do all of the reading but should not prevent students from trying to read on their own or from reading words they already know.

- **Activate Prior Knowledge.** Read the title of the selection and the author's and illustrator's names. At the beginning of each Big Book, read the title of the book and discuss what the whole book is about before going on to reading the first selection.
- **Discuss Prior Knowledge.** Initiate a brief discussion of any prior knowledge the students have that might help them understand the selection.
- **Browse the Selection.** Ask students to tell what they think the story might be about just from looking at the illustrations. This conversation should be brief so that the students can move on to a prereading discussion of print awareness.

> *Big Books offer all students crucial opportunities to confirm and expand their knowledge about print and reading.*

- **Develop Print Awareness.** The focus of browsing the Big Books is to develop awareness of print. Urge students to tell what words or letters they recognize rather than what they expect the selection to be about.

  To develop print awareness, have students look through the selection page by page and comment on whatever they notice in the text. Some students may know some of the words, while others may only recognize specific letters or sounds. The key is to get the students to look at the print separately from the illustrations even before they have heard the actual text content. This process isolates print awareness so that it is not influenced by content. It also gives you a clearer idea of what your students do or do not know about print.
- **Read Aloud.** Read the selection aloud expressively. The reading enables the students simply to hear and enjoy the text as it is read through once. With this reading, you will model behaviors and comprehension strategies that all students will need to develop to become successful readers—for example, asking questions; clarifying unfamiliar words, first by using the pictures and later by using context; or predicting what might happen next.
- **Reread.** Read the selection expressively again. During the second reading of the stories, you will focus on teaching comprehension skills. Also, to develop print awareness, point to each word as it is read, thus demonstrating that text proceeds from left to right and from top to bottom and helping advance the idea that words are individual spoken and written units. Invite the students to identify the rhyming words in a poem or chime in on repetitive parts of text as you point to the words. Or students can read with you on this second reading, depending on the text.
- **Discuss Print.** Return to print awareness by encouraging discussion of anything the students noticed about the words. Young students should begin to realize that you are reading separate words that are separated by spaces. Later, students will begin to see that each word is made up of a group of letters. The students should be encouraged to discuss anything related to the print. For example, you might ask students to point to a word or count the number of words on a line. Or you might connect the words to the illustrations by pointing to a word and saying it and then asking the students to find a picture of that word.
- **Responding.** Responding to a selection is a way of insuring comprehension. Invite students to tell about the story by asking them what they like about the poem or story or calling on a student to explain in his or her own words what the poem or story tells about. Call on others to add to the telling as needed. For nonfiction selections, this discussion might include asking students what they learned about the topic and what they thought was most interesting.

Tips for Using Big Books

- Make sure the entire group is able to see the book clearly while you are reading.
- If some students are able to read or predict words, encourage them to do so during the rereading.
- Encourage students to present and use their knowledge of print.
- Allow students to look at the Big Books whenever they wish.
- Provide small versions of the Big Books for students to browse through and try to read at their leisure.
- The reader of the Big Book should try to be part of the collaborative group of learners rather than the leader.

Using the Pre-Decodable Books

Purpose

Pre-Decodable Books play an important role in students' early literacy development by providing them with meaningful "reading" experiences before they are actually reading on their own and by expanding their awareness of the forms and uses of print. By following along as you read aloud a **Pre-Decodable Book,** students learn about the left-to-right and top-to-bottom progression of print on a page, the clues that indicate the beginnings and endings of sentences, the connections between pictures and words, and important book conventions, such as front and back covers, authors' and illustrators' names, title pages, and page numbers.

The **Pre-Decodable Books** provide students with opportunities to apply their growing knowledge of letter names, shapes, and sounds, and to become familiar with individual words.

Through retelling the story in a **Pre-Decodable Book,** predicting or wondering about what will happen, and asking and responding to questions about the book, students not only learn about the relationship between spoken and written language, they learn to think about what they have read.

About the Pre-Decodable Books

Each **Pre-Decodable Book** contains a story that engages students' interest as it provides them with opportunities to practice what they are learning in their lessons. These "Pre-Decodable" stories each contain several high-frequency words that most students already have in their spoken vocabularies and that are a basic part of all meaningful stories. Learning to identify high-frequency words quickly, accurately, and effortlessly is a critical part of students' development as fluent, independent readers. The inside back cover of each **Pre-Decodable Book** contains a list of high-frequency words.

How to Read the Pre-Decodable Books

- Before reading a **Pre-Decodable Book,** take time to familiarize students with any new **high-frequency words** in the book and to review previously introduced words. To reinforce the idea that it is important to know these words because they are used so often in print, always point out the words in context. For example, focus students' attention on the words in Big Book selections or on signs and posters around the classroom.

- Give each student a copy of the book. Tell students that you will read the book together. Hold up your book. Read the title. If the title has a rebus picture, point to it and tell the students what it is. Then point to the word beneath it and explain that the picture represents that word. Point to and read the names of the author and illustrator, reminding students that an author writes a book and an illustrator draws the pictures. Page through the book, pointing to and naming the rebus pictures. Have the students say the name of each rebus. To avoid confusion, always *tell* them the *exact* word that a rebus represents. *Don't encourage them to guess at its meaning.*

- Allow students time to browse through the book on their own, commenting on what they see in the illustrations and making predictions about what they think the book will be about. Encourage them to comment on anything special they notice about the story, the illustrations, or the words in the book.

- Help the students to find page 3. Read the book aloud without stopping. As you read, move your hand beneath the words to show the progression of print. Pause at each rebus as you say the word it represents, pointing first to the rebus, then to the word beneath it.

- Reread the book. This time, ask the students to point to and read the high-frequency words.

- Tell the students to follow along in their books as you read the story again. Read the title aloud, and then have the students read it with you. Reread page 3. Point to each rebus picture and ask a volunteer to "read" it. Point to the word beneath the picture and remind students that the picture shows what the word is. Continue through each page of the book, calling on volunteers to "read" and stopping as necessary to clarify and help students with words.

- After reading, answer any questions the students might have about the book. Encourage them to discuss the illustrations and to explain what is happening in each one.

Reading Decodables and Building Fluency

Purpose

The most urgent task of early reading instruction is to make written thoughts intelligible to students. This requires a balanced approach that includes systematic instruction in phonics as well as experiences with authentic literature. Thus, from the very beginning, *Open Court Reading* includes the reading of literature. At the beginning of first grade, when students are learning phonics and blending as a tool to access words, the teacher reads aloud. During this time students are working on using comprehension strategies and skills and discussing stories. As students learn the code and blend words, recognize critical sight words, and develop some level of fluency, they take more responsibility for the actual reading of the text.

This program has a systematic instruction in phonics that allows the students to begin reading independently. This instruction is supported by *Open Court Reading* Decodable Books.

Practice

The *Open Court Reading* Decodable Books are designed to help the students apply, review, and reinforce their expanding knowledge of sound/spelling correspondences. Each story supports instruction in new phonic elements and incorporates elements and words that have been learned earlier. There are eight page and sixteen page **Decodable Books.** Grade K has eight-page **Decodable Books.** In Grade 1 the eight-page books focus on the new element introduced in the lesson, while the sixteen-page books review and reinforce the elements that have been taught since the last sixteen-page book. They review sounds from several lessons and provide additional reading practice. Grades 2–3 have eight-page **Decodable Books** in Getting Started, and sixteen-page books in the first 4–5 units of the grade level. The primary purpose is to provide practice reading the words. It is important that the students also attach meaning to what they are reading. Questions are often included in the *Teacher's Edition* to check both understanding and attention to words.

Fluency

Fluency is the effortless ability to read or access words with seemingly little attention to decoding. It also involves grouping words into meaningful units and using expression appropriately. Fluency is critical but not sufficient for comprehension.

To become proficient readers who fully understand what they read, the whole process of decoding must become as automatic as possible. The students need to be so familiar with the

Reading Materials and Techniques (continued)

sound/spellings and with the most common nondecodable sight words that they automatically process the letters or spellings and expend most of their energy on comprehending the meaning of the text.

While fluency begins in first grade, many students will continue to need practice in building fluency in second and third grades. Initially, students can use the *Open Court Reading* **Decodable Books** in grades 2 and 3, but fluency practice should include using materials from actual literature the students are reading.

Procedure

Preparing to Read

■ Introduce and write on the board any nondecodable high-frequency or story words introduced or reviewed in the story. Tell the students how to pronounce any newly introduced high-frequency words. Then point to each new word and have the students say it. Have them read any previously introduced sight word in the Word Bank list. All of the *Open Court Reading* **Decodable Books** contain high-frequency words that may not be decodable. For example, the word *said* is a very common high-frequency word that is not decodable. Including words like *said* makes the language of the story flow smoothly and naturally. The students need to be able to recognize these words quickly and smoothly.

■ Read the title. At the beginning of the year, you may need to read the title of the book to the students, but as the year goes on, you should have a student read it whenever possible. The sixteen-page *Open Court Reading* **Decodable Books** contain two related chapters, each using the same sounds and spellings. In such cases, read the title of the **Decodable** book, and then point out the two individual chapter titles. Have volunteers read the title of the chapter you are about to read.

■ Browse the story. Have the students look through the story, commenting on whatever they notice in the text or illustrations and telling what they think the story will tell them.

Reading the Story

After this browsing, the students will read the story a page at a time. Again, these books are designed to support the learning of sounds and spellings. The focus should not be on comprehension. Students should understand what they are reading, and they should feel free to discuss anything in the story that interests them. Any areas of confusion are discussed and clarified as they arise, as described below.

■ Have the students read a page to themselves. Then call on one student to read the page aloud, or have the whole group read it aloud.

■ If a student has difficulty with a word that can be blended, help her or him blend the word. Remind the student to check the **Sound/Spelling Cards** for help. If a word cannot be blended using the sound/spellings learned so far, pronounce the word for the student.

■ If a student has trouble with a word or sentence, have the reader call on a classmate for help, and then continue reading after the word or sentence has been clarified. After something on a page has been clarified or discussed, have that page reread by a different student before moving on to the next page.

■ Repeat this procedure for each page.

■ Reread the story twice more, calling on different students to read or reading it in unison. These readings should go more quickly, with fewer stops for clarification.

Responding to the Story

Once the story has been read aloud a few times, have the students respond as follows:

■ Ask the students what hard words they found in the story and how they figured them out. They may mention high-frequency words they didn't recognize, words they had to blend, and words whose meanings they did not know.

■ Invite the students to tell about the story, retelling it in their own words, describing what they liked about it, or citing what they found interesting or surprising. Specific suggestions to use are listed in the *Teacher's Edition.*

■ Questions are provided in the *Teacher's Edition.* They are designed to focus the students' attention on the words and not just the pictures. The questions require answers that cannot be guessed by looking at the pictures alone, such as a name, a bit of dialogue, or an action or object that is not pictured. Have the students point to the words, phrases, or sentences that answer the questions.

Building Fluency

Buiding fluency is essential to gaining strong comprehension. The more fluent the students become, the more they can attend to the critical business of understanding the text. Opportunities for students to build fluency may include:

■ Have students "partner read" the most recent *Open Court Reading* Decodable Book twice, taking turns reading a page at a time. The partners should switch the second time through so they are reading different pages from the ones they read the first time. If there is time left, the partners should choose any of the previously read stories to read together. Use this time for diagnosis, having one student at a time read with you.

■ Making sure that the *Open Court Reading* **Decodable Books** are readily available in the classroom.

■ Reading **Decodable Books** with as many students as possible one at a time.

■ Reminding the students that they may read with partners during Workshop.

The only way the students can become fluent readers is to read as much and as often as possible.

Reading the Student Anthologies

Purpose

Reading is a complex process that requires students not only to decode what they read but also to understand and respond to it. The purpose of this section is to help you identify various reading behaviors used by good readers and to encourage those behaviors in your students.

Reading Behaviors and Comprehension Strategies

There are four basic behaviors that good readers engage in during reading. These behaviors include the application of certain comprehension strategies, which are modeled while reading the Student Anthology (Levels 1–6).

Setting Reading Goals and Expectations

Good readers set reading goals and expectations before they begin reading. This behavior involves a variety of strategies that will help students prepare to read the text.

- **Activate prior knowledge.** When good readers approach a new text, they consider what they already know about the subject or what their experiences have been in reading similar material.
- **Browse the text.** To get an idea of what to expect from a text, good readers look at the title and the illustrations. They may look for potential problems, such as difficult words. When browsing a unit, have students glance quickly at each selection, looking briefly at the illustrations and the print. Have them tell what they think they might be learning about as they read the unit.
- **Decide what they expect from the text.** When reading for pleasure, good readers anticipate enjoying the story or the language. When reading to learn something, they ask themselves what they expect to find out.

Responding to Text

Good readers are active readers. They interact with text by using the following strategies:

- **Making connections.** Good readers make connections between what they read and what they already know. They pay attention to elements in the text that remind them of their own experiences.
- **Visualizing, or picturing.** Good readers visualize what is happening in the text. They form mental images as they read. They picture the setting, the characters, and the action in a story. When reading expository text, good

readers picture the objects, processes, or events described. Visualizing helps readers understand descriptions of complex activities or processes.

- **Asking questions.** Good readers ask questions that may prepare them for what they will learn. If their questions are not answered in the text, they may try to find answers elsewhere and thus add even more to their store of knowledge.
- **Predicting.** Good readers predict what will happen next. When reading fiction, they make predictions about what they are reading and then confirm or revise those predictions as they go.
- **Thinking about how the text makes you feel.** Well-written fiction touches readers' emotions; it sparks ideas.

Checking Understanding

One of the most important behaviors good readers exhibit is the refusal to continue reading when something fails to make sense. Good readers continually assess their understanding of the text with strategies such as:

- **Interpreting.** As they read, good readers make inferences that help them understand and appreciate what they are reading.
- **Summing up.** Good readers sum up to check their understanding as they read. Sometimes they reread to fill in gaps in their understanding.
- **Monitoring and adjusting reading speed.** Good readers monitor their understanding of what they read. They slow down as they come to difficult words and passages. They speed up as they read easier passages.

Monitoring and Clarifying Unfamiliar Words and Passages

- **Apply decoding skills** to sound out unknown words.
- **Determine what is unclear** to find the source of the confusion.
- **Apply context clues** in text and illustrations to figure out the meanings of words or passages.
- **Reread the passage** to make sure the passage makes sense.
- **Check a dictionary or the glossary** to understand the meanings of words not clarified by clues or rereading.

Procedures

Modeling and Thinking Aloud

Modeling and encouraging students to think aloud as they attempt to understand text can demonstrate for everyone how reading behaviors are put into practice. The most effective models will be those that come from your own reading. Using questions such as the following, as well as your students' questions and comments, will

make both the text and the strategic reading process more meaningful to students.

- What kinds of things did you wonder about?
- What kinds of things surprised you?
- What new information did you learn?
- What was confusing until you reread or read further?

Model comprehension strategies in a natural way, and choose questions and comments that fit the text you are reading. Present a variety of ways to respond to text.

- Pose questions that you really do wonder about.
- Identify with characters by comparing them with yourself.
- React emotionally by showing joy, sadness, amusement, or surprise.
- Show empathy with or sympathy for characters.
- Relate the text to something that has happened to you or to something you already know.
- Show interest in the text ideas.
- Question the meaning or clarity of the author's words and ideas.

Encouraging Students' Responses and Use of Strategies

Most students will typically remain silent as they try to figure out an unfamiliar word or a confusing passage. Encourage students to identify specifically what they are having difficulty with. Once the problem has been identified, ask the students to suggest a strategy for dealing with the problem. Remind students to:

- Treat problems encountered in text as interesting learning opportunities.
- Think out loud about text challenges.
- Help each other build meaning. Rather than tell what a word is, students should tell how they figured out the meanings of challenging words and passages.
- Consider reading a selection again with a partner after reading it once alone. Partner reading provides valuable practice in reading for fluency.
- Make as many connections as they can between what they are reading and what they already know.
- Visualize to clarify meanings or enjoy descriptions.
- Ask questions about what they are reading.
- Notice how the text makes them feel.

Reading Materials and Techniques (continued)

Reading Techniques

Reading Aloud

Purpose

Adults read a variety of materials aloud to students. These include Big Books, picture books, and novels. Research has shown that students who are read to are more likely to develop the skills they need to read successfully on their own.

In every grade level of **Open Court Reading** there are opportunities for teachers to read aloud to students. At the beginning of each unit is a Read-Aloud selection tied to the unit theme. This Read-Aloud selection allows students the opportunity to think about the unit theme before reading selections on their own.

Reading aloud at any age serves multiple purposes. Reading aloud:

- Provokes students' curiosity about text.
- Conveys an awareness that text has meaning.
- Demonstrates the various reasons for reading text (to find out about the world around them, to learn useful new information and new skills, or simply for pleasure).
- Exposes students to the "language of literature," which is more complex than the language they ordinarily use and hear.
- Provides an opportunity to teach the problem-solving strategies that good readers employ. As the students observe you interacting with the text, expressing your own enthusiasm, and modeling your thinking aloud, they perceive these as valid responses and begin to respond to text in similar ways.

Procedures

The following set of general procedures for reading aloud is designed to help you maximize the effectiveness of Read-Aloud sessions.

- **Read-aloud sessions.** Set aside time each day to read aloud.
- **Introduce the story.** Tell the students that you are going to read a story aloud to them. Tell its title and briefly comment on the topic. To allow the students to anticipate what will happen in the story, be careful not to summarize.
- **Activate prior knowledge.** Ask whether anyone has already heard the story. If so, ask them to see if this version is the same as the one they have heard. If not, activate prior knowledge by saying, "First, let's talk a little about _____." If the story is being read in two (or more) parts, before reading the second part, ask the students to recall the first part.
- **Before reading.** Invite students to interrupt your reading if there are any words they do not understand or ideas they find puzzling. Throughout the reading, encourage them to do this.
- **Read the story expressively.** Occasionally react verbally to the story by showing surprise, asking questions, giving an opinion, expressing pleasure, or predicting events. Think-aloud suggestions are outlined below.
- **Use Comprehension Strategies.** While reading aloud to the students, model the use of comprehension strategies in a natural, authentic way. Remember to try to present a variety of ways to respond to text. These include visualizing, asking questions, predicting, making connections, clarifying, and summarizing.
- **Retell.** When you have finished reading the story, call on volunteers to retell it.
- **Discuss.** After reading, discuss with the students their own reactions: how the story reminded them of things that have happened to them, what they thought of the story, and what they liked best about the story.
- **Reread.** You may wish to reread the selection on subsequent occasions focusing the discussion on the unit theme.

Think-Aloud Responses

The following options for modeling thinking aloud will be useful for reading any story aloud. Choose responses that are most appropriate for the selection you are reading.

- **React emotionally** by showing joy, sadness, amusement, or surprise.
- **Ask questions** about ideas in the text. This should be done when there are points or ideas that you really do wonder about.
- **Identify with characters** by comparing them to yourself.
- **Show empathy with or sympathy for** characters.
- **Relate the text to something** you already know or something that has happened to you.
- **Show interest** in the text ideas.
- **Question the meaning and/or clarity** of the author's words and ideas.

Questions to Help Students Respond

At reasonable stopping points in reading, ask the students general questions in order to get them to express their own ideas and to focus their attention on the text.

- What do you already know about this?
- What seems really important here? Why do you think so?
- Was there anything that you didn't understand? What?
- What did you like best about this?
- What new ideas did you learn from this?
- What does this make you wonder about?

Reading Roundtable

Purpose

Adult readers discuss their reading, give opinions on it, and recommend books to each other. Reading Roundtable, an activity students may choose to participate in during **Workshop**, provides the same opportunity for students in the classroom. Sessions can be small or large. During Reading Roundtable, students share the reading they do on their own. They can discuss a book they have all read, or one person can review a book for the others and answer questions from the group.

During Reading Roundtable, students can discuss and review a variety of books:

- Full-length versions of Anthology selections.
- Classroom Library selections.
- Books that students learn about when discussing authors and illustrators.
- Books related to the investigations of unit concepts can be shared with others who might want to read them.
- Interesting articles from magazines, newspapers, and other sources.

Procedures

Encouraging Reading

- Read aloud to your students regularly. You can read Classroom Library selections or full-length versions of Student Anthology selections.
- Provide a time each day for students to read silently. This time can be as short as 10–15 minutes but should be strictly observed. You should stop what you are doing and read. Students should be allowed to choose their own reading materials during this time and record their reactions in the Response Journal section of their Writer's Notebook.
- Establish a classroom library and reading center with books from the school or local library or ask for donations of books from students, parents, and community members.
- Take your students to the school library or to the public library.

Conducting a Reading Roundtable

- When a student reviews a book others have not read, he or she can use some of the sentence starters to tell about the book. These may include, "This book is about . . . , I chose this book because. . . , What I really like/don't like about this book is . . . " and so on.
- When several students read the same book and discuss it during Reading Roundtable, they can use discussion starters. If the book is from the Classroom Library, they can discuss how it relates to the unit concepts.

Purpose

In *SRA/Open Court Reading*, students learn to relate sounds to letters in Kindergarten through the use of thirty-one **Alphabet Sound Cards** (Level K). In the upper grade levels, **Sound Spelling Cards** (Levels 1–3) are used to relate sounds and spellings. The purpose of the **Alphabet Sound Cards** is to remind the students of the sounds of the English language and their letter correspondences. These cards are a resource for the students to use to remember sound-letter associations for both reading and writing.

Each card contains the capital and small letter, and a picture that shows the sound being produced. For instance, the **Monkey** card introduces the /m/ sound and shows a monkey looking at bananas and saying */m/ /m/ /m/*. The name of the picture on each card contains the target sound at the beginning of the word for the consonants and in the middle for most of the vowels. Vowel letters are printed in red and consonants are printed in black. In addition, the picture associates a sound with an action. This action-sound association is introduced through a short, interactive story found in the *Teacher's Edition* in which the pictured object or character "makes" the sound of the letter. Long vowels are represented by a tall—or "long"— picture of the letters themselves, rather than by a picture for action-sound association.

Procedures

- Display the cards 1–26 with the picture sides to the wall. Initially post the first twenty-six cards in alphabetical order so that only the alphabet letters show. The short vowel cards may be posted as they are introduced later. As you introduce the letter sound, you will turn the card to show the picture and the letter on the other side. Once the cards are posted, do not change their positions so that the students can locate the cards quickly.

- Before turning a card, point to the letter. Ask students to tell what they know about the letter. For example, they are likely to know its name and possibly its sound if the letter is one they have already worked with.

- Turn the card and show the picture. Tell the students the name of the card, and explain that it will help them to remember the sound the letter makes.

- Read the story that goes with the letter. Read it expressively, emphasizing the words with the target sound and the isolated sound when it occurs. Have the students join in to produce the sound.

- Repeat the story a few times, encouraging all students to say the sound along with you.

- Follow the story with the cards for the target sound. (These are listed within the lessons.)

- Name each picture, and have students listen for the target sound at the beginning of the word. Ask students to repeat the words and the sound.

- For every letter sound, a listening activity follows the introduction of the cards. Lead the students in the "Listening for the Sound" activity to reinforce the letter sound.

- To link the sound and the letter, demonstrate how to form the uppercase and lowercase letter by writing on the board or on an overhead transparency. The students practice forming the letter and saying the sound as they write.

Alphabet Sound Cards

The pictures and letters on the **Alphabet Sound Cards (Wall Cards)** also appear on the small sets of **Alphabet Sound Cards (Individual)**. The Teacher's Edition specifically suggests that you use the **Individual Alphabet Sound Cards** for some activities. You may also use the small cards for review and for small-group reteaching and practice sessions. Have sets of the cards available for the students to use during **Workshop** either alone or with partners. Add each small card to the Activity Center after you have taught the lesson in which the corresponding **Alphabet Sound Card** is introduced. Here are some suggestions for activities using the **Alphabet Sound Cards**:

1. **Saying sounds from pictures.** The leader flashes pictures as the others say the sound each picture represents.

2. **Saying sounds.** The leader flashes the letters on the cards as the others say the sound that the letters represent.

3. **Naming words from pictures.** The leader flashes pictures. The others say the sound, and then say a word beginning with that sound.

4. **Writing letters from the pictures.** Working alone, a student looks at a picture and then writes the letter for the sound that picture represents.

Tips

- Throughout the beginning lessons, help students remember that vowels are special by reminding them that vowels sometimes say their names in words. For example, the picture of the *a* on the long *a* **Alphabet Sound Card** is long because the long *a* says its name. The short *a* **Alphabet Sound Card** pictures the lamb, because the lamb makes the short *a* sound, and you can hear the sound in the word, *lamb*. In the later lessons, students will use both sets of cards to help them remember that the vowels have both a short and a long sound.

- From the very beginning, encourage students to use the **Alphabet Sound Cards** as a resource to help them with their work.

- Mastery of letter recognition is the goal students should reach so that they will be prepared to link each letter with its associated sound. If students have not yet mastered the names of the letters, it is important to work with them individually in **Workshop**, or at other times during the day.

- The *Kk* card is a little tricky. A camera makes the /k/ sound when it clicks, and the word *camera* begins with the /k/ sound. However, the word *camera* is not spelled with a *k*. While you need not dwell on this, be aware that some students may be confused by the fact that the *Cc* and *Kk* cards have the same picture.

- The picture on the *Qq* card depicts ducks, *quacking ducks*. Make sure that the students consistently call them *quacking ducks*, not *ducks*, and that they focus on the /kw/ sound.

The Alphabetic Principle: How the Alphabet Works

The Alphabetic Principle

Purpose

A major emphasis in the kindergarten program is on letter recognition and attending to sounds. Students need to learn the alphabetic principle: that letters work together in a systematic way to connect spoken language to written words. This understanding is the foundation for reading. Students are not expected to master letter/sound correspondence at the beginning of kindergarten, nor are they expected to blend sounds into words themselves. They are only expected to become an "expert" on their Special Letter as they learn how the alphabet works. Through this introduction to the alphabetic principle, the students will have the basic understanding required to work through the alphabet letter by letter, attaching sounds to each.

Key concepts of the Alphabetic Principle include:

- A limited number of letters combine in different ways to make many different words.
- Words are composed of sounds and letters represent those sounds.
- Anything that can be pronounced can be spelled.
- Letters and sounds can be used to identify words.
- Meaning can be obtained by using letters and sounds to figure out words.

Procedures for Kindergarten

The following steps can be used for introducing letters and sounds in Kindergarten. These steps may be adapted for students at other grades if they do not understand the alphabetic principle. The tone of these activities should be informal, fun, and fast-paced. The purpose of these activities is to familiarize the students with how the alphabet works by having them participate in group play with letters and sounds.

Introducing Letters

- Reinforce the idea that anything that can be pronounced can be spelled with the letters of the alphabet.
- Tell the students that you can spell any word. Have them give you words to spell.
- Write the words on the board, and show students that the words contain the letters displayed on the **Alphabet Sound Cards**.
- Have students help you spell the words by pointing to letters as you say them and then write them.
- Encourage students to spell each word letter by letter.

Letter Expert Groups

- Have **Letter Cards** (Levels K and 1) available for the following set of letters: *b, d, f, h, l, m, n, p, s, t.* You will need two or three cards for each letter. (You will not need the **Alphabet Sound Cards** until later.)
- You will be the letter expert for the vowels.
- Divide the class into groups of two or three and assign each group a letter. Give each student the appropriate **Letter Card**.
- Tell the students that they are now in their Letter Expert groups and that they are going to become experts on their Special Letter's name, shape, and sound.

> *Students need to learn the alphabetic principle: that letters work together in a systematic way to connect spoken language to written words. This understanding is the foundation for reading.*

Making Words

- Begin each lesson with a rehearsal of each group's letter name.
- Demonstrate how letters work by writing a word in large letters on the board.
- Tell the students the experts for each letter in the word should hold up their **Letter Cards** and name the letter. One member of the group should stand in front of their letter on the board.
- Continue until all letters in the word are accounted for. Remember that you are responsible for the vowels.
- Demonstrate that you can make different words by changing a letter or by changing the letter order.

Identifying Sounds in Words

- Use the **Alphabet Sound Cards** to demonstrate that every letter has at least one sound.
- Give each student the **Alphabet Sound Card** for his or her Special Letter.
- Point out the pictures on the cards. Explain that each card has a picture of something that makes the letter's sound. The picture will help them remember the sound.
- Tell each group the sound for its letter. (Remember, you are the expert for the vowels.)

- Quickly have each group rehearse its letter's name and sound.
- Write a word on the board in large letters. Say the word first sound-by-sound and then blend the word.
- For each letter/sound in the word, have one student from each Letter Expert group come forward, stand in front of the appropriate letter, and hold their cards. Although only one member of the group may come forward with the **Letter Card** or **Alphabet Sound Card,** all students in a Special Letter group should say the name and/or sound of their letter when it occurs in words.
- Say the word again, pointing to the **Alphabet Sound Cards**.
- Ask students who are not already standing to help you hold the vowel cards.
- Vary the activity by changing one letter sound and having an expert for that letter come forward.
- End the activity for each word by saying the sounds in the words one by one and then saying the entire word. Encourage the students to participate.

Tips

- Remind the students to use the picture on the **Alphabet Sound Card** for their Special Letter to help them remember the letter's sound. The students are expected only to "master" their own Special Letter and share the information with their classmates. At this point in the year, they are not expected to blend and read the words by themselves. These are group activities in which you work with the students to help them gain insight into the alphabet.
- Have students note that what they learn about the letters and words applies to the words they work with in Big Book selections.
- Occasionally, have students find their special letters in a Big Book selection. Play some of the letter replacement and rearrangement games with words encountered in the Big Books.

Developing the Alphabetic Principle

Purpose

The following activities are extended to provide kindergarten students with a more thorough understanding of how sounds "work" in words. In this group of exercises, the students are introduced to specific letter/sound correspondences, consonants and short vowels. The students have previously been introduced to vowels and their special characteristics. This understanding is extended by introducing students to the convention that a vowel has a short sound in addition to its long sound. With this information and a carefully structured set of activities, the students can begin to explore and understand the alphabetic principle in a straightforward and thorough manner. The students not only listen for sounds in specified positions in words; they also link sounds to their corresponding letters. The activities in this group of lessons lay the groundwork for students to work their way through the entire alphabet as they learn letter-sound associations and to understand the purpose and the value of this learning.

Move the students quickly through these activities. Do not wait for all the students to master each letter/sound correspondence before going on. The students will have more opportunities to achieve mastery. The goal of these activities is for the students to obtain a basic understanding of the alphabetic principle.

Procedures

Introducing Consonant Letters and Sounds

- Point to the **Alphabet Sound Card** and name the letter.
- Point to the picture. Tell the students the sound of the letter and how the picture helps them to remember the sound. Repeat the sound several times.
- Tell the students you will read them the short story or an alliterative sentence to help them remember the sound of the letter. Read the story several times, emphasizing the words with the target sound. Have the students join in and say the sound.
- After introducing and reviewing a letter/sound correspondence, summarize the information on the **Alphabet Sound Card**.

Generating Words with the Target Sound

- Brainstorm to create a list of words that begin with the target sound. Write the words on the board or on a chart. Include any of the students' names that begin with the target sound.
- Play the *I'm Thinking of Something That Starts With* game. Begin with the target sound and add clues until the students guess the word. If the students guess a word that does not begin with the target sound, emphasize the beginning sound and ask if the word begins with the target sound.
- Silly Sentences. Make silly sentences with the students that include many words with the target sound. Encourage the students to participate by extending the sentences: *Mary mopes. Mary mopes on Monday. Mary and Michael mope on Monday in Miami.*

Listening for Initial Sounds

- Give each student a **Letter Card** for the target sound, /s/.
- Point to the picture on the **Alphabet Sound Card**, and have the students give the sound, /s/.
- Tell the students to listen for the first sound in each word you say. If it is /s/, they should hold up their *s* cards. Establish a signal so that the students know when to respond.
- Read a list of words, some beginning with /s/, some beginning with other sounds.

Listening for Final Sounds

The procedure for listening for the final sound of a word is the same as that for listening for the initial sound. The students may need to be reminded throughout the activity to pay attention to the *final* sound.

- Read a list of words, some ending with the target sound and some ending with other sounds. Avoid words that begin with the target sound.

Linking the Sound to the Letter

- **Word Pairs (initial sounds).** Write pairs of words on the board. One of each pair should begin with the target sound. Say the word beginning with the target sound, and ask the students to identify it. Remind them to listen for the target sound at the beginning of the word, to think about which letter makes that sound, and to find the word that begins with that letter. For example,
Target sound: /s/
Word pair: *fit sit*
Which word is *sit*?

- **Word Pairs (final sounds).** Follow the same procedure used for initial sounds, and direct the students to think about the sound that they hear at the end of the word. Since it is often more difficult for the students to attend to the ending sound, you may need to lead them through several pairs of words. Remind the students to listen for the target sound and to think about which letter makes that sound.
- **Writing Letters.** Using either of the handwriting systems outlined in the Program Appendix of *SRA/Open Court Reading*, or the system in use at your school, have students practice writing uppercase and lowercase letters. Remind the students about the letter sound, and have them repeat it.

Comparing Initial Consonant Sounds

This activity is exactly like **Listening for Initial Sounds** except that the students must discriminate between two sounds. They are given **Letter Cards** for both sounds and must hold up the appropriate card when they hear the sound.

Comparing Final Consonant Sounds

This activity is exactly like listening for final sounds except that the students must discriminate between two sounds. They are given **Letter Cards** for both sounds and must hold up the appropriate card when they hear the sound.

Linking the Consonant Sound to the Letter

In this activity to help students link sounds and letters, the students will make words either by adding initial consonants to selected word parts or by adding a different final consonant to a consonant-vowel-consonant combination.

The Alphabetic Principle: How the Alphabet Works (continued)

PROGRAM APPENDIX

Introducing Short Vowel Sounds

- Tell the students that the vowels are printed in red to remind them that they are special letters. (They are not special because they are printed in red.) They are special because they have more than one sound, and every word must have a vowel sound.
- Point to the long *Aa* **Alphabet Sound Card,** and remind the students that this letter is called a *vowel*. Vowels sometimes say their names in words: for example, *say, day, tray*. This vowel sound is called long *a*.
- Have the students repeat the sound.
- Sometimes vowels say different sounds. Point to the picture of the lamb on the short *Aa* card, and tell students that *a* also makes the sound heard in the middle of *lamb*. This is the short *a*. Read the short vowel story to help the students remember the short *a*.
- Have all the students join in saying /a/ /a/ /a/.

Listening for Short Vowel Sounds Versus Long Vowel Sounds

- Tell the students that you will read words with long *a* and short *a*. Review the two sounds.
- Give the students a signal to indicate when they hear the vowel sound. You may want one signal for short *a*, such as scrunching down, and another for long *a*, such as stretching up tall.
- Continue with lists of words such as: *add, back, aid, tan, bake, tame.*

Linking the Vowel Sound to the Letter

- Writing Letters. Have students practice writing the letter and review the sound of the letter.
- In this activity to help students link sounds and letters, the students will make words either by adding initial consonants to selected word parts or by adding a different final consonant to a consonant-vowel-consonant combination. Change the beginning of the word or the word ending, but retain the vowel sound to make new words:

at	hat	mat	pat
ap	map	tap	sap
am	Sam	Pam	ham

Comparing Short Vowel Sounds

This activity requires students to discriminate between short vowel sounds in the middle of words. Review the vowel sounds.

- Say a word, and have the students repeat it. Establish a signal to indicate whether they hear short *a* or short *o* in the middle of the word. For example, they can hold up the appropriate **Letter Card** when they hear a sound. Sample words: *cap, cot, rat, rot, rack, rock.*

Linking the Sound to the Letter

- In this activity write a word on the board, and help the students say it.
- Change the word by changing the vowel. Help the students say the new word, for example, *map, mop; hot, hat; pot, pat.*
- For a variation of this activity, write the pairs of words, and simply have the students say which word is the target word. For example, the students see *tap* and *top*. Ask which word *top* is, directing the students' attention to the vowel.

Tips

- Lead and model the exercises as necessary until the students begin to catch on and can participate with confidence.
- To keep the students focused on the various activities, have them tell you the task for each activity. For example, after telling the students to listen for final sounds, ask the students what they will be listening for.
- Actively involve the students by giving them opportunities to tell what they know rather than supplying the information for them. Do they know the letter name? Do they know the sound? Can they think of words that begin with the sound?
- Keeping the students focused on the idea that they are learning about sounds and letters so they can read these books themselves makes the lessons more relevant for the students.

The basic purpose of providing structured practice in phonemic awareness is to help the students hear and understand the sounds from which words are made. Before students can be expected to understand the sound/symbol correspondence that forms the base of written English, they need to have a strong working knowledge of the sound relationships that make up the spoken language. This understanding of spoken language lays the foundation for the transition to written language.

Phonemic awareness activities provide the students with easy practice in discriminating the sounds that make up words. Phonemic awareness consists of quick, gamelike activities designed to help students understand that speech is made up of distinct, identifiable sounds. The playful nature of the activities makes them appealing and engaging, while giving the students practice and support for learning about language. Once the students begin reading and writing, this experience with manipulating sounds will help them use what they know about sounds and letters to sound out and spell unfamiliar words when they read and write.

The two main formats for teaching phonemic awareness are oral blending and segmentation. These are supported by occasional discrimination activities and general wordplay. Oral blending encourages students to combine sounds to make words. Segmentation, conversely, requires them to isolate sounds from words. Other activities support discrimination, or recognition, of particular sounds. Sometimes simple songs, rhymes, or games engage students in wordplay. In these, the students manipulate words in a variety of ways. From these playful activities, the students derive serious knowledge about language.

As the students progress through different phonemic awareness activities, they will become proficient at listening for and reproducing the sounds they hear. It is essential for their progression to phonics and reading that they are able to hear the sounds and the patterns used to make up recognizable words. The phonemic awareness activities support the phonics instruction, but the activities are oral and do not focus on sound/spelling correspondences. Because the students are not expected to read the words they are experimenting with, any consonant and vowel sounds may be used, even if the students have not been formally taught the sound and its spellings.

Oral Blending

Purpose

In oral blending, the students are led through a progression of activities designed to help them hear how sounds are put together to make words.

Until students develop an awareness of the component parts of words, they have no tools with which to decode words or put letters together to form words. Oral blending helps students master these component parts of words, from syllables down to single sounds, or phonemes. Oral blending is not to be confused with the formal blending of specific sounds whose spellings the students will be taught through phonics instruction. Oral blending does not depend on the recognition of written words; it focuses instead on hearing the sounds.

Oral blending focuses on hearing sounds through a sequence that introduces the most easily distinguished word parts and then systematically moves to sound blending that contains all the challenges of phonic decoding (except letter recognition). This sequence provides support for the least-prepared student—one who comes to school with no concept of words or sounds within words. At the same time, the lively pace and playful nature of oral blending activities hold the interest of students who already have some familiarity with words and letters.

Oral blending prepares students for phonics instruction by developing an awareness of the separate sounds that make up speech. Oral blending activities then continue in concert with phonics instruction to reinforce and extend new learning. And, because these activities involve simply listening to and reproducing sounds, oral blending need not be restricted to the sounds students have been or will be taught in phonics.

The tone of the activities should be playful and informal and should move quickly. Although these activities will provide information about student progress, they are not diagnostic tools. Do not expect mastery. Those students who have not caught on will be helped more by varied experiences than by more drilling on the same activity.

Procedures

Following is a description of the progression of oral blending activities.

Syllable Blending

Syllables are easier to distinguish than individual sounds (phonemes), so students can quickly experience success in forming meaningful words. Tell the students that you are going to say some words in two parts. Tell them to listen carefully so that they can discover what the words are. Read each word, pronouncing each part distinctly with a definite pause between syllables broken by. . . . The lists of words that follow are arranged in sequence from easy to harder. They cover different types of cues. At any point where they fit in the sequence, include multisyllable names of students in the class.

Model

TEACHER: *dino . . . saur. What's the word?*

STUDENTS: *dinosaur*

Example Words

- First part of the word cues the whole word:
  vita . . . min　　*vaca . . . tion*
  hippopot . . . amus　　*ambu . . . lance*
- Two distinct words easily combined:
  butter. . . fly　　*straw. . . berry*
  surf . . . board　*basket . . . ball*

Phonemic Awareness (continued)

- Two distinct words, but first word could cue the wrong ending:
  tooth . . . ache   tooth . . . paste
  water . . . fall   water . . . melon
- First part, consonant + vowel, not enough to guess whole word:
  re . . . member   re . . . frigerator
  bi . . . cycle   bi . . . ology
- Identifying clues in second part:
  light . . . ning   sub . . . ject   in . . . sect
- Last part, consonant + vowel sound, carries essential information:
  yester . . . day   rain . . . bow
  noi . . . sy   pota . . . to
- Changing the final part changes the word:
  start . . . ing   start . . . er   start . . . ed

Initial Consonant Sounds

Initial consonant blending prepares students for consonant replacement activities that will come later. Tell the students that you will ask them to put some sounds together to make words. Pronounce each word part distinctly, and make a definite pause at the breaks indicated. When a letter is surrounded by slash marks, pronounce the letter's sound, not its name. When you see /s/, for example, you will say "ssss," not "ess." The words that follow are arranged from easy to harder. At any point where they fit in the sequence, include names of students in the class.

Model

TEACHER: /t/ . . . iger. What's the word?
STUDENTS: tiger

Example Words

- Separated consonant blend, with rest of word giving strong cue to word identity:
  /b/ . . . roccoli   /k/ . . . racker
  /f/ . . . lashlight   /k/ . . . reature
- Held consonant that is easy for students to hear, with rest of word giving strong cue:
  /s/ . . . innamon   /l/ . . . adybug
  /s/ . . . eventeen   /n/ . . . ewspaper
- Stop consonant that is harder for students to hear preceding vowel, with rest of word giving strong cue:
  /t/ . . . adpole   /p/ . . . iggybank
  /d/ . . . ragonfly   /b/ . . . arbecue
- Single-syllable words and words in which the second part gives a weaker cue:
  /s/ . . . ing   /l/ . . . augh   /v/ . . . ase

Final Consonant Sounds

In this phase of oral blending, the last sound in the word is separated.

Model

TEACHER: cabba . . . /j/. What's the word?
STUDENTS: cabbage

Example Words

- Words that are easily recognized even before the final consonant is pronounced:
  bubblegu . . . /m/   Columbu . . . /s/
  crocodi . . . /l/   submari . . . /n/
- Multisyllable words that need the final consonant for recognition:
  colle . . . /j/ (college)   come . . . /t/ (comet)
- Single-syllable words:
  sa . . . /d/   gra . . . /s/   snai . . . /l/

Initial Consonant Sound Replacement

This level of oral blending further develops awareness of initial consonant sounds. The activity begins with a common word, then quickly changes its initial consonant sound. Most of the words produced are nonsense words, which helps keep the focus on the sounds in the word. Note that the words are written on the board, but the students are not expected to read them. The writing is to help the students see that when the sounds change, the letters change, and vice versa.

Model

TEACHER: [Writes word on board.] This word is *magazine*. What is it?
STUDENTS: *magazine*
TEACHER: Now I'm going to change it. [Erases initial consonant.] Now it doesn't start with /m/, it's going to start with /b/. What's the new word?
STUDENTS: *bagazine*
TEACHER: That's right . . . [Writes b where m had been.] It's *bagazine*. Now I'm going to change it again. . . .

Repeat with different consonant sounds. Then do the same with other words, such as: *remember, Saturday, tomorrow, lotion,* and *million.* Continue with single-syllable words, such as: *take, big, boot, cot, seat, look, tap, ride,* and *late.* There are two stages in using written letters:

- The replacement letter is not written until *after* the new "word" has been identified.
- Later, the replacement letter is written *at the same time* the change in the initial phoneme is announced. For example, the teacher erases *d* and writes *m* while saying, "Now it doesn't start with /d/, it starts with /m/."

You may wish to alter the procedure when the consonants used have already been introduced in phonics by writing the replacement letter and having students sound out the new word. Feel free to switch between the two procedures within a single exercise. If the students are not responding orally to written spellings that have been introduced in phonics, don't force it. Proceed by saying the word before writing the letter, and wait until another time to move on to writing before pronouncing.

One-Syllable Words

The students now begin blending individual phonemes to form words. This important step can be continued well into the year. Continued repetitions of this activity will help the students realize how they can use the sound/spellings they are learning to read and write real words.

At first, the blended words are presented in a story context that helps the students identify the words. They soon recognize that they are actually decoding meaningful words. However, the context must not be so strong that the students can guess the word without listening to the phonemic cues. Any vowel sounds and irregularly spelled words may be used, since there is no writing involved.

Model

TEACHER: *When I looked out the window, I saw a /l/ /ī/ /t/. What did I see?*
STUDENTS: *A light.*
TEACHER: *Yes, I saw a light. At first I thought it was the /m/ /oo͞/ /n/. What did I think it was?*
STUDENTS: *The moon.*
TEACHER: *But it didn't really look like the moon. Suddenly I thought, maybe it's a space /sh/ /i/ /p/. What did I think it might be?*
STUDENTS: *A space ship!*

Once the students are familiar with this phase of oral blending, they can move to blending one-syllable words without the story context.

Example Words

- CVC (consonant/vowel/consonant) words beginning with easily blended consonant sounds (/sh/, /h/, /r/, /v/, /s/, /n/, /z/, /f/, /l/, /m/):
  nip   nap
- CVC words beginning with any consonant:
  ten   bug   lip
- Add CCVC words:
  flap   step
- Add CVCC words:
  most   band   went
- Add CCVCC words:
  stamp   grand   scuffs

Final Consonant Sound Replacement

Final consonant sounds are typically more difficult for students to use than initial consonants.

- Begin with multisyllable words, and move to one-syllable words.
- As with initial consonants, first write the changed consonant after students have pronounced the new word.
- Then write the consonant as they pronounce it.
- For sound/spellings introduced in phonics instruction, write the new consonant spelling, and have students identify and pronounce it.

Model

TEACHER: *[Writes word on board.] This word is* teapot. *What is it?*

STUDENTS: *teapot*

TEACHER: *Now I'm going to change it. [Erases final consonant.] Now it doesn't end with /t/, it ends with /p/. What's the word now?*

STUDENTS: *teapop*

TEACHER: *That's right . . . [Writes p where t had been.] It's* teapop. *Now I'm going to change it again. . . .*

Example Words

- Words that are easily recognized even before the final consonant is pronounced:
  *picnic   picnit   picnis   picnil
  picnid
  airplane   airplate   airplabe   airplafe*

- Multisyllable words that need the final consonant for recognition:
  *muffin   muffil   muffim   muffip   muffit
  amaze   amate   amake   amale   amade*

- Single-syllable words:
  *neat   nean   neap   neam   neaj   nead
  neaf
  broom   broot   brood   broof   broop
  broon*

Initial Vowel Replacement

Up to now, oral blending has concentrated on consonant sounds because they are easier to hear than vowels. As you move to vowel play, remember that the focus is still on the sounds, not the spellings. Use any vowel sounds.

Model

TEACHER: *[Writes word on board.] This word is* elephant. *What is it?*

STUDENTS: *elephant*

TEACHER: *Now I'm going to change it. [Erases initial vowel.] Now it doesn't start with /e/, it starts with /a/. What's the word now?*

STUDENTS: *alephant*

TEACHER: *That's right . . . [Writes a where e had been.] It's* alephant. *Now I'm going to change it again. . . .*

Example Words

- Multisyllable words:
  *angry   ingry   oongry   ungry   engry
  ivy   avy   oovy   evy   ovy   oivy*

- One-syllable words:
  *ink   ank   oonk   unk   onk   oink
  add   odd   idd   oudd   edd   udd*

Segmentation

Purpose

Segmentation and oral blending complement each other: Oral blending puts sounds together to make words, while segmentation separates words into sounds. Oral blending will provide valuable support for decoding when students begin reading independently.

Procedure

Syllables

The earliest segmentation activities focus on syllables, which are easier to distinguish than individual sounds, or phonemes. Start with students' names, then use other words. As with the oral blending activities, remember to move quickly through these activities. Do not hold the class back waiting for all students to catch on. Individual progress will vary, but drilling on one activity is less helpful than going on to others. Return to the same activity often. Frequent repetition is very beneficial and allows students additional opportunities to catch on.

- Say, for example, "Let's clap out Amanda's name. A-man-da."

- Have the students clap and say the syllables along with you. Count the claps.

- Tell the students that these word parts are called *syllables*. Don't try to explain; the idea will develop with practice. Once you have provided the term, simply say, "How many syllables?" after the students clap and count.

- Mix one-syllable and multisyllable words:
  *fantastic   tambourine   good
  imaginary   stand   afraid*

Comparative Length of Words

Unlike most phonemic awareness activities, this one involves writing on the board or on an overhead transparency. Remember, though, that the students are not expected to read what is written. They are merely noticing that words that take longer to say generally look longer when written.

- Start with students' names. Choose two names, one short and one long, with the same first initial (for example, *Joe* and *Jonathan*).

- Write the two names on the board, one above the other, so that the difference is obvious.

- Tell the students that one name is *Jonathan* and one is *Joe*. Have them pronounce and clap each name. Then, have them tell which written word they think says *Joe*.

- Move your finger under each name as they clap and say it, syllable by syllable.

- Repeat with other pairs of names and words, such as: *tea/telephone, cat/caterpillar,*

butterfly/bug. Be sure not to give false clues. For example, sometimes write the longer word on top, sometimes the shorter one; sometimes ask for the shorter word, sometimes the longer; sometimes ask for the top word, sometimes the bottom; sometimes point to a word and ask the students to name it, and sometimes name the word and ask the students to point to it.

Listen for Individual Sounds

Activities using a puppet help the students listen for individual sounds in words. Use any puppet you have on hand. When you introduce the puppet, tell the students that it likes to play word games. Each new activity begins with the teacher speaking to and for the puppet until the students determine the pattern. Next, students either speak for the puppet or correct the puppet. To make sure all the students are participating, alternate randomly between having the whole group or individuals respond. The activities focus on particular parts of words, according to the following sequence:

1. **Repeating last part of word.** Use words beginning with easy-to-hear consonants, such as *f, l, m, n, r, s,* and *z*. The puppet repeats only the rime, the part of the syllable after the initial consonant.

Model

TEACHER: *farm*

PUPPET: *arm*

Once the pattern is established, the students respond for the puppet.

TEACHER: *rope*

STUDENTS: *ope*

Example Words

Use words such as the following: *mine . . . ine   soup . . . oup   feet . . . eet*

2. **Restoring initial phonemes.** Now the students correct the puppet. Be sure to acknowledge the correction.

Model

TEACHER: *lake*

PUPPET: *ake*

TEACHER: *No, lllake. You forgot the /l/.*

TEACHER: *real*

PUPPET: *eal*

TEACHER: *What did the puppet leave off?*

STUDENTS: */r/. It's supposed to be* real.

TEACHER: *That's right. The word is* real.

Example Words

Use words such as the following:

look . . . ook   mouse . . . ouse   sand . . . and

3. **Segmenting initial consonants.** The puppet pronounces only the initial consonant.

Phonemic Awareness (continued)

Model

TEACHER: *pay*

PUPPET: /p/

Example Words

Use words such as the following:

moon . . . /m/   *nose* . . . /n/   *bell* . . . /b/

4. Restoring final consonants. The students correct the puppet. Prompt if necessary: *"What's the word? What did the puppet leave off?"*

Model

TEACHER: *run*

PUPPET: *ru*

STUDENTS: *It's run! You left off the /n/.*

TEACHER: *That's right. The word is* run.

Example Words

Use words such as the following:

meet. . . mee   cool . . . coo   boot. . . boo

5. Isolating final consonants. The puppet pronounces only the final consonant.

Model

TEACHER: *green*

PUPPET: /n/

Example Words

Use words such as the following:

glass . . . /s/   *boom* . . . /m/   *mice* . . . /s/

6. Segmenting initial consonant blends. The sounds in blends are emphasized.

Model

TEACHER: *clap*

PUPPET: *lap*

Next have students correct the puppet.

TEACHER: *stain*

PUPPET: *tain*

STUDENTS: *It's stain! You left off the /s/.*

TEACHER: *That's right. The word is* stain.

Example Words

Use words such as the following:

blaze . . . laze   draw. . . raw   proud . . . roud

Discrimination

Purpose

Discrimination activities help students focus on particular sounds in words.

Listening for long vowel sounds is the earliest discrimination activity. Vowel sounds are necessary for decoding, but young students do not hear them easily. This is evident in students' invented spellings, where vowels are often omitted. Early in the year, the students listen for long vowel sounds, which are more easily distinguished than short vowel sounds:

- Explain to the students that vowels are special, because sometimes they say their names in words.
- Tell the students which vowel sound to listen for.
- Have them repeat the sound when they hear it in a word. For example, if the target vowel sound is long e, the students will say long e when you say *leaf* but they should not respond when you say *loaf*.
- Initially the students should listen for one long vowel sound at a time. Later they can listen for two vowel sounds. All **Example Words**, however, should contain one of the target vowels.

Procedure

Listening for short vowel sounds discrimination activities should be done once the short vowels /a/ and /i/ have been introduced. Short vowels are very useful in reading. They are generally more regular in spelling than long vowels, and they appear in many short, simple words. However, their sounds are less easily distinguished than those of long vowels. Thus, the activities focus only on /a/ and /i/. All the words provided have one or the other of these sounds. Either have the students repeat the sound of a specified vowel, or vary the activity as follows: Write an *a* on one side of the board and an *i* on the other. Ask the students to point to the *a* when they hear a word with the /a/ sound and point to the *i* when they hear a word with the /i/ sound. Use words such as the following:

bat	mat	sat	sit	spit
pit	pat	pan	pin	spin

Consonant sounds in multisyllable words. Discriminating these sounds helps students attend to consonant sounds in the middle of words.

- Say the word *rib*, and have the students repeat it. Ask where they hear the /b/ in *rib*.
- Then say *ribbon* and ask the students where they hear the /b/ in *ribbon*.
- Tell the students that you will say some words and they will repeat each word.
- After they repeat each word, ask what consonant sound they hear in the middle of that word. Use words such as the following:

famous	message	picky
jogger	flavor	zipper

Phonemic Play

Purpose

Wordplay activities help the students focus on and manipulate sounds, thus supporting the idea that words are made of specific sounds that can be taken apart, put together, or changed to make new words. Through wordplay, students gain important knowledge about language.

Procedure

Producing rhymes. Many phonemic play activities focus on producing rhymes. A familiar or easily learned rhyme or song is introduced, and the students are encouraged to substitute words or sounds. An example is "*Willaby Wallaby Woo*," in which students change the rhyming words in the couplet "*Willaby Wallaby Woo/An elephant sat on you*" so that the second line ends with a student's name and the first line ends with a rhyme beginning with W (for example, "*Willaby Wallaby Wissy/An elephant sat on Missy*").

Generate alliterative words. Students can also say as many words as they can think of that begin with a given consonant sound. This is a valuable complement to discrimination activities in which the teacher produces the words and the students identify them.

The purpose of phonics instruction is to teach students the association between the sounds of the language and the written symbols—spellings—that have been chosen to represent those sounds.

As with all alphabetic languages, English has a limited number of symbols—twenty-six—that are combined and recombined to make the written language. These written symbols are a visual representation of the speech sounds we use to communicate. This is simply a code. The faster the students learn the code and how it works, the faster the whole world of reading opens to them.

Students are introduced to the sounds and spellings of English in a very systematic, sequential manner. This allows them to continually build on what they learned the day before. As each sound/symbol relationship is introduced, students learn about and practice with words containing the target sound/spelling and then reinforce their learning through the use of engaging text specifically written for this purpose.

It can be very difficult for students to hear the individual sounds, or phonemes, that make up words. When phonics instruction is explicit—students are told the sounds associated with the different written symbols—there is no guesswork involved. They know that this sound /b/ is spelled *b*. Therefore, students in an SRA/Open Court Reading classroom spend time learning to discriminate individual speech sounds, and then they learn the spellings of those sounds. This systematic, explicit approach affords students the very best chance for early and continuing success.

Sound/Spelling Cards

Purpose

The purpose of the **Sound/Spelling Cards** (Levels 1–3) is to remind the students of the sounds of English and their spellings. The name of the picture on each card contains the target sound at the beginning for the consonants and in the middle for most vowels. In addition, the picture associates a sound with an action. This association is introduced through an interactive story in which the pictured object or character "makes" the sound. These cards are a resource for the students to use to remember sound/spelling associations for both reading and writing.

Procedure

Posting the Cards

Initially, post the first twenty-six cards with the picture to the wall so that only the alphabet letters on the backs show. As you introduce each card, you will turn it to show the picture and the spellings on the front of the card. If, however, most of your students already have some knowledge of the letters—this is a second- or third-grade classroom and students are reviewing what they learned the year before—you may want to go ahead and place the cards with the picture and the spellings facing forward to provide support as they begin writing. Make sure that the cards are positioned so that you can touch them with your hand or with a pointer when you refer to them and so that all of the students can see them easily. The cards should be placed where the students can readily see them during reading and writing.

Special Devices

■ Vowel spellings are printed in red to draw attention to them. Consonants are printed in black. The blank line in a spelling indicates that a letter will take the place of the blank in a word. For example, the replacement of the blank with *t* in the spelling *a_e* makes the word *ate*. The blank lines may also indicate the position of a spelling in a word or a syllable. The blank in *h_* for example, means that the spelling occurs at the beginning of a word or a syllable.

■ The blanks in *_ie_* indicate that the *ie* spelling comes in the middle of a word or a syllable, while the blank in *_oy* shows that the *oy* spelling comes at the end of a word or a syllable. Uses of blanks in specific spellings are in the lessons. Please note now, however, that when you write a spelling of a sound on the board or an overhead transparency, you should include the blanks.

■ The color of the background behind the spellings also has a meaning. Consonants have a white background. The colors behind vowel spellings are pronunciation clues. Short vowel spellings have a green background, which corresponds to the green box that appears before some consonant spellings. Thus, before *ck* or *x* you will see a green box, which indicates that a short vowel always precedes that spelling. Long vowel spellings have a yellow background; other vowel spellings, such as r-controlled vowels and diphthongs, have a blue background. The color code reinforces the idea that vowels are special and have different pronunciations.

Introducing the Sound/Spelling Cards

In first grade, each sound and spelling is introduced by using a see/hear/say/write sequence. In grades two and three the same sequence is used in the review of the cards.

1. **See:** Students see the spelling or spellings on the **Sound/Spelling Card** and the board or an overhead transparency.
2. **Hear:** Students hear the sound used in words and in isolation in the story. The sound is, of course, related to the picture (and the action) shown on the **Sound/Spelling Card.**
3. **Say:** Students say the sound.
4. **Write:** Students write the spelling(s) for the sound.

There are a number of important points to remember about this technique.

■ The first item written on the board or an overhead transparency is the spelling of the sound being introduced. This gives the spelling a special emphasis in the mind of the student. It is the "see" part of the sequence.

■ One of the causes of blending failure is the failure to teach sounds thoroughly during introduction of the **Sound/Spelling Card** and during initial sounding and blending. To help ensure success for all students, make certain that every student is able to see the board or screen.

■ After you present the sound and spelling, have several students go to the board to write the spelling. Have them say the sound as they write the spelling. After they have written the spelling of the sound, give them a chance to proofread their own work. Then give the other

Explicit, Systematic Phonics (continued)

students the opportunity to help with proofreading by noting what is good about the spelling and then suggesting how to make it better.

Sample Lesson, Using the Letter m and the Sound /m/

- Point to the **Sound/Spelling Card 13 Monkey** and have students tell you whether it is a vowel or a consonant. Have them tell the name of the card. If they do not know it, tell them it is Monkey. Point to the *monkey* in the picture and say the word monkey, emphasizing the initial consonant sound—*mmmonkey*.

- Point to the spelling *m*. Tell students that /m/ is spelled *m*.

- If you wish, make up an alliterative sentence about the Monkey, or use the alliterative story that accompanies the card. (In first grade this story is printed on the page on which the card is introduced and in the Appendix. In grades two and three, the cards are printed in the Appendix of the **Teacher's Edition**.) For example, *When Muzzie the monkey munches bananas, the sound she makes is /mmmmmm/.*

- If students had **SRA/Open Court Reading** before, you can ask them if they learned an action such as rubbing their tummies to help them remember the sound. If your students don't have an action they associate with the cards already, make some up with your students. They will have fun, and it will be another way for them to remember the sound/spelling relationships.

- Write *m* on the board or on an overhead transparency and say the sound. Write the letter again and ask the students to say the sound with you as they write the letter on slates, on paper, or with their index finger on a surface. Repeat this activity several times.

- Have the students listen for words beginning with /m/, indicating by some signal, such as thumbs-up or thumbs-down, whether they hear the /m/ sound and saying /m/ when they hear it in a word. Repeat with the sound in various positions in words. Encourage students to tell you and the class words with /m/ at the beginning and end as well as in the middle of words.

- Check students' learning by pointing to the card. Have students identify the sound, name the spelling, and discuss how the card can help them remember the sound.

Individual Sound/Spelling Cards

Use the **Individual Sound/Spelling Cards** for review and for small-group reteaching and practice sessions. Students can use them alone or with partners. Here are some suggestions for activities using the **Individual Sound/Spelling Cards**:

1. **Saying sounds from pictures.** The leader flashes pictures as the others say the sound each picture represents.

2. **Saying sounds.** The leader flashes the spellings on the cards as the others say the sound that the spellings represent.

> *The faster the students learn the code and how it works, the faster the whole world of reading opens to them.*

3. **Naming spellings from pictures.** The leader flashes pictures. The others name the card, say the sound, and then name as many spellings as they can.

4. **Writing spellings from the pictures.** Working alone, a student looks at a picture and then writes as many spellings for that **Sound/Spelling Card** as he or she can remember.

5. **Saying words from pictures.** The leader presents a series of pictures. The others form words by blending the sounds represented.

Blending

Purpose

The purpose of blending is to teach the students a strategy for figuring out unfamiliar words. Initially, students will be blending sound by sound. Ultimately, the students will sound and blend only those words that they cannot read. Eventually, the blending process will become quick and comfortable for them.

Procedure

Learning the sounds and their spellings is only the first step in learning to read and write. The second step is learning to blend the sounds into words.

Blending Techniques

Blending lines are written on the board or an overhead transparency as the students watch and participate. The lines and sentences should not be written out before class begins. It is through the sound-by-sound blending of the words and the sentences that the students learn the blending process.

Sound-by-Sound Blending

- Write the spelling of the first sound in the word. Point to the spelling, and say the sound.

- Have the students say the sound with you as you say the sound again. Write the spelling of the next sound. Point to the spelling, and say the sound. Have the students say the sound with you as you say the sound again. After you have written the vowel spelling, blend through the vowel (unless the vowel is the first letter of the word), making the blending motion—a smooth sweeping of the hand beneath the sounds, linking them from left to right, for example, *ba*. As you make the blending motion, make sure that your hand is under the letter that corresponds to the sound you are saying at the moment.

- Have the students blend through the vowel. Write the spelling of the next sound. Point to the spelling and say the sound. Have the students say the sound with you as you touch the letter and say the sound again.

- Continue as described above through the word. After pronouncing the final sound in the word, make the blending motion from left to right under the word as you blend the sounds. Then have the students blend the word. Let them be the first to pronounce the word normally.

- Ask a student to read the word again and use it in a sentence. Ask another student to extend the sentence—that is, make it longer by giving more information. Help the student by asking an appropriate question about the sentence, using, for example, *How? When? Where?* or *Why?* Continue blending the rest of the words.

Whole-Word Blending

Once students are comfortable with sound-by-sound blending, they are ready for whole-word blending.

- Write the whole word to be blended on the board or an overhead transparency.
- Ask the students to blend the sounds as you point to them.
- Then have the students say the whole word.
- Ask the students to use the word in a sentence and then to extend the sentence.
- When all of the words have been blended, point to words randomly and ask individuals to read them.

Blending Syllables

In reading the **Student Anthologies,** students will often encounter multisyllabic words. Some students are intimidated by long words, yet many multisyllabic words are easily read by reading and blending the syllables rather than the individual sounds. Following a set of rules for syllables is difficult since so many of the rules have exceptions. Students need to remember that each syllable in a word contains one vowel sound.

- Have students identify the vowel sounds in the word.
- Have students blend the first syllable sound by sound if necessary or read the first syllable.
- Handle the remaining syllables the same way.
- Have students blend the syllables together to read the word.

Blending Sentences

Blending sentences is the logical extension of blending words. Blending sentences helps students develop fluency, which is critical to comprehension. Encourage students to reread sentences with phrasing and natural intonation.

- Write the sentence on the board or on a transparency, underlining any high-frequency sight words—words that the students cannot decode either because they are irregular or because they contain sounds or spellings that the students have not yet learned or reviewed. If the students have not read these words before, write the words on the board or an overhead transparency and introduce them before writing the sentence. These words should not be blended but read as whole words.

Building for Success

A primary cause of students' blending failure is their failure to understand how to use the **Sound/Spelling Cards.** Students need to practice sounds and spellings when the **Sound/Spelling Cards** are introduced and during initial blending. They also need to understand that if they are not sure of how to pronounce a spelling, they can check the cards.

Early blending may be frustrating. You must lead the group almost constantly. Soon, however, leaders in the group will take over. Watch to see whether any students are having trouble during the blending. Include them in small-group instruction sessions. At that time you may want to use the vowel-first procedure described below to reteach blending lines.

Extra Help

In working with small groups during **Workshop,** you may want to use some of the following suggestions to support students who need help with blending.

Vowel-First Blending

Vowel-first blending is an alternative to sound-by-sound and whole-word blending for students who need special help. Used in small-group sessions, this technique helps students who have difficulty with the other two types of blending to focus on the most important part of each word, the vowels, and to do only one thing at a time. These students are not expected to say a sound and blend it with another at virtually the same time. The steps to use in vowel-first blending follow:

> *Blending is the heart of phonics instruction and the key strategy students must learn to open the world of written language.*

1. Across the board or on an overhead transparency, write the vowel spelling in each of the words in the line. For a short vowel, the line may look like this:
   a a a
   For a long vowel, the line may look like this:
   ee ea ea
2. Point to the spelling as the students say the sound for the spelling.
3. Begin blending around the vowels. In front of the first vowel spelling, add the spelling for the beginning sound of the word. Make the blending motion, and have the students blend through the vowel, adding a blank to indicate that the word is still incomplete. Repeat this procedure for each partial word in the line until the line looks like this:
   ma__ sa__ pa__
   see__ mea__ tea__
4. Have the students blend the partial word again as you make the blending motion and then add the spelling for the ending sound.

5. Make the blending motion, and have the students blend the completed word—for example, *mat* or *seed*.
6. Ask a student to repeat the word and use it in a sentence. Then have another student extend the sentence.
7. Repeat steps 4, 5, and 6 for each word in the line, which might look like this:
   mat sad pan
   or
   seed meat team

Tips

- In the early lessons, do blending with as much direction and dialogue as is necessary for success. Reduce your directions to a minimum as soon as possible. You have made good progress when you no longer have to say, "Sound—Sound—Blend," because the students automatically sound and blend as you write.
- Unless the line is used to introduce or to reinforce a spelling pattern, always ask a student to use a word in a sentence and then to extend the sentence immediately after you've developed the word. If the line is used to introduce or to reinforce a spelling pattern, however, ask the students to give sentences at the end of the line. Students will naturally extend sentences by adding phrases to the ends of the sentences. Encourage them to add phrases at the beginning or in the middle of the sentence.
- Use the vowel-first procedure in small group preteaching or reteaching sessions with students who are having a lot of trouble with blending. Remember that you must adapt the blending lines in the lessons to the vowel-first method.
- The sight words in the sentences cannot be blended. The students must approach them as sight words to be memorized. If students are having problems reading sight words, tell them the words.
- Cue marks written over the vowels may help students.
  - ✓ Straight line cue for long vowels
    EXAMPLES: *āpe, mē, fīne, sō, ūse*
  - ✓ Curved line cue for short vowels
    EXAMPLES: *căt, pĕt, wĭn, hŏt, tŭg*
  - ✓ Tent cue for variations of a and o
    EXAMPLES: *âll, ôff*
  - ✓ Dot cue for schwa sound with multiple-syllable words
    EXAMPLES: *salȧd, planėt, pencil, wagȯn*

Dictation and Spelling

Purpose

The purpose of dictation is to teach the students to spell words based on the sounds and spellings. In addition, learning dictation gives students a new strategy for reflecting on the sounds they hear in words to help them with their own writing.

As the students learn that sounds and spellings are connected to form words and that words form sentences, they begin to learn the standard spellings that will enable others to read their writing. As students learn to encode correctly, they develop their visual memory for words (spelling ability) and hence increase their writing fluency. Reinforcing the association between sounds and spellings and words through dictation gives students a spelling strategy that provides support and reassurance for writing independently. Reflecting on the sounds they hear in words will help students develop writing fluency as they apply the strategy to writing unfamiliar words.

A dictation activity is a learning experience; it is not a test. The students should be encouraged to ask for as much help as they need. The proofreading techniques are an integral part of dictation. Students' errors lead to self-correction and, if need be, to reteaching. The dictation activities must not become a frustrating ordeal. The students should receive reinforcement and feedback.

There are two kinds of dictation: Sounds-in-Sequence Dictation and Whole-Word Dictation. The two types differ mainly in the amount of help they give the students in spelling the words. The instructions vary for each type.

Procedure

Sounds-in-Sequence Dictation

Sounds-in-Sequence Dictation gives the students the opportunity to spell words sound by sound, left to right, checking the spelling of each sound as they write. (Many students write words as they think they hear and say the words, not as the words are actually pronounced or written.)

- Pronounce the first word to be spelled. Use the word in a sentence and say the word again (word/sentence/word). Have students say the word.
- Tell students to think about the sounds they hear in the word. Ask, "What's the first sound in the word?"
- Have students say the sound.
- Point to the **Sound/Spelling Card**, and direct the students to check the card. Ask what the spelling is. The students should say the spelling and then write it.

- Proceed in this manner until the word is complete.
- Proofread. You can write the word on the board as a model, or have a student do it. Check the work by referring to the **Sound/Spelling Cards**. If a word is misspelled, have the students circle the word and write it correctly, either above the word or next to it.

Whole-Word Dictation

Whole-Word Dictation gives the students the opportunity to practice this spelling strategy with less help from the teacher.

- Pronounce the word, use the word in a sentence, and then repeat the word (word/sentence/word). Have the students repeat the word. Tell the students to think about the word. Remind the students to check the **Sound/Spelling Cards** for spellings and to write the word.
- Proofread. Write or have a volunteer write the word on the board as a model. Check the word by referring to the **Sound/Spelling Cards**.

Sentence Dictation

Writing dictated sentences. Help students apply this spelling strategy to writing sentences. Dictation supports the development of fluent and independent writing. Dictation of a sentence will also help the students apply conventions of written language, such as capitalization and punctuation.

- Say the complete sentence aloud.
- Dictate one word at a time following the procedure for Sounds-in-Sequence Dictation.

Continue this procedure for the rest of the words in the sentence. Remind the students to put a period at the end. Then proofread the sentence, sound by sound, or word by word. When sentences contain sight words, the sight words should be dictated as whole words, not sound by sound. As the students learn to write more independently, the whole sentence can be dictated word by word.

Proofreading

Whenever the students write, whether at the board or on paper, they should proofread their work. Proofreading is an important technique because it allows the students to learn by self-correction and it gives them an immediate second chance for success. It is the same skill students will use as they proofread their writing. Students should proofread by circling—not by erasing—each error. After they circle an error, they should write the correction beside the circle. This type of correction allows you and the students to see the error as well as the correct form. Students also can see what needs to be changed and how they have made their own work better.

You may want to have students use a colored pencil to circle and write in the correction. This will make it easier for them to see the changes.

Procedure for Proofreading

- Have a student write the word or sentence on the board or on an overhead transparency.
- Have students tell what is good.
- Have students identify anything that can be made better.
- If there is a mistake, have the student circle it and write it correctly.
- Have the rest of the class proofread their own work.

The Word Building Game

The major reason for developing writing alongside reading is that reading and writing are complementary communicative processes. Decoding requires that students blend the phonemes together into familiar cohesive words. Spelling requires that students segment familiar cohesive words into separate phonemes. Both help students develop an understanding of how the alphabetic principle works.

The Word Building game gives the students a chance to exercise their segmentation abilities and to practice using the sounds and spellings they are learning. The game is a fast-paced activity in which the students spell related sets of words with the teacher's guidance. (Each successive word in the list differs from the previous one by one sound.)

For the Word Building game, the students use their **Individual Letter Cards** (Levels K and 1) to build the words. (As an alternative they can use pencil and paper.) You will be writing at the board.

Give the students the appropriate **Letter Cards.** For example, if the list for the Word Building game is *am*, *at*, *mat*, they will need their *a*, *m*, and *t* **Letter Cards.**

- Say the first word, such as *am*. (Use it in a sentence if you wish.) Have the students repeat the word. Say the word slowly, sound by sound. Tell the students to look at the **Sound/Spelling Cards** to find the letters that spell the sounds. Touch the first sound's card, in this case the Lamb card, and have students say the sound. Continue the process with the second sound. Write the word on the board while the students use their **Letter Cards** to spell it. Have students compare their words with your word, make changes as needed, and then blend and read the word with you.
- The students will then change the first word to make a different word. Say the next word in the list, (*at*). Segment the sounds of the word, and have students find the **Sound/Spelling Cards** that correspond. Write the new word (*at*) under the first word (*am*) on the board and have the students change their cards to spell the new word. Have them compare their words to yours and make changes as needed. Blend and read the word with the students. Continue in a like manner through the word list.

Spelling Strategies

Spelling

Many people find English difficult, because English sound/spelling patterns seem to have a million exceptions. The key to becoming a good speller, however, is not just memorization. The key is recognizing and internalizing English spelling patterns. Some people do this naturally as they read and develop large vocabularies. They intuitively recognize spelling patterns and apply them appropriately. Others need explicit and direct teaching of vocabulary and spelling strategies and spelling patterns before they develop spelling consciousness.

Purpose

Spelling is a fundamental skill in written communication. Although a writer may have wonderful ideas, he or she may find it difficult to communicate those ideas without spelling skills. Learning to spell requires much exposure to text and writing. For many it requires a methodical presentation of English spelling patterns.

English Spelling Patterns

A basic understanding of English spelling patterns will help provide efficient and effective spelling instruction. Just as the goal of phonics instruction is to enable students to read fluently, the goal of spelling instruction is to enable students to write fluently so they can concentrate on ideas rather than spelling.

- **Sound Patterns** Many words are spelled the way they sound. Most consonants and short vowels are very regular. Once a student learns the sound/spelling relationships, he or she has the key to spelling many words.

- **Structural Patterns** Structural patterns are employed when adding endings to words. Examples of structural patterns include doubling the final consonant, adding –s or –es to form plurals, and dropping the final e before adding –ing, -ed, -er, or –est. Often these structural patterns are very regular in their application. Many students have little trouble learning these patterns.

- **Meaning Patterns** Many spelling patterns in English are *morphological*; in other words, the meaning relationship is maintained regardless of how a sound may change. Prefixes, suffixes, and root words that retain their spellings regardless of how they are pronounced are further examples of meaning patterns.

- **Foreign Language Patterns** Many English words are derived from foreign words and retain those language patterns. For example, *kindergarten* (German), *boulevard* (French), and *ballet* (French from Italian) are foreign language patterns at work in English.

Developmental Stages of Spelling

The most important finding in spelling research in the past thirty years is that students learn to spell in a predictable developmental sequence, much as they learn to read. It appears to take the average student three to six years to progress through the developmental stages and emerge as a fairly competent, mature speller.

Prephonemic The first stage is the *prephonemic* stage, characterized by random letters arranged either in continuous lines or in word-like clusters. Only the writer can "read" it, and it may be "read" differently on different days.

Semiphonemic As emergent readers learn that letters stand for sounds, they use particular letters specifically to represent the initial consonant sound and sometimes a few other very salient sounds. This marks the discovery of *phonemic awareness* that letters represent speech sounds in writing.

Phonemic When students can represent most of the sounds they hear in words, they have entered the *phonemic* stage of spelling. They spell what they hear, using everything they know about letter sounds, letter names, and familiar words. Many remedial spellers never develop beyond this stage and spell a word the way it sounds whenever they encounter a word they can't spell.

Transitional or Within Word Pattern As they are exposed to more difficult words, students discover that not all words are spelled as they sound. They learn that they must include silent letters, spell past tenses with –ed, include a vowel even in unstressed syllables, and remember how words look. The *transitional* stage represents the transition from primarily phonemic strategies to rule-bound spelling.

Derivational The *derivational* stage occurs as transitional spellers accumulate a large spelling vocabulary and gain control over affixes, contractions, homophones and other meaning patterns. They discover that related or derived forms of words share spelling features even if they do not sound the same. As spellers gain control over these subtle word features and spell most words correctly, they become conventional spellers.

Procedures

The spelling lessons are organized around different spelling patterns, beginning with phonetic spelling patterns and progressing to other types of spelling patterns in a logical sequence. Word lists including words from the literature selection focus on the particular patterns in each lesson. In general, the sound patterns occur in the first units at each grade, followed by structural patterns, meaning patterns, and foreign language patterns in the upper grade levels.

- As you begin each new spelling lesson, have students identify the spelling pattern and how it is like and different from other patterns.
- Give the pretest to help students focus on the lesson pattern.
- Have students proofread their own pretests immediately after the test, crossing out any misspellings and writing the correct spelling.
- Have them diagnose whether the errors they made were in the lesson pattern or in another part of the word. Help students determine where they made errors and what type of pattern they should work on to correct them.
- As students work through the spelling pages from the *Spelling and Vocabulary Skills* book, encourage them to practice the different spelling strategies in the exercises.

Sound Pattern Strategies

✓ **Pronunciation Strategy** As students encounter an unknown word, have them say the word carefully to hear each sound. Encourage them to check the **Sound/Spelling Cards.** Then have them spell each sound. (/s/ + /i/ + /t/: *sit*)

✓ **Consonant Substitution** Have students switch consonants. The vowel spelling usually remains the same. (*bat, hat, rat, flat, splat*)

✓ **Vowel Substitution** Have students switch vowels. The consonant spellings usually remain the same. (CVC: *hit, hat, hut, hot;* CVCV: *mane, mine;* CVVC: *boat, beat, bait, beet*)

✓ **Rhyming Word Strategy** Have students think of rhyming words and the rimes that spell a particular sound. Often the sound will be spelled the same way in another word. (*cub, tub, rub*)

Structural Pattern Strategies

✓ **Conventions Strategy** Have students learn the rule and exceptions for adding endings to words (dropping *y*, dropping *e*, doubling the final consonant, and so on).

✓ **Proofreading Strategy** Many spelling errors occur because of simple mistakes. Have students check their writing carefully and specifically for spelling.

✓ **Visualization Strategy** Have students think about how a word looks. Sometimes words "look" wrong because a wrong spelling pattern has been written. Have them double-check the spelling of any word that looks wrong.

Meaning Pattern Strategies

✓ **Family Strategy** When students are not sure of a spelling, have them think of how words from the same base word family are spelled. (*critic, criticize, critical; sign, signal, signature*)

Spelling and Vocabulary Strategies (continued)

✓ **Meaning Strategy** Have students determine a homophone's meaning to make sure they are using the right word. Knowing prefixes, suffixes, and base words will also help.

✓ **Compound Word Strategy** Tell students to break a compound apart and spell each word. Compounds may not follow conventions rules for adding endings. *(homework, nonetheless)*

✓ **Foreign Language Strategy** Have students think of foreign language spellings that are different from English spelling patterns. *(ballet, boulevard, sauerkraut)*

✓ **Dictionary Strategy** Ask students to look up the word in a dictionary to make sure their spelling is correct. If they do not know how to spell a word, have them try a few different spellings and look them up to see which one is correct. *(fotograph, photograph)* This develops a spelling consciousness.

Use the Final Test to determine understanding of the lesson spelling pattern and to identify any other spelling pattern problems. Encourage student understanding of spelling patterns and use of spelling strategies in all their writing to help transfer spelling skills to writing.

Vocabulary Strategies

Purpose

Strong vocabulary skills are correlated to achievement throughout school. The purpose of vocabulary strategy instruction is to teach students a range of strategies for learning, remembering, and incorporating unknown vocabulary words into their existing reading, writing, speaking, and listening vocabularies.

Procedures

The selection vocabulary instruction in the first and second part of the lesson focuses on teaching specific vocabulary necessary for understanding the literature selection more completely. The weekly vocabulary instruction in the Language Arts part of each lesson is geared toward teaching vocabulary skills and strategies to build and secure vocabulary through word relationships or develop vocabulary strategies for unknown words.

General Strategies

There is no question that having students read and reading to students are effective vocabulary instructional strategies. Most word learning occurs through exposure to words in listening and reading. Multiple exposures to words, particularly when students hear, see, say, and write words, is also effective. Word play, including meaning and dictionary games, helps to develop a word consciousness as well.

Vocabulary Skills and Strategies

Word Relationships People effectively learn new words by relating them to words they already know. An understanding of different word relationships enables students to quickly and efficiently secure new vocabulary. The weekly vocabulary lessons are organized around these types of word groups. Word relationships include:

■ **Antonyms** Words with opposite or nearly opposite meanings. *(hot/cold)*

■ **Synonyms** Words with similar meanings. *(cup, mug, glass)*

■ **Multiple Meanings** Words that have more than one meaning. *(run, dressing, bowl)*

■ **Shades of Meaning** Words that express degrees of a concept or quality. *(like, love, worship)*

■ **Levels of Specificity** Words that describe at different levels of precision. *(living thing, plant, flower, daffodil)*

■ **Analogies** Pairs of words that have the same relationship. *(ball is to baseball as puck is to hockey)*

■ **Compound Words** Words comprised of two or more words. *(daylight)*

■ **Homographs** Words that are spelled the same but have different meanings and come from different root words. *(bear, count)*

■ **Homophones** Words that sound the same but have different spellings and meanings. *(mane/main, to/two/too)*

■ **Base Word Families** Words that have the same base word. *(care, careless, careful, uncaring, carefree)*

■ **Prefixes** An affix attached before a base word that changes the meaning of the word. *(misspell)*

■ **Suffixes** An affix attached to the end of a base word that changes the meaning of the word. *(careless)*

■ **Concept Vocabulary** Words that help develop understanding of a concept. *(space, sun, Earth, satellite, planet, asteroid)*

■ **Classification and Categorization** Sorting words by related meanings. *(colors, shapes, animals, foods)*

Contextual Word Lists Teaching vocabulary in context is another way to secure understanding of unknown words. Grouping words by subject area such as science, social studies, math, descriptive words, new words, and so on enables students to connect word meanings and build vocabulary understanding.

■ **Figurative Language** Idioms, metaphors, similes, personification, puns, and novel meanings need to be specifically taught, especially for English language learners.

■ **Derivational Word Lists** Presenting groups of words derived from particular languages or with specific roots or affixes is an effective way to reinforce meanings and spellings of foreign words and word parts.

Vocabulary Strategies for Unknown Words

Different strategies have been shown to be particularly effective for learning completely new words. These strategies are included in the *Spelling and Vocabulary Skills* activities.

Key Word This strategy involves providing or having students create a mnemonic clue for unknown vocabulary. For example, the word *mole* is defined in chemistry as a "gram molecule." By relating *mole* to *molecule*, students have a key to the meaning of the word.

Definitions Copying a definition from a dictionary is somewhat effective in learning new vocabulary. Combining this with using the word in writing and speaking adds to the effectiveness of this strategy. Requiring students to explain a word or use it in a novel sentence helps to ensure that the meaning is understood.

Context Clues Many words are learned from context, particularly with repeated exposure to words in reading and listening. Without specific instruction in consciously using context clues, however, unknown words are often ignored.

■ **Syntax** How a word is used in a sentence provides some clue to its meaning.

■ **External Context Clues** Hints about a word's meaning may appear in the setting, words, phrases, or sentences surrounding a word in text. Other known words in the text may be descriptive, may provide a definition (apposition), may be compared or contrasted, or may be used synonymously in context. Modeling and teaching students to use context to infer a word's meaning can help in learning unknown words.

Word Structure Examining the affixes and roots of a word may provide some clue to its meaning. Knowing the meaning of at least part of the word can provide a clue to its meaning. (For example, *unenforceable* can be broken down into meaningful word parts.)

Semantic Mapping Having students create a semantic map of an unknown word after learning its definition helps them to learn it. Have students write the new word and then list in a map or web all words they can think of that are related to it.

Semantic Feature Analysis A semantic feature analysis helps students compare and contrast similar types of words within a category to help secure unknown words. Have students chart, for example, the similarities and differences between different types of sports, including new vocabulary such as *lacrosse* and *cricket*.

Developing Vocabulary

Purpose

Vocabulary is closely connected to comprehension. Considerable vocabulary growth occurs incidentally during reading. A clear connection exists between vocabulary development and the amount of reading a person does, and there are strong indications that vocabulary instruction is important and that understanding the meaning of key words helps with comprehension.

In *Open Court Reading,* vocabulary is addressed before, during, and after reading. Before reading, the teacher presents vocabulary words from the selection. Students use skills such as context clues, apposition, and structural analysis to figure out the meaning of the words. These selection vocabulary words are not only important to understanding the text but are also high-utility words that can be used in discussing and writing about the unit theme.

During reading, students monitor their understanding of words and text. When they do not understand something, they stop and clarify what they have read. Students will use these same skills—context clues, apposition, structural elements, and the like—to clarify the meanings of additional words encountered while reading. Figuring out the meanings of words while reading prepares students for the demands of independent reading both in and out of school.

After reading, students review the vocabulary words that they learned before reading the selection. They also review any interesting words that they identified and discussed during reading. Students record in their Writer's Notebook both the selection vocabulary words and the interesting words they identified during their reading and are encouraged to use both sets of words in discussion and in writing.

Procedure

Before students read a selection, the teacher uses an overhead transparency to introduce the selection vocabulary to the class. The transparency contains two sentences for each selection vocabulary word. Students must use context clues, apposition, or word structure in the sentences to figure out the meaning of the underlined vocabulary words. If students cannot figure out the meaning of the word using one of these skills, they can consult the glossary or dictionary.

Below are suggestions for modeling the use of context clues, apposition, or word structure to figure out the meaning of a word.

Modeling Using Context Clues

Have students read the sentences on the transparency. Explain to students that they will use *context clues,* or other words in the sentence, to figure out the meaning of the underlined word. For example, if the word is "treacherous," the sentences might include:

1. Mrs. Frisby must undertake a <u>treacherous</u> journey to bring her son some medicine.

2. We took a <u>treacherous</u> walk near a swamp filled with crocodiles.

Have students look for clues in the sentences that might help them understand the meaning of the underlined word. Point out that a good clue in the second sentence is "near a swamp filled with crocodiles." This clue should help them understand that *treacherous* probably has something to do with danger. Guide students until they can give a reasonable definition of *treacherous.* To consolidate understanding of the word, ask another student to use the definition in a sentence.

Modeling Using Apposition

Have students read the sentences on the transparency. Explain to students that they will use *apposition* to figure out the meaning of the word. In apposition, the word is followed by the definition, which is set off by commas. For example, if the word is "abolitionist," the sentences might include the following:

1. The conductor thought he was an <u>abolitionist</u>, a person who wanted to end slavery.

2. John Brown was a famous <u>abolitionist</u>, a person who wanted to end slavery.

It should be pretty clear to students using apposition that the definition of the word *abolitionist* is "a person who wanted to end slavery."

Modeling Using Word Structure

Have students read the sentences on the transparency. Explain to students that they will use *word structure,* or parts of the selection vocabulary word, to figure out the meaning. For example, if the word is "uncharted," the sentences might include:

1. The strong wind blew Ivan's ship away into <u>uncharted</u> seas.

2. The explorers Lewis and Clark went into <u>uncharted</u> territory.

Have students look at the word *uncharted* and break it into parts: the prefix *un-, chart,* and the suffix *–ed.* Students should know that the suffix *un-* means "not," and that the suffix *–ed* usually indicates the past tense of a verb. However, you may need to remind students about the meanings of these affixes. Ask students for the meaning of the word *chart.*

Students should know that a chart could be a "map" or a "table." Guide them as they put together the definitions of the word parts, *un-* (not), *charted* (mapped or tabled). They should be able to come up with the definition "not mapped" or "unmapped" or even "unknown." Have them substitute their definition in the sentences to see if the definition makes sense. So, for instance, the first sentence would read "The strong wind blew Ivan's ship away into unmapped (or unknown) seas." Confirm with students that the new sentence makes sense, and then repeat the same process for the second sentence.

Reading Comprehension

Everything the students learn about phonemic awareness, phonics, and decoding has one primary goal—to help them understand what they are reading. Without comprehension, there is no reading.

Reading Comprehension Strategies

Purpose

The primary aim of reading is comprehension. Without comprehension, neither intellectual nor emotional responses to reading are possible—other than the response of frustration. Good readers are problem solvers. They bring their critical faculties to bear on everything they read. Experienced readers generally understand most of what they read, but just as importantly, they recognize when they do not understand, and they have at their command an assortment of strategies for monitoring and furthering their understanding.

The goal of comprehension strategy instruction is to turn responsibility for using strategies over to the students as soon as possible. Research has shown that students' comprehension and learning problems are not a matter of mental capacity but rather their inability to use strategies to help them learn. Good readers use a variety of strategies to help them make sense of the text and get the most out of what they read. Trained to use a variety of comprehension strategies, students dramatically improve their learning performance. In order to do this, the teacher models strategy use and gradually incorporates different kinds of prompts and possible student think-alouds as examples of the types of thinking students might do as they read to comprehend what they are reading.

Setting Reading Goals

Even before they begin reading and using comprehension strategies, good readers set reading goals and expectations. Readers who have set their own goals and have definite expectations about the text they are about to read are more engaged in their reading and notice more in what they read. Having determined a purpose for reading, they are better able to evaluate a text and determine whether it meets their needs. Even when the reading is assigned, the reader's engagement is enhanced when he or she has determined ahead of time what information might be gathered from the selection or how the selection might interest him or her.

Comprehension Strategies

Descriptions of strategies good readers use to comprehend the text follow.

Summarizing

Good readers sum up to check their understanding as they read. Sometimes they reread to fill in gaps in their understanding. Good readers use the strategy of summarizing to keep track of what they are reading and to focus their minds on important information. The process of putting the information in one's own words not only helps good readers remember what they have read, but also prompts them to evaluate how well they understand the information. Sometimes the summary reveals that one's understanding is incomplete, in which case it might be appropriate to reread the previous section to fill in the gaps. Good readers usually find that the strategy of summarizing is particularly helpful when they are reading long or complicated text.

Monitoring and Clarifying

Good readers constantly monitor themselves as they read in order to make sure they understand what they are reading. They note the characteristics of the text, such as whether it is difficult to read or whether some sections are more challenging or more important than others are. In addition, when good readers become aware that they do not understand, they take appropriate action, such as rereading, in order to understand the text better. As they read, good readers stay alert for problem signs such as loss of concentration, unfamiliar vocabulary, or lack of sufficient background knowledge to comprehend the text. This ability to self-monitor and identify aspects of the text that hinder comprehension is crucial to becoming a proficient reader.

Asking Questions

Good readers ask questions that may prepare them for what they will learn. If their questions are not answered in the text, they may try to find answers elsewhere and thus add even more to their store of knowledge. Certain kinds of questions occur naturally to a reader, such as clearing up confusion or wondering why something in the text is as it is. Intentional readers take this somewhat informal questioning one step further by formulating questions with the specific intent of checking their understanding. They literally test themselves by thinking of questions a teacher might ask and then by determining answers to those questions.

Predicting

Good readers predict what will happen next. When reading fiction, they make predictions about what they are reading and then confirm or revise those predictions as they go.

Making Connections

Good readers make connections between what they are reading and what they already know from past experience or previous reading.

Visualizing

Good readers visualize what is happening in the text. They form mental images as they read. They picture the setting, the characters, and the action in a story. Visualizing can also be helpful when reading expository text. Visualizing helps readers understand descriptions of complex activities or processes. When a complex process or an event is being described, the reader can follow the process or the event better by visualizing each step or episode. Sometimes an author or an editor helps the reader by providing illustrations, diagrams, or maps. If no visual aids have been provided, it may help the reader to create one.

Monitoring and Adjusting Reading Speed

Good readers understand that not all text is equal. Because of this, good readers continuously monitor what they are reading and adjust their reading speed accordingly. They skim parts of the text that are not important or relevant to their reading goals and they purposely slow down when they encounter difficulty in understanding the text.

Procedures

Modeling and Thinking Aloud

One of the most effective ways to help students use and understand the strategies good readers use is to make strategic thinking public. Modeling these behaviors and encouraging students to think aloud as they attempt to understand text can demonstrate for everyone in a class how these behaviors are put into practice. Suggestions for think-alouds are provided throughout the **Teacher's Edition.**

The most effective models you can offer will be those that come from your own reading experiences. What kinds of questions did you ask yourself? What kinds of things surprised you the first time you read a story? What kinds of new information did you learn? What kinds of things were confusing until you reread or read further? Drawing on these questions and on your students' questions and comments as they read will make the strategic reading process more meaningful to the students. Below are suggestions for modeling each of the comprehension strategies.

- **Modeling Setting Reading Goals.** To model setting reading goals, engage students in the following:

■ **Activate prior knowledge.** As you approach a new text, consider aloud what you already know about the subject or what your experiences have been in reading similar material.

■ **Browse the text.** To get an idea of what to expect from a text, look at the title and the illustrations. Look for potential problems, such as difficult words. Have students glance quickly at the selection, looking briefly at the illustrations and the print. Have them tell what they think they might be learning about as they read the selection.

■ **Decide what to expect from the text.** Anticipate enjoying the story, the language of the text, or the new information you expect to gain from the selection.

■ **Modeling Summarizing.** Just as the strategy of summarizing the plot and then predicting what will happen next can enhance a student's reading of fiction, so too can the same procedure be used to the student's advantage in reading nonfiction. In expository text, it is particularly logical to stop and summarize at the end of a chapter or section before going on to the next. One way to model the valuable exercise of making predictions and at the same time expand knowledge is to summarize information learned from a piece of expository writing and then predict what the next step or category will be. Appropriate times to stop and summarize include the following:

■ when a narrative text has covered a long period of time or a number of events

■ when many facts have been presented

■ when an especially critical scene has occurred

■ when a complex process has been described

■ any time there is the potential for confusion about what has happened or what has been presented in the text

■ when returning to a selection

■ **Modeling Monitoring and Clarifying.** A reader may need clarification at any point in the reading. Model this strategy by stopping at points that confuse you or that may confuse your students. Indicate that you are experiencing some confusion and need to stop and make sure you understand what is being read. Difficulty may arise from a challenging or unknown word or phrase. It may also stem from the manner in which the information is presented. Perhaps the author did not supply needed information. As you model this strategy, vary the reasons for stopping to clarify so that the students understand that good readers do not simply skip over difficult or confusing material—they stop and figure out what they don't understand.

■ **Modeling Asking Questions.** Learning to ask productive questions is not an easy task. Students' earliest experiences with this strategy take the form of answering teacher-generated questions. However, students should be able to move fairly quickly to asking questions like those a teacher might ask. Questions that can be answered with a simple yes or no are not typically very useful for helping them remember and understand what they have read. Many students find it helpful to ask questions beginning with *Who? What? When? Where? How?* or *Why?* As students become more accustomed to asking and answering questions, they will naturally become more adept at phrasing their questions. As their question-asking becomes more sophisticated, they progress from simple questions that can be answered with explicit information in the text to questions that require making inferences based on the text.

> *Good readers use a variety of strategies to help them make sense of the text and get the most out of what they read.*

■ **Modeling Predicting.** Predicting can be appropriate at the beginning of a selection—on the basis of the titles and the illustrations—or at any point while reading a selection. At first, your modeling will take the form of speculation about what might happen next, but tell students from the start what clues in the text or illustrations helped you predict, in order to make it clear that predicting is not just guessing. When a student makes a prediction—especially a far-fetched one—ask what in the selection or in his or her own experience the prediction is based on. If the student can back up the prediction, let the prediction stand; otherwise, suggest that the student make another prediction on the basis of what he or she already knows. Often it is appropriate to sum up before making a prediction. This will help students consider what has come before as they make their predictions about what will happen next. When reading aloud, stop whenever a student's prediction has been confirmed or contradicted. Have students tell whether the prediction was correct. If students seem comfortable with the idea of making predictions but rarely do so on their own, encourage them to discuss how to find clues in the text that will help them.

■ **Modeling Making Connections.** To model making connections, share with students any thoughts or memories that come to mind as you read the selection. Perhaps a character in a story reminds you of a childhood friend, allowing you to better identify with interactions between characters. Perhaps information in an article on Native-American life in the Old West reminds you of an article that you have read on the importance of the bison to Native Americans. Sharing your connections will help students become aware of the dynamic nature of reading and show them another way of being intentional, active learners.

■ **Modeling Visualizing.** Model visualizing by describing the mental images that occur to you as you read. A well-described scene is relatively easy to visualize, and if no one does so voluntarily, you may want to prompt students to express their own visualizations. If the author has not provided a description of a scene, but a picture of the scene would make the story more interesting or comprehensible, you might want to model visualizing as follows: "Let's see. The author says that the street was busy, and we know that this story is set during the colonial period. From what I already know about those times, there were no cars, and the roads were different from the roads of today. The street may have been paved with cobblestones. Horses would have been pulling carriages or wagons. I can almost hear the horses' hoofs going clip-clop over the stones." Remind students that different readers may picture the same scene quite differently, which is fine. Every reader responds to a story in her or his own way.

■ **Modeling Monitoring and Adjusting Reading Speed.** Just as readers need to monitor for problems, they need to be aware that different texts can be approached in different ways. For example, if reading a story or novel for enjoyment, the reader will typically read at a relaxed speed that is neither so fast as to be missing information nor as slow as they might read a textbook. If on the other hand, the reader is reading a textbook, he or she will probably decrease speed to assure understanding and make sure that all important information is read and understood. When modeling this strategy, be sure you indicate why you, as the reader, have chosen to slow down or speed up. Good readers continually monitor their speed and ability to understand throughout reading.

Reading Comprehension (continued)

Reading Aloud

At the beginning of the year, students should be encouraged to read selections aloud. This practice will help you and them understand some of the challenges posed by the text and how different students approach these challenges.

Reading aloud helps students build fluency, which in turn will aid their comprehension. Students in grades K–3 can use **Decodable Books** to build fluency, while students in grades 4–6 can use the literature from the **Student Anthologies.** Fluent second graders read between 82 and 124 words per minute with accuracy and understanding, depending on the time of the year (fall/spring). Fluent third graders can be expected to read between 107 and 142 words per minute; fourth (125/143); fifth (126/151); sixth (127/153).

Make sure that you set aside time to hear each student read during the first few days of class—the days devoted to Getting Started are perfect for this—so that you can determine students' abilities and needs. **Workshop** is also a good time to listen to any students who do not get to read aloud while the class is reading the selection together.

If your students have not previously engaged in the sort of strategic thinking aloud that is promoted throughout the *SRA/Open Court Reading* program, you will have to do all or most of the modeling at first, but encourage the students to participate as soon as possible.

As the year progresses, students should continue reading aloud often, especially with particularly challenging text. Model your own use of strategies, not only to help students better understand how to use strategies, but also to help them understand that actively using strategies is something that good, mature readers do constantly.

Most students are unaccustomed to thinking out loud. They will typically stand mute as they try to figure out an unfamiliar word or deal with a confusing passage. When this happens, students should be encouraged to identify specifically what they are having difficulty with. A student might identify a particular word, or he or she may note that the individual words are familiar but the meaning of the passage is unclear.

Active Response

Not only are good readers active in their reading when they encounter problems, but they respond constantly to whatever they read. In this way they make the text their own. As students read they should be encouraged to:

- Make as many connections as they can between what they are reading and what they already know.

- Visualize passages to help clarify their meanings or simply to picture appealing descriptions.
- Ask questions about what they are reading. The questions that go through their minds during reading will help them to examine, and thus better understand, the text. Doing so may also interest them in pursuing their own investigations. The questions may also provide a direction for students' research or exploration.
- Summarize and make predictions as a check on how well they understand what they are reading.

Tips

- Remember that the goal of all reading strategies is comprehension. If a story or article does not make sense, the reader needs to choose whatever strategies will help make sense of it. If one strategy does not work, the reader should try another.
- Always treat problems encountered in text as interesting learning opportunities rather than something to be avoided or dreaded.
- Encourage students to think out loud about text challenges.
- Encourage students to help each other build meaning from text. Rather than telling each other what a word is or what a passage means, students should tell each other how they figured out the meanings of challenging words and passages.
- Assure students that these are not the only strategies that can be used while reading. Any strategy that they find helpful in understanding text is a good useful strategy.
- Encourage students to freely share strategies they have devised on their own. You might want to write these on a large sheet of paper and tape them to the board.
- An absence of questions does not necessarily indicate that students understand what they are reading. Be especially alert to students who never seem to ask questions. Be sure to spend tutorial time with these students occasionally, and encourage them to discuss specific selections in the context of difficulties they might have encountered and how they solved them as well as their thoughts about unit concepts.
- Observing students' responses to text will enable you to ascertain not only how well they understand a particular selection but also their facility in choosing and applying appropriate strategies. Take note of the following:

- ✓ Whether the strategies a student uses are effective in the particular situation.
- ✓ Whether the student chooses from a variety of appropriate strategies or uses the same few over and over.
- ✓ Whether the student can explain to classmates which strategies to use in a particular situation and why.
- ✓ Whether the student can identify alternative resources to pursue when the strategies she or he has tried are not effective.
- ✓ Whether students' application of a given strategy is becoming more effective over a period of time.

Becoming familiar and comfortable with these self-monitoring techniques gives readers the confidence to tackle material that is progressively more difficult. A good, mature reader knows that he or she will know when understanding what he or she is reading is becoming a problem and can take steps to correct the situation.

Reading Comprehension Skills

Purpose

An important purpose of writing is to communicate thoughts from one person to another. The goal of instruction in reading comprehension skills is to make students aware of the logic behind the structure of a written piece. If the reader can discern the logic of the structure, he or she will be more able to understand the author's logic and gain knowledge both of the facts and the intent of the selection. By keeping the organization of a piece in mind and considering the author's purpose for writing, the reader can go beyond the actual words on the page and make inferences or draw conclusions based on what was read. Strong, mature readers utilize these "between the lines" skills to get a complete picture of not only what the writer is saying, but what the writer is trying to say.

Effective comprehension skills include:

Author's Point of View

Point of view involves identifying who is telling the story. If a character in the story is telling the story, that one character describes the action and tells what the other characters are like. This is first-person point of view. In such a story, one character will do the talking and use the pronouns *I, my, me*. All other characters' thoughts, feelings, and emotions will be reported through this one character.

If the story is told in third-person point of view, someone outside the story who is aware of all of the characters' thoughts and feelings and actions is relating them to the reader. All of the characters are referred to by their names or the pronouns *he/she, him/her, it.*

If students stay aware of who is telling a story, they will know whether they are getting the full picture or the picture of events as seen through the eyes of only one character.

Sequence

The reader can't make any decisions about relationships or events if he or she has no idea in which order the events take place. The reader needs to pay attention to how the writer is conveying the sequence. Is it simply stated that first this happened and then that happened? Does the writer present the end of the story first and then go back and let the reader know the sequence of events? Knowing what the sequence is and how it is presented helps the reader follow the writer's line of thought.

Fact and Opinion

Learning to distinguish fact from opinion is essential to critical reading and thinking. Students learn what factors need to be present in order for a statement to be provable. They also learn that an opinion, while not provable itself, should be based on fact. Readers use this knowledge to determine for themselves the validity of the ideas presented in their reading.

Main Idea and Details

An author always has something specific to say to his or her reader. The author may state this main idea in different ways, but the reader should always be able to tell what the writing is about.

To strengthen the main point or main idea of a piece, the author provides details to help the reader understand. For example, the author may use comparison and contrast to make a point, provide examples, provide facts, give opinions, give descriptions, give reasons or causes, or give definitions. The reader needs to know what kinds of details he or she is dealing with before making a judgment about the main idea.

Compare and Contrast

Using comparison and contrast is one of the most common and easiest ways a writer uses to get his or her reader to understand a subject. Comparing and contrasting unfamiliar thoughts, ideas, or things with familiar thoughts, ideas, and things gives the reader something within his or her own experience base to use in understanding.

Cause and Effect

What made this happen? Why did this character act the way he or she did? Knowing the causes of events helps the reader to see the whole story. Using this information to identify the probable outcomes (effects) of events or actions will help the reader anticipate the story or article.

Classify and Categorize

The relationships of actions, events, characters, outcomes, and such in a selection should be clear enough for the reader to see the relationships. Putting like things or ideas together can help the reader understand the relationships set up by the writer.

Author's Purpose

Everything that is written is written for a purpose. That purpose may be to entertain, to persuade, or to inform. Knowing why a piece is written—what purpose the author had for writing the piece—gives the reader an idea of what to expect and perhaps some prior idea of what the author is going to say.

If a writer is writing to entertain, then the reader can generally just relax and let the writer carry him or her away. If, on the other hand, the purpose is to persuade, it will help the reader understand and keep perspective if he or she knows that the purpose is to persuade. The reader can be prepared for whatever argument the writer delivers.

Drawing Conclusions

Often, writers do not directly state everything—they take for granted their audience's ability to "read between the lines." Readers draw conclusions when they take from the text small pieces of information about a character or event and use this information to make a statement about that character or event.

Making Inferences

Readers make inferences about characters and events to understand the total picture in a story. When making inferences, readers use information from the text, along with personal experience or knowledge, to gain a deeper understanding of a story event and its implications.

Procedure

Read the Selection

First, have students read the selection using whatever strategies they need to help them make sense of the selection. Then discuss the selection to assure that students did, indeed, understand what they read. Talk about any confusion they may have, and make any necessary clarifications.

Reread

Revisiting or rereading a selection allows the reader to note specific techniques that authors use to organize and present information in narratives and expository genres. Once students have a basic understanding of the piece, have them reread the selection in whole or in part, concentrating on selected skills. Choose examples of how the writer organized the piece to help the reader understand.

Limit this concentration on specific comprehension/writing skills to one or two that can be clearly identified in the piece. Trying to concentrate on too many things will just confuse students and make it harder for them to identify any of the organizational devices used by the writer. If a piece has many good examples of several different aspects, then go back to the piece several times over a span of days.

Write

Solidify the connection between how an author writes and how readers make sense of a selection by encouraging students to incorporate these organizational devices into their own writing. As they attempt to use these devices, they will get a clearer understanding of how to identify them when they are reading.

Remind students often that the purpose of any skill exercise is to give them tools to use when they are reading and writing. Unless students learn to apply the skills to their own reading—in every area of reading and study— then they are not gaining a full understanding of the purpose of the exercise.

Grammar, Usage, and Mechanics

Writing is a complicated process. A writer uses handwriting, spelling, vocabulary, grammar, usage, genre structures, and mechanics skills with ideas to create readable text. In addition, a writer must know how to generate content, or ideas, and understand genre structures in order to effectively present ideas in writing. Many students never progress beyond producing a written text that duplicates their everyday speech patterns. Mature writers, however, take composition beyond conversation. They understand the importance of audience and purpose for writing. They organize their thoughts, eliminating those that do not advance their main ideas, and elaborating on those that do so that their readers can follow a logical progression of ideas in an essay or story. Mature writers also know and can use the conventions of grammar, usage, spelling, and mechanics. They proofread and edit for these conventions, so their readers are not distracted by errors.

Purpose

The Study of English Conventions

Over the years the study of grammar, usage, and mechanics has gone in and out of favor. In the past century much research has been done to demonstrate the effectiveness of traditional types of instruction in the conventions of English. Experience and research have shown that learning grammatical terms and completing grammar exercises have little effect on the student's practical application of these skills in the context of speaking or writing. These skills, in and of themselves, do not play a significant role in the way students use language to generate and express their ideas—for example during the prewriting and drafting phases of the writing process. In fact, emphasis on correct conventions has been shown to have a damaging effect when it is the sole focus of writing instruction. If students are evaluated only on the proper use of spelling, grammar, and punctuation, they tend to write fewer and less complex sentences.

Knowledge of English conventions is, however, vitally important in the editing and proofreading phases of the writing process. A paper riddled with mistakes in grammar, usage, or mechanics is quickly discounted. Many immature writers never revise or edit. They finish the last sentence and turn their papers in to the teacher. Mature writers employ their knowledge of English language conventions in the editing phase to refine and polish their ideas.

The study of grammar, usage, and mechanics is important for two reasons.

1. Educated people need to know and understand the structure of their language, which in large part defines their culture.

2. Knowledge of grammar gives teachers and students a common vocabulary for talking about language and makes discussions of writing tasks more efficient and clearer.

Procedure

The key issue in learning grammar, usage, and mechanics is *how* to do it. On the one hand, teaching these skills in isolation from writing has been shown to be ineffective and even detrimental if too much emphasis is placed on them. On the other hand, not teaching these skills and having students write without concern for conventions is equally ineffective. The answer is to teach the skills in a context that allows students to directly apply them to a reading or writing activity. Students should be taught proper use of punctuation or subject/verb agreement at the same time they are taught to proofread for those conventions. As they learn to apply their knowledge of conventions during the final stages of the writing process, they will begin to see that *correcting* errors is an editorial, rather than a composition skill.

History of English

A basic understanding of the history and structure of the English language helps students understand the rich but complex resource they have for writing.

Old English

The English language began about AD 450 when the Angles, Jutes, and Saxons—three tribes that lived in northern Europe—invaded the British Isles. Much of their language included words that had to do with farming (*sheep, dirt, tree, earth*). Many of their words are the most frequently used words in the English language today. Because of Latin influences, English became the first of the European languages to be written down.

Middle English

In 1066 William the Conqueror invaded England and brought Norman French with him. Slowly Old English and Norman French came together, and Middle English began to appear. Today 40% of Modern English comes from French. With the introduction of the printing press English became more widespread.

Modern English

With the Renaissance and its rediscovery of classical Greek and Latin, many new words were created from Greek and Latin word elements. This continued intensively during the Early Modern English period. This rich language was used in the writings of Shakespeare and his contemporaries and profoundly influenced the nature and vocabulary of English. With dictionaries and spelling books, the English language became more standardized, although it continues to be influenced by other languages and new words and trends. These influences continue to make English a living, dynamic language.

Punctuation

Early writing had no punctuation or even spaces between words. English punctuation had its beginning in ancient Greece and Rome. Early punctuation reflected speaking, rather than reading. By the end of the eighteenth century, after the invention of printing, most of the rules for punctuation were established, although they were not the same in all languages.

The Structure of English

Grammar is the sound, structure, and meaning system of language. People who speak the same language are able to communicate because they intuitively know the grammar system of that language, the rules of making meaning. All languages have grammar, and yet each language has its own grammar.

Traditional grammar study usually involves two areas:

- **Parts of speech** (nouns, verbs, adjectives, adverbs, pronouns, prepositions, conjunctions) are typically considered the content of grammar. The parts of speech involve the *form* of English words.

- **Sentence structure** (subjects, predicates, objects, clauses, phrases) is also included in grammar study. Sentence structure involves the *function* of English.

Mechanics involves the conventions of punctuation and capitalization. Punctuation helps readers understand writers' messages. Proper punctuation involves marking off sentences according to grammatical structure. In speech students can produce sentences as easily and unconsciously as they can walk, but in writing they must think about what is and what is not a sentence.

In English there are about 14 punctuation marks (period, comma, quotation marks, question mark, exclamation point, colon, semicolon, apostrophe, hyphen, ellipsis, parentheses, brackets, dash, and underscore). Most immature writers use only three: period, comma, and question mark. The experienced writer or poet with the command of punctuation adds both flexibility and meaning to his or her sentences through his or her use of punctuation.

Usage is the way in which we speak in a given community. Language varies over time, across national and geographical boundaries, by gender, across age groups, and by socioeconomic status. When the variation occurs within a given language, the different versions of the same language are called *dialects*. Every language has a *prestige dialect* associated with education and financial success. In the United States, this *dialect* is known as Standard English and is the language of school and business.

Usage involves the word choices people make when speaking certain dialects. Word choices that are perfectly acceptable in conversation among friends may be unacceptable in writing. Usage is often the most obvious indicator of the difference between conversation and composition. Errors in word usage can make a writer seem ignorant and thus jeopardize his or her credibility, no matter how valid or important his or her overall message might be. Usage depends on a student's cultural and linguistic heritage. If the dialect students have learned is not the formal language of school settings or if it is not English, students must master another dialect or language in order to write Standard English.

The English Language Conventions lessons in *Open Court Reading* are structured to focus on grammar and usage or mechanics skills presented in a logical sequence. A skill is introduced on the first day of the lesson with appropriate models and then practiced in reading and writing on subsequent days to ensure that skills are not taught in isolation. Encourage students to use the focused English language convention presented in each lesson as they complete each Writing Process Strategies activity. Also encourage them to reread their writing, checking for proper use of the conventions taught. With practice, students should be able to apply their knowledge of conventions to any writing they do.

Tips

- Some of the errors students make in writing are the result simply of not carefully reading their final drafts. Many errors occur because the writer's train of thought was interrupted and a sentence is not complete or a word is skipped. These may look like huge errors that a simple rereading can remedy. Most often the writer can correct these types of errors on his or her own. A major emphasis of any English composition program should be to teach the editing and proofreading phases of the writing process so students can eliminate these types of errors themselves. This involves a shift in perception—from thinking of grammar as a set of discrete skills that involve mastery of individual rules, to understanding grammar as it applies to the act of communicating in writing.

- As students learn English language conventions, they should be expected to incorporate them into their written work. A cumulative student checklist of the grammar, usage, and mechanics skills covered in a grade level appears in the back of the *Writer's Workbook.*

- Sometimes, students write sentences that raise grammatically complex problems that require a deep understanding of English grammar. Use the Sentence Lifting strategies outlined in the **Proofreading** part of the Appendix to identify and discuss these more sophisticated types of errors that can include:

  - **Faulty Parallelism.** Parts of a sentence parallel in meaning are not parallel in structure.
  - **Nonsequitors.** A statement does not follow logically from something said previously.
  - **Dangling Modifiers.** A phrase or clause does not logically modify the word next to it.
  - **Awkwardness.** Sentences are not written simply.
  - **Wordiness.** Thoughts are not written in as few words as possible.
  - **Vocabulary.** Precise words are not used.

Listening, Speaking, Viewing

Some people are naturally good listeners, and others have no trouble speaking in front of groups. Many people, however, need explicit instruction on how to tune in for important details and how to organize and make an oral presentation. While some people naturally critique what they read, hear, and see, many others need specific guidance to develop skills for analyzing what they encounter in images and the media. The abilities to listen appropriately and to speak in conversations and in groups, as well as to critically evaluate the information with which they are presented, are fundamental skills that will serve students throughout their lives.

Purpose

In addition to reading and writing, listening, speaking, and viewing complete the language arts picture. Through the development of these language arts skills, students gain flexibility in communicating orally, visually, and in writing. When speaking and listening skills are neglected, many students have difficulty speaking in front of groups, organizing a speech, or distinguishing important information they hear. A top anxiety for many adults is speaking in front of groups. Much of this anxiety would not exist if listening, speaking, and viewing skills were taught from the early years.

The Listening, Speaking, and Viewing instruction focuses on the literature selection or the Writing Process Strategies to provide context, reinforce other elements of the lesson, and integrate the other language arts. Many of the Listening, Speaking, and Viewing skills are very similar to reading or writing skills. For

example, listening for details is the same type of skill as reading for details. Preparing an oral report employs many of the same skills as preparing a written report. Learning to use these skills effectively gives students flexibility in how they approach a task.

Procedure

Listening, speaking, and viewing skills are presented with increasing sophistication throughout every grade level of *Open Court Reading* in the Language Arts part of each lesson. Every unit includes at least one lesson on each of the following skills so that students encounter the skills again and again throughout a grade level:

- **Listening.** Listening skills include comprehending what one hears and listening for different purposes, such as to identify sequence or details, to summarize or draw conclusions, or to follow directions.
- **Speaking.** Speaking skills include speaking formally and conversationally, using appropriate volume, giving oral presentations, and using effective grammar. Speaking skills also include using descriptive words, using figurative language, and using formal and informal language.
- **Viewing.** Viewing skills include comprehending main ideas and messages in images, mass media, and other multimedia.
- **Interaction.** Interaction instruction focuses on a combination of listening and speaking skills. These include asking and responding to questions, nonverbal cues such as eye contact, facial expression, and posture, and contributing to and interacting in group settings.
- **Presenting Information.** The last Listening, Speaking, and Viewing lesson in every unit usually focuses on presentation skills. These include sharing ideas, relating experiences or stories, organizing information, and preparing for speeches. These lessons often parallel the Writing Process Strategies instruction, so that students can prepare their information in written or oral form.

Tips

- Point out the parallels among the language arts skills: providing written and oral directions, telling or writing a narrative, and so on. Encourage students to see that they have choices for communicating. Discuss the similarities and differences between different forms of communication, and determine whether one is preferable in a given situation.
- Ensure that all students have opportunities to speak in small groups and whole-class situations.
- Provide and teach students to allow appropriate wait time before someone answers a question.

Writing

The ability to write with clarity and coherence is essential to students' success in school as well as in life. Communicating through writing is becoming more and more important in this age of computers. Yet, writing remains a major problem for students at all levels, as well as adults in the workplace.

Purpose

Writing is a complex process. It requires the ability to use a variety of skills (penmanship, grammar, usage, mechanics, spelling, vocabulary) fluently and appropriately at the same time one's creative and critical thinking processes create and structure an idea. Familiarity with the structures of writing and different genres, audiences, and purposes is necessary to write appropriately as well. The art of writing well also involves writer's craft, the ability to manipulate words and sentences for effect.

As strange as it may seem, the better a writer is, the *harder* he or she works at writing. The best writers are not the best because they are naturally talented. They are the best usually because they work the hardest. Good writers really do take *more* time than others in the planning and revising stages of the writing process. Poorer writers make writing look easy by writing without planning and typically build a composition sentence by sentence. They turn in their papers with little or no correction.

The goals of writing instruction have many facets:

- To model and practice writing in a variety of writing genres so that students can choose and write in an appropriate form.
- To model and practice a writing process to help students develop routines for planning their work and then revising and editing it.
- To practice using spelling, vocabulary, and English language conventions skills in writing so that students can use them fluently.
- To develop writing traits: ideas, organization, voice, word choice, sentence fluency, and presentation so that students become effective writers.

Just as the goal of phonics instruction is to teach students to read, the Writing Process Strategies instruction in **Open Court Reading** focuses on skills, structures, and strategies for writing. The goal of this instruction is to learn how to write, rather than to develop a particular idea. From this instruction, students will have a comprehensive bank of tools for writing, which they can then employ in the development of their Research and Inquiry investigations in each unit or in any other writing application.

Procedures

Writing Genres

There are several different genres students are typically asked to write. These usually

The best writers are not the best because they are naturally talented. They are the best usually because they work the hardest. Good writers really do take more time than others in the planning and revising stages of the writing process.

include many creative stories and a few reports. The only narrative writing most adults do, however, is summaries of meetings. The bulk of adult writing consists of writing reports, letters, analyses, memos, and proposals. College students, as well, typically write research reports or critiques. A literate student needs to be able to choose and write in an appropriate genre.

- Narrative writing is story writing, which has a beginning, middle, and end. It includes myth, realistic fiction, historical fiction, biography, science fiction, fantasy, folktale, and legend.
- Expository writing is informational writing. It includes research reports, scientific investigation, summaries, and explanations of a process.
- Descriptive writing is observational writing that includes details. It has descriptive paragraphs that may be part of narrative or expository writing.
- Poetry writing involves particular attention to word choice and rhythm. Poetry may be free form, ballad, rhyming, or a variety of other forms.
- Personal writing is functional writing to help record ideas, thoughts, or feelings or to communicate with others and may include E-mail, journals, lists, and messages.
- Persuasive writing involves the development of a persuasive argument. It includes posters, persuasive essays, and advertisements.

In **Open Court Reading** the first unit of every grade teaches the writing process and traits of writing. Each subsequent unit focuses on a particular genre appropriate for the unit content. Expository and persuasive writing are typically in the units with research themes such as medicine or business; personal, narrative, descriptive, and poetry writing are in units with universal themes, such as friendship and courage. Exemplary models of each form of writing are included either in the literature selection, on the **Language Arts**

Transparencies, or in the **Language Arts Handbook.**

Each genre has its own form and function. For example:

- A personal narrative is probably best ordered as a straightforward chronological retelling of events. Dialogue may help to tell the story.
- A process description should be told in a step-by-step order. The draft should include as much information as possible; each step must be clear. If the piece needs cutting, the student can always do it later.
- A persuasive piece appeals to feelings. It requires facts as well as expert opinions.
- An interview could be written as a series of questions and answers.
- The order of details in a descriptive piece must be easy to follow—from left to right, top to bottom, or whatever order makes sense.
- A fictional story must include details describing characters, setting, and the characters' actions. Dialogue also helps to tell the story.

The goal is not to develop full-blown novels and compositions, but to experience the structures of different forms of writing.

Structures of Writing

Structures of writing involve the effective development of sentences, paragraphs, and compositions. In **Open Court Reading** structures of writing are taught within the context of the Writing Process Strategies activities rather than in isolation, so that students integrate their practice of writing structures as they develop different writing genres.

Writer's Craft

Writer's Craft involves the elements and choices writers make to add drama, suspense, or lightheartedness to a written work. These elements may include foreshadowing, use of figurative language, dialogue, or enhancement of setting or use of description to affect the mood and tone. In **Open Court Reading,** along with structures of writing, the writer's craft is pointed out in the literature selection and then taught and practiced within the context of the Writing Process Strategies activities.

Writing Traits

Writing traits are those elements and qualities in a composition that enhance the effectiveness of the writing. These include:

- Ideas/Content. Not only the quality of the idea, but the development, support, and focus of the idea makes a strong composition.

- Organization. In quality writing, the organization develops the central idea. The order and structure move the reader through the text easily. The beginning grabs the reader's attention and the conclusion adds impact.
- Voice. Voice is the overall tone of a piece of writing. Good writers choose a voice appropriate for the topic, purpose, and audience. As students develop writing skills, a unique style begins to emerge. The writing is expressive, engaging, or sincere, demonstrating a strong commitment to the topic.
- Word Choice. In quality writing words convey the intended message in an interesting, precise, and natural way appropriate to audience and purpose.
- Sentence Fluency. Sentence fluency enhances the flow and rhythm of a composition. In good writing sentence patterns are somewhat varied, contributing to ease in oral reading.
- Conventions. Good writers demonstrate consistent use and awareness of English language conventions.
- Presentation. A quality piece of writing includes an impressive presentation with attention to format, style, illustration, and clarity.

In *Open Court Reading,* the traits of writing are taught in the first unit and then practiced in every Writing Process Strategies activity as an integral part of the writing process.

The Writing Process

Providing a routine or process for students to follow will help them to learn a systematic approach to writing. By following the steps of the writing process, students will learn to approach everything they write with purpose and thought. They learn that although writing takes time and thought, there are steps they can take to make their writing clear, coherent, and appealing to their audience.

In *Open Court Reading,* the first unit of every grade provides an overview and teaching of the writing process, including strategies and examples for getting ideas, determining audience and purpose for writing, organizing writing, drafting, revising, editing, and presenting. The vehicle used to apply this instruction is a student autobiography. The autobiographies can be collected in a school portfolio to assess writing development over the course of the elementary years.

Prewriting

Purpose

Prewriting is that phase of the writing process when students think through an idea they want to write about. To improve their writing, students should think about their ideas, discuss them, and plan how they want readers to respond. It is important for students to take time before writing to plan ahead so that they can proceed from one phase of the writing process to another without spending unnecessary time making decisions that should have been made earlier. Prewriting is the most time-consuming phase of the writing process, but it may be the most important.

> *The goal is not to develop full-blown novels and compositions, but to familiarize and practice the structures of different forms of writing.*

Procedure

Good student writers

- Listen to advice about time requirements and plan time accordingly.
- Spend time choosing, thinking about, and planning the topic.
- Spend time narrowing the topic.
- Determine the purpose for writing.
- Consider the audience and what readers already know about the topic.
- Conduct research, if necessary, before writing.
- Get information from a lot of different sources.
- Use models for different types of writing, but develop individual plans.
- Organize the resource information.
- Make a plan for writing that shows how the ideas will be organized.
- Elaborate on a plan and evaluate and alter ideas as writing proceeds.

Noting Writing Ideas

Students can make notes of writing ideas at any time, with a special time being set aside following the discussion of each reading selection. The writing ideas students get from a discussion might be concerned with the topic of the selection they just read or with an aspect of the author's style. You should keep such a list of writing ideas also, and think aloud occasionally as you make writing idea notes.

Students must make many decisions during the prewriting phase of the writing process. Most students can benefit from talking with a partner or a small group of classmates about these decisions. They may want to discuss some of the following points.

- **Genre** or format of each writing piece. Having decided to use a writing idea such as "a misunderstanding on the first day of school," the student must decide how to use

it—for example, as a personal narrative, a realistic fiction story, a poem, a fantasy story, a play, a letter, and so on.
- **Audience**. Although students' writing pieces will be shared with classmates and with you, some may ultimately be intended for other audiences.
- **Writing Purpose**. Each student should write a sentence that tells the purpose of the piece he or she plans to write. The purpose statement should name the intended audience and the effect the writer hopes to have on that audience. For example, a writer may want to describe her first day in school. The intended audience is kindergarten students, and she intends her story to be humorous. Her purpose statement would read, "I want to write a funny story for other students about my first day in kindergarten."
- **Planning**. Some writers may find it helpful to brainstorm with a partner or small group to list words and phrases they might use in a piece of writing. Sometimes this list can be organized into webs of related ideas or details. This kind of prewriting activity might be particularly useful for planning a descriptive piece. For planning a comparison/contrast piece, a writer might use another kind of visual organizer, such as a Venn diagram. Students planning fiction pieces might use a story frame or plot line.

Tips

- Circulate as students make notes on writing ideas or work in small groups on prewriting activities.
- Notice which students are having difficulty coming up with writing ideas. It may help to pair these students with students who have many ideas.
- Do not worry if this phase of the process seems noisy and somewhat chaotic. Students must be allowed to let their imaginations roam in free association and to play around with words and ideas until they hit on something that seems right. They must be permitted to share ideas and help each other.
- Do not worry if, in the early sessions, the class as a whole seems to have few ideas. Through the reading and discussion of selections in the reading anthology, most students will soon have more writing ideas than they can use.

PROGRAM APPENDIX

Drafting

Purpose

During the drafting phase of the writing process, students shape their planning notes into main ideas and details. They devote their time and effort to getting words down on paper. Whether students are drafting on scrap paper or on computer screens, your role is to encourage each writer to "get it all down." You must also provide a suitable writing environment with the expectation that there will be revision to the draft and to the original plan.

Good Student Writers

- Express all their ideas in the first draft.
- Stop and think about what is being written while drafting.
- Evaluate and alter ideas while drafting.
- Change or elaborate on original plans while drafting.
- Discover that they need more information about certain parts of their writing.
- Learn a lot more about the topic while drafting.

Procedure

Here are some points to share with students before they begin drafting:

- Drafting is putting your ideas down on paper for your own use. Writers do not need to worry about spelling or exact words. They just need to get their ideas down.
- Write on every other line so that you will have room to make revisions.
- Write on only one side of a page so that when you revise you can see all of your draft at once.
- As you draft, keep in mind your purpose for writing this piece and your intended audience.
- Use your plan and your notes from research to add details.

Using Word Processors for Drafting

Many students enjoy drafting on the screen of a computer more than drafting on paper. Once they have mastered the keyboard, they may find it easier to think as they write. Their first attempts look less sloppy, and they are often more willing to make changes and experiment as they draft. They will certainly find it neater to use the delete key on the word processor than to correct their mistakes by crossing out. The Basic Computer Skills instruction in the Language Arts Overview of every lesson provides instruction on using the computer.

Tips

Sometimes the hardest part of drafting is getting the first sentence down on paper. It may help a student even before she or he starts writing to begin a story in the middle or to write the word "Draft" in big letters at the top of the paper.

- If a student feels stuck during drafting, he or she may need to go back and try a different prewriting technique.
- After an initial fifteen or twenty minutes of imposed silence, some students may work better and come up with more ideas if they share as they write.
- You may find that it is difficult to get students to "loosen up" as they draft. Remember, most students have been encouraged to be neat and to erase mistakes when they write. It may help to share some of your own marked-up manuscripts with students.

Revising

Purpose

The purpose of revising is to make sure that a piece of writing expresses the writer's ideas clearly and completely. It has been said that there is no good writing, just good rewriting. A major distinction between good writers and poor writers is the amount of time and effort they put into revision. Poor writers look for spelling and grammatical errors if they do read their work.

Good Student writers

- Evaluate what has been written.
- Read the draft as a reader, not the writer.
- Identify problems with focus, giving enough information, clarity, and order.
- Think of solutions to problems and understand when solutions will and won't work.
- Recognize when and how the text needs to be reorganized.
- Eliminate sentences or paragraphs that don't fit the main idea.
- Identify ideas that need elaboration.
- Do more research if needed to support or add ideas.
- Identify and eliminate unnecessary details.
- Ask for feedback from peer and teacher conferences.
- Take advantage of classroom and outside resources.
- Check the accuracy of facts and details.
- Give credit for any ideas from other people or sources.

Procedure

Model asking questions like the following when revising various kinds of writing:

- About a narrative:
  ✓ Does my first sentence get my readers' attention?
  ✓ Are events in the story told in an order that makes sense?
  ✓ Have I included dialogue to help move the story along?
  ✓ Does the story have a clear focus?
- About a description:
  ✓ Have I used details that appeal to the senses?
- About a comparison/contrast piece:
  ✓ Have I made a separate paragraph for each subject discussed?
- About an explanation:
  ✓ Will readers understand what I am saying?
  ✓ Are the steps of the explanation in a clear order?
  ✓ Have I made effective use of signal words?
  ✓ Have I included enough information?
- About fiction:
  ✓ Have I described my characters and setting?
  ✓ Does the plot include a problem, build to a climax, and then describe the resolution of the problem?
- About persuasive writing:
  ✓ Have I made my position clear?
  ✓ Does my evidence support my position?
  ✓ Have I used opinions as well as facts, and have I said whose opinions I used?
  ✓ Have I directed my writing to my audience?

Help students understand the value of asking questions such as the following as they revise:

- About each paragraph:
  ✓ Does each sentence belong in it?
  ✓ Does each sentence connect smoothly with the next?
  ✓ Does each sentence say something about the main idea?
- About each sentence:
  ✓ Do the sentences read smoothly?
  ✓ Have I combined sentences that were too short?
  ✓ Have I broken sentences that were too long into two shorter sentences?
  ✓ Have I varied the beginnings of the sentences?
- About the words:
  ✓ Have I changed words that were repeated too often?
  ✓ Do transition words connect ideas?

Tips

- Use the student Writing Folder to review student progress. Check first drafts against revised versions to see how each student is able to apply revision strategies.

- You may find that some students are reluctant to revise. You might then try the following:

  ✓ If a student doesn't see anything that needs to be changed or doesn't want to change anything, get him or her to do something to the paper—number the details in a description or the steps in a process, circle exact words, underline the best parts of the paper. Once a paper is marked, the student may not be so reluctant to change it.

  ✓ One reason many students do not like to revise is that they think they must recopy everything. This is not always necessary. Sometimes writers can cut and paste sections that they want to move. Or they can use carets and deletion marks to show additions and subtractions from a piece.

  ✓ Give an especially reluctant student a deadline by which she or he must revise a piece or lose the chance to publish it.

  ✓ Students will hopefully be writing in other classes and on a variety of topics. Revision techniques can be used to improve writing in any curriculum area. Stress to students the importance of focusing on their intended audience as they revise.

Proofreading

Purpose

Writing that is free of grammatical, spelling, and technical mistakes is clearer and easier for readers to understand. By proofreading their pieces, students will also notice which errors they make repeatedly and will learn not to make them in the future.

After a piece of writing has been revised for content and style, students must read it carefully line by line to make sure that it contains no errors. This activity, the fourth phase of the writing process, is called proofreading and is a critical step that must occur before a piece of writing can be published. Students can begin proofreading a piece when they feel that it has been sufficiently revised.

Good Student Writers

- Edit the work to allow the reader to understand and enjoy the words.
- Correct most errors in English language conventions.
- Use resources or seek assistance to address any uncertainties in English language conventions.

Procedure

Using What They Have Learned

Students should be expected to proofread at a level appropriate to their grade. Young authors should not be held responsible for skills they have not yet learned. Older students will be able to check for a greater variety of errors than younger students and should be expected to take greater responsibility for their proofreading. For example, students in first grade can be expected to check for and correct omitted capital letters at the beginning of sentences, but they should not necessarily be expected to understand and correct capital letters in proper nouns or in names of organizations. Older students will have mastered many more grammatical, mechanical, usage, and spelling skills and can be expected to perform accordingly. When you spot an error related to a skill beyond a student's level, make clear to the student that you do not expect her or him to be responsible for the mistake, but do explain that the error still needs to be corrected. The following suggestions may be useful as you introduce proofreading to the students and help them develop their proofreading skills.

Proofreading Checklist

Have students use a proofreading checklist similar to the one shown here to help them remember the steps for effective proofreading.

✓ Read each sentence.

✓ Does each sentence begin with a capital letter and end with correct punctuation?

✓ Do you notice any sentence fragments or run-on sentences?

✓ Are words missing from the sentence?

✓ Is any punctuation or capitalization missing from within the sentence?

✓ Do you notice any incorrect grammar or incorrect word usage in the sentence?

✓ Do you notice any misspelled words?

✓ Are the paragraphs indented?

✓ Can very long paragraphs be broken into two paragraphs?

✓ Can very short paragraphs be combined into one paragraph?

Tips

- **Proofreader's Marks** Students should use standard Proofreader's Marks to indicate the changes they wish to make. Explain to students that these marks are a kind of code used to show which alterations to make without a long explanation. Students may also be interested to know that professional writers, editors, and proofreaders use these same marks. You may want to review these marks one by one, illustrating on the board how to use them. For example, they may insert a word or a phrase by using a caret (^). If students wish to insert more text than will fit above the line, they may write in the margin or attach another sheet of paper. It may be a good idea, when such extensive corrections are made, for students to proofread their final copy carefully to make sure they have included all their alterations.

- **Sentence lifting** is a very effective method of showing students how to proofread their own work. Because students are working on their own sentences, they will be more inclined to both pay attention to what is going on and better understand the corrections that are made.

  ✓ Choose several pieces of student writing and look for common errors.

  ✓ On an overhead transparency, write several sentences. Include at least one sentence that has no errors.

  ✓ Tell students that you are going to concentrate on one type of error at a time. For example, first you will concentrate on spelling.

  ✓ Ask students to read the first sentence and point out any words they feel are spelled incorrectly. Do not erase errors. Cross them out and write the correctly spelled word above the crossed out word.

  ✓ Next move to a different type of error. Ask students to check for capitalization and punctuation.

  ✓ Continue in this way, correcting errors as you go through the sample sentences.

- **Using a Word Processor.** If the students are using a word processor to write their pieces, they may wish to run a spell check on their document. Caution them, however, that even the most sophisticated computer cannot catch every spelling error. Misuse of homophones and typographical errors may not be caught by the computer if the misused words appear in the computer's dictionary. For example, if a student types *form* instead of *from*, the computer will not register a mistake because *form* is also a word.

Circulate as students are proofreading on their own or in pairs.

✓ Are students able to check references when they are unsure of a spelling or usage?

✓ Are students criticizing each other's work constructively?

✓ Does a student no longer omit end punctuation because he or she noticed this error repeatedly during proofreading?

✓ Note students who are having difficulty. You may wish to address these difficulties during individual conferences.

Publishing

Purpose

Publishing is the process of bringing private writing to the reading public. The purpose of writing is to communicate. Unless students are writing in a journal, they will want to present their writing to the public. Such sharing helps students to learn about themselves and others, provides an opportunity for them to take pride in their hard work, and thus motivates them to further writing.

Publishing their work helps motivate students to improve such skills as spelling, grammar, and handwriting. Publishing can be as simple as displaying papers on a bulletin board or as elaborate as creating a class newspaper. Publishing will not—indeed should not—always require large blocks of class time. Students will wish to spend more time elaborately presenting their favorite pieces and less time on other works. If students take an inordinate amount of time to publish their work, you may want to coach them on how to speed up the process.

Good Student Writers

- Present the work in a way that makes it easy to read and understand.
- Consider format, style, illustration, and clarity in the presentation of the work.
- Show pride in the finished work.

Procedure

Preparing the Final Copy

When students feel that they have thoroughly proofread their pieces, they should copy the work onto another sheet of paper, using their best handwriting, or type the work on a computer or typewriter. They should then check this copy against the proofread copy to make sure that they made all the changes correctly and did not introduce any new errors. You may need to proofread and correct students' papers one final time before publishing to make sure that they have caught all errors.

Publishing Choices

In publishing, students need to decide

✓ how to prepare the piece for publication.

✓ what form the published work should take.

✓ whether to illustrate their writing with photographs, drawings, or charts with captions, as necessary.

✓ where to place any art they are using.

Publishing Checklist

The following checklist will help students when they are publishing their work. (Not every question applies to every form of publishing.)

✓ Have I revised my work to make it better?

✓ Have I proofread it carefully?

✓ Have I decided upon my illustrations?

✓ Have I recopied my piece carefully and illustrated it?

✓ Have I numbered the pages?

✓ Have I made a cover that tells the title and my name?

Tips

- Read through the piece, and tell the student if any corrections still need to be made. Also make some suggestions about the best way to publish a piece if a student has trouble coming up with an idea.

- Make suggestions and give criticism as needed, but remember that students must retain ownership of their publishing. Leave final decisions about form and design of their work up to individual students.

- Remind students to think about their intended audience when they are deciding on the form for their published piece. Will the form they have selected present their ideas effectively to the people they want to reach?

Writing Seminar

Purpose

The purpose of Writing Seminar (Levels 1–6) is for students to discuss their work in progress and to share ideas for improving it.

Writing Seminar is one of the activities in which students may choose to participate during Workshop. Students will meet in small groups to read and discuss one another's writing. One student reads a piece in progress. Other students comment on the writing and ask questions about the ideas behind the writing. The student whose work is being critiqued writes down the comments made by his or her classmates and decides how to use these comments to make the writing better.

Procedure

To begin the seminar, have one student writer read his or her revised draft as other students listen carefully. When the student has finished, invite other students to retell the story in their own words. If they have trouble retelling the story, the writer knows that he or she must make some ideas clearer.

Then have listeners who wish to comment raise their hands. The writer calls on each in turn. The listeners ask questions or make comments about the writing, telling, for example, what they like about it or what they might change to make it better. After several comments have been made, the writer notes any information that she or he might use. Another student then reads his or her piece.

Guidelines for Peer Conferencing

In an early session, work with students to establish guidelines for peer conferencing. You might suggest rules such as the following:

✓ Listen quietly while someone else is speaking.

✓ Think carefully before you comment on another person's work.

✓ Make your comments specific.

✓ Comment on something that you like about the piece before you comment on something that needs to be improved.

✓ Discuss your work quietly so as not to disturb the rest of the class.

Modeling Seminar Behavior

You may need to model meaningful comments and questions. For example:

✓ What was your favorite part?

✓ I like the part where (or when)

✓ I like the way you describe

✓ What happened after . . . ?

✓ I'd like to know more about

✓ Why did _____ happen?

✓ What do you think is the most important part?

Teacher Conferencing

During Writing Seminar, you will want to schedule individual conferences with students to help them evaluate their writing so that they can recognize problems and find ways to solve them. Teacher conferences are useful during all phases of the writing process, but they are crucial during the revising phase. Conferences give you an opportunity to observe students as they evaluate their writing, solve problems, make decisions about their work, and take responsibility for the development and completion of their work. The basic procedure for conferences is:

- Have the student read his or her work aloud.
- Review any feedback the student has received so far.
- Identify positive elements of the work.
- Use one or more of these strategies to help the student improve his or her work.

  ✓ Have students explain how they got their ideas.

  ✓ Have students think aloud about how they will address the feedback they have received.

  ✓ Ask students to help you understand any confusion you may have about their writing.

  ✓ Have the student add, delete, or rearrange something in the work and ask how it affects the whole piece.

  ✓ Think aloud while you do a part of what the student was asked to do. Ask the student to compare what you did to what he or she did.

  ✓ Have the student prescribe as if to a younger student how to revise the work.

- Ask two or three questions to guide students through revising (see below).
- Conclude by having the student state a plan for continuing work on the piece.

Writing Conference Questions

Ideas

- Who is your audience?
- What is your purpose for writing?
- How does the reader know the purpose?
- Is there enough information about the topic?
- Do you like one part of your work more than the rest? Why?
- Is your main idea clear?
- Is there a better way to express this idea?
- Is this a good topic sentence?
- Is your introduction engaging?
- Are any important details left out?
- Are any not-so-important details left in?
- Do you use specific details and examples?
- Are your ideas accurate and, if necessary, supported by research?
- Does your conclusion sum up or restate your purpose for writing?
- What might be another way to end the work?

Organization

- Is the writing organized in a way that makes the most sense based on the main idea?
- Is the structure clear for the reader? Is there a clear beginning, middle, and end?
- Are there smooth transitions from one part to the next?
- Are supporting details ordered in the most logical way?
- Can you combine any smaller paragraphs or separate larger ones?

Voice

- Do you sound confident and knowledgeable?
- Does the voice you use reflect the purpose of your writing? Does your writing sound funny or serious when you want it to be?
- Is your voice appropriate for your audience?
- Do you sound interested in the subject?
- Have you confidently stated your opinion? Have you used the pronoun "I" if appropriate?
- Does your writing sound like you?
- Is your voice too formal or informal?
- Will this writing get a strong response from the reader?
- Does your writing make the reader care about your topic?

Word Choice

- Do you use the same word/phrase repeatedly?
- Could you say the same thing with different words?

- Have you defined words your audience may not understand?
- Have you used precise words to describe or explain?
- Is there a better word to express this idea?
- Have you used your own words when summarizing information from another text?
- Do you use time and order words such as *first, next, then,* and *last* to help the reader understand when events take place?

Sentence Fluency

- Are your sentences clear and to the point?
- Have you used different kinds and lengths of sentences to effectively present your ideas?
- Could any of your sentences be combined?
- Is there a rhythm to your sentences?
- Does each sentence introduce a new idea or a new piece of information?
- Do some sentences repeat what has already been stated? If so, cut or change them.
- Have you used transition words such as *in contrast, however,* and *on the other hand* to move smoothly from one subject to the other?
- Have you used transitional phrases, such as *according to, in addition to,* or *at the same time* to link sentences?
- Have you used conjunctions such as *and, but,* and *or* to combine short, choppy sentences?

Tips

- Completed pieces as well as works in progress can be shared during Writing Seminar.
- Concentrate on one phase of the writing process at a time.
- Remember to keep conferences brief and to the point. If you are calling the conference, prepare your comments in advance. Be sure that you confer regularly with every student if only to check that each one is continuing to write, revise, and publish.
- During teacher conferences, you might use the following responses to student writing.
  - ✓ To open communication with the writer:
    - How is the writing going?
    - Tell me about your piece.
    - How did you get your ideas?
  - ✓ To give encouragement:
    - I like the part where . . . .
    - I like the way you open your piece by . . . .
    - I like your description of . . . .
  - ✓ To get the writer to clarify meaning:
    - I wonder about . . . .
    - What happened after . . . .
    - Why did . . . ?
  - ✓ To get the writer to think about direction and about writing strategies:

- What do you plan to do with your piece?
- How will you go about doing that?
- What could I do to help you?

- As you confer with students, also recognize growth—evidence in the text that a student has applied what he or she learned in earlier conferences to another piece of writing.
- Some cues to look for when evaluating a student's growth as a writer include:
  - ✓ The writer identifies problems.
  - ✓ The writer thinks of solutions to a problem.
  - ✓ The writer recognizes when and how the text needs to be reorganized.
  - ✓ The writer identifies ideas in the text that need elaboration.
  - ✓ The writer makes thoughtful changes and pays attention to detail.
  - ✓ The writer takes advantage of peer and teacher conferences, books, and other resources to improve his or her writing.

Teaching Strategies for Writing

The teacher's role in writing instruction is critical. Certain strategies have been shown to be particularly effective in teaching writing.

Teacher Modeling Students learn best when they have good models. Models for the forms of writing appear in the literature selections, *Language Arts Transparencies,* and *Language Arts Handbook.* The Writing Process Strategies include instruction and models for all phases of the writing process. Teachers can also model the writing process for students every time they write.

Feedback. The most effective writing instruction is the feedback good teachers give to individual student work. Unfortunately many teachers simply mark errors in spelling, grammar, usage, and mechanics. The *Routine Card* and the *Writer's Workbook* provide questions that teachers can consider to offer constructive and meaningful feedback to students.

Clear Assignments. A well-written assignment makes clear to students what they are supposed to do, how they are supposed to do it, who the students are writing for, and what constitutes a successful response. When students have this information, they can plan, organize, and produce more effective work.

Instruction. Having students write a lot does not make them good writers. Few people become good writers, no matter how much they write. For many, the effect of years of practice is simply to produce increasingly fluent bad writing. Students need specific instruction and practice on different forms of writing and on different phases of the writing process, which they receive with instruction, modeling, practice, and feedback.

Classroom Discussion

The more students are able to discuss what they are learning, voice their confusions, and compare perceptions of what they are learning, the deeper and more meaningful their learning becomes.

Purpose

It is in discussions that students are exposed to points of view different from their own, and it is through discussion that they learn how to express their thoughts and opinions coherently. Through discussion, students add to their own knowledge that of their classmates and learn to explain themselves coherently. They also begin to ask insightful questions that help them better understand what they have read and all that they are learning through their inquiry/research and explorations. The purpose of classroom discussion is to provide a sequence through which discussion can proceed.

Procedure

Reflecting on the Selection

After students have finished reading a selection, provide an opportunity for them to engage in **whole-group** discussion about the selection. Students should:

- Check to see whether the questions they asked before reading have been answered. Encourage them to discuss whether any unanswered questions should still be answered and if so have them add those questions to the Concept/Question Board.

- Discuss any new questions that have arisen because of the reading. Encourage students to decide which of these questions should go on the Concept/Question Board.

- Share what they expected to learn from reading the selection and tell whether expectations were met.

- Talk about whatever has come to mind while reading the selection. This discussion should be an informal sharing of impressions of, or opinions about, the selection; it should never take on the aspects of a question-and-answer session about the selection.

- Give students ample opportunity to ask questions and share their thoughts about the selection. Participate as an active member of the group, making your own observations about information in a selection or modeling your own appreciation of a story. Be especially aware of unusual and interesting insights suggested by students so that these insights can be recognized and discussed. To help students learn to keep the discussion student-centered, have each student choose the next speaker instead of handing the discussion back to you.

Recording Ideas

As students finish discussions about their reactions to a selection, they should be encouraged to record their thoughts, feelings, reactions, and ideas about the selection or the subject of the selection in their Writer's Notebooks. This will not only help keep the selections fresh in students' minds; it will strengthen their writing abilities and help them learn how to write about their thoughts and feelings.

Students may find that the selection gave them ideas for their own writing, or it could have reminded them of some person or incident in their own lives. Perhaps the selection answered a question that has been on their minds or raised a question they had never thought before. Good, mature writers—especially professional writers—learn the value of recording such thoughts and impressions quickly before they fade. Students should be encouraged to do this also.

Handing Off

Handing off (Levels 1–6) is a method of turning over to students the primary responsibility for controlling discussion. Often, students who are taking responsibility for controlling a discussion tend to have all "turns" go through the teacher. The teacher is the one to whom attention is transferred when a speaker finishes, and the teacher is the one who is expected to call on the next speaker—the result being that the teacher remains the pivotal figure in the discussion.

Having the students "hand off" the discussion to other students instead of the teacher encourages them to retain complete control of the discussion and to become more actively involved in the learning process. When a student finishes his or her comments, that student should choose (hand the discussion off to) the next speaker. In this way, students maintain a discussion without relying on the teacher to decide who speaks.

When handing off is in place, the teacher's main roles are to occasionally remind students to hand off and to monitor the discussion to ensure that everyone gets a chance to contribute. The teacher may say, for example, "Remember, not just boys (or girls)," or "Try to choose someone who has not had a chance to talk yet."

In order for handing off to work effectively, a seating arrangement that allows students to see one another is essential. A circle or a semicircle is effective. In addition, all of the students need to have copies of the materials being discussed.

Actively encourage this handing-off process by letting students know that they, not you, are in control of the discussion.

If students want to remember thoughts about, or reactions to, a selection, suggest that they record these in the Writing Journal section of the Writer's Notebook. Encourage students to record the thoughts, feelings, or reactions that are elicited by any reading they do.

Exploring Concepts Within the Selection

To provide an opportunity for collaborative learning and to focus on the concepts, have students form small groups and spend time discussing what they have learned about the concepts from this selection. Topics may include new information that they have acquired or new ideas that they have had.

Students should always base their discussions on postings from the Concept/Question Board as well as on previous discussions of the concept. The small-group discussions should be ongoing throughout the unit; during this time students should continue to compare and contrast any new information with their previous ideas, opinions, and impressions about the concepts. Does this selection help confirm their ideas? Does it contradict their thinking? Has it changed their outlook?

As students discuss the concepts in small groups, circulate around the room to make sure that each group stays focused upon the selection and the concepts. After students have had some time to discuss the information and the ideas in the selection, encourage each group to formulate some statements about the concept that apply to the selection.

Sharing Ideas about Concepts

Have a representative from each group report and explain the group's ideas to the rest of the class. Then have the class formulate one or more general statements related to the unit concepts and write these statements on the Concept/Question Board. As students progress through the unit, they will gain more and more confidence in suggesting additions to the Concept/Question Board.

Visual Aids During this part of the discussion, you may find it helpful to use visual aids to help students as they build the connections to the unit concepts. Not all units or concepts will lend themselves to this type of treatment; however, aids such as time lines, charts, graphs, or pictographs may help students see how each new selection adds to their growing knowledge of the concepts.

Encourage students to ask questions about the concepts that the selection may have raised. Have students list on the Concept/Question Board those questions that cannot be answered immediately and that they want to explore further.

Exploring Concepts Across Selections

As each new selection is read, encourage students to discuss its connection with the other selections and with the unit concepts. Also encourage students to think about selections that they have read from other units and how they relate to the concepts for this unit.

Ultimately, it is this ability to make connections between past knowledge and new knowledge that allows any learner to gain insights into what is being studied. The goal of the work with concepts and the discussions is to help students to start thinking in terms of connections—how is this like what I have learned before? Does this information confirm, contradict, or add a completely different layer to that which I already know about this concept? How can the others in the class have such different ideas than I do when we just read the same selection? Why is so much written about this subject?

Learning to make connections and to delve deeper through self-generated questions gives students the tools they need to become effective, efficient, lifelong learners.

Tips

■ Discussions offer a prime opportunity for you to introduce, or seed, new ideas about the concepts. New ideas can come from a variety of sources: students may draw on their own experiences or on the books or videos they are studying; you may introduce new ideas into the discussion; or you may, at times, invite experts to speak to the class.

■ If students do not mention an important idea that is necessary to the understanding of some larger issue, you may "drop" that idea into the conversation and, indeed, repeat it several times to make sure that it does get picked up. This seeding may be subtle ("I think that might be important here.") or quite direct ("This is a big idea, one that we will definitely need to understand and one that we will return to regularly.").

Discussion is an integral part of learning.

■ In order to facilitate this process for each unit, you must be aware of the unit concepts and be able to recognize and reinforce them when they arise spontaneously in discussions. If central unit concepts do not arise naturally, then, and only then, will you seed these ideas by direct modeling. The more you turn

discussions over to students, the more involved they will become, and the more responsibility they will take for their own learning. Make it your goal to become a participant in, rather than the leader of, class discussions.

■ Help students to see that they are responsible for carrying on the discussion. After a question is asked, always wait instead of jumping in with a comment or an explanation. Although this wait time may be uncomfortable at first, students will come to understand that the discussion is their responsibility and that you will not jump in every time there is a hesitation.

■ As the year progresses, students will become more and more adept at conducting and participating in meaningful discussions about what they have read. These discussions will greatly enhance students' understanding of the concepts that they are exploring.

Discussion Starters

■ I didn't know that . . . .
■ Does anyone know . . . .
■ I figured out that . . . .
■ I liked the part where . . . .
■ I'm still confused about . . . .
■ This made me think . . . .
■ I agree with _____ because . . . .
■ I disagree with _____ because . . . .
■ The reason I think . . . .

Inquiry and Investigation

Research and Investigation form the heart of the *SRA/Open Court Reading* program. In order to encourage students to understand how reading can enhance their lives and help them to become mature, educated adults, they are asked in each unit to use what they are learning in the unit as the basis for further exploration and research. The unit information is simply the base for their investigations.

There are two types of units in the *SRA/Open Court Reading* program—units based on universal topics of interest such as Friendship, Perseverance, and Courage and research units that provide students a very solid base of information upon which they can begin their own inquiry and research. Units delving into such areas as fossils, astronomy, and medicine invite students to become true researchers by choosing definite areas of interest—problems or questions to research in small cooperative groups and then to present to their classmates. In this way, students gain much more knowledge of the subject than they would have simply by reading the selections in the unit.

The selections in the units are organized so that each selection will add more information or a different perspective to students' growing bodies of knowledge.

Investigating through Reflective Activities

Purpose

The units in *SRA/Open Court Reading* that deal with universal topics will be explored through reflective activities. These units—such as Courage, Friendship, and Risks and Consequences—are organized to help students expand their perspectives in familiar areas. As they explore and discuss the unit concepts related to each topic, students are involved in activities that extend their experiences and offer opportunities for reflection. Such activities include writing, drama, art, interviews, debates, and panel discussions. Throughout each unit, students may be involved in a single ongoing investigative activity, or they may participate in a number of different activities. They may choose to produce a final written project or a visual aid. They will share with the rest of the class the new knowledge that they have gained from their reflective activities. During **Workshop** students will work individually or in collaborative groups on their investigation and/or projects.

The reflective activities will be activities of students' own choosing that allow them to explore the unit concepts more fully. They are free, of course, to make other choices or to devise activities of their own.

Procedure

Choosing an Area to Investigate

Students may work on activities alone, in pairs, or in small groups. They have the option of writing about or presenting their findings to the whole group upon completion. Before choosing a reflective activity, students should decide what concept-related question or problem they wish to explore. Generally, it is better for students to generate questions or problems after they have engaged in some discussion but before they have had a chance to consult source materials. This approach is more likely to bring forth ideas that students actually wonder about or wish to understand. Students may also look at the questions posted on the Concept/Question Board or introduce fresh ideas inspired by material they have just finished reading. Students who are working in pairs or in small groups should confer with one another before making a decision about what to explore. Some of the students may need your assistance in deciding upon, or narrowing down, a question or a problem so that it can be explored more easily. A good way to model this process for students is to make webs for a few of your own ideas on the board and to narrow these ideas down to a workable question or problem.

Organizing the Group

After a question or a problem has been chosen, the students may choose an activity that will help them to investigate that problem or question. The students' next responsibility is to decide who is going to investigate which facet of the question or the problem (when they are conducting a literature search, for example) or who is going to perform which task related to the particular reflective activity (when they are writing and performing an original playlet or puppet show, for example). Lastly, students need to decide how, or if, they want to present their findings. For instance, after conducting a literature search, some students may want to read and discuss passages from a book with a plot or theme that relates to a unit concept. Other students may prefer acting out and discussing scenes from the book.

Deciding How to Investigate

The following suggestions may help you and your students choose ways in which to pursue their investigations. You may want to post this list in the classroom so that groups have access to it as they decide what they want to investigate and how they want to proceed.

Investigation Activities

- Conduct a literature search to pursue a question or a problem. Discussion or writing may follow.
- Write and produce an original playlet or puppet show based on situations related to the concepts.
- Play a role-playing game to work out a problem related to the concepts.
- Stage a panel discussion with audience participation on a question or problem.
- Hold a debate on an issue related to the concept.
- Write an advice column dealing with problems related to the concepts.
- Write a personal-experience story related to the concepts.
- Invite experts to class. Formulate questions to ask.
- Conduct an interview with someone on a subject related to the concepts.
- Produce and carry out a survey on an issue or question related to the concept.
- Produce a picture or photo essay about the concept.

EXAMPLE: In the Heritage unit in grade 5 of *SRA/Open Court Reading,* students read "In Two Worlds: A Yup'ik Eskimo Family." This selection is about how three generations of Eskimos living in Alaska near the Arctic strive to adopt the best of modern ways without abandoning their traditional values. During the class discussion, some students may note that Alice and Billy Rivers want their students to learn both the new and the old ways of living. As the discussion continues, many students may conclude from the story that the older generations hope that future generations will continue to value their roots and their cultural traditions. Students then relate this story to their own heritage. Some students may share information about their customs or traditions.

Students choose some reflective activities that will help them learn more about family heritage and that will answer some of their questions about the unit concepts. Some students may be interested in interviewing family members or close family friends about their cultural traditions and heritages. These students review what they know about interviewing. They proceed by:

- Contacting in advance the person(s) they want to interview.
- Preparing a list of questions to ask.
- Preparing a list of subjects to discuss, deciding how to record the interview (by audiotape, videotape, or taking notes).
- Deciding whether to photograph the person and, if so, getting permission to do so in advance—collecting the equipment necessary for conducting the interview.

After they conduct the interviews, students decide how they wish to present the information that they have collected.

> *Investigating through reflective activities allows students to gain a wider perspective on a concept by relating it to their own experiences. Students quickly become aware that it is their responsibility to learn and to help their peers learn more about the unit concepts.*

EXAMPLE: Another group of students in the same fifth-grade class may be more interested in planning a photo essay about one family or about a neighborhood with many families belonging to a particular culture. These students may decide to re-examine "In Two Worlds" to notice how the text and the photographs complement each other and what information is conveyed in each photograph. They may also decide to examine some photo essays listed in the unit bibliography. These students will need to make some advance preparations as well. They proceed by:

- Determining which neighborhood and which family or families to photograph.
- Contacting in advance the persons to be interviewed and photographed.
- Touring the neighborhood in advance of the photo shoot.
- Making a list of questions to ask the family or families about their heritage or about their neighborhood.

- Thinking about what information to include in their essay so that they can determine what photographs to take.
- Collecting the equipment necessary for conducting interviews and photographing subjects.

After students collect the information and take photographs, they may write and organize the photo essay and present it to the class. The teacher should remind students of the phases of the writing process, and encourage them to revise and proofread their work until they are completely pleased with it. Students can continue discussing family heritage and raising any new questions that they wish to investigate. The teacher should remind them that as they read further, they may think of a variety of ways to explore the unit concepts. The teacher should then ask students to post on the Concept/Question Board any new questions they have about family heritage. Students should sign or initial their questions so that they can identify classmates with similar interests and exchange ideas with them. The teacher should encourage students to feel free to write an answer or a note on someone else's question or to consult the board for ideas for their own explorations. From time to time, the teacher should post his or her own questions on the Concept/Question Board.

Tips

- The *Leveled Classroom Library* contains books related to the unit concepts. Remind students that these are good sources of information and that they should consult them regularly— especially when they are investigating concept-related ideas and questions.
- Some students work better within a specified time frame. Whenever they are beginning a new activity, discuss with the students a reasonable period of time within which they will be expected to complete their investigations. Post the completion date somewhere in the classroom so that students can refer to it and pace themselves accordingly. At first, you may have to help them determine a suitable deadline, but eventually they should be able to make this judgment on their own.

Inquiry and Investigation (continued)

Investigating through Research

Purpose

Students come to school with a wealth of fascinating questions. Educators need to capitalize on this excitement for learning and natural curiosity. A classroom in which only correct answers are accepted and students are not allowed to make errors and consider alternative possibilities to questions can quickly deaden this natural curiosity and enthusiasm. The purpose of the research aspect of this program is to capitalize on students' questions and natural curiosity by using a proven structure. This structure helps students to not get lost or bogged down but at the same time to preserve the open-ended character of real research, which can lead to unexpected findings and to questions that were not originally considered.

There is a conventional approach to school research papers that can be found, with minor variations, in countless textbooks. It consists of a series of steps such as the following: select a topic, narrow the topic, collect materials, take notes, outline, and write. By following these steps, a student may produce a presentable paper, but the procedure does not constitute research in a meaningful sense and indeed gives students a distorted notion of what research is about. We see students in universities and even in graduate schools still following this procedure when they do library research papers or literature reviews; we see their dismay when their professors regard such work as mere cutting and pasting and ask them where their original contribution is.

Even elementary school students can produce works of genuine research—research that seeks answers to real questions or solutions to real problems. This skill in collecting and analyzing information is a valuable tool in the adult world in which adults, as consumers, are constantly analyzing new information and making informed decisions on the basis of this information. Preparing students for the analytic demands of adult life and teaching them how to find answers to their questions are goals of education.

Procedure

In order to make the research productive, the following important principles are embodied in this approach:

1. Research is focused on problems, not topics.
2. Conjectures—opinions based on less than complete evidence or proof—guide the research; the research does not simply produce conjectures.

3. New information is gathered to test and revise conjectures.
4. Discussion, ongoing feedback, and constructive criticism are important in all phases of the research but especially in the revising of problems and conjectures.
5. The cycle of true research is essentially endless, although presentations of findings are made from time to time; new findings give rise to new problems and conjectures and thus to new cycles of research.

Following a Process

While working with the research units, students are encouraged to follow a set pattern or cycle in order to keep their research activities focused and on track. Students may go through these steps many times before they come to the end of their research. Certainly for adult researchers, this cycle of question, conjecture, research, and reevaluation can go on for years and in some cases lifetimes.

This cycle uses the following process:

1. **Decide on a problem or question to research.** Students should identify a question or problem that they truly wonder about or wish to understand and then form research groups with other students who have the same interests.
   - My problem or question is _____
2. **Formulate an idea or conjecture about the research problem.** Students should think about and discuss with classmates possible answers to their research problems or questions and meet with their research groups to discuss and record their ideas or conjectures.
   - My idea/conjecture/theory about this question or problem is _____
3. **Identify needs and make plans.** Students should identify knowledge needs related to their conjectures and meet with their research groups to determine which resources to consult and to make individual job assignments. Students should also meet periodically with the teacher, other classmates, and research groups to present preliminary findings and make revisions to their problems and conjectures on the basis of these findings.
   - I need to find out _____
   - To do this, I will need these resources _____
   - My role in the group is _____
   - This is what I have learned so far _____
   - This is what happened when we presented our findings _____

4. **Reevaluate the problem or question based on what we have learned so far and the feedback we have received.**
   - My revised problem or question is _____
5. **Revise the idea or conjecture.**
   - My new conjecture about this problem is _____
6. **Identify new needs and make new plans.**
   - Based on what I found out, I still need to know _____
   - To do this, I will need these resources _____
   - This is what I have learned _____
   - This is what happened when we presented our new findings _____

Procedure for Choosing a Problem to Research

1. Discuss with students the nature of the unit. Explain to students that the unit they are reading is a research unit and that they will produce and publish in some way the results of their explorations. They are free to decide what problems or questions they wish to explore, with whom they want to work, and how they want to present their finished products. They may publish a piece of writing, produce a poster, write and perform a play, or use any other means to present the results of their investigations and research. They may work with partners or in small groups.
2. Discuss with students the schedule you have planned for their investigations: how long the project is expected to take, how much time will be available for research, when the first presentation will be due. This schedule will partly determine the nature of the problems that students should be encouraged to work on and the depth of the inquiry students will be encouraged to pursue.
3. Have students talk about things they wonder about that are related to the unit subject. For example, in the grade 3 unit, Money, students might wonder where money in the money machine comes from or how prices are determined. Conduct a free-floating discussion of questions about the unit subject.
4. Brainstorm possible questions for students to think about. It is essential that the students' own ideas and questions be the starting point of all inquiry. *Helpful hint:* For the first research unit, you might wish to generate a list of your own ideas, having students add to this list and having them choose from it.

5. Using their wonderings, model for students the difference between a research topic and a research problem or question by providing several examples. For example, have them consider the difference between the topic California and the problem, *Why do so many people move to California?* Explain to them that if they choose to research the topic California, everything they look up under the subject heading or index entry *California* will be related in some way to their topic. Therefore, it will be quite difficult to choose which information to record. This excess of information also creates problems in organizing their research. Clearly, then, this topic is too broad and general. Choosing a specific question or problem, one that particularly interests them, helps them narrow their exploration and advance their understanding. Some possible ideas for questions can be found in the unit introduction. Ideas can also be generated as you and your students create a web of their questions or problems related to the unit concept. For example, questions related to the subject California might include the following:

■ Why do so many people move to California?

■ How have the different groups of people living in California affected the state?

6. A good research problem or question not only requires students to consult a variety of sources but is engaging and adds to the groups' knowledge of the concepts. Furthermore, good problems generate more questions. Help students understand that the question, *Why do so many people move to California?* is an easy one to research. Many sources will contribute to an answer to the question, and all information located can be easily evaluated in terms of usefulness in answering the question. *Helpful hint:* Students' initial responses may indeed be topics instead of problems or questions. If so, the following questions might be helpful:

■ What aspect of the topic really interests you?

■ Can you turn that idea into a question?

7. Remember that this initial problem or question serves only as a guide for research. As students begin collecting information and collaborating with classmates, their ideas will change, and they can revise their research problem or question. Frequently, students do not sufficiently revise their problems until after they have had time to consider their conjectures and collect information.

8. As students begin formulating their research problems, have them elaborate on their reasons for wanting to research their stated problems. They should go beyond simple expressions of interest or liking and indicate what is puzzling, important, or potentially informative, and so forth, about the problems they have chosen.

9. At this stage, students' ideas will be of a very vague and limited sort. The important thing is to start them thinking about what really interests them and what value it has to them and the class.

10. Have students present their proposed problems or questions, along with reasons for their choices, and have an open discussion of how promising proposed problems are. As students present their proposed problems, ask them what new things they think they will be learning from their investigations and how that will add to the group's growing knowledge of the concepts. This constant emphasis on group knowledge building will help set a clear purpose for students' research.

> *Even elementary school students can produce works of genuine research— research that seeks answers to real questions or solutions to real problems.*

11. Form research groups. To make it easier for students to form groups, they may record their problems on the board or on self-sticking notes. Final groups should be constituted in the way you find best for your class—by self-selection, by assignment on the basis of common interests, or by some combination of methods. Students can then meet during **Workshop** to agree on a precise statement of their research problem, the nature of their expected research contributions, and lists of related questions that may help later in assigning individual roles. They should also record any scheduling information that can be added to the planning calendar.

Using Technology

The **Research Assistant CD-ROM** (Levels 2–6), an interactive software program, supports student research by helping them plan, organize, present, and assess their research.

Students and teachers can access the Web site **www.sra4kids.com** to find information about the themes in their grade level.

Tips

■ If students are careful about the problems or questions they choose to research, they should have few problems in following through with the research. If the problem is too broad or too narrow, they will have problems.

■ Have students take sufficient time in assessing their needs—both knowledge needs and physical needs in relation to their research. Careful preplanning can help the research progress smoothly with great results.

■ Encourage students to reevaluate their needs often so they are not wasting time finding things they already have or ignoring needs that they haven't noticed.

■ Interim presentations of material are every bit as important, if not more so, than final presentations. It is during interim presentations that students have the opportunity to rethink and reevaluate their work and change direction or decide to carry on with their planned research.

Workshop

Every teacher and every student needs time during the day to organize, take stock of work that is done, make plans for work that needs doing, and finish up incomplete projects. In addition, time is needed for differentiating instruction and for peer conferencing.

Purpose

Workshop is the period of time each day in which students work independently or collaboratively to practice and review material taught in the lessons.

A variety of activities may occur during this time. Students may work on a specific daily assignment, complete an ongoing project, work on unit exploration activities, focus on writing, or choose from among a wide range of possibilities. With lots of guidance and encouragement, students gradually learn to make decisions about their use of time and materials and to collaborate with their peers.

A goal of **Workshop** is to get students to work independently. This is essential since **Workshop** is also the time during which the teacher can work with individuals or groups of students to reinforce learning, to provide extra help for those having difficulties, to extend learning, or to assess the progress of the class or of individuals.

Procedure

Initially, for many students, you will need to structure **Workshop** carefully. Eventually, students will automatically go to the appropriate areas, take up ongoing projects, and get the materials they will need. **Workshop** will evolve slowly from a very structured period to a time when students make choices and move freely from one activity to the next.

Adhere firmly to **Workshop** guidelines. By the time the students have completed the first few weeks of school, they should feel confident during **Workshop**. If not, continue to structure the time and limit options. For young students, early periods of **Workshop** may run no more than five to eight minutes. The time can gradually increase to fifteen minutes or longer as the students gain independence. Older students may be able to work longer and independently from the very beginning of the school year.

Introducing Workshop

Introduce **Workshop** to students by telling them that every day there will be a time when they are expected to work on activities on their own or in small groups. For young students in the beginning, you will assign the **Workshop** activities to help them learn to work on their own. Point out the shelf or area of the classroom where **Workshop** materials are stored. Tell students that when they finish working with the materials for one activity, they will choose something else from the **Workshop** shelf. New activity materials will be added to the shelf from time to time. Make sure that the students know that they may always look at books during **Workshop**.

Tell older students that they will have an opportunity each day to work on their unit explorations, their writing, and other projects. Students will be working independently and collaboratively during this time.

Guidelines

- Make sure each student knows what he or she needs to do during **Workshop**.
- Demonstrate for the whole group any activity assigned for **Workshop**; for example, teaching the students a new game, introducing new materials or projects, or explaining different areas.
- For young students, it is essential to introduce and demonstrate different activities and games before the students do them on their own. With games, you may want to have several students play while the others watch. Make sure that all the students know exactly what is expected of them.
- In the beginning, plan to circulate among the students providing encouragement and help as necessary.
- Once students are engaged in appropriate activities and can work independently, meet with those students who need your particular attention. This may include individual students or small groups.
- Let the students know that they need to ask questions and clarify assignments during **Workshop** introduction, so that you are free to work with small groups.
- Be sure that students know what they are to do when they have finished an activity and where to put their finished work.

Establish and discuss rules for **Workshop** with the students. Keep them simple and straightforward. You may want to write the finalized rules on the board or on a poster. You may want to review these rules each day at the beginning of **Workshop** for the first few lessons or so. You may also wish to revisit and revise the rules from time to time. Suggested rules include:

✓ Be polite.
✓ Share.
✓ Whisper.
✓ Take only the materials you need.
✓ Return materials.

Setting Up Your Classroom for Workshop

Carefully setting up your classroom to accommodate different **Workshop** activities will help assure that the **Workshop** period progresses smoothly and effectively. While setting up your classroom, keep the primary **Workshop** activities in mind. During **Workshop** the students will be doing independent and collaborative activities. In kindergarten and first grade, these activities may include letter recognition and phonemic awareness activities and writing or illustrating stories or projects. In addition, they will be working on individual or small group projects.

Many classrooms have centers that the students visit on a regular or rotating basis. Center time can be easily and efficiently incorporated into the **Workshop** concept. For example, the activities suggested during **Workshop** can be incorporated into reading and writing areas. Other typical classroom areas include an art center, math center, science table, play area, etc.

The following are suggestions for space and materials for use during **Workshop**:

1. **Reading Area** supplied with books and magazines. The materials in the Reading Area should be dynamic—changing with students' abilities and reflecting unit themes they are reading. You may wish to add books suggested in the *Leveled Classroom Libraries* and unit bibliographies available with each unit.

2. **Writing Area** stocked with various types and sizes of lined and unlined paper, pencils, erasers, markers, crayons, small slates, and chalk. The area should also have various **Letter Cards**, other handwriting models, and worksheets for those students who want to practice letter formation or handwriting. Students should know that this is where they come for writing supplies. In addition to the supplies described above, the Writing Area can also have supplies to encourage the students to create and write on their own:

✓ magazines and catalogs to cut up for pictures; stickers, paint, glue, glitter, etc. to decorate books and book covers; precut and stapled blank books for the students to write in. (Some can be plain and some cut in special shapes.)

✓ cardboard, tag board, construction paper, etc., for making book covers. (Provide some samples.)

✓ tape, scissors, yarn, hole punches for binding books.

✓ picture dictionaries, dictionaries, thesaurus, word lists, and other materials that may encourage independence.

3. **Listening Area** supplied with tape recorder, CD player, optional headphones, and tapes of stories, poems, and songs for the students to listen to and react to. You might also want to provide blank tapes and encourage the students to retell and record their favorite stories or make up and tell stories for their classmates to listen to on tape. You may also want to make available the *Listening Library Audiocassettes/CDs* that are available with the program.

4. **Workshop Activity Center** supplied with **Alphabet Flash Cards,** individual **Alphabet Sound Card** sets (Kindergarten), **Individual Sound/Spelling Cards** and **High-Frequency Word Flash Cards** (Grades 1-3), and other materials that enhance what the students are learning. Other commonly used classroom materials that enhance reading can be included (for example, plastic letters, puzzles, workbooks).

Since students will be working on their inquiry/investigations during **Workshop**, make sure there are adequate supplies to help them with their research. These might include dictionaries, encyclopedias, magazines, newspapers, and computers—preferably with Internet capability.

> *Workshop is the period of time each day in which students work independently or collaboratively to practice and review material taught in the lessons.*

Students thrive in an environment that provides structure, repetition, and routine. Within a sound structure, the students will gain confidence and independence. This setting allows you to differentiate instruction in order to provide opportunities for flexibility and individual choice. This will allow students to develop their strengths, abilities, and talents to the fullest.

Suggestions for English Language Learners

Workshop affords students who are English Language Learners a wealth of opportunities for gaining proficiency in English. It also encourages them to share their backgrounds with peers. Since you will be working with all students individually and in small groups regardless of their reading ability, students who need special help with language will not feel self-conscious about working with you. In addition, working in small groups made up of students with the same interests rather than the same abilities will provide them with the opportunity to learn about language from their peers during the regular course of **Workshop** activities.

Some suggestions for meeting the special needs of students with diverse backgrounds follow:

■ Preread a selection with English Language Learners to help them identify words and ideas they wish to talk about. This will prepare them for discussions with the whole group.

■ Preteach vocabulary and develop selection concepts that may be a challenge for students.

■ Negotiate the meaning of selections by asking questions, checking for comprehension, and speaking with English Language Learners as much as possible.

■ Draw English Language Learners into small group discussions to give them a sense that their ideas are valid and worth attention.

■ Pair English Language Learners with native English speakers to share their experiences and provide new knowledge to other students.

■ Have English Language Learners draw or dictate to you or another student a description of a new idea they may have during **Workshop** activities.

Workshop Management Tips

Use the following **Workshop** management tips to ensure that **Workshop** runs smoothly. Note that these suggestions for a weekly unit/lesson may not exactly correspond to a particular unit/lesson in a given grade level, but will give you a sense of how **Workshop** should progress.

Unit 1, Lesson 1 Introduce **Workshop** to students. Make sure they know where materials are located. Post the rules on the board or other prominent place in the classroom. Keep **Workshop** time short (less than thirty minutes) and very directed during the first few weeks until students can work independently.

Unit 1, Lesson 2 Discuss using small groups for pre/reteaching purposes and how you will indicate who will be in the groups. Start by forming one small group randomly and having other students do something specific such as a writing assignment. When you have finished with the small group, send them to do independent work. Call another small group of students to work with you. Continue this each day until students are accustomed to forming groups and working independently.

Unit 1, Lesson 3 Reading Roundtable is a student-formed and student-run book discussion. Encourage students participating in Reading Roundtable to choose a book that they all will read and discuss. Several different Reading Roundtable groups may form on the basis of the books students choose.

Unit 1, Lesson 4 For the first few weeks of the school year, make sure each student has a plan for using **Workshop** time.

Unit 1, Lesson 5 Allot time for presentation and discussion of research activities. Use a whole **Workshop** day and have all groups present their findings, or split the presentations over several days, depending on the small-group needs of your class.

Unit 1, Lesson 6 Review how students have used **Workshop** during this unit. Have they used their time well? Do they have the materials they need? Discuss suggestions for improving their use of this time. Take a few minutes at the beginning of each **Workshop** to make sure students know what they will be doing.

Unit 2, Lesson 1 Form small extra-practice groups with the more advanced students from time to time, as they also need special attention.

Unit 2, Lesson 2 To keep the whole class informed about the independent research being done, every other day or so invite a research group to explain what it is doing, how the research is going, and any problems they are encountering.

Workshop (continued)

Unit 2, Lesson 3 Discuss the use of **Workshop** time for doing inquiry and research projects. Introduce students to the activities provided for use with this unit at **www.sra4kids.com.**

Unit 2, Lesson 4 Make sure small extra-practice groups are formed based on your observations of students' work on the different daily lessons. Small groups should be fluid and based on demonstrated need rather than becoming static and unchanging.

Unit 2, Lesson 5 One purpose of **Workshop** is to help students learn independence and responsibility. Assign students to monitor **Workshop** materials. They should alert you whenever materials are running low or missing, and they can be responsible for checking on return dates of library books and making sure the books are either returned or renewed.

Unit 2, Lesson 6 Students sometimes have difficulty starting discussions in Reading Roundtable. Try some of these discussion starters with students, and print them on a poster paper for student use.

I didn't know that . . .   I liked the part where . . .

Does anyone know . . .   I'm still confused by . . .

I figured out that . . .   This made me think . . .

I agree/disagree with _____ because . . .

Unit 3, Lesson 1 By this time students should be accustomed to the routines, rules, expectations, and usage of **Workshop** time and be moving smoothly from small teacher-led groups to independent work. Monitor small groups occasionally to see that they are on task and making progress on their activities.

Unit 3, Lesson 2 Make a practice of reading aloud to students. All students enjoy being read to, no matter their age or grade. Encourage them to discuss the shared reading in Reading Roundtable groups and to bring books and read them aloud to their classmates.

Unit 3, Lesson 3 Encourage cooperation and collaboration by providing students with opportunities to engage in small groups.

Unit 3, Lesson 4 Spend a few minutes each day circulating around the room and monitoring what students are doing independently or in small groups. Students can then share any questions or problems they are having with you on a timely basis.

Unit 3, Lesson 5 Take note of different small groups. Make sure that quieter students are able to participate in the discussions. Often the stronger, more confident students dominate such discussions. Encourage them to give all participants a chance to share their ideas.

Unit 3, Lesson 6 If students are not productive during **Workshop**, keep them in the small group you are working with until they can successfully benefit from independent work.

Discuss strategies they could use to become more independent.

Unit 4, Lesson 1 Different students can monitor **Workshop** materials and alert you when materials or supplies are running low or missing and can check that library books are either returned or renewed.

Unit 4, Lesson 2 From time to time, join a Reading Roundtable group, and take part in their discussion. Make sure students lead the discussion.

Unit 4, Lesson 3 Encourage responsibility and independence by reminding students to show respect for each other and the materials provided.

Unit 4, Lesson 4 Be sure students discuss during Reading Roundtable what they like or dislike about a book, why they wanted to read it, and how the book either lived up to their expectations or disappointed them. Discussions should not be about basic comprehension but should help students think more deeply about the ideas presented in the book.

Unit 4, Lesson 5 Make sure students continue to use the activities provided for use with this unit at **www.sra4kids.com.**

Unit 4, Lesson 6 If students are not productive in **Workshop**, keep them in the small group you are working with until they can successfully benefit from independent work. Discuss strategies they could use to become more independent.

Unit 5, Lesson 1 Students often make great tutors for other students. They are uniquely qualified to understand problems that others might be having. Encourage students to pair up during **Workshop** to help each other with their daily lessons.

Unit 5, Lesson 2 Form small extra-practice groups with the more advanced students from time to time, as they also need special attention.

Unit 5, Lesson 3 In order to keep the whole class informed about the independent research being done, every other day or so, invite a research/investigation group to explain what it is doing, how the research is going, and any problems they are encountering.

Unit 5, Lesson 4 Most of the authors of the student anthology selections are well known and have written many, many pieces of fine literature. Encourage students who enjoy the anthology selections to find other books by the same author. Encourage them to think about and discuss what about that particular author's work attracts them.

Unit 5, Lesson 5 Share your impressions of books from the ***Leveled Classroom Library*** or other reading during Reading Roundtable. Note which students initiate sharing and which are reluctant to share.

Unit 5, Lesson 6 Review with students the time they have used in **Workshop**. Have they used their time well? Do they have the materials they need? Discuss suggestions for improving the use of this time.

Unit 6, Lesson 1 Spend a few minutes each day circulating around the room and monitoring what students are doing independently or in small groups. Students can share any questions or problems they are having with you on a timely basis.

Unit 6, Lesson 2 Students should be accustomed to the routines, rules, expectations, and usage of **Workshop** time and be moving smoothly from small teacher-led groups to independent work. Make sure to monitor small groups occasionally to see that they are on task and making progress with their activities.

Unit 6, Lesson 3 Make sure students continue to use the activities provided for use with this unit at **www.sra4kids.com.**

Unit 6, Lesson 4 Allot time for presentation and discussion of research activities. You may want to use a whole **Workshop** day and have all groups present their findings or split the presentations over several days, depending on the urgency of the small-group instruction your class needs.

Unit 6, Lesson 5 Students often make great tutors for other students. The fact that they too are just learning the materials makes them uniquely qualified to understand problems that others might be having. Encourage students to pair up during **Workshop** to help each other on their daily lessons.

Unit 6, Lesson 6 If the reading selection is an excerpt from a longer piece, encourage students to read the book from which the excerpt is taken and discuss how the excerpt fits into the larger work.

Assessment can be one of your most effective teaching tools if it is used with the purpose of informing instruction and highlighting areas that need special attention.

Purpose

Assessment is a tool the teacher uses to monitor students' progress and to detect students' strengths and weaknesses. Evaluation of student learning is addressed in two ways: Informal Assessment and Formal Assessment. Informal, observational assessment, or a quick check of students' written work, is presented in the *Teacher's Edition* in the form of assessment suggestions. Formal Assessment consists of performance assessment (both reading and writing) and objective tests (multiple choice and essay).

Procedure

Informal Assessment

Observation

Observing students as they go about their regular classwork is probably the single most effective way to learn in depth your students' strengths and areas of need. The more students become accustomed to you jotting down informal notes about their work, the more it will become just another part of classroom life that they accept and take little note of. This gives you the opportunity to assess their progress constantly without the interference and possible drawback of formal testing situations.

In order to make informal assessment of student progress a part of your everyday classroom routine, you might want to start by preparing the materials you will need on hand.

- Enter students' names in the Teacher's Observation Log, found in *Program Assessment.*
- Before each day's lesson begins, decide which students you will observe.
- Keep the Teacher's Observation Log available so that you can easily record your observations.
- Decide what aspect of the students' learning you wish to monitor.
- During each lesson, observe this aspect in the performances of several students.
- Record your observations.
- It may take four to five days to make sure you have observed and recorded the performance of each student. If you need more information about performance in a particular area for some of your students, you may want to observe them more than once.

Progress Assessment

Written Work

Students are writing one thing or another all day long. Each of these pieces of writing can provide you with valuable information about your students' progress. Two very helpful resources that students will work in daily are the *Comprehension and Language Arts Skills* (Levels 1–6) and the *Inquiry Journal* (Levels 2–6).

- The *Comprehension and Language Arts Skills* include skills practice lessons that act as practice and reinforcement for the skills lessons taught during the reading of the lesson or in conjunction with the Language Arts lesson. These skill pages give you a clear picture of students' understanding of the skills taught. Use them as a daily assessment of student progress in the particular skills taught through the program. In *Phonemic Awareness and Phonics Skills* (K), and *Phonics Skills* (1), students practice each of the skills taught in Part 1 of the program.

- The *Inquiry Journal* can give you invaluable information on how students are progressing in many different areas. In the *Inquiry Journal,* students

  ✓ Record what they know about the concepts and what they learn. You will be able to monitor their growing ability to make connections and use their prior knowledge to help them understand new concepts.

  ✓ Keep a record of their research: what resources they need, what they have used, where they have looked, and what they have found. You can keep track of students' growing ability to find the resources and knowledge base they need to answer the questions they pose.

  ✓ Keep track of their work with their collaborative groups. This will give you a good idea of students' growing ability to work with peers for a common goal—the acquisition of new knowledge.

  ✓ Practice study and research skills that will help them in all of their schooling. You can easily keep track of how well they are learning to use such things as library resources, reference books, visual organizers, and much, much more.

Dictation

In grades 1–3, students use dictation to practice the sound/spelling associations they are learning and/or reviewing. Collect the dictation papers and look through them to see how the students are doing with writing and with proofreading their words. Record notes on the papers and keep them in the student portfolios.

Portfolios

Portfolios are more than just a collection bin or gathering place for student projects and records. They add balance to an assessment program by providing unique benefits to teachers, students, and families.

- Portfolios help build self-confidence and increase self-esteem as students come to appreciate the value of their work. More importantly, portfolios allow students to reflect on what they know and what they need to learn. At the end of the school year, each student will be able to go through their portfolios and write about their progress.

- Portfolios provide the teacher with an authentic record of what students can do. Just as important, portfolios give students a concrete example of their own progress and development. Thus, portfolios become a valuable source of information for making instructional decisions.

- Portfolios allow families to judge student performance directly. Portfolios are an ideal starting point for discussions about a student's achievements and future goals during teacher/family conferences.

You will find that there are many opportunities to add to students' portfolios.

Assessment (continued)

Reading

- During partner reading, during **Workshop**, or at other times of the day, invite students, one at a time, to sit with you and read a story from an appropriate *Decodable Book* (grades 1–3) or from the *Student Anthology.*

- As each student reads to you, follow along and make note of any recurring problems the student has while reading. Note students' ability to decode unknown words as well as any attempt—successful or not—to use strategies to clarify or otherwise make sense of what they are reading. From time to time, check students' fluency by timing their reading and noting how well they are able to sustain the oral reading without faltering.

- If the student has trouble reading a particular **Decodable Book**, encourage the student to read the story a few times on her or his own before reading it aloud to you. If the **Decodable Book** has two stories, use the alternate story to reassess the student a day or two later.

- If after practicing with a particular **Decodable Book** and reading it on his or her own a few times, a student is still experiencing difficulty, try the following:

  - Drop back two **Decodable Books.** (Continue to drop back until the student is able to read a story with no trouble.) If the student can read that book without problems, move up one book.

  - Continue the process until the student is able to read the current Decodable Book.

Preparing for Formal Assessment
Written Tests

- Have the students clear their desks.
- Make sure the students can hear and see clearly.
- Explain the instructions and complete one or two examples with students before each test to make sure they understand what to do.
- Give students ample time to finish each test.

> *Observing students as they go about their regular classwork is probably the single most effective way to learn in depth your students' strengths and areas of need.*

The assessment components of **Open Court Reading** are designed to help teachers make appropriate instructional decisions. The variety of assessments is intended to be used continuously and formatively. That is, students should be assessed regularly as a follow-up to instructional activities, and the results of the assessment should be used to inform subsequent instruction.

Program Assessment

The Program Assessment is a series of three broad measures that are meant to be administered at the beginning of the school year, at midyear, and at the end of the year.

- The Pretest gives teachers a snapshot of students' entry-level skills. This information allows the teacher to provide supplemental instruction to students who have not mastered critical skills and to offer more challenging material to students who demonstrate advanced abilities. In addition, this Pretest can serve as a baseline against which to measure students' progress throughout the year.

- The Midyear Test reviews skills that were taught in the first half of the school year, allowing teachers to determine how well students are retaining what they have learned. In addition, the Midyear Test contains "anchor items" similar to those that appeared on the pretest. These items will allow teachers to measure student progress from the beginning of the year to the middle of the year.

- The Posttest is a review of the content that was taught throughout the year and is a summative measure that reflects exit-level skills. The Posttest also contains anchor items, so it is possible to compare students' performance on specific skills at three points in the school year.

In addition to the Pretest, Midyear Test, and Posttest, the Program Assessment also contains a Teacher's Observation Log. Informal assessment is a part of the everyday classroom routine. Teachers can record information quickly on this observation sheet, and they may extend their observations over several days, until they have had a chance to observe each student's performance in a particular area.

Unit Assessments

Unit Assessments, as the name implies, reflect the instructional content and reading selections in each unit. The various measures within a unit assessment allow the teacher to see how well students have learned the skills that have recently been taught and to provide any additional instruction that is necessary.

Unit Assessments include a variety of measures that vary in form and difficulty so they are both motivating and challenging. Some of the questions are relatively easy, and most students should answer them correctly. Others are more difficult, but none are beyond the abilities of the majority of the students in a class. The skills featured on unit assessments are tied to reading success and reflect both state and national standards.

Unit Assessments include:

- Individual lesson assessments that assess the skills taught in each lesson immediately after instruction is delivered. These assessments will help you determine how well students are grasping the skills and concepts as they are taught.

- End-of-unit assessments that assess all of the skills taught throughout the unit. These assessments will help determine the students' ability and growing bank of knowledge as well as their ability to retain concepts over a limited period of time—generally six to eight weeks per unit.

Diagnostic Assessments

For the majority of the students in a class, the Program Assessment component of **Open Court Reading** will provide the teacher with all the information needed to make appropriate instructional decisions. In certain circumstances, however, it may be necessary to gather additional information in order to provide students with appropriate instruction. Some students, for example, may have specific skill deficits that prevent them from making adequate progress. Other students may enter the class after the beginning of the school year. A third situation is when the teacher might want to group students who have the same skill deficit. For these circumstances, we provide Diagnostic Assessments.

The Diagnostic Assessments offer a variety of measures that allow the teacher to identify students' strengths and weaknesses. The results of the assessment can help the teacher develop intervention strategies and choose the right supplemental instruction that will meet each student's needs. General and specific instructions are provided so that the teacher can use the Diagnostic Assessments efficiently without disrupting the instructional routine.

Tips

- When observing students, do not pull them aside; rather, observe students as part of the regular lesson, either with the whole class or in small groups.

- Encourage students to express any confusion they may be experiencing. The questions students ask can give you valuable insight into their progress and development.

- The more comfortable students become with standardized-test formats—usually multiple choice—the more confident you and they will be in the fact that the test is testing their knowledge of a subject rather than their test-taking skills.

- Make sure students know that the ultimate purpose of assessment is to keep track of their progress and to help them continue to do better.

Assessment

Rubrics

A rubric is an established rule or criterion. Rubrics provide criteria for different levels of performance. Rubrics established before an assignment is given are extremely helpful in evaluating the assignment. When students know what the rubrics for a particular assignment are, they can focus their energies on the key issues.

Using Comprehension Strategies Rubrics

The following rubrics can be used to gauge the students' growing knowledge of the comprehension strategies and how adept they are becoming in their use. The rubrics are simply a guide. Students may and probably will develop strategies of their own. The important thing to consider is whether or not students are becoming strategic, active readers—do they employ these and other strategies, or do they continue to simply plough through text unaware of any problems they might be having? The rubrics indicate the types of behaviors strategic readers use and will help you identify the growing facility your students can gain in dealing with text of all sorts.

Grade 1: Comprehension Strategies Rubrics

Predicting

■ The student makes predictions about what the text is about.

■ The student updates predictions during reading, based on information in the text.

Visualizing

■ The student visualizes ideas or scenes described in the text.

Grades 2-6: Comprehension Strategies Rubrics

Summarizing

■ The student paraphrases text, reporting main ideas and a summary of what is in the text.

■ The student decides which parts of the text are important in his/her summary.

■ The student draws conclusions from the text.

■ The student makes global interpretations of the text, such as recognizing the genre.

Asking Questions

■ The student asks questions about ideas or facts presented in the text and attempts to answer these questions by reading the text.

Predicting

■ The student makes predictions about what the text is about.

■ The student updates predictions during reading, based on information in the text.

Making Connections

■ The student activates prior knowledge and related knowledge.

■ The student uses prior knowledge to explain something encountered in text.

■ The student connects ideas presented later in the text to ideas presented earlier in the text.

■ The student notes ideas in the text that are new to him/her or conflict with what he/she thought previously.

Visualizing

■ The student visualizes ideas or scenes described in the text.

Monitoring and Clarifying

■ The student notes characteristics of the text, such as whether it is difficult to read or whether some sections are more challenging or more important than others are.

■ The student shows awareness of whether he/she understands the text and takes appropriate action, such as rereading, in order to understand the text better.

■ The student rereads to reconsider something presented earlier in the text.

■ The student recognizes problems during reading, such as a loss of concentration, unfamiliar vocabulary, or a lack of sufficient background knowledge to comprehend the text.

Monitoring and Adjusting Reading Speed

The student changes reading speed in reaction to text, exhibiting such behavior as

■ Skimming parts of the text that are not important or relevant.

■ Purposely reading more slowly because of difficulty in comprehending the text.

Research Rubrics

Throughout each unit, students engage in research and inquiry activities based on the unit concepts. They will present the findings of their research to the class. In this way they exhibit the wealth of knowledge and understanding they have gained about that particular concept. In addition to gaining knowledge about the concepts, students will be honing their research skills. With each unit, they will progress with their research in the same manner in which professional researchers do.

With each new unit of study, students should also become more and more sophisticated in their ability to formulate questions, make conjectures about those questions, recognize their own information needs, conduct research to find that information, reevaluate their questions and conjectures as new information is added to their knowledge base, and communicate their findings effectively. In addition, they will become more and more adept at working as a team and being aware of the progress being made as individuals and as a group. The Research Rubrics will help you to assess the students' progress as researchers and as members of collaborative teams.

Formulating Research Questions and Problems

1. With help, identifies things she/he wonders about in relation to a topic.

2. Expresses curiosity about topics; with help, translates this into specific questions.

3. Poses an interesting problem or question for research; with help, refines it into a researchable question.

4. Identifies something she/he genuinely wonders about and translates it into a researchable question.

Making Conjectures

1. Offers conjectures that are mainly expressions of fact or opinion. ("I think the Anasazi lived a long time ago." "I think tigers should be protected.")

2. Offers conjectures that partially address the research question. ("I think germs make you sick because they get your body upset." "I think germs make you sick because they multiply really fast.")

3. Offers conjectures that address the research question with guesses. ("I think the Anasazi were wiped out by a meteor.")

4. Offers reasonable conjectures that address the question and that can be improved through further research.

Recognizing Information Needs

1. Identifies topics about which more needs to be learned. ("I need to learn more about the brain.")

2. Identifies information needs that are relevant though not essential to the research question. ("To understand how Leeuwenhoek invented the microscope, I need to know what size germs are.")

3. Identifies questions that are deeper than the one originally asked. (Original question: "How does the heart work?" Deeper question: "Why does blood need to circulate?")

Finding Needed Information

1. Collects information loosely related to topic.

2. Collects information clearly related to topic.

3. Collects information helpful in advancing on a research problem.

4. Collects problem-relevant information from varied sources and notices inconsistencies and missing pieces.

5. Collects useful information, paying attention to the reliability of sources and reviewing information critically.

Revising Problems and Conjectures

1. No revision.

2. Produces new problems or conjectures with little relation to earlier ones.

3. Tends to lift problems and conjectures directly from reference material.

4. Progresses to deeper, more refined problems and conjectures.

Communicating Research Progress and Results

1. Reporting is sparse and fragmentary.

2. Report is factual; communicates findings but not the thinking behind them.

3. Report provides a good picture of the research problem, of how original conjectures were modified in light of new information, and of difficulties and unresolved issues.

4. A report that not only interests and informs the audience but also draws helpful commentary from them.

Overall Assessment of Research

1. A collection of facts related in miscellaneous ways to a topic.

2. An organized collection of facts relevant to the research problem.

3. A thoughtful effort to tackle a research problem, with some indication of progress toward solving it.

4. Significant progress on a challenging problem of understanding.

Collaborative Group Work

1. Group members work on separate tasks with little interaction.

2. Work-related decisions are made by the group, but there is little interaction related to ideas.

3. Information and ideas are shared, but there is little discussion concerned with advancing understanding.

4. The group clearly progresses in its thinking beyond where individual students could have gone.

Participation in Collaborative Inquiry

1. Does not contribute ideas or information to team or class.

2. Makes contributions to Concept/Question Board or class discussions when specifically called upon to do so.

3. Occasionally contributes ideas or information to other students' inquiries.

4. Takes an active interest in the success of the whole class's knowledge-building efforts.

Writing Rubrics

Rubrics are particularly effective for writing assignments, which do not have simple right or wrong answers. The rubrics included in the *Unit Assessments* for writing cover different elements of the writing. They are intended to help teachers provide criteria and feedback to students.

Open Court Reading provides four-point rubrics for writing in each of four areas. This enables teachers to clearly distinguish among different levels of performance.

1. Point score indicates that a student is performing below basic level.

2. Point score indicates that a student's abilities are emerging.

3. Point score indicates that a student's work is adequate and achieving expectations.

4. Point score indicates that a student is exceeding expectations.

Conventions

The conventions rubrics provide criteria for evaluating a student's understanding and ability to use English language conventions, which include:

- Grammar and Usage
- Mechanics: Punctuation
- Mechanics: Capitalization
- Sentence Structure
- Spelling
- Overall grammar, usage, mechanics, and spelling

Genre

Genre rubrics, found in the *Unit Assessment,* enable evaluation of students' grasp of the different structures and elements of each of these different forms of writing:

- Descriptive Writing
- Expository Structure
- Genre
- Narrative
- Narrative Character
- Narrative Plot
- Narrative Setting
- Persuasive
- Personal
- Poetry

Writing Process

Writing process rubrics allow teachers to evaluate students' abilities in these areas:

- Getting Ideas
- Prewriting—Organizing Writing
- Drafting
- Revising
- Editing
- Presentation/Publishing

- Self-Management
- Language Resources

Writing Traits

Writing traits rubrics, found in the *Unit Assessment,* provide criteria for different elements of written composition to identify a student's strengths and weaknesses.

- Audience
- Citing Sources
- Elaboration (supporting details and examples that develop the main idea)
- Focus
- Ideas/Content
- Organization
- Sentence Fluency
- Voice
- Word Choice

Audiovisual and Technology Resource Directory

This directory is provided for the convenience of ordering the Technology Resources listed on the Technology pages in each Unit Overview.

BFA Educational Media Coronet/MTI

Phoenix Learning Group
2349 Chaffee Drive
St. Louis, MO 63146
800-221-1274

Dorling Kindersley

95 Madison Avenue
New York, NY 10016
212-213-4800
FAX: 212-213-5240
www.dk.com

Great Plains National Instructional Television Library

GPN Educational Media
University of Nebraska-Lincoln
1800 North 33rd Street
Lincoln, NE 68583
402-472-4076
http://gpn.unl.edu

Grolier Incorporated

90 Sherman Turnpike
Danbury, CT 06816
800-353-3140
www.grolier.com

Innovative Educators

P.O. Box 520
Montezuma, GA 31063
1-888-252-KIDS
FAX: 888-536-8553
http://www.innovative-educators.com

Library Video Company

P.O. Box 580
Wynnewood, PA 19096
800-843-3620
FAX: 610-645-4040
http://www.libraryvideo.com

Live Oak Media

P.O. Box 652
Pine Plains, NY 12567
800-788-1121
FAX: 866-398-1070
http://www.liveoakmedia.com

Macmillan/McGraw-Hill

220 East Danieldale Road
DeSoto, TX 75115-9960
800-442-9685
FAX: 972-228-1982
www.mhschool.com

MCA Video MCA Records/Universal Studios

100 Universal City Plaza
Universal City, CA 91608
818-777-1000

Mindscape, Inc.

The Learning Company
88 Rowland Way
Novato, California 94945
415-895-2000
Fax: 415-895-2102
www.mindscape.com

Multicom Publishing

Multimedia 2000
2017 Eighth Avenue, 3rd Floor
Seattle, WA 98101
800-850-7272
Fax: 206-622-4380
www.m-2K.com

Orange Cherry Software

P.O. Box 390
69 Westchester Ave.
Pound Ridge, NY 10576
914-764-4104
Fax: 914-764-0104
www.orangecherry.com

Paramount

780 N. Gower
Hollywood, CA 90038
800-699-1085
www.paramount.com

Queue, Inc.

338 Commerce Drive
Fairfield, CT 06432
800-232-2224
Fax: 203-336-2481
www.queueinc.com

Scholastic

555 Broadway
New York, NY 10012-3999
800-SCHOLASTIC
http://www.scholastic.com

Sony Wonder

Sony Corporation of America
550 Madison Avenue
Floor 19
New York, NY 10022
212-833-6800
http://www.sonywonder.com

SRA/McGraw-Hill

220 East Danieldale Road
DeSoto, TX 75115-9960
888-SRA-4543
Fax: 972-228-1982
www.sra4kids.com

Tom Snyder Productions

80 Coolidge Hill Road
Watertown, MA 02472
800-342-0236
Fax: 800-304-1254
www.tomsnyder.com

Scope and Sequence

Reading

	Level						
	K	1	2	3	4	5	6
Print/Book Awareness (Recognize and understand the conventions of print and books)							
Capitalization	✔	✔	✔			✔	✔
Constancy of Words						✔	
End Punctuation	✔	✔				✔	✔
Follow Left-to-right, Top-to-bottom	✔	✔					
Letter Recognition and Formation	✔	✔					
Page Numbering		✔					
Picture/Text Relationship	✔				✔		
Quotation Marks	✔	✔	✔			✔	✔
Relationship Between Spoken and Printed Language		✔					
Sentence Recognition							
Table of Contents	✔	✔					
Word Length	✔						
Word Boundaries		✔					
Phonemic Awareness (Recognize discrete sounds in words)							
Oral Blending: Words/Word Parts	✔	✔	✔				
Oral Blending: Initial Consonants/Blends	✔	✔	✔	✔			
Oral Blending: Final Consonants	✔	✔	✔	✔			
Oral Blending: Initial Vowels		✔					
Oral Blending: Syllables		✔			✔		
Oral Blending: Vowel Replacement					✔		
Segmentation: Initial Consonants/Blends	✔	✔	✔	✔		✔	
Segmentation: Final Consonants	✔	✔	✔	✔			
Segmentation: Words/Word Parts	✔	✔	✔	✔	✔	✔	
Rhyming	✔	✔			✔	✔	
How the Alphabet Works							
Letter Knowledge	✔	✔	✔	✔			
Letter Order (Alphabetic Order)	✔	✔					
Letter Sounds	✔	✔	✔	✔	✔		
Sounds in Words	✔	✔	✔	✔	✔		
Phonics (Associate sounds and spellings to read words)							
Blending Sounds into Words	✔	✔					
Consonant Clusters		✔		✔			
Consonant Digraphs		✔		✔	✔		
Consonant Sounds and Spellings	✔	✔	✔	✔			
Phonograms	✔	✔		✔			✔
Syllables	✔	✔			✔		
Vowel Diphthongs		✔		✔			✔
Vowels: Long Sounds and Spellings	✔	✔	✔	✔	✔	✔	✔
Vowels: r-controlled		✔	✔	✔	✔	✔	✔
Vowels: Short Sounds and Spellings	✔	✔	✔	✔	✔	✔	✔

☐ Skills, strategies, and other teaching opportunities   ✔ Formal, progress, or informal testing opportunities

Reading (continued)

	K	1	2	3	4	5	6
Comprehension Strategies							
Asking Questions/Answering Questions		✔	✔	✔	✔	✔	✔
Making Connections		✔	✔	✔	✔	✔	✔
Monitoring and Clarifying		✔	✔	✔	✔	✔	✔
Monitoring and Adjusting Reading Speed			✔	✔	✔	✔	✔
Predicting/Confirming Predictions	✔	✔	✔	✔	✔	✔	✔
Summarizing		✔	✔	✔	✔	✔	✔
Visualizing		✔	✔	✔	✔	✔	✔
Comprehension Skills							
Author's Point of View			✔	✔	✔	✔	✔
Author's Purpose			✔	✔	✔	✔	✔
Cause and Effect	✔	✔	✔	✔	✔	✔	✔
Classify and Categorize	✔	✔	✔	✔	✔	✔	✔
Compare and Contrast	✔	✔	✔	✔	✔	✔	✔
Drawing Conclusions	✔	✔	✔	✔	✔	✔	✔
Fact and Opinion			✔	✔	✔	✔	✔
Main Idea and Details	✔	✔	✔	✔	✔	✔	✔
Making Inferences		✔	✔	✔	✔	✔	✔
Reality/Fantasy	✔	✔	✔	✔			
Sequence		✔	✔	✔	✔	✔	✔
Vocabulary							
Antonyms	✔	✔	✔	✔	✔	✔	✔
Comparatives/Superlatives		✔	✔	✔	✔	✔	✔
Compound Words	✔	✔	✔	✔	✔	✔	✔
Connecting Words (Transition Words)						✔	✔
Context Clues		✔	✔	✔	✔	✔	✔
Contractions			✔	✔	✔		
Figurative Language				✔		✔	
Greek and Latin Roots				✔	✔		
High-Frequency Words	✔	✔	✔	✔	✔	✔	✔
Homographs			✔	✔	✔	✔	
Homophones/Homonyms		✔	✔	✔	✔		✔
Idioms					✔	✔	✔
Inflectional Endings		✔	✔	✔	✔	✔	✔
Irregular Plurals				✔		✔	✔
Multiple Meaning Words			✔	✔	✔	✔	✔
Multisyllabic Words			✔	✔		✔	
Position Words	✔	✔				✔	
Prefixes			✔	✔	✔	✔	✔
Question Words		✔					
Base or Root Words		✔	✔	✔	✔	✔	✔
Selection Vocabulary	✔	✔	✔	✔	✔	✔	✔
Suffixes		✔	✔	✔	✔	✔	✔
Synonyms		✔	✔	✔	✔	✔	✔
Time and Order Words (Creating Sequence)					✔	✔	✔
Utility Words (Colors, Classroom Objects, etc.)	✔	✔					
Word Families			✔	✔	✔	✔	✔

Inquiry and Research

PROGRAM APPENDIX

Study Skills	K	1	2	3	4	5	6
Charts, Graphs, and Diagrams/Visual Aids			✔		✔	✔	✔
Collaborative Inquiry			✔	✔	✔	✔	✔
Communicating Research Progress Results			✔	✔	✔	✔	✔
Compile Notes						✔	✔
Conducting an Interview							✔
Finding Needed Information			✔	✔	✔	✔	✔
Follow Directions	✔			✔			
Formulate Questions for Inquiry and Research			✔			✔	✔
Give Reports					✔	✔	✔
Make Outlines				✔		✔	✔
Making Conjectures			✔	✔	✔	✔	✔
Maps and Globes					✔		✔
Note Taking			✔	✔	✔	✔	✔
Parts of a Book			✔	✔	✔		
Planning Investigation			✔	✔	✔	✔	✔
Recognizing Information Needs			✔	✔	✔	✔	✔
Revising Questions and Conjectures			✔	✔	✔	✔	✔
Summarize and Organize Information					✔	✔	✔
Time Lines					✔	✔	✔
Use Appropriate Resources (Media Source, Reference Books, Experts, Internet)					✔	✔	✔
Using a Dictionary/Glossary		✔	✔	✔	✔	✔	✔
Using a Media Center/Library					✔		✔
Using a Thesaurus			✔	✔	✔	✔	✔
Using an Encyclopedia					✔		✔
Using Newspapers and Magazines					✔		✔
Using Technology							

Skills, strategies, and other teaching opportunities   ✔ Formal, progress, or informal testing opportunities

Language Arts
Writing/Composition

	K	1	2	3	4	5	6
Approaches							
Collaborative Writing		✔					
Group Writing							
Process							
Brainstorming/Prewriting	✔	✔		✔	✔	✔	
Drafting	✔	✔		✔	✔	✔	
Revising	✔	✔		✔	✔	✔	
Proofreading	✔	✔		✔	✔	✔	
Publishing	✔	✔		✔	✔	✔	
Forms							
Biography/Autobiography	✔	✔	✔	✔	✔	✔	✔
Business Letter				✔	✔	✔	✔
Describe a Process		✔	✔	✔	✔		✔
Descriptive Writing	✔	✔	✔	✔	✔	✔	✔
Expository/Informational Text	✔	✔	✔	✔	✔	✔	✔
Folklore (Folktales, Fairy Tales, Tall Tales, Legends, Myths)			✔	✔	✔		
Friendly Letter		✔	✔	✔	✔	✔	✔
Historical Fiction						✔	✔
Journal Writing		✔	✔	✔	✔	✔	✔
Narrative		✔	✔	✔	✔	✔	✔
Personal Writing		✔	✔	✔	✔	✔	✔
Persuasive Writing	✔	✔	✔	✔	✔		✔
Play/Dramatization				✔	✔	✔	✔
Poetry		✔	✔	✔	✔	✔	✔
Realistic Story				✔			
Writer's Craft							
Characterization			✔	✔	✔	✔	✔
Descriptive Writing	✔	✔	✔	✔	✔	✔	✔
Dialogue		✔	✔	✔	✔	✔	✔
Effective Beginnings			✔	✔	✔	✔	✔
Effective Endings			✔	✔	✔	✔	✔
Event Sequence		✔	✔	✔	✔	✔	✔
Figurative Language	✔		✔	✔	✔	✔	✔
Identifying Thoughts and Feelings	✔		✔	✔	✔	✔	✔
Mood and Tone				✔	✔	✔	✔
Plot (Problem/Solutions)	✔	✔	✔	✔	✔	✔	✔
Point of View				✔	✔	✔	
Rhyme	✔	✔	✔	✔	✔	✔	
Sensory Details				✔		✔	✔
Sentence Variety				✔		✔	✔
Sentence Elaboration				✔		✔	✔
Setting	✔		✔	✔		✔	✔
Suspense and Surprise			✔	✔	✔	✔	
Topic Sentences			✔	✔	✔	✔	✔
Using Comparisons						✔	
Purposes							
Determining Purposes for Writing	✔	✔				✔	

Scope and Sequence (continued)

Language Arts

Grammar

	Level K	1	2	3	4	5	6
Parts of Speech							
Adjectives	✔	✔	✔	✔	✔	✔	✔
Adverbs			✔	✔	✔	✔	✔
Conjunctions			✔	✔	✔	✔	✔
Nouns	✔	✔	✔	✔	✔	✔	✔
Prepositions	✔			✔	✔	✔	✔
Pronouns	✔	✔	✔	✔	✔	✔	✔
Verbs	✔	✔	✔	✔	✔	✔	✔
Sentences							
Fragments					✔	✔	✔
Parts (Subjects/Predicates)		✔	✔	✔	✔	✔	✔
Subject/Verb Agreement	✔	✔	✔	✔	✔	✔	✔
Structure (Simple, Compound, Complex)				✔	✔	✔	✔
Types (Declarative, Interrogative, Exclamatory, Imperatives)	✔	✔	✔	✔	✔	✔	✔
Verb Tenses	✔	✔	✔	✔	✔	✔	✔
Verbs (Action, Helping, Linking, Regular/Irregular)	✔	✔	✔	✔	✔	✔	✔
Usage							
Adjectives	✔	✔	✔	✔	✔	✔	✔
Adverbs			✔	✔	✔	✔	✔
Articles	✔	✔	✔	✔	✔	✔	✔
Nouns	✔	✔	✔	✔	✔	✔	✔
Pronouns	✔	✔	✔	✔	✔	✔	✔
Verbs	✔	✔	✔	✔	✔	✔	✔
Mechanics							
Capitalization (Sentence, Proper Nouns, Titles, Direct Address, Pronoun "I")	✔	✔	✔	✔	✔	✔	✔
Punctuation (End Punctuation, Comma Use, Quotation Marks, Apostrophe, Colon, Semicolon, Hyphen, Parentheses)	✔	✔	✔	✔	✔	✔	✔
Spelling							
Contractions		✔	✔	✔		✔	
Inflectional Endings			✔	✔	✔	✔	
Irregular Plurals			✔	✔	✔	✔	✔
Long Vowel Patterns		✔	✔	✔	✔	✔	✔
Multisyllabic Words			✔	✔		✔	
Phonograms		✔	✔	✔			✔
r-controlled Vowel Spellings		✔	✔	✔	✔	✔	✔
Short Vowel Spellings		✔	✔	✔	✔	✔	✔
Silent Letters				✔			
Sound/Letter Relationships		✔	✔	✔			
Special Spelling Patterns (-ough, -augh, -all, -al, -alk, -ion, -sion, -tion)		✔	✔	✔	✔	✔	✔

▨ Skills, strategies, and other teaching opportunities ✔ Formal, progress, or informal testing opportunities

Language Arts (continued)

Listening/Speaking/Viewing

	Level K	1	2	3	4	5	6
Listening/Speaking							
Analyze/Evaluate Intent and Content of Speaker's Message		✔	✔	✔	✔	✔	✔
Ask and Answer Questions	✔	✔	✔	✔	✔	✔	✔
Determine Purposes for Listening			✔	✔	✔		
Follow Directions	✔	✔	✔	✔	✔	✔	✔
Learn about Different Cultures through Discussion					✔	✔	✔
Listen for Poetic Language (Rhythm/Rhyme)	✔	✔	✔	✔			
Participate in Group Discussions		✔	✔	✔	✔	✔	✔
Respond to Speaker	✔	✔	✔	✔	✔	✔	✔
Use Nonverbal Communication Techniques	✔	✔	✔	✔	✔	✔	✔
Speaking							
Describe Ideas and Feelings	✔	✔	✔	✔	✔	✔	✔
Give Directions					✔	✔	✔
Learn about Different Cultures through Discussion					✔	✔	✔
Participate in Group Discussions	✔	✔	✔	✔	✔	✔	✔
Present Oral Reports			✔	✔	✔	✔	✔
Read Fluently with Expression, Phrasing, and Intonation			✔	✔	✔	✔	✔
Read Orally		✔	✔	✔	✔	✔	✔
Share Information	✔	✔	✔	✔	✔	✔	✔
Speak Clearly at Appropriate Volume	✔	✔	✔	✔	✔	✔	✔
Summarize/Retell Stories	✔	✔	✔	✔	✔	✔	✔
Understand Formal and Informal Language	✔	✔	✔	✔	✔	✔	✔
Use Appropriate Vocabulary for Audience		✔	✔	✔	✔	✔	✔
Use Elements of Grammar in Speech			✔	✔	✔	✔	✔
Viewing							
Analyze Purposes and Techniques of the Media				✔	✔	✔	✔
Appreciate/Interpret Artist's Techniques							
Compare Visual and Written Material on the Same Subject	✔				✔		
Gather Information from Visual Images	✔	✔	✔	✔	✔	✔	✔
View Critically		✔	✔	✔	✔	✔	✔
View Culturally Rich Materials	✔	✔	✔		✔	✔	✔
Penmanship							
Cursive Letters			✔	✔	✔	✔	✔
Manuscript Letters	✔	✔	✔				
Numbers	✔	✔	✔	✔			

Unit Themes

	LEVEL K	LEVEL 1	LEVEL 2
Unit 1	School	Let's Read!	Sharing Stories
Unit 2	Shadows	Animals	Kindness
Unit 3	Finding Friends	Things That Go	Look Again
Unit 4	The Wind	Our Neighborhood at Work	Fossils
Unit 5	Stick to It	Weather	Courage
Unit 6	Red, White, and Blue	Journeys	Our Country and Its People
Unit 7	Teamwork	Keep Trying	
Unit 8	By the Sea	Games	
Unit 9		Being Afraid	
Unit 10		Homes	

LEVEL 3	LEVEL 4	LEVEL 5	LEVEL 6
Friendship	Risks and Consequences	Cooperation and Competition	Perseverance
City Wildlife	Dollars and Sense	Astronomy	Ancient Civilizations
Imagination	From Mystery to Medicine	Heritage	Taking a Stand
Money	Survival	Making a New Nation	Beyond the Notes
Storytelling	Communication	Going West	Ecology
Country Life	A Changing America	Journeys and Quests	A Question of Value

Leveled Classroom Library Books

LEVEL K

Unit I School: *Mouse Views: What the Class Pet Saw; The 100ᵗʰ Day of School; Billy and the Big New School; Vera's First Day of School; Bea and Mr. Jones; The Kissing Hand*

Unit 2 Shadows: *Footprints and Shadows; Shadows Are About; I Have a Friend; My Shadow; What Makes Day and Night?; Sun Up, Sun Down*

Unit 3 Finding Friends: *My Friends; Yo! Yes?; Will You Be My Friend?; George and Martha One Fine Day; Friends; May I Bring a Friend?*

Unit 4 The Wind: *The Wind Blew; One Windy Wednesday; The Sun, the Wind, and the Rain; What Makes the Wind?; Millicent and the Wind; Feel the Wind*

Unit 5 Stick to It: *The Carrot Seed; Leo the Late Bloomer; You'll Soon Grow into Them, Titch; JoJo's Flying Side Kick; Paul Bunyan: A Tall Tale; Liang and the Magic Paintbrush*

Unit 6 Red, White, and Blue: *The Pledge of Allegiance; 'Night, America; This Land Is Your Land; Happy Birthday, America; The Flag We Love; Mr. Lincoln's Whiskers*

Unit 7 Teamwork: *Can I Help?; Animal Orchestra; Tippy Bear Hunts for Honey; Helping Out; Stone Soup; The Great Trash Bash*

Unit 8 By the Sea: *Oceans; In the Ocean; Tacky the Penguin; Fish Faces; The Seashore Book; Commotion in the Ocean*

LEVEL I

Unit I Let's Read!: *America: My Land Your Land Our Land; I Read Signs; Miss Malarkey Doesn't Live in Room 10; The Old Woman Who Loved to Read; A Cake for Herbie; More Than Anything Else*

Unit 2 Animals: *Sweet Dreams: How Animals Sleep; Moo Moo, Brown Cow; Here Is the African Savanna; Is Your Mama a Llama?; A Pinky Is a Baby Mouse; Wolf Watch*

Unit 3 Things That Go: *I Spy a Freight Train; Wheels Around; This Plane; This Is the Way We Go to School; The Listening Walk; Firehorse Max*

Unit 4 Our Neighborhood at Work: *Communities; Night Shift Daddy; My Town; One Afternoon; Career Day; Mommy Works, Daddy Works*

Unit 5 Weather: *Snow; Snowballs; Rain; Red Rubber Boot Day; Twister; Snow Is Falling*

Unit 6 Journeys: *Rosie's Walk; The Train Ride; Amelia's Fantastic Flight; I'm Not Moving, Mama!; Ferryboat Ride!; The Josefina Story Quilt*

Unit 7 Keep Trying: *Flap Your Wings and Try; The Chick and the Duckling; One Duck Stuck; One Fine Day; The Purple Coat; The Story of a Blue Bird*

Unit 8 Games: *This Is Baseball; Take Me Out to the Ballgame; What's What? A Guessing Game; Leon and Bob; Moongame; James and the Rain*

Unit 9 Being Afraid: *Sheila Rae, the Brave; Henry and Mudge and the Bedtime Thumps; First Day Jitters; Let's Go Home Little Bear; Can't You Sleep, Little Bear?; Feelings*

Unit I0 Homes: *My House Mi Casa: A Book in Two Languages; To Market, To Market; The Someday House; Homeplace; The Little House; Livingstone Mouse*

LEVEL 2

Unit I Sharing Stories: *Just Like Me; Mouse Tales; The Wednesday Surprise; Dear Annie; Jeremiah Learns to Read; Painted Words*

Unit 2 Kindness: *Abe Lincoln's Hat; Jamaica's Find; The Bat in the Boot; The Giving Tree; Uncle Willie and the Soup Kitchen; A Chair for My Mother*

Unit 3 Look Again: *The Trek; Who's Hiding Here?; The Mixed-Up Chameleon; A Color of His Own; What Do You Do When Something Wants to Eat You?; Hiding Out*

Unit 4 Fossils: *Dinosaur Babies; The Day of the Dinosaur; A Boy Wants a Dinosaur; If the Dinosaurs Came Back; Archaeologists Dig for Clues; How Big Were the Dinosaurs?*

Unit 5 Courage: *White Dynamite and Curly Kidd; What's Under My Bed?; Ruth Law Thrills a Nation; Jamaica and the Substitute Teacher; Birdie's Lighthouse; The Buffalo Jump*

Unit 6 Our Country and Its People: *Dancing with the Indians; A Picnic in October; Amelia's Road; Dragon Parade; The Lotus Seed; Dumpling Soup*

LEVEL 3

Unit I Friendship: *Charlotte's Web; And To Think That We Thought That We'd Never Be Friends; Best Friends; Amigo; The Mountain that Loved a Bird; Alex Is My Friend*

Unit 2 City Wildlife: *Wild in the City; Come Back, Salmon: How a Group of Dedicated Kids Adopted Pigeon Creek and Brought It Back to Life; Farewell to Shady Glade; Coyotes in the Crosswalk: True Tales of Animal Life in the Wilds of the City!; City Park; Birds, Nests and Eggs*

Unit 3 Imagination: *Behind the Couch; My Life with the Wave; Maria's Comet; Frederick; How I Spent My Summer Vacation; Crocodile's Masterpiece*

Unit 4 Money: *Lemonade for Sale; Round and Round the Money Goes; Saturday Sancocho; The Treasure; Our Money; Screen of Frogs*

Unit 5 Storytelling: *Tell Me a Story, Mama; The Worry Stone; May'naise Sandwiches & Sunshine Tea; One Grain of Rice; A Storyteller's Story; Firetalking*

Unit 6 Country Life: *The Raft; Night in the Country; Mowing; Winter Wheat; A River Ran Wild; Unseen Rainbows, Silent Songs: The World Beyond Human Senses*

LEVEL 4

Unit 1 Risks and Consequences: *The Big Balloon Race; A Day's Work; Poppy; Sarah, Plain and Tall; The Landry News; From the Mixed-Up Files of Mrs. Basil E. Frankweiler*

Unit 2 Dollars and Sense: *Max Malone Makes a Million; What's Cooking, Jenny Archer?; The Toothpaste Millionaire; Brainstorm! The Stories of Twenty American Kid Inventors; Odd Jobs; Better Than a Lemonade Stand!*

Unit 3 From Mystery to Medicine: *Germs Make Me Sick!; Pasteur's Fight Against Microbes; Marie Curie and the Discovery of Radium; Kids to the Rescue! First Aid Techniques for Kids; The First Woman Doctor; Fever: 1793*

Unit 4 Survival: *Harry the Poisonous Centipede; My Grandmother's Journey; Whichaway; Frozen Fire; Island of the Blue Dolphins; The Voyage of the Frog*

Unit 5 Communication: *Prairie Dogs Kiss and Lobsters Wave: How Animals Say Hello; Burton and Stanley; Dear Mr. Henshaw; The Chimpanzee Family Book; The Cat's Elbow and Other Secret Languages; Julie's Wolf Pack*

Unit 6 A Changing America: *Sleds on Boston Common: A Story from the American Revolution; The Discovery of the Americas; Stranded at Plimoth Plantation, 1626; . . . If You Traveled West in a Covered Wagon; The Louisiana Purchase; Gold Rush! The Young Prospector's Guide to Striking It Rich*

LEVEL 5

Unit 1 Cooperation and Competition: *The Big Bike Race; The Kid Who Ran For President; The Wheel on the School; Iditarod Dream: Dusty and His Sled Dogs Compete in Alaska's Jr. Iditarod; The View From Saturday; A World in Our Hands: In Honor of the 50th Anniversary of the United Nations*

Unit 2 Astronomy: *The Planets; Comets, Meteors, and Asteroids; Adventure in Space: The Flight to Fix the Hubble; The Young Astronomer; Edwin Hubble: American Astronomer; Tales of the Shimmering Sky: Ten Global Folktales with Activities*

Unit 3 Heritage: *Appalachia: The Voices of Sleeping Birds; This Land Is My Land; Going Back Home: An Artist Returns to the South; In the Year of the Boar and Jackie Robinson; The Great Ancestor Hunt: The Fun of Finding Out Who You Are; Do People Grow on Family Trees?*

Unit 4 Making a New Nation: *Samuel's Choice; Toliver's Secret; Johnny Tremain; A Young Patriot: The American Revolution as Experienced by One Boy; Mr. Revere and I; Come All You Brave Soldiers: Blacks in the Revolutionary War*

Unit 5 Going West: *Boom Town; Striking It Rich: The Story of the California Gold Rush; Black-Eyed Susan; By the Great Horn Spoon!; Children of the Wild West; Caddie Woodlawn*

Unit 6 Journeys and Quests: *Alicia's Treasure; Grass Sandals: The Travels of Basho; El Güero; Coast to Coast; Orphan Train Rider: One Boy's True Story; Call It Courage*

LEVEL 6

Unit 1 Perseverance: *The Most Beautiful Place in the World; Wilma Unlimited: How Wilma Rudolph Became the World's Fastest Woman; Littlejim's Dreams; The Circuit: Stories from the Life of a Migrant Child; Where the Lilies Bloom; The Wright Brothers: How They Invented the Airplane*

Unit 2 Ancient Civilizations: *Androcles and the Lion; Ancient Romans at a Glance; Painters of the Caves; Pyramids!; Dig This! How Archaeologists Uncover Our Past; Religions of the World*

Unit 3 Taking a Stand: *Aunt Harriet's Underground Railroad in the Sky; Jane Addams: Pioneer Social Worker; Number the Stars; Run Away Home; Kids at Work: Lewis Hine and the Crusade Against Child Labor; Red Scarf Girl: A Memoir of the Cultural Revolution*

Unit 4 Beyond the Notes: *The Jazz Man; A Mouse Called Wolf; Play Me a Story: Nine Tales about Musical Instruments; The Sea King's Daughter: A Russian Legend; Dragonsong; Music*

Unit 5 Ecology: *The Great Kapok Tree; Lifetimes; Elephant Woman: Cynthia Moss Explores the World of Elephants; The Missing 'Gator of Gumbo Limbo; Ecology for Every Kid: Easy Activities that Make Learning Science Fun; The Most Beautiful Roof in the World*

Unit 6 A Question of Value: *Abuelita's Heart; The Golden Bracelet; Lily's Crossing; The Black Pearl; The Monkey Thief; Wringer*

Glossary of Reading Terms

This glossary includes linguistic, grammatical, comprehension, and literary terms that may be helpful in understanding reading instruction.

acronym a word formed from the initial letter of words in a phrase, **scuba** (**self-contained underwater breathing apparatus**).

acrostic a kind of puzzle in which lines of a poem are arranged so that words or phrases are formed when certain letters from each line are used in a sequence.

adjective a word or group of words that modifies a noun.

adventure story a narrative that features the unknown or unexpected with elements of excitement, danger, and risk.

adverb a word or group of words that modifies a verb, adjective, or other adverb.

affective domain the psychological field of emotional activity.

affix a word part, either a prefix or a suffix, that changes the meaning or function of a word root or stem.

affricate a speech sound that starts as a stop but ends as a fricative, the /ch/ in **catch**.

agreement the correspondence of syntactically related words; subjects and predicates are in agreement when both are singular or plural.

alliteration the repetition of the initial sounds in neighboring words or stressed syllables.

alphabet the complete set of letters representing speech sounds used in writing a language.

alphabet book a book for helping young children learn the alphabet by pairing letters with pictures whose sounds they represent.

alphabetic principle the principle that there is an association between sounds and the letters that represent them in alphabetic writing systems.

alveolar a consonant speech sound made when the tongue and the ridge of the upper and lower jaw stop to constrict the air flow, as /t/.

anagram a word or phrase whose letters form other words or phrases when rearranged, for example, **add** and **dad**.

analogy a likeness or similarity.

analytic phonics also deductive phonics, a whole-to-part approach to phonics in which a student is taught a number of sight words and then phonetic generalizations that can be applied to other words.

antonym a word that is opposite in meaning to another word.

appositive a word that restates or modifies a preceding noun. For example, **my daughter**, **Charlotte**.

aspirate an unvoiced speech sound produced by a puff of air, as /h/ in **heart**.

aspirated stop a stop consonant sound released with a puff of air, as /k/, /p/, and /t/.

auditory discrimination the ability to hear phonetic likenesses and differences in phonemes and words.

author's purpose the motive or reason for which an author writes, includes to entertain, inform, persuade, and explain how.

automaticity fluent processing of information, requiring little effort or attention.

auxiliary verb a verb that precedes another verb to express time, mood, or voice, includes verbs such as **has**, **is**, **will**.

ballad a narrative poem, composed of short verses to be sung or recited, usually containing elements of drama and often tragic in tone.

base word a word to which affixes may be added to create related words.

blank verse unrhymed verse, especially unrhymed iambic pentameter.

blend the joining of the sounds of two or more letters with little change in those sounds, for example /spr/ in **spring**, also **consonant blend** or **consonant cluster**.

blending to combine the sounds represented by letters to sound out or pronounce a word, contrast with **oral blending**.

breve the symbol placed above a vowel to indicate that it is a short vowel.

browse to skim through or look over in search of something of interest.

canon in literature, the body of major works that a culture considers important at a given time.

case a grammatical category that indicates the syntactic/semantic role of a noun phrase in a sentence.

cause-effect relationship a stated or implied association between an outcome and the conditions that brought it about, also the comprehension skill associated with recognizing this type of relationship as an organizing principle in text.

chapter book a book long enough to be divided into chapters, but not long or complex enough to be considered a novel.

characterization the way in which an author presents a character in a story, including describing words, actions, thoughts, and impressions of that character.

choral reading oral group reading to develop oral fluency by modeling.

cinquain a stanza of five lines, specifically one that has successive lines of two, four, six, eight, and two syllables.

cipher a system for writing in code.

clarifying a comprehension strategy in which the reader rereads text, uses a dictionary, uses decoding skills, or uses context clues to comprehend something that is unclear.

clause a group of words with a subject and a predicate used to form a part of or a whole sentence, a dependent clause modifies an independent clause, which can stand alone as a complete sentence.

collaborative learning learning by working together in small groups.

command a sentence that asks for action and usually ends with a period.

common noun in contrast to **proper noun**, a noun that denotes a class rather than a unique or specific thing.

comprehension the understanding of what is written or said.

comprehension skill a skill that aids in understanding text, including identifying **author's purpose**, **comprehending cause and effect relationships**, **comparing and contrasting** items and events, **drawing conclusions**, distinguishing **fact from opinion**, identifying **main ideas**, making **inferences**, distinguishing **reality from fantasy**, and understanding **sequence**.

comprehension strategy a sequence of steps for understanding text, includes asking questions, clarifying, making connections, predicting, summarizing, and visualizing.

conjugation the complete set of all possible inflected forms of a verb.

conjunction a part of speech used to connect words, phrases, clauses, or sentences, including the words **and, but, or**.

consonant a speech sound, and the alphabet letter that represents that sound, made by partial or complete closure of part of the vocal tract, which obstructs air flow and causes audible friction.

context clue information from the immediate text that helps identify a word.

contraction a short version of a written or spoken expression in which letters are omitted, for example, **can't**.

convention an accepted practice in spoken or written language, usually referring to spelling, mechanics, or grammar rules.

cooperative learning a classroom organization that allows students to work together to achieve their individual goals.

creative writing prose and poetic forms of writing that express the writer's thoughts and feelings imaginatively.

cuing system any of the various sources of information that help to identify an unrecognizable word in reading, including phonetic, semantic, and syntactical information.

cumulative tale a story, such as The Gingerbread Man, in which details are repeated until the climax.

dangling modifier usually a participle that because of its placement in a sentence modifies the wrong object.

decodable text text materials controlled to include a majority of words whose sound/spelling relationships are known by the reader.

decode to analyze spoken or graphic symbols for meaning.

diacritical mark a mark, such as a breve or macron, added to a letter or graphic character, to indicate a specific pronunciation.

dialect a regional variety of a particular language with phonological, grammatical, and lexical patterns that distinguish it from other varieties.

dialogue a piece of writing written as conversation, usually punctuated by quotation marks.

digraph two letters that represent one speech sound, for example /sh/ or /ch/.

diphthong a vowel sound produced when the tongue glides from one vowel sound toward another in the same syllable, for example /oi/ or /ou/.

direct object the person or thing that receives the action of a verb in a sentence, for example, the word **cake** in this sentence: **Madeline baked a cake.**

drafting the process of writing ideas in rough form to record them.

drama a story in the form of a play, written to be performed.

edit in the writing process, to revise or correct a manuscript.

emergent literacy the development of the association of meaning and print that continues until a child reaches the stage of conventional reading and writing.

emergent reading a child's early interaction with books and print before the ability to decode text.

encode to change a message into symbols, for example, to change speech into writing.

epic a long narrative poem, usually about a hero.

exclamatory sentence a sentence that shows strong emotion and ends with an exclamation mark.

expository writing or **exposition** a composition in writing that explains an event or process.

fable a short tale that teaches a moral.

fantasy a highly imaginative story about characters, places, and events that do not exist.

fiction imaginative narrative designed to entertain rather than to explain, persuade, or describe.

figure of speech the expressive, nonliteral use of language usually through metaphor, simile, or personification.

fluency freedom from word-identification problems that hinder comprehension in reading.

folktale a narrative form of genre such as an epic, myth, or fable that is well-known through repeated storytellings.

foreshadowing giving clues to upcoming events in a story.

free verse verse with irregular metrical pattern.

freewriting writing that is not limited in form, style, content, or purpose, designed to encourage students to write.

genre a classification of literary works, including tragedy, comedy, novel, essay, short story, mystery, realistic fiction, poetry.

grammar the study of the classes of words, their inflections, and their functions and relations in sentences; includes phonological, morphological, syntactic, and semantic descriptions of a language.

grapheme a written or printed representation of a phoneme, such as **c** for /k/.

guided reading reading instruction in which the teacher provides the structure and purpose for reading and responding to the material read.

handing off a method of turning over to the students the primary responsibility for controlling discussion.

indirect object in a sentence, the person or thing to or for whom an action is done, for example, the word **dog** in this sentence: **Madeline gave the dog a treat**.

inference a conclusion based on facts, data, or evidence.

infinitive the base form of a verb, usually with the infinitive marker, for example, **to go**.

inflectional ending an ending that expresses a plural or possessive form of a noun, the tense of a verb, or the comparative or superlative form of an adjective or adverb.

interrogative word a word that marks a clause or sentence as a question, including **interrogative pronouns who**, **what**, **which**, **where**.

intervention a strategy or program designed to supplement or substitute instruction, especially for those students who fall behind.

invented spelling the result of an attempt to spell a word based on the writer's knowledge of the spelling system and how it works, often with overemphasis on sound/symbol relationships.

irony a figure of speech in which the literal meaning of the words is the opposite of their intended meaning.

journal a written record of daily events or responses.

juvenile book a book written for children or adolescents.

legend a traditional tale handed down from generation to generation.

leitmotif a repeated expression, event, or idea used to unify a work of art such as writing.

letter one of a set of graphic symbols that forms an alphabet and is used alone or in combination to represent a phoneme, also **grapheme**.

linguistics the study of the nature and structure of language and communication.

literary elements the elements of a story such as **setting**, **plot**, and **characterization** that create the structure of a narrative.

macron a diacritical mark placed above a vowel to indicate a long vowel sound.

main idea the central thought or chief topic of a passage.

mechanics the conventions of capitalization and punctuation.

metacognition awareness and knowledge of one's mental processes or thinking about what one is thinking about.

metaphor a figure of speech in which a comparison is implied but not stated, for example, **She is a jewel**.

miscue a deviation from text during oral reading in an attempt to make sense of the text.

modeling an instructional technique in which the teacher serves as an example of behavior.

mood the literary element that conveys the emotional atmosphere of a story.

morpheme a meaningful linguistic unit that cannot be divided into smaller units, for example, **word**; **a bound morpheme** is a morpheme that cannot stand alone as an independent word, for example, the prefix **re-**; **a free morpheme** can stand alone, for example, **dog**.

myth a story designed to explain the mysteries of life.

narrative writing or **narration** a composition in writing that tells a story or gives an account of an event.

nonfiction prose designed to explain, argue, or describe rather than to entertain with a factual emphasis, includes biography and autobiography.

noun a part of speech that denotes persons, places, things, qualities, or acts.

novel an extended fictional prose narration.

onomatopoeia the use of a word whose sound suggests its meaning, for example, **purr**.

oral blending the ability to fuse discrete phonemes into recognizable words; oral blending puts sounds together to make a word, **see also segmentation**.

orthography correct or standardized spelling according to established usage in a language.

oxymoron a figure of speech in which contrasting or contradictory words are brought together for emphasis.

paragraph a subdivision of a written composition that consists of one or more sentences, deals with one point, or gives the words of one speaker, usually beginning with an indented line.

participle a verb form used as an adjective, for example, **the skating party**.

personification a figure of speech in which animals, ideas, or things take on human characteristics.

persuasive writing a composition intended to persuade the reader to adopt the writer's point of view.

phoneme the smallest sound unit of speech, for example, the /k/ in **book**.

phonemic awareness the ability to recognize that spoken words are made up of discrete sounds and that those sounds can be manipulated.

Glossary of Reading Terms (continued)

phonetic spelling the respelling of entry words in a dictionary according to a pronunciation key.

phonetics the study of speech sounds.

phonics a way of teaching reading that addresses sound/symbol relationships, especially in beginning instruction.

phonogram a letter or symbol that represents a phonetic sound.

plot the literary element that provides the structure of the action of a story, which may include rising action, climax, and falling action leading to a resolution or denouement.

plural a grammatical form of a word that refers to more than one in number; an **irregular plural** is one that does not follow normal patterns for inflectional endings.

poetic license the liberty taken by writers to ignore conventions.

poetry a metrical form of composition in which language is chosen and arranged to create a powerful response through meaning, sound, or rhythm.

possessive showing ownership either through the use of an adjective, an adjectival pronoun, or the possessive form of a noun.

predicate the part of the sentence that expresses something about the subject and includes the verb phrase; a **complete predicate** includes the principal verb in a sentence and all its modifiers or subordinate parts.

predicting a comprehension strategy in which the reader attempts to figure out what will happen and then confirms predictions as the text is read.

prefix an affix attached before a base word that changes the meaning of the word.

preposition a part of speech in the class of function words, such as **of**, **on**, **at**, that precede noun phrases to create prepositional phrases.

prewriting the planning stage of the writing process in which the writer formulates ideas, gathers information, and considers ways to organize them.

print awareness in emergent literacy, a child's growing recognition of conventions and characteristics of written language, including reading from left to right and top to bottom in English, and that words are separated by spaces.

pronoun a part of speech used as a substitute for a noun or noun phrase.

proofreading the act of reading with the intent to correct, clarify, or improve text.

pseudonym an assumed name used by an author, a pen name or nom de plume.

publishing the process of preparing written material for presentation.

punctuation graphic marks such as comma, period, quotation marks, and brackets used to clarify meaning and give speech characteristics to written language.

question an interrogative sentence that asks a question and ends with a question mark.

realistic fiction a story that attempts to portray characters and events as they actually are.

rebus the use of a picture or symbol to suggest a word or syllable.

revise in the writing process, to change or correct a manuscript to make its message more clear.

rhyme identical or very similar recurring final sounds in words, often at the ends of lines of poetry.

rime a vowel and any following consonants of a syllable.

segmentation the ability to break words into individual sounds; **see also oral blending**.

semantic mapping a graphic display of a group of words that are meaningfully related to support vocabulary instruction.

semantics the study of meaning in language, including the meanings of words, phrases, sentences, and texts.

sentence a grammatical unit that expresses a statement, question, or command; a **simple sentence** is a sentence with one subject and one predicate; a **compound sentence** is a sentence with two or more independent clauses usually separated by a comma and conjunction, but no dependent clause; a **complex sentence** is a sentence with one independent and one or more dependent clauses.

sentence combining a teaching technique in which complex sentence chunks and paragraphs are built from basic sentences.

sentence lifting the process of using sentences from children's writing to illustrate what is wrong or right to develop children's editing and proofreading skills.

sequence the order of elements or events.

setting the literary element that includes the time, place, and physical and psychological background in which a story takes place.

sight word a word that is taught to be read as a whole word, usually words that are phonetically irregular.

simile a figure of speech in which a comparison of two things that are unlike is directly stated usually with the words **like** or **as**, for example, **She is like a jewel**.

spelling the process of representing language by means of a writing system.

statement a sentence that tells something and ends with a period.

study skills a general term for the techniques and strategies that help readers comprehend text with the intent to remember, includes following directions, organizing, locating, and using graphic aids.

style the characteristics of a work that reflect the author's particular way of writing.

subject the main topic of a sentence to which a predicate refers, including the principal noun; a **complete subject** includes the principal noun in a sentence and all its modifiers.

suffix an affix attached at the end of a base word that changes the meaning of the word.

summarizing a comprehension strategy in which the reader constructs a brief statement that contains the essential ideas of a passage.

syllable a minimal unit of sequential speech sounds comprised of a vowel sound or a vowel-sound combination.

symbolism the use of one thing to represent something else in order to represent an idea in a concrete way.

synonym a word that means the same as another word.

syntax the grammatical pattern or structure of word order in sentences, clauses, and phrases.

tense the way in which verbs indicate past, present, and future time of action.

text structure the various patterns of ideas that are built into the organization of a written work.

theme a major idea or proposition that provides an organizing concept through which by study, students gain depth of understanding.

topic sentence a sentence intended to express the main idea of a paragraph or passage.

tragedy a literary work, often a play, in which the main character suffers conflicts and which presents a serious theme and has an unfortunate ending.

usage the way in which a native language or dialect is used by the members of the community.

verb a word that expresses an action or state that occurs in a predicate of a sentence; an **irregular verb** is a verb that does not follow normal patterns of inflectional endings that reflect past, present, or future verb tense.

visualizing a comprehension strategy in which the reader constructs a mental picture of a character, setting, or process.

vowel a voiced speech sound and the alphabet letter that represents that sound, made without stoppage or friction of the air flow as it passes through the vocal tract.

vowel digraph a spelling pattern in which two or more letters represent a single vowel sound.

word calling proficiency in decoding with little or no attention to word meaning.

writing also **composition** the process or result of organizing ideas in writing to form a clear message, includes persuasive, expository, narrative, and descriptive forms.

writing process the many aspects of the complex act of producing a piece of writing, including prewriting, drafting, revising, proofreading, and publishing.

Open Court Reading develops handwriting skills through weekly Penmanship lessons. The instruction for these lessons appears in the Language Arts part of the lesson in every grade level. The purpose of these lessons is to develop important handwriting skills necessary for producing legible, properly spaced documents. Penmanship practice reinforces the vocabulary in the lesson selection.

In addition to the board, the overhead projector can be a very effective device for teaching penmanship. Students can move their pencils at the same time the teacher forms letters on the transparency. It also helps to recite the descriptions or chants that go with each letter.

Penmanship in Levels K to 2

Beginning in kindergarten, the Penmanship lessons expand on the sound/spelling instruction by introducing letters the students study in Sounds and Letters. Students learn that those letters are made of four basic lines: curved lines, horizontal lines, vertical lines, and slanted lines.

Next, students learn letter and number formation. The students practice letter formation by writing the letter being studied and then words from the literature selection that contain the particular letter. This instruction continues in Level 1 and is tied to the letter formation instruction in Phonics and Fluency.

Cursive Handwriting Models

Penmanship is developed and practiced through Level 6, with cursive instruction beginning in the final unit of Level 2. Students are taught that most cursive letters are comprised of four strokes: undercurve, downcurve, overcurve, and slanted lines. These lessons teach students the essentials of cursive handwriting, such as proper slant; loops; joining; and spacing between letters, words, and sentences. As in the earlier levels, the students practice letter formation by writing the letters in the Writer's Notebook and then words from the literature selection that contain the particular letter.

The writing exercises progress with each level. Students begin writing words in kindergarten and graduate to writing sentences by the end of Level 1 and into Level 2. Level 3 eases students into cursive by having them practice words from the literature, with a transition to sentences in Level 4, and paragraphs in Levels 5 and 6.

Hand and Paper Positioning

The **hand and paper positioning** models are for teachers' reference and enhance the written instruction of positioning lessons. The diagrams give teachers a visual aid so that they may better understand and demonstrate an effective technique of positioning.

A right-handed student should hold the pencil loosely about one inch above the point, between the thumb and middle finger. A left-handed student should hold the pencil the same way, but up to one half inch farther away from the point. The index fingers of both writers should rest lightly on the top of the pencil. The wrist should be level and just slightly raised from the desk.

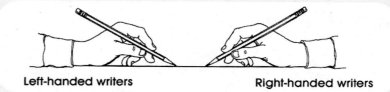

Left-handed writers   Right-handed writers

For both kinds of writers, the paper should lie straight in front of the student with the edges parallel to the edges of the desk. A left-handed writer may find it easier to slant the paper slightly to the right and parallel to the left forearm. A right-handed writer's writing hand should be kept well below the writing. The left hand should hold down the paper.

Left-handed writers   Right-handed writers

Penmanship (continued)

Cursive Handwriting Models

The models of cursive handwriting provide teachers with a systematic method for teaching students to form uppercase and lowercase letters of the alphabet. The dots on the letters indicate starting points for the students. The numbered arrows show the students in what order and what direction the line should go to form the particular letter. Teachers may use the chants to describe the letter step by step as he or she models the formation on the board. Students may also say the chants in unison as they practice the formation, whether they are writing the letter or tracing it on the board.

The four basic cursive strokes diagram aids teachers by giving examples of the strokes that recur frequently in cursive handwriting. Students can form most cursive letters by using one or more of these strokes. The letters in the Penmanship lessons are grouped according to the strokes particular to each letter.

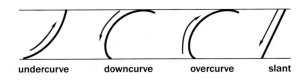

undercurve   downcurve   overcurve   slant

Undercurve letters

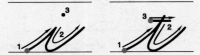

i Starting point, undercurve
Slant down, undercurve to endpoint, dot exactly above: small *i*

t Starting point, undercurve
Slant down, undercurve to endpoint
Starting point, straight across: small *t*

u Starting point, undercurve
Slant down, undercurve
Slant down, undercurve: small *u*

w Starting point, undercurve
Slant down, undercurve, slant down, undercurve, small curve to right: small *w*

r Starting point, undercurve
Slant right
Slant down, undercurve: small *r*

s Starting point, undercurve
Curve down and back, undercurve: small *s*

Downcurve letters

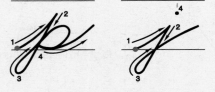

p Starting point, undercurve
Slant, loop back
Overcurve
Curve back, undercurve: small *p*

j Starting point, undercurve
Slant down
Loop back
Overcurve to endpoint
Dot exactly above: small *j*

a Starting point, downcurve
Undercurve to starting point
Slant down, undercurve: small *a*

c Starting point, downcurve
Undercurve: small *c*

d Starting point, downcurve
Undercurve past starting point
Slant down, undercurve: small *d*

q Starting point, downcurve
Undercurve to starting point
Slant down and loop forward, undercurve: small *q*

g Starting point, downcurve
Undercurve to starting point
Slant down and loop back, overcurve: small *g*

o Starting point, downcurve
Undercurve
Small curve to right: small *o*

Penmanship (continued)

Cursive Handwriting Models

Overcurve letters

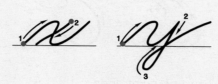

n Starting point, overcurve
Slant down, overcurve
Slant down, undercurve: small *n*

m Starting point, overcurve
Slant down, overcurve
Slant down, overcurve
Slant down, undercurve: small *m*

x Starting point, overcurve
Slant down, undercurve to endpoint
Starting point slant down: small *x*

y Starting point, overcurve
Slant down
Undercurve, slant down
Loop back into overcurve: small *y*

z Starting point, overcurve
Slant down, overcurve, down
Loop into overcurve: small *z*

v Starting point, overcurve
Slant down
Undercurve
Small curve to right: small *v*

Letters with loops

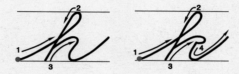

e Starting point, undercurve
Loop back, slant down
Undercurve: small *e*

l Starting point, undercurve
Loop back, slant down
Undercurve: small *l*

h Starting point, undercurve
Loop back, slant down
Overcurve, slant down
Undercurve: small *h*

k Starting point, undercurve
Loop back, slant down
Overcurve, curve forward and under
Slant down, undercurve: small *k*

f Starting point, undercurve
Loop back, slant down
Loop forward into undercurve: small *f*

b Starting point, undercurve
Loop back, slant down
Undercurve, small curve to right:
small *b*

Penmanship (continued)

Cursive Handwriting Models

Downcurve letters

A Starting point, downcurve
Undercurve to starting point
Slant down, undercurve: capital *A*

C Starting point, loop
Downcurve, undercurve: capital *C*

E Starting point, loop
Downcurve
Loop back, downcurve
Undercurve: capital *E*

O Starting point, downcurve
left into undercurve
Loop and curve right: capital *O*

Curve forward letters

N Starting point, loop
Curve forward
Slant down
Retrace up slant
Overcurve down into undercurve: capital *N*

M Starting point, loop
Curve forward, slant down
Retrace up slant, overcurve
Slant down, retrace up slant
Overcurve down into undercurve: capital *M*

Curve forward letters

K Starting point, loop
Curve forward, slant down to end point
Starting point
Doublecurve back to slant
Curve forward
Undercurve up: capital *K*

H Starting point, loop
Curve forward, slant down to end point
Starting point
Curve back and slant down
Retrace up slant, loop left and
curve right: capital *H*

U Starting point, loop
Curve forward, slant down into
undercurve
Slant down, undercurve: capital *U*

Y Starting point, loop
Curve forward, slant down
Undercurve up, slant down
Loop back, overcurve: capital *Y*

Z Starting point, loop
Curve forward, slant down
Overcurve, curve down
Loop into overcurve: capital *Z*

V Starting point, loop
Curve forward and slant down,
undercurve up and overcurve:
capital *V*

Cursive Handwriting Models

Doublecurve letters

Overcurve letters

X Starting point, loop
Curve forward, slant down
Undercurve to end point
Starting point, slant down: capital *X*

W Starting point, loop
Curve forward, slant down into
undercurve
Slant down into undercurve
Overcurve: capital *W*

F Starting point, loop
Curve forward and right to endpoint
Starting point
Doublecurve, curve up
Curve right, slant down: capital *F*

T Starting point, loop
Curve forward to endpoint
Starting point
Doublecurve, curve up
Curve right: capital *T*

I Starting point, overcurve
Curve down and up
Curve right: capital *I*

J Starting point, overcurve
Slant down and loop back
Overcurve: capital *J*

Letters with loops

  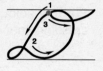

Q Starting point, loop
Curve forward, slant down
Loop back, curve under: capital *Q*

G Starting point, undercurve
Loop, curve up
Double curve, curve up
Curve right: capital G

S Starting point, undercurve
Loop, curve down and up
Curve right: capital *S*

L Starting point, undercurve
Loop, curve down and loop
Curve under: capital *L*

D Starting point, slant down
Loop, curve down and up
Loop and curve right: capital *D*

Undercurve-slant letters

P Starting point, undercurve
Slant down, retrace up
Curve forward and back: capital *P*

R Starting point, undercurve
Slant down, retrace up
Curve forward to slant
Curve forward
Undercurve: capital *R*

B Starting point, undercurve
Slant down, retrace up
Curve forward, loop
Curve forward and back
Curve right: capital *B*

Penmanship (continued)

Numbers

1 Starting point, straight down: *1*

2 Starting point, around right, slanting left and straight across right: *2*

3 Starting point, around right, in at the middle, around right: *3*

4 Starting point, straight down
Straight across right
Starting point, straight down, crossing line: *4*

5 Starting point, curving around right and up
Starting point, straight across right: *5*

6 Starting point, slanting left, around the bottom curving up around right and into the curve: *6*

7 Starting point, straight across right, slanting down left: *7*

8 Starting point, curving left, curving down and around right, slanting up right to starting point: *8*

9 Starting point, curving around left all the way, straight down: *9*

10 Starting point, straight down
Starting point, curving left all the way around to starting point: *10*

! Starting point, straight down
Dot exactly below: exclamation point

? Starting point, curving around right, straight down
Dot exactly below: question mark

Index (continued)

INDEX

Index (continued)

INDEX

Notes

Use this page to record lessons or elements that work well
or need to be adjusted for future reference.

Lessons that work well.

_____
_____
_____
_____
_____
_____
_____
_____
_____
_____
_____
_____
_____

Lessons that need adjustments.

_____
_____
_____
_____
_____
_____
_____
_____
_____
_____
_____
_____
_____
_____
_____
_____

Notes

Use this page to record lessons or elements that work well
or need to be adjusted for future reference.

Lessons that work well.

_____
_____
_____
_____
_____
_____
_____
_____
_____
_____
_____
_____
_____
_____

Lessons that need adjustments.

_____
_____
_____
_____
_____
_____
_____
_____
_____
_____
_____
_____
_____
_____
_____

Notes

Use this page to record lessons or elements that work well
or need to be adjusted for future reference.

Lessons that work well.

_____
_____
_____
_____
_____
_____
_____
_____
_____
_____
_____
_____

Lessons that need adjustments.

_____
_____
_____
_____
_____
_____
_____
_____
_____
_____
_____
_____
_____